THE BUTCHER OF AMRITSAR

The Butcher of Amritsar

General Reginald Dyer

Nigel Collett

Hambledon and London
London and New York

Hambledon and London
102 Gloucester Avenue, London NW1 8HX

175 Fifth Avenue
New York, NY 10010
USA

First published 2005

ISBN 1 85285 457 X

A description of this book is available from the
British Library and from the Library of Congress.

Typeset by Egan-Reid Ltd, Auckland, New Zealand,
and printed in Great Britain by Cambridge University Press.

Distributed in the United States and Canada
exclusively by Palgrave Macmillan,
a division of St Martin's Press.

Contents

Illustrations

Plates

Text Illustrations

Illustration Acknowledgements

The author and the publishers are grateful to the following for permission to reproduce illustrations: the British Library, plates 14–21; Martin Dyer, plates 1, 3 and 7; the National Army Museum, plates 13, 27 and 28.

Introduction

On the evening of 13 April 1919, Brigadier-General Reginald Dyer ordered the shooting of an unarmed and peaceful crowd, estimated to number over twenty thousand men, women and children, at Amritsar in the Punjab. His troops fired continuously at the panic-stricken and fleeing crowd for between ten and fifteen minutes. The Jallianwala Bagh, where this massacre took place, was a walled enclosure, a trap with no easy exit, and the crowd could not escape. By the time Dyer ordered a ceasefire his men had killed many hundreds of Indians and wounded perhaps a thousand more. He then marched his troops back to base, leaving the dead and wounded where they lay. Most of these were not rescued until the following morning, due to the curfew that Dyer had imposed. Many died where they lay overnight. In the weeks that followed, under the martial law which he administered in the city, Dyer proclaimed what became notorious as the 'crawling order', which closed the street where a British woman missionary had been assaulted and made those who wished to proceed down it crawl its whole length on their bellies.

It is difficult to exaggerate the effects of what Dyer did. His deeds, and other similar, if less drastic, acts carried out by British officers elsewhere in the Punjab, alienated all shades of Indian opinion. The failure of the British Government to punish or disown the perpetrators, and the huge support given them by much of the British public, was a critical factor in the metamorphosis of key leaders of the Indian National Congress, in particular of Gandhi, from loyal subjects of the King Emperor into implacable nationalists who came to reject every facet of the British connection. The massacre at the Jallianwala Bagh led directly to the bitterness and bloodshed of Indian independence and partition nearly thirty years later.

The man who perpetrated this disaster was made a hero by his British supporters, who idolised him as the 'Saviour of India'. To almost all Indians, then and now, Dyer was a monster. Yet this was a man, born in India, who was more of a stranger to the English than he ever was to the Indians amongst whom he lived almost all his life. He was a man upon whom was conferred the unheard of honour of being made a Sikh in the Golden Temple at Amritsar. He was an officer revered, even loved, by his Indian troops, and a man whose name retained such a hold on the Indian soldiers with whom he served that decades after he died they would come to pay their respects to his son and to shake his hand.

Dyer stands alone in modern British history. Nowhere in the world since the Indian Mutiny of 1857 have the British turned such violence upon a civilian population. Not since 1919 has anything approaching what he did been repeated. In his deeds, as in the circumstances of his life, Dyer was unique. Attempts to explain what he did at Amritsar by recourse to generalisations about imperialism, racism, gender or class founder upon the fact, frequently remarked by his contemporaries, that he was just not like everybody else. It is therefore to his life that we must turn for an understanding of one of the most infamous events in Indian and British history, and for an explanation of what it was that persuaded Dyer to act as he did, and to maintain for the remainder of his life that he had been right.

Discovering the real Dyer, however, is not easily done. His last years were lived in a glare of publicity, and his career included some of the best-documented events in the history of the time, but he remains elusive. He himself wrote little of a personal nature and, after his death, his wife, Annie, was careful to ensure that even less survived to reveal her husband to posterity. We possess no diaries, very few letters and only a handful of mementos to give an insight into his character and mind. Words of his we have in plenty, but they are official ones, in the dispatches from his campaigns and in his many statements of his case. These, by their nature, give an unbalanced and partial view. Nor are we helped in this by Dyer's official biography, written in 1929 by the right-wing journalist and writer Ian Colvin, which remains almost our only source for many episodes in his life. Colvin's book was the principal means through which Annie Dyer built and perpetuated her husband's legend. Its contents were those she chose to include and it is not an impartial source. The evidence that it presents has been sifted and arranged to present the public of the day with a picture that many wished to see. Colvin paints a portrait of a hero. Where his facts can be checked, Colvin is indeed almost always accurate, but his omissions warn us to take care both in relying on him as a source and in believing the portrait he drew.

Even Colvin could not alter the facts of what his subject had done. The records of Dyer's deeds remain the main guide to his character. His own words reveal what it was that drove him to a conception of his duty held by no other man then or since. It is to both that we must turn to understand the man. It is well that we are able to do so, for in some ways we are unable to get close to him at this distance. Yet in other ways we know him very well indeed, more than we can most of his contemporaries. We know in enormous detail what he did. His deeds are inscribed in the official records. We also have his own published account of his major campaign. From these, from his own many pronouncements about what he had done, and from his background, we can come close to his mindset, work out what it was he was trying to achieve, and draw out the imperatives that were urging him on. To understand what he did at Amritsar, this is enough.

Dyer lived at a time when one era was giving way to another. The settled, privileged, hierarchical world of the British Empire was imperceptibly ebbing away and being replaced by a world that valued self-determination, democracy and dynamic change. The First World War quickened this process as much in India as it did in Europe, setting in motion forces which those who were subject to them could barely comprehend, and against which many, including Dyer, set their faces. He was not alone in this, but it was his misfortune that, on that April evening in Amritsar, he unleashed the forces that were to destroy the India he had spent his life trying to preserve.

Acknowledgements

I wish to express my warm thanks to Jackie Harris, Margaret Surzyn and all the staff of the library of the University of Buckingham, where it was a very great pleasure to work. They have been a tremendous help to me in writing this book. I also owe a very considerable debt of gratitude to Steve Grant and his team at the Buckingham Library, in particular Judith Baines, Alison Bone, Jenny Chidley, Pam Gowen, Julian Handley, Clare Krajnyk and Marion Wedley, who spent a large amount of time in searching for my requests and put up with my typing in the library.

I wish to thank all those by whom my research in various libraries has been made enjoyable and comfortable: Brigadier Christopher Bullock, Curator of the Gurkha Museum, Winchester; Malcolm Davis of the Brotherton Library, Leeds University; Kevin Greenbank of the Centre for South Asian Studies, Cambridge; Deborah Hayward-Eaton at the Library, St Edmund Hall, Oxford; Oliver House at the Bodleian Library; Mr D. Lawrence of the India Office Collection in the British Library; Dr Alastair Massie of the National Army Museum; Colm McLaughlin of the National Library of Scotland; Kate O'Brien of the Liddell Hart Centre of the Library of King's College, London; Tony Richards of the Imperial War Museum; Jonathan Smith of the Library of Trinity College, Cambridge; and Christine Turton of the Bingham Library, Cirencester.

It gives me tremendous pleasure to thank Squadron-Leader Rana Chhina of the United Services Institute Centre for Armed Forces Historical Research, India, for his help with all aspects of my research on the Indian Army and for hosting me so generously during my stay in Delhi. I would like to thank the Colonels Commandant and Commanding Officers of 7th Cavalry, 1st Guards, the Dogra Regiment and the Punjab Regiment for the information they sent me of the regiments which were their antecedents. I also thank Mrs Jaya Ravindra and the staff of the National Archives of India for their help in discovering many of the official records still extant there. I am grateful to the Headmasters of Dyer's schools, Kabir Kumar Mustaphi of Bishop Cotton's School, Shimla, and Brian Cairns of Midleton College, County Cork, for their advice and help.

I also want to thank those who helped me with searches and references in their records: Miss S. Berry at the Somerset Record Office; the late Ruth Poole, the historian of Long Ashton, who sadly died before I was able to show her the results of my research; Valerie Bond and Mr Norman (who knew Annie Dyer) at Long Ashton; Rebecca Cheney at the Royal Engineers Museum, Chatham; Stephen Connelly, Curator of the Staff College Museum, Camberley; Paul Evans, Librarian of Firepower, the Royal Artillery Museum, Woolwich; Mr P.R. Evans at the Gloucestershire Record Office; Martyn Henderson at the Wiltshire and Swindon Record Office; Sheila Lang at the Bristol Record Office; Phil Martin at Companies House; Judy Mills at the Corinium Museum, Cirencester; Sandra Rowley at Cirencester College Library; Helle Savage, Secretary of the Anglo-Danish Society; Dr Peter Thwaites, Curator of the Sandhurst Collection; and John Wilson, Editor of the *British Army Review*.

For permission to quote papers in their possession, I gratefully acknowledge the Bingham Library, Cirencester, for excerpts from the Bull Club papers; the British Library Oriental and India Office Collections, for excerpts from the papers of Sir Harcourt Butler, Lord Chelmsford, Reginald Howgego, Edwin Montagu, Sir J.P. Thompson and Sir George White; the Brotherton Library, Leeds University, for excerpts from the Glenesk-Bathurst papers and the Liddle Collection; the Churchill Archives Centre, Churchill College, Cambridge, for excerpts from the Churchill papers; the Gurkha Museum, for excerpts from the Villiers-Stuart papers and from *Man of Iron* by T.L. Hughes; the Trustees of the Imperial War Museum for allowing access to the collections, and to the copyright holders of the papers of P.W. Ellis, Lieutenant-Colonel M.H.L. Morgan, Captain H. Nisbet and Field-Marshal Sir Henry Wilson; the Liddell Hart Centre, King's College, London, for excerpts from the Edmonds, Liddell Hart and Sclater papers; the Trustees of the National Library of Scotland, for excerpts from the Blackwood papers; and the Master and Fellows of Trinity College, Cambridge, for excerpts from the Edwin Montagu papers. I am grateful for the permission of the Controller of HMSO and the Queen's Printer for Scotland to quote from Crown copyright papers: the papers of Winston Churchill as Secretary of State for War in the Churchill Archives Centre; India Office papers and the papers of Lord Chelmsford as Viceroy and Edwin Montagu as Secretary of State for India in the Oriental and India Office Collections of the British Library; the papers of Edwin Montagu as Secretary of State for India at Trinity College, Cambridge; and Cabinet Office and War Office papers in the National Archive.

I am most grateful to Professor Josef Elfenbein, who gave me guidance on Baluchistan and the Baluch in my chapters on the Sarhadd. For permission to quote from his mother's diary and letters, I especially wish to thank the Reverend Mark Wathen, upon whose Indian table I read his mother's letters and diary, who was in Amritsar when the events I describe unfolded, and whose father, Gerard Wathen, was one of the few to have emerged from Amritsar with honour enough to show how things could have been in India had events at Amritsar taken another, better road.

In 2001-2 I attended a most enjoyable and stimulating course on biography run by Dr Jane Ridley at the University of Buckingham. I am very grateful to Jane for her guidance and for the encouragement she gave me to continue my research into Dyer's life and to write this book.

I owe a special debt of gratitude to Martin Dyer, great-grandson of the General, who allowed me to see the items still held by the family and put up with much questioning with great good humour and patience. He has generously given me permission to quote from the family tree and memorial book in his possession and to publish his photographs of his great-grandfather.

I warmly thank my friend, David Harding, late of 10th Princess Mary's Own Gurkha Rifles, who spent many days guiding me through the India Office collection and who saved me from much error by advising me on the military background to Dyer's career. When he reviewed this book's final draft, he also helped iron out the inconsistencies and errors in its text, and much of it bears his imprint.

Without the committed support of my publisher, Martin Sheppard, this book would not have seen the light of day. For the wise advice he has given me in the course of bringing it to print, I offer my heartfelt thanks. Any mistakes within the book that remain, despite his strenuous efforts to shape and polish it, are my own.

I leave my final thanks to my partner, Austin, who has been my companion through every stage of the writing of this book, as he is of my life.

Abbreviations

AAG	Assistant Adjutant-General
AG	Adjutant-General
AICC	All India Congress Committee
AMS	Assistant Military Secretary
CB	Companion of the Bath
CBE	Companion of the British Empire
CGS	Chief of the General Staff
CID	Criminal Investigation Department
CIE	Companion of the Indian Empire
CIGS	Chief of the Imperial General Staff
C-in-C	Commander-in-Chief
CO	Commanding Officer of a battalion or regiment
CSI	Companion of the Star of India
DAAG	Deputy Assistant Adjutant-General
DAG	Deputy Adjutant-General
DCIGS	Deputy Chief of the Imperial General Staff
DSO	Distinguished Service Order
DSP	Deputy Superintendent of Police
GOC	General Officer Commanding
GP	General Practitioner
GOC-in-C	General Officer Commanding-in-Chief
GSO	General Staff Officer
HQ	Headquarters
HMG	Her/His Majesty's Government
HMSO	Her/His Majesty's Stationery Office
IA	Indian Army
ICS	Indian Civil Service
IDSM	Indian Distinguished Service Medal
INC	Indian National Congress
IO	India Office
ISC	Indian Staff Corps
LSE	London School of Economics
MID	Mention in Despatches

MP	Member of Parliament
MS	Military Secretary
NCO	Non-Commissioned Officer
NMML	Nehru Memorial Museum and Library
OC	Officer Commanding a company or squadron
PSC	Passed Staff College, the Army qualification to work as a staff officer (usually written psc)
Q Exam	Qualifying Examination for promotion to lieutenant-colonel
QMG	Quartermaster-General
RAF	Royal Air Force
RFA	Royal Field Artillery
RHA	Royal Horse Artillery
RMA	Royal Military Academy, Woolwich
RMC	Royal Military College, Sandhurst
RSM	Regimental Sergeant-Major of a battalion or regiment
SSI	Secretary of State for India
USI	United Service Institute
USS	Under-Secretary of State

PART ONE

A Soldier's Life

'He did his duty as he saw it.'

Rudyard Kipling

Simla

The Dyer family were in India from the 1820s. John Dyer, the first of the family to live there, was an officer in the East India Company's naval service, serving in the Bengal Presidency. He sailed out of Calcutta, and captained ships as far afield as Burma and the Malay Archipelago, where he fought the pirates who infested the coasts and preyed upon the sea lanes. Piracy had been a part of life in the East Indies since time immemorial, sponsored and financed by the still independent Malay rajahs and by the aristocracy of their petty states, who paid for the boats and took a share of the proceeds of their raids. The available alternative styles of life were unattractive, a living cut from the jungle on infertile river estuaries or fishing out at sea, so as late as 1836 the pirates swarmed, irrepressibly, along the Malay coasts and even around the colony of Singapore. Fleets of up to two hundred pirate *prahus*, some reaching over fifty feet in length, and propelled by both oars and sails, swept the seas from the sultanates of Brunei and Sulu, preying on both local and European merchant shipping across the South China Sea. Their great voyages lasted three years or more and reached as far as the coasts of India, from where they were pursued back to their island bases by John Company's ships. The pirates were formidable seamen and brave foes, and their menace was far from eradicated in John Dyer's day, when the British were gradually extending their influence into Burma and along the Malay Straits.

It was at this time, in 1839, that James Brooke arrived in Singapore in his privateer the *Royalist* to begin the campaigns in North Borneo which heralded the end of Bruneian piracy and which were to secure his White Rajah's crown in Sarawak. John Dyer's service was one of exciting chases and battles at sea, of raids deep into the jungle up broad, muddy rivers, searching out pirate stockades, then mounting short, violent attacks which invariably ended with the firing of settlements and the summary dispatch of their defenders. His was a hard if manly life, and one in which he followed his family's tradition. His father, Edward, had served before him in the Royal Navy, and would have seen many of the same small campaigns as his son on the seas of the world as the eighteenth turned to the nineteenth century.[1]

The family came from Pilton, a small place just outside the town of Barnstaple in Devon. Mary Dyer, Edward's wife, gave birth to John at Stoke Damerel, near Plymouth, on 7 April 1799. It was back in Barnstaple, though, that John found his own wife, Julia Oxenham, who was born there on 25 April 1804. She went out to India to marry him in St John's Cathedral in Calcutta on 24 March 1827, and she survived the heat and humidity of Bengal to give him ten children. Matthew was the first-born son, and there were four others, Alfred, James, John and Edward, and five daughters. It was to Pilton that the couple returned when John retired from the East India Company sometime in the 1840s. By then, India had entered the Dyer blood, and two of their boys were to return there to establish their own careers. John Dyer made himself a man of means in the company's service, probably in part through the prize money he had won capturing pirate ships, and he could provide well for the futures of his numerous children. There is no record of what happened to the first two sons, but the third, James, went into one of the Services, and retired with the rank of captain to live until well into the next century at Westfield near Lymington in Hampshire. The fourth son, John, became a barrister and went out to India to practise in Mussoorie, a hill station in the Himalayan foothills of Kumaon near Dehra Dun. Edward was the youngest son; he was educated in England and was destined by his family for the Army, probably for the Royal Engineers, as he trained as an engineer and acquired a knowledge of physics and chemistry which was to give him his later livelihood. It is possible that Edward did, in fact, serve in the Army. Lord Hailey, who served as a civil servant in Simla, recorded that the Dyer family was well known to him, and that Edward had been a Quartermaster-Sergeant in a British regiment. The information is hard to reconcile; perhaps it was Mini's father that Lord Hailey recalled. Like his father before him, he fell in love with, and succeeded in marrying, a Barnstaple girl. She was named Mary Passmore, Mini within the family. The newly married Edward, or perhaps his newly-wed wife, rejected the idea of a military career, and Edward persuaded his father to allow him to use the money which had been intended for his commission and his place at the Royal Military Academy at Woolwich to finance his travel to India to begin a new life as an engineer. He set out leaving Mary, for the time being, at home in Devon.[2]

Edward reached India sometime about the year 1850, and travelled up country to his brother John's home at Mussoorie. There together they reviewed the prospects of an engineer in India. John had been out there for long enough by then to have spotted an opportunity, and he suggested to his brother that he start up the brewing of English beer. At that time, beer came out from home on the long sea journey round the Cape of Good Hope, and so it was prohibitively expensive. As late as 1870, decades after the establishment of Indian breweries had opened up competition and so reduced the price, English beer was still costing between seven and ten rupees a bottle as against the five rupees charged for the locally brewed equivalent. By the time Edward reached India only one attempt had been made to brew beer there, at Kasauli, in the foothills below

Simla, to the west of Mussoorie, and this had failed in the 1840s. Edward was a man of some strength of character who was prepared to take a risk, and he resolved to try his hand at this new field of business. He returned to England to learn the trade, and on reaching India once more in 1855 he settled at Kasauli, where he set up his first brewery on the ruins of the earlier enterprise. He installed the most modern technology, and managed, contrary to the expectations of his fellow expatriates, to prove that beer brewing in India could be a success. After some time at Kasauli, Edward sent home for Mary, who, according to family recollection, came out in the best cabin of an East Indiaman, and reached Kasauli just before the Mutiny erupted in 1857. For over a year, the plains below their home were engulfed in flame and carnage.[3]

The Mutiny's shadow darkened the Dyer family's lives, as it darkened almost everything in British India. The echoes of its fears and hatreds, and the prejudices to which they gave rise, were to reverberate through their and their children's futures. Edward and Mary's home was very close to the plains. Kasauli was the first place reached on the way to the hill station at Simla, and was only a few hours up the narrow mountain road from the last lowland terminus at Kalka, and although it was not touched directly by the violence of the Mutiny, it became a refuge for those escaping the horrors unfolding below. It had a sanitarium, and a depot for British soldiers recuperating from sickness and wounds, some of whom no doubt furnished Edward with custom for his beer.[4] From these, and from the fugitives fleeing through Kasauli onwards to Simla and further into the hills, Edward and Mary heard stories of the massacres of the garrisons on the plains below, of the murder of families at Meerut, of the atrocities against women and children at Cawnpore, of the horrors of the sieges of Delhi and Lucknow, and of the ghastly and merciless retribution visited upon the mutineers by the avenging British. Throughout British India, confidence in the survival of the Raj, in the personal safety of its British population, and in the inevitable progress of Christian and western civilisation in India, were all severely shaken by the Mutiny. Gone, in the decades which followed, were the old, easy superiority and the indulgence of racial and cultural differences which had hitherto eased the relations between rulers and ruled. In their place came a rigid segregation and a widespread suspicion of what had come to be seen as the unfathomable native Indians. Worst of all came a fear, which at times of crisis was to break out into a terror, of the dishonour of European womanhood at native hands. The young couple in Kasauli, only recently arrived in India, isolated in their small hill station and totally surrounded by Indians both at home and at work, must have felt themselves very vulnerable. Their fear, and the fear felt by their friends and the society of which they were a part, permeated the atmosphere in which their children were to grow up.

Their children were not long in coming. The growing success of the brewery allowed Edward and Mary to start what was to be a very large family. They were eventually to have nine children, five girls and four boys, and at least the first three of these, Clare, Arthur and Edward, were probably born at Kasauli. At the time, Edward's reputation was spreading, and sometime around 1860 he was approached by the partners of the Murree Brewery Company, General Cantley (who had earlier been one of the developers of the Ganges Canal) and Lieutenant-Colonel Oliphants VC, to become the manager of their business. Edward accepted the offer, and did not disappoint his new employers, for he made as much of a success of the Murree Brewery as he had of his own. This entailed a move for his family to Murree, which was in the hills of the Pir Panjal Range, north east of Rawalpindi on the Kashmir border. It was there that their next three children were born in quick succession, first Walter, then Alice, and, on 9 October 1864, Reginald, the youngest son and sixth child. From the start the family called him Rex. By the year of his birth, his father had become the Managing Partner of the company.[5]

It is unlikely that Rex retained any memories of Murree, for the family left it in 1866 when he was less than two years old. They moved to Simla, where Edward Dyer set up a brewery at a new site on a hillside near St George's School, in Chota (or lower) Simla Bazaar. It is not clear whether this was an independent enterprise; about this time he left the Murree Brewery Company to start out again on his own, and this may have coincided with the move to Simla. Edward was attracted to the town by its growing market and by the fact that an earlier brewery (known in Simla as the Old Brewery, built in former years by a local businessman and philanthropist named Barratt) had gone out of business some three years before. The European population of the town was very much in favour of establishing a local source of beer. Carey's *Guide to Simla* of 1870 recorded that 'all Simla hopes to drive out English beer', despite the fact which it also wrily noted that the locally brewed variety 'requires one to get used to it'. Edward's brewery, which became known as the New Brewery, was not without competition, for in 1869 a consortium leased the Old Brewery from the Simla Bank which had repossessed it six years before, and under the management of 'a practical brewer', H.G. Meakin, recommenced its operations. Every six months they managed to brew some five hundred hogsheads of an ale 'much liked and sought after', and this must have been something of a threat to Edward's business in its early years. However, Meakin did not prove as successful a businessman as he was a brewer, and by 1870 his brewery, which had cost 150,000 rupees to build, was again being offered for sale to the public at half that price. We do not know the size of Edward's investment in the New Brewery, but the cost of Meakin's competing establishment shows that even by 1866 Edward had managed to multiply the sums of money he had been given by his father, and that he had become a wealthy man.[6]

Dyer Family Tree

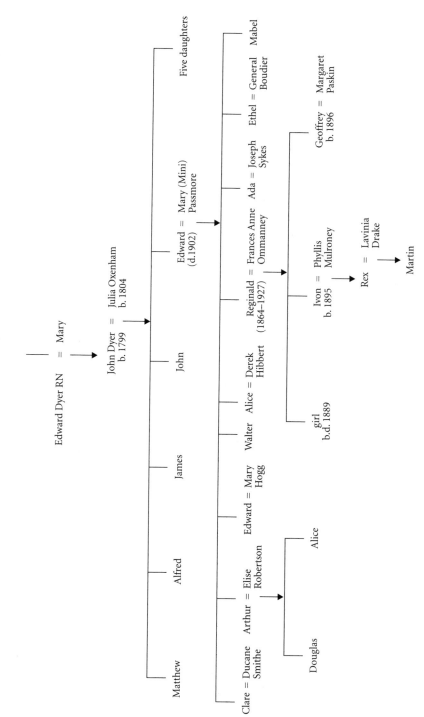

Edward purchased a house named Ladyhill, not far from the brewery and also in Chota Simla, several miles from the main part of the town. It was built, as was much of the Simla of the day, in the style of Surrey rather than of India, and was surrounded by a large garden full of English fruits and flowers; chrysanthemum, dahlia, delphinium, iris and other English plants flourished in the Simla soil and climate. By 1870, the estate of which the house was the principal part had been retitled 'Dyerton', and Carey's *Guide* of that year records that its annual rent was 900 rupees, which although not the greatest rent payable in the area was nevertheless a respectable sum. Dyerton lay on the side of a ridge with spectacular west-facing views, looking out across the valley to the road which wound up to Simla from the plains. The town was itself in clear view from the estate, straggling along the ridge on the other side of a deep, intervening chasm. In the other direction, about a mile and a half away around the hill, was Bishop Cotton's School, and further up the slope from the house was 'Woodville', the first Simla residence of the Commanders-in-Chief in India. That grand house had been built by the then Commander-in-Chief, General Sir William Rose Mansfield, only a year before the Dyers arrived, and it was to be occupied by his next four successors until the fifth moved to the larger and more conveniently located 'Snowdon' in 1881. The area in which the Dyers settled was thus a desirable one, and their purchase of a property there was an indication of the status to which they aspired.[7]

The family's last three children were born at about the time of the move to Simla and in the years just afterwards. All were daughters, and they were christened Ada, Ethel and Mabel. Their mother had let neither the succession of home moves nor the uncertainties of her husband's new enterprise prevent her completing their large, characteristically mid-Victorian family. Mini Dyer was a robust and determined woman.

Simla had long been popular as a hill station where those working in the capital, Calcutta, or in the Ganges plains, could sit out the summer heat. Lord Amherst, when Viceroy, had set the trend with a visit there in 1827, and his successor, Lord William Bentinck, had built himself Bentinck Castle in the town in 1832. A later Viceroy, Lord Auckland, summered there in 1841. The town grew rapidly as a result of this patronage, and became the first municipality incorporated in the Punjab in 1850. The Dyers' arrival coincided with the formal establishment of Simla as the summer capital of India by Sir John Lawrence, who was Viceroy from 1863–69. From his time on, the start of the summer was marked by the arrival of a swarm of civil servants and clerks, who brought in their wake bullock cartloads of their files and ledgers. Army Headquarters soon followed the Government of India, adding to the population large numbers of senior officers and their staffs, and not long afterwards these were joined for every summer season by the Government of the Punjab, in whose province Simla lay. The town developed the dual aspect it was to retain until the end of the Raj, a somewhat incongruous mix of the serious and sententious with the idle and pleasure-seeking, the latter there solely for relaxation and the pursuit of pleasure in the rarefied air of the hills. As Edward Buck put it in 1925, 'There are two communities – the bees and the butterflies'. In the 1860s all of this was causing a rapid growth in the number of both Europeans and Indians living in and around the town, which in turn increased the size of the booming local market for bottled beer.[8]

Edward's company made rapid progress, and at some point in the 1870s he built another, and this time much larger, brewery on a more convenient site at Solon, lower down the road from Simla to the plains. This site had an abundant supply of spring water and was closer to the roadhead at Kalka from where supplies of coal had to be hauled up the mountain by the Kashmiri labourers employed on the road, all of which made the manufacture of beer cheaper there than further up the road in Simla. The Solon brewery was to prove more successful than Dyer's earlier site at Simla, which went out of use sometime later.

As a market, Simla was crucial to the massive commercial success of Edward Dyer's company, but living there was not, for his family, without its own peculiar disadvantages. By settling in Simla, the Dyers had placed themselves in a society of which they could only and forever remain on the periphery. Any pretensions to social status on the part of 'unofficials', the members of the commercial class, received little, if any, recognition by the 'officials', the Government servants who dominated the Simla of that day. The Dyer family could with much justice claim a respectable social position: their forebears had served in both the Royal Naval and the East India Company, and they were considerably wealthier than many of their neighbours. Yet they would have found only condescension from the 'officials', whose attitude towards 'box-wallahs', as those who were in trade were derogatively called, was one of contempt. Mary Dyer had social ambitions for her family. She intended, for instance, that Rex join a smart cavalry regiment, something she and Edward would have had to subsidise very heavily had her wish been fulfilled. Two of her daughters were to marry Service officers. Yet the Dyers' estimate of their own social position would not have been accepted by the society in which they lived, and they must have found irksome and infuriating the rigid conformity to the rules of social protocol which governed everything polite in the town and which inexorably relegated them to the rear. The *Times* correspondent, William Russell, had written of Simla society under a decade before, 'Neither wealth, wit nor desirable connections could guarantee an individual breaking through the sacred barrier which keeps the non-official world from the high society of the services.' Little had changed ten years later. It is highly unlikely, for instance, that the Dyers were ever guests of their military neighbour at Woodville; geographical propinquity in no way implied social proximity. By taking up the life of an entrepreneur and by placing his family at Simla, Edward had condemned them to an outsider status which must have rankled severely with a woman as strong-willed as his wife.[9]

On the other hand, British Indian society granted those whose social aspirations it frustrated some compensation in the form of the inviolable superiority they enjoyed in their relations with their inferiors; and most of these inferiors were, of course, Indian. Between the British and the Indian in Simla there was a chasm which it is unlikely that the Dyers, who have left no sign of any propensity for nonconformity, ever tried to bridge. The family's experience of Indians was confined to their extensive domestic staff and to the workforce at their breweries. Simla society of the day was so open in the arrogance and insularity that it displayed towards Indians that it shocked many visitors out from England. It rigorously excluded Indians, for instance, from the better hotels and from the clubs frequented by the British. In British minds the fears generated by the Mutiny had transmogrified into the theory that the maintenance of British prestige was necessary to ensure that the Empire continued at all, and so the maintenance of that prestige came to replace almost all other considerations. 'Fraternisation', it was thought, could only take place at the expense of prestige and so was to be avoided at all costs. As late as 1918, Edwin Montagu, the Secretary of State for India, was told when he visited Simla that he should never to talk to his servants as it was harmful to prestige. At its worst, this self-generated insularity encouraged ill-manners, arrogance and even physical brutality towards native Indians, an ill-natured atmosphere for children to imbibe. The harvest of ill-will this would cause, particularly amongst the growing educated and professional Indian classes, was to be a major factor in the development of nationalist politics over the next few decades.[10]

It seems that this milieu was one which caused Mary Dyer no discomfort. She was noted, even amongst her family, for holding, and for forthrightly expounding, the arrogant and segregationist views that were characteristic of much of British Indian society of the day.

> When, for example, Edward Dyer, recounting his travels and by way of conversation, said that he had once lit a cigarette from a Burma girl's cheroot, his wife expressed her disapprobation in words that laid a damp of silence not only over him but over the whole dinner party. 'That sort of looseness', she said, 'is what has peopled Simla with thirty thousand Eurasians.'[11]

By all remaining accounts, Mary Dyer was a very formidable woman, and it would appear that she wore the trousers in the family. Her influence was increased by the fact that her husband was often away from home, travelling all over India developing markets for the products of his brewery. Edward's absences were to increase after he moved the brewing operations to Solon, which was over thirty miles from Dyerton, many hours away by horse or carriage on the sole steep and winding mountain road. Edward could not have commuted daily to work, so it is likely that he stayed over at the brewery, perhaps coming home only at weekends. Later, in about 1880, his absences from home increased again, as he established a distillery at Lucknow, where he made use of his knowledge of chemistry and refrigeration to develop processes which allowed the making of liquor in the heat of the plains. In this he was widely credited with instigating something of a renaissance in Indian brewing, hitherto an industry pretty much in the doldrums. He was both a highly successful technician and an entrepreneur, as his obituary in the *Pioneer* makes clear. It characterises him as a scrupulous businessman, and comments on the role he played in advising the Government of India on brewing issues, recalling that his sound advice had always benefited the relations between it and industry. By his later years he came to be regarded as 'the senior and most important representative' of the brewing industry in India. Those who knew him also remembered 'his warm hospitality, old fashioned courteous manners and kind welcome to friends and guests', as well as his character of 'a high minded gentleman'. He possessed a strong physique coupled with physical courage: he had been a boxer and a wrestler in his youth in Devon, so it is sure that Rex's stamina and bravery were Edward's gift to his son; as were his shyness, his reserve and the reverence he showed towards womenfolk, characteristics which had allowed Mary to become the dominant partner in the marriage. She ruled, as her children later remembered, not only her family but beyond, the centre of a much wider circle which she entertained by the means provided by her husband's wealth. Her dominance may have surprised some of her contemporaries, who on first acquaintance might have thought her of nervous disposition, for she spoke with a marked stammer, but mastered it by deliberately speaking slowly and firmly. This defect, and the stubborn will which overcame it, was the inheritance she passed on to Rex.

Mary's social prowess is not really surprising. The social circle which she was able to collect would have largely consisted of those she would have deemed her social inferiors: tradesmen from Simla, local hoteliers, clergymen, schoolmasters and their wives. These were the few who remained in Simla all year round, in their number all those excluded by Society in the town in the summer. With the Dyer family roots and with Edward's wealth, Mary could sit comfortably at the pinnacle of her own small society, which must have been something at least of a compensation for the way she was treated by the rest.[12]

So, in this hilltop household ruled by over by Mini Dyer, her children grew up. They found in the hills around Simla a playground full of delight and adventure. They ran free with their Indian servants amongst the oak and deodar forests and the thickets of rhododendron and white roses, brambles and barberry. The Simla of that day was still a wild and enchanting place. Much of the station lay at an altitude of over 7500 feet, so the weather was cool all year round, cold enough in the winter months for deep snow to fall and cut off all communication with the plains and the world outside. At that time of the year Simla was largely deserted by its summer inhabitants, and the town became as empty as a holiday resort out of season. Wildlife returned then to the paths around the bazaar, and to the walks frequented in the summer by the fashionable. In broad daylight, leopard hunted the pie dogs of the bazaar, jackal and fox scavenged in the outskirts and lynx and bear roamed the hillsides around the town. Hyenas, less bold than the leopards, prowled the night to take domestic animals, and it was one of these beasts which provided the occasion of the first recorded incident in Rex's life, one which was to set the pattern of consistent bravery characteristic of him throughout his life. Walking through the forest to escort his sisters home from school, he came across a hyena blocking his path. Rex remembered that animals were said to fear the human eye, so he stared steadily at the ugly beast as he walked past it on the narrow trail. Keeping his eye fixed upon it until he was past, quickly turning and all the while holding the hyena in his stare, he walked backwards until it was out of sight. Rex can have been little more than ten years of age at the time, and he was certainly little taller than the hyena. It was a very brave thing to do.[13]

All the Dyer children spoke Hindustani with the Indians of their household, as was customary with British children in India at that time. They had all been brought up by an Indian *ayah*. With his siblings, Rex learned to ride on the donkeys of the family's *dhobis*, and, as they grew older, they made longer and longer expeditions together to camp out in the surrounding hills. Accompanied by the family's old *chaprasi*, who carried the guns, Rex went out hunting and learned to shoot at a very young age. He also acquired early on something highly unusual for a boy of his time, an aversion to hunting animals. Shooting birds one day, he hit a female monkey by mistake. He was close enough to his target see the tears of pain streaming down the monkey's face as it tried to wipe the blood from its breast with a handful of leaves. Catching sight of Rex, the monkey looked at him so reproachfully that his dreams were troubled by the sight for months afterwards. From that day, he would never hunt for pleasure, only for necessity or for the pot. He did not extend this sympathy to all creatures, though, for he fearlessly caught and killed snakes with a cane. On one occasion he both startled then amused his family by pulling one particularly large snake by its tail out of the hole into which it was rapidly trying to disappear. The snake hung fast, then suddenly gave way, and both Rex and snake tumbled together down the hillside. Even at such a young age, Rex had a good deal of carelessness about the consequences of his bravado.[14]

Every day Rex walked with his brothers the few miles to Bishop Cotton's School, where he enrolled in 1869 or 1870. The school was further round the

THE INDIAN EMPIRE

AFGHANISTAN

PERSIA

THE CHINESE EMPIRE

TIBET

GILGIT

JAMMU

KASHMIR

N.-W. FRONTIER PROVINCE

Peshawar

Rawalpindi

Dharamsala

Dalhousie

Amritsar

Jullundur

Simla

Chakrata

Mussoorie

Naini Tal

Multan

Lahore

PUNJAB

Delhi

Meerut

Aligarh

NEPAL

SIKKIM

BHUTAN

N.-E. FRONTIER

ASSAM

OUDH

Lucknow

Cawnpore

Jhansi

RAJPUTANA

SIND

Karachi

Quetta

BALUCHISTAN

BOMBAY

Bombay

HYDERABAD

BENGAL

Calcutta

UPPER BURMA

Mandalay

LOWER BURMA

Rangoon

FRENCH INDO-CHINA

SIAM

ANDAMAN ISLANDS

NICOBAR ISLANDS

MADRAS

Madras

CEYLON

Colombo

ridge on which their home stood, built upon a spur known as Knollswood, and facing south with a vast view which opened before it through the pine forests, ridge after serried ridge retreating in waves as far as the eye could see. Bishop Cotton's had only been built on this, its second site, in the year the Dyers had arrived in Simla. It was finished in 1868, so all was very fresh and new when Rex arrived. The estate on which the school was built was extensive, over fifty-four acres of hillside purchased by the Viceroy, who was *ex officio* the school's Visitor, from the local Rajah of Keontal. The buildings were of two storeys, with pitched roofs and sloping eaves, and of a style of architecture ecclesiastically Gothic. The plaque recording its first foundation of 1859 adorned the main school building, and another marking the new foundation of 1866 was affixed to the outside of the chapel wall.[15]

The first Headmaster, the Reverend Samuel Slater, was still in post when the Dyer boys were pupils. He had been a protégé of George Cotton, the Anglican Bishop of Calcutta and Metropolitan of India, Burma and Ceylon, who had himself been one of the masters trained by Thomas Arnold at Rugby. Slater aimed to replicate at Bishop Cotton's the systems both he and his mentor had known and had helped to develop at Rugby and Marlborough. The pupils were mostly the children of civil servants or of the richer commercial classes, though not of Army officers, whose sons usually attended St Edward's School, some distance away in the town.

Bishop Cotton's was very much a microcosm of British Indian society. It owed its very foundation to the Mutiny, still then only just over a decade in the past. The school had been established with money Bishop Cotton had raised by subscription as a thank offering to God for British victory in the Mutiny. It was closed to Indians – the first Indian pupil entered it in 1881, six years after Rex had left – and within it reproduced all the social prejudices and segregations of Simla itself. Its ethos of class and race, its emphasis upon a robust Christian religion, and its trust in a God who had saved British India from the frightfulness of the Mutiny, informed a great deal of its pupils' education. Upon its boys was imprinted the importance of adhering strictly to the codes by which British India had been saved and still lived, codes, paradoxically, by which families such as the Dyers were labelled inferior.[16]

Bishop Cotton's had two hundred boarders and twenty-five day boys, and as the Dyer boys were included among the latter, they were automatically outsiders. No doubt the petty snobberies their parents endured in Simla society were inflicted with interest upon their offspring at school. These difficulties, magnified for Rex by the stammer which afflicted him, were the cause of the scars that he frequently bore when he came home; his sisters recalled that he stubbornly fought his way through the five or six years in which he attended Bishop Cotton's. It cannot have been a very happy place for him. Although the school reinforced the conviction given him by his family of his personal superiority as a member of British society in India, it was probably also a factor in the development of his shyness and his inability to get on with his fellows. These were to be part of his character throughout his life. We do not know how Rex did at the school; none of his records have survived there. The school burned down in 1905, and if there were any records kept there of his school days, they vanished then.[17]

Yet any seeds of unhappiness which afflicted Rex at school, important as they may have been for his later development, probably had little visible effect on his life at the time. His large family, with its lavish estate and the grand house in which his parents entertained, their many servants, and their impressively wealthy style of life, gave the boy a more than usually good start in life. There could hardly have been a better place than Simla for an adventurous child like Rex to grow up. As well as his much-loved expeditions in the wilderness, there were visits to enjoy to the smart shops and plush hotels lining the Mall, and calls to make at the houses of his parents' friends, visits the quiet Rex, perhaps, would have found less enjoyable. Sunday was the day of attendance at the Anglican parish church at the end of Mall. This dominated the town and the surrounding hills from the highest point on the ridge, its tower visible for miles around. Though, in the summer at least, the Dyers would have been seated towards the rear of the simple Gothic church, Rex was able to see, particularly if he was lucky enough to be seated in the balcony, the Viceroy and his party in the front pews, with the Commander-in-Chief and the Lieutenant-Governor of the Punjab to the left and right in the row behind, their places marked by shining brass plates fixed to the pews.

His father must have taken him to the breweries at Simla and Solon to watch his Indian workers feeding the furnaces and mixing the contents of the brewing vats. The brewery would have fascinated Rex. It was much the largest industrial establishment in the hills and was impossible to miss on the road up to Simla, as its great chimneys belched out smoke over the hillside, its blackened sheds hummed and clanged with the noise of its hundreds of workers and the sweet smell which emanated from it permeated the valley around. It is likely that Rex's later fascination with applied mathematics and optics was the fruit of his father's own scientific skills, for Edward Dyer was highly skilful in the handling of the machinery which drove his enterprise. In such an isolated location there was no one else to roll up his sleeves, get his hands dirty and fix things if they went wrong. Rex saw his father working alongside his own artisans and labourers and this he did not forget. He himself would always show a willingness matched by a practical ability to pitch in and get the job done. Not for him the snobbery of many of his fellows, who denigrated honest toil and the use of their hands. Rex saw vividly that his family were at the forefront of change and progress in India. His father was an entrepreneur, a pioneer, albeit one whose success had given them a life of ease and refinement which contrasted starkly with the lives of the mass of the people among whom they lived. The Dyers were in the vanguard of what was modern in Simla and in India in their day, and must have regarded themselves as ultra-modern, at the forefront of what they thought the future was to bring to India.

In one matter, though, and that the most vital of all for Rex at the time, Edward Dyer failed his son. When Rex was eleven, Edward and Mini decided that he, with his brother Walter, who was thirteen, would be sent to boarding school back home. For some reason we do not know, they fixed for their sons' education upon a school in Ireland, Midleton College. The choice is, at this distance, inexplicable. The family seems to have had no connections there, and no relations or friends in Ireland who could have been asked to watch over the pair. The Dyers probably had little or no knowledge of the school, and not much more of the country, though they cannot have been wholly ignorant of the political turmoil to which Ireland had only recently been reduced and which it was about to endure again. There had been an abortive Fenian rising there in 1867, which had been rigorously suppressed, but the events of the succeeding years in Ireland had been highly controversial, and much argued about throughout the Empire. The suppression of the rising had been followed by attempts to ameliorate Irish conditions and to meet Irish aspirations. The Irish Church had been disestablished in 1869, and a year later the first Land Act gave tenants across Ireland control of their lands in all but the vital matters of rental and eviction. The power of the Protestant Ascendancy was weakening in Ireland, and its members were beginning to flee to England in search of greater security, a stream of well-heeled refugees which was gradually to turn into a flood. Those who stayed in Ireland were to become an even smaller minority in the country which they ruled.[18]

All of these issues were in the public mind when the Dyers made their decision to send their sons to Ireland; if they were aware of them, they can have given them little weight. Perhaps, though this can only be guessed at, they saw Midleton as a cheaper alternative to the more prestigious schools in England. Whatever their reasons, in 1875 Edward and Mary sent Walter and Rex to Ireland, alone by train and steamer half way across the world, in an exile from home which was to last for an unbroken twelve years. The golden age of Rex's boyhood ended in a moment. His ties with India, with the mountains which he loved, and most of all of with the close affection of his family, were all abruptly sundered. It was not to be until he was twenty-three years of age that he would see again his family, Simla and the scenes of his childhood.

2

Cork and Sandhurst

Midleton College stands in wide playing fields outside the small market town of which it bears the name, twelve miles north east of the city of Cork. It was founded by Elizabeth Villiers, Countess of Orkney, the mistress of King William III, who gave her all the Irish lands of the deposed Roman Catholic King James II after he conquered Ireland in 1689. From this enormous fortune she endowed Midleton College, appointing a board of governors on which she installed representatives of the ascendant Protestant aristocracy, including, *ex officio*, the Bishop of Cork. Like Bishop Cotton's, Midleton thus had its roots, though much longer ones, in imperial and ecclesiastical soil, and its strong links to the Church of Ireland were reinforced by the early appointment of another of its bishops, that of Cloyne, which was about ten miles south of Midleton, to the board of governors. Many of the college's masters were clergymen and many of its pupils entered the Church. The college went into decline in the first half of the nineteenth century, for some years admitting no pupils at all, and its buildings fell derelict, but in March 1863 a new Headmaster, the Reverend Thomas Moore, was brought over from Liverpool with his wife to begin what was to be a remarkable renaissance in the college's fortunes.[1]

When the Moores arrived at Midleton, they found its pupils had been reduced to a single boarder and three day boys, but in less than a year the new Headmaster's energetic recruitment and his growing name as a teacher increased this to forty boarders and twenty-two day pupils. In 1864, Moore's success persuaded the Irish Commissioners of Education to grant funds to the college to provide the growing number of pupils with a substantial new building housing a school room, a dormitory, masters' rooms, two classrooms and a bathroom, and all were built by the following year. The new School House was an imposing red-brick building of three storeys, with high walls and grey slate roofs. Mrs Moore's skills as a gardener were employed in improving the grounds, and in building the sunken area which was thereafter to be the Headmaster's garden. She took on the task of furnishing the new buildings, adding a woman's touch to the accommodation. Numbers carried on growing and by 1878, three years after Walter and Rex Dyer arrived, there were sixty boarders and fifty-one day pupils. That year, with more help from the Educational Commissioners, School House was extended to add two new classrooms with dormitories above. There was much building going on, and a real feeling of growth and progress, in the Dyer boys' early years at Midleton.

Mrs Moore had died before the Dyer boys reached Midleton, leaving her husband a widower for the remainder of his life, a personal tragedy which was to benefit his pupils as he henceforth devoted all his private time to his work, regularly tutoring them after hours. The school joined the front rank of Irish schools, and many of its boys gained scholarships to Oxford, Cambridge, Trinity College, Dublin and Queen's College, Belfast. Moore employed three resident teachers, one of them Standish O'Grady, who was to gain national eminence as a father of the Irish literary revival, as well as a non-resident assistant who ran a boarding house for pupils for whom there was no room in the school. It was perhaps the school's growing reputation which persuaded Edward and Mary Dyer to send their third and fourth sons to the college. There is, too, a possibility that Edward had heard of the school through his contacts in trade, for there was a distillery at Midleton, not far from the college, and it was famed for its brand of Irish whisky.

Walter and Rex arrived in 1875. They had taken over two months to get there, probably escorted at the start of their journey by the family's servants down the mountain road to the plains at Kalka and then on by train for over a day to Bombay. There they took the steamer to England, on their own for the long, six or seven week voyage, for their arrival in Southampton or London, for the train journey across England and Wales, and finally for the ferry to Cork. It must have seemed forever before the Midleton College trap met them at the quayside to whisk them away through the bustle of Cork into the quiet, green Irish country-side. It was an exciting journey; all at sea was new and interesting, and to the two boys from Simla the British Isles and its inhabitants would have been as exotic as India was to most of their countrymen. It must also have been a lonely, at times an alarming, journey. Their parents had equipped them with only a cheque book and a banker's draft to cover the costs of the travel and their first school fees. The clothes in which they had been packed off to Ireland showed how little their parents comprehended of the place they were sending them: the boys arrived in Midleton wearing solar topis and each with a *khukuri*, the traditional Gurkha knife, stuck in his cummerbund. Quite naturally, they were immediately christened 'the wild Indians'.

It would not, for them, have been an amusing or an auspicious start, and the boys must have found the dissonance between Ireland and India, and between the freedoms of home and the regulated life of a boarding school, a very painful shock. The strangeness of their dress and accents, and their complete unfamiliarity with the country and the ways of the school, made them ready victims for the taunts and bullying which inevitably befall the new boy at any school. Their difference was extreme, and Rex's stammer made his predicament worse, singling him out as a butt for many schoolboy cruelties. The first few months were hard going and both boys were bullied badly, until there was one occasion too many for Rex's stubborn spirit to stand. One of their larger tormentors chose to pick on Walter, and Rex went to his brother's aid. The bully turned on Rex, but between the two of them the brothers brought him down, and they at last established their place in the school.

Rex became known at Midleton as Reggie, and he was remembered years later by the Headmaster's daughters as a 'shy, gentle boy'. But he had another nickname, one given him out of respect by his fellows, that of 'Rags', which indicated different qualities, and referred to the prowess he showed in the school's traditional fights with the gangs of children from the town. These 'Baminines' as they were called, were wont to invade the college grounds, particularly through breaches in the wall by the football fields, and when discovered by the school 'there were Homeric fights with wickets, bats, fists, anything'. Most of the local boys were Roman Catholics whilst the school, or at least most of its boarders, were Protestants, and their fights no doubt mirrored the sectarian conflicts that were enveloping the Ireland around them. Already it is possible in this to discern a pattern in Rex's character. On the surface, what showed was a self-conscious diffidence with the female sex and a deference to those in authority, but this belied a stubborn toughness which made him quite capable of meting out rough treatment to his fellows and to his enemies.

At Midleton, work began at seven in the morning, and classes went on until three in the afternoon. After that the boys were free to play games or attend the tuition classes taken by the Headmaster; these went on even as late as midnight. The syllabus was conventional in its teaching of Latin, Greek and the Classics, none of which much interested Rex, and of Mathematics, for which he developed a notable aptitude under Moore's tuition. The school was innovative, however, in its teaching of Natural Philosophy (by which was meant Physics), Mechanics and Botany, all of which were subjects which suited Rex's practical bent. It is possible that the inclusion of these subjects in the syllabus had been a factor in Edward Dyer's choice of the school, and indeed the scientific bent of the curriculum was not lost on Rex. He was attracted to the practical solution of mechanical problems, and the lessons at Midleton gave him a firm foundation for his lifelong habit of building useful things, as well as for the pursuit of technical inventions which was to mark much of his later career.

Religious education was, unusually for the day, not part of the syllabus, for the college was deliberately non-sectarian in its teaching, despite its origins and the background of the majority of its pupils. Many of its day boys were Roman Catholics, and the college tried hard to avoid charges of sectarianism, removing, for instance, Morris's *History* from the college's textbooks because it treated the Reformation from a Protestant viewpoint and so offended Catholic parents. The college, like many public schools of its day, had an Army Class to prepare pupils interested in an Army career for the Preliminary Military Examination giving entry to Sandhurst; this was usually taken between the ages of fifteen and sixteen. Rex took this class and in it was taught military history by the Headmaster. Some of the larger public schools of the day also prepared their pupils for the second stage of Sandhurst entry, the Army Entrance Examination, known as the 'further' examination, but this was not the case at Midleton, which was too small to provide the more specialised tuition this would have required. Formal examinations in all subjects were first instituted in the school in Rex's day. In 1879, boys began to sit for the Intermediate Examinations, and Rex must have taken these, though we do not know with what success. No school records have survived at Midleton from Rex's day and if his examination results were stored in the Government records in Dublin, they were to be destroyed by fire in the troubles of the 1920s.

The school became the boys' home for the decade in which they passed through youth to manhood. It seems they stayed at Midleton for most of the time, and even during their holidays took no trips to England to stay with relatives in Devon or elsewhere. Nor did they return to India. Their parents do not seem to have visited Ireland, so contact with the family back at home in Simla could be maintained only by letter. Home, parents and siblings grew more and more distant, but Rex was not going to allow himself to forget the paradise of his childhood and was determined that one day he would go back there. He doggedly practised his Hindustani, using books sent out from India. In the holidays, perhaps, the boys may have been invited to the homes of friends who lived in Ireland, particularly when the school closed for Christmas, but their lives must have seemed an endlessly lonely sojourn to both of them at times. The solitude increased Rex's natural reserve. He walked alone in the woods around the college, and made use of these walks to eradicate his stammer. By dint of long, solitary practice, he drummed it out of himself, and there was no trace of it left after his time at the school.

Midleton was in the forefront in its day in offering a good deal of recreation in the form of sport. The school played cricket on a pitch at Cahermone, the nearby estate of Viscount Midleton, one of the college governors and an increasingly prominent Unionist politician. Lord Midleton's silver cup was presented annually to the college's best cricketer. It had an excellent cricket team, which played, and beat, the Cork 1st Eleven, and the Queen's College 2nd Eleven, and even on one occasion managed to tie with the Queen's 1st Eleven. Given the disparity in age and size between them and the students of Queen's, this was an achievement of which the boys of Midleton must have been very proud. Rugby was also played at the college, on occasion against the local Cork side. One of Rex's contemporaries, Tom Harrison, won three Irish caps as a full back between 1879 and 1881, and the school was one of the earliest to affiliate to the Irish Rugby Football Union, which was formed in 1874. The boys swam in the local river, and on Sundays the Protestant boys attended the local parish church of the Holy Trinity at East Ferry, of which the Reverend Moore was Rector and which he himself had built. Rex was a member of his Headmaster's congregation throughout his time at Midleton, and it is probable that Moore prepared him for confirmation. In almost every way Moore stood in for the father whom Rex no longer had.

It must have made it very painful to Rex that the times were propitious neither for the college, nor for the Protestant establishment of which it was a part. While Rex was a pupil, the college was buffeted by the storms of Irish politics from which even the skills of the energetic Moore were unable to protect it. Midleton began to fall into another decline, one which matched that of the landowning and commercial classes from which its pupils were largely drawn. The disturbances of the 1860s had given way to some years of economic prosperity in Ireland in the early 1870s, and this had drawn the sting to some extent of the underlying political grievances so that things had quietened down for a while. When Edward Dyer sent his two boys to Midleton he may well have thought that Ireland was securely at peace. This was a misjudgment. The middle years of the decade brought an industrial slump in England which led to economic catastrophe in Ireland after 1876, where agricultural prices plummeted by up to 50 per cent. Making matters worse in the countryside, the potato harvests of 1877–79 were disastrous; in the latter year, only a quarter of the normal yield could be harvested and famine ensued. Landlords once again turned to eviction to dispose of tenants who could not grow enough crops to pay their rents. By 1880, at the height of this period of steep economic decline, over two thousand Irish families were being evicted every year, and each eviction generated retaliatory outrages against the landlords and their agents. Ireland teetered on the brink of revolution. Across the country, the more radical members of the Land League, often men who had played a part in the Fenian rising of the 1860s, burned ricks, maimed animals and made attempts, some successful, on the lives of the ruling class. Murder and terror spread across Ireland: there were over 2590 outrages reported in 1880 alone. As Irish society increasingly disintegrated, the countryside around Midleton began to take on a threatening, dangerous aspect, and the Reverend Moore must have viewed with dismay and then despair the hardening of sectarian barriers against which his own small attempts at a tolerant middle way were totally powerless. He soldiered on amidst the slow ruin of his life's work and the air of sadness which pervaded Midleton during the last half of Rex's time there.

The establishment in Ireland struck back. The deteriorating situation in the countryside led to renewed coercion by Dublin Castle. By 1881, using rigorous police measures, the Government managed to suppress the Land League. It also made some attempt to respond to Irish grievances. A second Land Act was passed in 1881, but it failed to prevent the evictions which continued as before. Parnell, the leader of the Home Rule Party and of the Land League, went to gaol and outrages against landlords increased across the countryside. In May 1882, the Chief Secretary, Lord Frederick Cavendish, was assassinated in Phoenix Park in Dublin on his first day in office. The Government responded in kind. Armed with a new Coercion Act, the Viceroy, the 'Red Earl', Earl Spencer, introduced a savage repression which stabilised a situation that had seemed in danger of bringing English rule in Ireland to the brink of dissolution. There had very nearly been, in fact, a civil war. The lack of security across the country in these troubled years forced many Irish Protestant families to move to England and to send their children there to school; by 1885 it was estimated that at least a thousand Irish schoolboys were studying in England.[2]

Midleton College saw the same flight of its Protestant boarders as was being seen across Ireland, a loss worsened in its own case by the simultaneous withdrawal from the school of its mostly Catholic dayboys. By 1881, when Rex was in the upper part of the college, there were only fifty-five pupils of all types left. Moore resigned the next year, and his successor, the Reverend Albert Burd, was no better able to stop the rot. Burd explained to the Endowed Schools Commission in 1885 that until two years previously nearly half his day-boys had been Roman Catholics, but that increased sectarianism in national politics, coupled with the famine and the agrarian disturbances around Cork, had driven almost all of these to attend the Christian Brothers school in Midleton town. Two years after Rex left Midleton there were only fifteen pupils left.

Edward Dyer kept his two boys at the college throughout the troubles. It is difficult not accuse him of neglect of his sons' welfare and education. The effect of the disturbances upon the few remaining pupils must have been marked. Surrounded by a countryside in turmoil, with outrages committed against their families, with Government policy openly blamed by their parents for the destruction of their society and the victory of their nationalist enemies, Midleton's boys must have felt lost, betrayed and afraid of what the future was bringing. The experience, an unrelieved pressure over many years, must have marked Walter and Rex, who could see that they were in a country where there was no longer any security and whose very foundations were shaking. The vision of a society in terminal decay, with the loss and damage suffered by those on the losing side, his people, in effect, brought low by revolution and what they would have characterised as Government weakness, was something Rex would not forget. He clung tightly to his memory of India and its seemingly unchanging and unchallenged way of life. This must have sustained him through some dark and fearful times during the long years in which he grew up in Ireland. He was to spend his life in pursuit of the certainties which were lost to him there.

Rex left Midleton in late 1882 or early 1883 when he was eighteen years of age. Walter had departed a few years before to study medicine in Dublin. Both boys were seemingly left by their parents to decide their own careers, though no doubt there was correspondence between Midleton and Simla on the subject, for their father's money was needed to pay for whatever form their education was next to take, and his approval would have been required whatever course they chose. Rex had long been intended for the Army; his mother hoped for a commission in a cavalry regiment, one of the reasons for his attendance in Midleton's Army Class, but at this stage in his life he seems to have had second thoughts. Instead of going on with his Army entrance, he applied to join his brother as a medical student at the Royal College of Surgeons, and was accepted.[3]

Now followed a brief and happy interlude in the Dublin spring of 1883. It is not at all clear for how long he stuck at his medical studies, and in truth he seems to have enjoyed the city rather than devoting much time to his work. The Royal College stood right in the centre of Dublin, its imposing colonnade and portico dominating the corner of Stephen's Green and York Street. Many of its students were accommodated in the college. At the time, the Royal College was undergoing a period of reform and improvement under its capable Resident Surgeon, Thomas Myles. New subjects were being introduced, new exams instituted, and change was in the air. A new royal charter was granted to reflect all these improvements in the year Rex arrived. The college was becoming a seriously professional institution, and the pressure upon its students was increasing as it did so.

Despite the difficulties of his studies, and the clouds which continued to hang over Irish politics (two British governments fell over the Irish question during this brief period, and Fenian agitation continued to rack the countryside around the city and beyond), Rex's life was pleasant enough. He was young and healthy, for the first time in his life the delights of a cultivated city were open to him, and he was again in the company of his brother Walter, the only person he was close to, and so probably the cause of his decision to study in Dublin. They swam together often, on one occasion accomplishing the remarkable feat of a seven mile swim off the coast to Black Rock and back. Rex played chess with his fellow students and took up boxing, becoming proficient in a sport for which he was later to become noted and which would stand him in good stead in the Army. There is nothing to tell us whether he had any female company in the student life he was enjoying. The college at that date was a male preserve, but he would have met sisters of friends, and perhaps the daughters of his professors to drink tea with and dance with at parties. He was now of an age when it would have been quite natural to seek out his first experiences of sex. Dublin was notoriously well provided with brothels, and Rex was a member of a body of medical students which was notorious for frequenting them.

The first few months at the College of Surgeons were enough to persuade Rex that he would be better off following his mother's original plan, and he resolved to abandon his studies, giving as his reason the fact that he was sickened by the dissecting rooms. He therefore crossed the Irish Sea to England, in the second half of 1883, to enrol in London with a crammer named Ashton who was a well-known tutor for the Army Entrance Examination. The use of such a tutor was then commonplace: two years later, the Governor of the Military College at Sandhurst noted that 79 per cent of his cadets had passed their entrance exams with the help of a crammer; and as late as 1891 the figure was reportedly still as high as 50 per cent. Many crammers were retired Army officers, and they fulfilled a real need, for the entrance exam was stiff and the competition for places at Sandhurst fierce, only the top 25 per cent of applicants passing the exam. It was administered by the Civil Service Commission in London and was a heavily academic affair. It was divided into three classes. Class I, which was obligatory, included mathematics, arithmetic, algebra, Euclid, plane trigonometry, Latin, French or German and English history. Class II, from which candidates chose two subjects, included higher mathematics, German or French, Greek, English composition, chemistry, physics, physical geography and geology. Class III, which was obligatory, included freehand and geometrical drawing. The part of the Army for which a successful candidate found himself eligible depended on the result of the examination and a candidate needed high marks to enter Sandhurst on the infantry list. Rex sat for the exam in the autumn of 1883, intending to enter Sandhurst at the start of the next year, but fell ill with pleurisy on the eve of his examination. He was forced to resit the following spring, which must have en-tailed a good deal of waiting around in lodgings in London, all at his father's expense. He passed at the second attempt, and at a high enough level to allow him to join the infantry, gaining a place at Sandhurst for the September of 1884. This was a real achievement. In comparison, Winston Churchill, who tried for Sandhurst only a few years later, passed the exam below the level to gain a place on the infantry list, and made it later only as another candidate dropped out. If Rex had not been able enough to make the grade as a surgeon, it seemed he had a good future as an Army officer.[4]

Dyer's entry to Sandhurst and the inception of the career in which he was to spend most of his life are recorded in the college's Gentleman Cadet Register, which states that he was 5 feet 10 inches tall and aged nineteen years, nine months (this last slightly erroneously, as he was in reality one or two months older than that). As with all three of the educational establishments which he had attended, Dyer found the Royal Military College Sandhurst (which was known as the RMC to distinguish it from the RMA, the Royal Military Academy at Woolwich, which trained artillery and engineer officers) undergoing a development and reform typical of the times. The RMC had been training young officers at its site in Camberley since 1812, but it had a mixed record in its early years, and its irregular teaching, general lack of professionalism and lax discipline, so lax on occasion that there were outbreaks of disorder amongst its cadets, made it a target of the Army reforms introduced in the early 1870s by Edward Cardwell, Gladstone's Secretary of State for War. Cardwell reformed Sandhurst's establishment, replacing the cadets who had hitherto been its students with officers who had already been commissioned, and instituting a one year course of three terms, with two entries, one in February and one in September. Cardwell altered the syllabus, and instituted a final exam which a student had to pass in order to gain a commission. Thereafter, the place a student obtained in this exam fixed the date from which his commission was reckoned, an antedate of seniority being awarded for the top three grades. As this meant more pay and faster progress, it was a real incentive to do well.

The syllabus was fixed at this time with six sections: Queen's Regulations (which governed most areas of military activity in peace or war); regimental interior economy (administration and logistics), accounts and correspondence; military law; elements of tactics, field fortifications and elements of permanent fortifications; military topography and reconnaissance; and riding. A new wing was built at the college to house more students, the numbers of whom almost doubled. Cardwell's reforms did not prove a complete success, and some had been unpicked as early as 1879, when the rank of officer cadet abolished by Cardwell was reintroduced. Training at the RMC was further disrupted by the war then raging in Egypt and the Sudan, which between the years 1882 and 1885 drew in an ever-increasing number of troops and demanded more officers than could be trained. This was an emergency, and in the year before Dyer's arrival the course had to be shortened so that many cadets passed out after only six months' training. All of this threw both the syllabus and the systems of instruction into a confusion which, when Dyer arrived, had yet to be sorted out. It is unlikely, though, that he or his fellow cadets perceived much amiss; to them the military life was new, and its mysteries would have been made deliberately impenetrable by the college instructors, then as now adept at covering up for anything tending to chaos by loyalty, bluff or just plain military bull.

Dyer and his fellow cadets, of whom there were about 295 at the time (a number that increased slightly to 305 in the following year), and of whom half were on the same course as he was, had little time left to them to see through any cracks in the college's polished edifice. Their routine was a punishing one. Reveille was at 6.30 a.m., with the first period of study from 7 to 8 o'clock. Breakfast then followed, with sick parades before the college surgeon at 8.30. A parade from 9 to 10 o'clock, including occasional riding, preceded three periods of study up to 2.00 p.m., when the cadets ate a rapid lunch before setting off for an afternoon of drill and two classes of riding. This was taken very seriously at the college, though in Dyer's time the horses ridden by cadets were borrowed from local regiments and so were unlikely to have been the best mounts. Gymnastics followed at 4 o'clock, then sword exercises from 6 to 7 p.m. and dinner in the Mess at 8 o'clock. The library, financed by cadet subscriptions, was open for reading in the evening. Roll call was at 10 p.m., and the gaslights with which the college had by then been fitted were turned off an hour later. Sleep came quickly after such a day.

The cadets were divided into divisions when Dyer arrived at Sandhurst, and instruction was carried out by divisional officers, assisted by drill sergeants borrowed from the nearby garrison at Aldershot. At some point in Dyer's time, or just after it, the divisions were replaced by six companies, lettered A to F, each numbering about sixty cadets. The best cadets were promoted to the rank of under-officer and allowed to exercise discipline over their fellows. Everything at the college was designed to be highly competitive; in addition to competition for promotion and for a good place in the final examination, cadets competed for a sword which was presented on the passing out parade held at the end of each course, either the Anson Sword, presented in December, or the General Proficiency Sword, presented in August. Some of Dyer's contemporaries were formidable competitors: the cadet who was one day to become General Lord Rawlinson of Trent, and who was to be Commander-in-Chief in India just after Rex retired, passed out of Sandhurst in 1884. Douglas Haig, the future Field-Marshal and Earl, won the Anson Sword in December 1884. Rex would have at least seen the latter, though whether he knew him then we have no idea; there is no record of any friendship Rex made in his year at the RMC.

Rex did not win a prize at the end of his course, and there is little record of how he did in his studies, other than the Gentleman Cadet Register, which records that his conduct deteriorated from 'good' at the end of his first term in December 1884 to 'indifferent' by July 1885. He had, at some point, blotted his copybook. His final report mentioned sparingly that he had 'proficiency in Military Law and Tactics'. Some of Dyer's training was in the classroom, but much of it took place in the open air, on the heaths of the extensive training area known as Barossa attached to the college and in the grounds of its park. Tactical and field engineering training were taught, which gradually grew more advanced over the year, so that by its end he and his fellow cadets were able to form a battalion defensive square, assault an enemy position in company and battalion formation, bridge chasms and watercourses and build fortifications, from the parapets of which they practised fending off the mock attacks of their exercise 'enemies'.

Into this hectic schedule was inserted as much sport there was time for. Sandhurst was in the forefront of the great explosion of physical recreation which took place in the late Victorian era, for the Army viewed sport as a means to make its officers fit whilst fostering their leadership skills and testing their courage. Within the RMC much time and effort was expended in competitions, and the divisions and companies vied for many sporting cups and shields. Though at the time there were still only limited sports facilities at the College, Dyer, who was already something of a sportsman from his days at Midleton, was able to indulge his inclinations to the full. Recreational activities for the summer term included the annual sports meeting in May, with tug of war, cross country running and athletics. There were racquets and lawn tennis in the summer months, and all year round cadets could take part in boxing, fencing and sabres. Hockey, which was later to be one of Dyer's favourite sports, was not played while he was a cadet, but cricket was, and there was an annual fixture against the RMA at Lords. There was also an annual rugby match against the RMA, this time at the Oval.

In Dyer's day, shooting was treated as an optional recreational activity. The War Office did not believe it necessary for its officers to be taught to shoot, and allowed each cadet only twenty rounds for target practice for the year; there was not even an official rifle range at the college. The Martini Henry Rifles with which the cadets were armed were used almost exclusively for drill. A Rifle Club had been started at the RMC only some three years before Rex arrived, by the brother of the Kitchener then making his name in Egypt. Cadets had to pay a 10 shilling subscription for their ammunition. There was also a pistol club; more relevant, perhaps, as the revolver was the cadets' future side arm. Both clubs were very popular and almost all cadets were members. Fewer played polo, which was open to cadets rich enough to afford the sport, but many attended the gymkhanas and point to point races organised by the club. The sport was drawing many cadets into debt whilst Dyer was there, and it was banned eight years after he left.

Dyer and his fellows were dressed in a uniform of simple blue patrols with a soft, peaked cap, but for parades they also had a smarter red tunic, with white belts and a dark blue helmet. After the Cardwell reforms Sandhurst had been equipped to house officers rather than cadets, so when the latter were reinstituted they found the accommodation in the college unusually comfortable. Cadets now had carpets and rugs in their rooms, and enjoyed easy chairs and card tables in the anterooms where they could relax, read the papers and drink tea. It would have been quite a change from school and medical college.

Sandhurst was then, as now, a grand place in which to live and train. The college's famous front steps swept down beneath its colonnaded portico and opened out onto the vast platform of the parade ground. Surrounding the college building, gleaming white between the trees, was an extensive wooded park, through which a small stream ran into a large ornamental lake frequented by swans and geese. The college grounds were very beautiful to walk or ride in, and provided great stretches of open country, with grassy paths under the oaks and chestnuts of the park and amidst the rougher bracken on the open heathland of

Barossa, where sluggish streams and marshy bottoms criss-crossed long rides cut through birch wood and pine.

The impressiveness of the surroundings was mirrored by the formal ceremonial of drill and duties which took up much of the cadets' time, and by the elaborate pomp of the passing out parades and inspections which saw members of the royal family or field-marshals, generals and foreign dignitaries inspecting the college and presenting prizes. The Duke of Cambridge, still Commander-in-Chief of the British Army, paid his last visit to Sandhurst in Dyer's year. The Duke had visited almost annually since he had been appointed Commander-in-Chief, and took a keen interest in its affairs. On his last 'Duke's Day', as his visits were known, he watched the cadets performing tactical and physical exercises around the college, then, flanked by the college Governor, General Taylor, and the Commandant and Secretary, Colonel Flood, he addressed the cadets drawn up in a square around him, with the college staff and the wives standing behind. To the Duke, the Army was his family, and this was an occasion in which Rex would have been as caught up as the rest, one of the earliest exposures he had to the restrained emotion which was thereafter to imbue his life.

'Family' was the hallmark of the officer corps at this time, and Dyer met for the first time at Sandhurst a world of which so far he had only peripheral knowledge, the world of the British upper classes and of its officer caste. General Taylor noted in the year after Dyer left the college that of his three hundred and nine cadets, one hundred and forty were sons of Army officers. Not all cadets had rich fathers – forty-three were orphans, known as Queen's Cadets, studying at the college with reduced fees – but the backgrounds of most of the cadets were as affluent as Dyer's, and their education was generally at schools of better repute than his. In 1891, the RMC magazine was to publish a breakdown of the educational background and parentage of the cadets of that year. Only thirty-four of them were university graduates, but two hundred and seventy had attended public schools, sixty-four had studied at private schools and five had private tutors. Eton, Harrow, Rugby, Charterhouse and Westminster alone accounted for seventy-three cadets, and the newer establishments of Chelten-ham, Marlborough, Rossall, Radley, Wellington, Haileybury, Clifton, Malvern and Westward Ho! accounted for another one hundred and thirteen. Cadets with officer fathers predominated, with one hundred and eighty six in this category. Other fathers included eight titled aristocrats and forty-five private gentlemen, thirty-three civil servants, twenty-nine clergymen and twenty-one lawyers. Only seventeen were described as being employed in any form of commercial activity, and of these three were described as shipowners, and so were probably very rich indeed. Dyer's year was no doubt very similar, so that socially he found himself an outsider, both because of his Indian origins and because of his father's profession of brewer. He was without the contacts that would have given him entry to smart London circles or to any country house set. It is likely that he spent what spare time he had within the college, with perhaps an infrequent trip up to town by train.

If Dyer felt at a disadvantage at Sandhurst, he would have been bolstered by its training, which took as its aim the creation of an elite that was confident in its superiority, and whose rigid code of behaviour was designed to separate it from the civilian society which it existed to serve. Cadets were prepared for a life of physical hardship compensated by social privilege. With the toughness of their training went the inculcation of a mystique which set them apart, not only from the soldiers they were destined to command but from the entire civilian world from which the military deliberately fenced itself off. The cadets trained at Sandhurst were sent out into the Empire as the chivalric soldiers of a sacred mission, the spreading and maintenance of the blessings of British civilisation around the globe. Whatever their abilities, the officers of the *Pax Britannica* left Sandhurst sure that they were morally and technically superior to anything they would meet. This was an ethos to which Rex must have taken very readily, brought up as he had been in exactly those beliefs in India. After the unsettling days in Ireland, it must have been a great relief to him to be back in a society which believed in its invincible, God-given right to its position and to the exercise of its power. In this, at least, he must have felt completely at home.[5]

Dyer passed off the square in August 1885 and was commissioned into the 2nd Battalion of the Queen's (Royal West Surrey) Regiment. It is likely from what we know of his earlier mind that he had long intended to join the Indian Army, but to do this, according to the custom which pertained at the time, he had first to spend a couple of years in a British regiment. The 2nd Battalion of the Queen's was in India, suitably stationed at Fort William in Calcutta to provide Dyer with the apprenticeship from which he could make an eventual transfer to the Indian Army. Dyer had no personal link with the Queen's Regiment, having neither forebear nor relative in its officer ranks, nor was he, as were many of its officers, from Surrey or any of that county's schools. The Queen's was a proud and prestigious corps, the 2nd of Foot in the old numbering which Cardwell had recently replaced with the county title. The fact that Dyer was accepted by them shows that he had passed out well from Sandhurst and that he was reckoned as a man of some promise. It was a good start to his career, and one with which he could well have been very content.[6]

BURMA

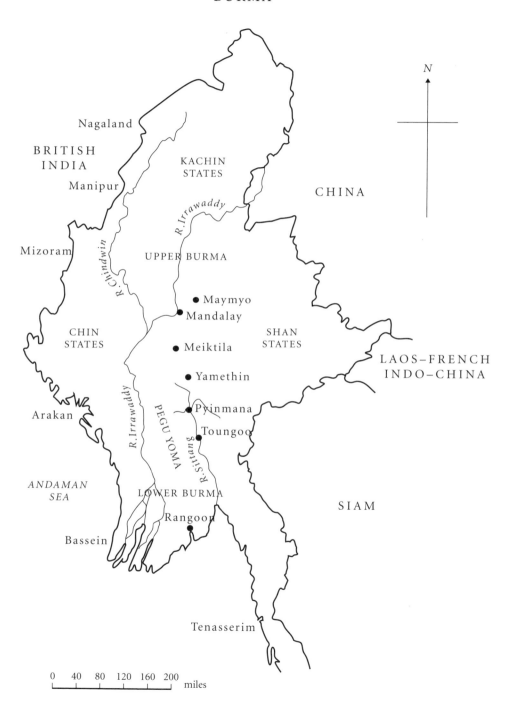

Nagaland

BRITISH
INDIA

Manipur

Mizoram

Arakan

*ANDAMAN
SEA*

Bassein

KACHIN
STATES

CHINA

R.Irrawaddy

R.Chindwin

UPPER BURMA

● Maymyo
● Mandalay

CHIN
STATES

● Meiktila

SHAN
STATES

● Yamethin

R.Irrawaddy

PEGU YOMA

● Pyinmana
● Toungoo

R.Sittang

LAOS–FRENCH
INDO–CHINA

LOWER BURMA

● Rangoon

SIAM

Tenasserim

N

```
 0   40  80  120 160 200
|—|—|—|—|—|—|  miles
```

3

Ireland and Burma

Cardwell's reforms, which had shaped Dyer's life at Sandhurst, gave each infantry regiment two battalions, one of which was posted overseas to garrison the Empire, one of which remained at home. The home battalion's was the less glamorous role, but was ideal for a young officer to learn the basics of his profession before meeting the greater tests he would find overseas. The 1st Battalion of the Queen's was at that time in Ireland, and so it was to the country where he had grown up that Rex now found himself posted. His battalion was based in Cork, where it had already been stationed for a year, only twelve miles from where he had been at school. Once again he took the Cork ferry, and once again he was met upon the quayside, this time by his battalion's transport. His return to Ireland must have occasioned some very mixed feelings.[1]

There was much to absorb in his first days in the battalion. He needed to learn fast the names and characters of his brother officers and of his men, and in particular of those of whom he needed to be careful (the twin figures of his OC, the Officer Commanding his company and his old-sweat Company Sergeant Major would have figured large here) and which to avoid entirely if he could (the CO, the battalion's Commanding Officer, his Adjutant and the Regimental Sergeant Major, any summons to whose offices in Battalion Headquarters all newly joined subalterns dreaded). He had to get to know the composition of the different companies and departments, where they were housed in the barracks and what they did. He had to acquire, rapidly if his life was to be tolerable, the customs of the Mess in which he lived and dined, and all the other rules and standing orders by which the 1st Battalion governed its life. For all but the exceptionally quick-witted, which, from what we know of Dyer he was not, there were sufficient pitfalls in this learning process to keep a young officer in hot water and extra duty punishments for many months. His arrival gave, as it always did, his fellow officers the opportunity to have some fun at his expense, not least in the rituals of his first night at dinner in the Mess, which invariably called for an initiate to make a fool of himself, and just as invariably involved the intake of a large amount of alcohol. That Dyer was not overtly clever, in fact was rather shy, but that he was something of a sportsman would have eased his passage into this new life. His boxing skills were particularly useful here, and he taught at least one of his fellow subalterns to box, a man his senior by some five years, named

Charles Monro. The two were to meet in less happy circumstances some thirty-five years later when Monro had reached the pinnacle of Commander-in-Chief in India.

Dyer had little authority at first, but gradually, as he learned his profession, more trust was given him and he received a steadily growing number of assignments to command small groups of soldiers, probably including those in the outstation the battalion manned on Spike Island off the Irish coast. By the following year, when the battalion entrained for a new station in Dublin, Dyer had begun to make his way. He was lucky that he had time to settle in before he met with in any serious soldiering. Operations in aid of the civil power were never long in coming in Ireland, and it was only in June 1886, a few months after the Queen's arrived in Dublin, that rioting erupted in Belfast and nearly three hundred men of the battalion were rushed there to help keep the peace.[2]

The cause of the outbreak was Gladstone's first Home Rule Bill, which had been introduced into Parliament earlier that year, and the failure of which was to lead to the fall of the Government later that month. Pre-empting the result of the vote in the Commons, Protestant Unionists in Belfast's Harland and Wolff shipyard attacked their fellow Roman Catholic workers and then went on the rampage across the city in violent protest against Home Rule. Violence was to go on until September in what was to become the worst outbreak of rioting in Ireland in the nineteenth century. Belfast suffered many deaths and huge damage. Three thousand Catholics were evicted from their employment, and twenty-eight of their public houses were burned down by Protestant mobs; in retaliation, the Catholics managed to burn only two. The authorities found the prosecution of Protestant rioters impossible, as juries composed largely of their coreligionists returned a series of not-guilty verdicts. This, with the pressure on the police on the streets, led to the breakdown of law and order. The Chief Secretary, John Morley, reinforced Belfast with police from Dublin; the Protestants christened them 'Morley's Murderers' and made sure that matters were soon beyond their capacity to control. The anniversary of the Battle of the Boyne caused pitched fighting, and three policemen were killed. Morley sent in troops, which included the first detachment of the Queen's, but their numbers were insufficient to make much difference to the situation, and they found themselves in the painful position of being fired on by Protestant gunmen. The election which followed the fall of Gladstone's administration resulted in the Conservatives taking power, and after the arrival in Dublin in August of the new Conservative Chief Secretary, Sir Michael Hicks Beach, the forces of law and order began to get the upper hand. He reinforced the Belfast garrison, gave the soldiers a freer hand, and banned all meetings. He was cordially hated by the Protestants, who dubbed him 'Black Michael', but by September the troubles were over.

Dyer arrived in Belfast in the middle of this chaos, either with the first party his battalion sent there in June or with the reinforcements that were dispatched on 8 August, just in time for the second major outbreak of fighting in the city. The battalion patrolled the streets, protecting the Catholic population and dispersing crowds on both sides. It was an unpleasant, confusing campaign for a young officer, involved in attempting to suppress, and being violently resisted by, Protestants who were seeking to maintain their links with Britain and the Empire, people whose loyalties were very similar to his own. Dyer and his colleagues found themselves protecting those whose sympathies lay with the Home Rulers they doubtless deprecated and despised. The task they were called on to perform on the streets of Belfast was a hard one, both physically wearing and mentally taxing. Small patrols of ill-equipped infantry patrolled squalid, debris-strewn streets and mounted guard at flash points in troubled areas. Bottles, stones, brickbats and on occasion bullets flew from both sides at the troops sandwiched between them. The battalion lost a soldier killed by a revolver bullet in one of these attacks.

Peace was, however, eventually restored, and a month or so later Dyer was posted to the Queen's 2nd Battalion, which had just had orders to deploy to Burma from its station in Fort William, Calcutta. His period of regimental apprentice-ship over, and blooded in Belfast, Dyer now put Ireland behind him forever. He would not forget the scenes of his first active operations. From Ireland he drew a stark warning of the chaos that civil weakness could let slip. He would remember these lessons when his own society in India was faced with similar turmoil and what he thought was a similar threat.

On 6 October 1886 Dyer sailed for Burma. The voyage to the East was a long one, taking over a month. This was his first return to India since he had come to Ireland half his life time before, and the excitement of going back to his own world was increased by his knowledge that this time he was on his way to take part in a war. This was the Third Burma War, which had broken out in its second and most bitter phase whilst Dyer was on the streets of Belfast. It was to be a campaign of a totally different sort from what he had experienced so far, imperialism at its flood, half a world and what must have seemed a whole era away from the imperial ebb that he had lived through in Ireland. Dyer's ship reached Calcutta on 2 November, and there he transshipped to another vessel which, by the 27th of the month, brought him to Rangoon.[3]

The Third Burma War was the last major act of imperial expansion under-taken by the British Government of India, the culmination of over a century of adding vast swathes of territory to the Raj. The campaign had been mounted the year before by the Viceroy, Lord Dufferin, to absorb the remaining third of a Burmese state which had been gradually losing its territory to the British since the days when Dyer's grandfather had sailed the waters off its coasts. The British

already held Lower Burma with its capital at Rangoon and Tenasserim to its
south, but inland at Mandalay in Upper Burma King Thibaw still ruled. Buddhist,
cruel, corrupt and independent, in all reality Thibaw was of little threat to the
British, who had, though, a lively fear of the growing influence of the French,
who had established themselves close by in Indo-China and who were whispering
words of a protectorate in Thibaw's ears. Burma was India's immediate eastern
neighbour, and the Government in Calcutta was determined to pre-empt the
appearance of French power on India's borders. In this it was supported by the
Conservative Government in London. Lord Randolph Churchill was at the India
Office, a driving force behind extending British power, and his imperial ambitions were egged on by British commercial interests in Rangoon. Stories of King
Thibaw's violence and degeneracy (he had massacred most of his family on his
accession), and petty quarrels over the logging rights of the Bombay-Burma
Trading Corporation, gave the British an excuse to present the Burmese with an
ultimatum which was tantamount to the removal of their independence. They
rejected this, and in October 1885 a British force of ten thousand men under
General Prendergast sailed up the Irrawaddy river and within ten days swept
away the Burmese feudal levies who opposed them. Thibaw and his family were
packed off to exile, leaving an immediate vacuum in authority across the country
which the British had not prepared themselves to fill. There had been no real
post-war plan. The soldiers of the Burmese army, still in possession of their arms,
slipped into the jungle, and claimants to the throne began to emerge all over
Burma to lead them. Some of these were of genuine royal blood, some were old
royal officials or priests, and others were *dacoit* chiefs who had for long time past
ravaged the hinterland untroubled by Burma's ineffectual kings. The loss of their
own king, the abolition of the traditional organs of government, and the heavy-
handed behaviour of the British in Mandalay all combined to create a patriotic
reaction, and by the time the British officially annexed the country in January
1886, the second, far more difficult, phase of resistance was upon them.[4]

The situation was exacerbated in the first few months of the annexation by
the drastic measures the British took against their Burmese opponents, all of
whom they insisted on denigrating as *dacoits*. Any caught with weapons were
shot out of hand. Punishment was exacted from any village that was the site of
guerilla attacks or that was suspected of harbouring Burmese resistance. Kipling's
poem 'The Grave of the Hundred Head', which he based on a British raid upon
the village of Pabengmay in Bassein District of Lower Burma, gives the flavour
of this time. A young British subaltern has been shot by a sniper there, and his
men wreak retaliation:

Long was the morn of slaughter,
Long was the list of slain,
Five score heads were taken,
Five score heads and twain;
And the men of the First Shikaris
Went back to their grave again,

Each man bearing a basket
Red as his palms that day,
Red as the blazing village –
The village of Pabengmay.
And the '*drip-drip-drip*' from the baskets
Reddened the grass by the way.[5]

The dead in Pabengmay had included women and children. Grattan Geary, the editor of the *Bombay Gazette*, who was in Burma at the time, reported that villages were shelled from the rivers by naval launches, and that at one village twelve men were executed one by one to terrify the other villagers. Those killed were decapitated, and their heads exhibited on stakes. Floggings were common in Mandalay, and the Provost Marshal, Colonel Hooper, carried out executions by firing squad. On one occasion, in order to extract a confession, Hooper had a man named Nga Neing tied to a stake and placed in a pile of dead Burmese. While the firing squad was readied in front of the man, Hooper set up his personal camera on a tripod, and only when he had carefully arranged his lens and plate did he give the order to fire, a deed which earned him the name in Mandalay of 'The Ogre with the Camera'. Despite protests in the London press, Hooper was not punished. General Prendergast only belatedly realised the counter-productive effect of these atrocities and issued orders to stop them, too late to prevent himself being relieved of command. His successor, Major-General Sir George White, who had served under Prendergast, wrote to his wife, 'I am the one man opposed to the system and made a stand against the wholesale executions the moment I took command'. But it was too late by then to prevent the bitterness and the more determined resistance that was its fruit. From the Burmese point of view, despite the end of arbitrary shootings, little changed, as the new policy merely substituted a quick summary trial, by whichever official was on the spot, followed by execution with a rope, for a swifter death by firing squad. It was to be many months, years in places, before the apparatus of the law could be extended into the depths of the jungle and the hills.[6]

As a result of this, almost half the Burmese aristocracy had taken the field against the British by the middle of 1886, and almost every village family had a member under arms in the jungle. British forces proved too few to fight the type of suppressive campaign that was now required, and large reinforcements had to be brought from India. General White wrote to his wife in April: 'I have been quite taken aback by the energy developed by the organization against us in the country … The outposts have been attacked everywhere, and there has been one continued cry for reinforcements.' On 15 May he wrote again 'the resistance to our authority is much more persistent than I had anticipated … The men are breaking down very fast.' By the summer it was clear that the cheap conquest originally envisaged was slipping through British fingers. By then there were 17,022 troops scattered around Upper Burma in forty-three posts, and 7162 more in Lower Burma, and these were proving far from sufficient to hold the country down. The British lost control of almost all the territory between the centres of population, and in these they held on by the skin of their teeth. The Burmese raided into the cities at night, and burned down large parts of them, not a difficult feat as they consisted for the most part of closely-packed wooden buildings. As reinforcements arrived, the British spread out into the provinces, garrisoning the major towns and establishing small, mutually supporting stockades on the routes between them, which were mostly along the rivers. Their initial plan was to work up the main river systems, principally the Irrawaddy and the Chindwin, and gradually to gain control of the country along their banks. Static posts were supplemented by river patrols using large flotillas of steamers. Throughout the summer there were daily skirmishes around many of these posts, and the deteriorating situation frightened the Government in Calcutta, causing it to send out one of the most senior officers in India to take over, the Commander-in-Chief of the Army of the Madras Presidency, Lieutenant-General Sir Herbert Macpherson. Almost immediately after his arrival, on 2 October, he died of malaria, and General White was left to carry on as before. By late 1886, the two brigades operating in the country had increased to three, and the 3rd Brigade, commanded by Brigadier-General Lockhart, was set up at Nyingan, later renamed Pyinmana, on the Sittang river north of Toungoo, about one hundred and fifty miles south of Mandalay.[7] Pyinmana was strategically sited on the only land route to the capital from the coast at Rangoon. It was here that 2nd Queen's were posted in November 1886.[8]

Dyer joined them shortly afterwards, travelling up from Rangoon for twelve hours on a slow, rickety train to the railhead at Toungoo, then another fifty miles by boat up the Sittang to the jetty at Sinthawa, from where the final short leg was by road to Pyinmana. He found his battalion stationed alongside Brigade Headquarters and reported there to his new Commanding Officer, Lieutenant-Colonel William Holt. The battalion was at that stage spread out in outposts of company-size and smaller along the river and in the more important local villages on its banks. The Sittang was massive at this point, half a mile wide in places, flowing south through the jungle between the Pegu Yoma hills to the west, and the Shan hills to the east. The Queen's area was a principal focus of Burmese resistance in what was considered the most lawless and difficult tract in Upper Burma.[9]

The Burmese in the area, who had been led by the Myinzaing Prince until he had died a few months before, and were now led by a royalist official, Maung Gyi, and a Buddhist monk, U Paung, harried the British hard. There were other Burmese leaders active in the regiment's area. A self-styled member of the royal family known as the Kyimyindaing Prince was leading resistance around Toungoo. Three local royal officials had not abandoned their posts but had taken up arms: the Laywun, or Le Wun, who had been the Burmese Governor of Yamethin, was in the field at Kinywa in the east; the Thanegon Thugyi, or Theingon, who had also been a Government officer at Yamethin, dominated Chinzu in the south west; and Myat Hmon, also known as Hmyat Maung, operated around Wundwin. Also in the area were two old *dacoit bos*, Budda Yaza and Thiya Yaza, who had taken advantage of the breakdown of order to stake political claims, and who boldly raided around the Brigade Headquarters at Pyinmana itself. The bands they led consisted of old royal retainers, soldiers from the Burmese army, civilians who had fled from town and village, and fighting Buddhist monks, the *pongyi bos*. The district was in turmoil and the British hold on Pyinmana was far from secure. The town had been occupied since November of 1885 but in the year since then the British had only managed to occupy a few of the surrounding villages. There had been a serious rising in the town in June 1886, which had been suppressed with difficulty, and the town remained in effect under a state of semi-permanent siege. The countryside was very difficult to control: in the north there was open country, which required mounted troops, of which the British had none at that stage to deploy, but the rest was dense jungle. Across the whole area there was no real civil administration. The inhabitants saw few British troops and no Government servants. They feared the impermanence of the new regime, and preferred to pay their taxes to the old officials or to the *dacoits* rather than to the British. At best they stayed aloof from the struggle; more often than not they actively aided the resistance with food and information.[10]

The 2nd Battalion's posting to Pyinmana had just preceded the visit to Burma of the Commander-in-Chief, India, General Sir Frederick Roberts, who at the time held authority over all three Indian Presidency armies, and who arrived in Mandalay with the Viceroy, Lord Dufferin. Roberts found the situation serious enough to stay on after the Viceroy went back to India, and to take personal command of operations until February of the following year.[11] His energy and careful planning had a remarkable effect and in the few months in which he was present the back of the Burmese resistance was broken. Using his own authority, he was able to order a growing number of reinforcements from India, which increased the forces in Burma to 32,000. Troop numbers continued to rise.

By April 1888 the total of the military and police forces in Burma had reached 34,712.

Roberts masterminded a classic campaign of suppression. He introduced five battalions of paramilitary police recruited in the Punjab and on the North-West Frontier to take over policing functions and to hold small intermediate posts, releasing troops for operations. He increased the number of cavalry and mounted infantry units which were needed to pursue fleeing guerillas. He set his forces to operate first against the major Burmese resistance groups, patrolling in ever-widening circles spreading outwards from the occupied posts. He ensured that garrisons were strong enough that none were ever taken by the Burmese, and he ordered the jungle to be cleared for a hundred yards either side of the tracks to prevent ambushes. During the last part of 1886, his priority was the break up of the larger Burmese bands, and this was so successful that by 1887 he was able to turn his attention to the surviving smaller groups. Though there was hardly any open fighting, the relentless, sustained pursuit driven by Roberts ground down the resistance, removing its leaders, drying up its sources of recruits, and inexorably reducing Burmese strength.

The policies Roberts enforced were harsh. In his *Instructions for the Guidance of General and Other Officers Commanding Columns in Burma*, issued on 20 November 1886, he put his force on the offensive:

> When there is an enemy in arms against British rule, all arrangements must be made not only to drive him from his position, but also to surround the position so as to inflict the heaviest loss possible. Resistance overcome without inflicting punishment on the enemy only emboldens him to repeat the game, and thus, by protracting operations, costs more lives than a severe lesson promptly administered.

The enemy was to be surrounded before being attacked in order to create the greatest number of casualties. Judicial power was given to Army officers, who, unaccompanied by a civilian officer, had the power to award up to two years' imprisonment and thirty lashes. This was a real improvement on the summary execution that had been exercised before, and only three captured *bos* were executed after Roberts imposed his new policies, though many were imprisoned or exiled. Measures were also implemented to win the hearts and minds of the Burmese. Their religion and customs were respected, their chiefs and villager leaders honoured and given local authority, punitive measures were prohibited, the troops were forbidden to touch Burmese property, and an amnesty was offered to those willing to surrender. Those who did were often given appointments in the local administration, and these men were turned to bring their comrades to book. As the war dragged on, and as the size and capabilities of the groups resisting the British deteriorated, more and more Burmese found these measures persuasive. They began to lay down their arms, to pass information to the British, and eventually to kill surviving *dacoits* themselves. Yet it was to take a full five years before all organised resistance ceased.[12]

Dyer's battalion formed many of the flying columns sent out around Pyinmana to chase guerillas who had attacked outposts or villages, and to follow up information about their bases. At first, this information was hard to come by, as the villagers were rightly frightened of both sides: punished by the British if they aided the guerillas; punished by the Burmese if they did not. Theirs was an unenviable lot at this stage. The Burmese resistance levied taxes, food and all forms of logistic support from the villagers and extracted it forcibly if it was not offered. They dealt with informants harshly, and British columns, likened by the Burmese to buffalos lurching through elephant grass, would often arrive too late to catch the vanishing enemy. In their place they would find those suspected of betrayal crucified on stakes outside the village gates. Not surprisingly, the British found guides were difficult to get early in the campaign, and those dragooned into this role were liable to lose their ears or worse at the hands of their compatriots. Dyer saw all of this at first hand, and inevitably participated in the horrors of this war. He was soon given command of a detachment of men in an isolated post, and so was pitched straight into the effort to create local networks of informants. He took swiftly to this work and had a liking for it. This was to be the start of a great deal of work of this type in which he involved himself later in his career. It was an exciting game of bluff and bluster, calling for cunning and the exercise of a good deal of savvy. It was also a game which could make a name for the man who kept his head amongst the dangers and subterfuges with which it was cloaked. It appealed both to Rex's appetite for adventure as well as to his ambitious streak. He was lucky at so early a stage in his career in being in a theatre of war in which he was left much to his own devices – there were few campaigns in which so much initiative was left to the junior officers.[13] Roberts called it 'a subaltern's war'. This was something Dyer relished; it gave him a lifelong taste for acting on his own and for avoiding close supervision.

The Queens's regimental history gives the flavour of those days in the heat and the rotting, mildewed damp of the jungle:

> A rapid night march was usually made, the locality was surrounded at daybreak, and if the rebel chief was not killed or captured, he finally wearied of such a precarious existence and made his submission. Or if the Burman force was too strong to be dealt with in this manner, the concentric march of several columns always sufficed for its dispersion. Much hard marching by night through swampy, fever-haunted jungles, therefore fell to the lot of the troops, but there was little fighting; and the diseases inherent in the damp, marshy country were responsible for most of the casualties.[14]

On 12 November, the battalion attacked the camp of the Kyimyindaing Prince and took it. The Prince fled, abandoning his wife to be killed. He, like all the others of his kind, had conducted resistance according to Burmese custom, which tended to limit the effectiveness of the guerilla war he waged. The Burmese had great reverence for royal blood and the Buddhist religion, and even in the jungle, no matter to what level of destitution they had been reduced, they did their utmost to observe the protocol due to royal status, real or otherwise. All their bands fought under the national peacock banner of Burma:

> Court ceremonies were maintained in their bands; ministers were appointed; royal orders were issued, scratched in proper form on tapering palmyra leaves; proclamations were issued stamped with lion, rabbit or peacock seals; huts in which the leaders lived were called temporary palaces and the bands royal armies. If there was no gold or silver plate, they ate off plantain leaves, for royalty alone should eat off such a leaf.[15]

At the end of 1886, Burmese attacks in the north of the battalion area were still disrupting communications on the Yamethin road, and convoys sustained heavy losses. After one such attack, which had caused the death of a British lieutenant-colonel, the Queen's attacked the Burmese rifle pits overlooking the road at Kanha on 17 November. Their attack cleared the road, but another British officer lost his life in the process. Three days later, Rex's Commanding Officer took two hundred and eighty men on a thirty-two mile march through the jungle to the village of Posoundong. They accomplished this in only twenty-seven hours, surprising and killing a *dacoit* named Tha Haman along with his son and many of his men. The battalion received a reward of 1000 rupees for the action, and earned the Commanding Officer a recommendation for an award from his Brigadier, Lockhart: 'On all occasions he and his regiment have done admirably. His successful attack on Tha Man, in which that leader fell on 20 November 1886, struck a heavy blow at rebel gatherings in this district.'[16] Their first month in theatre was a very busy time for the Queen's. In another attack in November, the battalion assaulted a village stockade at Sekhungyi which was held by a *dacoit* called San Pe, routing the *bo* but losing nine men in the action. Again, near Toungbo, on 22 November a detachment under Captain Rose surprised *dacoits* who were attacking the village, and managed to kill four and capture eight of them.[17]

Buddha Yaza, who had been terrorising the district since King Thibaw's days, proved the battalion's most difficult opponent. He was attacked on 23 November by a column commanded by Major Beale, but he escaped into the jungle on an elephant, leaving part of his force commanded by his deputy, Bo Htum, to be captured whilst covering his flight. Kipling's 'The Ballad of Boh Da Thone' could almost have been written of Buddha Yaza:

He crucified noble, he scarified mean,
He filled old ladies with kerosene ...

And sooth, if pursuit in possession ends,
The Boh and his trackers were best of friends.

The word of a scout – a march by night –
A rush through the mist – a scattering fight –

A volley from cover – a corpse in the clearing –
A glimpse of a loin cloth and heavy jade earring –

The flare of a village – the tally of slain –
And ... the Boh was abroad on the raid again.[18]

On 5 December, 119 men of the Queen's forming part of a composite force attacked Nga Hamat at Yadan, destroying most of his band but narrowly missing the leader himself. By keeping up an incessant pressure of marching and attack, the battalion succeeded in clearing the entire eastern part of their district by 14 December. In the centre, around their Headquarters at Pyinmana, where troops had not yet been concentrated, operations had to continue over the Christmas, as columns carried on the pursuit of the elusive Buddha Yaza, forcing him to flee at last into the wilderness of the Pegu Yoma. The Kyimyindaing Prince was tracked down and killed on New Year's Day 1887, and this marked the end of that phase of the operations.

The battalion was then divided up, four hundred men remaining at Pyinmana and two hundred marching north to Yamethin on the Sinthe river, further up the route to the capital. It was many days' march away, and they found some opposition in the town after they had occupied it; they repulsed an attack there on 18 February. A company of the Queen's marched through the jungle north west to a small town named Hlaingdet, near Meiktila on the Samon river, whilst another company went west to Yendaw. All this stretched the battalion across over a hundred miles of jungle, scrub and river, making command difficult and necessitating the delegation of local responsibility to commanders on the spot. The battalion's dispersion meant that the area under British control was gradually extended westwards. The land around Hlawbone and Meiktila was cleared and garrisoned by 1 February, and by that stage only the Bo San Pe was left with any following in the district. In March, operations reached for the first time as far as the boundaries of the battalion's area of responsibility; Major Ilderton with a column of two companies formed the right-hand column of a neighbouring brigade's assault on Hmaw-aing in a pincer movement aimed to encircle the Burmese there. This small but gruelling campaign lasted until May and ended with the death of the *bo* Tok Gyaw. Major Ilderton and his two companies moved on from there to attack and destroyed Myat Hmon's group at Wundwin on 2 May. Surrenders of principal *bos* then began to accelerate, and the elusive San Pe was killed that month.[19]

By now disease and debilitation, caused by the ever-present humidity, heat and leeches, were proving more of an enemy than the Burmese. The British lost more casualties through the campaign to ill health than to enemy action. In the year before Dyer's time in Burma, from November 1885 to October 1886, ninety British troops were killed in action across the province, whilst 930 died of disease, and 2032 had to be invalided out of Burma due to ill health. The Queen's were as afflicted as any by this. By 1 February 1888, when they returned to Calcutta, their casualty totals were to reach seventy-one deaths through disease or accident, but only one man killed and seven wounded as a result of enemy action. On 14 December 1886, cholera broke out at Yamethin, and Lieutenant Shaw, a brother subaltern of Dyer, died of the disease. Dyer was at Yamethin at the time. Although he escaped the ravages of cholera, he became a casualty from another cause. Two weeks before the cholera outbreak, on 3 December, Dyer was riding behind a fellow subaltern named Fullerton, and both put their horses at a hedge. Fullerton fell, and was killed instantly when his head hit a tree stump. Dyer did little better, and as he fell his head hit the same stump, but he proved the luckier of the two and escaped with concussion. He had sufficiently recovered to take command soon after of a platoon in a small, isolated stockade at Taungnyo, north of Pyinmana and west of the Sinthe river. He remained there until March when the battalion received orders to move into the Shan hills to the east. Rex's small force marched in from Taungnyo and rejoined the battalion for its campaign.

By this time, the area was well on the way to pacification; Yamethin was almost free of resistance, though the area around Pyinmana was only brought under control by June. To facilitate the gradual spread of British power, roads were being built and the railway was being extended north. The battalion's attention could now be safely turned to the warlike Shan tribes who inhabited the hill tracts east of the Sittang river. These had never been more than feudatories of the Burmese Crown and were to all intents and purposes independent. The campaign against them was correspondingly sharp, for the tribes were fighting for a freedom they had long enjoyed. The columns had to press home attacks on stockades built on steep slopes in the cover of thick jungle. The paths approaching these were narrow and precipitous, easily blocked by tree trunks and branches, and reinforced with stakes and bristling thickets of thorn. From behind these and from the heights above, the Shan showered the advancing British with *jingal* balls, arrows and rocks. They were, however, neither strong enough nor well organised enough to offer any lengthy resistance, and by May, after incessant British attacks, many of them began to surrender, picked off one by one.

Operations continued in the hills throughout the year, and the last Shan tribe surrendered on 25 November 1887.

Dyer was not there to see this final success, having left Burma some months before, making his way back down the Sittang to Toungoo then on by steamer to Rangoon. He sailed for India on 12 August, ostensibly to go on leave, but actually to arrange his transfer to the Indian Army, a transfer he must have applied for some time before. He left Burma with his first campaign medal, and two clasps, and with a reputation for bravery and dash which was quite exceptional for a subaltern of his years, and which was to remain with him throughout his service.[20] Nine years later, in 1896, a fellow student told the Commandant of the Staff College: 'His reputation in India is that he does not know what fear means, and is happiest when crawling over a Burmese stockade with a revolver hanging from his teeth.'[21] He had done well in his first regiment and his career seemed one of promise.

His journey to India was, however, marred by an incident on the river steamer he took to Rangoon. On deck, in the oppressive heat which frayed tempers and made men murderous, his bearer got into a religious argument with the crew, who set upon him and began to beat him so severely it seemed they would kill him. Dyer was dozing in the cabin below, and awakened by the tumult he went to his man's aid, standing over his fallen body, and fending off his assailants with his fists. His skill as a boxer made him more than a match for the lighter Burmese, and he knocked out those who made the mistake of getting too close. The rest, including the captain, fled and took refuge in the poop and in the deckhouse from which they were reduced to begging abjectly for mercy. When they docked in Rangoon, the steamer's captain lodged a case for assault against Dyer in a civil court. The court referred the complaint to Army Headquarters.[22]

We do not possess the full details of the incident, and have no way of telling if this was a heroic action by Dyer in defence of the vulnerable victim of an attempted murder, and a native Burmese at that, or rather a brawl that got out of hand and led to his beating and intimidation of much of the crew. That Dyer may have gone too far in his action is an inference that might be drawn from the fact that Army Headquarters in Rangoon took note of the charge and sent it on to India behind him. It was ominous that as Dyer left Burma, and the British Regiment in which he had so notably started his Army service, a doubt had been entered on his record indicating an inability to prevent his temper turning to violence against native Indians.

THE NORTH-WEST FRONTIER

RUSSIAN
EMPIRE

WAKHAN

KAFIRISTAN

R. Kashgar

CHITRAL

GILGIT

Chitral

AFGHANISTAN

KOHISTAN

N

Chak Darra

YUSUFZAI

SWAT

Agror

BATAUR

R. Kunar

*Malakand
Pass*

*Black
Mountain*

Oghi

R. Kabul

MOHMAND

Amb

Abbotabad

Kabul

Jellalabad

Landi Kotal

Khyber Pass

Nowshera

HAZARA

Jamrud

Peshawar

Attock

Parachinar

AFRIDIS

KURRAM   TIRAH

Ghazni

ORAKZAIS

Kohat

Matun

Thal

Rawalpindi

Samana

Hangu

KHOST

Khatak

Tochi Pass

KOHAT

R. Indus

R. Jhelum

R. Chenab

Bannu

MAHSUD

BANNU

WAZIRISTAN

Goma Pass

R. Indus

PUNJAB

Chuarkei Pass

Dera Ismail
Khan

PATHAN TRIBES

R. Chenab

New Chaman

BALUCHISTAN

Quetta

Multan

R. Sutlej

*Bolan
Pass*

BALUCH TRIBES

Dera Ghazi
Khan

Sibi

Kalat

0   20   40   60   80   100   120
miles

BAHAWALPUR

4

The Black Mountain

Rex Dyer reached India in the late August of 1887 and went up to Simla. Reunited with his family for the first time in over twelve years, he found them even more prosperous than he had left them. His father had expanded his business empire, and had opened a new establishment at Rawalpindi in the Punjab, where his new brewery found a ready market in the huge garrison of the North-West Frontier. He was shortly to do the same in Mandalay, the occasion for his wife's disapproval of his method of lighting his cheroot. At about the time of Rex's return home, his father sold his two breweries at Solon and Simla to his rival, Meakin, so there was no longer a need to stay all year round in the hills. The family began to spend the winter months down on the plains in Lucknow, where they lived in one half of an old rajah's palace on the banks of the River Gumti. In the other half Edward Dyer installed a new distillery.[1]

There were fewer of the family at home now. Arthur was in England, where he had married a girl named Elise Robertson and settled down to produce what was to be a family of seven children. He took no part in the brewery and left his younger brother Edward to assist his father and eventually inherit the business. Probably by this time Edward had married Mary Irma Hogg, who was eventually to bear him six children. Walter was pursuing his medical career back in Britain; he was to be wedded to his profession and remained a bachelor throughout his life. Of Rex's sisters, only Mabel, the youngest, was never to marry, and so she at least was at home to greet Rex, but it is likely that the others were already gone. It was a considerably quieter place than the home he had left.[2]

Rex settled down for a brief time. He and his parents had pretty much to start anew, for the memories they had of each other were by then remote, and Rex had grown up from boyhood to manhood by the time he returned. He was still troubled by the inquiry into the affray onboard the Sittang steamer. General Headquarters required a report, and his father helped him write it. It was easy to submit this, as the Headquarters was still in Simla for the summer. Family legend had it that the report eventually reached the desk of Roberts, who was still Commander-in-Chief and had not long returned from Burma. Whether Roberts approved or not, the report was successful in ending the affair, and the inquiry was dropped. Rex now had the leisure to sit and pass the exam for the Higher Standard of Native Languages in Urdu, something he needed for his future career in the Indian Army. His application for transfer went through without a hitch, and he was granted a probationary commission as a lieutenant in the Bengal Staff Corps. This was the invariable procedure at the time. The Indian Army wished to assess its new officers in post, despite their having already completed a period of apprenticeship with a British regiment, and would only confirm an officer's commission after a year's service with Indian troops. An officer joining the Indian Army was not commissioned directly into a regiment but into one of the three armies – Bengal, Bombay and Madras – which had survived (at least in name) the evolution at the end of the Mutiny of the East India Company's three Presidencies. Rex's transfer did not please his mother, who had set her heart on a commission in a smart cavalry regiment, and had been prepared to promise Rex whatever it took from his father's purse to finance her dream. Rex was not tempted, and stood his ground, defying his mother, and very sensibly insisting that he remain in the infantry. He had seen enough of the Army to know that he was not cut out for the cavalry, where neither his temperament nor background would have suited the expensive and socially exclusive life its officers led. So when he received his first posting to the 39th Bengal Infantry, he set off happily to join them. When he arrived towards the end of 1887 at their station in Cawnpore, which was on the Ganges not far from Lucknow, he found that things were far from what he had hoped.[3]

The 39th were under a cloud. It was a regiment of a type common before the Mutiny, which it had survived only to find that it fitted uncomfortably in the Indian Army that was being reshaped. Its men were Hindus from around Aligarh, a town south east of Delhi in the plains of Oudh, and from which sprung the regiment's original name, the Aligarh Levy. The soldiers were of the sort who were gradually being weeded out of the three Indian Armies and replaced by men regarded in the fashion of the day as better soldiers, men from the 'martial castes' of the Punjab and the North-West Frontier. This was General Roberts's personal policy. 'The first step', he wrote when describing his assumption of command, 'was to substitute men of the more warlike and hardy races for the Hindustani sepoys of Bengal, the Tamils and Telegus of Madras and the so-called Mahrattas of Bombay.' 'No comparison,' he went on, 'can be made between the martial races of a regiment recruited amongst the Gurkhas of Nepal or the warlike races of northern India and of one recruited among the effeminate races of the south.'[4] Perhaps the men of the 39th had seen the writing on the wall, and morale had suffered. It cannot have been easy to serve in the face of such openly expressed contempt. Poor morale easily shows itself in ill-discipline, and the 39th showed both in spectacular fashion. At the recent Rawalpindi review, the Viceroy, Lord Dufferin, had taken the salute. As the regiments began to march past him, the skies opened up, but the parade carried on, and as the wheels and horses of the artillery were followed past the saluting dais by cavalry mounts and finally by elephants, the ground became a sticky morass of mud. The infantry, as is always their lot, marched past last. The British lost step but kept going, as did the Indian regiments who followed them, but the 39th had shoes, not boots, and many sepoys left the ranks to retrieve footwear which had become stuck in the mud. This was bad enough, but the crowning disgrace was committed by the Indian officer carrying the Queen's Colour, one of the regiment's two standards, which by custom are treated as almost sacred. As the regiment marched past, he was seen using the tip of the pole carrying the colour to extract his shoes from the mud. The regiment was placed under review, its commanding officer removed, and a veteran officer, Lieutenant-Colonel Edmund Pippon Ommanney, was posted in to see whether it could be saved.

The unit's state was sufficiently bad to receive special adverse comment from General Headquarters, India, in a letter to the Secretary of State. According to this, the regiment's musketry (its skill with firearms) and its overall general condition were bad, and the regiment was teetering on the brink of disbandment. It was inspected at Jhansi on 5 February 1888, just after Dyer joined it, and did not redeem itself. The inspecting officer, Brigadier-General Marter, commented that the native officers (that is the Indian officers; the term 'native' had been officially discarded three years before this, but old habits died hard in the Army, and the word continued in use for decades) were 'an indifferent set'. Marter concluded: 'The regiment is evidently in bad order. The native officers and non-commissioned officers are an inferior lot, but there are signs of improvement.' Even Colonel Ommanney did not emerge completely free of criticism. Something had happened to the regimental funds, leading Marter to add: 'It is unfortunate that the new commanding officer should now be in difficulties regarding the funds of the regiment; but this matter has not yet been investigated.' General Roberts had the last word: 'Most unsatisfactory. The musketry of the regiment is very bad', a particularly damning failing in his eyes. He still hoped for an improvement, but it was not to be. The following year, after Dyer had left the regiment, the Commander-in-Chief minuted: 'As at present composed, the regiment could not stand the test of service, and the retention of these men of low caste is a waste of money far exceeding their own pay.' In 1889 all ranks of the 39th were discharged the service and replaced by Garhwalis, soldiers considered to be of a martial caste and who were akin to the Gurkhas, their neighbours in the hills. The regiment was completely reformed.[5]

When Dyer joined them, the 39th were at Cawnpore, which was redolent of the Mutiny and the site of its most horrific event, the massacre of the British women and children collected in the Bibighar after the surrender of the British garrison. By Dyer's day there was a memorial there which had become a place of pilgrimage for the British, as was the room with its bloodstains around the hooks in the wall upon which the children were impaled and the well into which their bodies, many still living, had been thrown. Dyer must have visited the site whilst he was stationed nearby and it is probable that it affected him deeply. Throughout his life he displayed an extremely chivalric attitude to women, one in which he was far from alone in holding in India, but one which was growing steadily outdated back in England. Cawnpore was a place that he would not have forgotten. The regiment was about to depart for their new station at Jhansi, which was an isolated site in central India and one not yet reached by railway; the march there was to be part of the regiment's assessment for survival. Jhansi was another site vividly associated with the Mutiny, for its Rani had been one of the key opponents of the British and had gained the notoriety of an Indian Boadicea.

Dyer was not long at Cawnpore, for the regiment commenced its march on the long road to Jhansi just after he arrived. It was a journey of over a hundred miles and took them over a week, the column's progress tied to the slowest of the baggage train, so the stages were short and much time was spent in camps along the way. It was the cool season, so a pleasant one to be marching through India and living under canvas at night. Colonel Ommanney was almost at the end of his long service in India, and was accompanied on the march by his wife and two daughters, the elder named Frances Anne Trevor, Annie to her friends, and the younger Helen Violet, who was usually called Henrietta. The road and the campsite were ideal places for romance to blossom. The regiment's officers had few pressing responsibilities and were free to pay their attentions to the Ommanney girls. Helen was courted by a young officer named Edward Willoughby Richards, whom she was to marry in Simla the following year.[6] Rex set his cap at Annie, and the friendship they initiated on the march continued at Jhansi, where they began to spend much time in each other's company, wandering together in the countryside surrounding the camp. A hill overlooking the lines was their favourite haunt, and their visits there were so well known that for years it was known as Dyer's Hill. Perhaps it was there that Rex proposed and was accepted sometime in the new year of 1888. It had been a whirlwind romance, typical of Rex in its impetuosity, but also typical of him in its commitment, for he and Annie were to be inseparable for the next forty years. Annie was to stay by Rex's side through all the dusty stations of his career, and to endure with him the marches and expeditions in the jungle, and the discomfort and lack of privacy of camp life. Rex saw women as a sex to be reverenced; we can guess that he treated Annie with gentleness and consideration, but neither diaries nor letters between them have survived to tell us how they felt for each other. We have to read between the lines of what they went through together to see that they loved each other very much.

Annie's family had a record of distinguished service both at home and in India. Her surname was apt to mislead, for it was not the Irish name it was generally assumed to be but an English one spelt at various times as Omenie and Ampney.

This confused their contemporaries; Annie's sister's name is given as O'mmanney in the marriage register. Of Annie's many uncles, one, Captain Francis Metcalfe Ommanney, was a successful officer in the Royal Navy; another, Sir Montagu Frederick Ommanney, a prominent member of the Indian Civil Service; and a third, Charles Henry Ommanney, a diplomat. Annie's great-grandfather, Sir Francis Molyneux Ommanney, had been Member of Parliament for Barnstaple, and two of his brothers had reached the rank of admiral in the Navy. There were other senior naval officers in the family. Two of Annie's more distant relatives, Sir Erasmus Ommanney and Sir Nelson Ommanney, also achieved the rank of admiral. Her most famous relative in India was her great-uncle Manaton Collingwood Ommanney, the Commissioner for Oudh who was killed at the siege of Lucknow during the Mutiny. The Ommanneys were thus several cuts above the Dyers, but the Colonel seems to have accepted Annie's choice of partner without demur. He may have been susceptible to a little romance at this stage in his life, having not long since married again after the death of Annie's mother, Fanny; it was the Colonel's second wife, also Annie, who was with him at Jhansi. Sadly, she too died not long after, and Annie's father was to marry a third time, to Marion Gannon, a marriage which gave Dyer a family of step-in-laws to complicate his family tree, and which provided him with a step-brother in law, Jack Gannon, who was to become a close friend for the rest of his life.[7] Rex and Annie were to treat the Ommanney home as their own in the future.

Strangely, the Ommanney family's ready acceptance of their prospective son-in-law was not reciprocated by the Dyers. Rex wrote home to tell his father of his engagement, only to receive the reply that if he persisted with the match he would be cut off without a penny. Quite why this was so is not clear. Annie's family was at least as good, if not better, than those of any other of the families into which the Dyer children were to marry. Had Mary Dyer rubbed up against the Ommanneys at some point in Simla? Or had some whiff of financial impropriety attached itself to Rex's prospective father-in-law? Perhaps she already had another match in mind, and this defiance of her plans for a second time was just too much for her to stomach. Rex and Annie were under no illusion that it was Mary Dyer who was the source of opposition to their marriage. It was an opposition Annie was not prepared to forgive as long as she lived.

Annie's father granted Rex ten days' leave to have it out with his parents in Lucknow, where they were spending the winter. It was a miserable trip home. The interview with his mother and father lasted an afternoon, and Rex and his mother were both stubbornly angry, words were heated and they parted in acrimony. Neither mother nor son would yield. That night Rex, unable to sleep, went out into the garden of the Imam Bara to sit by the great water tank under the moon and think through what he had to do. After a while he noticed another figure not far off, also sitting dejected, head bowed, and he realised it was his father. Both crept home without speaking, but in the morning all three met again, and Rex tried to win by gentle persuasion what he had failed to win by blunt assertion the day before, this time using every argument he could summon, including a promise to abandon the betting which was at the time one of the faults for which his mother berated him. His father was softened, but Mary Dyer was not, and her final pronouncement was that Rex might have 100 rupees a month for his first year of marriage, if marry Annie Ommanney he would, but after that he would be on his own.

Rex returned to Jhansi to defy his mother, and, buying a lump of gold in the bazaar, had a ring hammered into shape by a goldsmith. He married Annie on 4 April 1888. Her parents, her sister and Rex's brother officers of the 39th were there, but none of the Dyers.[8] The couple managed a short honeymoon in Lucknow, living in the Dyers' house next to the newly established brewery in the old rajah's palace. By then, the Dyers had moved back to the cool of Simla, so there was no need for them to meet their new daughter-in-law. The city was yet another place full of memories of the Mutiny, having been famously besieged and relieved twice, and the battered Residency where Annie's uncle had died still stood, pock-marked by shot and shell as a memorial to what had taken place there. Annie hated her honeymoon. Forty years later, her sensitivity on this subject was still evident to Ian Colvin, who had at first headed this page of his biography of Rex 'Honeymoon at Lucknow', but deleted the heading when he found she would object.[9] In the heat of April, Rex and Annie sheltered in the decrepit mansion, whose garish stucco housed the icicle-fringed vats of refriger-ated beer. It was a suitably Gothic end to Rex's connection with his parents. There is no record that he ever saw them again.

The couple did not return to Jhansi, as Dyer's transfer out of the 39th had come through on their wedding day, a wedding present, in part, from Annie's father, who had probably come to the conclusion by then that his regiment was doomed and so helped Dyer find a better and more permanent home for the next stage of his career. Their honeymoon had been snatched en route to their new station, and within twenty-four days of their wedding they joined the 29th Punjab Infantry at Peshawar in the Punjab, several hundred miles to the north west.[10]

Peshawar was the largest garrison close to the North-West Frontier, a station laid out in a pleasant valley, surrounded by wooded hills providing a gentle back-drop to the orderly rows of English buildings and bungalows shaded by leafy trees which formed the cantonments. This peaceful, almost suburban, appear-ance was deceptive, for Peshawar was the centre of almost continuous operations against the Frontier tribes. Less than forty miles from Afghanistan as the crow flies, and at the foot of the main road to Kabul through the Khyber Pass, it was itself at times the scene of military action. It was not unknown for raiding tribesmen to sneak into the town to kidnap, loot and snipe at the garrison. The year after the Dyers arrived, a young officer of the 29th, Lieutenant Stephens, was stabbed to death at the railway station. It was necessary to be vigilant in Peshawar. The garrison contained not only many of the units but also the Headquarters of the part of the Army which controlled the Frontier. Alongside it was a native town which was a crossroads for traders and travellers of all the races and religions to be met on the Frontier. Its bazaar was a place to buy horses, cloth, weapons, fruit and grain from Afghanistan, Kashmir and the rich plains of the Punjab. Peshawar was an exciting town, just the place for an officer like Dyer who wanted (and indeed by force of personal circumstances now needed) to get ahead.

Luckily for Dyer, the regiment he was joining was just the right home for an officer with ambition. The 29th Punjabis had a great deal of style, a reputation for being highly efficient at their work and a title acquired over many years as the best shots in the Indian Army. The regiment had been raised at Jullundur in the Punjab during the Mutiny thirty years before, and its men were a mix of Sikhs, Dogras (Hindus from the northern Punjab hills) and Punjabi Musulmans (or Muhammadans, as Muslims were then known by the British), all of whom were recruited from the martial castes so highly prized by Roberts. Its commanding officer, Colonel Beddy, was famed for his handling of his men. 'Colonel Beddy Sahib Bahadur', as he was called by his troops, was still 'spoken of thirty years after retirement with love and reverence by the Sikhs'. Two months before the Dyers arrived, on 8 February, the 29th had been inspected at Peshawar by their Brigade Commander, Brigadier-General Keen. He reported that the British officers were a sound team, and he gave the regiment a good grade. Roberts, still the Commander-in-Chief, a good judge of soldiers and not the easiest man to please, was fulsome in the remarks with which he closed the report:

> The Commander-in-Chief is glad to find that the 29th Punjab Infantry maintains its good name and that it is reported on to be thoroughly efficient. This result reflects great credit on Colonel Beddy and all under his command. The regiment has for years past headed the list in musketry, and its splendid shooting again this year shows how carefully this part of the instruction is attended to. All ranks are to be congratulated on the proud position the regiment holds.

Roberts was particularly keen on raising the standard of shooting in the Army, and the 29th were a regiment of which he took particular notice.[11] Rex Dyer would have his work cut out to make his mark in such a fine school.

For the third time in as many years Dyer now faced settling into a new regiment. This time, as he and Annie occupied a bungalow in the cantonment, it was a different sort of process. No longer living in the Mess, Dyer was somewhat distant from his young fellow officers, many of whom, following the custom of the day, remained unmarried until a later age. It was not usual to arrive in a regiment already married, and this may have added a degree of awkwardness to the settling in process for both Rex and Annie. Social life began immediately, with the arrival of invitations from couples senior to Rex both in the rank of the husband and in years. Rex's shyness no doubt made this an uncomfortable time for him, though Annie probably coped better; the Dyers were inevitably thrown more closely together as a result. They may have found it all rather lonely and weary going at first.

Whilst Rex was on duty, Annie got to know the regimental wives, and perhaps some of those of the garrison, beginning the dreary life of an army wife in barracks, a round of coffee mornings, lunches, tea parties and dinners, interspersed with walks and rides around the cantonment and the occasional game of tennis. On the other hand, it was a life in which she had grown up, so she would not have been too disappointed by the way things had worked out. Dyer began work again as a wing officer, training his men, who were Sikhs, on the rifle ranges in the cantonment and in the hills around the base, drilling them on the square, and exercising with them in the *khud*.[12] He now met for the first time the Sikhs with whom he was to form the closest comradeships of his service, and whose lives and characters were to resonate most strongly throughout his career. In Peshawar, he gained his first knowledge of the Sikh religion and began to learn the Punjabi language his men spoke, gradually coming to know a way of life which, like many British officers, he came to admire. Now, however, he had only a short time to get to know his men, for five months after the Dyers' arrival in Peshawar, the 29th were called out on operations on the frontier over a hundred miles to the north.

At that time, and indeed until the end of British rule in India, the North-West Frontier included a very large no man's land lying inside the international border with Afghanistan but outside British administered territory. The tribes living within this area, many of whom were Pathans, whose tribal areas spread across the border into neighbouring parts of Afghanistan, were almost entirely Muslim and were independent of any government. Many of them were bound by treaties preventing depredations inside British territory, treaties which were often breached and which were almost impossible to enforce, for the tribesmen were fiercely independent and their leaders held little powers of discipline and usually less desire to exercise what they had. The country was mountainous, mostly barren, bare of much vegetation and unrelieved by rainfall, and life within it was rugged and hard. Raiding the richer, and therefore perpetually tempting, territory of the plains had been a way of life there throughout history. The border was long and indefensible, and the British, ruling an area they could never fully protect, found it easier to exclude the wilder areas beyond their administrative frontiers, sallying occasionally across them to punish tribal raiders who were getting out of hand. It was a system that achieved only occasional peace and was marred by perpetual, if sporadic, outbreaks of violence.

The trouble which now drew Dyer to the Frontier for the first time had arisen in an area known as the Black Mountain, tribal lands across the administrative frontier west of the District of Hazara, the northernmost British-administered territory in the Punjab. The Black Mountain took its name from the dark forests of berbery and acacia which clothed its lower slopes, and of Himalayan silver fir which grew up to 8000 feet on its ridge lines. It was cut off from the rest of tribal territory by the River Indus, which flowed through ravines around three of its sides. The British administrative frontier made a fourth, so the area was in effect an island. The Black Mountain massif was a series of spurs running up to a central, dominating ridge line, which at its highest, the peak of Machai Sar, reached 9817 feet. Along this ridge ran the line beyond which the British writ did not run, though the local tribes lived on both sides regardless. The area was not on the road to anywhere and the British had been happy to let it be; unfortunately, the inhabitants were not inclined to let them do so. These were an unusually mixed group of tribes, not particularly large or powerful, although combined they could put between six and seven thousand men in the field, but warlike, and, in some cases, religiously inspired against the infidel British. Politically, they were nominally under the influence of two independent princelings, the Nawab of Amb and the Wali of Swat, but these exercised little real power in the hills. On the eastern slopes of the mountain, nearest British territory, lived Swatis who pretended to be Pathans, but fooled neither their neighbours nor the British, and were so little regarded that they were described by a contemporary as 'cowardly, deceptive, cruel, grasping, lazy. Replacing the bold frank manner of the Pathan by the hang-dog look of the whipped cur.'[13] On the western flanks of the Black Mountains, and on either side of the Indus river which ran around it, lived men the British regarded as of better stock, Isazai Pathans of the Yusufzai tribe. Among these lived a section of fanatical Muslim extremists, remnants of a group known to the British as the Hindustani Fanatics, who had settled in villages near the Indus. These were Indian Wahhabis, who had been crushed by the British in the Ambela Campaign of 1863 and had fled to the Black Mountain, from where they, with some local colonies of Piarai Saiyids, who claimed descent from the Prophet Mohammed, continued to be a hotbed of anti-British agitation.[14]

The Black Mountain tribes had been raiding across the border over many decades, and British punitive expeditions in 1863 and 1875 had procured no lasting effect. In 1884, the Punjab Government had blockaded the Piarai Saiyids and the tribes after they had attacked the town of Agror, seeking by economic sanction to bring them to heel, but this was ineffective and raiding continued.[15] The Punjab Government was prevented from mounting another punitive expedition

by the Government of India, so the ineffective blockade was maintained and
extended.

The occasion for the outbreak of the campaign upon which Dyer now found
himself was, however, the result of a disastrous error of judgment on the part of
the British themselves. On 17 June 1888, Major Battye, officiating Commandant
of 2nd Battalion 5th Gurkha Rifles, visited the post held by his unit at Oghi on
the Agror frontier below the Black Mountain. He was accompanied by a friend,
Captain Urmston of 6th Punjabis, who for some offence that is no longer
recorded was at that time under arrest, but who had nevertheless been permitted
by the Commander of the Punjab Frontier Force, Brigadier-General McQueen,
to accompany Battye 'in consequence of [his] bad health and depressed spirits'.[16]
Major Battye sent the young subaltern of his regiment commanding the fort
back to base and took over command himself, then immediately decided to carry
out in person a highly provocative march along the administrative frontier which
ran along the ridge of the Black Mountain. This was specifically forbidden in the
standing orders for the post, and why he determined on this almost suicidal
course of action was never discovered.[17] The subsequent inquiry could only comment that 'Major Battye seems to have acted very injudiciously', and speculated
that he seemed to have thought that the post orders only applied to officers junior
in rank to himself. When he announced his intentions to the local police force,
five of whom he intended to take with him on his walk, he was advised by the
police inspector not to take his intended route 'as there would be great loss, and
that the Gujar village was a very dangerous place no white sahib had ever visited
before.' Battye ignored this and, after breakfast the following day, led his considerable force towards the summit of the Black Mountain. At a small spot named
Chitabat he left most of his party, sixty men of 5th Gurkhas and nineteen
policemen, just below the crest, and with Urmston and a few men walked up to
the ridge. He was spotted immediately, and the tribesmen reacted violently to
his presence, opening fire on Battye's party from a distance and rapidly advancing
towards them. For some unaccountable reason (perhaps because he knew he
was in the wrong), Battye did not order a return of fire but carried on walking
towards the tribesmen.[18] One of his party, a *havildar*, was hit and fell, and when
the two British officers went to rescue him carrying a stretcher they were charged
by tribesmen and killed in hand to hand fighting. Four Gurkhas were killed in
the ensuing struggle to recover the bodies, and six rifles were lost. Six of the
tribesmen were also killed. The party had to fight its way back down the
mountain, and in the immediate aftermath the tribes began to collect on the
Black Mountain ridge. Soon, intelligence reached the British that they were
making plans to attack Agror, and they were joined on 27 June by the Maulvi
Abdulla leading 120 Hindustani Fanatics from the village of Palosi, which was
across the Indus. It seems the tribes were under the impression they were to

be attacked; for, when it became clear to them that this was not the case, they dispersed.

It is possible at this distance to see the pattern of misconception on both sides that led to the final conflict. The Punjab Government felt obliged to avenge the slaying of two British officers, no matter how foolish their actions had been, and had now enough ammunition to gain agreement from Simla to deal more firmly with the Black Mountain tribes. The Hindustani Fanatics were included in the ongoing blockade, and on 31 July the Khan of Agror, Ali Gauhar Khan, was arrested as he was suspected of supporting the blockaded tribes and as his troops had watched the 5th Gurkha party being attacked without going to their aid. On 29 August a decision was taken to send a punitive expedition to punish the tribes and pacify the Agror frontier, with the mission of 'coercion into submission of the Akazais and the Khan Khel division of the Hassanzais with the punishment of any clans or divisions which might assist these tribesmen in their opposition'. An ultimatum was issued to the tribes to submit by 2 October. It was ignored.[19]

This had been anticipated, for, almost a month before, on 7 September, the Hazara Field Force had formed under the recently promoted Major-General McQueen, who was allotted two brigades and a force a little over 9400 strong including four British and nine Indian battalions of infantry, and three mountain batteries of guns. Attached as Political Officer to McQueen, and responsible for dealing with the tribes, was Colonel Ommanney, Rex's father-in-law, by then released from the burden of the 39th. The troops concentrated on the Agror frontier at Oghi, a British fort on the Unhar river at the foot of the Black Mountains. The plan of campaign was for three of the four columns into which the force was divided to march independently up to the summit of the ridge, dispersing the tribes by a multi-directional pincer movement. The other column, Number Four, part of Brigadier-General Galbraith's 2nd Brigade, concentrated separately at the small town of Darband on the Indus to the south of the Black Mountain. Its tasks were:

1. If possible to sever the connection between the Cis and Trans Indus tribes.

2. In co-operation with the columns on the ridge, to dominate the country of the disaffected tribes, and carry out the punitive object of the expedition.[20]

The commander of this column, which became known as the River Column, was Colonel Crookshank, Commanding Officer of the 34th Pioneers, and it was to his force that 29th Punjabis was attached. The scheme of operations had the River Column starting a few days earlier than the rest, due to the rugged country it faced.

Nine officers and 618 men of the 29th, with six horses, left Peshawar by train on 19 September, and reached the camp at Darband on the 29th. The first part of the journey was by train to Taroo and Nowshera, which they reached after a day; then they marched for a week via Attock along the road up the banks of the Indus, their baggage carried on two hundred and seventy mules. On the 21st, at Akora, they met the 2nd Battalion Royal Irish, and marched with them the rest of the way. They found the River Column in camp on the riverbank at Darband, just below where the Indus, several hundred yards wide at that point, disgorged from the narrow ravine in which it ran around the Black Mountain. Already in the camp were their fellow 4th Punjabis and the 34th Pioneers, whose Commanding Officer was doubling as the Column Commander. With them were two mountain guns manned by Scottish gunners, and the Brigade Headquarters of Brigadier-General Galbraith, who had attached himself to Crookshank's Column, probably much to the latter's chagrin, for he now had the eye of his superior looking directly over his shoulder.[21]

Hostilities began four days later, on 2 October, when the tribes on the high ground overlooking the camp got in the first blow and attacked a picquet protecting the water point. Captain McLeod of the 29th took a company and drove them off.[22] The next day, Crookshank pushed the 4th Punjabis forward onto the point on the Chamb ridge from which they had earlier been shot at, to secure the high ground overlooking the single narrow footpath which wound its way, clinging to the hillside, up the east bank of the river. In the advance which now began, the 29th were assigned the unglamorous role of baggage and ammunition guard, and so brought up the rear of the column as it snaked its way up the narrow path. At first this was still just within the administrative frontier, but this line was crossed on the 4th by the Royal Irish, who spent the early part of the morning almost in single file working their way up the path cut from the cliffs along the river bank. Covered to their rear and right flank by the picquets of the 4th Punjabis, who had scrambled up the adjacent ridgeline just before the tribesmen reached it, the Irishmen emerged from the ravine and advanced into Shingri, the first village on their route.

Opening out before them they found a gravelly flood plain which gave two or more miles of uninterrupted view to the next village, Tawara. There the Indus ravine again narrowed to a defile, and there the tribes had prepared their defence at the narrowest point, placing their men in stone sangars along on the ridge for a mile behind the village, stretching in much depth to their rear as far as the next village up the valley, Kotkai. The tribes had effectively closed off the east bank and the path. They were supported by snipers who had been sited on the west bank of the river to provide fire across it. It was a very strong position. The Brigadier himself came forward to carry out a reconnaissance of the ground in front of Tawara, and directed Crookshank to clear both his flanks in order to prepare for an attack across the open ground in the centre. The 4th Punjabis seized the high ground to the right, and commenced to pour fire down onto the tribes in Tawara. The 34th had the more difficult job of clearing the boulder-strewn outcrops on the edge of the river, and so came under fire from both left and right. Galbraith directed their advance from a distance, and at one point sent one of his staff officers, Captain Beley, to gallop across to them with orders. It was an ill-timed mission, for as Beley galloped across the open ground he found himself in the path of a counter-attack by a group of Hindustani Fanatic *ghazis* who had lain concealed in a gully off to the flank and who now surged forward armed with swords intending to attack the 34th. Beley's horse was cut from under him, and the British front lines watched helplessly as he stood sword in hand surrounded by the tribesmen. He was cut to pieces in full view of the column. The *ghazis* then suffered the same fate, shot down almost to a man by the Royal Irish for whom they formed a perfect target at close range, and by the Gatlings sited on high ground with the 4th. Eighty-eight of their bodies were found at this spot after the battle. The artillery and Gatling gun fire then switched to rake the tribesmen's position in the village, and the Royal Irish charged across the plain, 'as steadily as if on parade', straight into Tawara, the surviving tribesmen fleeing before them and leaving their standard behind in the rout. Galbraith immediately sent the 4th and the 29th in pursuit of the fleeing enemy; the mountain guns carried on a quick rate of fire from the rear, the gatling guns deployed with the 4th swept the ridges in front of them, and by 3.30 p.m. the enemy had abandoned all their positions along the path as far as Kotkai and were in full flight towards Kanar, two miles further north.

Kotkai was the key to the Indus valley, 'perched on top of a high conical peak of rocks on the left bank of the river [where it] completely closes the valley at this point'. It was shelled, and Colonel Crookshank took four companies of the 29th and a wing of the Royal Irish to climb the ridge and assault it at 4.30 p.m. Rex Dyer was in the forefront of the charge, and seeing the remaining tribesmen jumping over the opposite walls of the village, he and the few of his men who could keep up with him chased them closely down the slope on the other side. He was spotted by his regiment haring off into the distance, unsupported by any other troops, and had to be recalled by bugle. When he got back, he was ticked off for 'surmounting an obstacle without knowing what was on the other side', something he would do more than once in his career. Another officer of the 29th, Major Alexander Reid, was luckier, and was awarded a DSO and later a brevet lieutenant-colonelcy for capturing the standard the tribes had left in the village.[23] Brigadier Galbraith came up to Kotkai just after the attack and established his brigade headquarters there. The day's fighting had resulted in some two hundred enemy dead for the loss of five killed (including Captain Beley and the Subadar-Major, the senior Indian officer, of the 34th) and ten wounded on the British side. The guns and Gatlings had made this an uneven contest, but there was no doubt of the courage and dash shown by the troops of the column, and not least of all by Dyer. It had been a most successful start to the campaign, and the troops had their tails up.

The column stayed in Kotkai until the 10th, carrying out daily forays to local villages to disperse groups of enemy thought to be in the vicinity. Much time and a good deal of hard labour was spent ferrying supplies up the path from Darband. The track was too narrow in places for even a camel to pass, and supplies had to be carried by men on foot or brought up the river in boats supplied by the Nawab of Amb. A minor disaster struck on the evening of 5 October, when Colonel Crookshank, leading a column north along the river to Kanar, was forced to retreat under rifle fire from the other side of the Indus and fell wounded. Dyer's Commanding Officer, Colonel Beddy, took temporary command of the column. Beddy does not seem to have pleased his Brigadier. He was recommended for none of the awards made after the campaign, and Galbraith's praise of the man who eventually took over the column from Beddy made his view of the latter clear: 'his timely arrival relieved me of much anxiety'. The wounded Crookshank was evacuated, and lingered on until 24 October when he confounded the optimistic reports of his doctors and died.[24] Whilst he exercised command over the next few days, Colonel Beddy sent troops to climb the three thousand feet of the nearest ridge to Kunarai and Tilli. On the 9th, Major Reid of the 29th led two companies two miles north to occupy Kanar. Using the boats supplied by the Nawab of Amb, troops were ferried over the Indus to raid on the west bank, destroying the village of Garhi opposite Kanar and raiding above the Hindustani Fanatics' base at Palosi on the 10th. Although some resistance was still offered by the tribes across the river, the fight had gone out of the tribes to its east, and the last shot fired on the east bank was on the 7th. Four days later the advance north resumed and Kanar became the column's base. Leaving the Royal Irish there, the column pushed on another mile or so further up the canyon to Ghazikot, Galbraith crossing the Indus with 1200 troops and attacking the Hindustani Fanatics' fort at Maidan. He destroyed it in an unopposed assault, and occupied their base at Palosi, after which he returned across the river to meet his fellow brigade commander, Brigadier-General Channer, who had brought the 5th Column down the ridge to meet up with the River Column at Kanar. The troops again crossed the river on the 16th, on this occasion burning down half of Palosi village, and the next day, back on the east bank, they pushed north to occupy the village of Diliaroi high on the ridge line.

By this time there was no fight left in the tribes. Operations became a desultory destruction of fortifications and villages, crops and grain. All the tribesmen had fled. On the 20th, the Akazais sent a separate deputation seeking to surrender and accepting all the terms imposed upon them. Peace was made with them on the 26 October, but, as the other tribes did not come in, the campaign continued and columns pushed into the valleys leading off the main canyon, one reaching as far as the village of Ledh, about six miles north of Kanar, the furthest north reached by the River Column. On 24 October, Pirzada Bela, a hamlet on the west bank of the Indus opposite Kanar was destroyed, and the next day, its neighbour, Garhi, was burned. On the 29th, the village of Kotkai was razed to the ground. At that point, on the 30th, the tribes of the valley surrendered their sole surviving prisoner and paid their fine of 7500 rupees. The tribes in the northern parts of the Black Mountain, which had so far not been reached by the columns, continued to hold out, so the River Column remained in its positions along the Indus until the rest of the force had dealt with them, and until the tribal *jirgha* had reached Oghi and agreed to terms.

Eventually, peace was agreed, the tribes accepting all the terms imposed on them and paying their fines, and on 11 November the column began to withdraw back down the valley, reaching Darband two days later without a shot being fired. From there it dispersed back to base, and the 29th were back in Peshawar by 29 November. In this expedition, the Hazara Field Force lost twenty-five men dead and fifty-four wounded, against a tally of about four hundred enemy dead. The operation could be counted a success, though not a lasting one, as the whole thing had to be done again three years later in 1891, when peace was finally and permanently enforced. The River Column had seen the hardest fighting of the campaign, facing the greatest concentration of enemy, and having had to mount the only set-piece attacks. Dyer had cut his teeth on the Frontier in a sharp, successful and, for the British, not particularly costly operation, which was concluded within a few months. From the military point of view, which would not have been greatly concerned with the origins of the campaign, nor with its political outcome, it had been a job neatly done, something of a classic of its kind. It set the pattern for the type of work Dyer was to be engaged in for the next twenty years.[25] He now owned a third clasp, 'Hazara, 1888', for the India General Service Medal he had earned in Burma.[26] Despite the reprimand he had received – which was one a young officer would have been unlikely to have felt left any stain on his character – he was proud of himself, and particularly of his part in the action at Kotkai, which was considered sufficiently worthy to be entered formally upon his record.[27]

Almost immediately the 29th reached its barracks it was inspected by the Commander-in-Chief. Had this been a regular inspection, the 29th might have felt a little aggrieved to be visited so soon, but it is likely that Roberts wanted to see them to congratulate them on their conduct in the campaign. They came through the snap visit with flying colours. It was recorded that: 'When the Commander-in-Chief inspected the regiment at Peshawar last November, His Excellency was much pleased.' It is very likely that on this occasion the young Dyer met his Commander-in-Chief, a man held in awe by the Army. Although Roberts was not the sort of man to have forgotten Dyer's part in the riverboat affair, nor to have failed to notice his headlong rush down the hill at Kotkai, he was just the sort of officer to appreciate the reputation for courage that the tongue-tied young man before him was fast establishing in his as yet very short career.[28]

5

The Relief of Chitral

Back in base at Peshawar and reunited with Annie, Rex Dyer now had time to settle properly into the 29th Punjabis. Up to now he had been fortunate in his service: three exciting years and a campaign in each of them. This was not a typical pattern of regimental soldiering, even in the Victorian Army, and Rex's career now reverted to something closer to the norm of long periods of peacetime garrison soldiering relieved by the occasional dash of active service. It was a style of life, however, which offered a man like Dyer many compensations: manly companionship with the soldiers of his company; a life spent outdoors on the firing range or the hillside; and the almost daily physical activity of route march or sports field to keep a man healthy and strong. It could be a satisfying, stretching, even a stimulating life, but it had its frustrations. The snail's pace of peacetime preferment could grow to gnaw at the vitals of an ambitious or impecunious man. Promotion was a necessity if a man was to clear the debts accumulated in his youth, provide a reasonable life for his family, educate his children, and ultimately accumulate enough money for a pension on which to retire home. Dyer was certainly impecunious, and his ambitions were sharpened by the need to prove himself to his parents if not also to himself. He lacked any source of financial support other than his pay; and, since he had, at an early age it seems, acquired a gambling habit, he had probably accumulated the debts that usually went with it. Married life in the regiment would tend to produce more. The Dyers could neither avoid the expense of equipping a home nor avoid entertaining in it. They would have needed to maintain a household with at least a few servants, an inevitably expensive drain no matter how little these were paid. It may have been an indication of their need for frugality that Rex and Annie were so careful in their family planning, and indeed there is no record of Dyer's being in debt. Later, when he was commanding his own battalion and writing reports on his young officers, he frequently made disapproving comments on those who let their finances get out of hand.[1] Officer indebtedness was widespread at the time:

> Junior officers with expensive tastes and a small private income (or none at all) found it impossible to keep out of debt in cantonments, and sought refuge in Frontier wars where free rations were provided and the opportunities for spending money severely restricted.[2]

Dyer's battalion was no stranger to this problem. In 1889, the Captain McLeod who had acted so creditably on the Black Mountain expedition was superseded for the post of battalion second-in-command, a job which held responsibility for many the unit's finances, as he was hopelessly in debt.[3] That Rex and Annie did not let themselves get into such a parlous state of affairs speaks creditably of the careful way they managed their lives, and particularly of Annie's skills at household management. It also indicates the quiet way in which they had to live.

Dyer spent much of his spare time sitting on the verandah of his balcony with his Persian teacher, whom he had found in the Peshawar bazaar advertising for students to rake together the money for his return journey home. In this way he gained a colloquial grasp of the language, enough for it to be of some use to him when he served in Persia eighteen years later. He had passed the Army's lower level examination in Persian by late 1892. His knowledge of Punjabi improved at the same time, and he became able to work effectively in the language and to use it to get to know his men. He took and passed the obligatory exam in the language.[4] Rex still had with him the bearer he had brought from the 39th, an old soldier named Maheshar Ram, a *poorbeia* from the plains of Oudh, and they could only communicate with each other in the Hindustani Rex had first known as a child. Service in the Punjab was a polyglot affair.

Much of Rex's time was spent with his men on the range, honing the skills which had won the 29th first place in the annual Indian Army Snider Rifle competition eight times out of the last eleven entries and second place on the other three occasions. This was a remarkable achievement and to maintain such dominance the regiment's shooting team had to be firing on the range for much of the year. The standard of shooting within the companies from which the team was drawn needed to be correspondingly high, and this meant much target practice for everybody. The 29th was a regiment that took great pride in its sporting achievements, particularly those of its tug-of-war team. This was composed of Sikhs, men usually of greater size than the other members of the regiment, who trained daily by pulling on a rope attached to a heavy block of iron suspended from a tree branch. The 29th's great rivals were the 14th (Ferozepore) Sikh Infantry, which only recruited Sikhs and so had a much bigger pool from which to draw its team. About the year 1889, a contest took place between the two regiments in the final of the Peshawar garrison competition, one that was to be long remembered. Cheered on by crowds of spectators, the teams

> dug their naked feet into the hot sand and pulled without relaxing the strain for a space of one hour and nine minutes. When the last man of the 14th Sikhs was hauled over the line, both teams fell in their tracks and lay where they fell. They were carried to hospital, where one died, and it was found that most of them had strained their hearts, and that none of them had any skin left on the soles of their feet.[5]

Dyer's initial probationary period came to a successful close in late 1888 and, as he had hoped, he was permitted to remain with the 29th.[6] In about 1889 he was given responsibility for the regimental training team, which instructed cadres of recently joined recruits and assessed men seeking promotion.[7] It was at about this time that an incident occurred which once again cast a cloud over his career, and provided an uncomfortable reminder of the affray on the Burmese river-boat.[8] For some reason, perhaps for training or duty in some frontier post, Dyer and the Sikhs of his company travelled by train to Nowshera, the next town east of Peshawar on the main trunk line from the Frontier. The party detrained at the station and Dyer secured the only *thika ghari* in the station forecourt to carry his baggage, then went back to the platform to watch his men assemble. He returned to the yard to see the trap disappearing towards the town carrying an Indian passenger, so he ran back to the train, brought his horse out of the horse box in which it had travelled with the party, and galloped in pursuit of the *ghari* down the road towards Nowshera bazaar. There he caught up with the trap, and found that its occupant was the local *tehsildar*, who refused to vacate the vehicle. Who first pushed whom is not clear, but after some altercation Dyer pulled the *tehsildar* from the trap, and a scrimmage developed as the enraged official called for help and the local people came to his aid. Dyer managed to knock several down, but was pushed back against the trap and began to be assaulted from all sides. The *tehsildar* was urging on the crowd, so Dyer grabbed him by the head, and demanded that he tell the locals to back off. This enraged them the more and Dyer was assailed from the roof of the *ghari* by a man wielding a *lathi* and from between its wheels by someone trying to trip him up. He was taking a severe beating and about to fall when his men came running from the station to his rescue. The crowd melted away, and the party got back to their nearby campsite, where Dyer stripped off his clothes and found himself covered in bruises from the waist upwards.

The *tehsildar* brought an action against him in the Nowshera magistrates' court, where the local magistrate was an Indian. Rex appeared with his lawyer, to be faced by the *tehsildar*, who pulled off the cloth covering his head to reveal a battered and discoloured face.

'And now', said the judge, 'we are to deal with this disgraceful assault'. He got no further. Dyer there and then took the case out of the hands of his legal adviser. 'I protest', he said, 'against this prejudgment of the case. I ask it to be noted that the court has spoken of a disgraceful assault before hearing the evidence. I refuse in these circumstances to submit to its jurisdiction, and give notice of appeal.' The judge saw that he had committed an indiscretion. If, as Dyer's lawyer believed, he had intended to find for the plaintiff on grounds of friendship and interest, he changed his mind. The case was dismissed.[9]

Quite how much of this story, transmitted through several partial informants to Dyer's biographer, Ian Colvin, are we to believe? Elements of it smack of elaboration by its protagonist, who, with his wife and friends, clearly believed that he had come out of it well. The alternative view of his behaviour, and one more likely perhaps to strike us at this distance, is that he had been at best foolhardy and at worst had conducted himself in a manner unbecoming an officer. He had readily used his fists against a civilian Indian, and, although it should perhaps make little difference to the case, one who held an official position. The humiliation of local Indian officials and magistrates was clearly something which Dyer found amusing. It is unlikely that his Commanding Officer would have been able to take other than a dim view of this escapade, though we do not know what, if anything, he did about it. The episode does not do Dyer much credit.

This year was to be a sombre one. The Dyers made their first attempt at starting a family at around the time of their arrival at Peshawar, or at the latest just after Rex returned from the Black Mountain campaign. Their first child, a daughter, was born in 1889 but died the same year. There is no record of her name or of what caused her death. The sadness of her brief life must have lingered with the Dyers for a long time – their next child did not come until six more years had passed – so when the regiment moved to Jhelum in the spring of 1890 it was probably a relief. Rex and Annie could, to some extent, leave behind in Peshawar the unhappiness that had struck them there.

Jhelum was a town in the north of the Punjab, lying to the east of Rawalpindi and a considerable distance from the Frontier, a quieter spot with a smaller garrison than Peshawar's. It was where the 29th had its depot for enlisting and training recruits, so the battalion was for a while united with its small depot staff. The town took its name from the Jhelum river, one of the five main rivers of the Punjab, upon the banks of which it was built, and lay below the foothills of the Pir Panjal range that formed the border with Kashmir. The Commanding Officer of the 29th doubled as the station commander.

The battalion settled in to its new post. Their new brigade commander visited, and there was the inevitable parade. The Mess invited the locally important people to dine to enable those who were useful to get to know the regiment's officers. Visiting cards were dropped in the boxes at the gates of the driveways of the garrison officers' bungalows, initial calls were paid and invitations issued in return. The 29th arrived in good shape; Brigadier-General Keen, their brigade commander back at Peshawar, had just inspected them and had been highly complimentary in his report. General Roberts, clearly still fond of the regiment, added to their annual report that the 29th was: 'Excellent in every respect … It is composed of a fine body of men and is in admirable order. As regards musketry, the regiment is second to none.'[10] The Jhelum garrison no doubt welcomed them.

The Dyers had not long been in the new station before they decided on an expedition. On 15 April 1890 Rex took leave, and he and Annie both set out to cross the hundred or so miles of the Pir Panjal range which separated them from Kashmir. It was too early in the year for the roads to be properly open, but if Rex was aware of this he did not let it deter him. They struggled across a pass at 11,400 feet in the midst of a blizzard, and only just made the refuge of a rest house on the summit before the snow overwhelmed them. More adventures awaited them on the way back. They took a different route, and returned through the small hill state of Poonch, where they were entertained by its young Raja to a tiger hunt. They rode out on elephant back, fording the flooded Surran river on their way to the hunting grounds, Annie perched high on a slippery *howdah*, and as they forded the river, she saw all but the tip of the elephant's trunk and the *mahout* sitting behind its ears disappear under the muddy waters. During the shoot,

> the tiger broke back through the beaters; the Raja cursed his men; the head *shikari* led up an old fellow, and dramatically throwing aside a cloth which covered his head, revealed a face stripped to the skull by a blow of the tiger's paw as he passed through the line; a handful of rupees from the Raja; salaams from an old man.

Dyer formed the idea of making it back to Jhelum by boat, as the Surran was a tributary of the Jhelum river, and with the help of the Raja, he arranged a boat and boatmen. They took off on a river swollen with melting snow and flew

> dizzily along the flooded stream, through wild ravines, and down no less than eighty-seven rapids, until at the last and worst, at the place called Tangrote where the Poonch [the Surran river] rushes over rocks to join the Jehlam, the boat capsized, and Mrs Dyer was only saved by the prevision of her husband, who at that point had rigged a rope from the boat to a team on the shore.[11]

The couple made it back to Jhelum no worse for the expedition, which must have been more than enough to blow away any cobwebs remaining from Peshawar. The river trip had whetted Dyer's taste for boating, and when they got back he spent his leisure time in constructing his own boat, which he built with a draught of three inches, shallow enough to enable him to explore the shores and islands of the river. They had also brought back with them from Poonch a bearer who would stay with them for the rest of their time in India, a man named Allah Dad Khan who replaced Maheshar Ram when the old man retired.[12]

In November and December of 1890, the 29th took part in the Army exercises at Attock on the Indus, the area through which they had marched to the Black Mountain two years before. General Sir Frederick Roberts, still Commander-in-Chief, saw the battalion in action there, and recorded in the next annual report: 'I was much pleased with what I saw of it at the Attock Manoeuvres.'[13]

On 10 December, immediately as the exercise ended, Rex and Annie set out to take a year's leave in England. Rex had now been serving for just over five years, and so was entitled to home furlough.[14] The couple started the long passage back from Bombay, and reached England only late in the following January or February. They may have stayed in Brooke House, the house of Annie's father at West Malling in Kent. They were to do so in the future, and it was not far from Chatham, where Dyer meant to attend courses during this leave. They spent the first half of their leave separated whilst Rex studied in the School of Military Engineering. He had enrolled himself on a course in field works to start in the spring of 1891. This is one of the earliest indications that Dyer had ambitions beyond the usual, and that he had committed himself to studying hard at his profession, for the course was not one attended by the majority of infantry officers, and for it he would have needed to volunteer his name. He worked hard on the course and got a distinction in May. He followed this up with another course at Chatham, this time in topography, also a voluntary course. This was a subject involving sketching in the field, an important skill for an officer making a reconnaissance of a position. Dyer achieved another distinction when that course ended in July.[15] That left him and Annie with under four months together to enjoy England before they embarked for India.

They reached Bombay in December and were back in Jhelum by the 10th. They found on their return that there had been a few changes. Colonel Beddy had retired and had been replaced by Lieutenant-Colonel A.J.F. 'Jock' Reid, the officer who had distinguished himself at Kotkai three years before. The Bengal Staff Corps into which Rex had been commissioned in 1888 had also gone, merged with the other two Presidency Staff Corps into one Indian Staff Corps the previous year, so that from now on Rex was a member of the Indian rather than the Bengal Staff Corps. He had, to his chagrin, missed an entire campaign, for the 29th had been called out, not long after the Dyers had left for England, and had joined the force carrying out a punitive expedition into the Miranzai valley in the Tirah, south of the Khyber Pass. The Commander-in-Chief had noted their achievements during the campaign, and in his report for that year coupled a compliment upon their conduct to the usual praise he bestowed upon their shooting: 'The Regiment did well during the recent Miranzai Expedition … The musketry state of the 29th Punjab Infantry is all that could be wished.'[16] To have taken leave just before his regiment was deployed to a border campaign in which it had caught the eye of the Commander-in-Chief must have been both disappointing for Dyer and the source for a certain amount of ribaldry from his brother officers. He must have felt it an unlucky start to his next tour of duty.

Change was also to take place in Dyer's employment within the unit, for almost immediately he arrived he assumed the post of Quartermaster, and so became responsible for the battalion's equipment, uniform, ammunition, stores, catering and rations.[17] This was a heavy load, but a vital one for the well being of the regiment and its soldiers, so the post was usually held by a promising young officer; Dyer would have regarded it as a good career move. Whether the book keeping and counting of socks can have improved his temper is open to doubt; the post removed him from working directly with the regiment's soldiers and left him no opportunity for training in the field. It did, however, allow him time to study, and he took his next professional qualification, the Officers Extra Certificate in Musketry, in the spring of 1892, achieving a first-class pass at the School of Musketry at Chungla Gully, the Punjab's small arms school.[18] The certificate was something all young officers were obliged to pass to enable them to plan and conduct firing practices on ranges and in the field; Rex clearly had an aptitude for this type of work, and, as always, applied himself sufficiently thoroughly to make sure that he did well.

When he got back to Jhelum, his prospects looked even better, as the Commanding Officer appointed him to officiate as Adjutant while the regular incumbent was away from his post for a few months. The Adjutant's job was reserved for the best officer of each generation, and carried a prestige and a power within the battalion second only to that of the Colonel. He was the Commanding Officer's right-hand man for all disciplinary, ceremonial and personnel matters, and much else besides, and many an Adjutant became the personal confidant and often the friend of his Commanding Officer before going on to greater things. In this case, the post carried a double authority, as the regiment's Adjutant acted as station staff officer for the Jhelum Garrison. Its holder had a finger in almost every matter affecting the officers, soldiers and families of the station. At this point, though, something went badly wrong. There is no clear record of what or why; the only indication we have is a cryptic line let slip by Colvin, who says that Dyer 'might have been Adjutant but for a condition proposed by the Colonel which he felt himself in honour bound to reject'. As this is almost certainly information passed to Colvin by Annie Dyer, the issue had to have been one she understood in these terms, so rather than a matter related purely to the duties of the post it is more likely that this was one affecting the Dyers' personal circumstances. The point most probably at issue was Rex Dyer's married status; it is quite likely that the Commanding Officer believed that the duties of the Adjutant's post were so onerous, and required such a commitment to the regiment, that they were best conducted by a single man. If such was the case, he may have asked Dyer to send Annie home for the duration of his tour of duty, and Dyer's refusal to be separated from Annie, if such were the case, even though it meant the dashing of his career hopes, speaks very creditably for his devotion to his wife. Whatever the point at issue, the outcome was serious. The adjutancy was lost irrevocably, and Dyer's career began to stagnate in a way that is quite likely to have been an indication of at best a malign neglect, and at worst of a deliberate decision by his Commanding Officer to make sure he would never command the battalion. That Colonel Reid did bear some hostility towards Dyer was picked up some twenty-seven years later by Brigadier-General Villiers-Stuart, a Gurkha officer, a bachelor and a martinet, but a renowned Frontier soldier who was Inspector of Infantry in India and so well placed to hear gossip about his contemporaries (though it has to be said that he was also a man who was neither very circumspect nor accurate in retailing what he heard). He related that:

> Old Jock Reid (who commanded the 29th P.I. for so long and made it such a good regiment particularly in shooting, the 29th. P.I. being Dyer's regiment) could not stand him, and following the custom at that time pushed him off on staff billets whenever he came near the regiment.[19]

Villiers-Stuart, who wrote long after the events he purports to report, and would not have known Reid closely, could only have been at best right in part of this. Rex Dyer was not posted away while Reid commanded, and remained with the 29th for almost another decade before being exiled to a series of unattractive posts. But any hostility at all on the part of the Commanding Officer would have been a source of anguish to Rex and Annie, and one which perhaps they had no alternative but to abide if they were to go on living together. It was something which would have thrown them even closer together.

Dyer may have still been acting as Adjutant when the battalion was inspected for the last occasion in Jhelum. On 26 February 1892, the GOC, Major-General Sir W.K. Elles, visited and gave the battalion 'A very satisfactory report in all aspects'. He noted that all but three British officers were well reported on by their Commanding Officer, so that, although Dyer's own report does not survive, it can be accepted that it was a satisfactory one. Those who had not done so well were named, and included Captain McLeod, who was still in debt. General Roberts added his usual encomium to the report on what was clearly one of his favourite regiments. Recalling his visit to the battalion during the campaign which Dyer had missed the previous year, he wrote:

> I inspected the 29th Punjab Infantry on the Samana last November, and was much pleased with the turn out and general appearance. I was also much pleased to hear a very favourable report of the regiment's behaviour during the Miranzai expedition from Major-General Sir William Lockhart. The shooting has been maintained, the regiment being fifth in the order of merit. It has won my prize. The Assistant Adjutant General for Musketry reports fire discipline not quite what it was; Lieutenant-Colonel Reid will pay attention.[20]

The campaign on the Frontier had no doubt taken the edge off the shooting team's consistency, a small and temporary blot on the regiment's record.

When the Adjutant returned to duty, Dyer returned to his Quartermaster's post. He was to hold this, with an occasional tour of temporary duty away from it, for a total of four years. The 29th moved station in January 1893, a busy time for Dyer as his department was involved for months in packing, moving then unpacking the battalion's equipment, as well as in handing over their old camp to their successors, and in taking over the new barracks from their predecessors. A testing time, too, as names were to be lost or won, and usually the former, in what went on at such a time. Losses accumulated during a tour had to be hidden, new terms had to be negotiated with wily local camp contractors, and the deceptions of the quartermasters of the other regiments had to be avoided. Dyer, no doubt supported by the tried hands with many years experience of this sort of skulduggery in his department, seems to have managed in this tricky school with no loss of reputation.

Their new posting was Meerut, a large station in the Bengal Command in the comparative quiet of the United Provinces, well away from the Frontier and only some fifty miles from Delhi (not yet the capital of India, which was still at that time at Calcutta). Meerut was another site ineradicably linked with the Mutiny, the place where it had all begun on 10 May 1857 when the 3rd Bengal Light Cavalry had risen late in a sleepy, hot Sunday afternoon to kill as many of their officers and wives as they could find before marching on Delhi. The remembrance would have been enough cause for an occasional shiver down the backbone of any officer like Dyer whose wife was with him there.

The 29th had scarcely had time to unpack before they received their annual inspection. Over two days, 16 and 17 February 1893, the local commander, Major-General Nairne, put them through their paces. He found he liked Colonel Reid but thought little of Majors Mainwaring and McLeod, who were still 'not well reported on', and classed 'the rest average'. He concluded, somewhat stereotypically, 'this regiment heads the musketry list of the Native Army, and is in all other respects in excellent order'. General Roberts, forgetting the organisational changes he had himself introduced, added: 'This is a most satisfactory report and I congratulate Lieutenant-Colonel Reid and all ranks under his command on the efficiency of the regiment, especially in musketry, in which it holds first place in the armies of the three presidencies.'[21]

Once he had, for a second time, settled the battalion into a new barracks, and once the excitements of the inspection were over, Dyer turned again to his own studies. In October that year he took and passed the exam for captain, though it was to be several years before he reached sufficient seniority to be actually promoted.[22]

Early in 1894, Dyer handed his Quartermaster's office over to a temporary relief and with Annie made the trip home to England, this time to use his leave to study for the Staff College exam. It was only some three years since they had last gone home, so this, and the fact that Dyer's intention to take the exam was an unusual one for an infantry officer (many of the ambitious didn't bother, as it was quite possible at the time to rise to high rank without attending the college, and many of the rest regarded it as an unutterably careerist thing to do), is yet another indication of the care with which he was planning his career, and his seriousness about his profession. It is also an indication that Colonel Reid was generous enough to give him time to study.

The Staff College entrance exam was academically weighted, involving languages, military law and a good deal of history, and an officer was on his own in mugging it all up. The Dyers left Meerut on 28 March 1894. On arriving in Europe, landing at Marseille, they went first to Paris for some months of the summer to enable Rex to learn French. The couple then crossed the Channel to Kent, and stayed with Annie's parents in West Malling. Rex studied hard at law and military history, and covered the walls of the room the Ommanneys gave him for a study with self-drawn maps of the campaigns of Napoleon.[23] He also spent money on a crammer, as he had done for his Sandhurst entry.[24] Ivan Reginald, their first surviving child, who was always to be known as Ivon rather than Ivan, was born there on 8 March.[25] His father's studies were interrupted, though, by events back on the North-West Frontier, where the tiny British garrison of Chitral found itself under siege on 3 March 1895.

The story of the siege and relief of Chitral is one of the best-known romances of the North-West Frontier. Five hundred and forty-three men, most of them Kashmiris, some Gurkhas and the rest Sikhs, penned inside a mud and timber walled fort of seventy square yards under a handful of British officers, of whom the most senior was the Surgeon Major, Robinson; beyond its ramparts, tribesmen too numerous to count, and the nearest British forces and all hope of relief over a hundred miles away; on the makeshift flagpole the battered and bullet-holed Union flag fluttering defiantly throughout. As the two Younghusband brothers put it in the book they rushed into print immediately it was all over: 'Since Lord Roberts made his famous march from Kabul to Kandahar the Indian Army has perhaps taken part in no campaign so rapid, brilliant and successful as the operations which resulted in the relief of the severely pressed garrison of Chitral.'[26] The campaign was an epic of the high watermark of imperialism, and the public showered adulation on the few who were lucky enough to have taken part in it. No fewer than four accounts were published within a year of the campaign, and young officers made reputations there that carried them through the long remainder of their careers.[27]

Once again Dyer found himself on the wrong side of the world when events involved his battalion in the active service that might have led him to medals and promotion. He was not going to be left out this time and, as soon as he heard news of the campaign he took ship for India, leaving Annie and baby Ivon with the Ommanneys. He was back with the 29th on the frontier by 26 April, but he was too late to see anything but the close of the fighting. Chitral had been relieved six days before, and when Dyer reached the 29th they were garrisoning the Malakand Pass.

Chitral was the most northerly of any British garrison on the frontier, just south of the Afghan panhandle of Wakhan that separated British India from the Russians in the Pamirs to the north. It was about 120 miles in a direct line north of Peshawar, but there were no roads to give direct access there. The small British garrison, in place only since 1893, was supplied and relieved over a mountain track which wound west from Gilgit, itself a fabulously difficult place to get in and out of, as it lay in secluded valleys to the far north of Jammu, which was then ruled by the Maharajah of Kashmir. Chitral, in the minds of those occupied with the Great Game, was a potential route for a Russian army invading India; in truth, it was an impassable backwater. The Chitralis were an independent race, and their ruler, the Mehtar, had traditionally spent much of his time at war with the Pathans and Kashmiris who surrounded his country. It was local feuding which involved the British on this occasion; in 1895, the young and recently crowned Mehtar, Nizam, was murdered by his step-brother, Amir-ul-Mulk, under the eyes of the British Political Agent and at the behest of his uncle, Sher Afzul, who had been passed over by the British for the succession. Immediately, the most powerful local Pathan ruler, Umra Khan of Jandol, a local empire builder, conqueror of Dir and Bajaur, who had recently defeated the Amir of Afghanistan and conquered the Kunar valley just over the Afghan frontier, invaded the valley. With Sher Afzul, he surrounded the British and their new child appointee, the Mehtar Shuja, in the ramshackle fort.[28]

It took some time for this news to percolate through to the Government of India, and relief forces did not begin to assemble at Nowshera until 26 March, over three weeks after the fort was invested. The Chitral Relief Force was commanded by a hero of the Mutiny, Lieutenant-General Sir Robert Low, who had been at the sieges of Delhi and Lucknow, and who had later been with Roberts in Afghanistan. There was a very real possibility that the relief would be too late, for between Nowshera and Chitral lay unmapped territory which the British had never entered, and over which there were no proper roads. 15,000 troops supported by 28,000 baggage animals assembled by rail at Nowshera, and the 29th joined the force, being assigned to the lines of communication troops, whose task was to hold open the road as the forward three brigades forced a passage through the tribes. These were rightly assessed to be intent on preventing any incursion into their territory. The mission given the force was to relieve Chitral and to force Umra Khan of Jandol to submit, and its advance was to be a running fight over one hundred and fifty miles. It began on 1 April. The advance guard reached Jalala and Lundkwar that day, and the following day they met the first real obstacle, the Malakand Pass, where they were opposed by ten thousand tribesmen who rolled boulders down on them from the heights above. The pass was assaulted on the 3rd, and troops entered the Swat valley beyond it. By the 12th, the 29th was in place at the Malakand holding a defensive position, part of a strong force including a wing of the 34th Punjab Pioneers and two companies of the 30th Punjabis. Their task was to fight off attempts by the tribes to break the chain of supply and to prevent the frequent sniping attacks made on the slow columns of pack animals. Ahead of them the force made slow progress against bitter resistance, and it was still slowly advancing on the 21st when it heard the news that the siege had been lifted the day before. Lieutenant-Colonel Kelly, Commanding Officer of the 32nd Sikh Pioneers, with five hundred of his Sikhs, accompanied by only two mountain guns which had to be mostly man-oeuvred by hand, had marched unsupported from Gilgit, crossing the Shandur Pass at 12,000 feet, and had snatched the garrison from the jaws of defeat. He had also snatched the honour of their relief from Low and his men. After this anticlimax, the main column was forced to continue the advance against a tribal opposition which continued until the end of April.[29]

When Dyer reached the 29th, dug in around the Malakand Pass, he found that they had missed the major actions of the campaign and were still at the full strength at which they had started out, eleven British officers, seven hundred and thirty Indian officers and men.[30] They were at that stage under the command of Brigadier-General Bindon Blood, the Chief of Staff of the Force, but almost immediately Dyer arrived there was a reorganisation.[31] At the end of April, Major-General Stedman was made GOC Lines of Communications, and he formed up a new 4th Brigade on 19 May from his Lines of Communications troops. The 29th were included in this brigade under Brigadier-General Hammond. The next few months which Dyer spent at the Malakand Pass were mostly spent protecting convoys and constructing a road over the pass.

As things had now settled into some routine, Colonel Reid, still very indulgent in allowing Dyer time to study, granted him permission to travel back to the battalion's station at Meerut to sit the Staff College exam, which was to be held on 7 August. Rex returned to find the battalion had moved, this time to Chakdara, further north up the road to Chitral, where they were stationed with 1200 camels forming part of the supply relay system.[32] The battalion was inspected there in the field by Brigadier-General Waterfield, who gave it as good a report as usual. The Commander-in-Chief, by now the same General White who had been Dyer's Commander in Burma, concurred in his assessment: 'The condition of the 29th Punjab Infantry is very satisfactory.'[33] The Chitral Relief Force was still in the Swat and Chitral valleys, and the road had to be held open whilst the Political Officers organised the eventual political settlement.[34] In the meantime, the tribes, believing that their land was being annexed, continued to attack the troops and labourers, and punitive raids were mounted against their villages and lands. Orders had already been issued for a withdrawal before Dyer got back, and he returned to find the force withdrawing by stages back the way it had come.

By early October, the 29th were back in base at Meerut. It had been a frustrating campaign for them, with an unglamorous role in a relief force that had been beaten to its objective. It had nevertheless been a difficult and uncomfortable campaign, and they deserved the grant of the new India General Service Medal which all members of the battalion who had taken part in the campaign, including Dyer, received.[35] The campaign had been a great success. The wicked uncle Sher Afzul was carted off to prison in India. Umra Khan of Jandol fled to Afghanistan, where the Amir took his revenge for his earlier humiliation and clapped him in jail. Chitral became a partially sovereign state, with its local affairs left in the hands of the Mehtar, and its international relations and defence in the firm hands of the Political Agent appointed to his court by the Government of India. Chitral was properly pacified, and nothing further untoward was to occur there again, secured as it was by a permanent garrison of two battalions. This success was not mirrored further south, where troops had to be left permanently in place to guard the Malakand and Swat crossings on the road built during the campaign.[36] The road ran for 180 miles through tribal land, and the military posts, established in territory which was otherwise independent, and which until then had never suffered foreign invasion, were one of the irritants which were to set the Frontier ablaze in the biggest conflagration of the century only two years later in 1897. But for this next campaign Dyer was once more to be absent, for he was by then again in England.

6

Staff College and the Mahsud

In November 1895, Dyer heard that he had passed the Staff College exam and had won a place at Camberley for the following year. This was a double happiness: the Staff College place was a great feather in his cap, and attending it meant that he would be united in England with Annie and Ivon. The long course would allow them to be together for two uninterrupted years. A few weeks later, on 14 December, he set off from Meerut, and in the new year of 1896 was back in the house of his parents-in-law in Kent. He was not there long, as on 15 January he reported to Camberley to commence his two years at the Staff College.[1]

The College was a grand Italianate building of three storeys which stood in its own grounds, its yellow stone walls framed by the green of croquet lawns and the colour of flower beds, on a small knoll set back from the main entrance to the Royal Military College Sandhurst. This was familiar ground for Rex, though he had not been back there since he had passed off the square at Sandhurst nearly ten years before. Behind the college, hidden in the woods of beech and birch that ringed the park, were the married quarters in which Annie and Rex were to make their home for two years, not this time a bungalow with surrounding verandahs but a two-storey detached house of brick, partially hidden by overhanging branches and boxed in by hedges which quite hid the secluded lawn on which Ivon could take his first steps. It was a pleasant place to live, though society in the college was small and very different from what the Dyers were used to in India. Many of the couples who were their neighbours came from backgrounds of which Rex and Annie knew little. They may have felt more than a little isolated and unsure in Camberley, at least at the start. Brigadier-General Edmonds, the historian of the Great War, was one of Dyer's fellow students, and he recalled the tone set in their number by Captain Douglas Haig (the future field-marshal): 'He had rather outraged our finer feelings by writing in the Leave Book, on arrival, a request for three-days' leave, "to shoot, to meet the Prince of Wales".' But not all of those at Camberley moved in quite so exalted circles, and Edmonds also records that his thirty-two fellow students were 'more than half of them married, five recently', and that they 'were a cheery, sociable lot'. Dyer's handwritten list of students shows that Haig lived as a bachelor in a room on the first floor of the college, well away from the married quarters. Annie would have seen little of him. The four students from the Indian Army in Dyer's batch gave the Dyers at least a few couples with something in common. There may even, perhaps, have been one or two they had met before.[2]

The college had fallen somewhat behind the times in its instruction, and it was not in those years the intellectual powerhouse for which it had been intended and which it was later to become. The previous Commandant had spent much of his time in London, but his successor, Colonel (later General Sir Henry) Hildyard, was determined to improve things and set about reforming its syllabus. Hildyard was known in the college as 'Akela', the lone wolf of Kipling's *Jungle Book*, which had been published a year or so before; clearly, he was a man who walked by himself. Yet Hildyard had made little progress in revising the new syllabus by the time the Class of '96 arrived, and Edmonds for one found that in the first year he learned very little that he hadn't studied when he was a cadet at the Royal Academy Woolwich. The students even had to submit a certificate of horsemanship, so 'were put through the riding school again', which seemed rather pointless to most. There was study of tactics, field sketching, the minutiae of standard military organisations, and what abbreviations to put into a memo or a telegram, but the work did not seem, at least to Edmonds, very stretching. Significantly, he recalled, when reflecting later about his fellow student Rex Dyer, that they all received instruction in military law, and that this had included action in aid to the civil power:

> We had been carefully instructed at the Staff College that when soldiers are called out in aid of the civil power, the Riot Act must be read and no more force must be used than is absolutely necessary: thus in the case of a riot, if called on to fire by a magistrate, first only a single round should be fired; if this had no effect, five rounds might be fired; and so on.[3]

Edmonds had a very sharp mind and found the instruction easy, but other students were not so blessed. He records that Allenby (the future field-marshal) 'was a very popular member of the batch, though he had not much to say for himself, and was obviously out of his depth at Camberley', a strange comment in light of the fact that Allenby had gained first place in the entrance exam. Haig, on the other hand, may have had to work hard, as he was not gifted academically; he had failed the entrance exam completely (which puts Dyer's achievement in passing it into an even more favourable perspective), and had only got in when strings were pulled to give him one of the few places reserved for the deserving but dense.

The officers who attended the Staff College were of a much more varied, and generally far more junior, rank than those attending that institution today. Only three were already majors, twenty-seven were captains and five were lieutenants, and their ages ranged from twenty-five to thirty-seven. As a thirty-one-year-old lieutenant, Rex was one of the most junior officers on the course, a fact which must have reinforced his natural diffidence. He was only promoted captain in August of his first year at the college.[4] To make matters more difficult for him, this was a very talented intake. Edmonds recorded that 'The batch (or year) was a good one … it held the record for gaining the largest percentage of officers recommended for Staff appointments.'[5] Some of the students had other abilities beyond the usual. One Gurkha officer named Colomb was a musician and a writer as well as being an artist who sold his water colours in London. Another, W.J. Anderson, was a Turkish interpreter. Many years later, Edmonds compiled a list of what happened to his fellows in their subsequent service, a list which shows what the class of '96 was to achieve, and which supplies a yardstick against which to measure Rex's career:

Killed in action	4
Died of hardship in a theatre of war	2
Died before 1914 of disease contracted abroad	2
Invalided from 1914 War as Colonels	2
Field-Marshals and Peers (Haig and Allenby)	2
Generals and Knights	8
Generals, decorated but not knighted	6
Placed on the retired list for quelling a riot by machine-gun fire [sic] in India (Dyer)	1
Joined the Sudan Civil Service	1
Retired before 1914 on coming into money, one during and the other at the end of the Staff College course	2
Shot his mother-in-law and her lawyer and committed suicide	1
Last heard of keeping a brothel in Smyrna – his father married a Levantine during the Crimean War	1[6]

Dyer had his work cut out making an impression amongst this talented bunch, and did not find it easy. His wife later recalled to Colvin that he:

left but a slight impression on this brilliant assembly. He had not come from their schools; he was most terribly shy; the ways and customs of the south of England, its heaths and hedgerows, fox-hunts and country houses were all a sealed book to him. He got along, however, well enough, a quiet, silent, closely and carefully observant fellow, who took in a great deal more than his comrades and teachers supposed.[7]

She was concealing what must have been an uncomfortably difficult memory, the reality of which is revealed by Edmonds:

> After we had been there about six months, four of us … were summoned to the Commandant … Hildyard opened the proceedings by saying that he wanted our help: 'There is a very strange officer in your batch, Captain Dyer: I think him strange: my staff think him strange; I am minded to send him away: but last year when I sent an officer away I got into trouble with the War Office, and was told that if that kind of thing happened it would discourage officers from competing for the Staff College: I should like, therefore, before making any decision, to know what you think of Captain Dyer: Major Heath, will you tell me?' Heath replied that we had already discussed Dyer among ourselves: 'He shuns our society and is not a member of any syndicate … When we speak to Dyer he does not appear to grasp what we say, and looks at his questioner with uncomprehending eye: he does not appear to be all there: however … we will arrange to look after him, and at the end you need not recommend him for a psc.' The other three students agreed with Heath. I pointed out that Dyer had been born in India and had spent most of his youth and service there, had been very little in England, and was 'out of water' here: he could not pronounce a number of English words correctly, and fell down badly over place names. I had encountered him on Esher Common, enquiring the way to Esch..er'. So Dyer was allowed to stay. Haking's syndicate gave him hospitality, and others gave him help; but he continued to leave the impression that he only partially understood what was said to him. In the end, he received a psc.[8]

Dyer's life in India and in his school in Ireland had given him neither the contacts nor the social skills to make his way in the mainstream of the Army. It is probable that he was never aware of how close he came to failure; that he succeeded was due in great part to his dogged determination and penchant for hard work. His Staff College record shows only that he 'Passed. 21 December 1897', but pass he did, and could thereafter proudly add the letters psc after his name.[9] Colonel Hildyard's final report on him survives, and shows that he passed out twenty-eighth of thirty-two, not the worst on the course, albeit worse than his three fellow Indian Army officers, who passed out sequentially 19th to 21st (in this, as in their studies, it is noticeable that they seem to have stuck together without Dyer). Hildyard wrote:

> This officer has no more than average ability and he has got through his work at the Staff College by sheer plodding determination. He entered it singularly ill-equipped as regarded [sic] his knowledge of the arms [parts of the Army] other than his own, and of military subjects generally. In addition to this disadvantage, he suffered from liver, and he did not at first get on well with other officers. But he overcame these difficulties by

means of persistent effort, and during the second year of his course he made marked progress with his work. His leading characteristic is persistent determination and he has shown powers of persistence and application. By temperament he is shy and reserved and is lacking in influence on others; but he is trustworthy and to be depended on to do thoroughly to the extent of his powers, whatever he is entrusted with. He went through the voluntary course of Surveying satisfactorily, and is an accurate mathematician. He would make a useful Special Services Officer. H. Hildyard.[10]

The Commandant had accurately picked up on Dyer's aptitude for mathematics and surveying, as he had also noticed Dyer's interest in intelligence and political work. His reference to Dyer's 'liver' indicates that some occasion had arisen for a display of his quick temper, perhaps an argument with other students. Although he allowed the award of a psc, the Commandant did not specifically recommend Dyer for a staff appointment, and this was to be a major factor in the course his career was to take. Indeed, Rex had not made a good impression. He was remembered in the Army for not exactly relishing the intellectual aspects of the course (such as they were); the *Army Quarterly Review* remarked in its obituary of him: 'A fighting man in every sense of the word, little influenced by his two years at the Staff College, Camberley, when theory failed to interest him.'[11] But pass Staff College he did, and so could return with some pride to his regiment, perhaps even thinking, if he was not totally clear about the implications of the absence of a recommendation for a staff appointment, that he might hope for great things in his future career.

There was also something else about which he and Annie could rejoice in their time at Camberley, for a year before, on 29 December 1896, their second son was born. He was christened Geoffrey; he was always to be 'Geoff' in the family. All four Dyers sailed together for India in February 1898, just over a month after the course ended, and by the following April they were back with the 29th, who were by that time in Delhi having moved there the year before.[12]

This time Dyer did not return to his Quartermaster's post, but was once again designated a wing officer. He was now senior enough to be expected to exercise command on occasion of two or more of the wing's companies. His soldiers were once again Sikhs.[13] He, Annie and the boys settled back into another bungalow in the cantonment. At some stage they no doubt visited the Delhi Ridge, where they would have viewed its memorial to the legendary siege of the city during the Mutiny. They would have often passed by the Red Fort, seat of the last Moghul Emperor dethroned by the British at the bloody conclusion to the siege. The echoes of the Mutiny were as inescapable in the Dyers' lives as they were for all the British in India, who shuddered at the fear of a recurrence as they celebrated the victory which outwardly had made their position secure.

While Dyer had been in England, the 29th had been stuck in the Delhi Garrison and so had missed the major Frontier campaigns of 1897, fretting away their time in the heat of the city whilst almost everyone else, it must have seemed, was winning glory. So when he returned to the battalion Rex had not missed out this time on any active service. The 29th had continued to perform very well in their peacetime soldiering, and had achieved excellent reports in the two inspections carried out while Dyer was away. In his last report before vacating his post of Commander-in-Chief, General White echoed all the comments he, and Roberts before him, had made: 'A thoroughly satisfactory report on a very fine and efficient regiment. The 29th Punjab Infantry is the best shooting regiment of the Native army.'[14] The 29th was undoubtedly a very good regiment indeed.

Not long after the Dyers reached Delhi, the battalion was posted to Peshawar, and so was back once more to operational soldiering on the Frontier. They went by train and were routed through Amritsar, which was a key junction on the main line to the Frontier. The Golden Temple there was, and remains, the centre of the Sikh religion, the ultimate place of pilgrimage for all Sikhs, and the spot where the Sikh's holiest book, the *Grant Sahib*, is read continuously day and night. The Temple is extraordinarily beautiful, one of India's wonders. At its heart is an island on which stands a small pearl of a temple housing the *Grant Sahib*, its roof and walls a scintillating drop of gold from which shimmering light dances onto the calm waters of the lake and bathes the spotless white marble of the walls and pavements which surround it on four sides. It was a sight which the whole regiment, including the other ranks, wished to see, and it may have been for this reason that the train made a temporary halt in the city. When it drew into the station, and the troops had detrained to start erecting tents for their families alongside the railway tracks, Rex and Annie hired a *ghari* to tour the city's sites. They climbed a tower by the Golden Temple to watch the pilgrims at their devotions inside.

After they had descended the steps of the tower and were strolling through the crowded and narrow streets of the bazaar, they were distracted by the sound of shouting not far off. Something in the sound was recognisable to Rex, and he told Annie he believed his men were involved. Sending her back to the *ghari*, he ran off towards the source of the noise, and forcing his way through the crowd that he found gathered there, he saw a party of his men beating a local man who was down and howling on the ground. The soldiers, recognising Dyer, left off their beating, came to attention and saluted, but the crowd continued to grow in size, and was becoming more and more threatening. Dyer

held up his hand, obtained silence, and made the people a speech. These were his soldiers; he would inquire into their conduct, and if they had done wrong, he would punish them severely. This quieted the tumult, and Dyer marched his men off to the station. There the soldiers explained very simply the cause of their conduct. They had left their tents unguarded, and suddenly returning had found this rascal peeping at their women through the flaps of the tent ... Dyer, concluding from their evidence that their statement was true, held that they had acted under provocation, and did not punish them.[15]

On this occasion in Amritsar Dyer kept his head. The next day the party continued on its way to Peshawar, where they settled back into the cantonment. Rex and Annie occupied a bungalow at the end of the lines, which they nicknamed 'the last house in Asia'.[16] They resumed the round of garrison life, with its training, sport, society, relieved for Rex by the occasional spot of duty in isolated posts on the Frontier. In February 1899, the 29th found themselves back on the road to Chitral, which they had helped to hold four years before. Posts were still being manned along it in order to hold the route open, and the 29th took their turn at providing the garrison at a small place named Drosh, some thirty miles south of Chitral on the Kashgar river.[17] This was further north by over seventy miles than they had reached during the campaign of 1895. Colonel Reid was by now no longer Commandant, having finally reached the end of his long, nine-year tenure, and Captain A.B.H. Drew was temporarily in command. The regiment was inspected at Drosh on 13 February by Colonel Lorne Campbell, and the inspection proved the 29th's usual success. Lorne Campbell considered the British officers a 'Hard working good body of officers', and the 'Native Officers intelligent and good instructors'. This was perforce a rather perfunctory inspection due to the operational circumstances; most of the battalion would have been in small posts well out of the inspecting officer's reach, but even up here in the wildest of Frontier postings the 29th were clearly keeping up their standards.[18]

Back in barracks in Peshawar, Dyer played hockey, which on the hard, rocky ground was a rougher and faster game than that played back home on grass, and sometime that year he suffered a nasty injury. An inadvertent blow with a hockey stick wielded by a brother officer caused him to lose two teeth and to suffer a badly broken jaw and a smashed palate which laid him up and kept him off duty for several months.[19] There is no record of any lasting damage either to his speech, which was unaffected, or to his appearance, which was unscarred. Colleagues and friends remember him at the time, aged then about thirty-four, as:

A man rather big in build and of remarkable bodily strength, very clever with his hands, an eternal smoker of cigarettes, often carried in empty envelopes or loose in the pocket; of an absent-minded and casual habit in ordinary life; always deep in some absorbing subject, paying no heed to the small conventions of society, but forgiven all these little sins by reason of an engaging frankness, a perpetual overflow of merriment and good-nature.[20]

About that time, Peshawar suffered an outbreak of fire, allegedly (though uncertainly) started by a deliberate arson attack by Hindus on the Muslim quarters. Whole areas of the city went up in flames, and the conflagration was fed by explosions in the sugar factories which caused intense heat and massive destruction of the wooden houses and shops tightly-packed in the Indian quarters. The garrison turned out to fight the conflagration and to rescue as many of the inhabitants as they could get to safety, but they were not helped in this by Muslim house owners who stood in front of their doors with drawn swords to prevent their women being dishonoured by being seen, let alone touched, by infidel strangers. After a whole night fighting the fires, the 29th staggered exhausted back to barracks. Dyer came home to Annie 'black and singed, his eyes crimson, his veins almost bursting'.[21] She swiftly had him packed in ice and managed to ward off the heatstroke from which he was by then suffering. This was not to be the last occasion on which Rex Dyer drove himself until he dropped from the heat.

In the year 1899, Dyer was posted to the regimental depot. Such a posting was routine for any infantry officer, and not an unwelcome duty as it was a small independent command, giving an officer the opportunity to carry out his own ideas of how training should be conducted. Here Dyer was responsible for training recruits and for supervising the small team of Indian officers and NCOs seconded from the three units whose men they drilled into shape over a period of some six months or so. The depot was back in Jhelum, and Annie and the boys may have gone with him there, though if they were not able to do this it may have meant a small period of separation for the couple.[22]

Dyer was away from the battalion on 25 January 1900 when it was inspected by Brigadier-General McCall, Commander Peshawar District. The Commanding Officer was now Lieutenant-Colonel R.W. McLeod, who had managed to survive all the years of adverse reports on his debts, which he had presumably repaid at last. McLeod continued Colonel Reid's successful handling of the battalion, and Brigadier McCall reported that the British Officers were 'Professionally and socially an excellent lot, keen to keep up the credit of their corps [and who] pull very well together.' He judged the 29th to be 'A smart, well set up, and efficient regiment in every respect fit for active service.'[23]

By May 1900, Dyer was back with them at a time when a reform was instituted affecting the infantry of the entire Army.[24] The old wing system, with which Dyer had grown up, and which had been part of the reorganisations which had followed the Mutiny, was finally abolished. In its place, the eight rifle companies of the battalion were grouped in pairs, and a British officer placed in command of each two, which were now known as 'double companies'. Double companies were grouped by the caste of their men, so that there were Sikh, Dogra and Punjabi Musulman double companies, a segregated way to order a unit but one which made the observation of religion, custom and caste easier, and which ultimately made it more likely that a battalion would be reliable in all circumstances against any conceivable enemy. So Dyer found himself, albeit briefly, in command of two companies of the battalion.

There were other jobs for him to do as well. Officers of Dyer's age and experience could expect to pick up the occasional odd job in a garrison, especially in a large one like Peshawar, where, for instance, visiting dignitaries needing escorts were frequent. That year, Peshawar was visited by a Russian general. Why such a visitor was allowed on the Frontier of British India, to which the only major threat at the time was a Russian one, is unclear. Whatever the reason, the Peshawar garrison found a Russian in their midst, and Dyer was detailed off to be his minder. Visits to the Peshawar Club made an easy start to the tour, hard going on his escort though the Russian's heavy indulgence in its hospitality made them, but the subsequent trip to the Khyber Pass in a landau accompanied by a strong escort of troops was inevitably a trickier proposition. Things quickly turned sour when Dyer spotted a camera slung over his guest's shoulder and requested that he surrender it; the Russian flew into a rage, which did not intimidate Dyer, and matters remained at a standstill until General Ellis, the Peshawar Commander, himself descended from his Headquarters and confiscated the camera. The Russian departed in a huff by train for Rawalpindi and Dyer was relieved of his charge.[25]

The next year's inspection of the 29th was conducted on 8 February 1901 by Brigadier-General Stratford-Collins, Commander Peshawar District. He reported that the battalion was in good order and that Lieutenant-Colonel McLeod was a 'Strong Commanding Officer who learnt details of profession young, and kept them up. Commands with judgment. ... To be depended on. Socially all that can be desired.' The Brigadier tested the 29th with a snap drill parade, which was well performed under their Commanding Officer but less well under the junior officers he detailed off thereafter. In his report he stated: 'the British Officers are a hardworking lot who have considerable war experience. The native officers are a very fine set of men who command respect', and who were 'distinctly good in manoeuvres'. The inspection team found that the unit was 'a thoroughly well regulated corps in which a good system exists. Books up to date. Men's comfort looked after ... there is no crime. Musketry receives the greatest attention, the regiment produces some brilliant marksmen, and, as a whole, the shooting is very good.'

For the first time in the records, the Commanding Officer's reports on his British officers were appended to the review report, so we can see at last his opinion of Dyer, by then the third most senior captain of the battalion. McLeod wrote of him: 'Exceptionally clever and smart, thoroughly popular, keen sportsman, fond of games, joins in men's sports.' Dyer was evidently well thought of, and there is no echo here of anything that would justify a belief that the Commanding Officer would have preferred him to be away from the battalion. Dyer was a successful regimental soldier. The Brigadier knew him enough to add: 'I concur. By education above the average.' It would have been this reputation as an intellectual soldier which would have accounted for his selection as escort to the Russian visitor.[26]

Whilst the 29th was honing its peacetime skills, across the other side of the Indian Ocean the South African War was tying down large parts of the British Army, and the Boers were making it very plain to the world that much of that Army's organisation, training and equipment was defective. The Indian Army was not directly involved in this conflict but watched it carefully, and one of the lessons which it drew was that it had a lot to do to improve the standard of its officer corps. Army Headquarters directed that each military district (the geographical areas into which the garrisons were split for administrative, rather than operational, purposes) establish a school for its young officers, and these, being outside the military establishment then existing, were staffed and run from unit resources. Meerut District in the Bengal Command established a school in the foothills of the Himalayas at the small and isolated station of Chakrata, between Mussoorie and Simla, and Dyer was posted to command this school on 6 March 1901.[27] The posting, scheduled for five years, was the real start of the Dyers' exile from the 29th. It is noteworthy that it took place a year after Colonel McLeod took over, and it is really seems impossible to agree with Villiers-Stuart that he or his predecessor had shuffled Dyer out of the battalion. Colvin mentions that Colonel Macleod (the spelling of whose name seems to change at this time) was a friend of Dyer, and so we may assume that Annie considered him so.[28] But Dyer probably did view the job at Chakrata as a disappointing posting for a Staff College graduate. It was not the prestigious post at a key Headquarters, one carrying with it the chance of active service or close proximity to a commander who could assist his subsequent career, that he had worked so hard for at Staff College. Chakrata's Officer Commanding was in reality an instructor, and one in a school hidden away in the hills many miles from the regiment and right out of the mainstream of Army life. The five-year tenure attached to this post would block the chance any Staff appointment for a very long time. Now, at least, it must have become very clear to Dyer what his failure to achieve a recommendation for Staff duties really meant.

There were, though, compensations to be had at Chakrata. Dyer was undoubtedly suited for the job there and had both the knowledge and the skill to be a good instructor. The Army, unusually, had found a round peg for a round hole. Dyer found himself in command of his own unit and as far away from any interfering superior officer as it was possible to be. He found that he could run the school pretty much as he liked, and this, of course, suited his temperament perfectly. The subjects he had to teach were those he had specially studied on the extra courses he had attended (a fact which had been picked up from his record, no doubt, by the Adjutant General's branch when they looked for a suitable selection for Chakrata). Rex and Annie now had a certainty of five years together, and they could set up home in a way they had so far never been able to do. Ivon and Geoff, by now six and five years old, were going to be able to spend their childhood at home in the kind of Himalayan countryside in which Rex himself had grown up and which he loved so much. In the winter months, when the cold and snow made Chakrata impractical for training, the school moved down to Meerut, where there was some society for Annie to enjoy, perhaps even one or two people still whom they had known when they were stationed there six years before. Delhi was not far off for the occasional visit to sightsee or to shop in the bazaar. There could have been no better family posting than Chakrata, and as the Dyers settled in this must have sweetened the otherwise rather bitter pill.

The school taught three courses a year of field engineering, topography and fortification to subalterns mostly some ten or so years junior to Dyer, and they much appreciated the interest he took in them. This was recalled years later by a friend of Ian Colvin who was one of Rex's students in 1902:

when I was then a one of his Garrison Class of young officers. I have a great respect and affection for him – Major Dyer as he was then. He was very kind to and encouraged me much. I well remember his congratulating and encouraging me in my efforts in topographical sketches in the hills near Chukrata and know I pretty well mastered the subject under his able tuition. The knowledge I gained under him has stood me in good stead ever since. I remember too, the jolly expensive parties in the *khud*! We all loved Dyer I think. I remember one evening he dined at the Class Mess and we carried him shoulder high on the way home ... I met Dyer again ... before the Delhi Durbar and he knew me at once and gave me a cheery, kindly greeting. He was a fine type of British Soldier, Gentleman, and human friend.[29]

From this it appears that Dyer was given acting rank of major to command the school (he was not to be promoted to the substantive rank until this was due by time in August 1903), so this was another advantage the post had over a Staff billet, and one which brought with it a welcome increment of pay.[30]

Among the ways by which Dyer fostered his students' interest and gained a reputation as an instructor were the 'explosive picnics' he organised in the *khud*. On arrival in Chakrata, finding a large store of explosives in the camp, he determined to use it to demonstrate the effect of mines. He prepared targets on the slopes of a valley, on the opposite side of which he assembled his students' picnic party, which thus had a full view of the explosion and of the bits of *sangars*, rocks, deodar trees and dummies that flew through the air when he detonated the charges. He always lit the fuses himself and dealt with them himself when they failed to function; delegation, particularly of risky tasks, was not in Dyer's nature. The school covered less exciting subjects, too, and Dyer recalled later that he instructed for five years in military law, and that this instruction covered military assistance to the civil power during disturbances.[31] His reputation as an instructor grew to such an extent that his contemporaries began to ask him the favour of coaching them in their studies for the 'Q' exam, the examination for promotion to lieutenant-colonel, which Dyer himself had not taken and was not to pass until 1904.[32]

In the winter of 1901, Dyer was called back briefly to the 29th to take part in operations on the Frontier. Colonel Macleod, who had been appointed a Column Commander, needed a staff officer to help coordinate his force, and he sent for Dyer.[33] The area of operations they were headed for was Waziristan, much further south on the Frontier than Dyer had been before. It lay opposite the British district of Bannu, south of Peshawar and strategically placed between the Tochi and the Gomal passes through which ran the roads from the Indus Valley to Ghazni in Afghanistan. The usual desiccated and rugged Frontier terrain was occupied here by Pathan tribes, and in particular by the Mahsuds, one of the two great divisions of the Waziri, who lived in the isolated mountain valleys in a belt some seventy miles wide between the administrative frontier and the Afghan border. Waziristan was a running sore for the British and a problem they were never to solve. In part this was because of Waziri power; the Mahsud alone were estimated to have about ten thousand men capable of bearing arms and who habitually did so from childhood. The Waziri had been unlucky to have been empire building in this area just before the British arrived, and they resented having had their wings clipped by being made to relinquish the control they had established over other tribes, particularly those of the neighbouring plains. They were much under the influence of Muslim mullahs, whose diatribes often stirred up the tribesmen to wage religious war on the British infidel. They were highly proud of their individual style of life, and fiercely resistant to anything seen as a threat to it, for they considered themselves free men and lived very democratically. They begrudged every power granted to tribal chiefs, who were at the most spokesmen, and only very occasionally would the tribes acknowledge the joint power of a tribal council, or *jirga*. The British saw much that they liked in this kind of society, and were inclined to admire the rugged independence of their foes, men whom they found were not easily susceptible to any form of coercion.[34] The Mahsud's perpetuation of blood feuds over many generations, and their inveterate habit of pillaging their richer neighbours, whom they despised, made it scarcely surprising that the tribe could not live easily alongside the British border, nor that they bitterly resented the fortified posts which the British had inserted around, and in some places inside, their lands.

The British had already invaded Mahsud territory three times, but the punitive expeditions, 'the burn and scuttle policy' which seemed the only method of dealing with the tribes, settled nothing and left only bitterness to mix with the ashes of the houses and fruit trees burned in the raids. British attempts to appoint tribal leaders they could use to exercise control succeeded only in creating implacable enemies. One of these, the Mullah Powindah, was to be a particular thorn in the British side over many decades, and became so notorious that he was dubbed by no less a figure than Kitchener as that 'Pestilential Priest'.

Raiding into British territory had increased in the late 1890s, and the local British response almost encouraged it. The Indian Arms Act of 1899 prevented the carriage of weapons by any inhabitant of British territory but, as there were few troops on the Frontier, the disarmed border villagers now found themselves defenceless against the Mahsud. The Border Military Police whose job was to police the Frontier were so intimidated by the Mahsud, particularly by their habit of revenging shootings or arrests by assassination, that they preferred to let raiders give them the slip and notoriously aimed to miss fleeing targets. In January 1900, the Mahsud showed their contempt for the police by massacring a small garrison in an isolated post at Zam, and in 1901 they repeated this with at the similar post at Baran. At the same time they attacked a party making a survey of the Frontier and killed half of its members. By November 1900, the unpaid fines levied on the tribe for all this mayhem had reached 200,000 rupees. The British tried to levy this through a tribal *jirga* but were ignored.[35]

The Viceroy at the time was Lord Curzon, who had decided after the first small expedition he had allowed himself to be persuaded to mount that he would never allow another. He believed that the presence of military posts within tribal terri-tory was one of the causes of the perpetual unrest on the Frontier, so withdrew them, and he was proud of the reduction of military expenditure he achieved by curtailing local wars, boasting that whilst his predecessor had spent £4,500,000 on expeditions he had spent only £248,000. He was also notoriously con-temptuous of the military and was not inclined to adopt a course of action recommended by them unless it coincided with what was already his own view. Curzon would not agree to an expedition against the Mahsud, so instead, in December 1900, they were subjected to a blockade, their territory ringed by a force consisting of a cavalry regiment and three battalions which manned a cordon stretching some three hundred miles. Blockhouses were built and small mobile columns operated out of them to patrol the paths across the hills. The Mahsud's access to the plains was denied, any of them found there were deported and all supply of grain to the hills was prevented. This caused great difficulties in tribal territory: prices rose to famine levels, luxuries became unobtainable, as did staples such as salt, tobacco, cloth and ghee. The blockade seemed to be a success; after eighteen days all raiding ceased and the Mullah Powindah advised the tribes to pay the fine. About three quarters of it was actually collected, but factions within the tribe hostile to the Mullah dissuaded the tribes from completing the fine, and on 1 February 1901 the Mahsud *maliks* repudiated their responsibilities.

Raiding resumed, and whilst it had been found perfectly possible to prevent merchants moving supplies into the hills, it was not found at all possible to prevent small bodies of tribesmen slipping through the cordon to raid the plains. It was also discovered that the Mahsud had stocked up on grain in the expectation of British action, so the embargo proved less effective than had been anticipated. Yet Curzon would still not be pushed into mounting an expedition and insisted on maintaining the blockade, seeking to keep public opinion on his side by leaking financial justifications to the press; *The Times* of 17 August 1901 carried an article in which it was claimed that it cost only 1500 rupees per day to run the blockade against the 100,000 rupees a day that would be needed for an expedition (figures too suspiciously neat to be credible). By the end of the year, however, as the number of outrages perpetrated by the Mahsud continued to climb, and as the fines levied on them remained unpaid, even Curzon had to admit that his policy was not working and he was forced to authorise an expedition after all.

In late 1901, the cordon commander, Lieutenant-General Egerton, was given more troops, which he quietly distributed to four bases around the cordon to form four raiding columns. Egerton had the objective of punishing the Mahsud by demolishing all their defences, capturing prisoners and cattle, and destroying grain and fodder. His plan was to mount a simultaneous surprise attack from four directions, pushing the columns deep into tribal territory to slash and burn for three to four days, then withdraw before the tribes could mount a determined resistance. The troops would then rest and do the same again elsewhere. By November the troops were in place, and on the 25th, No. 3 Column, consisting of a thousand rifles of the 1st Punjab Infantry, the 35th Sikhs and the 29th Punjab Infantry, all under the command of Colonel Macleod, marched out of Sarwakai on the cordon and into tribal territory. Dyer rode with his Colonel through a bleak landscape, deserted of all but the enemy, who sniped from rock and crag then fled. They marched at first unopposed to the village of Shahur Tangi, where they spent two days destroying the defences and taking seven prisoners and five hundred head of cattle. Everything they could not take away they destroyed. The troops fanned out to hamlets in the nearby areas and destroyed them too. They then marched back outside the protection of the cordon. The Mahsud were taken completely by surprise. The report sent to London makes clear that there were no British casualties: 'Sarwekai column surprise complete. 57 prisoners including Malik Shah Salim. 8 large villages and 5 towers destroyed. 690 animals captured. Enemy killed about 20. Column returned 27 November.'[36]

A second series of raids began on 4 December. Brigadier-General Dening, Commander Derajat District, was given command of two columns, and left the cordon base of Jandola with 2500 men and four guns. Dyer was with one of these columns, still acting as Colonel Macleod's staff officer. The force invaded

Shingi Kot, where Dening divided his force into two to spread the effect of their punitive raids. Troops marched north west up the Tazar Tang, razing the villages of Dwe Shinkai and Guni Khel, then returned through Marghaband to Jandola, wreaking destruction as they went. The winter weather added to the difficulties of a terrain of which the altitude averaged between 5000 and 6000 feet. The men rode and marched muffled and huddled from the wind, and the cold was intense.[37] The surprise of the first British sortie could not be repeated on the second foray, and by now the Mahsud had recovered and gathered to oppose the columns. They fought bravely and lost many men. Calcutta telegraphed London on the 9th with the results of this operation, indicating that this time there had been British casualties, but still surprisingly few:

> Dening force moved to Dur Shinki [sic] and camped overnight. Mahsuds assembled at Karamma, six miles away. 5 December troops destroyed towers two miles from camp, returning to Gunikhel followed by Mahsuds. Rear guard action. That night Mullah Powindah arrived three miles from the camp, directed Mahsuds to go to higher ground with families and flocks. 6 December Dening halted Gunikhel, some sniping. 7 December Dening retired slowly to Marghaband, destroying villages, Mahsuds following as far as Kotshinghi, charging to close quarters once, severely repulsed. 8 December returned to Jandola, with part of force up Shaitak valley, destroyed several villages without opposition. Mahsuds disappeared. Total losses 13 killed, 18 wounded. Mahsud losses not known, thought severe. 15 villages, six towers, grain and fodder destroyed. Several maliks among the slain.[38]

Back in base, the columns reformed during December. No. 3 Column was adjusted to include the 23rd Pioneers and the 32nd Pioneers along with the 29th and Macleod was now superseded as Column Commander by Colonel Hogge, presumably one of the other battalion commanders more senior to him. It seems that Dyer was no longer needed as a staff officer and so went back to Chakrata. He had served for only three weeks on this campaign, and it looks very much that his posting to Macleod's column Headquarters was an informal and personal arrangement made at Macleod's own invitation. This adds to the impression that Macleod thought highly of him.[39]

After Dyer left, the tribes submitted on the 16th, paying the fine in full.[40] The blockade was lifted. The campaign had cost the Mahsud heavily, as they paid another *lakh* of rupees fine, lost all their customary allowances for fifteen months, along with rifles, animals, crops and fodder, all calculated as a total loss of 539,000 rupees. The British columns left behind them scores of derelict villages, ruined defensive towers and, most important of all, an estimated one hundred and thirty dead and two hundred and fifty wounded tribesmen. Yet even this did not succeed in suppressing the Mahsud; the British were to enter their territory to carry out another punitive expedition as early as 1904.

The campaign in Waziristan had been short but hard, and particularly during the second round of British raids Mahsud opposition had been fierce. Dyer saw a good deal of the action at reasonably close range, and he no doubt felt he had deserved the second clasp he was given for his India General Service Medal.[41]

7

Chakrata and Chungla Gully

Rex Dyer got back to Meerut after the Mahsud campaign in January 1902, and once again settled down to the routine of running his school. Life resumed its former steady pace, and he took the school up to Chakrata in the spring, when the weather became too hot on the plains. Once more in the hills, the Dyers watched their sons grow up, Ivon by now receiving whatever schooling was available at such a remote station. At Chakrata, Rex could show his sons the things he had grown up with and loved when he was a boy. The birds, monkeys, trees and flowers in the hills around their home were all very similar to those in the country around Simla. Rex had time to devote to his children; at home in the evenings, before the boys were put to bed, Rex would tell

> an endless serial story to his two small sons in the verandah of his little bungalow, a story which drew the officers of the garrison into the house to listen covertly behind the door, a story taken up where left off, in which current events were interwoven in the fable of beasts, prodigies, and monsters – the Tsar of Russia attacked by an octopus as big as a house, protectively swallowed by a fabulous 'arkjaw', and rescued by the King's Swordsman, not a hair the worse; an 'underground wallah' of portentous powers – all manner of facts and fancies turned into a tale for the delight of two children.[1]

Edward Dyer died in late April 1902.[2] Rex's brother, Edward, now took over the brewery, and inevitably there must have been some communication between the brothers at this time. We know they were in touch many years later in 1916, so it seems likely that the old family hostilities died with Rex's parents. They were not forgotten by Annie, however, who, when relating her family history to Ian Colvin, made no mention at all of the death of her parents-in-law.

Towards the end of 1902, as cooler weather again arrived on the plains below, the school packed up once more and took the trail down to Meerut. Dyer was called away once more to act as a temporary staff officer, this time in the post of DAAG, a major's post, in the headquarters of 4th Brigade. Peacetime headquarters always needed officers to supplement their staff when they went to war and when they practised for this it was the custom to coopt officers working in local training and garrison posts. On this occasion, 4th Brigade was on manoeuvres, involved in an imaginary scenario pitting them against another brigade. By a ruse, they managed to capture their opponent's commander and his staff, and so acquitted themselves creditably.[3]

After the exercise, the brigade's officers attended the Delhi Durbar, held that year to mark the coronation of King Edward VII. It was an occasion planned personally by Lord Curzon to show off to the whole world the magnificence of the Raj, and it was a hugely colourful and impressive display of British power in India which was attended by the entire British establishment and by most of India's native princes. British India, and the Empire of which it was the chief part, were now at their peak, and the panoply of power revealed at the Durbar must have had a strong effect upon Dyer. An impression of a somewhat different sort was made by the unprecedented reception of silence which the audience, mostly military, gave the Viceroy, and the contrasting cheers with which it greeted the contingent of the 9th Lancers who rode past him in review. Curzon was by this point in his tenure an extremely unpopular man, and had, in an issue involving the 9th Lancers, given much of the Army great offence. An Indian cook of the regiment had been brutally assaulted at the regiment's barracks in Sialkote and had died of his injuries. The culprits were never identified, though it would appear they were known to the regiment's commanding officer, and both General Headquarters and the Government of India felt that the 9th Lancers had made too little effort to track them down. The Commander-in-Chief indicated his view that there had been a cover up by ordering that the regiment forfeit its winter leave, hardly a draconian punishment but one which caused howls of protest in the popular press in England. The affair divided British India between those who castigated the Government for damaging British prestige by the unfair censure of an entire regiment, and those who believed that the Army could see so little wrong in the death of an innocent Indian at the hands of its soldiers that it had hidden the culprits. It was an ugly issue, and one made worse by Curzon's contemptuous treatment of his military staff. Very noticeable coughing interrupted his speech at the Durbar ceremony on New Year's Day, and a few days later Rex watched Curzon take the salute at the military review when the 9th Lancers, probably (as Curzon himself realised), including the two murderers, rode by to cheers not only from many of the military members of the crowd but, embarrassingly, also from the viceregal party.[4]

The cold weather gave way again to the heat of the summer of 1903, and the school moved back up to Chakrata to resume its work. The schedule of courses left plenty of time for recreation and adventure. Dyer was joined there by his step-brother-in-law, Jack Gannon, who seems to have been one of his few close friends, in an expedition to explore the River Tonse. This was an unmapped and violent river which joined the Jumna at Kalsi. The course of the river, which plunged through canyons in the hills west of Chakrata, disappearing both from view and from the map, ran between mountain cliffs capped by thick jungle, and was way off the usual routes. It had never been traversed. Dyer and Gannon built 'a coracle of split bamboo, covered with canvas, light yet strong, with a floor above the keel, a false keel of a tug-of-war rope and gunwales of canvas padded with straw'. In this they set off on the Tonse.

> They launched out upon a furious torrent, hurrying into long and frequent cataracts, round which they had to make painful portages. Then they found themselves going dizzily down a chute between precipitous cliffs, and as their pace increased, heard the roar ahead of an unforeseen cataract. Dyer was in front with the oars, Gannon behind with a double-bladed paddle. By desperate efforts they contrived to reach the side, when within sight of the fall; but as the rock rose precipitously from the river, they had to haul themselves upstream along the bank by the help of bushes and projections of the rock for some hours until at last they found a place where they could get themselves out of the water.

They were forced to keep going by portages and climbs. Their rations ran out after three days, and they found no game to shoot other than a single green pigeon, which they tried to cook but found almost inedible. Gannon fell sick, and after they had been out for eight days, they were both defeated at last by hunger. Abandoning their boat and its equipment on the river bank, they determined to climb their way out. After a steep, perilous climb up the sheer cliffs of the gorge, they emerged half way up onto a narrow mountain path leading out of the ravine. They began to wind their way along this, but turning a corner they found their path blocked by a large black bear: 'The hill rose sheer above and dropped sheer below. There was only one way out: they both fired their shot-guns at once into the face of the bear, which plunged over the *khud* into the torrent below.' At last at the summit, they found all the villages deserted, and so could get no food. At three in the morning of the ninth day they staggered in to the bungalow at Kalsi where Annie was anxiously awaiting them. She had sent out search parties of soldiers from the South Staffords days before, but the only report they had heard was from the locals who had seen what they thought were ghosts in the ravine and had fled from the Tonse (a fact which explained the deserted villages Dyer and Gannon had passed). The brave but failed attempt to chart the river had shown that the Tonse was indeed unnavigable. It was typical of Dyer's stubborn refusal to give up something on which he had set his mind that it took the pair five days without food to abandon the attempt.[5]

In August 1903, Dyer was at last promoted to major.[6] It was at about this time that he and his fellow Indian Army officers lost the post-nominal initials ISC, which had marked their membership of the Indian Staff Corps, and replaced them with the IA of the Indian Army, a more popular designation, though not one which had any real effect on their lives.[7] The weather at Chakrata again turned chill, and the school moved down the mountain to Meerut, where the

Dyers spent their last winter together in the cantonment. Ivon was now eight, Geoff seven, and their schooling was becoming a pressing issue. The Dyers were determined to avoid for their sons the kind of school life that Rex had suffered, and the separation from their parents that boarding school in England would mean. Indeed, the boys had to go home, but the Dyers resolved that Annie would go with them to be nearby and to be at home in Kent for their holidays. Given the way that Annie managed to stay by Dyer's side throughout his career, her acceptance of exile in England now is a real indication of the painful memories Rex had of his childhood. So, early in 1904, she set off with Ivon and Geoff on the long journey back to England, leaving Rex forlornly at his post. Left to himself, he filled the time not occupied in teaching his students by studying for the Q Exam which would qualify him for promotion to lieutenant-colonel. He was well placed for this, surrounded as he was with the facilities of the school, and with the free time its programme allowed him. He passed the exam sometime in 1904 or 1905.[8]

As Dyer whiled away the years in the hills around Chakrata and in the cantonment of Meerut, the Indian Army was going through an upheaval. In 1902, Curzon began to revise the scheme of Frontier defence he had inherited from his predecessors. He determined to remove from the Punjab a strip of territory west of the River Indus, including Peshawar and all the scenes of Dyer's Frontier campaigns, and established in 1904 a new North-West Frontier Province. Curzon also instigated detailed planning for a radical overhaul of the Army's deployments inside the administrative frontier, in effect a withdrawal from the forward positions held hitherto. Forts and isolated posts housing British troops in tribal territory were handed over to militia recruited from the tribes. The regular troops these relieved were drawn back into the interior, where they could be held in readiness to strike in many directions from central locations. The scheme was sensible, and was to survive on the Frontier for the next seventeen years.

A year after the implementation of these reforms, General Lord Kitchener, the hero of Omdurman and the conqueror of the Sudan, arrived to take post as Commander-in-Chief in India. Kitchener had his own ideas about the organisation of the Army, and it was his demands for reform of the Army Department and the abolition of the post of Military Member of the Viceroy's Council, demands aimed at centralising all military affairs in India under his own control, which were to bring him into conflict with the Viceroy.[9] Curzon resisted Kitchener's plans, but although he had much the better of the argument, and was to be proved right when Kitchener's system was found to be unworkable during the First World War, it was Kitchener's ability to manipulate his contacts in London which won the day. Outmanoeuvred and forced to accept Kitchener's proposals, Curzon resigned shortly afterwards in 1905. The Army was little saddened to see him go.

Kitchener also instituted, this time with Curzon's agreement, a series of reforms which dramatically improved the Army's operational capabilities and its readiness for war. He was not an old India hand, and disliked much of what he found there when he arrived, particularly the way in which the Army was deployed across the country in a fashion which he charcterised as designed 'to hold India against the Indians'. 129,000 British and Indian troops were tied down by internal duties, leaving only four divisions totalling 73,900 men to put into the field, insufficient for any real operational purpose. By centralising manpower, and by reducing its deployment on internal tasks, Kitchener managed to build a field army of nine infantry divisions and eight cavalry brigades, a total of 149,000 men, leaving only 85,566 earmarked for internal security. He reduced administrative overheads, cutting the four Commands established in 1895 to three.[10] A Northern Command was established to manage the Frontier, consisting of the 1st, 2nd and 3rd Divisions, with independent brigades in Kohat, Bannu and Derajat. Each division was organised on a war establishment, with a complete complement of infantry and a cavalry brigade. Divisional areas were allocated their own local defence troops and additional units for internal security or frontier defence.[11] The point of the new system was to produce an Army capable of countering a Russian attack, and, ironically, it almost perfectly matched Curzon's reforms of the Frontier; in this, at least, the two were in harmony.

Kitchener also turned his attention to the organisation of the infantry, giving each regiment a unique number, and making the numbers run consecutively. Thus in 1903, the 29th Punjab Infantry became the 29th Punjabis, which in their case was not a particularly great change.[12] Just before they were renamed, they left Peshawar and moved further south down the Frontier to Dera Ismail Khan, just below the Waziri country, where they were split up along the Frontier to man a series of isolated posts. This took them further away from Chakrata, and meant that Dyer now lost touch with them even more. Around this time, Colonel Macleod handed over command to Major A.B.H. Drew, and the latter, after a very short tour of two years, handed over in his turn to Lieutenant-Colonel W.B. Mullins. Dyer seems to have been close to neither. His links with the battalion were growing weaker and he would not again be called upon to do temporary duty with them. This put Dyer at a disadvantage in terms of his future, particularly as the Commanding Officer's power, the deciding factor in a regimental officer's career, was a notable feature of the 29th. The Commander Punjab, Lieutenant-General Sir Bindon Blood, who thought the battalion was 'an excellent one, quite one of our best', nevertheless commented in his review report for 1904–5: 'The 29th have been a one-man battalion for many years, and they have not yet got rid of that serious defect.' Kitchener agreed: 'More delegation of responsibility to subordinate Commanders, both British and Native, is required.' Being out of the Commanding Officer's sight was often equivalent to being out of his mind, and Dyer's long absence at Chakrata accumulated more and more disadvantages to frustrate his hopes as time passed.[13]

At last, in the early part of 1905, Dyer was relieved of command of the school, a year earlier than had originally been intended. He took this year to go home on leave to be with Annie and the boys. They spent part of their time together at Rhosneigr on the west coast of Anglesey, where Rex taught his sons to swim and handle boats.[14] For the family this was a quiet year together, spoiled by no courses or emergencies back in India. At the end of it, Rex returned to duty leaving Annie to look after Ivon and Geoff as before, and he reached Meerut some time at the start of 1906.[15] He rejoined the 29th as a double company commander; they were by then at Jullundur in the Punjab, with a detachment at Hoshiarpur some thirty miles to the north.[16] His annual report for that year was written on him by Colonel Mullins, who had a good opinion of him, although he wrote of him tersely enough to indicate he did not know him well: 'Major R.E.H. Dyer psc. Highly efficient. Thoroughly fitted for promotion.' The Brigade Commander did not know Dyer well enough to make any comment at all, but Lieutenant-General Walter Kitchener, the Commander-in-Chief's younger brother and Commander 3rd (Lahore) Division, agreed with Mullins that Dyer was 'Fit for promotion'. Dyer had caught the eye of Northern Command, the formation of which 3rd Division was a part, though even this did not turn out to his advantage. Lieutenant-General Barrow, standing in for General Sir Alfred Gaselee, Commander Northern Command, stated that: 'I have recently selected him for DAAG at the Musketry School. Fit for promotion.'[17] The success Dyer had achieved at the Chakrata school was frustratingly the cause of his again being posted away as an instructor. This must have been galling. Evidently Dyer had no patron to keep a watchful eye over his career, which must have seemed to him to be going nowhere.

By now, the 29th was no longer at the peak of efficiency it had maintained only a few years before. Its 1906 inspection did not go well, and the report was unusually scathing. General Pollock, the Jullundur Brigade Commander, even found that: 'field firing [is] not up to expectations; fire effect not good', and he awarded the battalion a grade of 'very good', one below the best. At 3rd Division, General Kitchener graded the 29th 'only fairly satisfactory', as did General Barrow at Command. The Commander-in-Chief was 'disappointed to see such a falling off in shooting. I cannot consider the present report satisfactory in view of the 29th's past success.'[18] The time spent on the Frontier at Dera Ismail Khan, where the battalion was split up into detachments and where shooting practice was difficult, had caused many of the 29th's old skills to go rusty. Dyer returned to the battalion in 1906 at an uncomfortable time as the Commanding Officer tightened discipline and rigorously retrained his men. The 29th worked hard during the year, and Mullins was successful in bringing them back to scratch by the next year's review, going on to achieve a report of the old standard in 1907.[19]

Nothing was going smoothly for Dyer at this time. Early in 1906, he received a telegram from England saying that Ivon was acutely ill and not expected to live. The boy had contracted pneumonia which had been followed by a congestion of the lungs. Dyer immediately applied for three months' emergency leave and returned in haste to England. It must have been a very long and anxious journey, but he was delighted to find when he got back that Ivon had already recovered. Colvin says that this trip cost Dyer the command of the 19th Punjabis, a post offered him as an accelerated promotion by General Walter Kitchener. According to this account, when Dyer refused the post in order to return home, Kitchener gave it to another and he 'was never quite forgiven by the General, who, like his brother, had little sympathy with the troubles of family men.'[20] If this story were true, it would indeed have meant a rapid promotion, as Dyer had been a major for only two years; although he was qualified and, at forty-two years old, of an age when he could have been promoted, his record had hardly been one to justify such acceleration. His confidential report for that year, though recommending promotion, says nothing about any of this, specifying rather that he was earmarked for the instructor post he eventually took up. It was not in the power of a divisional commander to appoint the commanding officer of an infantry battalion, a function reserved to the regiment and to General Headquarters. Colvin's comment also seems singularly inappropriate in the light of the fact that Kitchener's wife had died in his arms of disease in South Africa during the Boer War a few years before. It is likely that Annie, whose memory this must have been, remembered something which Dyer had discussed with his Divisional Commander before he hastened to England, something touching on his future. What the issue was remains unclear, though it may have been a question of a transfer to the 19th to prepare for eventual command (as was later to happen to Dyer with the 25th) rather than of immediate promotion. There is the hint again here that Annie believed her husband had been disadvantaged in his career by his devotion to his family.

Dyer returned to India to take up the new appointment at the School of Musketry at Chungla Gully, near Rawalpindi in the north of the Punjab. This was a permanent establishment and much larger than the school at Chakrata, and Dyer had taken his own musketry certificate here in 1892, getting the first class pass which was one of the causes for his selection now for the staff of the school. His title of DAAG was not indicative of his function, as he was in fact the school's second-in-command. Once again, he found himself in a post far from the mainstream, and once again in a unit neither properly funded nor established, with its officers carried on the strength of units in the Command, units which had to make do without their officers in peace time and could call upon them only in the event of war. Dyer was thus still on the strength of the 29th and was designated only as an 'additional' staff officer, which would not have made the rather bitter pill of his posting any sweeter. He took up post on 1 June 1906 and quickly found that Chungla Gully had its compensations. His superior, Colonel O'Donnell, left him much of the practical work, so Dyer was in fact, if not in name, the School's Chief Instructor.[21] As Annie and the boys were in England, he lived in the Mess.

He now had time on his hands again, and as always he used it for something constructive. Returning to his penchant for mathematics, and the feeling for technology he had absorbed from his father, he turned inventor, and set out to design a replacement for the inadequate, heavy and delicate Mekrometer artillery range-finder then in service with the Army. The calculation of the range to a target was vital if shell and bullet were to be properly brought to bear, but range finding was a particularly difficult problem at the time, and one which had not been mastered by the available technology. The technical difficulties involved abstruse matters including the physical differences between the eyes of observers, fluctuating atmospheric conditions upon the battlefield, and the engineering of prismatic devices capable of giving accurate readings. Other problems arose from the delicacy and bulk of the instruments themselves, for there was as yet no mechanical transport to carry them. The complicated nature of the calculations which operators were forced to carry out to operate the current device made their use by the average soldier inadvisable. The Boer War had made it clear just how impractical it was to try to carry, then slowly assemble, the heavy piece of machinery and to make the mathematical calculations its operation made necessary whilst all the time being shot at and shelled. The Army recognised this as a major problem, and wrestled with it over the first two decades of the century, testing many devices submitted by commercial companies and individuals. Dyer saw an opportunity to make a name for himself. He also relished the mathematical and practical challenges involved. The struggle to produce a new infantry range-finder was to occupy him for the next eight years and would cost him the expenditure of much time and much of his own money.

The posting at Chungla Gully enabled him to begin experiments using the principles then used in the service device. This measured the angle between two lines from the target to the base line between the observer's eyes, which allowed the construction of a triangle whose angles altered with the distance to the target. The shortness of the base line made accurate measurement of the angles difficult, so to overcome this the line was extended by prisms, and it was these prisms which made the devices delicate, and which made the machine itself bulky to protect them. In his first design, Rex experimented with a different method, placing two mirrors on a bar, both set at forty-five degree angles to the line of sight, one focussing on the target and the other on a fixed point at a known range, and channelling both to the observer through a telescopic sight mounted at the end of the bar. The mirrors could be moved to give readings on both target and fixed point, thus forming an angle that allowed the difference in range between the points to be calculated. At first, this was a very crude device, made with the materials Rex had to hand in the school, and it was not very effective. He worked hard to improve the design, and it was the beginning of what was to become a long, and impressive, series of inventions that were to occupy every spare moment of Dyer's life for many years to come.[22]

Dyer was a success as an instructor, and was well reported on in his first year at Chungla Gully. His report was written by Brigadier-General Barrett, DAG Northern Command: 'He appears to be quiet, hardworking and trustworthy, and likely to prove a success in his present employment.'[23]

1907 passed much as 1906 had done. At its start, Rex Dyer was travelling. From this time exists a letter to Ivon, datelined 'The Imperial Hotel, 23–1–07,' though which Imperial Hotel is not indicated. This is the only personal letter from Rex of which we have the complete text (other letters that survive are either fragments or business correspondence):

> Darling Old Ivon, What the —— is the matter with your writing. You must take more care with it, or I shan't be able to read it soon. Sorry to hear about your spill: I hope you were not very much hurt. I am getting very tired of being all alone, so you and Geoff had better hurry up and become soldiers, sailors, engineers, ploughboys, or, but no, thieves. If mother comes out, you must remember the promise you made me and look after Geoff like a man. You must keep to the right road as far as you can, and remember that it is only by trying hard we can manage this. Have your fun, but never be a sneak.
>
> I am giving you a long lecture, but as you must now depend on yourself for a time I don't think it is unnecessary to warn you, though I feel and believe that both you and Geoff have the makings of men in you. I don't so much care if you do not happen to be very learned when I meet you next, but I shall be very disappointed if you are not of the right sort.
>
> Enough, dear old boy. Best love. Your very loving DADDIE[24]

Rex was finding it hard to live apart from Annie; they had never been separated for such a long time, and from this letter it is evident that they were planning to be together again as soon as they judged it possible to leave the boys alone in England.

Dyer's life was now immersed in the routine of teaching, administration and, in his spare time, the range finder, a quiet life in a backwater shielded from the ominous changes which were beginning to affect India, changes which no doubt troubled him. He could not have known it, but he was watching shifts to the patterns which had prevailed throughout his life – the tide of European imperialism in the East was beginning to turn. To understand this, we need to make a backward glance at the more recent history of India.

In 1904–5, the Japanese had defeated the Russian Empire, the first time an Asian power had defeated a European, and an imperial, power for over a century, and this gave Asian nationalists hope that the imperialist structure might not be so immoveable as it seemed. Indian nationalism had been given an unintended impetus at the time, strangely by Curzon's own reforms. In 1904 he reorganised the Bengal university system and managed to alienate the Bengali educated middle classes, driving them into opposition to the Government. For the first time India saw political agitation, protest meetings, demonstrations and unsettling press attacks on the Government, which included the vilification of prominent British officials including the Viceroy himself. Whilst this was in progress, Curzon stuck a stick into the Bengali hive by announcing the redrawing of the province's boundaries, aiming to make by partition administrative sense of Bengal, then an enormous and unwieldy province of seventy-eight million inhabitants, but achieving merely the arousal of enormous popular opposition. Hindu Bengalis felt their nationality and their Hindu religion under threat, as the reorganisation threatened to reduce them to minority status in the two new provinces. Led by Surendranath Banerjea, they had boycotted British goods and publicly burned imported Lancashire cotton. A Bengali revolutionary movement emerged which began a campaign of terrorist outrages causing loss of life and damage to property, few in number but greatly effective in the fear and anger they created in a land which had all but forgotten political violence. By the time Curzon left India in 1905, the reforms he had instituted had also given real steel to what had hitherto been a malleable and quiescent Indian National Congress. He had spawned a violent nationalism that was, in one form or another, to continue to endanger British individuals, if not British rule, for as long as the Raj survived. Dyer's newspapers began to carry news of nationalist outrages and inflammatory speeches, and they began to disturb his belief that all was well with his world, a belief that was to become more and more difficult to sustain with every year that passed.

Troubles began to move closer than Bengal. In 1907, during Dyer's second year at Chungla Gully, an agrarian unrest broke out in the richly irrigated agricultural lands of the central Punjab around Lyallpur. The Lieutenant-Governor, Sir Denzil Ibbetson, had published a Colony Bill introducing various reforms affecting Crown Lands, and the Bill was widely taken as an attack on landholding rights. In the spring and summer of 1907 a serious agitation spread through the Punjab. Two nationalist politicians came to the fore in this movement: Lala Lajpat Rai, who was now at the start of a long career in nationalist politics, and Ajit Singh. The oratory both deployed around the province whipped up crowds which went on to riot in Lahore, Lyallpur and Rawalpindi. Much of the countryside became disaffected, something seen by the British as a particularly dangerous phenomenon, for the Punjab was the recruiting ground for much of the Army.

The agitation began to take on a religious tinge and to involve many members of the *Arya Samaj*, a reformist Hindu organisation seeking religious purity. The *Arya Samaj* was strongest in Lahore, and students who were its members were prominent in the rioting there. The Punjab Government responded energetically, as was its wont: Lajpat Rai and Ajit Singh were deported to Burma, and the newspaper which had given them the greatest support, the *Punjabi*, was prosecuted for sedition. Lord Minto, by now Viceroy, sensibly retreating from enacting the Colony Bill, drew the teeth of the opposition so that the agitation died away.[25] The outbreak worried the authorities and the signs that the Punjab was becoming as politicised as Bengal did not bode well for the future in a province so crucial to India's agricultural wealth and military might.

At Chungla Gully, Dyer watched these events unfold around him, but, though school life carried on undisturbed, uncomfortable echoes of the troubles surrounding Midleton College must have crossed his mind. He did not let these affect his work, and his confidential report for 1907 was complimentary, though it showed an even greater lack of knowledge about him on the part of his superiors than had been evident in previous years. This was one of the penalties of being stuck in an out of the way place like Chungla Gully, but was also some indication of the type of officer Dyer was, a man whose reserve tended to a shyness that prevented his giving of his best before senior officers, who did not come often to Chungla Gully, and who, when they did, scarcely noticed him. There was, however, something in the report this time in which Dyer could take comfort, an indication that his long time in the wilderness was at last drawing to a close. Major General Collins, Commander 2nd (Rawalpindi) Division, reported him to be 'An officer of much energy, considerable character', and went on:

> The Assistant Adjutant-General of Musketry speaks very highly of him as an Assistant. My personal knowledge is limited. I believe him to be satisfactory in all points mentioned on reverse. Is 2nd-in command of the 25th Punjabis; the present Commandant is time-expired 10th February 1910. I think he should rejoin his Regimental appointment.

Brigadier-General Poett, DAG Northern Army, wrote: 'I have not seen much of this officer, but he has impressed me as being capable and reliable'. By the time the Northern Army Commander wrote 'A satisfactory Staff Officer. About to rejoin his Regiment', his future had been decided.[26]

General Collins's report makes clear for the first time that sometime between the years 1906 and 1907 Rex had transferred regiment. Quite how this came about is unclear, but the change had taken place at the latest by October 1907.[27] What is likely is that the 29th had no vacancy as Commanding Officer for Dyer to fill. Colonel Mullins was still Commanding Officer and he had a few years left to run. It would seem that the 29th had decided that Mullins's successor was to be another man, and so Dyer was free to be offered up to General Headquarters as a candidate to command another battalion, one which was not at that time able to produce its own Commanding Officer. In such straits, it seems, were the 25th Punjabis.

In the Army, to fail to achieve command of one's own battalion is, to almost all those upon whom this fate befalls, a matter for sadness, and it is more than likely this was so for Dyer. He had spent nineteen years of his service in the 29th, at that point almost half his life. He had always had particularly warm relationships with his men, and over such a time many of them must have become something of an extended family to him. He must have hoped, if not expected, to command them; now these hopes had been dashed, and he would never serve with them again. No matter that the compensation of another command was offered, this had to be for Dyer something of an exile.

8

The Zakka Khel

The 25th Punjabis were another regiment with its origins in the Indian Mutiny, having been raised to fight it in Lahore, from which it took its name of the Lahore Battalion until 1861 when it became the 17th Bengal Native Infantry. This evolved into the 25th Punjabis in Kitchener's reform of 1903.[1] Dyer almost certainly knew some of its officers, including Brevet Colonel Hamilton, who had served with the regiment since 1882, and had been its Commanding Officer since 1902. The 25th had served alongside the 29th in both the Black Mountain Expedition of 1888 and the Relief of Chitral of 1895, so Dyer had probably met them then. He would have got to know some of their officers who were his students during his times as an instructor at both Chakrata and Chungla Gully. The regiment evidently knew of him and of his record, and would not have accepted him as a future Commandant (a term widely used for, and interchangeable with, Commanding Officer in the Indian Army) had they disliked the look of him. But his arrival may not have been welcome to all his brother officers. It is likely that there was at least one member of the 25th who imagined that Rex had taken his vacancy for command, and, as in any organisation in which people spend the whole of their working lives, there were probably others who resented any newcomer. Some would have heard of Rex's fiery temper, or even experienced it at first hand, and his arrival may have been looked upon rather warily by some of the regiment's more senior officers.

The 25th were not quite up to the exemplary standards of the 29th. There was nothing exactly wrong with them, but neither was there anything about them exactly outstanding. They always seemed to get by without feeling a need for the final effort that would have raised them beyond the run of the mill. The review report they received for 1907, the year before Rex and Annie Dyer arrived, had been good enough; their reviewing officer, Brigadier-General Powell, Commander Rawal Pindi Brigade, wrote: 'A useful regiment. The individuality of all ranks is properly encouraged and there is no tendency to over-centralize. The Native Officers are generally zealous and efficient. Fit.' He reported that Colonel Hamilton was 'quiet and unostentatious', with which the next superior officer, Major-General Stratford-Collins, Commander 2nd (Rawal Pindi) Division, agreed. He thought Hamilton 'of ordinary ability. Not much character, takes pains', and added that the 25th were 'A good serviceable battalion. I should like to see higher marks made in the test. The regiment is fit for service. Condition much the same as last year, as far as I can judge from the report.'[2] They were a regiment that did the job to hand, but made no particular splash about it, and they were not thought very noteworthy as a result.

There was much in the 25th that was familiar to Dyer. It was organised in the double companies instituted throughout the Indian infantry in 1900, though its caste system was somewhat different, for in addition to the companies of Sikhs, Punjabi Musulmans and Dogras which it had in common with the 29th, there was a company of Khattak Pathans. The battalion was organised as follows:

Double Company Number 1 – A and B Companies – Sikhs

Double Company Number 2 – C and D Companies – Dogras

Double Company Number 3 – E and F Companies – Punjabi Mussalmans

Double Company Number 4 – G Company (Khattaks) and H Company (Sikhs)[3]

Dyer was probably not very familiar with the Khattaks, though he had met them in the 29th, where, for some reason, there had been twelve of them. He found over one hundred in the 25th, and their presence meant that he had a new language to learn, the Pushtu which was the Pathan tribes' native tongue. He now studied with the men to add this to the other Indian languages he could speak.[4]

When Dyer arrived there were eleven British officers in the battalion, two other majors besides himself, three or four captains, and the remainder subalterns. The majors were men with whom Dyer was to serve for the rest of his regimental service. The first was a high-flier, who had been one of the lucky few to have taken part in Kelly's legendary march to relieve Chitral in 1895, and had won a DSO in the campaign. He was one who seemed destined, at least in the estimation of the regiment, for high rank. This was Major Moberly, who had been reported on by Colonel Hamilton in the year before Dyer arrived as 'exceptionally able'. The regiment was pushing Moberly on rather hard; the brigade commander, with maybe the slightest hint of irony, described him as 'very anxious to get on in the service', a remark which elicited the riposte from the Northern Army Commander that Moberly 'has already received special promotion. Recommended for staff.' Moberly had been judged too junior by General Headquarters, it would seem, to take over as Commandant from Hamilton. He had not spent all his service in the 25th; when he won his DSO, he was serving in the 37th Dogras, from which he transferred only in 1903, possibly to fill a vacant slot in the 25th and to get quicker promotion than that available in the 37th. With his Chitral record, the 25th would have seen him as a catch, but if anyone was in a position to be disadvantaged by Dyer's arrival it would have been Moberly. If he resented the newcomer at first, he overcame the feeling; he was to be the only member of the 25th to attend Dyer's funeral nearly thirty years later.[5]

The battalion's other major, and one who was at the opposite end of the scale of abilities from Moberly, was Major Paleologus. Colonel Hamilton had commented in his report that year: 'Has only recently joined. Seems energetic and capable, though very noisy and impatient with Native Ranks. Good horseman. Rather excitable and argumentative.' This was a judgment that echoed down the years of the irascible Paleologus's service; his career was that of a loose cannon-ball whose trajectory offended and upset everyone in its path. The 25th must have been very short indeed of officers in this generation to have accepted Paleologus, and in him they had acquired an irritant around whom no pearl would form. He had already come to the adverse notice of the Army Commander, and his previous regiment must have been very relieved to see his back.

Dyer did not have far to go to join the 25th, for they were at Rawalpindi, just up the road from his school, and he had probably already visited the battalion and dined in the Mess when he transferred regiment the previous year.[6] He reported to the battalion on 1 February 1908, having made arrangements for Annie to come out from England to join him.[7] It is likely that she arrived in Rawalpindi to find an empty barracks and to settle in by herself, for only two days after Dyer was posted in, on 3 February, the 25th took to the field as part of the force assembling to punish the Pathan tribe of the Zakka Khel in the wilderness near the Khyber Pass.

Trouble had been brewing for some time in this area of the Tirah, which flanked the Khyber Pass. Here the tribes had been gradually recovering from the punitive campaigns waged against them after their rising of 1897, and of these the Zakka Khel, who lived just to the south of the Khyber in the Bazar valley, had been particularly quick to return to their old habits of raiding. They were a sub-section of the Afridis, and in the remote fastnesses in which they lived were possessed of few resources from which to scratch a living. The Zakka Khel had an evil name for robbery and extortion, and their territory was a refuge for every kind of malcontent and exile from both sides of Frontier. They held up caravans in the Khyber Pass, they swept down on the settlements below their lands and made off with cattle and slaves, and they looted the goods of Hindu merchants and kidnapped them for ransom. They murdered and pillaged, quite without partiality, and were hated not only by the British and neighbouring tribes but also by the other Afridis, none of whom would trust a man of the Zakka Khel.[8] From 1905 to 1908, the Zakkha Khel terrorised the Frontier from Peshawar in the north to Kohat in the south, impoverishing and depopulating the country. The Peshawar Commissioner, Sir Harold Deane, reported to the Government in 1908 that in the previous seven years the Zakka Khel had murdered thirty-two British subjects, wounded another twenty-nine, and kidnapped thirty-seven for ransom. They and their lands were dangerously close to Afghanistan, and the tribal *maliks* paid court to its Amir; it seemed to the British that their activities were at least in part aimed at embroiling both countries in a war. Afghan territory provided a safe haven for Zakka Khel outlaws on the run, and a group of them, with an evil collection of other cut-throats and thieves, established themselves at Hazarnao, just inside Afghanistan, from which they operated into British territory with impunity.

Other *khels* of the Afridis, anxious to avoid war with the British, raided Zakka Khel territory to limit their activities, but with no lasting success. The Zakka Khel became increasingly arrogant, and began to develop ideas of political independence which made them dangerous in British eyes. In 1907, the Zakka Khel *malik* Khawas Khan, a charismatic leader who exercised a hypnotic effect on his followers, barged in uninvited on a *jirga* being held by Roos-Keppel, the Political Agent Khyber, at Landi Kotal in the Khyber Pass, and placed in the astonished agent's hands a paper containing a manifesto of the tribe's independence before vanishing back into the mountains as unexpectedly as he had come.

On 28 January 1908, the Zakka Khel finally went too far. They attacked Peshawar itself, mounting a raid that was particularly cheeky. One of their members, an ex-British sepoy, played the bugle call 'no parade', and succeeded in delaying a turn out of the garrison whilst his fellow raiders attempted to kidnap the British Assistant Commissioner. They failed, but less than a week later, on the night of 3 February, the house of a Hindu merchant named Ram Singh, who lived just outside Peshawar at Tirahi Bala, was robbed of cash and jewels worth 800 rupees by a gang of Zakka Khel.[9] The few remaining Hindu merchants who had not been so terrorised as to flee the district embarrassed the British by demonstrating outside the Chief Commissioner's bungalow about the lack of law and order.[10]

The Government of India was at last stirred to act. They hoped this time to make a permanent settlement of the Tirah Frontier, and proposed to London that they be allowed to occupy the Bazar valley permanently. Bizarrely, they had been invited to do this by the rest of the Afridis, who had had enough of their fellow tribesmen. But the Liberal Secretary of State for India, Lord Morley, seeking to avoid any more additions to British responsibilities, turned this down. He did, however, allow a punitive expedition, provided that the Afghan Amir were informed. This he duly was, and an expeditionary force swiftly assembled at Peshawar under the guise of 'the Nowshera Manoeuvres'. The commander of the Zakka Khel Field Force, Major-General Sir James Willcocks, the General Officer Commanding 1st Peshawar Division, was given orders by the Government that: 'The end in view is strictly limited to punishment of Zakka Khels and neither immediately nor ultimately, directly or indirectly, will there be occupation or annexation of tribal territory.'[11] Willcocks was to deploy his own division, the first time since Kitchener's reforms that a complete formation that had exercised together in peacetime was deployed on operations. It was armed for the first time, too, with the new ten-pounder mountain gun, a breech-loader using smokeless powder which was easy to operate and hard to spot. The success the Field Force achieved was to be a vindication of Kitchener's reforms. On 13 February, Willcocks departed from Peshawar with two brigades each of over 3300 men and headed for the Khyber, reaching Jamrud at the entrance to the pass the same night.[12]

The 25th were not part of the 1st Division, but joined the Field Force's divisional troops, whose role was to guard the lines of communication in the rear (much the same role, in fact, as had been allotted to the 29th during the Relief of Chitral). The divisional troops were over 4600 strong, an indication of the size of force needed to overcome the problems of logistics and communications on the Frontier. The 25th set out for the campaign with 766 officers and men and fifty-two followers, going up by rail to Peshawar, then marching on by road to Jamrud to take up positions picquetting the Khyber Pass as far as Ali Masjid, deep inside it.[13] Daily they guarded, observed and patrolled the road through the pass, both between Ali Masjid and Chora Kandao and between Ali Masjid and Jamrud, but there is no record that they saw any action.[14] The deployment was, however, quite the best way for Dyer to get to know the officers and men of the battalion. As second-in-command, he had to stand in for the Commandant from time to time and his role included supervising the battalion's administrative support. He took his turn visiting the picquets and posts deployed on crags and vantage points overlooking the road. The campaign saved him months of getting to know everyone back in barracks.

Up ahead of the 25th, deep by now into the hills, Willcocks's division made a rapid advance by the Chora Pass, and on 15 February poured into the Bazar valley, taking the Zakka Khel completely by surprise. From the 17th to the 24th of that month, the force punished whatever of the Zakka Khel they could find, killing seventy tribesmen and wounding many more, seizing large quantities of live-stock, and destroying many villages and much fodder. The British reckoned that in that short time the Zakka Khel suffered greater damage than the whole Afridi tribe had done during the war of 1897–98. The tribe was stunned, and a *jirga* came in to submit on the 23rd. Four days later, peace was signed, and the *jirga* of the Afridi tribe gave pledges for the future good behaviour of the Zakka Khel. Willcocks was able to withdraw from the Bazar valley on 29 February having completely accomplished his mission. During the campaign his force had lost only three men killed and thirty-seven wounded. No other Frontier tribe had been punished so effectively or so rapidly before.[15]

The 25th went back to Rawalpindi in early March, having watched their comrades of 1st Division march back home through the pass before themselves withdrawing. They left a frontier still ablaze, for the Mohmands to the north of the Khyber had risen in support of the Zakka Khel, and Willcocks's division marched north in April to deal with them, only to have to hasten back down the Khyber when tribesmen from inside Afghanistan threatened Landi Kotal. It seemed for a time that a war with Afghanistan was imminent, but Willcock's swift return prevented this. Having ejected the invading tribesmen, he marched north once gain, and by May he had defeated the Mohmands and the Frontier was again at peace.

Dyer received the India General Service Medal, 1908, newly issued for the campaign, with the clasp 'North West Frontier 1908'.[16] Despite the cold, the potential danger and the undoubted hardships of the campaign, he could not have asked for a better way of joining his new regiment.

Back to soldiering in barracks, Dyer put his regimental skills to good use, and settled in fast. He was fortunate in this, too, as the regiment's fiftieth birthday now brought all the serving and retired men of the 25th into the Rawalpindi barracks for the occasion. The regiment's pensioners flocked in from all over the Punjab to be entertained over a whole week from 10 to 17 March. The celebrations included a rifle meeting, no doubt with competitions between past and present crack shots, just the sort of event in which Dyer's experience could be put to good use. A special *durbar* was held at which all ranks present sat in a huge circle facing the Colonel of the Regiment, its Commandant and its Subadar-Major, the senior serving Indian officer. To the left and right of these were the regiment's British officers, and beyond them all the serving and retired Indian officers. There were speeches in Punjabi by the Colonel and the Subadar Major, and then others took their turn to rise and speak of the regiment's history, its battle honours and the campaigns they remembered, of the state of the regiment as it had been and as it now was, and where its future would take it. In the evenings, parties were held across the barracks by each company and mess, there was much feasting, and, in G Company at least, the wild Khattak dancing for which its men were famed. The Colonel of the Regiment took the salute at the inevitable parade, and there were displays of training and weapons, sporting competitions between all sections and a *mela* for the families. The organisation required for all this was prodigious: tents, stores, food and drink were needed in large quantity, and for each event there were rehearsals at least once before the day. The 25th had only about a week after they returned from Tirah to put the whole thing together, and much of this work fell to the second-in-command. Dyer was thrown into the arrangements immediately he returned, and spent long hours away from home just when he and Annie had hoped to spend time again with each other. But again this was an excellent chance to meet in just one week all the men of importance in his new regiment, and the chance, too, to show of what he was capable under the initially sceptical gaze of the Colonel of the Regiment and of his new Commanding Officer. He came through this test, and his welcome into the 25th was now complete.[17]

Even at this exceptionally busy time, Dyer continued to fill every spare moment with work on his range-finder. The designs which he dispatched to the patent office just as he went on campaign in February must have been finalised before he left Chungla Gully. He had now found a firm of consulting engineers, the firm of Marks & Clerk, who had offices in London, Birmingham and Manchester, to take on the drafting and the technical aspects of his designs. This represented a considerable drain on his resources, but Marks & Clerk were to continue to represent him from now on. They submitted Dyer's first patent application on 14 April 1908. This was a development of the ideas using sliding mirrors with which he had started work several years before. In the newly patented design, the bar on which the two mirrors were mounted could be swivelled to point at the target by a drum mounted beneath it. The viewing telescope had now been moved through forty-five degrees and was mounted at right angles to the bar, perhaps so that the operator did not have to lie directly behind the device and so make himself an obvious target for an enemy. It was still a fairly simple device and one which could be described in four pages of the patent, with eight figures to illustrate the text. It was accepted by the Patent Office at the start of the following year as his first patent, no. 9559 of 1908.

Some of the calculations and drawings must have accompanied Dyer in his baggage on the Zakka Khel campaign, as by June another set of his designs reached the Patent Office in London, though this time a shorter description with fewer figures, and his application embodied only modifications of the principles he had already employed. The most significant of these included the return of the telescopic sight to a position in line with the bar, and the replacement of the two moveable mirrors by a single mirror. He had to complete and post the drawings and application for this design from Nowshera, for the dust of the jubilee celebrations had scarcely had time to settle back over the drill square and sports pitches when the battalion was out of barracks again. During the operations which General Willcocks was conducting against the Mohmands in the aftermath of the Zakka Khel campaign, the 25th replaced troops of the Nowshera Brigade which had gone to the Frontier. The 25th performed local garrison duties there between 5 May and 6 June, and so Annie was once again left alone in their new quarter at Rawalpindi; she was having a pretty miserable time so far.[18] It was not until the 25th reached base again in June that the couple could at last settle down together for the first time in four years and make a home.

Dyer managed to find time in October for some local leave for them both, and it was from Naini Tal, a hill station and a Gurkha depot in the Himalayan foothills of Kumaon, that he submitted his next application for a patent for his range-finder, the third he had submitted that year. He was clearly determined to bring his designs as fast as possible to the state where he might offer them to the authorities. The new design was now more complicated than its predecessors: the telescopic sight remained at the end of the bar, and in line with it, but he had reverted once again to two mirrors. As before, the bar could be aimed at the target by a rotating drum, but there was now a large square plate between the bar and the drum, forming a table upon which calculations or maps might be placed. This was all rather unwieldy, and getting away from the easily portable, soldierly device he was seeking to perfect, so his next patent application, sent to London in December 1908, went back to basics, and the result was a lot lighter and simpler to construct. It was, however, based upon much the same principles as he had used so far. There was still a telescopic sight at the end of a bar on which were two moveable mirrors, but the drum and table had now been replaced by a two-armed swivel upon which the bar was mounted and which could rotate to aim at the target. This, a cruder looking device than the previous two, was accepted as Dyer's fourth patent in May of 1909. All of this work, and the device itself, must have impressed and perhaps more than a little bemused Dyer's fellow officers.[19]

The battalion was inspected at Rawalpindi in late 1908 by Brigadier-General Powell, Commander Rawalpindi Infantry Brigade. He did not think the 25th was as good as it should have been. The areas he and his team inspected were found to be only 'satisfactory' save musketry, for which the 25th managed the higher grade of 'very satisfactory'. Powell commented: 'Average standard maintained. Regiment should aim higher.' Major-General Martin, Commander 2nd Division, felt similarly; 'Regiment should aim at a higher standard', though he conceded that the 25th were 'A good looking lot of men.' Lieutenant-General Woodhouse, the Northern Army Commander, added: 'A higher state of smartness and effi-ciency could be got out of this fine battalion', and Kitchener, by now in his last year in post as Commander-in-Chief, indicated that he felt there was 'room for improvement'. Part of the 25th's problem was its rather lacklustre Commandant. Colonel Hamilton must have long realised that his career was not going any further, and maybe saw no point in making an effort to impress his superiors. Brigadier-General Powell reported that year: 'Brevet Colonel A. Hamilton – Average ability, conscientious, steady, no special qualification for higher command.' The Divisional Commander, General Martin, agreed: 'Rather wanting in strength of character, vacates command February 1910. Not recommended for further advancement.'

Hamilton, however, had taken to Dyer, and made an effort to push his career along. In his report he described a more mature Dyer than had been reported on before: 'Very capable, cool and self-reliant. Ability above the average, tactful and of even temper. Passed staff college, keen on musketry, and popular.' Brigadier-

General Powell had 'not seen sufficient of this officer to verify the above remarks', but General Martin knew Dyer from his time at the school at Chungla Gully, which was within his Rawalpindi Divisional area, and wrote: 'A good officer – fit for promotion.' Rex had made a good showing of his first year with the battalion, and had not disappointed his new regiment's intention that he would relieve Hamilton at the end of the latter's tour.[20]

Around Christmas of 1908, Rex and Annie took leave together, and sailed for England to be reunited with the boys. Their winter voyage on a ship of the Anchor Line was an eventful one:

> In the Suez Canal she ran into a fog so thick that the Bitter Lakes were packed with hooting and helpless steamers. In the Straits of Messina she was flicked by the tail of the great earthquake, which jolted her engines almost off their foundation plates. In the Straits of Bonifacio she met a blizzard so strong that driving against it made no headway for twenty-four hours. The Captain, standing on the bridge throughout the gale, never took his hands off the levers, and, or so at least it was currently reported and firmly believed among the passengers, he saved his ship by running full steam ahead up the slope and full steam astern down the slope of the waves. Dyer, who found savour in such things, watched the heroic little group on the tilting bridge – the Captain clenching the handles of his instruments, the First Officer sustaining him and occasionally feeding him with a spoon. Nor did adventure end at Marseilles, for the Dyers were snowed up on their way to Paris; and when at last they got to Boulogne, found a fog which stopped all shipping, so that they had to go to Calais, and there found the weather so thick that the boat made Folkestone instead of Dover.[21]

Their first stop was a rented house in London, at 14 Bedford Place in Bloomsbury, in early February 1909. Rex had brought with him the papers for his range-finder, and from here he sent in both the complete specification for his fourth patent, no. 27,022 of 1908, and twelve days later what was to be the application for his fifth. He used the time to visit his agents Marks & Clerk; this was the first time they had been able to meet face to face, everything so far having been managed between them by post. Now they were able to discuss his designs in detail. Because of this the resulting fifth patent, no. 4227 of 1909, was a much more impressive and workmanlike looking device. The principle, though, remained the same. The telescopic sight remained in line with the bar at the end of which it was mounted. The two mirrors, or now the alternative of a prism, were mounted in a moveable assembly which slid up and down the bar by means of a groove or a wire. The bar could be rotated for direction or tilted for height by means of a drum. An extra mirror was mounted to gauge the range of a moving target, a particularly difficult problem at the time for this type of device.[22]

The Dyers very quickly moved to the country, and by March had rented Helebridge House in the village of Marhamchurch, just inland from the coast south of Bude in Cornwall. There Rex could work in quiet on his designs, and they could both enjoy the fresh sea air. From here, almost as soon as they arrived, and with amazing speed, Rex submitted his next patent papers, posting them to Marks & Clerk for them to prepare the detailed application. This was again an amplification of his previous plans, with no change to the governing principles; it was to be the farthest that he would take this type of design.[23]

With the patent papers out of his hands, Dyer could relax, and the boys joined them from school for the summer holidays. Ivon was thirteen now, starting at Uppingham that year, and Geoff was eleven. Reunited for the first time for years, they all spent 'a joyous holiday at Bude – working on the range-finder, building a boat for the boys on novel principles out of old packing cases and canvas'.[24] Dyer occasionally took the train to London to visit his agents, and to meet Mr Conrad Beck, an optical instrument maker who was henceforth to work with him on the prisms and lenses with which the range-finder was fitted. It was probably following these meetings with Edward Marks, who handled his project at the agents, and with Beck that Dyer began to realise that the principles on which he was working would never be capable of the improvement in performance which he sought. A more radical departure from the principles behind the current service device and all his designs to date was needed if he were to win the prize of getting his range-finder accepted by the Army. The idea for a fresh approach came to him on the train. Watching the scenery moving past his carriage, he noticed the effect the glass of its window had upon his perception of the moving scene beyond it. This gave him the idea of using stereoscopic principles using lenses and prisms, focussing them upon a target and reading off a range from a scale on the eyepiece. Though Dyer was unaware of it, this was an idea which had been hit upon by others: it had been trialled earlier in Edinburgh University and was to be tried again by Zeiss, which went on to manufacture a range-finder on these lines for the German army. His notes of his reasoning give some indication of the principles involved:

(a) If two images of an object ranged on are cast from opposite ends of a base on to one and the same focal plane, these images are laterally displaced from one another in that plane by an amount which varies inversely as the range.

(b) The image formed by an object glass of an object ranged on is focussed not on the infinity point but beyond it – that is to say, nearer to the observer's eye. The amount of this focal displacement varies inversely as the range.

He thus proposed to measure displacements of the image on the focal plane and to construct a scale against which the range could be measured. He noted: 'I believe the methods I adopt are novel and open up a wide field for thought – a field so wide that there appears to be no finality.'[25] This new design was one he

1. Major Reginald Dyer at the Delhi Durbar, 1903. (*Martin Dyer*)

2. The Delhi Durbar, 1903.

3. Dyer was notably fond of cars. This was probably taken in 1917 when he was a Abbottabad; 'he used to drive about the mountain roads around Abbottabad with a car fu of ladies of the station, his great delight being to frighten them'. (*Martin Dyer*)

Picnicking in the Punjab in 1919; Rex Dyer with his wife Annie, his niece Alice and his rigade Major, Captain Briggs. Taken near Jullundur before the storm of the Punjab disturbances broke. (*Martin Dyer*)

5. The officers of the 25th Punjabis at the Delhi Durbar, 1911. Dyer is seated in the back row, fourth from the right. *Back row* (left to right): Major Paleologus, Captain Riley, Lieutenant Kennedy, Captain Hunt, Lieutenant Walker, Lieutenant-Colonel Dyer, Major Martin, Captain Passy, Lieutenant Gardner; *front row* (left to right) Lieutenant Steel, Captain Atkins, Lieutenant Coats, Captain Tyrrell.

6. Lieutenant-Colonel Reginald Dyer, 1911.

7. Reginald Dyer with his range-finder. The only surviving photograph of any of his designs. Dyer produced many variants and this photograph may have been taken perhaps as late as 1913. (*Martin Dyer*)

4227. Dyer, R. E. H. Feb. 20. [*Cognate Application,* 5169/09.]

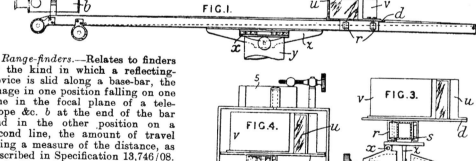

Range-finders.—Relates to finders of the kind in which a reflecting-device is slid along a base-bar, the image in one position falling on one line in the focal plane of a telescope &c. *b* at the end of the bar and in the other position on a second line, the amount of travel being a measure of the distance, as described in Specification 13,746/08. A double reflector consisting either of two mirrors *u, v* set at 45 degrees to one another, or of a reflecting-prism, is now used, the device being mounted on a carriage *d* travelling along the base-bar and provided with springs *s* on one side for keeping it in position and rollers *r* on the other for guiding. The instrument can be adjusted in azimuth on its stand *y,* and, by means of the screw 1 pressing against the depending bar *z*, the bar can be turned about its pivot *x* to enable objects at a higher or lower level to be observed. Alternatively, the reflectors only can be adjusted. In one modification, the carriage slides along a taut wire along the base; and in another, the hollow base is used as the body of the sighting-telescope. To enable the range of moving objects to be taken, a subsidiary reflector 5, Fig. 4, is adjustably mounted on a frame enclosing the bar. The main reflecting-device then being brought beneath it, the object is sighted when two images appear on the same sighting-line. As the object moves, the instrument is rotated to keep the image from the reflector 5 on this line, and the main device is traversed along the base till the other image coincides with the second sighting-line. Specification 27,022/08 is also referred to.

8. Range-finder, patent no. 4227

9. Dyer's car in difficulties between Nasratabad and Robat in Sistan.

10. The fort at Khwash, capital of the Sarhadd, which Dyer demolished.

11. The Durbar at Khwash, 1 June 1916. With Dyer are Major-General Grover, General Officer Commanding 4 Division, and Khan Bahadur Shakar Khan, Sarhadd-dar.

12. Dyer's column on the march towards Gusht, July 1916.

13. Brigadier-General Reginald Dyer CB (*National Army Museum*)

would follow down many frustrating paths for the next five years, and which now began to occupy what was left of his leave. Just as Annie had hoped that his sixth submission to the patent office would be his last, he dived back into his drawings and calculations and started all over again.

Events were moving in London that year which were to alter the Indian political scene, and were to put in place the first of the gradual series of reforms which would, in the distant future, lead to independence. Not that they were seen in this light at the time. Both in England and in India the steady, if slow, political emancipation initiated in the Indian Councils Act was viewed as a means by which India could be brought to eventual self-governance within the Empire, a Dominion even if not so far talked of as such. The Act, more usually known as the Morley-Minto reforms after its authors Viscount Morley, the Liberal Secretary of State for India, and Lord Minto, the Viceroy, increased the size of the Indian Imperial Legislative Council, for the first time opened provincial councils to Indians, and provided that some council members at both national and provincial levels be directly elected, though by a limited franchise. This gave a huge boost to the political groups formed from the educated, rich and professional Indian classes, whose numbers, if not yet greatly significant, were steadily growing. It also introduced electoral politics to the Raj.

The year in England sped by, with more work on the new form of the range-finder, which often called Dyer away to London for discussions with his advisers. By the time their leave was over, a new design had been achieved, though Dyer had to take the papers back to Rawalpindi to put the finishing touches before submitting a new patent application. He sent the provisional specification back to Marks & Clerk just as he rejoined the 25th, and the firm submitted the complete specification for him some months later. The range-finder was now a very different looking device. The bar with mirrors and its attached telescope were all gone. In their place were two tubes laid side by side in parallel, at one end of which the image of the target entered via prisms. Within the two tubes two offset prisms focussed the image onto a range-scale placed in front of the two eyepieces. The whole device was mounted on two tripods, one front, one back, which gave it the appearance of a set of elongated binoculars on legs. It was a remarkably workmanlike looking device and quite an achievement, the fruit of a year's hard work in England.[26]

Christmas came and went, and after the new year of 1910 Rex and Annie said their goodbyes once more to the boys and boarded ship for the month's trip back to India. This time, there was an excitement in their return which neither had known before, for Dyer was returning to take command of the battalion. At the age of forty-five, he had achieved the first pinnacle of an infantry officer's career.

When Rex and Annie Dyer arrived back in Rawalpindi, they found that Colonel Hamilton's health had broken down, and that he was no longer effectively exercising command. The handover began immediately, and Dyer plunged into a week or two of briefings and tours of all the companies and departments: accounts were presented; checks of all the unit's stores completed and signed; the barracks and its quarters and grounds inspected; and all the hidden functions of the battalion were for once brought forth for view by the new Commanding Officer. Dyer had a huge amount of things to do, so had little time for Annie, who was again left much on her own. He had operational plans to read, Brigade Headquarters to visit, and the important personalities of the garrison to call upon. In the evenings, and at the weekends, there was a succession of parties in the various Messes, British and Indian, to welcome the Dyers. The climax of all of this came on 25 February, when Colonel Hamilton was paraded out of barracks, and Dyer was at last on his own, and in command.[27] Soon there followed the battalion's first muster parade under its new CO, the first ceremonial report to the new Commandant by Moberly, his Second-in-Command, the first words of command spoken by Dyer, his first speech to his assembled men. These were for all, and especially for Dyer, heady, hopeful days, when all the officers and men of the battalion could look forward eagerly to the good things they expected from their new Commandant.

The 25th were in good shape despite Hamilton's sickness, but within the British Officers' Mess Dyer found personal divisions centred around the figure of Major Paleologus, divisions which Colonel Hamilton's superiors had sadly laid at his door and believed had led to a withdrawal of support for him by his officers. The annual review, conducted at Rawalpindi by Major-General Young, Commander Rawal Pindi (Infantry) Brigade, just before Dyer took over, showed an improvement in shooting but a deterioration in administration. Young pointedly, and rather cruelly in the light of the fact that Hamilton probably saw the report, wrote: 'Average standard of last year still exists, but change of Commanding Officer should improve this.' Much was clearly riding on Dyer's appointment. General Young wrote of Dyer: 'Recently rejoined from leave and taken over command of battalion. Gives me the impression of being a capable man, active in mind and body and fitted to command a battalion.' The General Officer Commanding 2 (Rawalpindi) Division agreed: 'Has been appointed commandant. A good sound officer, possessed of commonsense and a good professional knowledge. Should do well.'[28]

Within weeks of Dyer's assumption of command, the 25th moved to Multan, almost at the southern tip of the Punjab and about 270 miles from Rawalpindi. The garrison here was part of a brigade based at Ferozepore, hundreds of miles away in the central Punjab, so for Dyer the posting had the added advantage that his closest superior officer was a very long way away. Multan was near the banks of the River Chenab, one of the great rivers of the Punjab, here flowing broadly over a vast irrigated plain. Sixty miles to the east lay the great deserts of Bahawalpur, then one of the princely states of British India and not directly under British administration. Gone were the views of the mountains and the cool of the foothills; in their place, the unending flatness of the plain with its dust devils and shimmering mirages, and a midday sun that had to be avoided in the summer. Multan was a long way from the Frontier and was somewhere that would give Rex the time to hone his battalion's soldiering skills and to start to shake it out of the mediocrity upon which all its inspecting officers had commented.

He had a good team to help him do so. His second-in-command was particularly strong as Moberly was filling the post, no doubt attempting to shine well so that he could follow in Dyer's footsteps. Dyer's Adjutant, his right-hand man, and guardian of his outer office, was Captain Penton, who had held the post since 1905. He had knowledge and experience for Dyer to tap, but he was also the officer at whom the inspecting officers' barbs about deficiencies in routine and paperwork had been aimed, and Dyer replaced him that year with Lieutenant Walker, who was to serve as Adjutant until 1913 and of whom he had a very high opinion. Dyer made a clean sweep of the old regime; he replaced Hamilton's Quartermaster with Lieutenant Steel, whom he was also to keep in post until 1913. Major Paleologus was still there, gloweringly commanding one of the double companies, but was so far in hand, perhaps unsure enough of the new dispensation to make trouble. The weight of experience among Dyer's Indian officers was immense, as was repeatedly commented on by its inspecting officers. The senior serving Indian officer, Subadar-Major Sandhya Dass, who had been awarded the Order of British India second class in 1906, had been in post for over four years, and had probably served for over thirty in the Army by the time Dyer took over. The Bandmaster, Honorary Jemadar Santa Singh, had served in the band since 1893, and was to go on to serve in the regiment to 1937.[29] Dyer could rely upon, and make great use of, the store of regimental knowledge and operational experience represented by these men, and he would have taken pains to ensure he was seen to listen to their advice, if not always to take it. Dyer remained a major for the first few weeks in command until his promotion could be gazetted and his seniority date backdated to the day he took over. The appropriate entry appeared in the *Gazette of India* in June:

The King has approved of the following promotions of officers of the Indian Army, Indian Medical Service and Indian Subordinate Medical Department:

Majors to be Lieutenant-Colonels:

Dated 25th February 1910. Reginald Edward Harry Dyer, Commandant, 25th Punjabis.[30]

It was a very proud moment for both Rex and Annie, the proof that he had indeed made a success of his regimental career.

The 25th flourished under Dyer's command, his new broom evident everywhere in the battalion. Dyer looked after his officers, reporting on them in a way calculated to improve their chances of promotion, and they responded to the new treatment. Subadar-Major Sandhya Dass Bahadur was promoted to the first class of his Order of British India in 1910, and this would have been at Dyer's recommendation.[31] The men worked well for him, and the regiment improved its performance; inspired by his leadership, they rose to the demands he placed on them. He was popular, too; one of his Muslim officers made a remark at the time to another British officer, Claridge of the 28th Cavalry, who was later to serve with Dyer in Persia: 'I have only one God, but if I had two, Colonel Dyer Sahib would be the other.' Dyer made a determined effort to be fair to those who had caused his predecessor trouble, even ensuring that the Brigade Commander was given a favourable view of Major Paleologus: 'Able, energetic, vastly improved', was how he described this officer to Major-General Fasken, Commander Ferozepore Brigade, who visited the 25th at Multan in early 1911. Dyer had already improved the battalion's administration. His new Quartermaster had managed to reduce expenditure on recruits' clothing from the sum of just over 92 rupees paid out in his predecessor's day to just over 79 rupees, a considerable saving. Fasken summed up the 25th as: 'A good well set up regiment ably commanded by Lieutenant-Colonel Dyer, who now receives the proper support from his officers … A capable Commanding Officer. Fit for promotion on staff.'[32]

Dyer was able to settle down to work the battalion in the two areas at which he had always excelled, shooting, which he gradually improved, and sport. 'Dyer's ideal was to have every man in his regiment an athlete', and he fostered every form of competition in the battalion. Wrestling was a particularly noted sport amongst the Sikhs; few others could withstand men of their size and skill. At the Delhi Durbar of 1911 the 25th was to win the hockey cup, which must have gladdened Dyer's heart. At the same time their champion wrestler, Harman Singh, was to emerge victorious in the ring.[33] All this time, too, Dyer worked on his range-finder, corresponding with Marks and Beck back in England, ordering parts made to his own specifications, and himself directing the cutting of blocks of glass into shapes which could then be ground to the precise form for the prisms which his device required. As Commanding Officer he could make use of the armourers and workmen in the Multan garrison to help him with the mechanical work, and had unlimited access to the ranges he required to trial his working models, as well as to the fatigue parties of soldiers he needed to do the work of firing, fetching and carrying. He could not have been in a better position or place to further his work.[34]

In the wider world, India was seeing increasing political change. The year before, in 1909, Lord Minto's tour as Viceroy had come to an end and he had been replaced by Lord Hardinge, a man of liberal views who set out to work with the unofficial members of the Imperial Legislative Council to show that he intended to implement both the letter and the spirit of the Morley-Minto reforms.[35] Spreading from Bengal, the continuing outrages of the revolutionaries showed that terrorism was not under control, and the occasional murder, assault and bombing gave these years a sombre background and added a touch of real anxiety to the deeper fears of the British in India, fears which had never been totally stilled since the Mutiny and were now reviving. Dyer was among many in feeling that the direction of events was ominous and the future threatening, and he must have remembered, when he read the political reports, what had happened in Ireland in his youth.[36]

The accession of King George V was marked by the first visit to India of a reigning British sovereign, and the occasion was celebrated at Delhi in 1911 by an imperial *durbar* as magnificent as that which Curzon had staged seven years before. The pageantry of the occasion was matched by the optimism engendered by the political announcements made there. There was to be a new beginning in India, for the capital was to be moved to Delhi, at the heart of the country, and the old conflicts were to be put behind as the partition of Bengal which was Curzon's legacy was to be reversed and the province again united. The British were seen to be responding to Indian opinion, but also to be making a commitment to the future of a Raj in which imperial government was to be conducted with the participation of its subjects. For some, Hardinge's Viceroyalty was a time of hope and promise and the Delhi *durbar* its outward and visible sign. It is unlikely that Dyer saw things in this light, though he was able to hear the speeches which announced these changes at first hand, for at the *durbar* the 25th provided the guard of honour at the Royal Garden Party. Dyer was presented to the King and Queen Mary, and received signed portraits from them for the regiment, an occasion for which the battalion was presented with one hundred Durbar medals, one of which Dyer as Commanding Officer received.[37]

In the garden that day, Dyer and his officers, attired in blue full dress, and carrying white plumed solar topis, posed for their photograph. Thirteen officers gaze back at us from the plate, all dressed identically, save their medical officer who was in the uniform of the Indian Medical Corps. Dyer is at the centre of the group, his second-in-command, now Major Martin, standing to his left, Major Paleologus on his right. He looks relaxed, dignified, in untroubled command. Looking back at that day, with our ability to exercise hindsight, we can see it as the high watermark both of an era, the apogee of a way of life that was about to change, and of a career which, whilst not outstandingly successful, was one which had so far been without real blemish, and which had involved much solid achievement and a good deal of bravery. Dyer was entitled to be proud and more than a little content that day in the Delhi garden.[38]

He still found time during 1911 for work on the range-finder, though his responsibilities meant that he was unable to devote such concentrated periods to it as he had managed hitherto, and so the pace of development slowed. By the summer he got away another set of documents to his London agents describing his most recent ideas and asking them to apply again for a patent. His new design was of a significantly different shape; he had reduced the device to a single tube with two eyepieces at one end. Images of the target now entered through two prisms mounted at the end of arms which could be folded out to the sides of the single tube. The two target images were directed into the tube where a triangular prism placed in its centre directed them down the tube to focus at a scale. The stereoscopic effect of the two entry points, widened by the folding arms, gave a more accurate reading than that achieved in the earlier model. Marks had the specification completed during the year, and the patent was granted in 1912.[39]

As is the way in battalions, the initial honeymoon period the 25th enjoyed in Dyer's first year slowly gave way to a more mundane reality. The reforms he set in place became routine in their turn, and what had seemed new and attractive hardened in its turn into the stale and familiar. Old hostilities and antagonisms re-emerged and reasserted themselves, and the abrasive personality of Major Paleologus once again began to exercise its malign influence. Paleologus was at the root of a factionalism in the 25th which pitted its officers against both each other and against their Commanding Officer. There is no record of the incident that sparked the rupture. Whatever it was divided Dyer from his second-in-command, who had failed in some way. At the time, Dyer felt, and made public that he felt, that Paleologus had challenged not only his authority but also his honour. It was a sufficiently serious dispute to make Dyer's superiors come to believe that the two men would not be able to work together in the same unit, though they did not post Paleologus out.[40] He was to linger on in the battalion, trailing clouds of disaffection, until 1913. The second-in-command, Major Martin, also survived and went on to be promoted to lieutenant-colonel; he owed his future to Rex's handling of whatever it was that he had done. An issue with so much personal bad blood must have made life all but intolerable at times in such a small group of men as the 25th's British Officers' Mess, and would have made the social life in a small station like Multan very difficult indeed. For Annie this must have been so painful that when she came to recount her memories to Ian Colvin nearly twenty years later, she omitted not only any real account of the 25th but all detail of Multan and of the Paleologus affair.

9

Hong Kong

The effect of the internal conflicts which plagued the 25th is not made clear in any review report, for there was no time for an inspection that year. By the time the next report was written in 1912, the 25th were at sea, heading east for Hong Kong, on their way to reinforce the British garrison against threats from across the border with China, which was in the throes of revolution.[1] The year before, in 1911, nationalist generals had overthrown the Manchu dynasty and the imperial government, unleashing chaos across the country. The new government in Peking only slowly spread its authority over the country. Fighting with the old imperial garrisons broke out in many places, and counter revolutions by local warlords weakened central control causing huge numbers of people to flee. China was awash with refugees, many diseased, all destitute. The British Governor of Hong Kong, Sir Frederick Lugard, feared that the colony would be swamped by people fleeing over the border from neighbouring Canton, and that fighting might follow them into the New Territories, the British territory closest to China. The General Officer Commanding the Hong Kong garrison requested the Colonial Office in London to send out reinforcements, specifically requesting two Indian infantry battalions and a battery of mountain artillery, the need for which he had identified the previous year during exercises to test the defence of Hong Kong. The Colonial Office passed the request to the India Office, which forwarded the request to India the same day, and the Viceroy approved the request almost immediately.[2] A force consisting of the 25th and 26th Punjabis (the latter fortuitously on the way to Karachi at the time), and the 24th Hazara Mountain Battery, then stationed in Maymyo in Burma, was ordered to Hong Kong. Each man was ordered to be equipped with a thousand rounds of ammunition, and the units were to be accompanied by peacetime scales of camp followers (the Indian laundrymen, barbers, cleaners and the like who ministered to the daily needs of the units' soldiers).[3]

Dyer's battalion heard of their deployment within a day or so, all other duties ceased immediately, and preparations began for the move to the Far East. The 25th did not have much time, for within nine days they had to be entrained and bound for Karachi, where they were to board the troopship RIMS *Hardinge* for the voyage to China. This was not a light matter for the battalion, as none of the men had been onboard ship before and most had never seen the sea. The

Adjutant announced that anyone who was seasick would be left behind, and so would forfeit his chance of active service, and in the event no one allowed himself to be left in Multan.[4] The posting meant separation from the families, which were left behind along with a small rear party, but at the last moment a reprieve came for the British wives as the Government granted leave to take them to Hong Kong.[5] There was frantic packing and the making of travel arrangements for Annie and the four other wives who determined to go with their husbands for what seemed likely to very rough conditions and was likely to involve active soldiering. General Headquarters in India telegrammed the War Office on 25 January:

> 25th Punjabis embarked at Karachi on board the *Hardinge* January 22nd sailed same day for Hong Kong. Strength Officers 14, ladies 4, children 1, native officers 17, NCOs and men 783, followers 95, miscellaneous Warrant Officers 2, women 1, children 3, Transport Establishment 33, mules 55, horses 14.[6]

The 25th were expected to arrive in Hong Kong on 7 February, with the 26th Punjabis and the 24th Battery a little later, on the 13th and 14th of the month.[7] Dyer's men and the small party of wives, which Annie, being the senior, had to shepherd on the trip, found themselves couped up onboard for over two weeks on a journey around Cape Comorin, the southernmost point of India, and across the Indian Ocean to the Straits of Malacca. The ship touched Singapore before heading north across the South China Sea. It was a quiet time of the year to transit these waters, for the tempestuous and typhoon-laden monsoons of the summer were yet to come, but for those unused to the sea, or to such cramped quarters, it must have been an uncomfortable experience they were glad to complete. Their arrival in Hong Kong on the day expected was reported in the press on the 8th, the *Hong Kong Daily Press* informing its readers that 850 men of the 25th Punjabis, accompanied by thirty-three soldiers of the Supply and Transport Corps, had arrived at Holt's Wharf onboard the *Hardinge* captained by Commander C.M. Luck. The battalion was given temporary accommodation under canvas on reclaimed land near the Kowloon railway terminus.[8]

The newcomers must have been downcast at the campsite they had been allocated. Land had just been reclaimed from the sea on the tip of the Kowloon Peninsula to provide space for the construction of the new terminus of the Kowloon-Canton Railway and of the Eastern Hotel, and it was on this empty plot that the 25th was directed to pitch its tents. They were to stay here for three months, luckily during the cool, dry weather of the spring, but all the while living on the rock and mud which had been heaped into the sea. It was an arid wasteland where the sea breezes whipped up the dust making it impossible for anyone to stay clean for long. Mosquitoes, still in those days carrying the malaria endemic to the region, made life even more uncomfortable, a continuous struggle to keep arms and legs covered, and to keep the mosquito net tight around the camp bed at night to avoid the biting swarms of insects getting inside.

The men at least had their work to take their minds off the dreary discomfort of the campsite. The situation in the surrounding parts of China was tense, but so far there had been no incursions over the border, so the 25th were not immediately placed on any operational duty and could unpack and acclimatise themselves to this very strange environment. Yet the threat remained, as famine across China's central provinces increased the likelihood of large-scale movements of refugees, some of whom did make it as far as Hong Kong, reaching the colony overland and by ship, though not in the numbers feared. The political situation was turbulent in neighbouring Canton throughout the months of April and May as Chinese garrisons mutinied across the province.[9] Governor Sir Frederick Lugard had only one month left of his tour, and his successor, Sir Henry May, had been announced as the 25th arrived. Sir Henry was due to arrive in July, and was to prove wrong those in Hong Kong, and there were many, who had objected to the appointment of a man widely considered to be too junior for the post. He was to be a strong, active Governor who reformed and improved almost all aspects of life in the colony, and this was an exciting time to be stationed there.

At the time, Hong Kong was beset by disease; apart from the endemic malaria, which was particularly virulent in the wet summer months, epidemics of bubonic plague and smallpox ravaged the Chinese population.[10] The newspapers were full of complaints about the dumping of Chinese bodies in the streets overnight, something the authorities found it difficult to prevent in the tightly packed quarters of Hong Kong and Kowloon where the populace feared to handle the infected bodies. The 25th had their work cut out to stay healthy in the dust and mud of their building site, and it says much for Dyer's reform of their administration that they succeeded in doing so.

In such circumstances, it was wise to keep the battalion occupied, and there was in any case a need to tighten up on its training after the enforced idleness of the move, so Dyer quickly put his men back to work, concentrating, as usual, on shooting. At the end of March, the 25th carried out field firing below the hills between Grasscutters Pass and the Shatin Pass, near the Lion Rock to the north of Kowloon, an area still at that time devoid of settlement.[11] Before the hot and humid weather of the summer monsoon set in, the battalion was relieved to be moved to other accommodation, which was to prove a little better, though only marginally so, than their first billet; as always, Hong Kong residents were not eager to contribute taxes to make life comfortable for the troops who defended them and there was no prospect of proper barracks being built. In May, the battalion moved by sea up the west coast of the Kowloon Peninsula as far as the small fishing village of Lai Chi Kok, where they were given temporary barracks next to the Standard Company Oil godowns which had plenty of space and which their presence could serve to protect. This time the 25th was accommodated in corrugated iron sheds built, though never used, for the large amounts of Chinese indentured labour it had been planned to send to the gold and diamond mines in South Africa after the Boer War, plans abandoned after only 1500 coolies had been dispatched. The sheds had lain abandoned after that, rusting in the dank humidity of Hong Kong. Here the battalion unpacked again, cleaned up the debris of a decade of disuse, and settled into what was to be their home for the next two years. Lai Chi Kok was an isolated post, reached at that time only across the water of Hong Kong harbour or over a narrow and rugged footpath which snaked through the hills to Kowloon. They were cut off from the rest of the garrison and from the civilisation of Victoria, the city and main settlement of the colony on Hong Kong Island, which was a couple of hours away by ferry. Surrounding the camp were steep hillsides covered in thorny scrub and grass, bleak and dry in the winter, rain-swept in the monsoons of the summer. The 25th were lucky as they made their corrugated iron sheds habitable through the summer of their first year, for 1912 was the driest year on record, and dry weather kept the mosquitoes down. The New Territories lay around them, stretching over a dozen miles to the Chinese border to the north across rugged ridges flanked by paddy fields. These were lands which had only been absorbed by the colony some thirteen years before. The villagers there still seethed with resentment against the British encroachment into what they persisted in regarding as part of an undivided China. When British administration had moved into the New Territories in 1899, resistance had to be suppressed by force and the walled defences of the villages destroyed. The Chinese throughout Hong Kong, both urban and rural, remained deeply conservative; at the time respectable women, which meant all but the hawker or the sampan woman, did not allow themselves to be seen in public or even out of doors. British society in the colony was as one with the Chinese in its adherence to social rules, and segregation between the races was rigidly observed; this was the era of notices forbidding dogs and Chinese in the residential parts of the colony.

Piracy was as endemic in the seas surrounding the colony as malaria was on land, and the threat of a raid on the isolated buildings of Lai Chi Kok, or on the unescorted ferryboats which plied there, was enough for the guard on the camp to be much more than a ceremonial one. The British garrison still patrolled much of the New Territories. A single road had been pushed north from Kowloon as far as the small village of Tai Po, which lay many miles across the hills from the 25th's camp. Beyond Tai Po a road was under construction as far as the border, though as there were still no motor vehicles in the colony (and even horse-drawn carriages had by then largely given way to the more convenient rickshaws and chairs carried by coolies), the absence of roads had not been greatly felt. This was to change; Sir Henry May imported his own motor car, and was quickly followed by many of the rich, who were already abandoning the rickshaw for the combustion engine by the time the 25th sailed back to India in 1915. South west of Fanling, the area at Ping Kong, a place daringly near the frontier, was being cleared for the beginnings of a golf course. Monkey, wild cat, porcupine, anteater, boar and even tiger still stalked the hills around this, and the press carried the occasional report of tiger prints seen below the walls of Kowloon City.[12] As late as 1915, a tiger killed a Chinese villager and fatally wounded a European police sergeant at Sheung Shui near the frontier. The New Territories and Lai Chi Kok were quite as wild as any places Annie Dyer had suffered in India.[13]

A month before Sir Henry May took over, the administration had established a cordon of military posts along the frontier to protect the New Territories against bands of robbers raiding out of China. The 25th took their turn manning these, patrolling the difficult and at that time unmarked line of the border, mountainous and sheer in the east, marshy and mosquito-infested in the west. It was sticky, dirty work, especially in the summer, when temperatures were in the thirties and humidity was over 90 per cent. The battalion was also given the occasional task of patrolling the villages deep in the hills of the New Territories, and of manning observation posts along the frontier. The hills around the camp were steep and barren enough to allow their old North-West Frontier mountain skills to be kept honed, and the sea, with its myriad small islands and sandy inlets, made practice for amphibious warfare both easy and greatly enjoyable. As the 25th had their own jetty at the camp, the Royal Navy could pick up the troops from their own doorstep and take them off to land them on beaches along the coast. Dyer ensured that some sport was organised to occupy his men and keep them fit. He held swimming lessons off the jetty, and nearly managed to drown some of his men. The whole battalion was ordered to march down to the jetty and jump in; the water alongside was deep enough for an oil-carrying ship to berth and some of the men were pulled out just before they sank for the last time. All of them eventually learned to swim, and some even took up rowing.[14]

Dyer had the opportunity, with his unit armourers and the ranges conveniently to hand, to carry on work on the range-finder. By the summer, he had sent home to Marks & Clerk the provisional specification for the next development of the design. He had now refined the arrangements of the range-finder's internal prisms so that they initially reflected the image of the target away from the observer before bouncing it back to the eyepieces, thereby lengthening the distance covered in the transmission to the eye and making the final focus upon the scale more accurate. The new design also widened the separation of the eyepieces to allow them to be used more easily. Dyer was beginning to believe that he had a device which could be brought into service, and he determined to show it to the Army when he next went home on leave.[15]

The political turmoil in China proved to be much more alarming in prospect than it proved in reality, and Hong Kong was scarcely affected by events across the border. The battalion had time to make a reasonably comfortable home alongside the oil tanks at Lai Chi Kok, and, presumably by the combination of strenuous hygiene and by being well away from everyone else, avoided the epidemics that continued to ravage the colony.[16] Almost the only sign in Hong Kong of the political changes then underway in China was the universal abandonment by the population of the queue, the long plaited pigtail hitherto worn by all Chinese men as a sign of their subjection to the Manchu. This occurred in the year the 25th arrived, and, within weeks, anyone wearing a queue was in as much danger of losing his life from attack in the street as he had been under the imperial regime for not wearing one. After five months when it was quite clear that there was no emergency facing the battalion, Rex and Annie Dyer decided it was safe enough to take leave. They sailed to Japan, which was at that time an English ally, and which provided a secure location for a holiday then unavailable in China. Rex arranged to be joined in Japan by the regiment's champion wrestler, the Sikh Harman Singh, who had found no competition since he had arrived in Hong Kong and wanted to pit his strength against the sumo wrestlers he had heard about. This plan was spoiled, though, as the Emperor of Japan died on 31 July, casting the whole nation into mourning, and all wrestling bouts were banned until after the Dyers' leave was over and they were all back in Hong Kong.[17]

They returned to find that security in Hong Kong had deteriorated. Pirates had attacked shipping off Lantau Island, within the colony's waters, on 1 July. Three days later, Sir Henry and Lady May disembarked from their ship at the central pier on Hong Kong Island for their official welcome to the colony. Just after they had entered their official chairs for the short journey to the City Hall, a Chinese revolutionary stepped from the crowd and fired a single revolver shot. Both the intended victims were unharmed, but the bullet buried itself in Lady May's chair. Onlookers overpowered the assailant, the ceremony continued, and the couple was given an ovation when they reached the City Hall. The Dyers found the colony slightly less self-confident when they returned. Just after they did, on 21 August, the public was shocked by a very daring raid by a pirate gang, which sailed into Hong Kong from the nearby Pearl River delta and attacked the police station on the island of Cheung Chau, only a couple of miles west of Hong Kong Island. The three Indian police constables stationed there were killed and the by then defenceless islanders were terrorised and their property looted. The Governor determined that this outrage could not go unanswered. With the cooperation of the Portuguese administration in Macao, and with the consent of the powerless Chinese administration in Canton, Sir Henry ordered a punitive raid to destroy the gang. His plan to use force inside China received approval three days later from London.[18] Unfortunately for the 25th, the Indian battalion allocated to the expedition was the 26th, so Dyer missed out on the only operational task that came the garrison's way during his time in Hong Kong. Things now began to quieten down again and anxieties subsided.

Dyer had brought the 25th to a high degree of efficiency, as was shown by their review report covering the year 1912–13, which was issued in April of the latter year by Major-General Anderson, Commanding Troops, South China. The General liked the appearance of the battalion, which he thought a 'Good sturdy lot with plenty of endurance though not quite of the best type of the various classes recruited'. He gratifyingly concluded that the battalion's general efficiency was 'unquestionable'. He was content, too, with what he had seen of Dyer during his time in Hong Kong, describing him as 'A capable battalion commander as far as I have had the opportunity of judging'. By the time the report was made, Dyer was on leave, and Major Robinson of the 27th Punjabis had been posted in to command; clearly the authorities did not consider any of the 25th's serving officers, including Major Martin, the second-in-command, fit for this. The old trouble with Major Paleologus continued to cast a shadow, though Dyer had managed to establish a *modus vivendi*.[19]

The battalion was in good shape, the political and security situation was under control, but Annie had fallen ill. Rex was due leave, so they decided to take a year in England. What it was that had turned Annie into an invalid is not recorded, but her state of health continued to worsen for some years. The Hong Kong climate and the conditions in Lai Chi Kok may have made her illness worse, and it is likely that the Dyers decided that she would be better off in England. Dyer handed over to Major Robinson and left Hong Kong with Annie on 8 October 1912. They travelled across the Pacific to Vancouver, then on by the Canadian Pacific Railway over the Rockies and the enormous empty spaces of the North American prairies before taking ship again to cross the Atlantic. Soon after their arrival home in early December they lodged for a while at the Hotel Somerset in Portman Square, London, from where they set about finding a house to rent. Within a few weeks they had taken 'Tregenna' in Woking, and were reunited there at Christmas with the boys. Ivon had taken his London matriculation in January and was within a year of leaving Uppingham. They must have discussed what he was to do, perhaps deciding then that he should follow his father into the Army. Dyer used the time in London to visit Marks and Beck, and it was from the Hotel Somerset that he sent in another provisional specification for the range-finder, this time an elaboration on the new designs he had produced in Hong Kong.[20]

They had not long been home when news arrived from India of an attempt to assassinate the Viceroy. In December 1912, as Lord and Lady Hardinge made a state entry into Delhi, their carriage was bombed by revolutionaries. The Viceroy was not seriously wounded and was soon back at his duties, but the incident was disturbing to all of Dyer's caste. It was ironic that it was Hardinge who had been attacked. His liberal intentions and policies had resulted in the smooth implementation of the Morley-Minto reforms, and he was on good terms with leaders of the Indian National Congress. Dyer must have viewed the political developments in India that year with growing displeasure as Hardinge and the government in London pressed on with the appointment of the Royal Commission on the Public Services in India, announced on 31 August, with Lord Islington as its chairman and with terms aimed at introducing Indian members to the Indian Civil Service. Hardinge ensured the appointment of Gokhale, the Congress leader, to the Commission, something widely disapproved of by British India. To Dyer the attempted assassination was probably proof of what came of pandering to nationalists, and as if to further illustrate this, another bombing outrage, this time the successful assassination of a more junior official, took place in Lahore in May 1913.

The small house at Woking was conveniently near to the ranges at Bisley and Pirbright and Dyer could try out his range-finder there. He completed the specification for the patent for which two provisional specifications had been submitted the previous year, and these, his ninth and tenth patents, were granted later in the year. The work on the range-finder absorbed as much of his time on this furlough as it had on the last; Annie's sickness prevented their travelling much in any case. Ivon, now nearly eighteen, and Geoff, who was a year below his brother in school, were with them in the summer. By September 1913, they all moved to another rented house, Leitrim Lodge in the village of Hampton on Thames, Middlesex, not far from Hampton Court. While Annie was undergoing treatment, and the boys went back to school, Rex absorbed himself in perfecting the design of the range-finder. He now had the principles well worked out, but he had yet to assemble a fully working model. Despite this, he made the decision to demonstrate his ideas to the Inspection Department at the Royal Arsenal, Woolwich. The specification he wrote stated:

> What I claim as novel in my instrument is:
>
> 1. The method of sliding a scale whereby equal variations in range are indicated by equal spaces on the scale.
>
> 2. The methods whereby not only are the focal points of objects drawn back to the infinity point of focus, or pushed forward to some initial point of focus, but the images are also brought into coincidence.[21]

The Royal Arsenal deputed a Royal Engineers officer to view the device, but by the time he arrived at Bisley ranges the working model was still not assembled, and all Dyer had to show was a collection of lenses and prisms lined up on a table. The inspector was not impressed, either with the theory, which he believed overcomplex, or with the state of the device, and on his recommendation Dyer's design was rejected. This was a huge disappointment to Dyer after all his work. He had shot his bolt by seeking Army approval before he was ready, but he did not abandon the project, and worked on to improve the device and to produce a working model.[22] By the time he left England he had manufactured a very serviceable looking device, which Conrad Beck later described to Ian Colvin as:

> An extraordinarily good instrument, light, handy, and serviceable for distances up to about 3000 yards [and] of a handy size, which registered the distance of any object on which it was brought to bear. To such a pitch was it brought that the observer, following the flight of a bird, could see at the same time the scale moving along the index as it measured the distance in numbered hundreds of yards.

The only remaining photograph of the device testifies to its lightweight, easily portable appearance. Dyer submitted the provisional application for what was to be his final and eleventh patent for this model from the house at Hampton. It was a development of the principles upon which he had been working so far. The two extendable arms were now fitted with a scissors mechanism to open them, he had retained the top box with its prism taking the image of the target initially away from the observer, and the two eyepieces had now become one at the rear where the viewer lay. The whole device was supported on a tripod at the rear, and a bipod at the front, and stood some eighteen inches off the ground, so its low silhouette was perfectly suited to tactical use, and the observer was exposed as little as possible to enemy view. There was a leather strap attached to the centre of the tubes to carry the device.[23] Dyer's typically impetuous attempt to interest the Royal Arsenal before he had a workable model had prevented his work being given a fair viewing; had he demonstrated this model rather than an unassembled set of prisms, the outcome might well have been very different. Beck was impressed both with Dyer and his work, as he later told Colvin:

> Dyer, he tells me, had an excellent mathematical mind, which was, besides, open to ideas and of strong grasp. The object of all his endeavours was not to make money but to serve his Army and his country. 'He was', says Mr Beck, 'a high-minded public-spirited man, and it was a great pleasure to work with him.'[24]

At the end of the year, Dyer had to bid farewell to Annie, who was so sick by this time that she was unable to return to Hong Kong. He took her down to Bournemouth and placed her in a nursing home, then took ship once more to travel back to the East. He reached the colony by way of the Suez Canal and India in October 1913.

There had been a few changes while he had been away, but battalion routine had continued as normal. There was a new General Officer Commanding,

Major-General Kelly, a Royal Engineer who had served in Burma while Dyer was
there, and who had much experience of the North-West Frontier. Turmoil had
continued in China; in August a mutiny against the new republican administration had taken place up the Pearl River in Canton, but though the Chinese
had suppressed this only with great difficulty, it had not spilled over into Hong
Kong.[25] An historic change in Hong Kong's economic life had also taken place
that year, as India had announced that it would cease to export opium to the
colony. This led Sir Henry May to review the whole opium issue, and by 1915 he
was to end the system of private concessions and assume Government control of
trade in the drug. The flow of 'foreign mud', for so long a blot on the British
name in the East, was, however, to be some time coming to an end.[26]

Something very welcome which Dyer found on his return was the absence of
Major Paleologus, who had departed for England on 11 August finally to take his
retirement. That year, the Subadar-Major, Sandhya Dass *Sardar Bahadur*, also
went on pension, leaving for India in 1913. Dass was made an honorary captain
on his retirement, a promotion which would have been at Dyer's recommendation. The new Subadar-Major was Mula Singh, a Sikh, whose appointment was
Dyer's own choice.[27]

On 10 October, the War Office informed Army Headquarters in Hong Kong
of changes to the organisation of the infantry of the Army, ending the double
company system which had been instituted in 1900, and replacing the eight rifle
companies of the old dispensation with four, each of which was to consist of
four platoons. The changes were to be implemented by November, so the 25th
went through a considerable reorganisation during the intervening month. For
the first time British officers took over command of companies from their Indian
officers, all of whom now became, except in temporary or emergency circumstances, their subordinates. This reform reduced the power and influence wielded
until then by the regiment's Indian officers, and more than halved the number
of senior posts open to them; it is hardly likely to have been a reorganisation
popular amongst the Indians of the battalion.[28] In the midst of this upheaval,
the new General Officer Commanding, Major-General Kelly, decided to carry
out his first inspection. He had been slowly working his way around the garrison
since his arrival in Hong Kong in the summer and had left his visit to the 25th
until the last, probably to allow Dyer time to settle back in after his leave. Lai Chi
Kok was considered too far for the General to travel for the inspection, and
anyway it had no parade ground, so the 25th took barges to Hong Kong Island,
and joined the 26th Punjabis to parade before General Kelly on the open ground
between the Happy Valley race course and the sea. They had to stay there in
tented camps for two weeks to practise their drill; after such a long time in the
makeshift barracks at Lai Chi Kok they probably needed a good deal of work to
get back up to standard. The parade took place on 29 October, and the press

reported that the troops put on a fine display. They were cheered roundly by the watching crowds when they marched off parade for tiffin.[29]

Sometime after Dyer's return to duty, a fire broke out in a Standard Oil Company tank in the depot next to the lines. The men of the 25th saved the site from destruction, at great risk to themselves removing petrol tins by hand from a building near the blazing oil tanks. As a result, the battalion received Sir Henry May's official thanks for their gallantry. This was pretty much the only excitement that year. As 1913 moved towards 1914, peacetime life in the garrison seemed set in its usual round.[30]

Dyer still had time to devote to his range-finder, and in the early part of 1914, he sent the documents describing the complete specification for his last patent, no. 20,771 of 1913, back to Marks & Clerk. The patent was granted in September, but the opportunity that battalion command had given him to devote his energies to his invention was almost at an end. Sadly, Dyer had left it too late to influence the design which was destined to come into service for the Army during the forthcoming war, for in 1913 the Army chose a design based upon different, and simpler, principles designed by the company of Barr & Stroud. The chance to gain a part in this contract was now closed, and it would in any case be many years before Dyer had time to spare to take the work further. When he did try to return to it, circumstances would no longer be so propitious, and it was not after all to be for his achievements as an inventor that Dyer would be remembered by posterity.[31]

The 25th were inspected as usual in April 1914. In the review report for that year, Major-General Kelly was highly complimentary about almost all aspects of the battalion's performance. The battalion looked good to him: 'All that can be desired, all ranks being very hardy.' General Kelly was similarly complimentary about Dyer, and, though there had not really been much chance for him to show off his abilities, he had clearly made an impression.

A capable commanding officer. Has supported me loyally. His staff experience added to by considerable active service renders him a valuable officer. Fit for promotion and for advancement to command a Brigade. Will do well as a General Staff Officer 1st Grade of a Division.

These were the vital reports on Dyer whilst he was in command that he needed to ensure that he progressed to the next stages of his career, and were the most specific recommendations he had received to date. That they were based upon so slight an acquaintance is a comment upon the occasional vagaries of the military promotion system, but Dyer's good luck in this case was no different from that of countless others then and since, and good luck he had at last been granted.

The review report gives extracts from the confidential reports Dyer had written on his subordinates, and confirms the impression that he took care to further their careers. Now the irritant of Major Paleologus had been removed, things were happier in the battalion, and it was a much more cohesive unit. Dyer's second-in-command was once again Moberly, who had already been promoted to lieutenant-colonel. By that time he was Dyer's designated successor, which must have made for an unusual relationship between the two men, if not a strained one, but Dyer's report duly recommended Moberly to succeed him. The other officers of the battalion were also an able bunch. In these reports, Dyer's preferences regarding character come through clearly; a good officer, in his view, was dedicated to the service, intelligent, close to his soldiers and popular with them, fit, active and a sportsman; an unremarkable set of priorities for an infantry officer, perhaps, but a perfectly adequate one, and there is nothing here to distinguish Dyer from any other good Commanding Officer then or now.[32]

Ivon left Uppingham in the summer, having achieved the rank of colour-sergeant in the Officer Training Corps where he had enjoyed himself for five years. What it was he was to do is unclear, but he was evidently suited to be a soldier. For the time being he went home, and whatever his plans were, they were soon to be interrupted by the imminent outbreak of war. Through the year, though, news of events in Europe did not give much cause for alarm in Hong Kong, and inside the colony relations with the other Europeans who were present in the East remained good. The ships of the German fleet called in at Hong Kong and invited selected guests to parties onboard. The band of the cruiser *Emden* played in the City Hall, and the German Club on Kennedy Road flourished; it had hosted Prince Waldemar of Prussia when he visited in 1912, and its members included the many Austrian merchants working in the colony.[33] When war broke out in Europe in August, it was a shock to the population of Hong Kong to see HMS *Triumph* steaming out of the harbour to join the Japanese attack on the German fleet in Tsingtao. It is indicative of the lack of anxiety in the colony, and in the East in general, that Dyer took leave again in the summer and was once more in Japan when war broke out on 4 August 1914, having left the 25th in the hands of his second-in-command, Moberly.[34] When he heard of the war in Japan, Dyer hastened back to Hong Kong.

In the brief lead up to what was to become the First World War, the colony activated its defence plan, stage by stage, from the end of July. The first warning of impending hostilities had arrived from London by telegram as late as the 30th of that month.[35] On 4 August, the battalion was duly placed at four hours' notice to move, and Operation Order 1 was activated on the 5th. Hong Kong Garrison Order Number 167 published that day stated baldly: 'Declaration of War – War having been declared against Germany, the Defence Scheme of Hong Kong is put into force herewith.' The garrison was now on active service.[36] Two days later, full mobilisation was ordered, and Routine Order Number 2 issued that day instructed officers 'to wear uniform at all times … Martial Law having been proclaimed'. This new order made it clear that the GOC had already decided to change the original plan. It stated: 'Depots of Indian Units will be situated as follows:- 25th Punjabis – Victoria Barracks'. This was the central barracks on Hong Kong Island; the battalion's original destination in Kowloon had already been found to be overcrowded, as the 26th Punjabis and 40th Pathans had moved into Whitfield Barracks, and 74th Punjabis were accommodated in Whitfield Camp Barracks alongside them. It was then decided that 25th Punjabis were to go to the race course at Happy Valley, less one double company (the Headquarters staff had not altered their approach to infantry organisation despite the War Office order of the previous year) which was to be stationed in Victoria Barracks.[37] The battalion was now earmarked as part of General Reserve for Hong Kong, and Headquarters appointed Lieutenant-Colonel Moberly to command this Reserve from Victoria Barracks once Dyer returned from Japan, an awkward idea as it placed Dyer with the majority of his battalion under the command of his own second-in-command. Following these conflicting orders, the 25th moved in their vessels from Lai Chi Kok down to Hong Kong Island on the 7th.[38] They had packed up camp before they moved, leaving behind their heavy baggage in storage at Holt's Wharf. At Happy Valley, the conditions they found were primitive, as no real administrative arrangements had been made and the men had to sleep on the ground; it was not until 8 August that authorisation was given to issue them straw bedding. Their baggage was moved into Army stores on 21 August; by then it was clear to them that they would be in the field for a long time. Dyer returned at this point from Japan to find his men camping out on the racecourse and took over again from Moberly, who went off to Victoria Barracks to command the General Reserve.

As soon as Dyer arrived, he sent a typical telegram to Annie: 'Both boys join at once'. Ivon did so straight away, and by 4 November was training with the 3rd Dorsets as a second lieutenant with a wartime commission, but Geoff was still at school, and Annie wisely kept him there for another year.[39] Almost immediately, the battalion was put on standby to join the Japanese attack on Tientsin; it seemed that Dyer would at last get the chance to lead his battalion into battle. General Kelly later reported:

> Orders were received that one Indian Battalion was to be sent for special service to North China. I selected the 25th Punjabis ... To the very great disappointment of all concerned a cable was received on the 22nd August from the War Office cancelling the taking part in the operations in North China by any troops from here.[40]

The War and Colonial Offices had realised the vulnerability of Hong Kong; there was a strong German naval squadron at Tsingtao up the coast, and the area in and around the colony was far from secure. There was also some unrest amongst the Chinese population, 30,000 of whom left Hong Kong after war broke out, and Sir Henry May did not wish to see the garrison depleted. Dyer and his men, to their great disappointment, were stood down.[41] They remained on Hong Kong Island, though not under command of Moberly, at Victoria Barracks; Dyer had that idea scotched as soon as he got back.[42] Despite the mobilisation, there was not at first much to keep the troops occupied, so training was allowed to continue; the battalion was firing on Kowloon's A Ranges on 20 August.[43]

As time passed, it became clear that the 25th could not stay camped out on the racecourse for the duration of the war. Plans were made to return them to some form of accommodation with a roof over their heads. In September, they were assigned Murray Barracks, and A, B and H Blocks of Whitfield Barracks, both across the harbour in Kowloon. The battalion duly crossed over from Hong Kong Island to Kowloon by ferry on 6 October, and moved into Murray Barracks, the light baggage following to the jetty by mule. After it left Happy Valley the straw bedding they had been sleeping on was taken away to be disinfected; everything out in the open in the summer wetness at Happy Valley had begun to be a bit squalid.[44] Only the double company under Moberly was left behind on the island, and this transferred to Western Section of the Hong Kong Island garrison that day, forming what became known as Headquarters and General Reserve Section.[45]

By this stage, Dyer had little time left to serve with his battalion, and must have realised that his chances of commanding it in action were slipping away. The 25th as a whole felt less than pleased at being, as they saw it, cooped up in Hong Kong far away from the main theatres of war.[46] They were chagrined to be left with sentry duties and the guarding of prisoners, of whom there were growing numbers in the colony. By 12 September, the original prisoner of war camp on Stonecutters Island had to be moved to Hung Hom, near the railway terminus, and just up from the 25th's original campsite of two years before, as prisoner numbers had reached over a hundred and Stonecutters was too small to house them. Towards the end of October, the Governor decided to intern or deport all German and Austrian residents, who were, incredibly at that stage, still at liberty in the colony. Eighty-three were arrested and placed in the camp at Hung Hom, and forty-four more were deported with their families. The families of those interned (amounting to seventeen women and children) were housed in empty Army married quarters at Gun Club Hill Barracks in Austin Road, Kowloon, a few hundred yards from their husbands' prison. The GOC made use of Moberly, of whom he clearly thought very highly, as a temporary staff officer at Army Headquarters, where he stood in until 10 December for an officer who was sick, so that when Dyer's tour came to an end in November, he was unable to hand over the battalion directly to his successor. The unit he left was a depleted one; the strength of British officers with all the Indian battalions in the garrison had been reduced to seven each at the end of November when officers were drafted to Egypt to fill out units sent from India to face the threat from the Turks. All this must have been considerably frustrating to Dyer as he departed.

News that the *Emden*, the *Scharnhorst* and the *Gneisenau* had broken out of port and were at sea somewhere in the Western Pacific reached Hong Kong in a telegram on 20 October: 'German Destroyer Squadron broke out of Tsing Tau on evening 17 October. Direction unknown.'[47] This caused considerable anxiety in the colony until the *Emden* sailed into the Indian Ocean (making a highly daring attack on a Russian ship in Penang harbour as she did so) and until the other two German ships were sunk off the Falkland Islands on 8 December. Other anxieties were more local. During October, complaints began to come into Army Headquarters, some sent up by the Indian battalions, that revolutionary ideas were being circulated in the colony. Indians, mostly Sikhs, had arrived 'from America to propagate seditious teaching amongst the troops on outpost', causing the GOC to report that he had 'issued warning to Commanding Officers accordingly. I also heard of sedition being talked in the Gurdwara.'[48] Dyer, with his large number of Sikh troops, and through his Sikh officers with whom he got on so well, was probably one of the first to pick up this intelligence and pass it to Headquarters. He would not have known it at the time, but these were the first signs of the new Indian revolutionary movements that he was shortly to encounter in the Punjab, and which were in the fullness of time to alter the course of his life.

Sometime at the end of November, Dyer handed over the battalion to a temporary successor (this was perhaps Captain Riley, though no record exists).[49] It was not an easy situation in which to bid farewell and ceremonies must have been kept to a minimum. No doubt Moberly came down from Headquarters to meet Dyer before he left, but there was no time for the usual one or two week handover. For Dyer, the Hong Kong tour had been a frustrating start to the war, and he had not been able to achieve very much. The circumstances of his handover made this worse. Towards the end of his time in the colony, he had found himself overshadowed by Moberly, who had attracted the regard of the GOC in a way which Dyer had not been able to emulate. In his dispatch on operations during 1914, General Kelly mentioned ten officers by name as those whose services 'I desire particularly to bring to notice'; these officers would thereby receive the oak leaf cluster of the Mention in Despatches on their war medal, and they included Moberly. The list did not include Dyer. He, along with another sixteen officers of the garrison, had to be content with words: 'My thanks are also due to Lieutenant-Colonel R.E.H. Dyer, 25th Punjabis'. There was no award for this scant praise.[50] Yet Dyer handed Moberly a unit to be proud of. General Kelly himself stated in the next February's review report: 'The unit is in every way efficient and quite ready for service in the field. I do not think there is a better fighting unit in the Indian Army.'[51] This was Dyer's achievement over his five years in command, not Moberly's, and if General Kelly failed to acknowledge it, we may do so now.

Dyer put to sea, his ship avoided all contact with the *Emden*, and by 13 December 1914 he was once again in Rawalpindi.[52]

10

The First World War

Rex Dyer went back to India again at the start of 1915. Once more he was on his way to Rawalpindi where he had joined his regiment six years before, but this time he was on his own. Annie remained in England undergoing treatment for the illness that had confined her to a nursing home. Ivon was a subaltern in the Dorsets, shortly bound for the front in France, and Geoff was about to join up after he passed his eighteenth birthday, so for Dyer it was a lonely and worrying time. As he travelled back to India, he must have reflected that this journey was taking him away from regimental soldiering for the last time. His five years in command had left him very mixed recollections. To his credit, he had turned the 25th from a unit with a consistent record of under achievement into a fine battalion that had won plaudits for much of what it did. He had managed this in spite of the fact that he had come to its command as an outsider who had needed to force through reform whilst winning over his officers and men. He had faced down, and then lived with, the fractious and insubordinate senior officers who had divided his Mess and had given the 25th a reputation for internal strife, but these feuds had, despite his efforts, poisoned much of his tenure of command. Frustratingly, there had been no chance to prove himself as a leader in war or to show off his battalion on any active service. He had been forced by circumstances to leave the 25th without a proper handover to a successor who seemed destined to outshine him. These were uncomfortable thoughts to live with on the long journey home.

Looking ahead, Dyer could see his new post in two lights; on the one hand a compensation for the disappointments of the past, on the other itself a disappointment. He was about to take up the job of the senior staff officer in a divisional headquarters, at last the kind of post that had eluded him since Staff College, so seemingly he was still on track to gain higher rank. His division was in Rawalpindi, one of the formations created by Kitchener's reforms, which was no sleepy hollow but an active Headquarters in the heart of the Punjab and within reach of the Frontier. And yet, and this rankled with him, 2 Division was not in France, where the main theatre of war lay, and where there were by now two divisions of the Indian Army fighting in the British Expeditionary Force, nor was it in Egypt where some of his own battalion's officers had gone to face the Turks. Once again he was missing the main show. Worryingly, though this had happened to him before, for some reason his posting was annotated as 'temporary', and so his tenure was not fully secure; perhaps Army Headquarters was not totally sure of him, or had other plans for him in mind.[1]

When he arrived in Rawalpindi, Dyer found himself responsible for the running of the Divisional Headquarters, specifically for the allocation and management of its work and for the supervision of its junior officers and staff. To him fell the implementation of the GOC's orders, the writing of detailed operational plans, the organisation of aid to the civil power, the mobilisation and movement of the division's units, as well as recruiting and a multitude of smaller administrative tasks. The brigades and divisional troops which made up the 2nd Division, a force of some 12,000 or more men, reported through him to the GOC, so that to all intents and purposes he was the General's right-hand man. In the event, he made a success of this job and was well thought of by his GOC, Major-General Sir Gerald Kitson, who wrote later to Ian Colvin: 'He was an excellent staff officer, and, having been through the Staff College, was thoroughly trained. He was a very genial, pleasant companion, full of fun and humour, and I was very fond of him.'[2] That this was not polite praise is indicated by the boost which Kitson was to give Dyer's career, which took off after this time. He had at last found a mentor. It does seem that Dyer fitted the role of staff officer very well. It allowed him to invest his considerable energy in a mass of detailed work, something to which he was by nature inclined, without calling on him to make controversial decisions or to handle problems without recourse to a higher authority. It was a role in which he could excel without too much risk of getting things badly wrong or of making important errors of judgment.

Although Rawalpindi was far from the front line, it was in several respects at the heart of the First World War in India. The Punjab provided a far greater pool of recruits for the war than any other Indian province, and the 2nd Division played a crucial part in the sustained and energetic measures pursued throughout the province to fill the ranks of the new battalions raised for the war, and to replace those who were casualties. When war broke out, half of the Indian Army was already drawn from the Punjab and about 100,000 Punjabis were serving. By 1916, the Punjab alone had raised a further 110,000 men out of the total of 192,000 recruited throughout India.[3] At the time that Dyer was involved, the Army had sole control of recruitment, which was at that time fully voluntary. After 1917, when the civilian authorities took it over, things began to change to a more oppressive system, but in the year in which Dyer managed the system, the corrupt and repressive recruiting systems which later became notorious had yet to develop. Dyer's knowledge of the Punjab and its people, and his contacts with the retired senior men of both the 25th and the 29th Punjabis, were tremendous assets to him in this work, which took him on occasional tours all over the divisional area.

With Annie at home he had little to do but work and worry. Ivon reached the front in France in that summer of 1915, attached to 3rd Royal Fusiliers, and was to be a continuous source of anxiety during the next few months, for by now the casualty rates and the dismal life expectancy of young officers were becoming all too public. On 28 September, Ivon was wounded at the battle of Loos, where, despite the fact that he was still a second lieutenant, he was commanding a company. He was shot in the head, and when he regained consciousness he had lost his memory. He was evacuated to Dublin and hospitalised for some months. It seems that whilst recovering Ivon met an Irish girl; we cannot be sure of this, but he was to marry Phyllis Mulroney five years later, and in the intervening years of war he had little other chance of such a meeting. Ivon was back in England with the 3rd Dorsets by March 1916.[4]

By now, the Punjab was becoming increasingly disturbed by revolutionary nationalism, and Dyer's post at Rawalpindi had some of the responsibility for fighting it. Across his desk flowed all the intelligence reports circulated to higher Headquarters, which described daily the growing struggle being waged against the Raj by the disparate groups of Indian revolutionary nationalists who saw the war as an opportunity to attack the British whilst their attention and resources were directed elsewhere.

The threat posed by revolutionary violence emanating from Bengal had grown by the time Dyer reached India again and was steadily increasing. Fourteen terrorist outrages occurred in Bengal in 1914, deteriorating to a figure of thirty-six during 1915. The British were still far from in control of this problem. A more recent threat, and one more specific to the Punjab, was posed by a group of Sikh revolutionaries formed in California in 1911 by a revolutionary named Har Dayal, and named after the paper, the *Ghadr*, which he founded at Berkeley University.[5] They were strong in the USA and Canada, in both of which the children of richer classes studying at the universities found ready audiences amongst the Indian labourers who had emigrated there. At the start of the war, Ghadr leaders were contacted by the German Embassy in Washington and given funds and intelligence. In January 1915, they shipped 8000 rifles and four million rounds of ammunition to San Diego to load aboard the *Annie Larsen* which was to take the cargo to India. After a few weeks spent evading the Royal Navy in the Pacific, the ship was forced to return to Washington State where US agents seized her cargo. The Germans and the Ghadr also operated in Vancouver, but their plan to sabotage the Canadian railway there was broken up at the time of the seizure of the *Annie Larsen*. Whilst this was going on, the movement began a determined effort to transport very large numbers of revolutionary supporters back to India. The SS *Komagatu Maru*, the first of several ships which carried them, took four hundred Sikhs and sixty Muslims to Calcutta in 1915. The British had considerable notice of this, for the ship had been chartered by a notorious snakehead in Vancouver who was under Canadian surveillance, and she had already been refused landing in Canada, Shanghai and Hong Kong. Nevertheless, on reaching Calcutta, her passengers still managed to scramble ashore, taking their firearms with them. The British forces at hand ordered them to disarm and to entrain for the Punjab under escort, but the activists resisted, and a firefight ensued before most were rounded up. More returning emigrants arrived in Calcutta, Madras and Colombo, and many of these managed to escape into the interior. The SS *Tasu Maru* followed these to Calcutta carrying most of the Ghadr leadership, a rather stupid move at that stage, as all were immediately interned.

Yet the influx went on. Eight thousand Ghadr supporters are estimated to have returned to India, mostly to the Punjab, during the four years from 1914 to 1917. Once home, they aimed to raise the Punjab and to liberate Kashmir, using German-financed weapons shipped into India from Batavia in the Dutch East Indies and from Siam; the German Consul-General in Shanghai was a focus for the plot in the East. They also planned to liberate Burma and the Malay States, which were largely policed by Sikhs, and to infiltrate colonial garrisons outside India to cause disaffection amongst Indian troops. This was the disaffection which Dyer had begun to pick up in the temple attended by his men in the months before he left Hong Kong. The 26th Punjabis were found to have been badly subverted when they returned from Hong Kong in 1915. Dyer was no doubt proud of the fact that his own battalion, which had served alongside the 26th and returned to India with them, was not similarly affected. Others were: Sikhs of the Malay States Guides at Penang and Singapore became disaffected. The conspiracy was not publicised, but to those in the know it was highly worrying.

Terrorist attacks began in the Punjab in October 1914, and when Dyer returned to the province he was warned of the heightened state of operational alert. At about the time of his arrival, the railway bridge picquet at Amritsar was ambushed, a guard murdered and his weapons taken. Intelligence made him aware that Rash Behari Bose, an organiser of the outrages carried out at Delhi in 1912 and 1913, including the bomb attack on Lord Hardinge, had thrown in his lot with the Ghadr and set up his headquarters, first at Amritsar and later at Lahore; his group had caused forty-five serious outrages by February 1915. This, in a hitherto peaceful province, was a severe blow to the authorities, and, although many of the attacks were not very effective, the rate of ten incidents a month that this represents caused serious alarm and could not be concealed from the public. On 19 February the Ghadr mounted a rebellion which went off at half-cock in various Punjab centres after its ringleaders were arrested in Lahore. It was just a day after intelligence agents managed to penetrate the group; the authorities had been very lucky. This was followed in March by a Sikh rising in the countryside, though this was aimed at Hindu creditors and landlords rather than the Government, and subsequently by similar separate risings of Muslim peasantry in the Punjab districts of Multan, Muzaffargarh and Jhang. The province was obviously in a very febrile state indeed.

Agents of the Ghadr had managed to infiltrate many of the garrisons inside India, initially with some success. They attempted to subvert Sikhs of the 23rd Cavalry at Amritsar in November 1914, planning to use them to attack the magazine at Lahore, and they succeeded in inciting some of these troops to march on the town of Jhar Sahib, near Lahore, on 26 November, and to mount a raid on the treasury at Ferozepore four days later. All these conspirators were arrested, and twelve men of the 23rd Cavalry were executed after court martial. Ghadr agents again contacted the 26th Punjabis at their new station in Ferozepore, this time without success. Further east, at Meerut, the 12th Cavalry and the 128th Pioneers were approached by the Ghadr leader N.J. Pingle, who was arrested in their lines in possession of explosives and subsequently hanged. 21 February 1915 was fixed by the Ghadr for a coordinated rising amongst the troops, timed to coincide with the rising crushed by the authorities on the 19th, but informers gave their plans away and the regiments concerned were searched and disarmed. One hundred and eighty Sikh soldiers were arrested in Lahore, fourteen at Benares and five at Mandi. More seriously, the 8th Cavalry at Jhansi murdered its Commanding Officer and wounded some of its officers before being suppressed and disbanded. The conspiracy was also found to have reached as far afield as the Sikhs of the 12th Pioneers stationed in Aden, and in Burma seventeen Sikhs of the Burma Military Police stationed at Mandalay were arrested. In the extended follow up, which the British coordinated across several continents, twenty-one Sikhs were convicted in the United States of waging war against Great Britain, along with the eighteen American and German nationals who had been their link to the Imperial German Government.

It was not only the Sikhs who were a cause of anxiety. Muslim unrest, which began after the Sultan of Turkey joined the war on the German side in November 1914, added to British fears for the loyalty of their troops. The Turks issued five *fatwahs* that month calling for Indians to rise up in *jihad* against the British, and Indian troops were in some places affected. Nationalist revolutionaries used the war against Turkey as an issue with which to suborn Muslim troops. In Burma, Pathans of the 130th Baluch Regiment mutinied in Rangoon; half of the battalion's eight companies were found to be disaffected. This was the unit's second outbreak, as they had bayoneted a British officer when posted to East Africa on the outbreak of war. Over 190 men of this unit were court martialled; one Indian officer and one *havildar* were shot, and the remainder were transported for life to the Andaman Islands. In Singapore, *rangars* of the 5th Light Infantry broke out of their barracks one night and killed every European they could find. They were bloodily suppressed by a hastily collected force of sailors and civilians who had seized the nearest weapon and come to the aid of the authorities. Before the revolt was crushed, thirty-two Europeans had been killed. This was the most serious mutiny of the period; after its suppression, in which forty-six mutineers were killed, another thirty-seven men of the unit were shot and eighty-nine imprisoned. The Muslim teashop owner who had spread pro-Turkish propaganda amongst the troops in Singapore, a man named Kasim Ismail Mansur, was hanged. After Turkey joined the war, some Muslims began to desert in India, sometimes fleeing with their arms and many of them heading for Afghanistan. Signs of mutiny were detected amongst Muslims in some of the regiments stationed in northern India, and some Muslim soldiers deserted in France, from where the Germans sent them on to Afghanistan. The Indian divisions at the front were forced gradually to replace two predominantly Muslim units by others with more men of other faiths.

Civilian revolutionaries of many types added to the difficulties faced by the Punjab authorities. The Ghadr incident in Lahore in March 1915 was found to have involved Hindu fundamentalists led by Bhai Parma Nand, a professor of the *Arya Samaj* college in the town; he was arrested and sentenced to death. In February 1915, groups of Muslim students began to disappear from Lahore, Rawalpindi and Peshawar and were later spotted making their way to Kabul; one was captured and shot. As a whole, though, there was little public unrest in either the Muslim or Hindu communities. The Government exercised censorship of newspapers, closing down a few of the more radical ones, and in June 1915 the Viceroy confined the main Indian pan-Islamic Muslim leaders, the brothers Shaukat Ali and Mohamed Ali, to their villages, and this quietened the agitation. The Frontier remained largely peaceful, though the Hindustani Fanatics, the Wahabi Muslims whom Dyer had fought at the Black Mountain in 1888, carried out a few raids from Afghanistan during 1915.[6]

In the main, the Indian Army stayed solidly loyal, and the fight against the relatively few nationalist revolutionaries did much to stimulate the development of the British intelligence services and the mechanisms of state security, scarcely existent until then.[7] The Government of India passed the Defence of India Act in March 1915, a measure largely enacted at the insistence of Sir Michael O'Dwyer, the Lieutenant-Governor of the Punjab, who considered his province 'a powder magazine', and who initiated a series of rigidly authoritarian measures aimed at keeping order (including the banning of magazines and the barring of nationalist politicians from the Punjab), measures which the more liberal Viceroy, Lord Hardinge, feared were remedies worse than the disease they were meant to cure. The Defence of India Act gave the Indian and provincial governments powers of surveillance, search, arrest and internment, and legitimised methods of operation hitherto unavailable to the authorities, which had so far been fighting the revolutionaries with little success. They now began to get the upper hand. The number of outrages in Bengal declined steadily from the peak reached in 1915: there were twenty-four in 1916, eight in 1917, and six in 1918. The Ghadr revolt in the Punjab proved easier to eradicate, and was stamped out by August 1915. The revolutionaries there proved thoroughly incompetent, and had little general support outside their own groups. In Lahore, two hundred and twelve Ghadr members were charged, thirty-six of whom were sentenced to death, seventy-seven to transportation and fifteen to imprisonment. 1534 of the Ghadr members who had returned from America were temporarily restricted to their villages, but in the vast majority of cases, over six thousand, no police action was considered necessary at all, though the returnees were kept under surveillance. Their leaders fled abroad, Bose to Japan, many to Afghanistan.

During these campaigns, officials and senior military officers in positions such as that held by Dyer became accustomed to the need to look over their shoulders for foreign and revolutionary intrigue. They learned the efficacy of dealing sharply and swiftly with any outbreak of revolutionary violence, and this reinforced the beliefs that had been held in the Punjab since the Mutiny, that it was invariably best to strike swiftly and to strike hard to forestall greater trouble. It is understandable, then, that it was with great surprise that the British were to find only two years later that these lessons could no longer be so effectively applied.[8]

In the middle of his year at Rawalpindi, Dyer was promoted to full colonel, and so he passed finally out of regimental service and onto the general staff.[9] He was not to stay much longer in the Headquarters of 2nd Division, for in February 1916 he was relieved of his duties there and summoned to Delhi to meet General Kirkpatrick, Chief of the General Staff at Army Headquarters. There he was given instructions to take independent command of the Seistan Field Force, the British forces operating in East Persia in the area now known as Sistan.[10] This was a great opportunity for Dyer, who was at last being given a chance to do his bit for the war and to show that he was fit for higher command. The job was bound to give him the kind of action which he loved, and, to add to his undoubted pleasure on hearing all this, Sistan was so far from anywhere that he was to be almost completely free of control by any superior. It was a splendid post for an independently-minded officer like Dyer, and he had much in this for which to be grateful to General Kitson, who must have recommended him for the appointment.

The command in Sistan was to be the first defining moment of Dyer's career, and he was to see his work there as his greatest achievement. He published his experiences in his book *Raiders of the Sarhad* in 1921, intending the account to be the cornerstone of the Dyer legend he was by then assiduously fostering.[11] The book is a valuable insight into his mind and character, and shows what he preferred to have the world believe about him. Luckily, the military log sheets and correspondence of his campaign survive in abundance, and allow his deeds and movements to be traced almost by the hour. They enable us to check his account and to balance it with the evidence. The East Persian campaign provides the lens through which we can see Dyer develop the character, ideas and methods which were to carry him to the Jallianwala Bagh in Amritsar some two years later.

11

Sistan

In his Rolls Royce car, Dyer motored up from Rawalpindi to Delhi. Once at the Headquarters on 17 February he was briefed by General Kirkpatrick.[1] The Seistan Field Force, which was to be his first formation command, was deployed in east Persia, which at that date was an independent and ostensibly a neutral country, though one which had for some years been divided into areas of British and Russian influence. The British area included the Persian region of Sistan which bordered Afghanistan. Troops were there because of events not in Persia, but in Kabul, where the Germans had sent emissaries early in the war, aiming to use it as a base for revolutionaries to subvert India and to persuade the Amir of Afghanistan to enter the war on their side.[2] They were eventually to prove unsuccessful in both aims, as the Amir was too wily to depend upon the promises of such a faraway power. From 1915, though, the Germans infiltrated agents into Afghanistan through Persia, and in the latter country they sought to tie down troops and threaten British oil interests by creating trouble amongst the tribes.

Plans for the subversion of India were handled in Berlin by the Intelligence Bureau for the East, part of the German Ministry of Foreign Affairs. In August 1914, the junior official in charge of the Indian Department, Otto Günther von Wesendonck, set up an Indian Centre with an 'Indian Independence Committee' in Germany, consisting of student revolutionaries studying at European universities, and headed by Virendranath Chattopadhyaya, who had earlier been active in ineffectual revolutionary circles in London and Paris. In January 1915, the Ghadr leader Har Dayal joined them from the United States, fleeing from the American crackdown on his conspiracy. The committee aimed to arm the Bengal revolutionaries and to work with those Ghadr members who were infiltrating India.

After Turkey joined the war, the Turkish commander, Enver Pasha, set up an Indian Revolutionary Headquarters at Medina under Maulvi Mahmud Hassan, but this was a half-hearted affair, and the Turks made little effort to try to subvert Indian Muslim troops or to coordinate their work with the German Intelligence Bureau. The Germans, though, posed a considerable threat, and in February 1915 in the south of Persia, led by Wilhelm Wassmuss, the former Consul at Bushire, their agents began to create a great deal of trouble amongst the tribes of the interior. So successful was he at this that Wassmuss earned the sobriquet 'the

German Lawrence'. By March 1915, British troops had to be detached from the Army in Mesopotamia to deal with unrest behind their lines, and a small number of Indian troops were deployed from India across the hundreds of miles of open desert between British Baluchistan and Russian Turkistan. These formed a cordon which linked at one end with a similar force sent south by the Russians, and which attempted to prevent German agents getting into Afghanistan and the Russian Muslim khanates. Wassmuss was to remain at liberty and a thorn in the British side until they took Mesopotamia in 1917.

The German plan to foment trouble inside India centred on the deposed ruler of a tiny Indian state, Raja Kunwar Mahendra Pratap, who had fled earlier to Europe and who in April 1915 left Germany for Istanbul and Afghanistan in the company of the agent Werner von Hentig. In his hands went a letter in which the imperial German Government promised the Amir of Afghanistan all of India as far as Bombay. At the same time he carried conflicting letters promising the Indian princes their freedom. Joined in Mesopotamia by Maulvi Barkatullah and the German officer Oskar von Niedermayer, Kunwar reached Kabul in October 1915. Here the party worked with the Amir's brother, Nasrullah, and son, Amanullah, who were the leaders of the anti-British party in Kabul and were supported by a vociferous Afghan press. The Amir stalled masterfully, prolonging the negotiations until the German mission and its disparate nationalist allies started to break up under the weight of their own antagonisms. By the time Dyer was posted to Persia in February 1916, the danger was already on the wane, and the German agents in Kabul were looking for a way out.

The task of the British cordon was to round up the German agents in Persia and prevent their crossing the border.[3] The area through which their very thin red line stretched was one of the greatest wildernesses left on the planet, a region of dust, sand and rock, of scorching temperatures and infrequent rain. Its inhabitants were Baluch tribes whose ethnic and linguistic kin straddled the borders of the three countries.[4] In Sistan, they were nominally subjects of the Shah of Persia, but they affected to regard themselves as independent of any political control. Historically, the Baluch were all subjects of the Khan of Kalat, who had thrown off a dependency upon the Durrani Afghan monarchy in the late eighteenth century but was now under the protection of the British. The border between British India and Persia had only very recently been drawn (some forty years before) so as to include in Persia large areas formerly under the Baluch Khan's suzerainty. Due to the weakness of the Persian central authorities, these areas were now under no one's control, and the tribes there were very liable to be tempted by German gold.[5] In the upland wilderness of the Sarhadd, an area of about two hundred by eighty miles in extent inside Sistan, the livelihood of the Baluch tribes depended upon raiding.[6] The major tribal grouping there was the Damanis, though there were others such as the Rekis and Kurds, and these had little to depend upon for survival in these vast, almost waterless deserts other than stealing their neighbours' animals, crops and goods.[7] The number of troops allotted to the British cordon was insufficient to prevent both German infiltration and Baluch raiding, and the Sarhaddi Baluch, watching the weakly protected camel trains supplying the British cordon move slowly past their homeland, could not believe their luck. By 1916 the Sarhaddi Baluch had begun to have a severe effect on the cordon's supplies and thus to pose a threat to the entire operation. Mounted on swift-moving camels, appearing suddenly out of the sand clouds, descending upon caravans before any alarm could be raised then cutting out the laden camels and fleeing before any pursuit could be mounted, they had so far proved invincible.

Dyer would not have been surprised by much of General Kirkpatrick's briefing. Some of it concerning Afghanistan, Persia and the German infiltration was new to him, but he had had a year's experience of revolutionary Indian nationalism in the Punjab, and the threat it posed was familiar. We do not have a copy of the instructions he was given in Delhi, nor of the wording of his mission. Circumstances and subsequent events make plain, however, what these contained. The orders issued to Dyer's eventual successor in this post survive, and are worth quoting as they purport to repeat what he was told:

> The orders issued to your predecessor and which still hold good are to intercept, capture or destroy any German parties attempting to enter Afghanistan or Sistan ... A good system of intelligence is recommended to avoid detachments watching the whole road. You can spend freely for the purpose of organizing such an intelligence system ... So long as Persia maintains her neutrality, every endeavour must be made to act in a manner friendly to the Persians and in support of the Persian authorities. Persian subjects should not be interfered with, unless they are escorting hostile parties or unless there is reason to believe they are carrying dispatches for the Germans ... Avoid small detachments as they are liable to attack.[8]

It will become clear as events unfold that for one reason or another Dyer misunderstood, or chose to ignore, these instructions.

The officer then commanding the cordon, Colonel Wilkeley, was still in post but was too sick to carry out his duties for much longer, so there was a need for haste.[9] In his hurry to get away, Dyer's departure from Delhi almost degenerated into a farce reminiscent of his fracas on the riverboat in Burma and his attack on the *tehsildar* at Nowshera. The intervening years had not changed his style. His account of what happened at the station is in *Raiders of the Sarhad*:

> I hurried, with car and native chauffeur, to the railway station, and asked for a truck on which to place the car for entrainment to Nushki. The station master assured me I was asking for an impossibility. A great maharajah, then travelling, had commandeered every available truck for his suite, luggage and cars. I told him that the Government business

on which I had been sent was important, and by a little persuasion, soon had myself on the way to Pindi and the car on the way to Nushki.[10]

Dyer immediately returned to Rawalpindi, packed his bags, and with his orderly, Allah Dad, and the British driver he had borrowed from his GOC entrained for Quetta. General Kitson, very much his mentor at this stage, lent him his own driver, Corporal Allan of the 9th Middlesex. Dyer already had both an Indian and a British chauffeur, the latter being Corporal Allan's brother, but General Kitson allowed him to exchange the two brothers as his own man was the better driver.[11] The next stop for the party was Quetta, the seat of the Agent to the Governor General in Baluchistan (who was effectively the British Governor) and the Headquarters of Major-General Grover, the General Officer Commanding 4 Division, who was to be Dyer's nominal superior. Grover had the unenviable task of supporting Dyer's operations from a base over 450 miles to his rear whilst being unable to exercise any timely influence over them. Dyer's Headquarters reported by telegraph direct to Army Headquarters at Delhi and Simla, bypassing Quetta, which was exactly the sort of arrangement that was proving so disastrous for the British forces further away in Mesopotamia, which were also commanded from Simla. It is worth bearing in mind in the account of Dyer's operations which follows that his superiors in Army Headquarters had very much more on their minds than his small campaign, a factor which enabled him to do much as he pleased for a good deal of the time.

Dyer picked up more instructions from General Grover and acquired petrol and spare tyres for his car, then once again entrained, this time for the little town of Nushki where he arrived on 25 February. This was as far west as the railway went in those days, but it was still some 375 miles from the Persian frontier. At Nushki, he managed a swift line to Annie giving her the first news she had received about his new appointment:

> Just a line to let you know that I am off to Seistan from Nushki, and you may not hear from me for many a long day. My address will be OC Troops, Seistan, Robat, Baluchistan. All has been arranged in a great hurry, and I am delighted to say that I am at last doing something. I am very fit indeed, and hope I may remain so. Best love, dearest, to yourself and the boys.[12]

Dyer set off by car two days later, typically disregarding warnings given him by the political staff in Quetta that the road had been interrupted by Baluch raiders and that he would be wise to delay. He was unaccompanied and unescorted except by Corporal Allan and the orderly, Allah Dad Khan (the Indian chauffeur had thrown his hand in at Nushki when he saw what he was being asked to do, much to Dyer's disgust). They made for Robat, the cordon's first post on the Persian frontier. Dyer was not about to be put off his plans either by Baluch tribesmen or by the Politicals he despised, and of whose advice this was only the first piece of many he was to ignore: 'I saw no reason for altering previously made plans or for delaying my departure.' There was no road to Robat, only camel tracks through open sand and gravel desert over which no car had travelled before, and there were very few settlements or British posts on the way to offer protection against the raiders who infested the area. This was a brave journey, but a foolhardy one. They left Dyer's heavier luggage and his charger, Galahad, to follow with a camel train. As he made his way across the desert, perpetually bogging the car in sand dunes and occasionally running out of fuel, Dyer reflected: 'But upon one thing I made up my mind – even at that early stage – I would do my utmost to show these Raiders, who were doing us so much harm, that they could not do this with impunity.'[13] Already, his mind was set not on his main mission, but on punishing the Baluch.

Unlooked for rain made the soft going even worse, and water lay in wide shallow pools around which they were forced to detour. Losing his patience at what seemed to him the hundredth diversion they had met, Dyer ordered Corporal Allan to drive through a pool of water; up to its axles in mud, the Rolls bogged in and stuck fast. The three of them were unable to shift it, and Dyer had to bribe the riders of a passing caravan to dig him out. He had to do this twice, as the car bogged in again not much further on. This time they found that the petrol tap had been left on inadvertently and that a lot of their fuel was gone. Had they not found a miraculous dump of petrol cans at the rest house at the dusty nearby post of Yadgar, they would have had to walk the last few hundred miles; they never did discover how the petrol came to be there. Underway again, on the fourth day of the journey, they became lost and exhausted by continually having to dig the car out of the sand, so they decided to halt for the night. Alone and forgetting his revolver, Rex took a hurricane lamp and stumbled off into the desert to look for the camel track. Instead, he stumbled into the campsite of some Chagai Levies, who were part of the tribal militia recruited by the British from the local Baluch. It was a stroke of good fortune (of which they had many on that trip) which once again saved them, and that night the levies took them into the small mud fort manned by police at Saindak. They spent the next day there recovering, then guided by the levies they went on to reach Robat. It was 3 March and they had been five days alone on the road.[14]

In Robat, Dyer was met by Colonel Wilkeley, who as Commanding Officer of the 28th Light Cavalry had been *ex officio* Commander Seistan Field Force. He was very sick and had scarcely been able to hold on until he was relieved. Wilkeley had managed to make it down from his Headquarters at Nasratabad, which was further north and in the centre of the cordon, and he now handed over his task to Dyer, though he remained in the theatre, perhaps too sick to travel.[15] Dyer's arrival was a tonic to the cordon's rather dispirited Headquarters and troops.

Colvin quotes a letter he received from A.F. Fremantle, a subaltern there at the time:

> When General Dyer joined us in Seistan he immediately filled the place with an atmosphere of confidence, which made me at any rate as a subaltern understand what was meant by stories of the sight of Wellington's long nose being worth ten thousand men.[16]

Yeates, who was a Pioneer subaltern commanding the post at Kacha, felt similarly, describing Dyer affectionately as a

> sturdily built man, with a soft voice and kindly blue eyes ... Helpful and sympathetic; his simpleness and friendliness made one feel that one could unfold all one's difficulties to him and be sure of receiving wise advice. At the same time one felt that there was a great forcefulness latent in him, and that he was not a man to be wantonly provoked ... He had the knack of making us all feel at ease together ... His health was already somewhat shaken [but] Dyer revelled in unusual situations, and was always ready to step in himself and fill the breach when hands were short.[17]

Dyer set out to make the most of his new role, and to liven up what he clearly saw was a jaded group of men who were coping badly with their task. His first act in post was to review his forces, and as a result he redeployed elements of his force in the posts at Nasratabad, Shurgaz and Saindak, and also telegraphed Simla requesting four more cars and more machine guns. He immediately began to act upon his intention of bringing the sardars of the Sarhaddi Baluch to heel, though at the outset he did not make plain to his superiors what he intended to do. Instead, he made piecemeal requests for authority to implement parts of his scheme, a bit at a time, whilst feeding Army Headquarters small snippets of information as events developed. This was a technique he was to use repeatedly during his command in Sistan, presumably to avoid his plans being turned down. It was a rather less than honest way of proceeding and indicates that he was indeed aware what his real mission was, but was intent on doing something else.

He began this on 3 March, when he asked for sanction to bring the Sarhaddi sardars under British influence. 'I intend to bring Sarhadd Sardars under our control by inducement. By means of money and with the assistance of the present Political Authority at Robat this can now be accomplished; but if there is delay, it will be too late as every means to influence them are being used by the Germans.' This was sanctioned by Army Headquarters: 'Entire approval given to your proposal', though the caveat was added that 'As far as possible arrangements should be effected through Political Agent, Chagai, as we propose to bring Persian Baluchistan under political control of Baluchistan.'[18] Dyer followed this up on 6 March with the first sign that he intended to use force rather than inducements; he wrote to Army Headquarters: 'With a view to making the Germans pause in their activity towards Vasht and Bampur and also to give the Sarhadis courage, it is necessary for me to make a slight forward move during the time I am winning over the Sarhad-Sardars.'[19] At that stage the Government of India was very receptive to any proposal to deal with the Sarhaddi menace, and were quite prepared to go along with what they saw initially as limited operations.[20] The threat posed by the Sarhaddi Baluch was worsened by German involvement; the Germans had not missed the potential they had for causing trouble, and had contacted them. This suited Dyer, who coupled reports of these contacts with the words: 'I am proceeding to bring the Sarhad Sardars under our influence with all speed.'[21]

There was a good deal of necessity to justify Dyer's decision to deal immediately with the Sarhaddis. They were delaying and depleting the cordon's supplies, and were raiding in dangerously large numbers, four to five hundred in a band, with which it was beyond the capacity of the small bodies of troops spread out in isolated posts to deal. They posed a larger and much more immediate threat than the bands of Germans wandering back from Afghanistan. Something did, indeed, have to be done about them. Yet Dyer was badly hampered in taking any offensive by the forces at his disposal. The troops which he found manning the cordon were scarcely adequate to cover the enormous distances, some 350 miles, of open desert that stretched between British Baluchistan and Russian Central Asia. On his assumption of command, the Seistan Field Force consisted of 28th Light Cavalry, a section of mountain guns, the major part of the 19th Punjabis, the machine gun section of the 12th Pioneers, twenty rifles of the 106th Hazara Pioneers, and ten men of the Sappers and Miners.[22] There were also two hundred Hazara Levies and also some Chagai Levies attached to the force, but under the control of the civilian authorities. From the start of March, a strenuous effort was mounted to recruit more of these levies, and by the end of the month their numbers had reached six hundred.[23] The total manpower in the force was 1170 fighting troops.[24] As no reinforcements were on offer from India, which had its hands full in Mesopotamia and at home, the recruitment of levies was of urgent concern if the cordon was to be augmented.

The issue had been taken up before Dyer's arrival, but he quickly saw that rapid local recruitment was the only way open to him to deal effectively with his manning problems and to enable him to operate against the tribes. He fired the first shot in what was to be a campaign with his own political authorities in early March, as he sought both to increase recruitment (something in which he was supported by Army Headquarters) and to wrest control over the levies from the Politicals (something the Government of India and Army Headquarters would not countenance). Dyer wrote to Army Headquarters on 8 March:

I agree *in toto* with the idea of using fast moving detachments of cavalry and levies to hunt down wandering German parties. For this to be effective I must have good information quickly and perfect organization, to let detachments move out at once, and I can arrange this. If I trained levies as sowars or sepoys for a short period it would only detract from their fighting value at present juncture. As their mobility is already extraordinary I would on all possible occasions train them in shooting and that alone. With a stiffening of cavalry the Sarhadi levies will clearly make splendid fighters ... I think I can at once obtain requisite men who must meet Sarhad Sardars. ... Please rely on me to give my whole mind to the matter in hand to act with due caution where Political situation calls for it and with boldness on reliable information. Place them all under my orders and I will do the remainder ... I ask that the 500 levies mentioned above (except 100 at Sipi which are Sistan Baluchis raised by the Consul) and Major Keyes be put under my orders at any rate for the present.[25]

This last suggestion was blocked by the Foreign and Political Department whose Secretary minuted: 'I do not think that it is desirable to place the organization of the Levies under Colonel Dyer. This would merely increase his work and confuse the correspondence as they are civil forces. But they should be at his disposal for all operations necessary and under his orders when cooperating with troops.' The Viceroy himself agreed this line: 'Approved. H[ardinge]', but the rebuff did not prevent Dyer returning later to the idea and ultimately acting unilaterally to seize control of the levies.[26]

Dyer found that the Politicals got in his way not only in their control of the local levies, but also as they held the strings of political authority for any action he might take. This was a red rag to a bull, and in fighting political control Dyer was to take as much unscrupulous advantage as he could of the tenuous chains of political authority in his area. They were almost designed to cause confusion. The great distances which hampered up-to-date communications forced the Government of India to allow its men on the spot the exercise of a great deal of their own initiative, and where the man in question was not interested in making the system work, the system was not really operable.

On the Persian side of the international frontier control was exercised in theory by the British Minister in the embassy in Tehran, who was in telegraphic contact with his subordinate, the Consul for Seistan and Kain, Major F.B. Prideaux. This officer, the civilian counterpart to the Commander of the Seistan Field Force, was based sensibly in Nasratabad, the Persian town which up until Dyer's arrival had housed the headquarters of the cordon. His task was to arrange political support for the troops, and to liaise with the local Persian Governor of Khurasan, Hisam-ud-Daula, and his local representative in Sistan, Sardar Khudadad Khan. Also with him was a British Baluch Political Officer, the *Khan Bahadur* Shakar Khan, who held the title of Sarhadd-dar from the Khan of Kalat.[27] Prideaux was supposed to give Dyer political direction on any action taken inside Persia. His office also held responsibility for arranging local supplies for the cordon. Under Prideaux were several vice-consuls located at strategic posts along the Afghan border, such as Major Heron at Dehani Baghi. Complicating the issue from the Persian side was the fact that the Sarhadd fell to the responsibility of the Governor of Kirman, not of Khurasan, so Prideaux was not well placed to deal with the area. The situation at Kirman had fallen into confusion in late 1915 when a party of Persian democrats with the German Lieutenant Seiler had expelled the Persian Governor. Seiler had remained in control of Kirman until February 1916, and Persian authority there remained weak.

The political authority over the long border between the Persian governorate of Kirman and British Baluchistan, which was to the south of the cordon, was exercised by the Agent to the Governor General, Lieutenant-Colonel Sir John Ramsay, in far off Quetta. In theory he was the British Resident at the court of the Khan of Kalat, but in reality he exercised political control over the Kalat territories that were commonly, if strictly erroneously, labelled British Baluchistan. Under his authority were local Political Agents: Major W.G. Hutchinson, the Political Agent for Chagai, who was based at Robat and who was appointed to advise Dyer on local political matters including those affecting the Sarhadd (although the Sarhadd was across the border inside Persia and so might have been thought to come under the political control of Major Prideaux); and Major T.H. Keyes, the Political Agent for Sibi in Makran, whose responsibilities covered an area to Dyer's south. Keyes was not attached in any way to Dyer, and when Dyer arrived in post was conducting a roving mission inside Persian Baluchistan with a strong escort. He ranged from Gwadur in Makran to Khwash in the Sarhadd then back to Chahbar in Makran on a journey which was to take him from April 1916 to February 1917. His entry into the Sarhadd from the south added to the confusion in the lines of control. Keyes's immediate superior was Lieutenant-Colonel A.B. Dew, the Political Agent at Kalat, Baluchistan's capital, who was at that point conducting another independent mission in an area to the east of Keyes in the province of Jahlawan, inside British Baluchistan, suppressing a rebellion which had been stirred up there by the Germans against the Khan of Kalat.[28] Dew was mostly out of touch with Keyes. Finally, way south near the Persian Gulf, Lieutenant-Colonel Sir Percy Sykes operated independently out of the port of Bandar Abbas, exercising responsibility over the tribes of the interior of southern Persia. Dyer was directed to keep Sykes informed of his actions but invariably chose not to.[29]

One factor that was to prove important in the conflicts which followed was the relatively junior military rank held by both Consular staff and Political Agents. All were Army officers but far junior to Dyer, which made opposition by them to any instructions he issued difficult, even though they were in theory controlling his work. Dyer's early bid to take Major Keyes under his command was a sign of things to come.

Dyer further added to his own problems, and to his immediate difficulties with his political advisers, by objecting to the fact that all intelligence gathering was in their hands. He immediately set about creating a parallel intelligence organisation which reported directly to him. His confidence in his own skills in handling 'natives', and his evident enjoyment of this type of work, inevitably caused conflict with his political advisers and was at times to lead him dangerously up the garden path. His skills and powers of discernment did not prove as great as he imagined, and he had no knowledge at all of local conditions, something which those he chose as his intelligence agents seem to have taken early advantage of. On his arrival in Robat, without authority, he coopted as his Brigade Major, a post that did not actually exist, the officer employed there as the local intelligence gatherer, Captain Landon. Having attached him to his staff in this capacity, he then employed him to work as his own intelligence officer, an early example of Dyer getting his way by incremental steps whilst disguising his objective, and an arrangement that Army Headquarters was not eventually to sanction.[30] But for the meantime Landon set about organising a body of spies to bypass the political chain.

Dyer himself recruited a few locals who had caught his eye, including a member of the Baluch Reki tribe named Idu, one of the party of Chagai Levies who had come to his assistance in the sand dunes near Saindak.[31] In *Raiders of the Sarhad*, Dyer narrates that Idu claimed to have prevented his fellows shooting up Dyer's car, which he said they believed was a German airship. On the strength of this claim to have saved his life, Dyer immediately coopted Idu from the levies and appointed him as his personal aide. According to his own account, although he knew nothing of Idu other than their chance meeting in the night, he relied thereafter on his advice in preference to that of his political advisers; a somewhat haphazard way of running an intelligence operation.[32] He called Idu his 'head,' 'a man in a million', and the fact that Idu's advice seems to have been aimed in the main at doing damage to the enemies of his tribe was a point which Dyer seems to have missed. Idu was, it would seem, a relative of the sardar of the Reki tribe (and was in later days to be his successor), though he did not tell Dyer this. If he did, Dyer kept it quiet.[33] As a result of all this, from early March Dyer began to submit his own intelligence reports direct to Simla, bypassing the political chain, and the information he sent was often highly suspect. One of his first telegrams to Army Headquarters was a report, completely unfounded, concerning threats posed by the Sarhaddi raiders: 'Spy states Juma Khan has been offered [by the Germans] 100 krans per foot soldier and 200 krans per camel sowar and camels and rifles captured in last raid.[34] Reported that Juma has written to Jiand Khan asking him to join Germans.[35] Jiand planned to raid Panjgur first.'[36] Panjgur was hundreds of miles away in Makran, inside British protected territory, far away from the territory raided by the Sarhaddi Baluch. Dyer's interest in exaggerating the Sarhaddi threat had clearly been appreciated by his informants.

Whilst Dyer was getting to grips with his widely flung force, Sarhaddi raiders made the mistake of impinging directly upon his private arrangements. On 18 March, when the convoy bringing on his baggage reached the Borgah plain outside Nushki, the Baluch swooped upon it, killing the Chagai Levies who were mounting guard, stealing Dyer's luggage and shooting his horse. They robbed Dyer's groom of all his clothes, even ripping the rings from his ears, and the man reported to Dyer at Robat almost naked and in a state of abject terror.[37] The horse, Galahad, had been 'a fiery chestnut Arab, half trained and almost unmanageable', a present from his brother Edward, who was by that stage managing the brewery, and who had given him the cash to buy 'the best horse in Bombay presidency'. From that moment there was more than a little of the personal in Dyer's campaign against the Sarhaddi Baluch. Dyer immediately ordered the 28th Cavalry to Saindak to chase the raiders, but, though they found many tracks, the raiders got away.[38]

In Dyer's view, the importance of his new position and the rank of acting colonel which he held did not coincide. As he puts it in his book:

> Already I could see I was going to be badly handicapped by my lack of rank, and determined to make a bid for the rank which would give me more authority. With this object in view I sent a telegram to General Kirkpatrick … asking him to make me a General, and stating baldly that I considered it necessary … Meanwhile, though I was not yet a General I determined to act the part. The 28th Light Cavalry made crossed swords for my shoulders and the necessary red tabs.[39]

Luckily for Dyer, who would have lost some face had he needed to remove his home-made badges, Army Headquarters acquiesced in this bit of bravado and he was promoted to local brigadier-general with effect from 24 February, the date of his assumption of command.[40] Though it had been unable to allocate more troops to the cordon other than new levies, Army Headquarters had intended with Dyer's appointment to have a more senior officer in the post than his predecessor, so his request was in tune with their policy at the time.[41] Sykes was similarly promoted in Bandar Abbas.

Dyer then turned to his intended campaign against the Sarhaddis. He sent their sardars a message inviting them to a *darbar* at Kacha, a small post inside British territory halfway between Robat and Saindak. Simla was to spot this only three days after the day of the *darbar*. They reminded Dyer, too late, that he was to consult his Political Officers in all tribal matters.[42] He did not expect the chiefs to come, so in the meantime he and Landon drove off north to Nasratabad for his first visit, intending to remove some of its troops rather than to install himself and his Headquarters in the location from which his predecessors had operated.[43] Here he met the acting Commanding Officer of the 28th Light Cavalry, Major P.S.D. Claridge, and relieved him of a squadron of his regiment as well as of some of the infantry and stores in the base. These were sent to Robat, where Dyer now returned. Though he realised he could not strip the cordon north of Robat of any more troops than this, he showed no interest in the operations of those he left in place. He did not drive north of Nasratabad to visit the rest of the cordon, and in his entire tour as Commander Seistan Field Force never returned to the base. He resigned what his mission had made clear was the real work of his force to the few troops he left in the cordon, and delegated the watch for German agents to Colonel Wilkeley, his predecessor, who was now in Kacha. Dyer now turned his full attention to the Sarhadd.

On his return to the south, Dyer motored on past Robat to Kacha, and found that only one Baluch sardar, Taj Mahomed, the sardar of the Rekis, had come to the *darbar* scheduled for the end of March. The Rekis were already friendly to the British and were providing recruits for the Chagai Levies. They had historically been at enmity with the other Baluch of the Sarhadd, particularly with their chief tribe, the Damanis. Unsurprisingly, the Reki chief offered to attack the other Baluch in alliance with Dyer.

What did not become clear to any of the political authorities until over a month later was that without any assistance from, or even with the knowledge of, his Political Officers, Dyer had proceeded to reward the Rekis and their allied tribe, the Kurds, with a full-blown treaty of friendship. Dyer signed this and sent it as a *fait accompli* to Simla. He compounded this action, taken without advice or authority, by granting outrageously favourable terms to the Rekis. The fact that the treaty included provisions of which Dyer could have had no understanding makes it clear that it was in large part drafted by the Baluch. These were terms tantamount to a British recognition that the Sarhadd was an independent region and was to become a British protectorate, and Dyer promised on behalf of the British Government that they would pay the Reki and Kurd sardars an allowance similar to that then being paid to the major sardars of British Baluchistan.

Dyer's text, an 'Agreement Made at Kacha between Some Sarhaddi Sardars and Myself,' stated that the sardars, presenting themselves

> before General Dyer sahib Bahadur at Kacha … having taken allegiance to His Britannic Majesty's Government with all sincerity of heart, do hereby declare that we and all the people of our tribe are obedient and loyal to this Great British Kingdom … We have been independent since time immemorial … [Dyer has] granted rewards and fixed monthly pay for us and the people of our tribe.

In return for this they gave permission for the British to fix outposts in their territory and to take troops anywhere inside it, promised to help the British Government, 'which will have the same rights over us as it has over the Sardars of Sarwan and Jhalawan' (who were in British Baluchistan), and stated that 'we will serve the British Government in the same way as these Sardars do'.[44] They promised to hand over or report any enemy, and to report and punish any Sarhaddis attacking the British. Clause Five of the treaty embodied what was clearly Dyer's intentions regarding the long-term future of the Sarhadd, stating that, after the cessation of hostilities with the Germans, the Sarhaddis 'will ask for the same concessions and privileges as are enjoyed by the Sardars of Mekran, Sarwan and Jhalawan' (all of which were in British Baluchistan).[45] The treaty was signed at Kacha on 24 March 1916 by four sardars, twenty-one 'sarkardars' and by Dyer, Captain Landon and Lieutenant Yeates, but not by any Political Officer.

The treaty was unequivocally regarded by both the Persians and Baluch as having absorbed the Sarhadd into the Raj. The Consul for Seistan and Kain was told by the local Persian officer, Sardar Khudadad Khan, and by the local *thanadar*, that 'Dyer made Sarhaddi Sardars British subjects', and that the other Sarhaddi sardars had attacked the Rekis for signing the treaty. The consular politicals in Persia feared that the treaty would oblige the British to go to the aid of the Rekis in their quarrels with the other Baluch. Government of India file notes make clear the violence of the reaction when the treaty surfaced in Simla. The Foreign and Political Department objected that no Political Officer had been consulted, informed or present. They strongly objected to the Sarhaddi claim to independence 'since time immemorial', for the official view recognised that the Sarhaddis were Persian subjects. The Assistant Secretary, Denys Bray, who was an expert on the Baluch of some renown, saw long-term problems with the promise of a subsidy, and commented:

> The implied annexation of the country may be brushed aside, but the guaranteed rupees will be another matter … Without in any way belittling the work General Dyer has done in the Sarhad, one inclines to the conclusion that this work would have a more permanent character if he were assisted by a trained Political Officer … General Dyer's excess of zeal in concluding the high-sounding agreement with the Reki and others of the Sarhad is likely to lead to trouble … On the whole, the best policy seems for us to ignore the agreement at the present.

His superior, A.H. Grant, added: 'General Dyer's agreement is, of course, impossible as it stands', though he conceded it was useful 'to tide us over … We can always wriggle out on this'. The Agent to the Governor-General in Baluchistan telegraphed Simla when he received his copy on 11 May: 'I had not seen agreement. Dyer has suggested coming to see me, he might be instructed not to enter into further agreements until seeing me.' He telegraphed Simla again on 24 May: 'In my opinion it was not a wise [treaty] and a number of signatories are, according to Hutchinson, men of no importance whatever.' On 27 May he wrote Simla a stiff letter pulling Dyer's treaty to pieces: 'I think it is unfortunate that

General Dyer should have entered into this agreement without previous consultation with any Political Officer.' He quoted local advice that the treaty's signatories included only one real sardar (not the four Rekis who claimed that rank), that one of those pretending to be such was a Chagai Levy *khassadar* who had earlier been dismissed from his post at Robat as he was of bad character, and that only one tribe mentioned in the treaty was of any importance (the Rekis), since the Kurds 'are practically non-existent'. He was advised that the 'title of *sarkardar* is unknown to us' and that it was probably no more than a petty *lambardar* or *malik*. The wool, it seemed, had been well pulled over Dyer's eyes. At a meeting subsequently arranged in Simla, it was agreed to provide Dyer with a trained Political Officer to ensure that he made no more agreements without authority.[46]

Dyer's treaty of friendship with the Rekis was an absurd act of breathtaking arrogance. He had been in the country for less than a month, and his ignorance of the international and local political issues involved in his mission is obvious in the text of the agreement. It is clear that he was fooled by those with whom he seemed, to himself, to be negotiating from a position of such power. Indeed, it is the self-delusion of this action which stands out most clearly. He really did believe that he could handle everything by himself, and that his skills with 'the natives' made the presence of his advisers redundant. In this ill-conceived treaty it is not fanciful to see the first signs of the self-delusions which were increasingly to mar Dyer's view of his duty. On this and on subsequent important occasions in his life, he judged the efficacy of his actions not in terms of any real consequences they might have but according to how well they matched with the self-generated drama in which he saw himself playing the lead, the drama of the 'General Sahib Bahadur', the imperial warrior. His need to satisfy the dictates of self-image rather than those of the situation in which he found himself was to become highly dangerous when the conduct of events touching the lives of many lay in his hands.

On 30 March, Dyer telegraphed Simla announcing that he intended to attack the Sarhaddis, and seize their capital town, Khwash, which lay about fifty miles inside the Persian frontier. He was, this time, reasonably frank about at least his initial objectives:

> A quick method of drawing off the raids from the Line of Communications would, I think be for an advance to be made by me on Khwash. The Kurds and Rekis are amenable to attacking the Damanis. It should be easy to punish them and bring their lashkars back with us with as small backing of one troop cavalry and fifty infantry. On April 3rd two guns arrived here. May I do this?

Simla signalled back: 'The Chief has no objection but desires that you will ensure that the guns are sufficiently escorted.'[47] The die was cast for a campaign which was not to be the short raid Army Headquarters envisaged, but was to be a campaign lasting for the next six months. Yet the forces which Dyer had managed to scrape together for his mobile column were completely inadequate for the task he had set himself. He was joined at Robat, where he had returned after the failed *darbar*, by seventeen *sowars* of B Squadron of the 28th Light Cavalry and the two mountain guns from Nasratabad commanded by Major MacGowan, but he still could muster no infantry at all. To add to this minuscule force he had about fifteen Chagai Levies. He and Landon drove off to Kacha to collect what troops could be removed from the post. On 2 April, as they drove into the fort, the garrison turned out to meet them under Lieutenant E.P. Yeates of the 12th Pioneers. Amongst the company of the 19th who presented arms, Dyer found to his dismay only nine trained soldiers. All the rest were newly arrived recruits. He took the nine, added sixty-five of the recruits along with Yeates and his two Maxim machine guns, and left the fort at Kacha almost unmanned except for the long-suffering Colonel Wilkeley, who remained there to command the cordon. Dyer moved with these reinforcements to the border at Mirjawa, a fort manned by the Chagai Levies, where he had arranged a rendezvous with the troops he had left with Major MacGowan at Robat. They all met up on 6 April.

As Yeates later put it: 'General Dyer was not the man to be deterred by such trifles'; in other words he would pursue his objective irrespective of the troops he had to task. In these circumstances it was necessary that any use of force would have to be supplemented, and at times totally replaced, by stratagem.

> Now commenced a miniature campaign, conducted under heavy odds and difficulties, which was remarkable for its bluff and daring. With his boldness, initiative and profound knowledge of native psychology, General Dyer was an ideal leader for such an undertaking.[48]

It was as well that his troops thought him so.

Maps illustrating Dyer's campaign in the Sarhadd, from R.E.H. Dyer, *The Raiders of the Sarhadd* (1921).

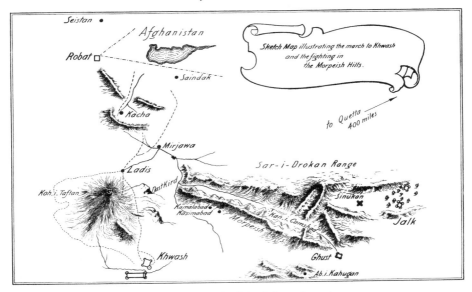

The Persian-Baluchi Afghan frontiers

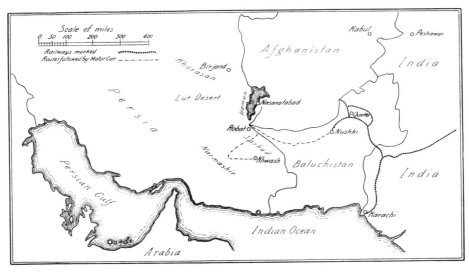

The campaign around Khwash

12

The Sarhadd

Dyer's small column moved across the Persian border on 7 April 1916, reaching the deserted fort at Ladis on the same day. This was in a comparatively well-watered valley on the north side of the Kuh-i Taftan, the mountain which dominated the border region.[1] Dyer left Colonel Wilkeley in charge at Kacha, as he had been told by Army Headquarters to delegate command of the cordon to him whilst in the field. He was not at all happy about this, but it was a sensible arrangement.[2] He could not have controlled the cordon whilst he was on the march and away from the line of the telegraph and, although the German position in Persia was reckoned to be collapsing in April, the trouble they had stirred up with the tribes had yet to subside. The column had a political agent with it in the shape of Sardar Shakar Khan, the Baluch Political Officer responsible for the area, who had come at the last moment, as the Persian officer, Sardar Khudadad Khan, had refused to cross the frontier with such a small force. Shakar Khan was to prove a great asset to Dyer over the next few months.[3] Dyer had with him the indispensable Idu, who had sent ahead some men of his Reki tribe to spread word of the great size of the force that was about to descend upon the Sarhadd, and to circulate rumours to confuse the Sarhaddis as to the direction in which they were heading.

As Dyer marched south, he was unaware that three parties of Sarhaddi raiders under the Sardar Juma Khan, chief of the Ismailzay (one of the sections of the Damani Baluch, the most powerful tribe in the Sarhadd), were on the move in the opposite direction. Juma Khan had set out himself to raid the area between Neh and Birjand, but was intercepted by C Squadron of the 28th Cavalry and a small force of 19th Punjabis. The infantry found the raiders first on 13 April and put Juma Khan's force of 550 camel riders to flight. The Baluch put up a fierce fight and charged close to the infantry before they were driven off, losing forty-five men dead. On the British side, 2nd Lieutenant Chalmers and eleven of his sepoys were killed, and another fifteen wounded. Embarrassingly, eighteen sepoys, as well as the levies accompanying the infantry, fled the field thinking the day was lost. The next day, the surviving raiders, encumbered by their loot, were attacked by C Squadron, who killed many of them and forced the rest to abandon their booty and flee. Some 2146 sheep were recaptured. Chagai Levies followed the fleeing Ismailzay and managed to kill another seven men.

This was a significant defeat for Juma Khan's tribe, and was enough to deter him from further action against the British, despite the success of his other two raiding parties. The second struck further east into British Baluchistan and ransacked the government rest house at Nok-Kundi, then attacked a convoy making its way from Nushki to supply the cordon. The escorting troops were unable to catch the raiders, and though patrols continued to hunt them until the last week of the month, the Baluch escaped back into the Sarhadd. The third party of Ismailzay under a raider named Ali Shah looted the telegraph office further north at Sipi on 20 April.[4] Troops were sent from Dehani Baghi to intercept them, but the levies refused to fire on fellow Muslims and discharged their rifles in the air.[5] If any further emphasis was required of the need to deal with the Sarhaddi Baluch, it was being delivered by them as Dyer marched into their country.

On 12 April, two days beyond Ladis at a place called Sangun, Dyer's column was approached by a force of Sarhaddi Baluch which had ridden out to meet them. These were led by Sardar Jihand Khan, chief of the Yar-Muhammadzay, the section of the Damani Baluch who controlled the Sarhadd capital at Khwash, and a raider famous in the border regions.[6] Jihand was an old man by this time, about sixty-five years of age, and held a certain tenuous pre-eminence amongst the uncontrollable Baluch tribes. He had been fighting Persian attempts to exercise control over his country since 1888, and so was an old hand at this type of warfare. The Persians had never subdued him, and they usually preferred to recognise him as Sultan of Khwash.[7]

Between the two opposing forces, the land lay in ridges running down from the mountain, which the track crossed at right angles to the slope. Jihand's force was large, Dyer estimated it at several thousand strong, and was drawn up across the track along one of these ridges. Dyer made the first move on the 13th and advanced to engage with the Baluch. Luckily for him, the ridges prevented the tribesmen seeing the size of his force, and the dust clouds kicked up by the six hundred camels carrying his column's baggage confirmed the Baluch raiders' expectations that they were facing a major attack. Dyer went forward to reconnoitre on foot, and deployed his force behind one of the ridge lines, the two mountain guns to the left, the troop of cavalry on the right, and his nine trained infantry soldiers with the two Maxim guns in the centre. He left the sixty-five untrained Punjabis guarding the camels behind the ridge; for all the weakness of his force, he clearly considered these would have been more dangerous in the front line. All were out of sight of the Baluch. As he finished drawing up this tiny force for battle, the Baluch sent an envoy across the open ground; he was recognised by the Sarhadd-dar as Shah Sawar, a famous raider of Jihand's tribe, who had been sent to propose that Dyer meet Jihand and engage in negotiations. Dyer was not about to do any such thing; he met Shah Sawar halfway between the forces, from where nothing could be seen of the British troops.

As he later recalled, he did not intend to give Shah Sawar any chance to take an advantage:

> How dare you come to a British General with any such proposal from a scoundrel like Jiand? Go back and tell him that I am coming, not half-way, but the whole way, and at once. I will then fire a shot into the air as the signal that hostilities have begun, and the attack, which will wipe you out, will commence.[8]

This bluster shook Shah Sawar, who sent his escort back to Jihand to repeat Dyer's message, then immediately surrendered himself. This was encouraging, so as soon as the envoy was back with the Baluch and had been given time to deliver his message, Dyer had the shot fired for the signal to attack. His cavalry appeared over the ridge (sitting on the skyline they appeared to be the impressive vanguard of a larger force), the mountain guns and Maxims opened up, and the nine men of the 19th, with a few of the Chagai Levies, charged in the centre. Jihand's men fled immediately in all directions, pursued by Dyer and Landon, who fired their pistols at the backs of the rapidly disappearing camel riders. Within minutes the field was empty, and the day was Dyer's. His force had only one casualty, a man wounded by friendly fire, and the enemy lost seven dead, including Jihand Khan's son. The sardar was to blame Dyer personally for this loss, and it ensured that his resistance remained embittered and unyielding. Such was the speed and chaos of the flight that Jihand believed he had lost seven hundred men killed.[9]

The column pursued Jihand's tracks for two days but was unable to keep up with the camel riders they were pursuing. When they reached the Yar-Muhammadzay winter grazing area at Kamalabad, where the tribe had its few cultivated fields, Dyer halted, and sent messengers out to spread the word that, if Jihand did not surrender, he would destroy the crops. This resulted in Jihand Khan's rapid arrival, and he was soon followed by the chief of the third section of the Damanis, the Gamshadzay.[10] This was Khalil Khan, who had been shaken by the news he had heard of Jihand's loss of seven hundred men.[11] They both surrendered to Dyer, who continued to maintain the bluff that the few troops they could actually see around him were only a part of the force which had defeated Jihand. The chiefs swore peace upon a copy of the Koran. Dyer demanded the return of the luggage which he had lost from the caravan from Nushki, and this Jihand promised to perform. On 18 April, the force marched on Khwash, and was met outside the walls of its ancient and dilapidated mud fort by its governor, Muhammad Hassan, who surrendered it to Dyer.

The campaign of bluff had resulted in something of a clean sweep. Dyer now had in his hands the capital town of the Sarhadd with its fort (though Khwash was little more than a small collection of fly-blown hovels grouped around an oasis), and two of the three Damani Baluch sardars. Only one section was still beyond his grasp, the Ismailzay under Sardar Juma Khan.[12] It was quite an achievement, though it was certainly a precarious one. Dyer held a *darbar* on the banks of the stream under the shade of the trees which grew just outside the fort, and harangued the Baluch about their mistaken choices in the current war.[13] Immediately afterwards, to capitalise on his success, he marched on the Ismailzay lands which lay to the north west of Khwash. With him marched the two surrendered sardars and their armed parties; these now outnumbered Dyer's troops, who were only sufficient on the march to guard the baggage train and to escort Dyer himself. Dyer had left five of his nine trained infantrymen and some of his Reki levies to garrison the fort in Khwash, telling the Sarhaddis it was held against their good behaviour.[14] He was dangerously overstretched. Now on the march he placed Shah Sawar in the front as advance guard, and kept Khalil Khan and the Gamshadzay on the left of the column separated from Jihand and the Yar-Muhammadzay on the right, all the while telling the Baluch that his force was out of sight. They took five days to reach Galugan, the centre of the Ismailzay lands, arriving there on the 24th. It turned out to be like Kamalabad, not a town but the ground where the tribe pitched their tents and where their crops were planted. Using the same threat of destruction, and because the combined force with him now looked an impressive one (though only because of the presence of large numbers of Baluch riders), Dyer swiftly secured Juma Khan's surrender. Juma's easy submission had much to do with his bloody defeat by the troops of the cordon on the 13 and 14 April, something about which Dyer still did not know; he had been very lucky.[15] Dyer's triumph in the Sarhadd now seemed complete.

To seal his victory, Dyer decided to take those he regarded as his prisoners – though they probably did not view themselves in that light at all – back to Kacha, the site of the *darbar* they had refused to attend at his earlier invitation. He intended this to rub their noses in their defeat, as he made plain in the story he unwisely gave out to his men. Yeates records that: 'General Dyer now decided that, in order that the chiefs should understand that his wishes were not to be flouted, they should accompany him back to Kacha, and thus obey the summons they had originally disregarded.'[16] There was of course a real need to arrange a political settlement and this was indeed best done back in territory firmly under British control. The march back to Kacha took another four days and was, towards its end, a nerve-racking affair, as the sardars feared they had been deceived and that they were riding to their deaths, and it was only by maintaining the appearance of complete confidence among the British party that the Baluch were not spooked into murdering them and escaping.[17]

Luck remained with Dyer and they made it into Kacha on the 28th. The troops settled into barracks and the Baluch camped around the absent British Political Officer's house. Dyer made his first real report to Simla in a month:

Arrived Kacha today and hold Durbar on 30th or 1st to impose strongest terms ... But it is still necessary to occupy Khwash strongly until Sarhaddi Sardars have settled down. I consider Khwash to be the true heart of the Sarhaddi country and operations very simple in (any?) direction from there. Propose making a temporary field fortification at Khwash where there is ample supply of good water. I must go there myself again.[18]

What Dyer really wanted to do, rather than abandon Khwash when the Sarhaddis had settled down, was to build it up into a base into which more of the forces from his cordon could be placed. He made this plain in a telegram to Army Headquarters on the next day:

By placing guns and the bulk of my cavalry at Khwash I can get Bursken grass good for the horses at annas six to annas eight per maund besides placing my troops in the most favourable position for checking the Sarhadis.[19]

At this date, Dyer's earlier agreement making the Rekis British subjects had still not surfaced back in Simla, and his intention to hold Khwash for a while seemed sensible to Army Headquarters and so gained support from the Government of India. The file was minuted: 'Sir John Ramsay is in favour of holding Khwash, the Damani headquarters, in strength and from there dominating the Damanis for the present.'[20] But Dyer was convinced he had already settled affairs in the Sarhadd, and was anxious to be off elsewhere. The next day he telegraphed Simla: 'More forces can be accumulated by the Sarhaddis than I anticipated, and they are in every way to be trusted. If it will assist General Sykes in any way, may I make a demonstration towards Regan, Bam or even Kirman?' Aside from his extraordinary confidence that his own personality and deeds had transformed the Sarhaddi raiders into a ready source of loyal levies, given the precarious strength of the forces at his disposal this was a foolhardy suggestion. Kirman lay about 300 miles to the west of the frontier, and the other two places mentioned were on the way to it. This was a hugely ambitious project for a man with such slender means. Dyer failed to tell Simla that he had already sent agents to Bampur (not to be confused with Bam), which was the Persian administrative centre for Baluchistan and lay to the south. It was ruled by Bahram Khan Baranzay, who had thrown off Persian control before the war, and earlier in the year had attacked a German party under Lieutenant Erich Zugmayer which was advancing on his territories from Bam. He was therefore a natural British ally, and was cultivated as such by Major Keyes, whose area of responsibility included the Khan's territory. The messengers sent by Dyer had been told to spread the rumour that his force was on its way, and the Khan, hearing of the abject collapse of the Sarhaddis, immediately fled to Makran and threw himself on the mercy of Colonel Dew. Simla turned down Dyer's plans for any foray out of his area on 10 May.[21]

Dyer's enthusiasm for spreading his net wider was in part connected with the rivalry which had developed between him and Brigadier-General Sykes in Bandar Abbas. Both vied with each other for control over areas in eastern Persia. Sykes was permitted by Simla to march a column of five hundred men from Bandar Abbas right across Dyer's front and into Kirman, and finally as far north as the Russian cordon.[22] This was galling to Dyer, whose own proposal of a similar march had received a veto. Sykes now telegraphed from Bandar Abbas that Bampur was in his area and was under control (which is not what its khan's flight to Makran seemed to indicate; Sykes, too, had grandiose ideas).

A second area of friction had already developed. Although the British Minister in Tehran was not adverse to Dyer's suggestion, thinking a British presence in Kirman might bring some order to the place, he had already come to the conclusion that Dyer was a loose cannon. After Dyer had taken Khwash, he acerbically telegraphed Simla: '*Very Confidential*. General Dyer appears not to be in touch with forces operating in Persia or with His Majesty's Consul in Sistan, at any rate this is second indication I have had of it. As far as I can see, General Dyer shows no wish to keep in touch with Consul, but I am instructing latter to keep him informed.' A few days later the Viceroy reported to London that, whilst it was necessary, due to the need for the force in Sistan to move away from telegraph lines, that Dyer 'should be given a free hand', Dyer was being reminded that he had to cooperate with the consular staff. He was to be sent a radio to keep him better in touch.[23]

Frustrated in his scheme for a campaign deep into Persia, Dyer now took up the cudgels again on the issues of levies and spies. His confused and perhaps deliberately confusing telegram to Simla of 3 May, one which it seems was meant to deflect criticism onto a man who was now his second-in-command, is a sad illustration of the methods he was developing, as well as of his propensity for failing to notice the spelling of his officers' names:

> When I went to Khwash I was obliged, much against my will, to delegate my authority to Colonel Wikeley [sic] as I was aware that he and the Consul were not acting in unison. When I came back I found to my annoyance that matters had gone from bad to worse. I think the Sarhaddi Chiefs, and also Khudadad Khan, Narui, who is closely connected with the Sarhaddis, should be placed under my control entirely as regards the raising of levies, and that all levies that are raised by this means in Sarhad or Sistan should, as a temporary measure, be placed under my command.[24] There would then be no doubt, when I delegate authority to my second-in-command, as to who should give the necessary orders for military operations. With the help of Major Landen I am organizing an intelligence system and want to include the Nahruis therein ... Any kind of friction at the present time is to be deprecated and to ensure that the great aim is not forgotten I am ready to do all in my power.[25]

He was to be disappointed in this, as the Politicals would not budge. The Consul for Seistan and Kain was scathing about Dyer's attempt to recruit members of the Narui tribe to the private intelligence network he and Major Landon were constructing. Dyer telegraphed the Consul on 30 April: 'Alishah Hajizai Narui will, I consider, be more than ordinarily useful if his services are enlisted in the Secret Service I am organizing.' The Consul forwarded this to Simla, with the comment that this man was Ali Shah Khan, Narui, 'the notorious ex-Telegraph Line Guard of Nasratabad Sipeh'. Dyer was eventually told that the Government would not pay the man; the Consul (by then intent on forwarding to Simla every piece of damaging information he could find about Dyer) told the Government of India in June that Dyer had written to him on 10 May saying that he had told Ali Shah to go away to try to redeem his character by helping his Intelligence Officer, Landon, and that he was not being paid. In other words, Dyer had refused to get rid of him.[26]

On 2 May, Dyer held the *darbar* at Kacha in the open air outside the Political Officer's house. As before, there was no British Political Officer present, though the Sarhadd-dar was there to represent the Baluch interest, and to issue money from bags of Indian rupees to the Sarhaddi sardars. Colonel Wilkeley rode down from Robat to be present.[27] Dyer harangued the sardars as he had at Khwash, then produced a document for them to sign. According to Dyer's own account: 'I called on the Chiefs to sign an agreement whereby they handed their country over to the Sirkar.' The sardars, who could not write, put their thumbprints to the document, swore an oath on the Koran to abide by the agreement it contained, then took their money and dispersed back to the Sarhadd. There is no record of this agreement, or in fact of any agreement having been made at all, in Government files, so it is possible that Dyer suppressed the document. This is likely, not so much for the embarrassing terms the agreement contained (for although it seems to have gone even further than his first treaty with the Reki in purporting to absorb some of Persia's territory, Dyer was still unaware of the view Simla was to take of his first treaty), but because it was embarrassingly quickly betrayed by two of its signatories, men whom Dyer had just told Simla were thoroughly trustworthy. Within a day, the Rekis reported to Dyer that only Juma Khan of the Ismailzay remained faithful to his word. The sardars Jihand Khan of the Yar-Muhammadzay and Khalil Khan of the Gamshadzay, having at last seen in Kacha how weak Dyer's force really was, had agreed between themselves to return home, to seize the fort at Khwash and to attack the British.[28] Raiding resumed almost immediately. On 19 May, a party of Baluch attacked a convoy north of Robat, wounding two men of the 19th in the escort and making off with twenty-six laden camels.[29]

Dyer realised that his house of cards had collapsed, and that the plans he had been making had been based only on the sands of his own overconfidence. Worse, the tiny garrison he had left at Khwash was now in serious danger, and were Khwash to fall, the British position in the Sarhadd would be irreparably damaged, Juma Khan would probably be induced to throw over his agreement, and raiding would resume. Dyer realised he had to get back to Khwash as fast as he could.[30] The embarrassment he felt in all this is clear in his failure to report it (none of the Government records has an account of the *darbar*, the treaty or its betrayal), and in his own log he recorded only the fact of his return to Khwash.[31] There is also evidence that he lied to Army Headquarters about his reasons for returning there; on 3 May he telegraphed: 'Tomorrow I leave on medical certificate for Khwash.'[32] He was pretending to be going there for the sake of his health.

His 'sick leave' required a larger escort than the force with which he had first entered the Sarhadd. The new column marched on the 4th under the command of Major Landon, and included a troop of B Squadron of the 28th Cavalry commanded by Second-Lieutenant Fremantle, two mountain guns commanded by Lieutenant English, seven sappers and miners, two Maxims under Lieutenant Yeates, and seventy-five men of the 19th Punjabis.[33] This was still a pretty small force, but was all Dyer could scrape together at the time. The strength of the cordon had not been increased, though the recruiting of the last month had raised the number of levies to 830 men; there was no one else to take.[34] The force moved painfully slowly at the speed of the marching infantry, making only nine miles on the first day. At this rate, there were seven stages ahead of them, and they were bound to be outstripped in the race to Khwash by the camel-riding Baluch. Dyer waited for Corporal Allan to motor his car down from Robat, then followed and caught up with his troops on the third day after another terrible journey of endless bogging-in and digging-out on the road to the rendezvous. There was little time left, and so Dyer decided on a desperate throw. He would go on to the fort in the car, alone except for Idu and Corporal Allan.

Even by car, the journey took several days, and was very much like the one he had made from Nushki two months before. They were lucky in finding a party of fifteen Reki tribesmen who could act as escorts, but the car continually sank in sand drifts, and its tyres were so cut up by the sharp rocks of the ridges across which they dragged it that in the last stages of the journey they had to pull it along on the rims of its wheels. Two days out of Khwash, their path crossed that of a group of Yar-Muhammadzay. They hid the car in a *nullah* while Idu went to talk with them. They turned out to be a band under the leadership of a chief named Izzat, a notorious slaver and raider, who were on their way to join Jihand Khan in his attack on the British troops in Khwash. Idu spun them a yarn about the magical powers of the car, which they had never seen, and told them that its radiator grill spat bullets in invincible numbers. They were sufficiently impressed to come and see it, and were so overawed that they agreed to accompany Dyer to

Khwash. On the way, the car again stuck in a steep-sided and narrow *nullah*; Dyer summoned the raiders to assist, and 'it was not long before they were straining at the drag ropes'. Dyer's erstwhile enemies pulled the car out and his small party continued the last stage of the journey through the night.[35] At dawn the car lurched into a gully, became hopelessly lodged in the sand and had to be abandoned. They rode the final five miles to Khwash on camels and headed straight for the fort, having no idea whether they would be met by their own men or by Jihand's tribesmen.

They were in luck: the fort was still in British hands and the party set to putting it in as good a state of defence as they could manage, placing the five infantrymen in the tallest of the four corner towers which they intended to hold as a last redoubt. Izzat and his party were placed under watch in the courtyard, and the car was brought in by the villagers. They had arrived just in time, for Shah Sawar was already encamped nearby, awaiting the arrival of Jihand and the main body of the tribe. Idu went out to meet Shah Sawar, and so overawed the man with bluff about the size of the British force and the mysterious powers of the car that Shah Sawar rode into Khwash to surrender again (for a notorious raider he was remarkably easily frightened). When Jihand arrived that night, it was to find two of his principal chiefs already under guard in the fort.

The next day Landon and the column marched in, preceded by the Sarhadd-dar, who rode ahead alone on his swift camel to find out whether the General was still alive. Jihand now thought better of his plan to seize the fort, and rode in to offer Dyer his compliments and the loyalty of his tribe. He rode out taking Izzat and Shah Sawar with him, and peace was restored for a while, though not in Shah Sawar's tent, where his wife, the *gul-bibi*, whose father was Muhammad Hassan, the governor of the fort, and who was reputed by the locals to be the most beautiful woman in the world, belittled her husband's cowardice, and as a gesture of contempt for him sent Dyer a gift of two goats. Dyer went to call on her the next day and was very struck by her beauty; unusually, she was not veiled. Dyer describes her as:

> Very fair for a Sarhadi, with regular, clean cut, almost Grecian features, and unusual-looking, big hazel eyes. She was evidently small-boned, and her limbs and hands were beautifully modelled. She was obviously aware of her own attractions and very animated. Her dress was white, embroidered in Persian colouring, and she wore a *chuddah* over her head, which fell in graceful folds, without, however, in any way concealing her face.[36]

Dyer had something of an eye for the ladies. She spoke to him in Persian, and presented him with a carpet, all the while making fun of her cowardly husband.

The situation now seemed once more under control, and Dyer determined to remain at Khwash. He requested stores, labourers and a tube well to be sent down from Quetta to make the fort habitable.[37] He had plans for the long term, and began to travel around the area looking for somewhere cooler to spend the summer. He found a site on higher ground at a place called Kosha, which had supplies of water sufficient for agriculture.[38] Instructions arrived allowing him to recruit the levies he had requested, but Simla maintained the line that: 'You may continue to make arrangements for raising levies, but they are to be eventually administered by the officers selected for the purpose.' He was ordered to discuss the issue with the Consul for Seistan, but made no attempt to do so. Instead, he set about recruiting the Sarhaddi Baluch into his new levy force.[39] He outlined his intentions in a telegram to Simla at the end of the month; if one accepted that the Sarhaddis could be relied upon (and the Consul for Seistan, for one, did not accept this) his ideas made some sense.

> The more Sarhaddis I enlist in the levies the less will become the fighting strength of the Sarhaddi Sardar concerned. If the Sarhaddis obtain no employment at the present juncture, they must live by other than fair means. As I have done serious damage to Jiand's crops, hardships in the food line will be inevitable. I propose enlisting 150 Rekis, including Gwgieh, 100 Ismailzais, 50 Gamshazas, 100 Yarmahomedzais … Actual strength at present is Rekis and Gwgieh 136, Yarmahomedzais 31, Gamshazai 3. Total 180.[40]

A second disappointment for Dyer came in dispatches that arrived by camel from the end of the telegraph line some days later. On 18 May, the Government of India made an attempt to clarify the lines of command which were causing the men in the field such irritation. It was not a successful one. Dyer was told that he had sole charge of operations, but that 'as Political Agent, Sarhad, and attached to your staff as Adviser for Political matters for Sarhad, a Political Officer will be appointed. On political matters you are always to consult this officer, and whenever his advice is not taken you should report.' Major Hutchinson, the Political Agent for Chagai, was appointed to this post. Dyer was reminded to keep the Agent to the Governor-General in Baluchistan and Brigadier Sykes at Bandar Abbas informed of his actions. He was to act on the advice of the Consul for Seistan and Kain for all affairs touching that region. He was not to be given control of the levies; the Seistan and Hazara Levies were to remain under the command of the Consul for Seistan and Kain for organisation and adminis-tration, and the Sarhadd Levy Corps which he was raising in Khwash was to be administered by the Political Agent Sarhadd. However, the training and the control of operations for all the levies was left to Dyer. His wider hopes were dashed, too. 'All arrangements you make with tribes are temporary.' Nothing permanent was to be done without Government authority. On every point he had taken up, Simla had ruled against him; on almost every point, Dyer proceeded to ignore their ruling.[41] It seems, however, as though he contemplated going back to Quetta and Simla in person to fight his corner. On 24 May, he signalled Simla asking the CGS if he could come to see him 'as situation is very complicated'. He also sought an interview with the Agent to the Governor-General in Baluchistan. Both requests were ignored.[42]

The German threat to the cordon had not yet evaporated. On 11 May, German letters were intercepted which sought to stir up trouble with the Sarhaddi chiefs. The German Consul, Zugmayer, urged Sardar Jihand Khan to 'combine and exterminate the enemies of your religion and country', and pressed him to attack the small cordon post at Dehani Baghi. Another letter to Sardar Juma Khan from a neighbouring sardar was intercepted, saying he had received the unbelievable news from the German Consul that a German army was coming to Nasratabad, and that he should collect his men and wait.[43] Nevertheless, Dyer's policy of dealing aggressively with the Sarhadd seemed to be paying off. Raiding on the cordon ceased, and peace descended on Khwash. Sardar Khalil Khan of the Gamshadzay came in and surrendered some looted rifles, camels and other property, and a few days later Jihand Khan again visited the fort to make peace. He bound himself 'to hand over certain tracts of land, if he failed to carry out the conditions imposed'. The full text of this agreement is not extant, but Dyer forwarded part of it by post to Simla, where it arrived nearly a month later. As Army Headquarters had not been informed of the earlier agreement made at Kacha, nor of its repudiation by the Sarhaddis, Dyer had to excuse the existence of a second: 'I found it necessary to make this agreement as my faith in him was very much shaken by various rumours regarding disloyal action on his part.' In the agreement Jihand Khan promised:

> I hereby promise and testify in writing that from to-day I … will remain under the orders of the British Government as subjects thereof. Signed Sardar Mir Jiand Khan 28 May 1916.

Dyer was still persisting with his annexation of the Sarhadd, despite the orders he had only just been given to the contrary. By the time Simla received their copy of this agreement, Jihand had again gone into revolt, and in a note on the file Secretary Grant minuted that the one satisfactory thing about the recent Jihand rebellion was that it made void any agreement with General Dyer.[44]

More cavalry reinforcements, C Squadron with a troop of B Squadron commanded by Major Claridge, arrived from Nasratabad.[45] Major Landon was finally relieved of his temporary role of Brigade Major as a properly appointed officer, Captain Saunders, now arrived to fill the post. Dyer had gun cotton and fuses brought forward from Kacha along with some barbed wire. He was unsuccessful, though, in his request for five Vickers machine guns to mount on his vehicles. By now, the forces at Khwash had swollen to a squadron and a half of cavalry, two mountain guns, one hundred rifles of the 19th Punjabis, and four Maxim machine guns.[46]

Major-General Grover came down from Quetta to set the seal on Dyer's victory, arriving on 30 May. It is likely that his visit was designed to make sure that Army Headquarters' recent orders on political issues were obeyed, as well as to check on the situation of Dyer's force. He met the Baluch sardars, inspected the new Sarhadd Levy Corps, with which he seemed pleased, then presided over a grand *darbar* held on 1 June. Dyer laid this on with some style. In the evening, a salute of thirteen guns was fired for Grover, then an exhibition of small arms fire was laid on to impress the Baluch. The Maxim guns opened up on dummy targets, and one of the machine guns, mounted on Dyer's car, fired from behind a wooden slat whilst the car was on the move, so demonstrating that the car did indeed spit bullets. All sat down on rugs in the open, the two British Generals made speeches, as did the Sarhadd-dar and the sardars after him. With General Grover present, Dyer presented no agreement for the chiefs to sign. They did, however, give formal assent to the recruitment of their men for the levies, which was just as well, as Dyer had already recruited, and was paying, some two hundred men of their tribes, men who would not have taken well to having their income cancelled at this stage. Jihand used the occasion to present Dyer with a large amount of loot taken in the raids on the cordon, including his own baggage and four tyres for his car.[47]

As the *darbar* dispersed, Sardar Khalil Khan made a request to leave to seek his family, which had taken refuge from the British in the hills behind his territory. Dyer let him go, but as he did so shouted out a less than diplomatic warning, one which the proud Baluch sardar would have keenly resented: 'Halil Khan, if you play me false, or ever raise your hand against me again, I will blow your head off.'[48] Several days later, Mir Madad Khan of Jalk, a town to the south east of the Sarhadd, came to pay his respects.[49] All this was indeed very gratifying.

Events were now seemingly under control, and the visiting General was now once more out of the way, so Dyer could turn his attention to the problem of supply which had begun to affect his expanded force, and which was, as the Baluch soon realised, to be much more of an obstacle to his plans for the Sarhadd than they were themselves. Dyer's daily log makes first mention of this on the day of the *darbar*: 'The supply question here has become critical – Officer Commanding Kacha reports having no *atta* to send us.' The troops were placed on half rations of bread, and meat was issued in lieu. The animals also went on half rations. The problem was twofold. Supplies were insufficient locally for any long-term occupation by large forces, so they had to be ordered through the Consul in Nasratabad from the more fertile areas of Sistan. Dyer sought to overturn this arrangement and to bring the system under his own control, but sensibly was not allowed to; the purchase of supplies was not something that could have been controlled from where he was. Careful planning with the prior dumping of supplies in depots at key sites would have eased his problems, but he had not thought of this. Secondly, all supplies had to be carried over huge distances by camel. The longer the distances, the more camels were needed, and the greater the necessity for a careful arrangement of fodder and water. Dyer had not thought this through either. General Grover took him to task over these issues during his visit:

> I found on 1 June Dyer had 2000 camels at his disposal, and 270 at Khwash, 525 en route Khwash to Kacha. Supplies are at main depots; problem is distribution … Any shortage at any place such as at Khwash appears to indicate a lack of foresight and bad staff work added to the fact that a considerable amount of military rations have been given to Sarhadi Sardars and their following and to newly enlisted levies on different occasions recently at Khwash. I discussed these points with General Dyer when I was at Khwash and believed that I had made the position clear both as regards supplies and transport and the necessity for co-ordination between staff and administration departments.[50]

The position improved with the arrival of a caravan on 10 June, and all went back onto full rations, but this was not to last. Reinforcing the garrison and raising more levies only made the problem worse. By 4 June, the number of 19th Punjabis at Khwash had increased to 134 officers and men. Dyer never did make any inroads into solving this problem, and it was the one which eventually defeated his plans entirely.

Although the overall strength of the Seistan Field Force had not been increased to compensate for this reinforcement of Khwash, throughout June Dyer drained resources from the north of the cordon down to Kacha in its south, and from Kacha he extracted them to Khwash.[51] This process caused alarm in Army Headquarters and even with the Russians, who objected to London that the force holding the cordon to their south was being depleted, prompting the Secretary of State for India to ask the Viceroy what was happening. Army Headquarters tried to stop the redeployment but, as usual, found out about it too late to prevent it. They had to be content with another ineffectual warning to Dyer to remember why he was in Sistan: 'You should remember … at the present juncture that the primary duty of your force is the capture of German parties'.[52]

Yet Dyer was intent on staying where he was. He started building a road from Khwash to the border post at Mirjawa, and carried on his reconnaissance for a summer station in the hills nearby. He began an eventually unsuccessful attempt to get Army Headquarters to provide khaki uniforms and modern weapons for his Sarhadd Levies; they refused both. He brought a gardener from Kacha to plant out a garden around the base, and recorded in his log of 3 June his decision to blow up the old fort and replace it with defensible emplacements. Three of the four corner towers and the curtain walls were demolished.[53] It is difficult to see any other reason for Dyer's remaining in Khwash in June save for his private plans to absorb the area into British Baluchistan. The situation in the Sarhadd now seemed stable, and his primary mission, the maintenance of the cordon, could now have been safely resumed. Had he left Khwash at that stage, his policy of dealing first with the Sarhaddi raiders might well have been vindicated, for their raids were now over. Yet he stayed, and so found himself sucked into a quagmire which was to ruin his tenure of command.

Jihand Khan had retired from Khwash to his territories in the hills. On the surface, he had accepted British rule, but he still wished to be rid of Dyer, and the garrison's tenuous supply situation gave him the opportunity to achieve this. The British began to buy up as much fodder and other supplies as they could find on the local market, and they arranged to buy fourteen bales of *bhusa* from a man named Murad Khan whose fields were in Jihand's lands at Dehbala, a day's march north of Khwash. On 13 June, the fodder was put to the torch by one of Jihand's men named Charag Khan. Dyer realised that this was more than arson, and that it was in effect an attack on his position. He lost his temper, as he makes clear, quite unabashed by it, in his book: 'As may be imagined, I was nearly beside myself with rage at the news.'[54] With a force which was half that of the garrison of Khwash, including his mountain guns and Maxims, and with ten days' rations, he set out to apprehend the culprit. Jihand was waiting for him to come, hoping to ambush him, but was taken aback by the size of the force with which he was met. Rather than take on more than he could deal with, he came to meet Dyer near the site of the arson. Dyer rode forward to meet him, accompanied by Captain Saunders, Lieutenant Yeates and an escort of twenty-seven men, leaving the majority of his force out of sight and hearing behind a low hill. The party sat under the shade of a tree outside the ruined fort at Karsimabad. Dyer began an interrogation into the burning of his supplies, and Murad Khan produced the man whom he had captured in the act.

Immediately, however, events began to slip out of control. About 150 heavily armed Baluch emerged from the nearby fort and from hiding places in the surrounding fields and encircled the tree where they sat. Yet undaunted by the arrival of the intimidating numbers of Baluch, who were draped with bandoliers of ammunition and carried rifles, pistols and swords, Dyer began to shout at the prisoner: 'How dare you burn my *bhusa*? What reason had you for doing it, and who told you to do it?' Before the man could reply, a cousin of Jihand's, Nur Mahommed, leapt up and shouted back at Dyer: 'The country is ours and everything in it. We will burn the *bhusa*, or burn anything we like.' Dyer told him to sit down, but he would not, and sneered at Dyer, taunting him for his inability to do anything about it. This was too much for Dyer's temper, and he ordered one of his sepoys to arrest the man.

What followed all happened in a flash. The *sepoy* had scarcely moved a step to obey when every one of Jiand's men leapt to their feet and brought their rifles to the present. I must confess to having acted automatically. Indeed, there was no time to think or do otherwise. I literally roared at them. 'How dare you, you dogs? Sit down this instant.' I reached my hands towards Jiand who was close to me, and in a paroxysm of rage, forced him down by my side. 'Sit down!' I roared again into the dark faces of the men surrounding us. Hesitation and doubt spread amongst that threatening crowd – and the bulk of them sat down.[55]

Dyer then ordered the troops to arrest the entire band of Baluch, and there was a scramble to catch those who were too slow to run away. Many of the Baluch took to their heels, but the troops succeeded in securing some sixty of them, of whom Dyer later released a few of the least important. With their captives, including Jihand Khan, secured with ropes, the column reached Khwash the next day. On the way back through the tribe's fields at Kamalabad they relieved Jihand of the sacks of wheat his people had hidden in the sand dunes, a recompense for the *bhusa* they had burned.

The problem now was what to do with the prisoners. There were thirty-nine of them, including the Sardar Jihand Khan, his cousin, Mir Nur Mahommed, whom Dyer described as 'dangerous' and an 'evil spirit'. The sepoys had also seized a motley collection of typical Baluch armament; forty-three rifles, a shield, ten swords, a pistol, fifteen knives and sixty-five bandoliers.[56] The log makes it clear that the arrests caused considerable ill-feeling locally, and holding that number of eminent men in the fort was asking for trouble.[57] They were bound to be a continuing source of friction, not least due to the treatment meted out to them by their guards, who were their fellow Baluch. On one occasion, Dyer saw some of the guards relieving prisoners of their personal possessions, and 'went off the deep end … he fell on them with his stick and belaboured everyone within reach'.[58] He signalled for authority to send the prisoners back to Quetta, and asked for an escort of one hundred men to be sent to bring them in. For the present, he put the prisoners to manual labour in the construction of his new fort.[59] They were not in the least accustomed to physical work, which was to them a degradation of their status, and to which they objected vociferously; Dyer took no notice. On 19 June, 4 Division ordered that the prisoners be sent on to Quetta, and instructed a detachment of three hundred 106th Hazara Pioneers, who were then at work on the road between Robat and Nushki, to march to Khwash to collect them. General Grover specifically instructed Dyer not to treat these troops as reinforcements, though he may as well not have bothered as Dyer was to ignore this order completely. The Agent to the Governor General in Baluchistan was quite pleased to have the senior Sarhaddis to keep as hostages for the future good behaviour of the tribes, but sent the prophetic advice: 'You will discourage attempts to rescue the prisoners if you let it be known that the escorts have orders to shoot prisoners rather than risk their escape.'[60]

Whilst this was going on, Dyer turned his attention to the slaves who had been seized by the Sarhaddis in their recent raids. Their fate had weighed on his conscience since he had first come to the Sarhadd. He ordered that they all be brought in to Khwash, and then returned to their homes. It is interesting that he records that he was opposed in this for the only time by the Reki, Idu. Sarhaddis of all tribes were notorious slavers, and their captives, sold on to Persian merchants, formed one of their principal sources of revenue. They also had a nasty reputation for maiming their captives to prevent their return home, and for killing those they couldn't sell.[61] Dyer had the slaves assembled in Khwash, and made the inhabitants clothe and feed them. He then devised a method of getting them back to their homes that could also be seen as a punishment which fitted the crime (he was very fond of this sort of stratagem). He ordered the Yar-Muhammadzay chief Izzat, who was a leading slaver (and whose men had pulled his car out of the dune during the race to Khwash), to form a caravan and take the captives home. To guard against Izzat selling the women, Dyer issued each slave with a letter to send back with Izzat certifying they had been delivered to their homes. He threatened Izzat that he would hang all his family if any of the slaves came to harm. Izzat did eventually return with all the letters signed. Dyer believed he had delivered his captives as ordered. Whether Izzat actually did this, we are entitled to some degree of doubt.[62]

The prisoner escort column from the 106th was marching on foot, and would take nearly two weeks to arrive at Khwash, so Dyer had to sit and wait for them. Despite his reinforced garrison, the presence of so many prisoners made security difficult, and they had to be fed, which added to the supply problems. Outside the fort, the resentment that the arrests had caused amongst the Baluch began to take worrying shape. On the 24th, four letters were intercepted sent by Shah Sawar to the Germans; in these, he sought their aid, renewed earlier offers of help, and promised them safe passage through the Sarhadd.[63] Whether this panicked Dyer can only be surmised, but on the next day he changed his plans, and, waiting no longer, sent all the prisoners with a strong guard of cavalry and infantry to march towards the 106th Pioneers and meet them on the road.

When the prisoners had gone, Dyer dealt next with Shah Sawar, summoning him to a drumhead court martial formed by himself and two of his officers. The letters to the Germans were produced in evidence along with the *mullah* who had written them, and Shah Sawar was found guilty and sentenced to be shot. Dyer announced that the sentence would be carried out immediately, but at that stage the *gul-bibi* arrived at the *darbar* tent and fell on her knees before Dyer, imploring mercy for her husband. Dyer relented and placed Shah Sawar in his wife's custody. The court martial was forgotten, which was just as well, as the proceeding had a very dubious basis even in military law, and the sentence of death was not one that could have been legally carried out without reference to Simla.[64]

The prisoners and their escort made their slow way towards the approaching column of the 106th, marching around the western flanks of the Kuh-i Taftan mountain. The escort was under the command of Captain James of the 28th Light Cavalry. With him were two troops of the 28th, one commanded by Lieutenant Uloth, and fifty men of the 19th Punjabis with a machine gun. The first night out of Khwash, they camped at a spot named Kalchat, and placed the prisoners inside a very thin barbed wire entanglement in a ruined enclosure. At eleven that night, the Baluch broke out, using their clothes to cover the wire so that they could scramble over it. In the mêlée which ensued a few rounds were fired, but thirty-four prisoners made their escape. Only Jihand Khan, his son and two others who had been kept in a separate cage failed to get away. This was disastrous news: the escape of such a large number of prisoners was a very bad blot on the conduct of Dyer's force, and the fact that a large number of by now very hostile Baluch were again at large was highly dangerous. Dyer went out himself the next day with another troop of the 28th and a second machine gun to meet James and work out what to do. They met in the desert late in the afternoon. Dyer was faced with several problems at once. There were still four prisoners to send back to Quetta. Also, many of Jihand Khan's men were at large and would probably be returning home to raise up their tribe for an attempt to release their sardar from captivity. Another small but imminent problem in Dyer's mind at the time was the very weak British party which was on the road from Ladis to Khwash, travelling around the other side of the Kuh-i Taftan on another route from that being taken by the 106th. This was escorting a consignment of gold coin and the wireless sent by Army Headquarters, and it was now at considerable risk.

Dyer claimed later that protecting the wireless party was now his priority and that he believed Captain James and his party of prisoners were less at risk. 'The best thing to be done at the moment was to order the prisoners' escort – who now had no one to escort! except Jiand and his son – to proceed instantly in the direction along which the wireless troop was coming.'[65] He says that he decided to try to draw off Jihand's men with his own party, to 'overawe the Yarmohommedzai country', and to deter any attempt by Khalil Khan and the Gamshadzay to join Jihand's men. To do this, and to augment the troops he had brought with him from Khwash, he took from James one troop of his cavalry and most of his infantry. His reasoning at this point is obscure. The idea of drawing the Yar-Muhammadzay, whose sardar was still in James's custody, away from James seems an unlikely one, and the reduction in James's force left him extremely vulnerable. Possibly Dyer had again lost his temper and wanted now to pursue the tribesmen towards the centre of their territory, where he assumed, wrongly, that they would have fled. There is no real way of knowing what was in his mind at the time.

At 4 a.m. the next morning he set off towards Jihand Khan's tribal centre at Kamalabad, and spent the next two days fruitlessly marching around it before returning to Khwash. Captain James, with his much reduced escort, and still with his four prisoners, marched east, making for the British border at Saindak. Unfortunately for him, the Baluch had not been fooled by Dyer's movements, and on 28 June, at Siah Jangal in the Laramba Pass, they ambushed his small party. The action was vicious and went on as a running fight throughout the day. The British desperately tried to draw clear, but the Baluch, who were up to two hundred in number, kept in close pursuit. Both James and Uloth were wounded in the first attack; though hit in the shoulder, and with his arm broken, Captain James managed to hold his force together till the Baluch left off at nightfall, but by then both Jihand Khan and his son had escaped. The other two Baluch prisoners were killed as they fled. This more than compounded the original loss of prisoners, as did the heavy British losses. Five of James's force were killed and eight of them wounded, including the two officers; twelve cavalry mounts were killed, fourteen were lost, and thirty-seven camels were killed or went missing. It was a heavily embarrassing defeat, and exposed to the Baluch just how fragile Dyer's hold over the Sarhadd really was.[66]

Immediately the news of James's defeat reached Khwash, Dyer sent Claridge, who had by now been promoted lieutenant-colonel, with C Squadron to Sangun, ordered to collect James's party and then to meet both the 106th Pioneers and the small party escorting the gold and the wireless and bring them in. This was bound to take some days; in the meantime, with his forces now very thinly spread indeed, Dyer was forced to sit it out inside the fort at Khwash, aware that Jihand Khan was gathering his forces in the nearby Gilikoh hills to attack him. What was on his mind, though, was exacting retribution for the damage done to his force. On the day that Claridge rode out of the fort, Dyer sent a message to Kacha, where Lieutenant-Colonel Dale, the Commanding Officer of 19th Punjabis, had recently taken over from Colonel Wilkeley in command of the cordon in Dyer's absence.[67] Dyer demanded that Dale send three companies of the 106th Pioneers to Khwash, claiming that GOC 4 Division had promised he could have them in an emergency; this was actually almost the opposite of the orders General Grover had given. Dyer told Dale he needed the Pioneers 'to punish the Damanis'. Dale did as ordered, and also sent Major Landon with fifty cavalrymen to Siah to find the wireless party.[68] At the same time, Dyer told Army Headquarters he was intending to go after Jihand's tribe as soon as he was reinforced.[69] In his reports to Simla, he attempted to make light of his reverse, telling them on 5 July that nothing really serious had occurred, that Jihand was neither powerful nor popular in the Sarhadd, and that there were in any event no Germans there. There never had been, of course, and it is doubtful if Simla could have taken the loss of prisoners so lightly. The Viceroy had been forced to inform the Secretary of State about it the day before.[70] The CGS could not understand why Dyer had relieved the prisoner escort of troops when he had met James on the 26th. Dyer was forced to explain that the problem was the protection of the wireless detachment:

> I took one troop of cavalry, thirty-six infantry and one machine gun from him at Kalchat night of 26/27 July. He took what he had left as escort of four prisoners … With a view to breaking up, as far as possible, the Yar Muhammadzai combination, and thus protecting Captain James and the wireless, I proceeded to Kamalabad. I am told that I succeeded fairly well, and that James was ambushed by thirty-five men only.[71]

This, particularly the last self-exculpatory sentence, must have made pretty unimpressive reading back in Simla. He worsened rather than improved matters in his fuller report, drawn up on 13 July, supposedly after he had convened a board of inquiry to inquire into the loss of his prisoners. The report (which is certainly not the report of a board of inquiry in either form or content) raises more questions than it answers. In it Dyer attempts to deflect the blame for the débâcle onto his subordinate, Captain James. Its text, here given in full, states:

> I have the honour to forward herewith the proceedings of a Court of Enquiry held on circumstances under which the Damani prisoners escaped on June the 25th and June 28th.
>
> 1. The day before Captain James left Khwash I saw him personally in my tent, and explained to him the vital necessity of safeguarding the prisoners he was to escort to Saindak. I gave him more troops than I could well spare from my small garrison at Khwash. He took with him to Kalchat three troops cavalry, one Indian officer and fifty men, 19th Punjabis, and one machine gun, 12th Pioneers, together with some six good Chagai Levies. That the prisoners were allowed to escape on the night of his departure with the extraordinary ease with which they apparently did, can only have been due to everybody including sentries and guard having gone to sleep. Men did not even fall in on their alarm posts for a practice alarm. Nor were the majority of the prisoners bound, though orders were apparently given to this effect.
>
> 2. That the escort under Captain James allowed itself to be ambushed on the 28 June by what now appears to have been only twenty-nine men, shows in my opinion a greater amount of carelessness than was shown on the night of the 25th–26th. The locality where the party was ambushed was known to me, and also to Captain James. Considering the repeated warnings he had received and the lesson he should have learnt on the night of the 25th–26th, only his lack of taking any ordinary military precautions could have enabled the enemy to carry out their very bold enterprise

with such complete success. No doubt the infantry he had were young and the two troops cavalry appeared to be too heavily armed, as they carry not only a lance and a rifle but also a sword and a bayonet, and apparently are accustomed to dismount leaving the rifle in the bucket. This may have been the cause of their losing so many rifles, which number I believe thirteen, but the final report of the losses of this action has not been received by me. I can only hope that the result of the escape of the prisoners may lead to a more perfect settling of the Damani and Gamshadzai tribes hereafter.[72]

Army Headquarters's opinion of this extraordinary document is not recorded. Despite Dyer's attempts to excuse his actions to Army Headquarters, he could not cover up completely the fact that he had made several serious mistakes. He had sent the prisoners prematurely from Khwash rather than await the arrival of their escort. He was later to claim in his book that he had been ordered to send them, but this contradicts the evidence of his log and of Moberly's official history of the campaign. After the majority of the prisoners had escaped, he had seriously depleted the escort, apparently not anticipating that the rescue of their sardar would now be the priority of the tribesmen, and had gone on a wild goose chase in the wrong direction. For this, he had given the unconvincing reason that he had wished to draw off the enemy. As a result, he had lost his prisoners, British prestige in the Sarhadd had been badly damaged, and his force had suffered casualties. Army Headquarters would also have raised an eyebrow at the way he handled the follow-up. His attempt at exonerating his position in what purported to be the report of a board of inquiry was a dishonourable one. He had tried to deflect all blame for the incident onto his subordinate, Captain James, and to evade it himself. The episode did not redound to his credit.

13

Khwash

At the beginning of July 1916, Dyer was again cooped up in Khwash with the bulk of his force scattered across the deserts to the border. Colonel Claridge, with most of the garrison's cavalry, was bringing in the three parties making their way to Kwash, whilst a camel convoy which had recently set out from Kacha was being brought in by the levies. It was now high summer, with temperatures regularly over 40 degrees Celsius, and the burning sun made any work impossible in the middle of the day. 'Flies in camp very bad', recorded the log. Whilst the garrison could keep their encampment clean, there was nothing they could do about the villagers living around it, whose squalor was the source of the clouds of flies. The Damanis were beginning to surround the fort, Jihand Khan and one group to the north east of the town, Shah Sawar to the south west. Dyer's troops maintained their routine of daily work outside the new emplacements, but at night drew back into the small part of it they could hold, manning the only surviving tower of the fort with the two Maxims. Dyer must have regretted blowing up the old fort before he had completed the new. One of their Reki levies was abducted on 3 July, and Dyer rode out on a fruitless attempt to rescue him the next day. His column bumped into the Damanis, and one of his men was injured, so he had to withdraw; he did not possess enough troops to be more aggressive.[1] On 7 July, some of Jihand's men infiltrated close to the fort and sniped at the garrison. The reliability of the Baluch inside the fort began to be suspect. Some of the camel *sowars* were discovered taking their camels out of the emplacement to sell to the Damanis. They were intent on a double profit, as they claimed the beasts had been stolen and demanded 120 rupees each from Dyer in compensation. Dyer managed to get his Reki levy back on the 8th when the Damanis negotiated an exchange for some of their men Dyer was holding, which probably accounts for the original kidnapping. The next day, they attacked the camp again and made a rush into the empty interior of the emplacement, presenting an easy target for the troops who fired down upon them from the tower. The Baluch fled.[2] Dyer was humiliated, seething, and forced to confine himself to relieving his feelings in his reports to Army Headquarters, as he did on the night of the 9th: 'When reinforcements arrive I will attack him [Jihand Khan], as other clans will follow him if I don't … He cannot run far and it would never do, in my opinion, to let him rest.'[3]

Whilst Dyer was stuck in Khwash, events were occurring in the north of the cordon. In early July, a patrol of the 28th Light Cavalry became lost in the desert near Bandan, and one man and three horses died of thirst before they were found. Dyer was unable to do anything about the problems of the rest of the Seistan Field Force, and was indeed usually completely ignorant of them.[4]

Claridge returned on the 10th, bringing with him the three companies of the 106th Hazara Pioneers, the wireless detachment with its boxes of gold specie, and Captain James's surviving prisoner escort party. He also brought with him the new Political Agent Sarhadd, Major Hutchinson, a reinforcement Dyer was less happy to receive. All of this was watched by the Damanis, who realised they now had no chance of retaking the fort, and withdrew deep into their summer pastures in the Sar-i Mulan valley between the Morpish and Sar-i Drukan ranges of hills.[5] This rugged area lay to the east of Khwash, beyond the Yar-Muhammadzay centre at Kamalabad. If he was to catch Jihand Khan, this was where Dyer needed to follow him. He now planned to attack the Sar-i Mulan from the south east, where Yar-Muhammadzay territory abutted that of the Gamshadzay, and so split the two sections of the Damanis. Although this involved a longer march, as the most direct route into the mountains was from the north west, it would give his force the advantage of surprise.[6]

Dyer gave his troops and pack animals little time to recover from their exertions. Only two days after their arrival, on 12 July, he marched out of Khwash, taking with him a strong column of two troops of the 28th Light Cavalry commanded by Lieutenant Brownlow, his two mountain guns under Lieutenant English, and the trusty Lieutenant Yeates with two Maxim machine guns. The bulk of the force was provided by all three companies of the 106th Hazara Pioneers commanded by their senior officer, Captain Lang, with Captain Moore-Lane and Lieutenant Bream commanding a company each. They took with them one month's rations carried on seven hundred camels; Dyer clearly thought this might be a long expedition. He left Colonel Claridge behind in Khwash to hold the fort with what was left of its garrison.

The column reached Kamalabad on the first night and camped. The northern road into the Sar-i Mulan ran from there through a narrow defile called the Dast Kird, and Dyer sent Brownlow with the cavalry to make a noisy feint towards it that night. The ruse worked, and Jihand Khan, inside the hills, moved his forces up to the Dast Kird to oppose what he thought was Dyer's advance. This left the column free to skirt along the outside of the Morpish hills to the other entrance, towards which Jihand had sent his flocks for safety; it marched south next day, seizing grain and animals as it went. Shepherds of one flock bravely objected to this and fired at the troops, and three of them were killed. It was a slow march, with the infantry on foot slogging through the sand at a rate of only eleven to fifteen miles a day. They could only march in the cooler hours, and little water was found, none at all on one of the days. On the 16th, they arrived at the mud fort of Gusht which guarded the mouth of the south-eastern defile. Its sardar, Jelal Khan Gushti, came hurrying out to greet Dyer when he saw the column deploying to attack.

Unaccountably, Dyer now paused. To the north of Gusht lay the Saragan Tangi defile into the Sar-i Mulan, which was so far undefended. He knew that Jihand Khan would have realised almost immediately that he had been fooled and would now be marching down the valley inside the hills; he was at the most thirty miles away. The Gamshadzay were also collecting under Sardar Khalil Khan to the east of Gusht. The wisest course was clearly to seize the defile immediately and pass through. This is indeed what Dyer says he intended, and in his book this is what he says he did: 'We spent a very short time in Gusht ... We passed through the defile that evening, though we had already had a long march, for I did not want to risk losing the advantage we had gained.'[7] His log, however, shows, as do the various regimental accounts written later, that the column halted at Gusht throughout the next day, the 17th. It would seem that Dyer had not sufficient information to proceed so spent this time gaining information on the paths into the hills and on the whereabouts of the tribes. He also went sightseeing guided by Sardar Jelal Khan, who took him to see a spring which he 'insisted on our seeing, and which was supposed to possess extraordinary qualities'. He was forced to bribe Jelal Khan for the required information.

That there was some indecision about entering the Sar-i Mulan is indicated in remarks Yeates made later to Ian Colvin; he recalled that Dyer had summoned the most senior Indian officer of the three Hazara Pioneer companies and sought his advice about whether his men were prepared for a march of some forty miles through unknown and defended mountains. The Subadar advised that his men could be depended on. Dyer's handling of his Indian troops was skilful and instinctive, and in this case they were to respond to his leadership. That they appreciated the way he treated and consulted them, and held him in some affection, was shown during this campaign when the cavalrymen of the 28th asked Colonel Claridge to persuade Dyer not to have the Union Jack pennant carried by a mounted orderly alongside him, something he was in the habit of doing and which marked him out as a clear target. The troops feared losing him, and thanked Claridge when he prevailed on the General to desist from this practice. Aside from consultation with his officers, Dyer may have had other reasons for delay. The hitherto stout-hearted Idu opposed the invasion of the Sar-i Mulan as he believed Khalil Khan would combine with Jihand Khan to block the defile. 'For once,' says Dyer, 'Idu had become a croaker, but we were not in the mood to listen to him.' Idu's remarks, though, may well have put some doubt into Dyer's mind.[8] A contributory factor in Dyer's indecision may have been his state of health. At the time he was suffering from dysentery and conjunctivitis, the beginning of the ailments that would eventually see him invalided back to India.[9]

They set out once more, but by the evening of the 18th they had progressed only three and a half miles to the north of Gusht and had come to a halt just beyond the fort of Kalag which stood at the mouth of the Saragan Tangi. Dyer had the sides of the defile picquetted with troops, but this did not prevent an attack on their position that night by the Yar-Muhammadzay, who had by now taken advantage of Dyer's hesitation and were in the defile in strength. When the column attempted to force a passage through the Saragan Tangi at 8 a.m. on the next day, it was rebuffed. The attack never really got going. In the early hours of the dawn, even before the start line was crossed, the picquets placed on the higher ground came under fire and immediately took casualties. It took three hours to get the wounded down. The attacking force then got lost on the way to the start line due to misleading information they were given by a guide. More picquets had to run up onto the heights, then the column began slowly to edge up the defile. By the end of the morning they had managed to advance only three miles up the track. It soon became clear that the Baluch had not only occupied every hilltop to their front, but had also circled round behind and had now held the very high ground on which the column's picquets had sat at the start of the day. It was also clear by now that Khalil Khan had brought his men to Jihand Khan's support. Sensibly, Dyer thought better of this operation, and ordered a retirement back to the start line. They had to fight their way back. 'Every hill being sprinkled with Yarmohomedzais', as Yeates puts it, the Hazara Pioneers had to attack and take each slope in order to clear the way. Two men of the column were killed and another injured that day, for a score of three enemy dead. Dyer later did his best to confuse both the chronology and the distance of this retreat. His book indicates that it all took place on the inside of the defile, and that his retreat did not pass back through it. The log, however, indicates that Dyer ended the 19th still outside its entrance.[10]

This was not very glorious, and things were made worse by the loss of the picquet position above the only waterhole at their camping site, which had been seized before their return by a group of Baluch. Dyer himself accompanied a party of a dozen cavalrymen led back by Lieutenant Brownlow to clear the ground. They dismounted in a hail of bullets and then rushed up the ridge to the picquet. Dyer went up behind his men, and inside a *sangar* found one of the cigarette boxes he had lost in the convoy from Nushki back in March; one suspects this was left there deliberately to taunt him. His men felt he led a charmed life that day; none of the heavy fire aimed at him found its target. The old camping ground was now untenable and the next day Dyer withdrew back towards Kalag, some way away from the mouth of the defile. He made light of this reverse in his report and in his briefings to his force: 'I decided to play with the enemy for a day or two in the hope of bringing them down to attack me and at any rate wasting their ammunition before forcing my way, according to circumstances, either to Saragan or Guz.'[11] In the event, this turned out to be a sensible and successful plan (though it was clearly one that Dyer arrived at by force of circumstances. He himself lets this slip in his book: 'We now fully realized we were in a very tight corner, and that there was nothing to be done but to stay and fight it out'). As the column withdrew for a second time on the 20th, the situation was indeed not looking good. The combined forces of the Damanis now heavily outnumbered the column and were estimated to be anything up to 2500 strong. They were all around the column and sniping at it from all sides. The Baluch had also managed to occupy a small ruined fort in their rear, one which dominated the path back to Kalag. The mountain guns were deployed to shell this, and quickly destroyed it, killing its four defenders, and the column passed through. As they went, the Baluch taunted them, calling upon them to surrender and cheekily using the very phrases Dyer had used to them in Khwash, and imitating the rat-tat-tat of the Maxims with their voices.[12] The force lost another sepoy and a mule killed before they took up a defensive position at Kalag. Here, they would make their stand.

After dark, Dyer sent two strong parties, each of fifty Hazara Pioneers, to picquet the hills commanding the approaches to their new camp. This turned out to be an excellent move, and it surprised the Baluch completely. Just as dawn was breaking on the 21st, a shot rang out, fired accidentally by a man in Khalil Khan's attack force, which was revealed by the sound to be in a valley below the picquets, sandwiched in a hollow between their fire and that of the defenders of the camp. As the light came up, the Baluch were clearly visible from above, and though they resisted stubbornly until 10 a.m., they were eventually forced to flee. Many of them were killed, including Sardar Khalil Khan, whose head, just as Dyer had warned at the darbar in Khwash, had indeed been blown off. Dyer ensured he was given a decent burial, much to the chagrin of the Hazaras, who wished to mutilate his body in revenge for the similar desecration the Baluch had carried out on their dead the day before. The positions in which the Gamshadzay had taken cover were found covered with blood, but they had got their dead away; the column guessed at about eighty enemy killed, though this was later realised to be an overestimate.[13] The Baluch were totally demoralised by this defeat; the two sections split up again, Jihand Khan's men fleeing north into the Sar-i Drukan, the Gamshadzay east into their own territories in the Kuh-i Safed. The road was at last clear to resume the advance.

The force re-entered the defile the next day, as before sending parties to climb the high ground on either side of the pass all the way along their route to provide protection to their flanks. This was exhausting in the heat as much of the climbing had to be done at the double, but this time not a shot was fired against them, and indeed for the Yar-Muhammadzay the defeat of the 21st marked the end of active opposition to Dyer's annexation. From now on, they withdrew into their fastnesses and kept out of his way. The column, threading its way through a defile so narrow that the men had to march in single file, found blood trails left by the wounded, but there were no bodies and they saw no tribesmen. They also found no water that day beyond one small spring that gave enough only for half a bucket each for eighteen of their horses. Their guide – and they had only a Reki guide with them, not a native Yar-Muhammadzay, as none had betrayed their tribe – had thought there was water there all year round, but this was summer and the pool had dried. The men got through that day with one water bottle each, and that was an emergency bottle given to each man from the camel train. The horses and mules were given one bucket of water each from the supply carried on the camels, which were themselves given none at all. The guide took the cavalry to water holes three miles off, but they were found 'fouled and bloodied, littered with rags and bandages, by the fleeing Biloch', so the party returned more thirsty than before.

On the 23rd, the column marched out in the cool before dawn, desperate to find a water supply that day, and came out into the open ground of the Gilikoh valley, which they crossed towards Kahan-i Gamshad, where they came upon the whole wealth of the Yar-Muhammadzay spread out before them, an amazing sight of twenty-five grazing flocks of nine to ten thousand sheep and goats. Moore-Lane described this sight as an 'enormous flock of sheep and goats (the finest I have seen in India)'. Three shepherds put up a suicidal resistance and were killed, and the column rounded up the flocks – 'the men greatly enjoyed this'. In the floor of the valley was 'a stream of cool, clear water', and the column was at last able to drink. Camped happily around the stream, the Hazaras slaughtered a sheep for each of their three hundred men as a record of their triumph over the Yar-Muhammadzay. They had time to cook a few of these, but almost all had to be left where they were butchered, littering the ground around their halting place when the column marched on in the afternoon. The troops went on through the heat of the day, herding the animals with them, and making a total of twelve miles before they pitched camp at Banderan at 11.15 that night. They were exhausted by now. The heat over the last few days had been severe, enough to begin to kill the pack animals; thirty-six camels had died in the last two days.

Dyer found it necessary to grant a day's rest to let the column recover. He himself was suffering along with the rest. Yeates gives a picture of him now which gives an unexpected slant on his character:

> The General, by this time worn and ill, and on the point of being placed on the sick list, had thrown himself down in the scanty shade of a stunted bush. After a time, desiring a

drink of water, he called out to his Indian bearer to bring his water-bottle. No reply came, however, so he looked around and saw that his bearer had gone off to sleep. The bearer was young and strong, and I quite expected that the General would arouse him with a shout. Instead of this, Dyer wearily and painfully got to his feet, walked over and quietly took the water-bottle from beside the sleeping boy, and returned carefully without waking him.[14]

On the 25th, they resumed their march, and by the evening reached Sar-i Drukan, the place from which the mountains to their east took their name. The troops were much affected by the 'deafening noise of flocks as the lambing season was just over, and the number presented an extraordinary spectacle'; so loud was the din that they found it difficult to sleep. They found very little water at the halting place, despite digging for it, and there was insufficient that night for the huge flocks of animals with them, and very little for the men, so they started the next day's march dry. This was to be an arduous march, often in single file, as their path took them through the Dast Kird pass, the north-western entrance to the valley which threaded its way through the Morpish hills. All of that day, the men made do with a single bottle of water, the pack animals and horses with only a bucketful each, and the sheep drank nothing at all. Many animals began to succumb to the heat and thirst. The ground they covered in the searing temperatures was terrible, scree and bare rocks which threw back the scorching heat of the sun. Dyer recalled in his report: 'Any reasonable opposition would have killed my force for want of water, and I can only congratulate myself that the enemy had been thoroughly frightened before I undertook this march.' He had indeed been exceedingly lucky, as had the force been opposed here it would have been in great difficulties. As it was, the troops were severely tested; forty to fifty picquets had to be manned every day, each man in the force carrying out this duty frequently. At every halt there was always a perimeter to be built around the camp and night picquets to be positioned beyond its perimeter. These were manned all night by troops who had marched all day and who were to march all the next. All this was accomplished on scarcely any water.

On the 26th they were at last outside the hills, and they found a waterhole at the end of their march that evening. Dyer described the scene:

> The sight of the captured herds reaching the small pool of water at Gulas is one to be remembered. The battery mules first smelt the water and made a dash for it, then the sheep came on and charged the watering horses in a mass, brushed aside the sowars and horses and sucked the stream dry for some twenty minutes. No amount of force on the part of my men could move them for a considerable time.

In the rush, the herds trampled down the small bank retaining the pool, and the stream reduced to a trickle, so much of the water was wasted. Two hundred sheep died in the camp that night. From now on, the column's path was marked by a trail of dead animals, as the livelihood of the Yar-Muhammadzay tribe was squandered along the way, the bones of their sheep left for the tribe to find. Dyer was now making straight for Khwash, as it was evident that the Yar-Muhammadzay had vanished. The 27th found the column in an area of winter cultivation at Gazu, and the column dug up stores of buried wheat and fodder, burning the tents that the Baluch had left there. Moore-Lane recalls the death of many hundreds of sheep and goats that day: 'All the females were in kid ... hundreds being born and dying on the road.' On the 28th, as the column crossed the open desert, the log recorded: 'Enormous losses amongst the sheep, due to the heat and long and arduous march.' Dyer's report for that day adds: '28 July Nokju, very hot, many sheep died on route, hundreds more on arrival in camp ... There was nothing to be done for the sheep, as I was anxious to reach Khwash.' More animals died even as the column marched into Khwash on the 29th, a day when the temperature reached 106 to 110 degrees in the shade, 'the road being strewn with dead and broken down sheep and goats. The sight was pitiable, but there was nothing for it but to push on'.[15] Of the 10,000 sheep and goats which began the journey, only 4000 were alive when the column reached Khwash. These were sold to the Rekis at four rupees each. A considerable number of camels had also been left for dead; the column lost seventy-four of the seven hundred with which they started. The losses to the force, though, had been comparatively few, five killed and fifteen wounded on the British side throughout this operation.[16]

At times, though, Dyer could behave in a quixotically humane fashion. Major Landon recalled:

> He had a great ability for understanding the point of view of the tribesmen he was fighting, and in general had great sympathy with them. His humanity was very marked, and caused wonderment in the tribes. For example, his refusal to bombard (with two guns) the remnant of the Yarmuhammadzais who had taken refuge in a bolt hole in the Morpeish Hills after their first defeat, and whose women and children could not climb out.[17]

One reason for Dyer's rush back to Khwash was the news that Shah Sawar was coming close to the town to recover grain he had buried and to collect his daughter-in-law. Before the column got back, Colonel Claridge had sent out two parties to try to intercept him. One of these, a patrol of six men of the 28th Light Cavalry commanded by Lieutenant Duncan, succeeded in ambushing Shah Sawar's group at night. Despite the small size of his force, Duncan bravely led a charge and killed five Baluch, but as he put the rest to flight he was shot in the stomach, and though he managed to remain in the saddle, saying nothing to his men about his wound, he died after the action. Two of his *sowars* also died, and three were wounded. The second patrol came to their assistance, and killed another four of the Baluch as they fled. It was a heavy price to pay for this small victory, but it was an effective one, and it was the last time the Yar-Muhammadzay came near Khwash during the campaign.[18]

Back in the fort, Dyer found that Claridge had pushed on with the building plans; the perimeter was now complete and foundations had been dug for some of the buildings planned inside it. Communications with the outside world had been made easier as the wireless now reached the levy post at Mirjawa on the border, from where a rider could carry a message by hand inside four hours to the telegraph at Saindak. Army Headquarters in Simla was therefore now only about five hours away, and this was to bring much greater attention to the force, something not in the least welcome to Dyer. He held a parade on the 30th to commend the members of his column on their three weeks' work.[19]

Dyer's men and animals badly needed rest, but they were not to get it, for within four days of his return he issued orders for a foray against the Gamshadzay. This was to have a disastrous effect on his camels. The log stated on the day his force marched out: 'Camels badly needed a long rest [but] military situation demands their being in use after a rest of only three days.'[20] The issue of supply was now becoming more and more difficult. No measures had been taken to improve the logistic organisation that had started to deteriorate back in June. Dyer signalled Simla on the morning he marched out of Khwash:

> Owing to hardships, many [camels] die or become unfit. Conditions since General Grover's visit totally changed. Besides supply convoys columns are constantly operating against Yarmahomedzais and Gamshadzais. It is essential to have at least 1000 camels for Khwash in addition to 4600 asked for by supply officer, Sistan.

The Government of India had found it impossible to fulfil his original request for 4600 camels, and now felt forced to authorise the extension of the railway beyond Nushki to Dalbandin to shorten supply routes and throw up spare camels from that sector.[21] That, of course, would take time, and for now there were no more camels to be had. The CGS's negative response to Dyer's latest demand came too late to reach him, as he had been gone two days when it arrived: 'Imperative to ensure economy in camel transport, as if demands continue at present rate it will shortly become impossible to comply with them.'

Dyer was now intent on going after the Gamshadzay, who, now that the Yar-Muhammmdzay were so beaten that they were rumoured to have taken refuge with Bahram Khan, the Khan of Bampur, were the only section of the Damanis holding out. He informed Army Headquarters on 31 July that he was moving south. In reply, the CGS telegraphed Dyer next day asking for his appreciation of the situation and for his plans. Despite receiving the telegram in Khwash, Dyer ignored it completely until he was again out in the field and beyond the reach of any orders that might have countermanded his plans.[22] That he was expecting

this may be surmised from the argument he was again having with his Political
Agents. Major Hutchinson had telegraphed Quetta on the 30th:

> I have advised Dyer to take such military measures against the Damanis as he sees fit
> with the proviso that his operations are not in the country [which?] Bahram Khan or
> any more southern Chief can claim as being under their [control. For fear of?]
> misadventure. I am going with Dyer. The Gamshadzais are to be given the chance to
> submit before being attacked, submission to include disarmament.

It seems that Dyer had again expressed to Hutchinson some intent of dealing
with the Khan of Bampur, who was now sheltering Jihand Khan and many of his
people, although he had earlier been forbidden to go that far. Hutchinson also
seems to have been trying to put some kind of restraint on Dyer's forceful
methods. Dyer had not seen eye to eye with Hutchinson when the latter was at
Robat, and now resented his presence in his camp. He preferred to rely on his
own sources of intelligence, and this inevitably sidelined the Political Agent and
made his role partially redundant. Yeates noticed that the Baluch 'brought their
information much more readily to the General than to the Political Agent or to
the Staff officers, with whom in the ordinary course of events they should have
dealt'.[23] Not content with antagonising one Political Officer, Dyer now set about
upsetting another, this time Major Keyes, who was responsible for the area to his
south. Dyer ordered him to a meeting at Gusht where he was now heading, again
indicating in his report of this to Simla that dealing with Bahram Khan of
Bampur was very much in his mind: 'I have directed Keyes to move to Gusht
where I meet him on August 5th … A combination of our forces at Gusht will I
think have salutary effect on Bahram Khan and others and I think the
Gamshadzais will submit.' Keyes was not under Dyer's command, but he
complied with this anyway. This turn of events alarmed the Agent to the
Governor-General back in Quetta:

> I recommend extreme caution and patience before sanctioning extension of military
> operations south. It is reported that Bahram Khan has strong forts and is much stronger
> than Damanis. His code of honour also compels him to shelter refugees at least pending
> negotiations. It would be a political calamity to have anything like a military reverse in
> East Persia.[24]

Dyer was already well on the road by the time this correspondence occurred.
His column departed from Khwash at 5.20 on the morning of 2 August. With
him went a troop of the 28th, two mountain guns, two Maxims, and the three
companies of the 106th, along with one hundred and fifty Chagai and Sarhadd
levies under the command of Major Hutchinson (all of them from the Reki
tribe), and 670 camels carrying a month's supplies.[25] Claridge was once again
left in command in Khwash.

The column's march was much as before. They found no water on the first day, but made good going, achieving between fourteen and seventeen miles a day in the early stages. On the third night, they camped at a *nullah* called the Ab-i Kahugan. The log takes up the story: 'Heavy rain fell in the evening for a short while, and the General Officer Commanding ordered all onto high ground owing to the threatening appearance of sky.' The Baluch objected, saying that it never rained in the Sarhadd in August (though it had just done so). The column halted, most of the men pitched their tents on the slopes above the riverbed, and on the next day, 5 August, rain fell in torrents all morning and the column stayed where it was. That night, at midnight, a spate of water some one hundred and fifty yards broad and many feet deep roared down the *nullah*, carrying before it all in its path. The Sarhadd-dar, Shakur Khan, was almost lost in the torrent and had to be rescued from an island in the streambed where he had climbed a tree. Dyer later commended the man who saved him, Ali Yar, a Chagai Levy, for a Royal Humane Society medal. The flood left a mess of sticky mud and debris. It had destroyed the well at the spot and had carried away three days of the column's rations along with some of their equipment. The troops needed time to sit in the sun and dry themselves out.[26] Dyer later elaborated his sensible order to camp on high ground, recounting that he was credited by the Hazaras with a presentiment, and that they credited him with being a *buzurg*. In his own despatch reporting the campaign to Army Headquarters, in his account in *Raiders of the Sarhad*, and in 28th Light Cavalry's regimental history, this claim is given credence by the omission of the fact stated in the log that it had already rained the day before. Thus was the Dyer legend written.[27]

It took a day to dry everything out before the march could be resumed. On 6 August, the column arrived at Kalag, their starting point for the advance into the Sar-i Mulan of the previous month. Dyer rode on to nearby Gusht, and was met by Major Keyes, who had reached this spot during the course of his very long perambulation through Persian Makran, his task being to win over its Baluch sardars by diplomatic and financial means. He had with him a platoon of the 1st/7th Gurkhas, two hundred rifles of Baluch Light Infantry and two muzzle-loading guns on camels manned by Hazara reservists, so his was quite a useful little force.[28] When the two men met, Dyer presented Keyes with a demand that he come under his command and an instruction that, when Dyer marched on to pursue the Gamshadzay around Jalk, Keyes and his force should remain at Gusht. He was, according to Dyer, to leave off his political work and hold Dyer's line of communication open to his base at Khwash. Dyer informed Army Headquarters:

Arrived at Gusht and seen Major Keyes. Have informed him he is under my orders, which he previously did not know, and I am using his force in my operations against the Gomshadzais, which I hope will terminate at Jalk very shortly.[29]

Dyer intended that Keyes's force should act as a backstop, as he makes clear in his dispatch, where he claims (deliberately misleadingly, for he was aware by the time he wrote it that he had gone too far) that at the *darbar* on the morrow: 'It was settled that during my absence, Major Keyes and his force should remain at Gusht to block the Damanis from breaking back and also to protect the extra supplies, sick and wounded left behind by me at Gusht.'[30] He had spotted that Keyes had a section of a Field Ambulance unit in his escort. Even for Dyer, this was an extraordinarily peremptory way to behave. Keyes was a Political Agent reporting to the Agent to the Governor General in Quetta, and it was not in Dyer's power to assume any control over him. Keyes's work was political liaison with the Baluch tribes of the border, not holding Dyer's line of march while he attacked one of them, and he immediately protested to Quetta, but the message took three days to get through, and in the meantime, the senior man on the spot got his way. Keyes was only a major, and, as he does not seem to have had sufficient character to deal with Dyer's bluster, he did as he was told.[31] In the event, he wasn't to get much back up from Quetta, as they inexplicably gave way this time, replying to Keyes on the 9th: 'You should recognize his supreme authority and consider yourself his Political Adviser for matters connected with Bahram Khan.'[32]

Keyes had arranged a meeting of the important sardars of Persian Baluchistan, and on the 7th a *darbar* was held at Gusht. This was the highest-powered meeting Dyer was to preside over in the course of his command, and it was an assemblage of all the chief men allied with the British. Jihand Khan was of course absent, as was the Khan of Bampur. From the Sarhadd, Sardar Juma Khan of the Ismailzay had travelled down ahead of Dyer's column, as had Taj Mahomed, the sardar of Idu's Reki tribe. From Persian Baluchistan, the sardars of Sib, Rask and Gusht were there, along with Sardar Bahadur Mehrab Khan of the powerful Gichki tribe.[33] It does not appear that Dyer was fully aware of the significance of this meeting, which was composed of men who might have made possible a political settlement of the region. Too intent on his own quest to chastise the Gamshadzay, he makes mention in his report of the meeting only of the fact that his two Political Agents both opposed his action against Jalk, which they told him was within Bahram Khan of Bampur's area of influence. Dyer claimed that by the end of the meeting he had talked them round to his point of view (which is not borne out by their subsequent reports, though in any case the two Politicals are unlikely to have voiced their opposition to him in an open meeting in front of the Baluch).[34]

After the meeting, Dyer returned to his column at Kalag, and, sitting in his tent, at last gave his attention to replying to the CGS's request for his appreciation of the situation. Army Headquarters had sought a clear indication from Dyer as to what he was doing with his command of the Seistan Field Force. They did not get one. Instead, they got a ramble about his current obsession with the Damanis and Khwash. Perhaps the heat had got to Dyer that evening; it had no doubt been a long day:

> Following is my appreciation of situation: Gamshadzais and Yarmohzais have taken our money and, after having made unprovoked assaults on our Line of Communications, broken their signed pledges; they must, therefore, be heavily punished or cleared out of the Sarhad. The Yarmohzais have been driven out of their fastnesses in the Morpish and Gildikoh Ranges, and are reported to have taken refuge under Bahram Khan of Bampur. I am proceeding against the Gamshadzais to drive them out of Safed Koh and bring them to book. As my quarrel is with Gamshadzais and Yarmohzais, I am in no way interfering with Bahram Khan and, if he chooses to give refuge to our enemies, I must ask your further orders. If the supply question can be settled satisfactorily, I think he will easily be brought to reason. I do not anticipate that he will take any active action against me. It is my opinion that Khwash? (H?) [sic] must not be evacuated and two more field forts should be made, one at Gusht, the other at Korin near Galugan, with secondary posts where necessary ... I anticipate Gamshadzais will yield before I reach Jalk and terms will not be light ones.[35]

It is clear that Dyer saw his mission as a campaign to punish the two sections of the Damani tribe which continued to defy him. This had been his theme ever since March, and his campaign against Jihand Khan in the previous month had indeed been of a totally punitive nature, much like all the campaigns of punishment in which he had participated on the North-West Frontier. He had forgotten that the entire point of dealing with the Damanis was to secure the lines of communication for the cordon, thereby furthering his main mission of preventing infiltration across the Afghan border. There is not one word of the latter in the appreciation he sent. His punitive intentions now went as far as depopulating the Sarhadd, and he was also making it very clear that he did not intend to relinquish Khwash.

This appreciation drew a swift reprimand from the CGS. It was not before time. He replied to Dyer on 10 August, indicating that he had expected a fuller appraisal from Dyer:

> The following is to be kept in mind when submitting your plans asked for in former telegram. The countering of German intrigue and activity and the capture or destruction of German parties was, in co-operation with the Russians, the object of the dispatch of troops to Eastern Persia. You were forced by hostility on the part of various Sarhaddi tribes and raids by them on your convoys to move southwards into their country and take retaliatory action. The permanent occupation of any area beyond our present border is not intended and all arrangements you make should therefore be of an entirely temporary nature. The breaking up of the tribal combination against you by such punishment as will ensure reasonable prospect of peace on our border is to be the object of the continuation of your present operations. The presence of regular troops in Sarhad

may be necessary for some time to come but as soon as Germans have been dealt with and political arrangements made for the control of the border, it is the desire of the Government of India to withdraw the troops. Since the capture of the German parties re-entering Persia from Afghanistan is still your main object, His Excellency the Commander-in-Chief considers that your Headquarters should be located, as soon as possible, in the Robat–Saindak–Kacha area, as this will allow you to supervise arrangements for this object and at the same time consultation with both your political advisers and colleagues will be facilitated thereby.[36]

In short, Khwash was not to be retained, and Dyer was to get back across the border as soon as possible. This was a message it was impossible to misconstrue. Denys Bray noted on his file copy that Dyer had been 'informed in clear terms that his arrangements in Sarhad must be regarded on a temporary basis'. Dyer did not receive the CGS's message for many days, and not until the column had got back from Jalk; yet, when he did, he continued to treat its contents as a matter for negotiation.

On 8 August, the column resumed its march towards Jalk, leaving the unfortunate Major Keyes and his men in camp at Gusht. Dyer's march was initially through a defile close to that by which he had advanced north the month before, and which was similarly narrow for a distance of about fifteen miles. The men and animals had to march through in single file, with the heights above picqueted in front and to the flanks. Rocks had to be blasted out of the path in places to enable the camels to pass through. The column halted on the following day, sending patrols out to gather information in the Kuh-i Safed, the Gamshadzay fastness. One of these was fired on, but it was clear that the tribe had fled. The column resumed its eastwards march and reached open ground again on the 10th, making better time now at about fourteen or fifteen miles a day, and seizing some goats and a bull as they went. As before, one of the marches was waterless, so the camels went dry again. On the 12th, the column reached Sinukan, the first settlement in the district of Jalk.

Here they were overtaken by a letter from Keyes, who had summoned up the courage to put on paper his opposition to Dyer's going to Jalk or anywhere near Bampur. He was sure that Dyer's march would upset Bahram Khan. He now made it plain that Dyer's apparent hostility to the latter was undermining Keyes's own hitherto good relations with Bahram Khan, and that if Dyer did not return as soon as possible after visiting Jalk, Bahram Khan was likely to break into opposition. In that case, he warned, 'you will be letting in Government for something very serious'. His letter enclosed a copy of a telegram from Colonel Dew, making it quite clear that Bahram Khan had been given guarantees as far back as April that the British would not interfere in his territory. Dyer's movements towards Jalk were coincidentally giving credence to the story cleverly retailed to Bahram

Khan by Jihand Khan that Dyer had suggested to him that they might jointly conquer Bampur. Bahram Khan was now highly nervous. Dyer denied the allegation, but he was not totally believed even by his own Politicals, who still suspected him of harbouring ambitions towards Bampur.[37] Dyer replied to Keyes, denying any intent on Bampur, but also to say that it was by now too late to stop his advance on Jalk from which he was only a day away.[38] He did admit in his later dispatch that Keyes's appeal had at last persuaded him that he had gone far enough, and that he should go no further than Jalk. Back in Simla, the CGS also had his suspicions about where Dyer was going. He telegraphed: 'Chief [Commander-in-Chief] directs that unless you receive express orders from Army Headquarters, you are not to enter Bahram Khan's territory.'[39]

The column marched on the next day, and covered the remaining nine miles to Jalk. They were met some five miles out of town by its *mir*, Madad Khan, who rode out of town with a bevy of local sardars. That night, a *darbar* was held with the Gamshadzay who had taken refuge in the forts in Jalk. Charag Khan, the brother of the Sardar Khalil Khan whom they had killed in the mountains the month before, came in and submitted to Dyer. On the 14th, another *darbar* was held and presents were given to all those who had been useful to the British. A third *darbar*, the major political gathering, was held on the 15th, and this was attended by the principal Gamshadzay chiefs opposing Dyer, including Khalil Khan's two brothers and his son. Both sides had agreed to leave their forces five miles from the fort at Jalk where the meeting was held. Dyer presented them with his demand for their submission, and his terms: they were to hand in one hundred breech-loading rifles, including five magazine rifles of small bore; to give Dyer three influential hostages against the good behaviour of the tribe; and to sell as many sheep as the forces at Khwash required at market rates. All the terms were to be performed within eleven days, but the Gamshadzay rejected them, and Dyer told them to leave Jalk. The two sides went back to their own encampments, and Mir Madad Khan told all his people to eject the Gamshadzay from his lands. He at least was frightened of Dyer.[40]

The chance to capture many of his principal enemies was not one which Dyer was content to let slip, and, although he recognised that Keyes's letter had made it necessary for him to return to Gusht, he was angry at being prevented from going after the Gamshadzay. He determined on one last throw to catch those of his enemies he knew were still being harboured in Jalk. As soon as he returned to his force at Sinukan, he instructed his Brigade Major to separate the fighting part of the column from the transport and baggage. Plans for the attack on Jalk were laid in such secret, and the force's departure from the camp was made so quietly that night, that 'the General's servant brought his tea next morning, to find his bed empty'.[41] At midnight, the camp was struck, and by dawn the force was outside Jalk. They surrounded the mud huts and date groves around the

forts, and at 5 a.m., at a prearranged signal, two columns, one commanded by
Major Moore-Lane, the other by Major Lang, charged in from different directions. Not a shot was fired. The Gamshadzay fled out the other side of the two
forts in which they had been sleeping, most managing to get away and leaving
Dyer's men, assisted by Mir Madad Khan, to round up whoever was too slow to
escape. This disappointingly turned out to be only six men, but also one hundred
and fifty women and children who had been abandoned by their men folk. The
force also seized ten rifles, and some donkeys, cows, sheep and property. Dyer
released the women and children, 'which magnanimity', he reported, 'I am told,
will bear excellent fruit hereafter', and restored their property to them (though
he destroyed some of it, burning their stores of dates). He sent them home, characteristically warning them that he would not deal so leniently with their
husbands if he caught them. It was all over very quickly; by 3 p.m., the force was
back in Sinukan. It had, for once, been a neat, swift and bloodless operation. The
next day the march began back to Khwash.[42]

On 19 August, Dyer reached Gusht, where he conferred with the two Political
Officers, and allowed the column to rest a day before pressing on to Khwash.
The latest instructions from Army Headquarters were waiting for him there.
Rather than comply with them, he sought to temporise, sending the following
reply on the 20th:

> There is no intention on my part of ever interfering with or attacking Bahram Khan
> without your sanction. A full appreciation will be sent to you as soon after I return to
> Khwash as possible. Until you have seen what I have to say I would ask that I be allowed
> to remain at Khwash.[43]

Keyes insisted on marching back to his base at Sibi to the south, and so moved
out of Dyer's clutches. He left Dyer again subject to less sensible advice, prey to
the information fed him by his Reki levies, as can be seen in a report he submitted
to Army Headquarters on the 22nd that joint forces of Jihand Khan and Bahram
Khan of Bampur were only two days march from Khwash, and that German
letters had been sent to them both. This spurious information can only have
been designed by whoever gave it to him (presumably the Rekis) to unleash his
forces against Bampur.[44] Simla wisely took no notice.

On the 23rd, by now not far from Khwash, the column came upon some flocks
belonging to the Yar-Muhammadzay. Dyer and his staff officers accompanied
the cavalry detachment under Lieutenant Brownlow and charged off to hunt
these down, killing one of the twelve Baluch shepherds they found there, wounding another, then rounding up the 583 sheep and goats in their charge. This flock
had been on the way from the Sar-i Mulan to join Jihand Khan's people, who
were now sheltering in the Kuh-i Birg in the Khan of Bampur's territory, a place
to which, as Dyer ruefully acknowledged in his dispatch, 'I understand I must

not at present follow them'. The only casualties suffered by the column in this small chase were three horses which died of heatstroke. The force was back in Khwash the next day.[45]

Once back in his Headquarters, Dyer found that the forces in the cordon had achieved a success on the Afghan border; weeks before, on 5 August, troops from the post at Birjand had captured a German, two Indians and some followers at Sehdeh, deep in the desert, apparently escaping from Afghanistan. The German turned out to be a lieutenant named Voigt who had worked under Niedermayer in Kabul, and one of the Indians, who claimed to be from East Africa, was discovered to be a Bombay Sikh who had been a chemistry student in Berlin in 1914. Ten bombs and some coin were found in their possession. They had been taken to Kacha for trial by a military court. It was becoming steadily more evident that the German effort in Persia and Afghanistan was on its last legs and that the members of the mission there were trying to get away.[46]

In Khwash, more progress had been made with Dyer's building programme. Three officer quarters of brick had been built, and the vegetable garden was already yielding produce. Despite the explicit orders he had received that his troops were to withdraw from Khwash, on 1 September he had them start on building barracks to house them in the winter months. A couple of days before, he had also sent troops to build a small outpost for sixteen men at Gazu, twenty-five miles to the north east. On 5 September, he gave instructions for an additional outpost to be built to house twenty men at Dolani, twenty-four miles west of Khwash, and on the next day he ordered a similar post to be built at Dehani Baghi. On the 7th, he went out to have a look at the road from Khwash to Saindak with a view to upgrading it for cars. The work of extending a screen of outposts around Khwash continued. Dyer gave orders that the fort at Kamalabad be repaired and made ready for a garrison of twenty men. All of this work occupied the men of the Hazara Pioneers, whom, it will be remembered, he had been specifically ordered not to retain, but who were put to work for close on two months in building fortifications and habitable accommodation for the troops.

Dyer was assuming, without any reply from Simla to justify his belief, that his request for a stay in the execution of the order to withdraw would be granted until he had made a further submission of his appreciation. In addition, he assumed that his second appreciation, which he dispatched by hand on 26 August, would persuade Simla to change its mind. These were unwarranted assumptions, but Dyer continued to act according to them, and, rather than take steps to evacuate the Sarhadd, he was taking steps to solidify British control.[47] News of his building plans reached as far away as Kabul, where the Afghan Amir became concerned that the British were annexing the Sarhadd, and ordered his commander on the border to investigate.[48] The Persian Government protested to the Government of India about the building of the fort in Khwash.[49]

Dyer was still champing at the bit to be off after the remaining Yar-Muhammadzay and Gamshadzay sheltering in Bampur territory. Contrary to the statements he makes in his book, in which he maintains that by the end of August the Sarhadd was completely pacified and that 'there was now nothing left to be done', his actions at the time show that he felt that his work was far from finished. He had not given up hopes of being permitted to carry the campaign to Bampur. He telegraphed Army Headquarters only two days after getting back to Khwash pushing for this, although he admitted that 'While at Gusht I was told by Major Keyes that he is of the opinion that Kuh-i Birg is out of Sarhad and that I shall bring on a collision with Bahranzais if I attack the Gamshazais or the Yarmahomedzais there. Under the circumstances, your further orders awaited'. Three days later the CGS again made it clear that this was out of the question. 'You are not to extend your operations beyond the Sarhad, in respect of the boundaries of which Major Keyes's advice is to guide you.'[50]

On his return to Khwash, Dyer found that his problems with supply had not gone away, in fact they had worsened inexorably, in part because of his last expedition to Jalk. He had not improved matters by further reinforcing the garrison at Khwash, where the Sarhadd Levy Corps had grown to a strength of two hundred.[51] The number of camels necessary to support this large force, and the numbers of these which were dying both on Dyer's punitive expeditions and on the routes into the Sarhadd, are revealed in a telegram he sent the CGS on 23 August, asking for another thousand camels in addition to the increment that he had already requested. A caravan of 235 camels sent recently between Khwash and Kacha had suffered thirty-six deaths, one of 480 camels travelling between Kacha and Khwash forty-one deaths, and a third of 432 camels going between Khwash and Kacha lost seventy-six. These losses exceeded any possibility of replacement; the wastage was simply unsustainable. Without camels, the supply of Khwash was impossible, and without supply the garrison could not long remain. Dyer's own deployments had brought this about, but he naively seemed to believe that Army Headquarters could pull camels out of hats to make his plans feasible. Pointing out to the CGS that the rationing strength at Khwash was 1550, he claimed: 'It must be recognized that the scale on which transport is based did not allow for the rationing of so large a force as the Khwash garrison nearly 300 miles away from Sistan where most supplies bought.' Precisely.[52]

The log for 29 August states: 'Atta and grain running short Khwash. Transport lacking to distribute supplies. 104 max temperature in the shade.' By 3 September the animals were back on half rations, and the next day Dyer found that he had to yield to the inevitable and send two troops of the 28th back to Saindak. Neither men nor horses could be fed any longer at Khwash, where there was no fodder available at all. Though it was not clear to the garrison at the time, this was the start of the British withdrawal from the Sarhadd. On 9 September, Major Hutchinson finally extracted himself from Dyer's close control; taking with him Sarhadd-dar Shukar Khan and the Chagai Levies, he rode off to Saindak.[53] Yet Dyer had still not given up: on 13 September he telegraphed the CGS demanding a monthly inflow of four hundred camels. Army Headquarters did what headquarters usually do in such cases. They stalled and asked for more data.[54] They were told by the logistics staff at Kacha that there was a need for a minimum of 4604 camels to supply the Seistan Field Force as it was deployed at that time.[55] Dyer tried again on the 14th, outlining plans to hold camels at each post, and asking for a thousand more animals than he had. He added unnecessarily: 'No transport camels can be procured in the Sarhad as the majority of the local tribes have lost many camels owing to the prevalence of disease in the Sarhad.'[56] By 29 September, Dyer had only 1200 effective camels left, and his force had to be loaned camels from the Baluchistan allocation held at Nushki. Between June and September, 3680 camels died while working with the force, a large proportion of them in the Sarhadd.[57] Brigadier-General Dickson, who took over from Dyer's successor, recalls in his account of his time in East Persia: 'When I went to the country later, the old route to Robat was literally marked out in places with camel skeletons every hundred yards or so.'[58]

There was no remedy for this save for withdrawal, but Dyer would not acknowledge the fact, and set his face against abandoning what he had conquered. He had telegraphed on the 14th:

> Any further reduction of the force at Khwash is not recommended as some sections of the Yar Mohammedzais and Gamshadzais are reported to be on the point of coming in to give up their arms and a show of strength is advisable at Khwash at present. As soon as ever reduction is possible, the Chief of the General Staff will be asked for orders.

He never was, and Dyer never brought himself to order the abandonment of the Sarhadd. Instead, he carried out a piecemeal withdrawal, clinging onto the fort at Khwash until the last. Dyer's own Headquarters finally bowed to the inevitable and left Khwash for Saindak on 19 September, but even then not to comply with the orders he had been receiving for months, but simply because he could not feed himself. 'It was,' he wrote in his book, 'with real regret that I said goodbye to Khwash.'[59] Even as he left, he spent a day looking at a site on the road near Ladis for a wireless station to communicate with the Khwash garrison. On 25 and 26 September, as supplies in Khwash ran out, Dyer was forced to order all the remaining cavalry, the mountain guns and some of the Hazara Pioneers to withdraw to Robat. The Maxim guns followed shortly afterwards. Yet even as late as 30 September Dyer was still seeking sanction to extend the telegraph line from Mirjawa on the border to Khwash.[60]

Despite Dyer's efforts over eight months, nothing really had been settled in the Sarhadd, where two sections of the Damanis were still refusing to submit. Despite the information which continued to come in that the 'Damanis are in great straits and suffering from sickness and want of food. Many camels dead', and that their people were 'starving and sick, most want to come in', only one surrendered, the raider chief, Izzat, who came in on 14 September.[61] In a telegram which must have irritated Dyer considerably, Army Headquarters informed him on 6 September that the Gamshadzay had approached Major Keyes through another Baluch sardar, Dost Mohamed of Dizak, the nephew of Bahram Khan, to make terms. Obviously, they would do anything to avoid placing themselves at Dyer's mercy, though they had also refused Keyes's terms by the time Dyer was told this.[62] To the end, Dyer continued to inform Headquarters of his expansionist plans; on the 7th, he signalled the CGS that the Damanis could not 'interfere with me' due to the posts he had built at Dolani and Gazu, and reported that he intended to extend the screen designed to protect the garrison by building posts at Muken, twenty-two miles to the south east of Khwash, and further afield at Gusht, though in the event these were never built.[63] Jihand Khan remained defiantly at large; on 26 September, his men fired on troops on the road south of Khwash. On 27 September, Dyer hopefully reported that 'the Yarahmadzai lashkars of Zulfikar and Pasand said to be coming in to accept terms, in which case I propose releasing the two', but this did not materialise.[64]

On the same day, Dyer heard that an action had taken place the day before at Kalmas in the north of the cordon, where a cavalry patrol had chanced upon a party of thirty Afghan gun runners. In the ensuing firefight, the patrol commander, Lieutenant Wahl, and an Indian NCO were killed, as were four of the smugglers. The troops took one prisoner and seized bundles of rifles.[65] Dyer had never been anywhere near this area, and he continued to concentrate on the Sarhadd.

On 3 October, he reported that 'The Yarmahomedzais are suffering much and many sections are inclined to accept my terms. A very humble letter has been written by Shah Sawar asking to be allowed to come in.' But Shah Sawar did not come in, and the Yar-Muhammadzay stuck it out until Sardar Jihand Khan brought his tribe in to make terms on 29 October. He finally surrendered at a *darbar* at Khwash on 4 November.[66]

By then, the man he had been so bitterly resisting had been gone for over a month, for Dyer had at last been relieved. In the end, despite all the reasons that might have given grounds for his removal, he brought his removal upon himself. On 31 August, he applied for sick leave to return to India. He envisaged being away a short time, and felt that, as the Sarhadd was now relatively peaceful, he could leave his command with good conscience. He describes the state of his health in his book: 'I had had eight months of continual work in the hot weather of the Sarhad and was very near the end of my tether.'[67] He sent a telegram to Simla: 'Owing to repeated attacks of Colitis, Medical Officers deems [sic] it absolutely necessary that I should have a change. He thinks that Captain Yates should be sent back on account of the same disease.[68] Have I your permission to come to Simla for a change and in order to see you? For the present the Damanis are likely to remain quiet.'[69] He must have been extremely taken aback to receive a telegram on 15 September nominating not the temporary stand-in he had asked for but a permanent successor, Colonel Tanner of the 127th Baluchis.[70]

Simla had initially gone along with the idea of a temporary relief, and had asked 4 Division at Quetta to nominate one; Tanner was their suggestion. But by 11 September, Army Headquarters had decided that the opportunity to be rid of Dyer was not to be passed up.[71] Considerable impetus was given to this decision by the Foreign and Political Department, which had convened a meeting in Simla on 2 September to discuss affairs in East Persia. General Kirkpatrick, the CGS, Grant and Bray of the Foreign and Political Department, and some officers with experience of Persia and Baluchistan were present. Grant pointed out that it would be an advantage to terminate operations against the Damanis and that the present moment seemed opportune. He believed that the 'Chiefs would come to terms if reasonably treated'. It is likely, though the minutes do not say so, that Dyer's future was discussed at this meeting, which shelved decisions on the policy to be adopted until they had reviewed Dyer's request to return to India and to come to Simla.[72]

In the background to their deliberations hung the hostility that had built up towards Dyer over the summer, a hostility shared by the Agent to the Governor-General, who telegraphed the Government of India on 15 September making his feelings about Dyer and his activities very clear. He said that he distrusted Dyer's intentions, and that he feared his further operations against the Damanis would involve his attacking Bampur, which would be against Government of India instructions. He wished Dyer to cease operations and allow the tribes to go home, and noted that Dyer had harassed Major Keyes in his mission.

> No doubt that General Dyer did not grasp the larger political situation and though he says he merely made the statement in chaff, he did actually ask Jahind [Jiand Khan] if he was prepared to assist him in an attack on Bampur, and this statement is now being used with full effect.

He pointed out that Dyer had gone too fast in raising levies, and that the levies he had raised had left the British with a heavily partisan role in Sarhaddi tribal politics. Two thirds of the levies were Reki, one third Ismailzay, a force in fact composed mostly of the hereditary enemies of the Yar-Muhammadzay and the Gamshadzay. Despite the fact that there was no reason to suppose that any of the levies had any real loyalty to the British, Dyer had promised them three years' service, and had planned to arm them with the latest rifles. It was clear from this telegram that the Agent to the Governor-General for one would not have supported Dyer's retention in post.[73]

The Agent's telegram forwarded the document which Dyer had written in Khwash and had sent on by hand back in August, his second stab at an appreciation which only now arrived in Simla. This, a ramshackle document, the product of a mind seemingly unable to organise its thoughts clearly or to present them succinctly on paper, was redolent of all the obsessions and self-justifications that had marked Dyer's tenure of command. With its jumbled flow and its unfortunate return to issues that he had been instructed to drop, this appreciation was enough in itself to seal the decision to remove Dyer from his command. The timing of its arrival was impeccably bad.

> When I arrived at Robat on March 3rd, I realized that what I had come out to prevent happening was really then in the process of happening, merely letters sent by certain Germans to the Damanis had been sufficient to induce them to raid our lines of communications, that if vigorous measures were not immediately taken in this direction the actual presence of the Germans in the Sarhad and in the Bampur District would immediately raise a much larger storm in Persian Baluchistan. Considering that the Russians were coming southwards, and that the Germans had been ousted from Kerman, I considered that the line between Birjand and Robat was fairly secure against Germans attempting to get through there, especially in view of the water difficulties in the summer across the Dasht-I-Lut ... That no Germans have tried to cross from Afghanistan into Bampur or Narmashir is, I think, due to the fact that I have created a belt of friendly territory enclosed in the rectangle Khwash–Mirjawa–Robat–Gurg Fort (in the Rud-Mahi) ... I have never lost sight for a moment of what I am out here for, and I laboured with the Ismailzais centred at Galugan, the Rekis, and the Damanis to secure what I considered the most vulnerable area of the line I had to defend, not only with a view to preventing the Germans from crossing, but also for securing my lines of communication. Future events and the cold weather coming on may render it necessary for me to look to the security of the Northern Line, and this I am watching for as carefully as I can.

He went on to state that the Damanis had now been driven out of the Sarhadd, and would not interfere with the Lines of Communication 'while my present force is at Khwash'. He claimed that Bahram Khan of Bampur was pretending to be scared of the new fort at Khwash, 'which fort after all is merely an entrenched camp defensible by a small force, thus releasing my movable column for active operations. Bampur can be dealt with in the future, so long as he does not take active measures against me.' He rashly added that he believed Major Keyes should not be allowed to go on with his peaceful mission in South Persia as the money he gave out would be used to purchase arms, and that this peaceful mission was emboldening Bahram Khan to 'be actively opposed to us'. Dyer indicated that he would like to bring Major Keyes to Khwash but regretted that he couldn't feed him there, nor at Gusht, and that it was for this reason alone that he had assented to his return to Sibi. He continued:

> I have said nothing about Birjand and the Russian to the north, as my time has been fully occupied in the Sarhad, and consequently I have had no opportunity of properly appreciating the situation in that direction. The greatest difficulty, I have to contend with, is that of Supply and Transport. The camels throughout the line have of necessity been over-worked nor do I anticipate any cessation of such work in future.

Dyer made plain here that he expected to go on the way he had done, and demanded three hundred fresh camels every month along with the posting in of a veterinary officer, or the building of a light railway to Robat. In enclosures to his appreciation, Dyer spent a very great deal of time airing more of his grievances with the Politicals, this time in correspondence aimed at the unfortunate Major Hutchinson, with whom he was quarrelling again over the control and training of the levies. He enclosed part of Hutchinson's correspondence with him on this matter, and thus elicited a note on the file from Denys Bray which revealed the way Dyer was regarded in Simla:

> There seems a deal of sober sense in Major Hutchinson's note, which is likely to appeal with more force to General Tanner than to General Dyer, in view of the former's experience of the Baluch, which will probably result in our being furnished with a completely fresh view of the whole situation before long. This we may await.[74]

In fact, since as far back as July there had been little doubt in the official mind as to what Dyer was up to in the Sarhadd. Sir Percy Sykes had telegraphed then from Bandar Abbas enquiring whether 'policy is to restore order to Persian Baluchistan in interests of Persia not to annex it as Dyer apparently wishes'.[75] Writing to the King Emperor four years later, the Viceroy, Lord Chelmsford, made plain what his view of Dyer's activities had been:

> At an early period of my Viceroyalty he was conducting a small campaign on the borders of Persia, and he carried it out with an energy and thoroughness which was beyond all praise. I had however some difficulty with him inasmuch as I found he was annexing large chunks of Persia – a neutral country – and as no remonstrances seemed to have any effect, I had to tell Sir Beauchamp Duff – the then Commander-in-Chief – that I could not tolerate this, and that I should have to recall General Dyer. Fortunately ill-health on General Dyer's part saved me from having to take this extreme step and he came back to India on leave.[76]

On 4 October, Colonel Tanner arrived at Saindak where Dyer had now established his Headquarters. There was scarcely a handover. Dyer was gone in his car the next day, taking with him Captain Yeates, who by then had been promoted, and who was suffering from the same colitis as his commander. Dyer had offered the young man a lift in his car. As on the journey out, Dyer travelled without escort, with only Yeates, Corporal Allan and the orderly Allah Dad Khan. The Seistan Field Force, however, had not quite seen the last of him, for the car broke down in drifting sand twenty-five miles from Mushki Chah on the day they departed, and they were back at Saindak on the 6th. No doubt Colonel Tanner's heart sank when he saw them drive back through the gate. On the 7th, they set off again early in the morning, and managed this time to complete the journey back to the railway at Nushki, partly by car, and, when that gave out, by camel.[77] Yeates described the journey back as 'a privilege which involved responsibilities when, as often happened, we stuck in a sand drift and both had to get out and push'.[78] Their homeward journey of four hundred miles took nearly five days.

Yeates describes the first day when they had to turn back. Twenty miles from the nearest well in a forty mile stretch of waterless desert, the car stuck in the sand.

> The General and I had to get out and put our shoulders to the back of the car ... After an hour or two of this heaving and pushing I felt nearly at the end of my tether, and the General did not look to be in a much better way.

Yeates suggested going back before the radiator became empty;

> Dyer, however, was not a man to be stopped easily and gave my suggestion scant consideration. We accordingly continued our exertions for what seemed an eternity, but I suppose was not really more than another hour, when the car settled the matter by breaking its axle-shaft.

Corporal Allan replaced the shaft, but they had made only a couple of hundred yards when the car stuck fast again.

> The General and I accordingly resumed our role of coolies, and staggered through the sand with bundles of bedding, provisions and spare parts. When we had completed this, we once more put our shoulders to the car and started to work it back over the ground we had so laboriously gained ... I had had an unforgettable demonstration of Dyer's bulldog tenacity once he had undertaken a course of action.[79]

It was these kind of qualities – mucking in with his sleeves rolled up, looking after his men, messing with his subalterns, never giving up – that endeared Dyer to his junior officers and troops. There is little doubt that, as much as some of his seniors and equals, along with the Politicals, came to detest him, he was very popular with his juniors. He took trouble with them, confided in them, consulted them, gave them demonstrations of his knowledge of Indian lore and languages, and on occasion shamelessly played up to them. Around the campfire at night, he would recount to them the stories of his car, his demand for general's rank, his capture of Jihand Khan, and his prediction of rain. His small band of eager and happily flattered young men soaked up every word, and recounted it all later, and with elaboration. There is an indication, too (from both his book and his log), that he secured at least a local promotion for some of the junior officers he took a shine to, and that as he had put up new rank badges, so, for the duration of the campaign, did they. He recommended his officers and soldiers for awards profusely; after one campaign recommending seventeen for a mention in dispatches. All this would have been vastly flattering to impressionable young men subjected to Dyer's bonhomie, and would easily have made up for his occasional outbursts of temper. Dyer had a habit of adopting young officers who caught his eye, extracting them from their real jobs and installing them amongst his staff. Landon he made his quite unofficial Brigade Major until he had to return him to his post of Intelligence Officer; Yeates, whom he found commanding a small border post, was whisked off to command his machine guns. He kept these young men close to him throughout the campaign. Yeates himself comments on the fact that at times on Dyer's expeditions he was, as a regimental officer and the only one present, outnumbered by the staff in the persons of the Brigadier and the Brigade Major. Dyer's tendency to coopt young men ran across racial boundaries. Idu, the aristocratic Reki, encountered on the road right at the start, stayed with Dyer till the end.

None of this, of course, would wash with anyone who had any responsibility for policy, or whose mission was at variance with the task to which Dyer had appointed himself. To these, Dyer was impossible to deal with, incapable of understanding the politics of the situation he was in, and a man swayed to partiality by the advisers he chose to have around him. He seemed, and often was, impervious to argument, and even resistant to direct orders he disliked even when given him by very senior superiors indeed. Adrift from his main mission and pursuing his obsessions in ever-tightening circles, Dyer had shown himself a man capable of acts of enormous high-handedness and arrogance, one with a skin as thick as a rhinoceros in the face of pressure from above, but as thin as paper when it came to perceived slights from those in his power.

Aside from the decimation of his camel force and the anguish of his superiors, what had he achieved by all his efforts? He had put a stop to the raiding which, when he arrived in post, had been bad enough to bring operations in the East Persian cordon to a halt. By August, the Sarhadd was quiet, and had by then become in large part just empty desert. But to do this, he had for the entire period of his command ignored his main mission; whether German agents or gun runners breached the line of his cordon was not something of which he had been even aware, let alone actively involved in preventing. To provide the forces to enable him to hold down the Sarhadd, he had stripped the cordon of troops,

thereby causing an international incident with the Russians. Despite six months'
continuous campaigning, two of the three sections of the Damanis had refused
to submit to him, and a political solution in this part of the border had been
impossible while he was there. The Viceroy, Lord Chelmsford, put it thus to his
predecessor, Lord Hardinge:

> We should have been able probably to have restored order in Kerman at an earlier date if
> General Dyer had not pursued a policy of adventure in Sarhad. General Dyer has now
> been withdrawn, and, within a month of his departure, his successor – General Tanner –
> and Major Keyes were able to compose all the difficulties which had existed in Dyer's
> time.[80]

The *de facto* annexation of the Sarhadd, the forts and buildings, the gardens
planted around them, all were to be abandoned within months of Dyer's departure. Due to Persian weakness, the British were forced to maintain agents in the
Sarhadd, and to pay the subsidy to its chiefs granted by Dyer, up until 1924 when
the Government of India handed control to the new Persian Government of
Reza Khan, later to become Reza Shah Pahlavi.[81]

The cost of Dyer's campaign to the Sarhaddi Baluch was carefully evaluated
by Dyer's Political Agent in a report which Dyer attached to his log for August,
proudly entitled 'Memorandum on Damage Done to the Damani by General
Officer Commanding April to End August 1916'. Hutchinson counted thirty
Damanis killed, including Sardar Khalil Khan of the Gamshadzay, and Wali
Mohammed, son of Sardar Jihand Khan of the Yar-Muhammadzay. Many
tribesmen had been wounded, though these could not be accounted for. The
operations had taken fifteen prisoners, along with sixty-five rifles, seventy
bandoliers, a pistol, sixteen swords, fourteen daggers, two belts, a shield, fifty-six
camels, 11,180 sheep and goats, fifty-three donkeys, twenty-six cattle, 184 maunds
of grain, 152 maunds of *bhusa*, crops worth 16,000 rupees, twenty tents (another
125 had been destroyed), miscellaneous rugs, blankets, domestic articles, and
thirty maunds of dates. Hutchinson calculated all this to be worth a total of
110,000 rupees. On top of this, the Damanis' losses included the mortality
amongst the flocks (over 6000 of the Yar-Muhammadzay sheep had died), and
the fact that, as they had been captured in the lambing season, all the lambs for
the next year had died. No winter dates, which were a staple for food and trade,
had been harvested, and all the local wood had been used up by the garrison in
Khwash. The British had also recovered property looted by the Damanis: sixty-
two rifles, a pistol, cloth, and fifty female and child slaves, who had been rescued
from their captivity and returned home to Narmashir. Two sections of the
Damanis had fled as refugees to neighbouring Bampur: the Yar-Muhammadzay,
who numbered about 1600 men, women and children, and the Gamshadzay, who
were about 1200.[82] These refugees were now starving and diseased and living on

the charity of their neighbours in Bampur, an area which the British had been trying to keep friendly.

What this devastation meant in the Sarhadd, where crops could be grown only in a few fortunately watered spots, where wealth and livelihood were measured in the size of a man's flocks, and where, in normal times, the usual way of supplementing subsistence was by raiding abroad, can be gauged by what happened there twelve years later. Then the Persian monarch Reza Shah Pahlavi finally took steps to bring the territory under central control. His war was a mirror image of Dyer's, and lasted bitterly for six years from 1928 to 1934. Amazingly, Jihand Khan, by then aged ninety-four, was still leading the resistance, and after he had been arrested (to die in captivity in Mashad) his son-in-law took the tribe into the wilderness near the British frontier, refusing all contact with the Government. As in Dyer's day, both the Ismailzay, still led by Juma Khan, and the Rekis, by then led by their new sardar, Idu Khan, submitted to the Government. Raiding finally ceased, but the result of the war and the pacification that followed was an economic depression in the Sarhadd that lasted until the 1940s.[83]

There is no record of what the Sarhadd was like after Dyer had left it. We know enough to guess that it was indeed bad enough to justify the words the Viceroy wrote five years later to George V:

But there was no mistaking the impression he made on those out-of-the-way parts of the world, and the story goes that to this day women hush their children with the name of General Dyer much as the Saracenic women used to frighten their crying babies with the name of Richard Coeur de Lion.[84]

PART TWO

The Amritsar Massacre

14

Abbottabad and Jullundur

The railway could now take Rex Dyer all the way from Nushki to Simla, where he was to report to General Kirkpatrick at Army Headquarters. This was the first time he had been back there since he had left home nearly twenty years before, so the railway, which had opened in 1903, was a novelty for him, and he would have found the journey up the narrow gauge track ascending 2800 feet over the sixty-three mile journey a great improvement over the road. The views from the carriage of the precipitous cliffs beneath and the mountains away in the distance were spectacular enough to take his mind off the impending interview, one to which he was unlikely to have been looking forward.[1] There is no record of what was said when he met the CGS. After the increasingly frosty telegrams Kirkpatrick had himself sent Dyer, it is unlikely that he was particularly polite. Dyer probably got a roasting. Later, he was sufficiently sensitive about this time to pull a veil over it in his book, where he ends his campaign in August, over a month before his relief, obfuscates the situation when he left the Sarhadd, and makes no mention of his reception in Simla. That he was aware of the displeasure of the Government of India is visible in what Annie told his biographer of the interview – Colvin describes their 'doubts and misapprehension'; according to him the Government of India was: 'Somewhat scared by the proffered annexation of a corner of Persia, and did not confirm that part of his policy. It was also a little disturbed by a protest received from the Persian Government.'[2] Strangely, Dyer also says nothing in his book about either his award of the Companion of the Bath or the Mention in Dispatches he was awarded for his services in Persia, though both were granted in mid 1917.[3] It is possible that it was made clear to him that his conduct in Sistan had forever blighted his prospects of promotion to substantive brigadier-general. Even if he was not told so directly, this was in fact the case.

From Simla, Dyer wrote home to Annie for the first time since he had pencilled his note from Nushki in March. By then, she had recovered enough to leave the nursing home, and was living in White Lodge, in Finningham, Suffolk, which she had taken as German air raids had brought rents down in the area. On 23 October 1916, she received a telegram saying: 'Arrived Simla after exciting time – Dyer.'[4] Quite why Rex had not written to Annie in all his months in Sistan is unclear; he had never treated her so cavalierly before, they were usually very close, and he must have known that she would worry about him very much. She later told Colvin that the telegram 'for the moment set the husband's share of her heart at ease', a clear if suppressed indication of her feelings. Ivon was now back at the front, having just returned to the 1st Dorsets in France, recovered from his wounds of the year before. Annie was on her own in a strange house, trying to make ends meet, worrying about both her husband and her son. Dyer's obsessions about the Sarhadd had been strong enough, it would seem, to blot all this out of his mind.

After his reception in Simla, he must have wondered what his next role would be, but a post was swiftly found for him which allowed him to keep his temporary rank. If he went back to Rawalpindi to perform any of the functions of the post of Station Commander, which, in theory, he held, it was only for a short time, enabling him to recover from his intestinal disorder and to collect his belongings together, for within a month at the most he was in Abbottabad. This was some fifty miles north of Rawalpindi, up towards the Kashmir border, and he was posted there as the brigade commander. He arrived sometime in November or December 1916. Dyer could have been very content with this posting, probably even very pleased with what he could see as a further step in his career, and it was certainly a surprising appointment given the mess that he had made in the Sarhadd. The post was in General Kitson's division, so it may very well have owed something to his recommendation, particularly as it was temporary; Dyer was sent in to hold the post until another incumbent could be found, and he was not promoted to substantive brigadier-general. Nevertheless, Dyer had got his brigade.[5]

He did not relate much about all this to Annie, or, if he did, she did not choose to recall it, and we have no detail of anything that Dyer did whilst in command at Abbottabad. The garrison was in the Hazara District, a little to the east of the Black Mountains where he had first served on the Frontier, and the garrison provided Frontier duties, but these were routine in 1917 as the tribes were mostly quiet. Abbottabad was well away from the Punjab, so the garrison had no operational role in support of the civil authorities there. The terrorist threat was now in any case abating, as was any residual threat from Afghanistan. In Kabul, squabbles had broken out amongst the German party, and during the summer of 1916 its various elements had gone their different ways. Of the revolutionaries, two remained there, Raja Mahendra Pratap Kunwar and Maulvi Barkatullah, who declared themselves respectively President and Prime Minister of a provisional Indian government. Their Home Minister, Obeidullah Sindi, who had been a teacher at the Islamic Deoband School in India, surrounded himself with the fundamentalist Indian Wahhabi Muslims then found in some numbers in Kabul. In the summer of 1916, while Dyer was in the Sarhadd, Obeidullah had been part of one final plot. He had tried to contact the headmaster of his old school in

---

India, another Wahhabi named Mahmud Hassan, who had fled to Mecca, and sent him letters for the Turks and the Sherif of Mecca (the plotters were not aware that the Sherif was by then a British ally), offering them posts in an 'Army of God' linking all the Muslim nations. The letters were written in Persian on silk, and were sewn into the clothes of the messenger who carried them. The messenger was betrayed in the Punjab, and, as a result of this 'Silk Letter Plot', the British arrested twenty conspirators in Lahore, Delhi and Calcutta.[6]

Dyer would have known of this, but was probably not involved in any action connected with it. He may also have been involved in watching for raids across the border by the Hindustani Fanatics, who sought unsuccessfully to raise the border in *jihad* against the British. In the event, he was not to remain long in Abbottabad, as on 29 March 1917 he had the second riding accident of his career.[7] This was something about which he was rather sensitive; Annie gave a full account of what caused it to Colvin:

It was not, therefore, on Galahad [killed in the desert by the Baluch] but on a casual mount that the accident occurred. General Dyer, with the other officers commanding brigades, regiments, and batteries of the 1st and 2nd Divisions, had assembled near the Artillery camp at Nowshera for a demonstration of the result of modern artillery fire on trenches. General Dyer, who was mounted on an artillery horse, rode up when the firing had stopped, and set his horse at a trench in his way; but the animal either slipping or balking on the crumbling edge, reared up and fell backwards on his rider. Now General Dyer was, as we have seen, a more than usually powerful man, and, lying on his back, with his open hands he held the shoulder of the horse from coming down upon his face. Thus he probably saved his life; but the full weight of the animal and the high and hard cantles of its artillery saddle came down upon him as far as the chest. When he was carried to hospital and stripped, his lower body was found to be one livid bruise.

One reason which Annie may have had for relating such a detailed account of this accident was that Dyer was probably aware of the talk circulating in the garrison about it, gossip recounted with relish by the vituperative Villiers-Stuart, who at this point was a lieutenant-colonel under Dyer's command. Villiers-Stuart had been given charge of the Nepalese Contingent which was on loan to the British for the duration of the war, and which was posted at Hassan Abdal in the hills of Dyer's district:

There was a calamity. Brigadier-General Dyer, an excitable lunatic of a man, was appointed to command the Abbottabad Brigade. At once he thought Hassan Abdal and the Contingent would be more fun than Abbottabad in winter, and so came down there and went into camp in the married British officers' camp. He knew nothing of his work. He was lazy – and spent most of his time listening to the strains of the Territorial band with the married ladies in his camp. He didn't know how to treat the [Nepalese] Generals. He would not be told about the Contingent and I was with the Contingent out of the

Luard [Dyer's predecessor] frying pan into the Dyer fire. The worst things he did were to order parades of Nepalese regiments and then tell them they were wrong when they were perfectly right. His ignorance was amazing – I can't attempt to explain it. When I was holding Staff Exercises *without* troops for the Nepalese Generals, he would appear, and tell me and the Generals off because there were no troops there. He had not got and had never seen Training and Manoeuvre [Regulations] or Field Service [Regulations] and expressed the wildest surprise and indignation when the Generals quoted from them in explanation of their plans. Matters were boiling up to a very bad row when the Artillery Practise [sic] Camp at Hatti on the way to Peshawar came on and he had to attend that. He had not bothered to buy himself any horses, so was provided with a field artillery 'hairy' and caused the greatest amusement at Hatti for he couldn't ride at all, galumphing about on the brute. At last he fell off one day and the horse rolled on him and he went off to Abbottabad with pneumonia. Ordered by the doctor on no account to get up he did so at once, and got worse. But he would not go sick for fear of losing pay and some-how got kept off the sick list. When convalescent later he used to drive about the mountain roads around Abbottabad with a car full of ladies of the station, his great delight being to frighten them by dangerous driving at which he was an expert. The man was insane.[8]

Villiers-Stuart was notorious both for his misogyny and for his sharp tongue, though he was also famed for his professionalism; his account is worth noting for what was being said, even if it is perhaps not entirely accurate in its details.

Whilst in hospital in Abbottabad, and before he was affected by the pleurisy Villiers-Stuart recounts as pneumonia, Rex Dyer dictated the following letter to Annie, one of his few to her to survive:

My horse fell on top of me at Akora and squashed the life out of me, but no bones broken, and I am making quick recovery. I do hope you are improving and are taking an interest in life as far as the awful state of things will allow you to do. It is possible I will come home shortly; but it depends on the Chief of the General Staff. I got Ivon's letter yesterday, and it was very good and thrilling, and am replying to it. Much love. Your affectionate husband – REX.[9]

Ivon was still at the front in France, where he was Battalion Signals Officer of the 1st Dorsets, and, so Annie had much to be anxious about. Dyer cabled her on 4 May to tell her he had been granted six months' leave in England, but he did not set out until 8 July due to the pleurisy that developed in his lungs. As he left India, he automatically forfeited the temporary rank of brigadier-general that had gone with his brigade command and reverted to colonel.[10] The news of the award of the CB and MID for his time in the Sarhadd must have reached him about now, either while he was in the hospital or on his way home.

He reached Annie at Finningham in the Autumn of 1917, a 'wreck of a man, able only to crawl a few steps with the help of two sticks'. It was a sad reunion, the family depleted, both Rex and Annie in ill health. But at least they were together again, for the first time now for four years, the longest they were ever apart. Rex's legs had been damaged in the accident, so he set himself to work, at first in their garden and then on the paths and roads beyond its walls, and by much practice he managed to regain a normal gait. He found riding much harder, and nearly fainted with pain when he first sat astride a horse. Concealing from the examining doctors the pain he was in, he bluffed his way through a medical board, in order, as he said to his wife, 'not to be out of it'. They passed him fit to return to India. He had time to see at least one of his sons, for Ivon was back with 3rd Dorsets in England between June and September. He was promoted lieutenant in July, and went back to France, this time to the 5th Dorsets, and in time to command a company at Poelcapelle in October. Whilst he was at the front, his father set out in midwinter aboard the P & O ship, *Ormonde*, on the wartime route to India via the Cape. It was an uneventful journey, and a lonely one, as Annie again stayed behind in England. During the voyage, Dyer prevented an outbreak of indiscipline onboard by an Australian contingent returning home unfit for duty. The men had refused orders and would not wear their uniform, but Dyer persuaded their ringleaders to comply with instructions until the ship docked at Bombay.[11]

Political events had moved on in India whilst he was convalescing. The Liberal Secretary of State, Edwin Montagu, announced in the House of Commons on 20 August 1917 that:

> The policy of His Majesty's Government … is that of the increasing association of Indians in every branch of the administration and the gradual development of self-governing institutions with a view to the progressive realization of responsible government in India as an integral part of the British Empire.

This announcement was the high watermark of Liberal intentions for reform in India, part of a tradition the party had followed sporadically since as far back as Macaulay in the early nineteenth century, and in it the Government acknowledged that India should gradually follow the white Dominions in achieving self-rule within the Empire. The announcement was also intended to indicate that the Empire would not forget the sacrifices India was making in the war. Montagu was himself in India over the winter of 1917–18, and so was there when Dyer got back to hear at first hand of the opposition and hostility Montagu's visit had aroused in much of British India. In April 1918, Montagu and the Viceroy, Lord Chelmsford, published for consultation the package of reforms which were to become known by both their names, and which they designed to take the Morley-Minto reforms of an earlier decade to a further stage. They planned to decentralise some Government functions to the provinces, and to add greater Indian representation at both central and local levels. Decentralisation was something supported by most of the provincial governors, who welcomed the addition of power it gave them, but wider Indian representation was not. The issue was fought hard by men such as Sir Michael O'Dwyer in the Punjab, and by much of the Indian Civil Service, which objected to the diminution of its power as well as to the fact that in some cases in the provinces they would from now on be working under Indians. The Montagu-Chelmsford Report had proposed that the less politically sensitive areas of provincial administration (education, local government and health) be handed over to Indian ministers, whilst the rest (particularly security and the police) be reserved to the Governor, a system characterised as 'dyarchy'. In the centre, the Indian Legislative Council was to be expanded and made more representative, though the powers of the Viceroy were to be left untrammelled and the Government of India was left responsible to Parliament back home. The proposed reforms also included an increase in the numbers of Indians to be recruited to the ICS. All these reforms were delayed, though, until the end of the war.[12] There was much here that was highly unpopular amongst the British in India, and to Dyer the proposals were no doubt largely anathema. They were, however, to provide the political backdrop for the remainder of his service in India.

By March 1918 Dyer was back in the Punjab, this time appointed to permanent command of an infantry brigade, the 45th at Jullundur.[13] He was once again a brigadier-general, even though once more just a temporary one. Whether he still held hopes of rising further is doubtful. Within the year (if he had not already had it) in his mail would have arrived a buff envelope from Army Headquarters containing a demi-official letter (as the military form of formal correspondence was known) from the Adjutant-General's Branch informing him that 'the Army Selection Board in India had decided that, on his military record, Dyer did not come up to the standard for promotion'.[14] It is possible that this was not issued to him until after the end of the war. If this was the case, as long as hostilities continued, he may still have hoped that his fortunes might change. In war time, anything was possible.

Dyer knew Jullundur from his days there in the 29th Punjabis. His brigade and the Jullundur garrison were part of 3rd (Lahore) Division and lay some way back from the Frontier in the east of the Punjab, astride the trunk routes to Delhi. The major town within the brigade area was Amritsar. 45th Brigade included both regular units, mostly infantry, and nine infantry depots, and so was an unusually large and unwieldy formation for a junior brigadier-general to command. The units, not all of which were stationed in the city, included a wartime British infantry battalion, the 1st/25th (County of London) Cyclist Battalion, the London Regiment (which consisted largely of men invalided from the front), gunners of the Royal Artillery, some Royal Engineer detachments, and two Indian infantry battalions, the 3rd Battalion 23rd Sikh Pioneers and the 2nd Battalion

151st Infantry Regiment. There were also many small ancillary units involved in matters such as transport and supply. The depots included those of the 51st, 52nd, 53rd and 54th Sikhs (Frontier Force), the 56th and 59th Rifles (Frontier Force), and two cavalry depots, those of the Guides and the 11th Bengal Lancers.[15] On the brigade headquarters staff when he arrived, Dyer found Captain F.C.C. Briggs, DSO, of the King's Liverpool Regiment, who was the Brigade Major, and, as Staff Captain, a territorial officer, Captain J.A. Bostock of 2nd County of London Yeomanry. The brigade's main role was the recruitment and training of men for the war. Dyer took over this task from his predecessor, Brigadier-General Peebles, on 16 March 1918.[16]

Dyer settled into Flagstaff House, the Brigade Commander's residence, somewhat forlornly at first as he rattled around in it by himself. Life in the brigade passed by in a routine of training, ceremonial, paperwork and social life, a frustrating style of life for a man who saw the only prospect of future advancement to be active service. He inspected the Londons at work on 6 July 1918. On 25 July he was in Simla to receive his CB from the Viceroy, Lord Chelmsford, at an informal investiture at the Viceregal Lodge.[17] Ivon arrived from England in August, having applied to join the Indian Army whilst he was serving with the 5th Dorsets in France the previous year. He had needed to wait a few months whilst the paperwork cleared through from the War Office to the India Office, but by March 1918 he had returned to England and was accepted for transfer. He applied for, but did not get, the 25th Punjabis, his father's regiment, and instead he joined the depot of the 82nd Sikhs. He was there only for a month, then was posted in September to the depot of the 53rd Sikhs (Frontier Force) in Jullundur, perhaps so that he could be close to his father. Somewhat unusually for a lieutenant on depot strength, he took up residence with his father in Flagstaff House.[18]

Some serious duties did fall to Dyer in his new position. He settled a quarrel between some sepoys and the citizens of the town in the summer of that year, and was thanked by 'a deputation of the elders of the city'.[19] The Londons recalled an incident later in the year when fifty of their men hurriedly occupied the police barracks at Phillour at two in the morning while Dyer settled a dispute between the Mohammedan and Sikh elements of the two police battalions station there. The Muslims had attacked their Sikh colleagues. It took him till dawn to accomplish this, but he did it without the use of force.[20] Influenza struck the garrison in October 1918; every member of the Londons got it, and seven of them died.[21]

At the Armistice, on 11 November 1918, the GOC, Major-General Sir William Beynon, was on an inspection tour and staying with Dyer in Flagstaff House when the telegram notifying him of the end of the war arrived there at 11 p.m. Dyer and Ivon piled into the car and took the news around the garrison, which returned the compliment by assembling outside Flagstaff House in the early hours of the morning shouting 'We want the General'. They were invited in, everyone was given a drink, and Beynon was awakened to make a speech. The next day, the Londons furnished the guard at Simla for the Viceroy and heard him read out the terms of the Armistice. The Londons went up by train not knowing why they were detailed for this duty until they got there, as the message announcing the Armistice had not reached their barracks before they entrained. They all got very happily drunk in a grand Simla hotel, courtesy of the Headquarters Staff, and when they marched back noisily to the station behind their Commanding Officer, there were not enough sober men left even to provide the leading file.[22]

On the 13th, a celebratory dinner was held at the Jullundur Club followed by a fancy dress ball, and at this Dyer played a trick on Superintendent Donald, Jullundur's Chief of Police. On an earlier occasion, whilst the war was still on, Donald had fooled Dyer into thinking he was a German, appearing at the club in disguise and behaving in a highly arrogant manner to Dyer, who lost his temper and was about to have him arrested when Donald's real identity was revealed. Dyer's revenge was a neat one. He arrived at the Club during the Armistice party dressed as a Baluch sardar, with two similarly dressed companions, all mounted on camels. One of his staff officers who had been primed beforehand rushed into the club to inform the Chief of Police that the sardar had cut off the head of a Jullundur policeman who had tried to arrest him. He was now outside demanding to see the General. Donald marched out bristling only to be made fun of in Persian and Urdu by Dyer and his two mounted companions, who demanded to be treated as befitted their rank. As the berated and bemused policeman ran back into the Club to get a chair for the sardar, he saw the faces of the members and their wives watching him from the windows and enjoying the joke at his expense.[23]

Dyer, as with all brigade commanders of the station, was *ex officio* a leading member of the Jullundur Club, so it must have been something of a shock to the station (and one which caused his junior officers some unease) when he tendered his resignation. He did this sometime in early 1919 in support of the admission of Indian officer members. This surprising event stemmed from the commissioning of Indian officers into certain regiments at that time.[24] The new officers had exactly the same status in the Army as that of their British counterparts, so club membership, hitherto strictly segregated, became a difficult issue across India. Many clubs refused to alter their rules and refused to admit Indian officers. Some members of both the military and civilian establishments resigned in protest. Lord Willingdon, when Governor of Bombay and then later of Madras, was the most prominent official to resign from a club, and went so far as to found Willingdon Clubs, open to Indians, in both places. Dyer's resignation is an indication that he viewed the status of a military officer as an issue of greater importance than that of the officer's race. In Dyer's mind, the division between military and civilian was more clear-cut and more fundamental than any division in the service based on race. Civilians were perennially the objects of his contempt. His resignation was indeed a brave gesture and must have cut him off to a great degree from the social life of the town. He did, however, remain a member of the Kasauli Club; his father had been a member before him, and presumably it now admitted Indian officers.[25]

Peacetime routine resumed, and Dyer set an exercise for the garrison from 3 to 12 December. As a brigade commander unaccompanied by his wife, Dyer could devote all his energy to keeping his troops on their toes, but many of the British troops in the garrison were awaiting demobilisation and were not much impressed by peacetime training. They could think only of going home, so Dyer started a garrison riding school to occupy them while they awaited demobili-sation, using horses loaned from the cavalry depots.[26] Captain Ulric Nisbet, a young officer who had been medically downgraded after service in France and had arrived in Jullundur on attachment to the 23rd Sikh Pioneers, recorded in his diary for 3 and 12 December:

> 3 December: Had to parade at 8 after an early brekker for the Moveable Column. Waited on the Brigade Parade Ground for two hours, then the General (Dyer, of Amritsar 'fame') called us all up. He asked me my name, luckily nothing else … 12 December: Same attack with various other parties thrown in. By this time everyone is completely fed up with it except, perhaps, Brigade HQ. We are going into camp on Saturday. Why can't disbanding orders come through?[27]

Yet it would seem that Dyer was liked by his officers and men. Colvin quotes an Indian officer of the garrison, who, he was told, pointed at his forehead as he said: 'There is something here in the General Sahib which makes us all love him'. Captain MacDougall, Dyer's Transport Officer in Jullundur, wrote to Colvin:

> I remember General Dyer speaking in their language to an Indian regiment. And I saw a most unusual sight on the faces down the ranks – a look of high appreciation and affection. After thirty years all over India I had rarely seen a native show his true feelings to this extent. And yet his remarks were not all praise; he let them have it on their weak points.[28]

Dyer had that rare knack of talking to his troops in a way they could immediately understand and warm to. 'We liked our Brigadier-General', wrote R. Moray Graham, at the time a young subaltern at the Depot of 53rd Sikhs, and a friend of Ivon. 'I met his father from time to time unofficially … He was a normal, kindly man *of his generation*.'[29] Dyer earned much of this affection by looking after his men; he was at the Londons' Christmas party, no doubt carrying out the time-honoured custom of serving the men lunch. Corporal Davis recorded that day: 'Splendid dinner and happy time for all. Commanding Officer and General visited us.'[30] On New Year's Day 1919, there was a Brigade 'Proclamation Parade' with a *feu de joie*. It went well, for the troops had been practising for several days, and Dyer was pleased enough with the drill and the turnout to compliment the troops. Ulrich Nisbet recorded: '1 January: Brigade Parade, 10 a.m. Everything went off very well. The *feu de joie* was dam' well done, so was the march past. We were complimented afterwards by General Dyer.'[31]

Less satisfying, and doubtless very embarrassing on the day to all concerned, was an occasion to which Dyer was subjected by his staff on 18 January:

> The General and two officers from each depot and regiment went, complete with band, to welcome three hundred repatriated men at the station. On arrival, they were greeted with cheers, and speeches were just about to start when Bostock dashed up to the General to say that these men were on leave only. Obviously a put up job![32]

The return to barracks must have been a bit forlorn.

Annie rejoined Rex that month, bringing out to India their niece, Alice Dyer, the daughter of Dyer's eldest brother, Arthur. She was to stay with them for several months.[33] Their timing was bad, for they arrived as clouds were gathering over India; the salad days of the announcement of the Montagu-Chelmsford reforms, still unenacted, were already over. Reaction had set in, and the provincial governors and members of the Indian Civil Service who were opposed to change were mounting an opposition to it using the threat of terror and revolution which India had experienced before and during the war. They maintained that the reforms would add to the disorder already endemic in India, and they persuaded the Government of India to arm itself with strong new powers to deal with the trouble they predicted. The Defence of India Act, which had kept the lid on domestic strife during the war, expired with the end of hostilities and pressure grew to replace it with a similar measure for peacetime. A commission was established under Mr Justice Rowlatt to investigate the threat to security in India. Its report made public the police's view of the seriousness of the existing threat to law and order. Whilst it acknowledged that terrorist outrages were declining, it attributed this to the success of the Defence of India Act, discounting the alternative interpretation that terrorism was waning, though waning in fact it was. In 1918, there had been thirteen terrorist incidents across India, but in 1919 there were only five.[34] The ease with which the police had smashed the Punjab plots was forgotten, as was the fact that Bengali terrorism was now a broken force, its cells infiltrated and destroyed by the police and its programme made irrelevant by Montagu's reforms. The Rowlatt Commission nevertheless recommended the enactment of measures to allow the Viceroy to take special powers in areas where emergencies had been declared due to terrorism. These powers included measures curtailing the usual legal process and permitting the internment of suspects by provincial governors, the first time the power of internment had been delegated to anyone below the Viceroy.[35]

There is no doubt that there was considerable anxiety amongst the British in India at the time, and that many felt that the Rowlatt measures were justified. To the continual fear of disaffection that had lingered since the Mutiny had been added the more recent memories of the revolutionary terrorism of the pre-war years and the mutinies and conspiracies that had been uncovered during the war itself. Even a man of as liberal views as Montagu believed at the time that the Rowlatt Acts were needed; on 22 May 1919, he was to state in Parliament that Rowlatt 'was necessary, ought to have been passed, and could not have been avoided'.[36] As time passed, however, the supporters of the Bills were to be proved wrong, and it became evident that the Rowlatt Acts had been imposed unnecessarily. The violent revolutionary terrorism that had reached its height in the war years was not to be seen again in India until another decade had passed. In 1920 there were just two incidents of revolutionary violence across the entire country. The figures for much of the decade were similar: three outrages in 1921, nine in 1922, ten in 1923, seven in 1924, one in 1925, three in 1926, and five in 1927. The Rowlatt Act placed on the statute book in 1919 was to be repealed in 1922, its provisions never having been used, but sadly long after the severe damage that its enactment had caused.[37]

The Government of India accepted the Rowlatt Report, and, under the guidance of the Secretary to the Home Department, Sir William Vincent, determined to enact the two Bills which became known as the Rowlatt Acts. The minor Bill, which was never in fact enacted, increased the severity of the law of sedition, adding to the length of sentences and imposing a fine for possessing seditious literature unless possession could proved to be for a lawful purpose. It allowed any earlier conviction, or even association with those who had earlier been convicted of this type of offence, to be used against a defendant in court. There were provisions that, on release from prison, prisoners were to execute a bond for good behaviour and keep their address notified to police. The second Bill, the major one, which was eventually passed as the Rowlatt Act, and which was characterised by the Indian opposition as 'na dalil, na vakil, na appeal' (no argument, no lawyer, no appeal), allowed courts to sit in camera, and to admit evidence which otherwise would have been ruled inadmissible. Three judges were to sit without a jury for such cases, and there were to be no preliminary proceedings for committal. Part two of the Act allowed suspects to be forced to place a bond against good behaviour, to notify their place of residence to the police, to abstain from any act ordered by the court, and to report to the police when ordered. Part three allowed arrest and search without a warrant and confinement without trial for up to a year, a period which was renewable. Although the Act obliged the Executive formally to declare 'the prevalence of anarchical or revolutionary movements' to put the Act into force in districts which it specified at the time, the measures allowed in the Act were widely viewed as draconian, especially by lawyers trained in the liberties of the English Common Law, as of course all Indian lawyers were.

The publication of the two Bills aroused unprecedented public opposition from all sections of Indian opinion, loyalist, moderate and extreme. When the first of the two Acts was debated in the Imperial Legislative Council, every Indian member voted against it, something that had never happened before. Indians viewed the Bills as a slap in the face to India after its loyal efforts in the war, and one which cast doubt on British intentions for India's future, intentions which had, since the publication of the Montagu-Chelmsford reforms, been widely respected as honourable. The Bills were also resented as an attempt to conciliate white opinion in India, which had largely been against reform.[38]

As opposition grew amongst the educated Indian classes, the Government of India's position hardened, and it refused to bend, believing it necessary to maintain the prestige upon which it believed British power was based. There was also a total disbelief in the ICS in the warnings of bloodshed given by Indian politicians. Sir Stanley Reed, an ex-Editor of the *Times of India*, who was at that time working for the Government, tried to warn the Home Department of the reality of the opposition to Rowlatt:

At that time I was winding up the Central Publicity Board which had carried out the task of explaining to the Indian people the basic issues in the war. I had travelled far and wide, and in contact with my Indian friends had learned how deep-seated was the hostility to the Act and how real the fears it inspired. Returning to Delhi, I warned the Member of Council in charge [Sir William Vincent] that he was under a delusion; this was no factious opposition, but a genuine movement, strong in the classes which had most at stake, normally the best supporters of law and order; and urged him to take the advice of those who said that where the special powers were necessary they should be taken out by Ordinance. 'I won't listen to you', he blurted out. 'I won't listen to any suggestion of any Ordinance.'[39]

A visitor to Delhi during the days on which the Legislative Council was discussing the Rowlatt Bills described the mood of the Government at the time:

I called on Mr Marris, Sir William Vincent's Secretary. I called also on Mr Srinavasa Sastri [a member of the Imperial Legislative Council]. With neither of them did I discuss the Bill; but in their rooms and wherever I went in Delhi the atmosphere had one even temperature of set determination: hope had fled from both sides. The Service was determined to vest the Executive with extraordinary powers to deal with sedition. The Indian Members refused to accept legislation which was a flagrant evidence of distrust, and, in the situation of that hour, with the Reform Bill on the anvil, an absolute insult to the whole nation. But the Service, represented at that time by Sir William Vincent, was relentless. It had gone too far to step back. Apparently the loss of prestige would be disastrous! [40]

There was a complete lack of appreciation by the Government of the need to persuade the Indian population of the need for the Act. This left the field to the opposition, which won the public relations war unopposed, and the distortions which appeared in the vituperative Indian press further hardened Government intransigence. Lurid press stories were followed by wild rumours which swept India, including stories that the police would be able to arrest two or three people walking together, that a tax of five rupees would be levied on all marriages and funerals, and that crops would be seized. It was not until 6 April 1919, over a month after the Acts were brought forward, that the Government of India began to try to make a public case for them. [41]

By then, Rowlatt had soured the atmosphere so carefully cultivated by Montagu and ensured that his reforms could not be introduced as he had hoped. Worse still, in the febrile atmosphere of the post-war years, Rowlatt was almost certain to lead to trouble. The Indians dubbed the Rowlatt Acts 'the Black Bills', and once the fight against them had been lost in the Legislative Council, many felt there was no alternative but to continue opposition by other means. [42] Mainstream Indian politicians were not, however, at that stage ready to make their opposition felt by methods outside the old course of establishment politics; they did not yet see themselves in the business of popular agitation. This left an opening which Gandhi moved to fill. He had gained experience of local mass politics in South Africa and India, and had developed the theory of semi-religious *satyagraha*, loosely translated as 'soul force', to enable the people, by the mass application of peaceful resistance, to circumvent the authorities' hold on the levers of power. Whilst Rowlatt was not an issue, perhaps, that initially affected the masses, it aroused Gandhi, who was a barrister, intensely. As he later wrote: 'When the Rowlatt Bills were published, I felt that they were so restrictive of human liberty that they must be resisted to the utmost.' [43]

Gandhi set up the *satyagraha sabha*, a central committee, in his *ashram* near Bombay, and began to build an organisation through the provinces using whatever local political resources were to hand: the Home Rule League, Moslem *khilafat* organisations supporting the Sultan of Turkey as the worldwide caliph, Hindu *Arya Samaj* committees and the like. He was initially opposed by many national politicians, including most of the leaders of the National Congress led by Annie Besant and Tilak, who warned him (correctly as it turned out) of the violence that his incitement of the masses would cause, but his *satyagraha* pledge caught the national mood, partly due to its semi-religious content, and partly because many groups across the country were beginning to jockey for position at the time to take whatever power the Montagu-Chelmsford reforms might offer them. Seeking a cause upon which to fight, they took up his call to oppose Rowlatt. They included the Hindu merchants and bankers of northern India who used their commercial power to pressurise local businessmen to take part in the movement.[44] The *satyagraha* pledge ran:

> Being conscientiously of the opinion that the Bills known as the Indian Criminal Law (Amendment) Bill No. 1 of 1919, and No. 2 of 1919 are unjust, subversive of the principle of liberty and justice and destructive of the elementary rights of individuals on which the safety of the community as a whole and the State itself is based, we solemnly affirm that, in the event of these Bills becoming law, we shall refuse civilly to obey these laws and such other laws as a committee, to be hereafter appointed, may think fit, and we further affirm that in the struggle we will faithfully follow truth, and refrain from violence of life, person, or property.

Gandhi's ability to put together a movement out of such disparate strands caught the British unawares, and surprised even himself. It led the British to suspect a more sinister revolutionary conspiracy beneath the surface, one which did not in fact exist; but it was the fear of such a conspiracy which led to the severe repression which was to follow. All their experience of dealing with revolutionary disorder led the British to the wrong conclusion this time. Moreover, the British had never faced a countrywide campaign of civil disobedience and were ill equipped to deal with it. There was no organ of central government in place to direct policy during a civil disturbance, and so such policy was largely left to individual provincial governors, which in one case was to prove disastrous.[45]

This was the Punjab, where the circumstances of the time and the personality of the Lieutenant-Governor, Sir Michael O'Dwyer, combined in an explosive mix. The province was weary after the war, for which so many of its men had been recruited, many of them, in the later years, by a good deal of coercion. It was widely alleged that war loans had been extorted in the province, though this was not proven. It was certain, however, that taxes there had risen sharply to cover war expenditure, and this had continued after the end of the war. Super Tax had come into force on 1 April 1917 and a new Income Tax on 1 April 1918. An Excess Profits Duty Act was enforced from 1 April 1919; all this meant that between 1918 and 1919 the tax taken in the province had increased, by 30 per cent in the provincial capital Lahore and by 55 per cent in Amritsar. At the same time, the cost of living had risen steadily while wages were stagnant. The war had created an unprecedented inflation in the province: between 1914 and 1919, wheat increased in price by 47 per cent, cotton by 310 per cent, sugar by 68 per cent and food grains by 93 per cent. Bad weather led to bad harvests, and there were looting and food robberies in the Punjab during 1918 and 1919. In Amritsar, the centre of the cloth trade, the end of the war had brought down the price of cloth, causing a panic in the cloth market and a run on postal savings banks. The lot of the industrial classes was miserable; real wages dropped by 2 per cent from 1900 to 1919. The rural population was mostly in debt, and had been horribly affected by influenza, which took five million lives in India in the autumn of 1918; in some villages, 25 per cent of the population died. The situation in the Punjab was made worse by a local epidemic of malaria following the torrential rains of 1918, the worst for forty-seven years. The urban population was worse affected than the rural, as the higher prices for grain the farmers had achieved in the war had at least supported some increase in prosperity. In the towns, industry and commerce had suffered from the war's dislocation of international trade and the disruptions and restrictions applied to provincial transport. The railway workers were particularly disaffected by 1919.[46] In sum, the province was in a sorry state.

The Punjab was similar to other provinces in that its education system had, over many decades, produced numerous educated professionals, particularly in cities such as Lahore and Amritsar. The political expectations of these new men had been severely repressed by Sir Michael O'Dwyer's operation of the Defence of India Act. During the war years, the Punjab regime had been noted by the rest of India as being particularly harsh. O'Dwyer had censored and closed local newspapers, and prevented the circulation of others from outside. He had laid internment or prevention of speaking orders against local politicians, and rubbed salt in their wounds by making frequent derogatory speeches denigrating the educated classes, who were not, in his view, reliable enough to be given responsible political roles, and who would, were he to allow it, seek to exploit the rural population. He notoriously spoke of them as 'grasshoppers under a fern who make the field ring with importunate cries'. He had never been forgiven for the bankruptcy in 1913 of the most prominent Indian-owned bank, the People's Bank of Lahore, which had financially affected many of the urban middle classes in the province.[47] He was hated by old money and new learning alike.

Disorder in the Punjab was very near the surface of public life. 'The powder being dry, the exaggerated reports of the provisions of the Rowlatt Act acted as a lighted torch.'[48] O'Dwyer's colleague, Sir William Harcourt Butler, then Lieutenant-Governor of the United Provinces, wrote at the time: 'Sir Michael O'Dwyer has sown the wind and reaped the whirlwind. For some time past it has been evident that the Punjab was utterly out of touch with the educated classes. We shall see what the end shall be.'[49] Dyer would have been aware, at least superficially, of the state of the Punjab, working as he was in Jullundur, but, like most Anglo-Indians, even those with access to intelligence reports, he would not have noticed a great deal of difference on the streets of the city, nor would he have been more than vaguely aware of the political developments which were about to engulf him. He saw press reports of the meeting at which Gandhi decided on his *satyagraha* movement on 24 February 1919. The *satyagraha* manifesto was published in the press on 2 March, and the newspapers carried the news that Gandhi had proclaimed that the 30th of the month would be the day of the first *hartal*. This was a closure of all work, including offices, shops and business; it had a semi-religious content, allowing time for prayer, fasting and contemplation, but was also a strike and a politically motivated, enforced closure of all commerce. The Rowlatt campaign was to revive this technique of a combined strike and lock out which had not been used in India since Moghul days; it was something the British had not had to face before.[50]

Dyer's growing unease was heightened by the reports he began to receive from Amritsar, the major city in his area of command. Amritsar was only a few hours from Jullundur by both road and rail, and the small garrison there was linked by telegraph and telephone to his Headquarters. He first began to be aware of the mounting excitement of political activism in Amritsar as early as 9 February, when the first of what was to be a long series of meetings in many of the public halls and open spaces of the city was held. These were to take place every two or three days throughout February and March, and had a variety of themes, some called to protest about Rowlatt, others about matters of more local interest. Elections for the town council were going on, which led to some intimidation in the city, and a campaign was being waged to reinstate the sale of station platform tickets to Indians, something which the railway company had recently prohibited. The meetings gradually took on more and more of a national complexion, in support of issues such as the *khilafat*, the movement agitating for the retention of the Sultan of Turkey as Caliph of the Sunni Muslim world. The local branch of the Punjab Indian National Congress was also becoming very active after the lifting of the restraints that had prevented much activity during the war.[51] It was organising itself for the important annual meeting of the All India National Congress which it was planned to hold in the city in November 1919. The town was in political ferment, so when Gandhi's call for *satyagraha* against the Rowlatt Acts was broadcast in the press, the local leaders in Amritsar, none of whom had met Gandhi or knew much of him, took up the call. An Amritsar paper, the *Waqt* ('*Time*'), campaigned actively against Rowlatt throughout March.

At first, military life in Jullundur went on unaffected by the maelstrom developing around it. Ulrich Nisbit records the daily tenor of life in February and March. Dyer inspected the 23rd Pioneers and set them a test exercise on 7 February. Annie Dyer presented prizes at the brigade sports day on 10 February, her first exposure to the garrison after her arrival. The Dyers accepted calls from their officers and wives at Flagstaff House, and held a tea and tennis party on 1 March, occasioning Nisbit to remark 'Mrs Dyer very nice'. On 18 March, amateur theatricals, in which Ivon played a part, were performed in the garrison theatre. That month, in a more serious vein, Dyer was called upon once again to sort out ill-disciplined troops, this time when a draft of sepoys being posted from Lahore to Singapore were reported to be looting sweet vendors' stalls at stations along their route. He had their train stopped at Jullundur, detrained the troops into local barracks, and restored order without any formal discipline being necessary before sending them on their way. Life seemed normal enough to Dyer, and the Punjab peaceful enough, to arrange a ten-day motoring holiday in March to show Alice around Delhi and Agra.[52] It was a bad time to take a holiday.

Leaving Lieutenant-Colonel Hynes of the Londons in charge in Jullundur, Dyer, his wife and Alice, driven by their Goanese chauffeur, set out on their motoring tour in an open-topped car. They drove through the heat of the pre-monsoon; Annie recalled frequent stops to pour water over their tyres to cool them down and prevent the rubber melting.[53] They drove via Umballa (Ambala) in the Punjab to Delhi and on 29 March put up at the Maidens Hotel, a smart and luxurious new establishment with whitewashed colonnades and *pankha*-cooled verandahs set among palm trees and lawns. The next day they departed in the comparative cool of the early morning for sightseeing amongst the monuments and ruins which lay all around Delhi. Dyer could scarcely have been unaware that Gandhi had announced that day as the first national *hartal*, but his surprise on meeting the 'large and unruly' crowds which they met already noisily thronging the streets of the native quarters indicates that he had not really paid much notice to what was happening.

Dyer drove on through what he believed that morning was a religious festival. It was a day that went tragically wrong in the capital, as crowds attempting to force sweet vendor stalls to close at the railway station were fired on and deaths ensued. The Dyers' car attracted attention in the streets. Unseen by Dyer, two men attempted to jump on its boot, scaring Annie and Alice, who were in the back seat. Luckily for the party, a mounted policeman was to hand and pulled the men off.[54] They continued with their sightseeing in the Kutub, the area around the city, and on getting back to Delhi found the gate guarded by troops and the city streets silent. Delhi stayed shut the next day, so the Dyers drove out to Agra and the Taj Mahal. That night they were back at the Maidens Hotel. By then, Gandhi's *satyagraha sabha* had announced a further day of *hartal* for 6 April, but the Dyers lingered in the city for a few days more before deciding to make for home. As they drove back to Jullundur, the effects which the continuous agitation and the new *satyagraha* movement were having in the Punjab became clear to them along their way. Their car was stoned between Ludhiana and Phillour where the Grand Trunk Road crossed the Sutlej river, and a log was pushed out in front of it. The driver managed to swerve in time, and they escaped unscathed, though shaken. The two assaults on the car, and thus on his wife and niece, disturbed Dyer deeply, and their memory seems to have underlain much of his thinking over the next few weeks.[55]

The Dyers were back in Jullundur on 6 April, the day of the next *hartal*.[56] It is difficult to see why they were so slow in going home; perhaps, again, they had not seen the press reports of Gandhi's plans. If he did read the papers, it would seem that Dyer was more confident about the situation than he later made out. There was indeed much reason by now for disquiet, for the events in Delhi had set off an avalanche which was picking up speed. Dyer does not seem to have been in touch with his Headquarters during this holiday. Had he telephoned them he would have heard that in Jullundur, although no *hartal* had taken place on the 30th, mass meetings had been held on 31 March and 2 April. In Amritsar the *hartal* had been generally observed on the 30th, although peacefully, and mass meetings had been held there both on that and the previous day, with crowds of between 25,000 and 30,000 gathering to hear the speakers calling for the repeal of the Rowlatt Act. More large gatherings had occurred in the open ground of the Jallianwala Bagh in the centre of the city on 2 April, when Swami Satya Deo lectured the crowds on *satyagraha* and non-violence. 16 Division (into which the 3 Division had been transformed after the war, and which had its Headquarters in Lahore) had issued the 45th Brigade instructions to reinforce the garrison at Amritsar with a platoon of soldiers to guard the railway station, as trouble was expected during the *hartal* planned for the 6th. An Indian officer and twenty men of 54th Sikhs had been sent down from their depot the previous evening by train. At the request of the Jullundur Commissioner, Lieutenant-Colonel Burlton, Captain Briggs had also stood by a squadron of cavalry and a company of infantry for operations in Jullundur for the 6th. [57]

The *hartal* that took place on 6 April was hugely successful in the Punjab. Jullundur and Amritsar both shut down completely. It put the wind up the British authorities across India; on that day Hindus and Muslims marched together, drank from the same cups, and in Delhi a prominent Hindu politician spoke in a mosque. Eerily, and the British felt very ominously, there was no violence at all, though in Amritsar a handbill was found by the police pinned to the Clock Tower calling on the people to 'Prepare to die and kill others'.[58] Back in his office late that day, Dyer got a full brief from his Brigade Major, and then set about acquiring information from his Sikh contacts in the city on the trouble that was afoot. He still had a network of old soldiers he could call upon for this, although there was on this occasion insufficient time to call many of them in to hear their views before events developed which made further consultation impossible. These informants were unlikely in any case to have been close to the political movements that were erupting, being by their nature loyal and conservative and unlikely to understand the political movements developing around them, so the benefit of their advice was limited.[59] Instructions arrived from Divisional Headquarters in Lahore to take steps to post guards on the stations, telegraph offices, bridges and culverts of the railway system that ran through the area; these were complied with.[60] The railway running through Dyer's area was of national importance, as the lines to the Frontier passed through the city.

Whilst Gandhi planned the next phase in the Rowlatt campaign, the white population began to fear that there was a widespread plot to overturn British rule. There was much loose talk of mutiny and rumours of attempts at the subversion of the troops and of death threats to Europeans, who began to fear for their lives. The military began to consider responses to a threat they did not understand. There was a general, if quiet, arming of the population, the civilian as well as the military, in early April. Captain Nisbet, writing of himself, recalls that at 'the beginning of the unrest in India … in Jullundur, he slept with a revolver under his pillow'.[61] The general feelings of foreboding were well placed, for Sir Michael O'Dwyer was about to light the match that set the tinder ablaze across his province.

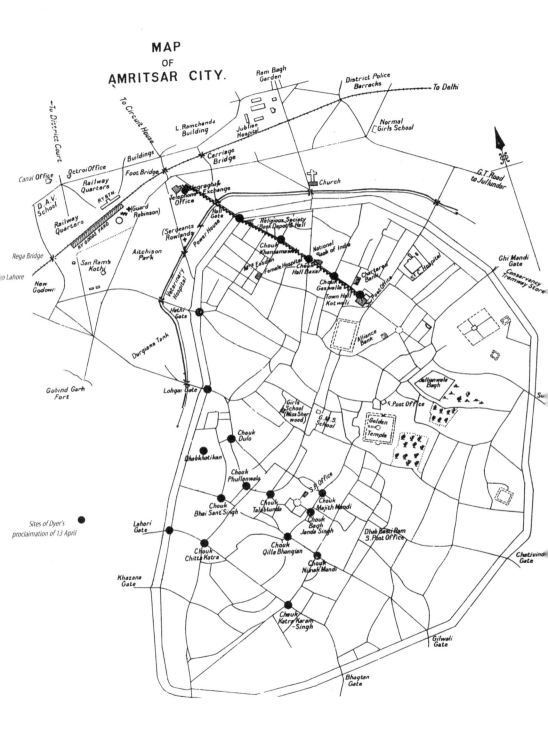

MAP
OF
AMRITSAR CITY.

To District Court

To Circuit House

L. Ramchands Building

Ram Bagh Garden

District Police Barracks

To Delhi

Normal Girls School

Canal Office

Octroi Office

Buildings

Carriage Bridge

Foot Bridge

Railway Quarters

RY. STN.

D.A.V. School

Railway Quarters

RY GOODS YARD

(Guard Robinson)

G.T. Road to Jullundar

Telegraph Office

Telephone Office

Hall Gate

Church

Religious Society Book Depot & Hall

Ghi Mandi Gate

Conservancy Tramway Store

(Sergeants Rowlands)

Power House

Rega Bridge

San Ram's Kothi

Aitchison Park

Veterinary Hospital

Chouk Khansamawali

Mrs Easdon

Female Hospital

Chouk Hall Bazar

National Bank of India

Chartered Bank

S.E.C. Hospital

To Lahore

New Godown

Hathi Gate

Chouk Gaswalla

Town Hall Kotwali

Post Office

Durgiana Tank

Alliance Bank

Gobind Garh Fort

Lohgal Gate

Girls School (Miss Sherwood)

G.M.S. School

Jallianwala Bagh

S. Post Office

Golden Temple

Su

Chouk Dula

Dhabkhatikan

Chouk Phullenwala

S.P. Office

Chouk Majith Mandi

Chouk Bhai Sant Singh

Chouk Talabtunda

Chouk Bagh Janda Singh

Dhab Basti Ram S. Post Office

Lahori Gate

Chouk Chitta Katra

Chouk Qilla Bhangian

Chouk Nisnak Mandi

Chativind Gate

Khazana Gate

Sites of Dyer's proclaimation of 13 April

Chouk Katra Karam-Singh

Gilwali Gate

Bhagtan Gate

15

Amritsar

Amritsar in 1919 was one of the principal cities of the Punjab with a population of 160,000, a centre of commerce, particularly for the cloth trade, and a mix of many races and beliefs: Sikh, Muslim and Hindu Punjabis, and outsiders like the Kashmiri Muslims and northern Indian Hindu merchants who had settled there to do business. The city was a major railway junction, but was principally known as the city of the Sikh's holiest site, the Golden Temple, which dated from the eighteenth century, when Sikhs had begun to gather there to celebrate their principal festival, Vaisakhi (or Baisakhi), their New Year's Day and a thanksgiving for harvest. On this day in 1699, the Sikh leader Guru Govind Singh had chosen the members of the first *khalsa*, his religious community.[1] After the British conquered the Punjab, they recognised the importance and sensitivity of the Golden Temple, and reserved the appointment of its manager in their gift.

Amritsar was in reality two cities: the old walled city with its civil population, a mass of narrow streets enveloping the Temple, congested with stalls and produce and lined with high, blank-faced houses shutting out the light; and the British cantonment outside the walls, spaciously laid out with wide boulevards lined with trees. The railway line segregated the new from the old as it did British master from Indian subject. The principal government sites were in the British lines; the only government buildings within the city were the municipal buildings alongside which was the police station, the *kotwali*. In the British lines was a small garrison, 184 infantrymen of 1st Garrison Battalion, the Somerset Light Infantry, commanded by Captain Massey, who acted as the Garrison Commander and answered to 45 Brigade at Jullundur. There were also about fifty mounted men of 12th Ammunition Column, Royal Field Artillery, under Captain Botting, who ran the ammunition depot there. At the Govindagarh Fort, an old Sikh fortification which lay outside the walls several miles from the cantonment, was half a company of Royal Garrison Artillery, numbering two officers and forty-four men under Lieutenant Shallow, who had charge of the fort. On the garrison strength there were also an officer and fifteen men of the Indian Defence Force, the territorial force consisting of European civilians. Amritsar was not of much military importance.[2]

The Deputy Commissioner, Miles Irving, had scarcely settled in since taking post as District Magistrate of Amritsar in February. He was by nature a retiring man, and throughout the events of that month he was to show as little confidence in himself as he inspired in others. The agitation of March had burst upon the city in his first month in post and had rattled him badly. Sir Michael O'Dwyer, the Lieutenant-Governor of the Punjab, treated him as peremptorily as he did most people; later, to the Hunter Committee, he condescendingly stated his opinion that Irving 'was not aware of the full situation'. Irving let himself be swayed in his handling of affairs by the old hands of the station, some of whom, grouped around the person of the Civil Surgeon, Lieutenant-Colonel Smith, were of reactionary views and had more of O'Dwyer's ear than Irving. During March and April, O'Dwyer and the Commissioner of Lahore Division, A.J.W. Kitchin, who was Irving's direct superior, issued instructions to Irving based as much on the information they were being fed by Smith and his friends as on Irving's own advice, and did not even consult the latter until the last minute about the fateful decision to deport leading agitators that was to start the violence in the city. O'Dwyer told the Hunter Committee:

> I may add that a day or two before the deportation Colonel Smith, the Civil Surgeon, who has a unique knowledge of Amritsar and great influence there, come [came] to see me at Lahore. I asked him if he thought the deportation would be likely to lead to any disturbance. His reply was that it would not, that the Khatris and Kashmiris [Hindus and Muslims] of Amritsar would not offer any open resistance.[3]

The Punjab Government began to lay orders against the principal leaders of the Amritsar agitation; on 29 March, Dr Satyapal was prohibited from public speaking, though he was a man who had hitherto only advocated non-violent civil disobedience and who had been the leader of the campaign to restore the sale of platform tickets to Indians at Amritsar station. Though he had served the Crown loyally in Aden as a lieutenant in the Army Medical Services during the war, he was a Hindu of strong beliefs, an active member of the *Arya Samaj* as well as of many Hindu charitable organisations. The restriction order did not prevent others speaking, and the atmosphere in the city worsened. British residents began to feel hostility towards them in the shops and streets, and ceased going into the city as a result.[4]

O'Dwyer decided to pre-empt Gandhi's *hartal* of 6 April by banning more Amritsar leaders from speaking in public. On 4 April, orders were served on Dr Kitchlew, Dina Nath, Swami Annubhava and Pandit Kotu Mal. Kitchlew, a Muslim barrister, was chairman of the Punjab *satyagraha sabha* and a rousing advocate of both political change and Gandhi's non-violent methods. He had been educated at Peterhouse, Cambridge, where he had been a friend of Jawarhalal Nehru, and also held a doctorate from Münster in Germany, which occasioned the British sneer that he was infected by German ideas. He was a prominent *khilafat* activist and the local National Congress leader, the man behind the invitation for the 1919 All India National Congress to be held in the city. Irving extracted a promise from the Congress leaders unaffected by the banning orders that the *hartal* would be cancelled, but Satyapal and Kitchlew, in private meetings, urged its continuance; so it went ahead as planned, peacefully and completely closing the city. The British garrison took no risks that day, parading through the city and picqueting the streets on the way to the church used by the Europeans, and they continued to be armed with rifles and ammunition when they attended church after that day in a fashion which recalled the days of the Mutiny. Yet, aside from the threatening handbill pasted to the Clock Tower and some verbal intimidation of Indian loyalists, nothing untoward occurred that day, though Irving took fright and began to see Satyapal and Kitchlew as representatives of some deeper conspiracy he did not understand. Anti-British feeling grew in the city; *tonga* drivers began to refuse to take English passengers or to pick them up at the station. Irving reported to Kitchin on 8 April:

> We cannot go on indefinitely with the policy of keeping out of the way, and congratulating ourselves that the mob has not forced us to interfere. Every time we do this the confidence of the mob increases; yet with our present force we have no alternative. I think we shall have to stand up for our authority sooner or later by prohibiting some strike or procession which endangers the public peace. But for this a really strong force will have to be brought in and we shall have to be ready to try conclusions to the end to see who governs Amritsar.

In the same report, Irving asked for reinforcements, as in any trouble 'we must abandon nine-tenths of the city to a riot'. This request for help, forwarded by the Punjab Government to the Army in the routine mail, reached the GOC of 16 Division only on the 11th, a day too late for it to do any good.[5] A day after he wrote this report, on the 9th, Irving was further shaken on Ram Naumi, the Hindu festival celebrating the birth of Ram, a holiday that this year saw unprecedented fraternisation by Hindus and Muslims in the streets and a parade which included Muslim boys dressed as Turkish soldiers who acted disrespectfully by clapping at the Deputy Commissioner when they passed him on the street. There was, however, still no violence, and the band accompanying the procession respectfully played 'God Save the King' when it saw Irving, who was saluted where he stood by all the different parts of the procession. A similar display of fraternisation took place in Jullundur that day, as it did in many places across India. The lack of violence added to the strangeness felt by the Europeans, who suspected subterranean currents but were unable to discern them, and this increased the tension. That day rumours began to circulate amongst the Europeans in Amritsar that there was a plot to kill them all on the 16th, when Gandhi was due to visit. To add to the anxiety, the city began to fill up with people arriving for the Baisakhi horse and cattle fair due to start on the 10th.[6]

O'Dwyer now decided to pre-empt the trouble he foresaw coming. All of his experience of service in the Punjab, where there was a tradition of nipping problems in the bud by decisive, aggressive action, and where he had himself successfully prevented trouble by pre-emptive arrests during earlier troubles, led him to act now. He later told the Hunter Committee: 'When confronted with a serious situation, I have generally found that prompt action is the best way of dealing with it.'[7] On the 9th, he ordered that Kitchlew and Satyapal be deported from Amritsar to another district within the Punjab. This was despite the fact that there was no suggestion they had broken their restriction orders; O'Dwyer later tried to make the case that they had evaded them, but the Government of India's evidence to the Hunter Committee belies this. Irving made no objection to carrying out the deportation and did not foresee that this act was in itself potentially highly inflammatory. Nor did anyone in Lahore. Both the Punjab Government and the 16th Division believed that the next day for which they would need to take precautions would be the 13th, the next Sunday holiday, and saw no need for anything to be done before that day. Accordingly, on the 10th, the 16th Division ordered the 45th Brigade to send one hundred Muslim troops to Amritsar as reinforcements to be ready for trouble on the 13th. From his position on the spot at Amritsar, Captain Massey was not so sanguine about what was about to happen, and he alone had the sense to telegraph to Lahore asking for reinforcements as soon as he was told of the planned arrests, which was late on the night of the 9th.[8] This was too late for the Army to respond, and in any case General Beynon took no immediate action on Massey's telegram, as he believed it was alarmist, merely passing it on to Dyer at Jullundur to action if he thought fit, and promising to send at some unspecified time some artillery troops from Lahore to bolster up the garrison of the fort.

At the time he ordered the deportations, O'Dwyer ordered the arrest of Gandhi, who was about to visit the Punjab. He had tried to persuade the Government of India to have Gandhi interned, but they had ruled this out, so he was taken off an inbound train at the railway station at Palwal on the borders of the province on the 9th and escorted back to Bombay.[9] As news of this action spread, it inflamed many parts of India.

In the Punjab, however, it was the arrest of Kitchlew and Satyapal on the morning of the 10th that sparked the conflagration. Fearing to arrest them openly, Irving invited them to a meeting at his bungalow and had them arrested there. They were then spirited away by car to Dharamsala in the hills, escorted by Mr Rehill, the Amritsar Superintendent of Police, an unfortunate choice of escort which left the Amritsar police force in the charge of his deputy, Plomer, throughout the turmoil which was to follow. The two men's attendants took the news of their arrest back into the city and within minutes Amritsar was in turmoil. About 50,000 people streamed out of the city towards the British lines, clamouring to see the Deputy Commissioner to demand the release of their leaders. The collision came at midday. Captain Massey, under written orders from the Deputy Commissioner to prevent any crowds crossing the railway, had placed troops on the bridges across the railway line, accompanied by three junior European magistrates. The crowd surged up against these, pushing them back off a footbridge by sheer weight of numbers. For some reason, a detachment of mounted men under Lieutenant Dickie had been placed on the narrow bridge, instead of infantry, and the horses would not stand. Assistant Commissioner Beckett, the magistrate with them, took immediate flight and galloped back to the lines to rescue his wife, spreading consternation as he went.[10] Back on the bridge, stones flew, the troops panicked and opened fire, and several people were killed. The crowd turned into a mob. Frustrated in their aim of crossing the bridge, surged in several directions, some towards the station further down the line and others back to the city. The station goods yard and sheds were looted and wrecked, and when the crowd found a British railwayman, Guard Robinson, sheltering there they beat him to death with *lathis*. Part of the mob reached the station and had to be driven off the platform by men of the 54th, just in time to save Station Master Bennett, who had been badly injured. The subadar in command of the 54th's detachment, Zardad Khan, bayoneted a man dragging the telegraph master, Mr Pinto, from his bedroom by his neck. Men of the Somersets under 2nd Lieutenant Brown opened fire near the station and drove the crowd off. Further down the track, Sergeant Rowlands, the garrison electrician, who had gone out to repair telegraph wires, was caught on his own in the open whilst trying to get back to safety and was beaten to death within sight of the fort.

The crowd which returned to the city flooded down the main street, the Hall Bazaar, and attacked the three British banks that stood there. Three British managers of two of the banks, Stewart and Scott of the National Bank and Thomson of the Alliance Bank, were inside, as they had been given no warning to stay at home that morning, for Irving's precautions had not extended to the non-official population.[11] They were cornered in their offices, attacked and thrown into the street where they were covered with their own furniture, doused with kerosene, then set alight. Ross and Thompson, the managers of the neighbouring Chartered Bank, were saved by their Indian clerks, who concealed them from the mob and sought help from the *kotwali* next door, where seventy-five Indian police were holed up. The police had been stationed there without any British officer in charge, and sat supinely by as the banks and town hall next door to them were looted and torched, and as churches, missionary buildings and all the post offices in the town were destroyed. Crowds made another attempt to cross the railway near the station at 2 p.m. but were repulsed with fire, this time after some warning. The garrison was severely stretched by this activity, but had the luck to be reinforced by a party of 260 men of the 1st Battalion, 9th Gurkhas led by Captain Crampton, who were moving their depot with its staff, recruits and families from Dehra Dun to Peshawar, and whose train was passing through the station when the mobs were by the line. They were detrained to help; as they had no rifles, one hundred of them were armed from the armoury in the fort. At the station, there was also a party of six men of the Londons, who had been waiting for a train when the riots began, and who were also absorbed into the garrison. In all that day, some ten Indians were killed and over thirty injured by the troops, who fired seventy-three rounds.[12]

Throughout the afternoon and evening, mobs sought out Europeans in the city. Mrs Easdon, a lady doctor at the Zenana Hospital, escaped from a mob by hiding in a closet; she was smuggled out of the city that night. Miss Marcella Sherwood, Superintendent of the Mission Day School for Girls, was caught by a mob whilst she was cycling round the city to close her five schools and get her girls home. She was assaulted in a narrow street named the Kucha Kurrichhan and, after several doors of houses where she sought refuge had been slammed in her face, was pulled to the ground by her hair, beaten, kicked and left for dead. She was rescued by some local Indians, including the father of one of her pupils, who bravely hid her from members of the mob who were searching for her and smuggled her to safety at the fort that night.[13] Colonel Smith took his ambulance into the city to rescue Europeans from the schools and hospitals, but was stoned and eventually had to desist. Those left behind managed to make their way to the *kotwali*. By the afternoon, Amritsar city had passed out of the control of the civil authorities, though all of the cantonment area was still in British hands. That evening, all the women and children from the lines were evacuated to the fort, where they were guarded by the Gurkhas, and where they were to remain for over two weeks, four hundred women, children and servants in unsanitary and cramped conditions, some grieving for dead husbands and fathers, many in terror of their lives. Gerard Wathen, the principal of the Khalsa College in the city, went there to see them: 'Never did I see horror so grimly written on any face except those who had come from the trenches … Most of them were weeping, many from sheer fatigue, and no one knew what the future would bring.'[14] The garrison and police held the railway line, but across the tracks the city smouldered and crowds carried on looting the damaged buildings until the evening.[15] Standpipes were smashed and the water supply was rumoured to be poisoned, so it was shut off that evening by the Municipal Engineer. As news of the outbreak spread in the country around Amritsar, mobs began to cut the telegraph and telephone wires along the railway lines connecting the city with the outside world.[16]

Captain Massey managed to get a telegram asking for reinforcements through to Dyer's Headquarters at 4 p.m., just before the wires were cut, and the 16th Division in Lahore got a message through to Dyer at the same time, as the

Government of the Punjab, warned by Irving that the city was out of his hands, had asked for military help. General Beynon ordered Dyer to send one hundred British and one hundred Indian troops immediately. Amritsar got another telegram through to Jullundur at 5 p.m. giving details of the events there, and this prompted Dyer to order an additional one hundred Indian troops to entrain.[17] He and Captain Briggs drove to the station and ordered the station master to commandeer the first available train for the troops; frustratingly, there was none available until after midnight. They then drove to the barracks of the 25th Londons and the 2nd/151st Infantry to give orders for the move, returning via the station, whence they wired Amritsar (the telegram having to go via Ludhiana and Lahore as the direct wires to Amritsar had been cut by then) that reinforcements were on the way. The troops assembled at the station, where Briggs saw them off at 1 a.m. on the 11th. They were a mixed company of the Londons commanded by the OC of A Company, Major F.S. Clarke, with 130 men of the 2nd/151st Infantry and a hundred men drawn from all the Frontier Force Regiment Depots in Jullundur, the majority from the 59th. A medical officer with a medical team was added. Briggs gave Clarke written instructions to get to Amritsar by any means and at all costs.[18]

That night the Dyers had guests at Flagstaff House for dinner. They carried on with the evening in order to keep up the appearance of normality, though Dyer and his staff took turns sitting by the phone. News had already reached Jullundur city of the events in Amritsar and there was some excitement in the bazaar. Overnight, telegraph and telephone lines were cut all around Amritsar, and railway tracks were pulled up on the lines to Lahore and Jullundur. The Bombay Mail arrived safely through Amritsar, but officers onboard it reported that crowds were assembling along the line shaking their fists at them. Railway police guards onboard the Calcutta Mail which arrived later said they had fired on a party trying to uproot the Lahore track near Amritsar, inadvertently saving the city waterworks which was about to be attacked. Railway stations at Bhagtanwala and Chheharta on the lines near Amritsar were attacked by mobs. The former was wrecked, and, as the train carrying the Jullundur reinforcements made its slow way to Amritsar, the troops looked out on looted railway buildings and wagons, and had to detrain several times where the line was torn up. It was repaired by an armoured train manned by men of the Indian Defence Force which travelled ahead of them. The slow progress meant that they didn't arrive in Amritsar until 5.15 a.m.[19]

The reinforcements which 16 Division was sending from Lahore (175 men of the 1st Battalion, 124th Baluch and 125 men of the 2/6th Battalion, Royal Sussex, commanded by the 1st/124th's second-in-command, Major MacDonald) got away before the party from Amritsar, leaving Lahore at 8.55 p.m. on the 10th, and so reached Amritsar very swiftly between 9.30 and 10.30 p.m. that night. MacDonald took over from Massey as the Officer Commanding in the city.[20] Another party from Lahore had preceded him by road: the Lahore Commissioner, Kitchin; Dyer's old friend Mr Donald, who was by now the Deputy Inspector-General of Police for the Punjab; and Mr Coode, Superintendent of Telegraphs, had been sent down by Sir Michael O'Dwyer. Kitchin now exercised control from the railway station where he had told Irving to establish his office; both by his mere presence and by his deliberate exercise of authority, Kitchin had superseded Irving to all intents and purposes, and seems to have ignored him for the most part from now on, issuing instructions in his own name. His description of his first action sets the tone for what followed: 'I fetched him [Irving] down to the Railway Station and established Headquarters at that place.'[21] Kitchin's evidence to the Hunter Committee later showed that his and O'Dwyer's adherence to the Punjab tradition extended only as far as the taking of rapid and draconian pre-emptive action. It did not extend to trusting the man on the spot, though Kitchin shied away from saying so:

> Question: On that very day you handed over charge. May I take it you deprived the Deputy Commissioner of all his authority?
>
> Answer: At the time I had no such intention ... It grew into that. It became that ultimately ... The Deputy Commissioner continued to exercise his powers.

The situation in which Major MacDonald found himself was thus one where the lines of civil authority were already growing confused, and this was now compounded as Kitchin verbally handed over control of the city to him. This was more than a request for military assistance to the civil power. Kitchin was not, however, at all clear in his instructions as to what he was handing over and what he expected MacDonald to do, and he seems to have intended to continue to exercise his own authority in civil matters, though he didn't say so at the time.

> I told him that the situation was beyond our control and that he must take such immediate steps as the military situation demanded ... Of course to act in consultation with me. On the 10th, I handed over charge to Major MacDonald of the military situation. He would take such steps as were required. I said nothing about civil administration ...
>
> Question: As regards the civil administration, the Deputy Commissioner was still in charge?
>
> Answer: Yes ... As a matter of fact my authority did not cease, because I continued to direct the affairs.[22]

It is, however, from that moment that martial law existed *de facto* in Amritsar. Captain Massey had refused to try to re-enter the city before reinforcements arrived, but just before midnight, in the midst of a dust storm which added its misery to the city, MacDonald, with a mixed party of two platoons each of the Sussex and the 1st/124th, marched into the city as far as the *kotwali* and rescued the four Europeans trapped there. He was accompanied only by Plomer, the Deputy Superintendent of Police, and not by any civil magistrate. Kitchin's excuse for this lack of civil presence was paper thin: 'I did not wish to embarrass the military officer in command with the presence of a civil officer senior to himself.' The troops returned at 3 a.m. with the bodies of the three murdered bank managers; they had found two of their corpses still in the street. The city was now quiet, the streets were deserted, but nothing was done that night to re-establish control.[23] Kitchin remained at the station overnight, and began what was to be a continual goading of the military to take violent measures against the populace. He pressed upon MacDonald the use of 'all military force' to prevent further processions, and wired O'Dwyer in Lahore that 'we intend to prohibit and break up such processions with military force. I have informed Officer Commanding that he is in charge and can use all military force.' The policy was approved the next morning by Sir Michael O'Dwyer, who promised to send aeroplanes and armoured cars. He asked General Beynon to do so.[24]

The reinforcements from Jullundur arrived in the dawn and Major Clarke handed them over to MacDonald before returning to Jullundur to brief Dyer about 'an unsatisfactory situation which the civil authorities had given up attempting to control'. The reinforcements relieved the garrison troops who were still guarding the railway line, and picquets were now also posted at all the entrances to the city. From this time, all exits from the city were in British hands.[25] At 7 a.m., two aeroplanes flew over the city, then landed on the open ground outside it, and an armoured train arrived a few hours later from Lahore carrying a party of twenty men of the Royal Garrison Artillery to reinforce the fort. Two armoured cars arrived during the day.[26] Irving, firmly under Kitchin's thumb, held a conference in a railway carriage at the station. Various hard-line courses of action were discussed, including bombing the city, as the aghast Gerard Wathen later told his wife:

> At 8 a.m. on Friday – Gerard heard that the commissioner was coming over and the troops were to march through the city, firing on every one they saw. He saw what a frightful blunder this would be, as of course hundreds of innocent people were out to look at the damage. He tore off to the station and for an hour argued with the authorities and at last got them to see that they must give warning, now that the actual mob had dispersed. The time appointed was 2 o'clock. If at that hour there was any meetings or crowds they would be immediately fired on … At 2 aeroplanes were to ascend and if the crowds still persisted bombs were to be dropt.[27]

Bombs and machine guns for the aircraft were in fact requested from Lahore by Major MacDonald in his last act as Officer Commanding Amritsar at 9.30 p.m.

that night. As a result of this conference, a proclamation was issued by Irving (though under Kitchin's instructions) prohibiting gatherings. It stated:

> The troops have orders to restore order in Amritsar and to use all force necessary. No gatherings of persons nor processions of any sorts will be allowed. All gatherings will be fired on. Any person leaving the city in groups of more than four will be fired on. Respectable persons should keep indoors.[28]

This was taken by the military as the instruction it was clearly meant to be, and was recorded as such in Jullundur in the brigade war diary:

> 0700 hours … troops received orders from Deputy Commissioner to restore order and use all force necessary, no gatherings or processions were allowed and all gatherings were to be fired on.[29]

It is certain that this entry, and probably the message itself, though this does not survive, was read by Dyer, and in the light of the lack of instructions he subsequently received from 16 Division, it is probable that he took this instruction as his mission at Amritsar. The proclamation was not circulated in the city, despite its lethal provisions, as Irving could think of no means of doing so. Instead, it was handed to a group of lawyers who visited the station, and to students of the Khalsa College. Kitchin told the Hunter Committee:

> I issued a proclamation on the morning of the 11th.
>
> *Question*: You simply said that you handed it over to some people who came to you?
>
> *Answer*: Yes.
>
> *Question*: That you think is sufficient?
>
> *Answer*: There was not sufficient time to make it known to the people of Amritsar. It was handed over to the citizens afterwards. College students were sent for … I asked the Principal of the Khalsa College who was thereabouts to send in his own students to tell the people that we considered that a state of war had broken out and they must settle down.[30]

The lawyers to whom Irving entrusted his proclamation had called on behalf of the families of those who had died the previous day, requesting permission to bury the corpses outside the city. Kitchin allowed this, and Irving issued the lawyers a note which stated:

> People will be allowed to bury their dead in number about 200 provided –
>
> (1)   Only Sultanwind and Chatiwind Gates used.
>
> (2)   All over by 2 p.m.

(3) At 2 p.m., warning by bugle.

(4) After 15 minutes fire.

(5) No *lathis*.

Miles Irving 11.4.19

The lawyers read out this note inside the city gates, and the instruction was, in the event, obeyed to the letter. Gerard Wathen's Indian professors also went through the city issuing Irving's warnings. The large crowds accompanying the bodies stopped inside the city, and, though the planes went aloft at 2 p.m., no bombs were dropped.[31]

Major MacDonald objected both to the means of the proclamation and to any attempt to force the military to interfere with the funerals.[32] Kitchin told the Hunter Committee: 'Major MacDonald said it was insufficient. He himself objected that the proclamation was not sufficiently known to the people, and he wished it better known.' That afternoon Kitchin wired Lahore: 'Officer Commanding Troops has given permission and has said that he will allow crowds to disperse. He does not want wholesale slaughter, which would be the result of earlier interference.' MacDonald waited until the funerals, which had to be held outside the city walls, had dispersed, which they all did peacefully. While this was going on, some of the British women and children were evacuated by train to Rawalpindi and the British buried their dead at the European cemetery.[33] Both sides regarded their dead as martyrs. The Indian dead were buried with 'colossal heaps of roses that have been withering due to the suspension of business'.[34] When MacDonald marched to the *kotwali* after the funerals with one hundred men, and posted some of them at junctions along the Hall Bazaar, the main road into the centre of the city, he found roses strewn in the streets and amongst the ruins. From this time, the main street and the part of the city which contained the municipal buildings were back in military hands.

Kitchin left Amritsar immediately after the funerals and before MacDonald marched into the city. He made his thinking clear at the inquiry: 'There was no time to ask the Magistrate to go and give the orders for firing. They would go and do it. I expected a fight that day.' He clearly expected the military to storm the town – 'I also advised that a party should go into the city at once and fight their way to the Kotwali' – and wanted the civilian officials out of the way while they did it. He was to be disappointed in the result, for the troops met no opposition.[35] Before he drove back to Lahore, Kitchin telephoned through a message indicating that the funerals had passed off quietly: 'the city is quiet and the shops will reopen soon. A message has come from the heads of the *Dharmsalas* that all is well.' He did not feel secure about the reliability of the Indian troops; along with others in the cantonment, he feared that the Indian soldiers would be subverted, though there was never any real sign of this, and he insisted that they be split up in small groups (which was just the way to ensure that they could be approached more easily had there been any attempt to subvert them).[36] Despite the fact that on the 11th there was no violence at all in Amritsar, the police made no attempt to reassert themselves, and were not to do so until the 14th. The situation remained very tense; the *hartal* was maintained in the city, intimidation of suspected loyalists occurred, rumours of revolts in other towns spread, and respectable citizens of the town were forced to make arrangements for the patrolling of their own streets. Ironically, Irving took this as a sign of continued disobedience.[37]

Commissioner Kitchin had reached Lahore later that afternoon, and briefed the Lieutenant-Governor.[38] He had been severely angered by MacDonald's resistance to his demands to take immediate and drastic action. He persuaded O'Dwyer to ask General Beynon to replace MacDonald with someone more willing to act aggressively. General Beynon ordered MacDonald's Commanding Officer, Lieutenant-Colonel Morgan, a man whose disposition was a good deal more fiery than that of his second-in-command, to go to Amritsar and take over himself.[39] Morgan described what took place:

> MacDonald had been less than forty-eight hours in Amritsar when I was summoned to the Divisional office. I was shown a letter from Kitchin, the commissioner, to General Beynon, saying 'Major Macdonald has done nothing to quell the rebellion. Please send an officer who is not afraid to act.' General Beynon decided that I was the officer. I was ordered to proceed as soon as possible to Amritsar ... 'Amritsar is in the hands of the rebels. It's your job to get it back.'[40]

Despite this, Dyer later claimed in his report to 16 Division that at 2 p.m. that afternoon, as the funerals were taking place, his Headquarters received a telegram from 16 Division telling him to go to Amritsar and take charge.[41] Yet there is no record of any instruction issued to Dyer, nor indeed of the telegram which he states ordered him to go there. Whilst it seems difficult to believe that he would have been brazen enough to report later to 16 Division that they had sent him a telegram they did not in fact send, there is considerable room for doubt that he was in fact ordered to go. The only evidence that he was sent there comes from his own, and his own Brigade Major's, statements. Contrary to what was normal practice, Dyer's Headquarters log makes no mention of a telegram, nor does the log of 16 Division, though the latter is careful to record the dispatch of Major Morgan to Amritsar at 8 p.m. that night. The ordering of Morgan to Amritsar after the dispatch of Brigadier-General Dyer calls into question why 16 Division would have simultaneously sent two commanders there, and particularly why the subsequent commander was junior to the first. Morgan later accounted for this by the confusion of the day, and stated that no one knew where Dyer was at

14. The Hall Gate, Amritsar. (*British Library*)

15. Iron footbridge over the railway, Amritsar, the scene of the start of the riots o[10 April 1919. (*British Library*)

16. The Jallianwala Bagh, 1919. (*British Library*)

7. The entrance to the Jallianwala Bagh through which Dyer marched his force, 1919. (*British Library*)

18. The firing point inside the Jallianwala Bagh, 1919. (*British Library*)

19. Inside the Jallianwala Bagh, 1919. (*British Library*)

20. The Kucha Kurrichhan, the site of the assault on Miss Sherwood, which wa closed by the crawling order. (*British Library*)

21. Men of the 25th Londons enforcing the crawling order. (*British Library*)

22. General Dyer lands at Southampton, 3 May 1920. He told the reporter who met him, 'And now I am told to go for doing my duty – my horrible, dirty duty'.

23. Mohandas Karamchand Gandhi.

24. Jawarharlal Nehru.

25. Sir Michael O'Dwyer.

26. Edwin Montagu.

27. Dyer's funeral procession passes the Guards Memorial, Horseguards, London, 28 July 1927. (*National Army Museum*)

28. Dyer's coffin, draped with the Union Jack that had flown over his Headquarters at Amritsar, is carried on a field gun and escorted by the Irish Guards. (*National Army Museum*)

the time he was himself posted there because the telegraph lines were down. There is no record, however, of any lines being cut between Jullundur and Lahore until the next day, the 12th. General Beynon, in his report to Army Headquarters, seems to have chosen his words carefully when stating what he had ordered, and what had merely occurred:

> (25) Owing to the importance of the Command at Amritsar, I deemed it advisable to send a more senior officer, and accordingly Major Morgan, DSO, Commanding, 1–124th Baluchis, proceeded to Amritsar on the night of the 11th April to take over command there.

> (26) *Arrival of Brigadier-General Dyer, C.B., at Amritsar* … General Dyer had, however, arrived at Amritsar at 21.00 hours and assumed personal command, in addition to establishing his Brigade Headquarters there.[42]

It looks very much as though Dyer made his own decision to move to Amritsar, and that he sought to conceal this later. His record in Sistan is there to remind us that he was not above manipulating the record in his own favour, even in this brazen fashion. If he did so here, however, and in fact made his own decision to go to Amritsar, this was not in itself a bad decision. Amritsar was the principal town in his area, reports from it spoke of open rebellion, and it would have been natural for him to go to the place which now seemed to be the crucial point in his area of command. Dyer could not have been criticised for taking command himself. In the light of what subsequently occurred, however, he may have felt it best to indicate that in going to Amritsar he was just doing his duty and obeying orders.

With or without instructions, Dyer and his Brigade Major called upon the Commissioner of Jullundur to ensure he was content with them leaving the city. Jullundur was closed by a peaceful *hartal* that day to protest at Gandhi's arrest, and troops had been deployed to the civil lines and the railway station, so this was not a foregone conclusion, but the Commissioner was persuaded that the situation in Amritsar was more grave. Dyer was nevertheless worried about an outbreak at Jullundur and pressed 16 Division to send British troops there to replace the Londons he had dispatched as reinforcements to Amritsar. 16 Division sent the 1/4th Battalion The Queen's from Ferozepore as soon as they could be moved. Lieutenant-Colonel Hynes of the Londons was again left in charge at Jullundur, and Dyer left by car at 6 p.m. with Captain Briggs and Captain Southey, a medical officer, and his bodyguard, Sergeant Anderson of the Londons, arriving three hours later in Amritsar.[43] Before leaving, Dyer took time to talk to his son; he told Ivon that Muslims and Hindus had united, and that 'there is a very big show coming … I must leave your mother and Alice in this house, although there is the same danger from Jullundur city. You will sleep under a tree beside the verandah near your mother and cousin. There will be Indian guards at both gates.'[44]

When he arrived at the railway station in Amritsar, Dyer found a tumult which he proceeded to restore to order. Finding a European crowd of 'would-be fugitives clamouring for railway transport', he said: 'Gentlemen, why are you here? Your place is to protect the ladies. You will report to me.' Inside he found Miles Irving and Plomer, the Deputy Superintendent of Police, along with Major MacDonald and Captain Massey. Irving looked to Dyer 'like a man broken by fatigue, anxiety, and the weight of responsibilities too heavy for his shoulders'.[45] Dyer was not at all impressed by Irving, and it is unlikely that he saw his own role as anything but that of replacing Irving from that time on. After a brief conference, Irving handed Dyer control; as Dyer put it, he 'gave over charge to me'. The vagueness about what powers were being handed over persisted. As Irving later said:

> I should regard myself as the adviser of the Military Commander, but I was, of course, carrying out a good number of duties of which he had no cognizance, and I was also reporting to my own official superiors. But I could do nothing against his orders and could not do very much without them.[46]

Dyer was not the sort of man to put too fine a shade of interpretation on exactly what powers he had, and from now on viewed himself as the supreme authority in Amritsar. As he put it to the Hunter Committee, 'The law was handed over to me at the time … The time for giving aid to the civil power had gone.' Irving handed him the proclamation issued that morning and signed by himself.[47]

Dyer automatically assumed command of all military forces from Major MacDonald, who returned to Lahore the next day. By now, there were 1185 troops in Amritsar. Half an hour after Dyer's arrival, Lieutenant-Colonel Morgan arrived from Lahore and met Dyer, whom he was surprised to see, but who prevailed upon him to remain to command the Indian troops. He recalled Dyer saying: 'I am the senior officer here so must take command.' Morgan said: 'My regiment is at Lahore so I had better return there', to which Dyer replied: 'I would like you to remain with me for the present.' True to form, Dyer was coopting an officer from another command without seeking any authority to do so.[48]

After this conference, at just gone midnight, Dyer and the Deputy Commissioner entered the city together, taking along Captain Massey and an escort of fifty troops, visiting the *kotwali* and bringing the Indian City Superintendent of Police, Ashraf Khan, back with them for discussions. As they marched through the city, they passed fires still burning in the looted banks. They returned to find that all the telegraph lines around the city had been cut. A second conference was held in a railway carriage in the early hours of the morning, and arrangements made for arrests to be made later that day, the 12th. Ashraf Khan briefed Dyer on what he described as the lawlessness then prevalent in the city, a lawlessness he was doing nothing about curbing as he and his men had remained huddled in the *kotwali*. He also alleged that the rebellion was being spread to surrounding villages by agents from the city, and that large numbers were coming into the city to form a *danda fauj* to drive the British out. There was, of course, no way that this was possible at the time as the troops had held all the gates since that morning. Before closing the conference at 2 a.m., Dyer ordered the electricity supply to the city to be cut off. Something that had seemingly not registered with any of them was that there had been no violence at all during the previous day.[49]

The night was short, and by 7 a.m. Dyer was moving his Headquarters out of the station to the open space of the Ram Bagh outside the city. This was a spacious park with many trees giving shade to the troops. In the centre of it was a lodge built by the Sikh Maharajah Ranjit Singh which provided Dyer a large and attractive building for his Headquarters and for the officers' mess for his force, one which was well away from the civil offices. He was clearly unimpressed by the arrangements that had been in place hitherto and was making a very visible statement that things were to be done differently now that he was in charge. He reduced the number of troops deployed on picquet duties along the railway line in order to have more forces available for 'a striking force', and his own Headquarters arrived from Jullundur during the day.[50]

News from elsewhere, of destruction of the railway and of telegraph and telephone wires, and of a further *hartal* at Jullundur, was coming in all the time now, adding to the tension and casting a black light on all local events.[51] At this point, Commissioner Kitchin returned with Mr Donald, bringing information he claimed to have picked up on the road from Lahore. Once again almost playing the role of *agent provocateur*, he told Dyer that rumours were spreading fast. 'I was advised on the road that the trouble would go further unless Amritsar riots were stopped at once.'[52] He passed on a rumour that two hundred armed Sikhs from the Manjha, the countryside surrounding Amritsar, were about to raid the city. This was despite the fact that he had driven down from Lahore that morning with no obstacle to the passage of his unescorted car. The Commissioner added that he 'did not put much reliance on this report'. Indeed it was untrue, though it did persuade Dyer to order the police to patrol against anyone seeking to enter the city.[53] As he had done before with Major MacDonald, Kitchin was making efforts to fire up the new Officer Commanding troops; he could not have been aware that his efforts in this direction were more than redundant, for he was dealing with a very different man. Interestingly, he later telephoned Lahore to give Sir Michael O'Dwyer a quieter picture than that which he had given Dyer: 'Troops have gone into the city to occupy and make arrests. General Dyer from Jullundur commanding. No news yet. Village peaceful. Headquarters now Rambagh. Message can be sent from station.'[54]

Using an aeroplane, Dyer discovered that crowds were gathering at the Sultanwind Gate, which was on the other side of the city. Typically, he decided to march immediately to deal with this, not knowing that it was another gathering of funeral processions for those who had died of their wounds from the firing on the 10th.[55] He was not corrected by the civil authorities or by the police in his belief that this gathering was another outbreak of the agitation; it is possible that they did not understand this either. If they did, they preferred to leave him in ignorance. Dyer assembled a large force of 125 British and 310 Indian troops, and with the two armoured cars rushed them around the northern perimeter of the city at about 10 a.m. He again took with him Irving and Captain Massey, and this time Mr Donald went along too. They reached the Sultanwind Gate and found the crowd milling about there, as had been reported.[56] Its members 'were most truculent and spat on the ground at us. "Hindi and Mussleman Ki Jai" was being shouted and it was with great difficulty that the mob was dispersed.' Dyer later made the point at the Hunter Commission that he had dispersed this crowd without violence, indicating that this was a measure of his restraint. He said: 'We had a little difficulty in dispersing them. So I considered the advisability of opening fire upon them. I thought it would not be quite right and that perhaps I had better issue a proclamation personally before I took that drastic measure.' Equally, the incident showed that crowds in the city could be dispersed without the use of force; Irving did not agree that there had been 'great difficulty' in clearing this crowd. There was no violence or even stone throwing, and Irving simply asked the crowds to disperse, which they eventually, if reluctantly, did. He later recalled that:

> A small crowd was repeatedly warned by me and Mr Donald to disperse but did not do so, and an unassailable legal ground for firing was given, but no one thought of doing so as no danger was threatened. And on the same day large crowds were streaming back from the mosques outside the city in defiance of orders but were not fired on for the same reason.[57]

The febrile atmosphere is made clearer in an account K.D. Malaviya had a few months later when he encountered a Mr Somdatt, who was one of those who returned from outside the city having attended the burials of the dead. He came across Irving and some military officers he did not recognise:

> The soldiers, however, were seated in the 'kneeling load' position pointing their rifles towards the crowd as if about to fire at it … Somdatt who was then in the last line found himself confronted by the Deputy Commissioner holding a loaded pistol in his hand. He almost lost his wits as the Deputy Commissioner raised the deadly weapon against his forehead and asked him to surrender. This gallant operation having been performed, Somdatt was asked to confess that he was Ratto [a man wanted for the crimes of the

10th] … The Deputy Commissioner and Mr Plomer were very insolent to Somdatt, calling him a liar. Plomer said that this was not the last funeral he would witness.[58]

The crowd dispersed and the force marched on into the city as far as the *kotwali*, now at a slower pace. The subaltern in charge of the Gurkha contingent, Lieutenant McCallum, remembered: 'As we went through the narrow streets angry faces looked down on us from the roof tops.' The column stopped occasionally 'to proclaim by beat of drum that any assembly over five was illegal'. The route was one not so far traversed by troops, and, after reaching the *kotwali*, the force sent out patrols which, guided by the police, made arrests of suspects. They searched houses and chased those who had escaped through the narrow streets, managing to grab two of the men they sought, Bugga and Dina Nath, both wanted for the murders of the 10th. The surviving bank managers were taken to see the ruins of their banks. Without success, the police tried to persuade the shopkeepers to open their shops; they would only do so, they said, when the two arrested leaders, Kitchlew and Satyapal, were returned to the city. Dyer's intention was to impress on the inhabitants that law and order had returned: 'I determined with a view to showing the inhabitants that I had sufficient military force to force them to law and order and also to arrest certain ringleaders.' The force returned to the Ram Bagh with their prisoners by 2 p.m., leaving the Gurkhas to guard the *kotwali* overnight, and on the way home down the Hall Bazaar passing the picquets placed there the day before by Major MacDonald. Once back in the Ram Bagh, they chained those they had arrested to a tree.[59]

In his palatial Headquarters, Dyer sat down to dictate to his Brigade Major the proclamation which he now saw was needed, as no proclamation of the assumption of control by the military, or indeed of any new regulations, had so far been given to the population. Known as Proclamation No. 1, this was not an informative notice:

> The inhabitants of Amritsar are hereby warned that if they will cause damage to any property or will commit any acts of violence in the environs of Amritsar, it will be taken for granted that such acts are due to the incitement in Amritsar City, and offenders will be punished according to military law. All meetings and gatherings are hereby prohibited and will be dispersed at once under Military Law.[60]

Briggs gave this to the Deputy Commissioner for translation and publication, but it was not promulgated in any way, for reasons similar to those which had prevented the publication of Irving's proclamation the day before. Irving later tried to maintain that this new proclamation had been read out during the morning of the 13th, but Dyer denied this.

Commissioner Kitchin, who remained at Amritsar throughout the 12th, also claimed to have issued new instructions that day: 'I issued orders prohibiting all gatherings in the streets and saying that all assemblies of more than five persons would be liable for dispersion without further warning.' Nobody else seems to have noticed that he did so (unless this is the proclamation remembered by Lieutenant McCallum); there is no copy extant of any such order, and no one mentioned it in reports or in the subsequent enquiry. Dyer certainly took no notice of it, and it is from this time that we can date the cessation of all civilian control over the military, and so over what was happening in Amritsar.[61]

The day of the 12th was a very busy one. Parties of troops were dispatched to show a presence in the neighbouring towns of Chheharta and Tarn Taran, and to rescue lady missionaries in a country school in Ashrapur. There were difficulties arranging for supply for the troops, as the locals would not sell to them, a problem which increased as more reinforcements arrived, this time of fifty sabres from the 11th Lancers at Jullundur. In the city, shops remained shut, but after the funeral crowds dispersed in the morning there were no more public gatherings that day. A meeting of the leaders of the agitation was held in the Hindu Sabha High School at 4 o'clock; they decided to observe the *hartal* until their leaders were released. Later that evening, another meeting was held in the Dhab Khatikan Mohalla where Hans Raj, an aide to Dr Kitchlew, announced that there would be a public meeting in the Jallianwala Bagh at 4 p.m. the next day, the 13th. He announced that this was to be organised by Dr Mohammed Bashir. It would be held under the chairmanship of an elderly and respected High Court lawyer, Lala Kanhyalal Bhatia, who was a Congress leader, but who was later to deny that he had been aware of this. A series of resolutions were drafted to be debated at the meeting. These show that without doubt this was to be a political meeting, but also make it clear that it was a meeting called not for a revolutionary or violent purpose but to pursue a political agenda similar to those of the agitation of the previous few months. The resolutions framed for debate the next day were:

1. This grand meeting of the inhabitants of Amritsar looks with extreme indignation and disapproval on all those revolutionary actions which are the inevitable result of the inappropriate and inequitable attitude on the part of the Government, and entertains apprehension that this despotic conduct of the Government might prove deleterious to the British Government.

2. This grand meeting of the inhabitants of Amritsar strongly protests against the despotic attitude which the Government adopted when the subject-people within the domain of law invited the attention of the British subjects by means of the only effective and last expedient, i.e., the Rowlatt Act, which was passed in disregard of the united voice of the public.

3. This grand meeting gives expression to its heartfelt and sincere sympathy with the families of the philanthropic and patriotic personages, Dr Saif ud Din Kitchlew and Dr Satya Pal, on their deportation by the Government, which is being naturally and inevitably felt by the members of those families.

4. This meeting gives expression to its feeling of displeasure on, and strongly protests against, the deportation of the popular patriots, Dr Saif ud Din Kitchlew and Dr Satya Pal, and, while keeping in view the injurious effects of the despotic attitude of the Government, which is simply based on one-sided and unauthenticated reports, requests that all the persons deported and interned may be released without further delay.

5. Copies of all resolutions to be sent to the Secretary of State, the Viceroy, the Lieutenant-Governor of the Punjab, and the Deputy Commissioner of Amritsar, and a copy of Resolution No. 4 be sent to the families of both the respective deported leaders.[62]

Dyer was aware of one of these two meetings held in the city on the 12th, probably of the earlier one, but there is no evidence that he was aware of the announcements made at the second.

Unrest continued to spread around Amritsar and throughout the Punjab. During the day, rails were again pulled up on the railway lines around the city, and rumours of outbreaks of violence, mutinies, the loss of Lahore Fort and the death of Sir Michael O'Dwyer were circulating everywhere. There was indeed violence in Lahore, and the small town of Kasur, south of Lahore, was engulfed in a riot; the crowds there attacking the station and the government buildings were strafed and bombed from the air as no troops were available to deal with the disturbance. In Jullundur, the shops stayed shut and telegraph wires were cut.[63]

In Amritsar, however, the evening and the night which followed were quiet, which makes it all the more strange that Dyer made no attempt to extend the area of the city which was in British hands. He did not continue Major MacDonald's policy of gradually winning back control of Amritsar, commenced the day before, first with the posts mounted at the gates to the city, then with the picquets extended up the Hall Bazaar to the *kotwali*. After his march through the city from the Sultanwind Gate, Dyer did not send patrols out into the rest of Amritsar. So far, although they lay quiet and exhibited no opposition to any return to law and order, the majority of the commercial and populated areas of the city, including the vital area around the Golden Temple, were left in a sort of limbo. By not expanding the area of control that day, Dyer lost the chance to regain the upper hand in much of the city. Had he done so, it is highly unlikely that crowds would have been able to gather the next day in defiance of the authorities, and it is not fanciful to suggest that the terrible events of the 13th might have been avoided altogether.

It is difficult to see why Dyer did not continue Major MacDonald's policy of gradually extending his control of the city. He had by now a large body of troops which could have been supplemented in duties in the city by the local police force. The likely root of this change in policy is a conceptual one. It seems, though we do not have the evidence to be sure, that Major MacDonald believed his mission was to resume control, and that such a mission was best answered by an incremental growth in the number of military positions spreading through the key points of the city, gradually allowing a reassertion of dominance over its population. To Dyer (and we have the evidence for his thinking in his own words to the Hunter Committee) the issue in Amritsar was the suppression of a rebellion and the punishment of 'mutineers'. Dyer came to Amritsar with the knowledge that unrest was widespread throughout the Punjab, and when he arrived he believed he had found the focus of a full-scale rebellion. In reply to Justice Rankin of the Hunter Committee, Dyer said this directly: 'I regret it [Amritsar] was in open rebellion.'[64] Nor was this only his own view, for it was one that had been repeatedly pressed upon him by the civil officials who had handed him control. Kitchin, Irving and most of those around them believed there was a revolution afoot in Amritsar and they did all they could to persuade the military to crush it. To Dyer's mind, the mission which he had been given called for far more drastic measures than any gradual restoration of civil authority; it was a mission that demanded the punitive techniques to which he had become very accustomed throughout his military career. It is worth recalling here that Dyer had not had experience of any operations in aid to the civil power in India, and indeed had only experienced such operations once in his life, and that over thirty years before in Ireland. Military aid to the civil power was not something in which he was versed.

In these two factors, Dyer's conception of his mission, and his lack of experience of the techniques for which it called, we may see an explanation for the tactics which Dyer employed: his occasional deployment of large mobile columns rather than frequent deployment of numerous and small bodies of troops; the search and arrest raids which were followed by the withdrawal of troops and so the abandonment of areas temporarily brought under control; and above all his ruthlessness in dealing with a civilian population which seemed to his mind to be composed of enemies rather than of fellow citizens. General Barrow, a member of the Hunter Committee, clarified this point with Dyer at the inquiry:

Question: In other words, you considered that war was being waged against the Crown and that you had a right to anticipate the proclamation of martial law?

Answer: Yes, Sir.[65]

To Dyer, Amritsar had become enemy territory, whose inhabitants were rebels who had to be defeated before law could be reimposed, and who deserved punishment. Amritsar was not, to Dyer, just a city which it was his duty to return to normality.

Commissioner Kitchin drove back to Lahore late that day and briefed O'Dwyer. He later said: 'I had already on an earlier occasion, probably in the evening of 12 April, told the Lieutenant-Governor that, in my opinion, Martial Law was inevitable.' Given the situation pertaining in Amritsar, and Kitchin's own view, expressed in his evidence to the Hunter Committee, that the city was now back under control – 'We lost control of Amritsar on 10th April, and did not recover control of the city till 12th April, when the first arrests were made' – his recommendation of the imposition of martial law is remarkable, and must have been based on a view of the situation wider than that applying in the city alone. In explanation, he later gave the Hunter Committee his, and one assumes the Punjab Government's, reasons for imposing martial law:

> The real need for Martial Law was to prevent the spread of disorders. In no place had the Civil Government, aided by military forces, actually lost and failed to regain control … The towns were in open insurrection, but the townspeople have no military value at all. It was necessary to strike quickly and strike hard in order to save the rural people and above all to save the Army from infection.[66]

This, too, is neither particularly cogent nor convincing, though it has its own logic in the light of the earlier revolutionary conspiracies in the province. It was as much as the Punjab Government was ever to reveal in public of its motives.

Kitchin's return to Lahore led to a declaration, made at 4 p.m. the next day, that the Seditious Meetings Act of 1911 now applied to Amritsar. This banned the holding of meetings without permission if the subject of the meeting were likely to cause a disturbance or public excitement.[67] It is probable that Kitchin had discussed his views and plans with Dyer before he left; if so, this must have had a significant effect on Dyer's own reasoning and actions in what followed.

Dyer was still up working in the early hours of the morning, this time on a new and longer proclamation to be issued later on the 13th; this was the second night on which he got little sleep. The proclamation he now drafted, known as No. 2 Proclamation, was again handed to Irving to translate into Urdu, and this was done by the morning.[68] Dyer phoned in a report to 16 Division, the first he had sent since he had arrived, in the early hours of the 13th: 'I marched in force through the city yesterday. In combination with arrests made this apparently had a very good effect. Am going to occupy important points in the city today and issue proclamation.'[69] It is quite clear that he had no idea at this stage of what was to happen the next day.

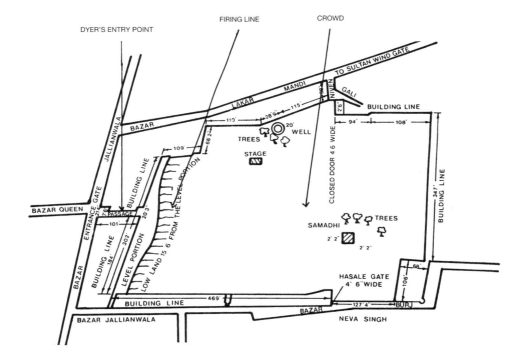

THE JALLIANWALA BAGH

16

The Jallianwala Bagh

It seemed to Dyer when he rose early on the 13th that he and his force were being steadily and deliberately cut off from the outside world; rail and wires had again been torn up overnight all around Amritsar, and more railway track was destroyed on the line to Lahore during the day, derailing a goods train and forcing communications with Lahore to be maintained by aeroplane. As he later put it:

> I thought they were trying to isolate me and my forces. Every thing pointed to the fact that there was a widespread movement, and that it was not confined to Amritsar alone. I looked upon these men as rebels who were trying to isolate my forces and cut me off from other supplies.[1]

He sent an armoured train to patrol along the line and effect repairs, and to disperse the parties of saboteurs armed with *lathis* seen along the tracks. The Treasury at nearby Tarn Taran had been attacked overnight, although it had been successfully defended by local police, so during the morning Dyer dispatched a platoon of the 1st/124th and seven cavalrymen to garrison the place. His troops were further depleted first thing when the men of the 2/6th Battalion, Royal Sussex entrained to return to Lahore, where 16 Division considered that the disturbances that had been raging for several days made their presence more necessary than in Amritsar. Back in Dyer's base, in Jullundur, a fire in an office in the military cantonment gave rise, though without cause as it turned out, to fears of subversion of the Indian soldiers there.[2]

Dyer's intention was now to make a demonstration of strength. At about 9 a.m., he formed up a column in the Ram Bagh then marched into the city. It was led by an armoured car, and the City Superintendent, Ashraf Khan, and his Sub-Inspector, Obaidullah, both on horseback, followed by Malik Fateh Khan, the city *Naib-tahsildar*, seated in a *duggiwalla*. With him was the town crier, who carried a drum that he beat loudly at each place they halted. Behind these came troops on foot, then a car carrying Dyer and Irving and another with the two British police officers, Rehill, who had by now returned from delivering his two prisoners to Dharamsala, and Plomer. It must have been an impressive parade. Only Lieutenant-Colonel Morgan was left behind, ordered by Dyer to come and extract the column if it got into difficulties: 'If we are not back by 2 p.m. you must come into the city with the rest of the troops and look for us.'[3] The column wended its way through the city, stopping at nineteen key spots and road junctions, although it did not go through the area containing the Jallianwala Bagh and the Golden Temple. This, although at the heart of the city, was omitted for some reason which has never been adequately explained. There was indeed no need to go the Bagh, which was just an empty space, but it should have been obvious that they needed to make an announcement near the Temple where the maximum numbers were; perhaps it was felt too sensitive a site to approach. Dyer later pleaded ignorance of the geography of the city to excuse these omissions:

> I thought we had gone a long way. We went to many places. I do not know Amritsar very well. We did a great deal in the way of reading out the Proclamation, and I understood that, after I had finished, perhaps a little more was going to be done in that way. I thought I had done quite enough. I confess I do not know how far we had penetrated into the city. I do not know the city very well.

Yet he had visited the city before, and seen its main sights, so he must have realised that he had missed the Temple. Whilst it was open to him, as a newly-arrived man, to make this plea, the excuse was not available to the Deputy Commissioner and the local police. Plomer, who was guiding the column, later showed a surprising lack of interest in his job that day:

> *Question*: You thought that was sufficient notice for a town like Amritsar to give an important proclamation?
>
> *Answer*: I did not think anything. When it was too hot to walk in the city I took the nearest route out.
>
> *Question*: You did not suggest to the General that a longer time might be given?
>
> *Answer*: No. When we got to the Majid *mandir* the General remarked that it was getting too hot for the troops so I took the route to Lohgar Gate.
>
> *Question*: And then this proclamation was stopped?
>
> *Answer*: Yes.[4]

At each place the proclamation was read out by the *Naib-tahsildar* in English and Urdu, and explained in Punjabi or Hindustani. Printed copies of the Urdu text were also distributed. The proclamation still did not make it clear that the city was under martial law; rather it gave the impression that the Deputy Commissioner remained in charge. Its first clause listed the officials from whom passes had to be obtained to leave the city, and all these were civilian. It then went on:

2. No person residing in Amritsar City is permitted to leave his house after 8.0 p.m. Any persons found in the streets after 8.0 p.m. are liable to be shot.

3. No procession of any kind is permitted to parade in the streets in the city or any part of the city or outside it at any time. Any such processions or any gathering of four men will be looked upon and treated as an unlawful assembly and dispersed by force of arms, if necessary.[5]

The march lasted for about four and a half hours, all through the morning until just before 1 p.m. The drum was beaten at each of the locations at which a halt was called and time given for a crowd to form. There was considerable noise. Dyer 'could see that they were laughing and that they were not behaving very well evidently. I was told that they were saying "this is all bluff, he won't fire", "not to be afraid" and words to that effect'. Men in the crowds shouted out that 'the British "Raj" was at an end and not to be afraid of being fired at', and that the British 'had no shoes'. Behind the military column walked a couple of men, Guran Ditta, a *bania*, and Balo, a *halwai*, beating an empty kerosene drum and giving out a counter proclamation that a meeting would be held in the Jallianwala Bagh that afternoon.[6] The police heard people in the crowds speaking of this. Inspector Obaidullah told them they would be fired on if they gathered illegally; they replied: 'We will hold a meeting; let us be fired on.' Arrests of seven of the rowdiest were made, though there seems to have been no attempt to catch those banging the kerosene drum. The police once more tried to get shopkeepers to open their shops, but were again unsuccessful. How many heard the proclamation is impossible to assess; the Minority Hunter Report estimated that only between 8000 and 10,000 people could have heard it, less than 10 per cent of the population, not counting the outsiders who were then in the city for the Baisakhi fair. However, there is no doubt that the news was spread by word of mouth throughout the city and that many more became aware of it during the day.[7]

As Dyer made his way back to the Ram Bagh at about 12.40 p.m., he was told by the police that, despite his proclamation, a meeting would be held at 4.30 p.m. in the Jallianwala Bagh. The information was given by the CID, whose men were lurking in the crowds, to Rehill; he passed it on to Dyer. Back in base by about 1.30, Dyer began to draw up his plans to deal with this.[8]

It was Baisakhi, the Sikh New Year's Day, and throughout it worshippers thronged into the Golden Temple. Before returning home in the cooler evening, some rested, as was customary, in the nearby open space of the Jallianwala Bagh. The Bagh was an open area of six to seven acres, dry ground at that time of the year, and surrounded with the high walls of local houses and compounds. It was about two hundred yards long, slightly less wide. It had five narrow entrances, some with locked gates; 'five crevices or shabby lanes on different sides which for the purposes of ingress and egress to it, may be exalted to the dignity of doors [which] lead to small lanes that are anything but wide and moreover, full of sewer *nalies*'. In the centre of the open ground stood a small domed *samadhi* and a very large well, some twenty feet or more in diameter with water up to a level twenty feet below its parapet. Both were shaded by a few trees; otherwise, the Bagh was bare, waiting for the rains when it would be planted with crops, and so it got frequent use as a place for gatherings of many kinds. It was completely surrounded by walls at least ten feet high, either of gardens, or more frequently of the three- or four-storey houses backing onto it, many of which had balconies and flat roof tops looking out over the Bagh. There were windows and some doors opening into the Bagh, but all were barred and locked.

Outside the city, the annual Baisakhi fair continued until the police closed it at 2 p.m. and sent away all those they found there. The fair customarily attracted a large number of farmers from the local area, as well as from further afield. With the fair closed, some of these straggled into the Jallianwala Bagh during the afternoon. They found that local political activists had been busy there from early in the day, setting up a wooden platform for the speakers. There is no doubt that the political nature of the meeting to be held there must have been known, or quickly became so, to most of the twenty or twenty-five thousand or so people who were crowded into the Bagh by the late afternoon. Many, however, were unaware of Dyer's proclamation. The gathering was very far from being a mob, and was a quieter crowd of a different composition from those that had been responsible for the mayhem of three days before. Some of the men there carried *lathis*, but most did not. There were also a few women there that day, and many children were with their fathers or had come from the local houses; for these the Bagh was their usual playground. During the afternoon, a funeral procession wound its way through the Bagh, accompanying the bodies of more of those who had died of injuries received on the 10th. This was followed out by about five thousand of the crowd, whose lives were thus saved. Plain clothes policemen, including the CID Inspector Jowahar Lal, mingled with the people, two of them even talking with the organisers of the meeting. Three policemen set up an observation post in a house overlooking the Bagh, where they set a guard at its front door; this man told a friend he saw there not to go into the Bagh as there was to be firing. It seems as if the police were aware of Dyer's intentions. An aeroplane flew over at some point, spooking the people, but they settled down again after it flew away.[9]

Neither Dyer nor the Deputy Commissioner thought it necessary to try to prevent this meeting, which they were by now well aware was about to take place. No police were sent to prevent entrance to the Bagh or to warn those there to leave. No military post was placed there, and none of the printed Urdu notices were posted on the entrances. Irving later claimed he thought the meeting would not take place; an insufficient reason for failing to act, and a conclusion which he is unlikely to have come to given his belief that the city was in open rebellion. Dyer's detailed preparations over the next three hours make it clear that he believed in at least the possibility of the meeting from the time he was first told of it, and acted on that belief. As he later put it: 'I personally had ample time to consider the nature of the painful duty I might be faced with.' Dyer's plans were not made on the spur of the moment. Moreover, his view of the purpose of his operations in Amritsar had not changed since the day before; on the contrary, it is likely that his view had been reinforced by his encounter with the defiant crowds in the streets. He was sure that what he was about was destroying and punishing a rebellion, and he had been puzzling how to do this, as the very nature of his opponents made them difficult to identify and to attack. As Annie Dyer, who had this from her husband, explained it later:

> How was he to fight the rebels, how was he to bring them to decisive action in the narrow streets and winding lanes of Amritsar? It was a problem ... which seemed to him, with his little force, insoluble, unless, indeed, he could get them somehow in the open. And that seemed too much to hope for ... But this unexpected gift of fortune, this unhoped for defiance, this concentration of the rebels in an open space – it gave him such an opportunity as he could not have devised. It separated the guilty from the innocent, it placed them where he would have wished them to be – within reach of his sword.[10]

The orders which he now gave, and the explanations he gave after the event, make it clear that he intended to deal with any crowd he met not, as he had the day before, by ordering it to disperse, but by dispersing it with force, and by punishing its members for defying his proclamation. It is clear that he believed he was going to strike a blow at a conspiracy which he imagined stretched across India and of which one of the principal centres seemed to be Amritsar. The casualties which the crowds in the city had suffered on earlier occasions had evidently been insufficient to do more than enrage the 'mutineers'. He was now faced, he thought, with the need to do something more drastic, to raise the level of violence to a mark sufficient to put a stop to the conspiracy and to punish its supporters.

As he had sent an aeroplane to seek out and assess the size of the meeting, and had information and advice being fed to him by the local police throughout the afternoon, he was not unaware of the fact that he faced a crowd of a considerable size in an enclosed space. This was not, though, something which gave him much concern, for whilst dispersal of a crowd always called for leaving it the maximum number of routes and space to escape, punishment of a crowd called for different tactics, in effect its entrapment. His plan had two elements; first, a 'special force' with considerable firepower: twenty-five 1st/9th Gurkhas and twenty-five Indian soldiers, mostly Baluch and Pathan, from the depots of two Frontier Force regiments, the 54th Sikhs and the 59th Scinde Rifles, a total of fifty men armed with rifles. As escort, he took with this party another forty Gurkhas armed only with *khukuris*; Captain Crampton, the Gurkhas' Officer Commanding, was ordered to command all the Indian troops, as the senior officer with the Frontier Force men was an Indian. With these ninety men Dyer intended to confront the crowd. Secondly, he detailed off five parties of troops, each of fifty men, which were to be placed around the area of his intended action and outside the city walls. He called these picquets, and said they were to hold the various gates of the city. This could not have been their real function; the gates were already held (unless Dyer had earlier withdrawn MacDonald's picquets; this is unlikely, but there is no record which makes this point clear), there were thirteen of them, and fifty men was too large a party to be needed at each gate. Unfortunately, we do not have Dyer's orders that day to tell us his intentions, so there is doubt here as to what the task of these picquets was. There are two possibilities: first, the groups may have been meant to assist his special force to extract itself if it got into difficulties, by coming to its rescue or by holding areas in force through which it might withdraw. Secondly, the picquets may have been 'backstops', designed to destroy an enemy fleeing from inside an area that had been sealed off. Both possibilities indicate that there was more than dispersion of the crowd on Dyer's mind.

The composition of the special force, one carefully chosen by Dyer, is significant. It had no British soldiers, and most of its Indian troops were men of nationalities foreign to India or recruited from its fringes. A local businessman, Girdhari Lal, stated that he saw the force leave the Ram Bagh, and describes them as Gurkhas and 'Baluchees'. Gurkhas were from the independent kingdom of Nepal and had little love for Indians. The Baluch were from the fringes of Sind and the wilds of Baluchistan. Lieutenant-Colonel Morgan, however, states that the depot troops were Pathans; as the Commanding Officer of a Baluch Regiment he should have been able to recognise these. For Dyer's purposes, Pathans from the North-West Frontier had similar advantages to the Baluch; neither would have had much compunction at shooting Punjabi civilians. He did not detail any men of the Somersets, the Londons, or the Indians of the 2nd/151st Infantry. By selecting native troops, but troops who were not liable to recoil from action against the locals, Dyer was making the statement that his troops were loyal natives whilst ensuring that the task he gave them was carried out. Also significantly, he decided to lead the small party himself. This was neither necessary nor usual, as the size of the special force he had assembled could easily have been delegated to a major. Yet Dyer dismissed the more senior British company officers of the men he chose: 'But when the Company Commanders reported to him – Major Inskip and two others unnamed – he told them to their surprise that they would not be going with him. "If there's anything to be done,

I'll do it alone"'. Captain Briggs later told his friend, Major Smyth, who was
Brigade Major of a brigade in Lahore, that 'General Dyer had no intention of
saddling a subordinate with what he knew might be a difficult and hateful
assignment'. When Dyer dismissed the company commanders, he told them 'he
had sent a message to the crowd, warning it to disperse, but now learned that it
was assembling in great numbers'. By dismissing these middle-ranking officers,
Dyer ensured that there would be no officers present who might baulk at his
plans. His choice of both commanders and troops argues for the deliberate nature
of what was to follow.[11]

Dyer knew that if he followed his plan, made as it was without any order from
his superiors (although one can guess it was a plan which would have had at the
least the tacit approval of the local civilian authorities) and derived solely from
his own judgment of the situation, he was about to break the law. He made this
plain to his Brigade Major before they marched to the Bagh: 'Briggs, I shall be
cashiered for this probably, but I've *got* to do it.'[12] From Dyer's record in the
Sarhadd, it is clear that he was quite capable of formulating his own mission
based upon erroneous information and upon a mistaken appreciation of the
situation. He had shown there on more than one occasion that he was capable of
following the logic of his misappreciation to tragic limits. That he should do so
now in Amritsar should not give cause for surprise.

Dyer was nervous of the potential for causing another backlash such as the
city had suffered on the 10th. He determined to avoid Irving's omission of that
first day, and ordered that all the Europeans not already in safety were to be
collected that afternoon by the 11th Lancers and brought under military guard.
Gerard Wathen, who with his family had been guarded since the first outbreak
of violence by his Sikh pupils and staff, and who was then at the Khalsa College
enrolling forty students as special constables, 'was in the grounds on the 13th
when a young officer galloped up and ordered him and Armstrong and Hervey
[his two British members of staff] to go, bag and baggage to the General's
camp'. Shortly after this, at about 4 p.m., Dyer was informed by Rehill that the
meeting in the Jallianwala Bagh had started. The Brigade Intelligence Officer
also received a letter to that effect from Mr Lewis, Manager of the Crown Cinema,
who had been walking around the city in disguise.[13] At this point the Deputy
Commissioner, according to his own account, decided to go to the fort and so to
absent himself throughout what followed.

> We heard certain rumours that a meeting would take place, but did not attach any great
> importance to that. I asked General Dyer if he could spare me as I wanted to go to the
> Fort. I had hardly gone (at about 4) when General Dyer received the news that a crowd
> was actually collecting in the Jallianwala Bagh … I did not think that the meeting would
> be held, or if held would disperse, so I asked the General to excuse me as I wanted to go
> to the Fort.

Some light on Irving's dereliction of duty was shed later by J.W. Fletcher, who replaced one of the dead managers of the National Bank. Irving told him a few days after the shooting that he had had no sleep for four days and went back to his bungalow to sleep on the afternoon of 13 April, staying there till 5 p.m. He told Fletcher he believed Dyer could not fire without warning as there had been no proclamation of martial law. It is difficult not to conclude that Irving was deliberately absenting himself from an event he had no wish to see. Dyer was later asked by the Hunter Committee whether he had considered consulting the Deputy Commissioner before opening fire. His dismissive answer can be taken to indicate his opinion of the man: 'There was no Deputy Commissioner there to consult at the time.'[14]

Almost immediately he had confirmation of the meeting, at about 4.15 p.m., Dyer's column marched out of the Ram Bagh and moved at walking pace through the narrow streets of the city towards the Jallianwala Bagh, dropping off the picquets as it went. Dyer travelled by car with Lieutenant-Colonel Morgan, Briggs, his Brigade Major, and his two British bodyguards, Sergeants Anderson and Pizzey of the Londons. The troops marched to the front and rear of his car. In another car behind him were the two policemen, Rehill and Plomer. With the column were two armoured cars. As he drove up the Hall Bazaar, past the looted banks and the ruined town hall, Dyer mulled over what he was about to do: 'My mind was made up as I came along in my motor car – if my orders were not obeyed, I would fire immediately.'[15] Dyer did not mean by this that he would fire if the crowd disobeyed any orders he gave it to disperse. He meant that he would fire if they had disobeyed his orders by gathering for the meeting. Before the Hunter Committee he made this crystal clear:

Question: And for the reasons you have explained to us, you had made up your mind to open fire at the crowd for having assembled at all?

Answer: Quite right.[16]

Guided by a policeman, the column 'arrived at a small alley just about broad enough for two men walking abreast'. The armoured cars had to be left outside, as they were too wide to drive in; a small guard, including two mounted Muslim police officers, perhaps again Ashraf Khan and Obaidullah, was left with them and the motor cars. This prevented the use of their machine guns. Briggs describes what happened next: 'The General Officer Commanding, Colonel Morgan, Mr Rehill and myself got out of the motor and advanced up the alley, the troops following us. Coming to the end of the alley we saw an immense crowd of men'.[17]

As soon as Dyer saw the crowd, he made up his mind to fire; he later told J.P. Thompson, the Chief Secretary to the Punjab Government, that this took him no more than three seconds. He immediately ordered his troops into the Bagh, Gurkhas right, Frontier Force left. He asked Briggs how many people he thought there were there; Briggs replied he thought five thousand or so. The troops deployed on either side of Dyer's small party, and took up standing firing positions on a low rise at the west end of the Bagh. The crowd was dense and was very close, most of it only a hundred yards away, and the closest people on its fringes were only eight or nine yards from the troops. The people were listening in silence to a speaker on the platform, who was seen by the troops to be gesticulating with his hands. This was Pandit Durga Dass, editor of the Amritsar newspaper, *Waqt*, who was the eighth speaker and who had just taken the rostrum from Brij Gopinath, a clerk from one of the looted banks who had guided the mob to murder his manager, and who had just finished reciting his poem, *Faryad*, to the crowd. Dass was now moving the third resolution of the meeting against the Rowlatt Bills, condemning the actions of the authorities in Amritsar since the 10th. The platform on which he stood was only fifty or sixty yards from the position the troops took up. Seeing the soldiers, many in the crowd took fright, but Dass, and one of the meeting's organisers, Hans Raj, shouted out that the British would not fire, and that if they did the bullets would be blanks. This did not stop the panic, however, and people began to run. Without any warning to the crowd, Dyer gave the order to fire. The order was repeated by Captain Crampton, whistles rang out, and immediately the troops opened fire.[18]

Havoc ensued. The crowd ran in terror in all directions but found few exits by which to escape. People crammed into the entrances to the narrow passageways, frantically seeking to force their way out. The troops were directed to fire on these, killing many, and causing more to be trodden underfoot or crushed under the mounds of bodies that eventually built up ten or twelve deep. Many tried to climb the walls, and were picked off as they did so. Crowds huddled in the corners of the garden with no way out at all and were shot down where they stood. Retired soldiers in the crowd shouted out that people should lie on the ground to avoid the bullets, and many did so only to be shot as they lay. At times the crowd seemed to the troops to be gathering to rush forward at the firing line; Briggs drew Dyer's attention to this perceived threat. 'The men sometimes collected in knots instead of bolting and he thought they meditated attack.' These knots of men were mown down. The firing ceased occasionally, whilst the men reloaded and targets were adjusted; more whistles blew, and firing started again. Dyer ordered reloading after the men emptied their first magazines, then ordered 'independent rapid fire', personally directing fire at the densest parts of the crowd. By now the troops were kneeling or lying prone to get the best point of aim. Colonel Morgan recalled that: 'Fire was opened once more on one man, a fellow with a red beard who was trying to rally the remnants against us. I regret to say he was not hit, but our little force was not one of marksmen. We did not know if the Gurkha recruits had ever fired a rifle.' Although Briggs later denied that any soldiers hesitated or deliberately fired high to miss, many of the soldiers seem to have been severely frightened by what was happening. An officer of the 59th, R. Moray Graham, pieced together an account when his men got back to the Depot:

> The small number of soldiers taken into the Bagh were [facing the mob] and they were very frightened. Who would not be? [The crowd] rushed to the gate where they saw the soldiers arrive only in the hope of being able to get out, away from the trouble. The soldiers, naturally enough, thought that they were being stormed by a riotous mob which vastly outnumbered them. And the mob were violently propelled forward by those who thought they could not run away out of the back of the Bagh.

Others with more experience were less easily frightened. Sergeant Anderson, standing alongside his brigadier, recalled:

> When fire was opened, the whole crowd seemed to sink to the ground, a flutter of white garments, with however a spreading out towards the main gateway, and some individuals could be seen climbing the high wall. There was little movement except for the climbers. The gateway would soon be jammed. I saw no sign of a rush towards the troops ... After a bit, I noticed that Captain Briggs was drawing up his face as if in pain, and was plucking at the General's elbow ... The fire control and discipline of the native troops was first class. The officer in charge kept his eye on the General, gave his fire and cease fire orders to his men, and they obeyed him implicitly: there was no wild sporadic firing ... Dyer seemed quite calm and rational. Personally, I wasn't afraid. I saw nothing to be afraid about. I'd no fear that the crowd would come at us.[19]

At least some of the Gurkha detachment were similarly unafraid. Two of them were later questioned by a member of the ICS they met in Darjeeling while they were on leave. Asked what they thought of the Jallianwala Bagh shooting, they said with relish, 'Sahib, while it lasted it was splendid; we fired every round we had.'[20]

Under the hail of bullets in the Bagh, people tried to hide behind the well or to jump into it, many drowning and dying in the crush inside. Many of those who had lain flat to escape the bullets were shot when they tried to take advantage of a pause in the firing to make a run for it; Dyer directed firing at what he described as the 'better targets' of those who were standing, as well as at a peepul tree behind and around which many were trying to shelter. Some people in the surrounding houses were also hit, perhaps by ricochets, though there is evidence that some of the troops fired at the onlookers. Girdhari Lal, who watched the scene with binoculars from a nearby house, saw that 'There was not a corner left of the garden facing the firing line, where people did not die in large numbers. Many got trampled under the feet of the rushing crowds and thus lost their lives. Blood was pouring in profusion.'[21] Maulvi Gholam Jilani was caught in the firing:

I ran towards a wall and fell on a mass of dead and wounded persons. Many others fell on me. Many of those who fell on me were hit and died. There was a heap of the dead and wounded over me, under and all around me. I felt suffocated. I thought I was going to die.[22]

Among the children there, Madan Mohau, the thirteen-year-old son of the local Dr Mani Ram, who 'along with his playmates used to visit this open square for play almost daily' was shot in the head; the bullet fractured his skull, he bled profusely and died instantaneously.[23]

The firing continued for between ten and fifteen minutes. The noise in the Bagh was a cacophony of rifle crack, bullets thumping into flesh and walls, ricochets screeching off the brickwork, the screams of 25,000 people in terror and the cries of the wounded. So loud was the noise that Dyer and Briggs were later to maintain that they had some difficulty in stopping the troops firing, though this was denied by Sergeant Anderson.[24] The sight was one of horror. The vast crowd staggered aimlessly; the air filled with dust and blood; flesh flew everywhere; men and children fell with limbs broken, eyes shot out, internal organs exposed. Rehill and Inspector Jowahar Lal, standing behind the troops, were unable to stand watching the massacre and went out of the Bagh whilst it was going on. Rehill was so badly affected that he later denied having seen anything at all. Plomer, built of stronger or more vindictive stuff, remarked to Dyer during a pause for reloading that 'he had taught the crowd a lesson it would never forget'. Dyer did not appear to hear.[25]

When Dyer finally decided to stop the firing, which was only when the troops had only enough ammunition left, according to his calculation, to enable them to defend themselves during the march back to base, much of the crowd was still up against the opposite wall, trying to scrabble its way out of the Bagh.[26] Those Gurkhas who were armed only with *khukuris*, which they now drew, were sent by Captain Crampton down to the *hansli* drain that crossed the Bagh to check on those hiding there. They were then ordered back. Dyer gave orders to withdraw, walked back to his car, then led his troops back to the Ram Bagh the way they had come. He neither inspected the destruction he had caused, nor made any arrangements to tend the wounded.

Dyer's belief was that he was still in the midst of a rebellious city and that the forces opposed to him might now retaliate; he had, in truth, as yet no comprehension of the crushing effect he had achieved. He felt it unsafe to do anything to help the wounded in the Bagh, and believed he needed to leave the city as soon as possible. As he put it: 'I had to be most careful of not at the last giving up the victory.' He had, however, no interest at all in succouring those he believed to be his enemies and was callous about what happened to those he had shot: 'It was not my job. But the hospitals were open and the medical officers were there. The wounded only had to apply for help.'[27] As a result, he had no idea of the casualties he had caused, and in his report of the action was forced to estimate the number of dead by the number of rounds he later found his men had fired. When the unfired cartridges and the empty cases the troops had picked up were counted back at the Ram Bagh, this proved to be 1650. It is possible that more rounds were fired; all of the empty cases could not have been picked up from the ground before the troops left the Bagh. Dyer calculated that between two hundred and three hundred people had been killed, but he later accepted that it was quite possible that he had killed between four and five hundred.[28]

The destruction of the crowd in the Bagh had been watched by a very large number of Indians from properties around its edge. The surrounding streets were strewn with the bodies of those who had escaped but had succumbed outside. Onlookers and family members tried to rescue the wounded and to bring succour to those still left alive. Many of them recounted to the INC inquiry the scenes of devastation they found when they entered the Bagh after the shooting. Mohammed Ismail, a butcher, had watched the massacre from the roof of a house:

> After the Gurkhas had left, I went to the Bagh to look for my maternal uncle's son. Corpses were lying all over. There were some wounded also. My estimate of the persons I saw lying was 1500. There were specially large heaps of corpses at the corners on both sides of Riazul Hasan's house near the well, as also at the corner near Meva Singh's Burj and along the well facing the platform from where the troops had fired. At several places, the corpses were ten or twelve thick. I saw some children lying dead. Khair-ud-Din Teli of Mandi had his child, six or seven months old, in his arm.[29]

Sardar Partap Singh gave this account:

> Dead bodies were lying on all sides near the enclosure walls. When I entered, a dying man asked for water. There is a drain that carries water from the canal to Darbar Sahib [the Golden Temple]. It is called Hansli. The drain is covered, but there is a pit connected with it which is about four feet square. When I tried to take water from that pit, I saw many dead bodies floating in it. Some living men had also hid themselves in it, and they asked me, 'Are they (i.e. soldiers) gone?' When I told them that they had gone, they came out of it and ran away. Then I went out into the middle of the Bagh to find out my son. There were about 800 or 1000 wounded and dead lying near the walls of the Bagh, besides others who ran away wounded and died either in their own houses or in the surrounding lanes. I remained there from fifteen to twenty minutes, but could not find my son. I heard the wailing of those shot and who were crying for water.[30]

The curfew came into force at 8 p.m., so the wounded were left in the Bagh until the next morning, when the work of clearing the bodies was resumed. There is no way of knowing how many people died there. Neither Irving nor Sir Michael O'Dwyer made any inquiry about the casualties, and the local government's first attempt to find out the numbers involved was initiated only on 25th June, over two months later. The Punjab government did not get around to making a proclamation inviting the population to submit the names of casualties until 7th August; even then many were still too frightened to come forward for fear of being identified as rebels. By 3 September, F.C. Puckle, who stood in as Deputy Commissioner in Amritsar after Irving was sent on leave to recover his nerve, was only able to account for 291 dead. He found in his investigations that two women were among those killed, though this fact was lost in subsequent tallies; it is not known if these were inside or outside the Bagh. The official number of deaths gradually grew: the Government of India announced a figure of 301 in the Imperial Legislative Council debate of 10 September 1919; F.H. Burton, the Punjab Assistant Commissioner charged with working out the casualties, told J.P. Thompson in November that year that, based on figures collated by the Amritsar Health Officer, Dr Rozdon, 'deaths proved or probable in the Jallewalian Bagh were about 415'. But this was not a full figure, and Burton received more, 480 names in all, on 22 October from V.N. Tivraj, the Secretary of the Allahabad *sewa samiti*, a social service league which had voluntarily undertaken the task of finding out how many had died. Irving eventually came to believe the figure was between 400 and 500 dead. Other estimates were larger; V.N. Tivraj concluded finally that 530 had died. J.P. Thompson recorded a guess of 800 to 1800 dead made by a colleague in the Punjab ICS, a Mr Bayley, who visited Amritsar on 20 April 1919. Bihar leader Hasan Immam claimed to have collected details of 941 dead. Pandit Madan Malaviya put the figure at a thousand in the Imperial Legislative Council on 12 September. Swami Shraddhanand wrote to Gandhi of over fifteen hundred dead.

Despite this, a figure of 379 identified dead was agreed upon by the Hunter Committee, based upon cases which had been proved by the time they sat in November 1919. These comprised 337 men, forty-one boys and a baby six weeks old. The Hunter Committee believed that the wounded would have been 'probably three times as great as the number of killed', and settled for a thousand as a guess. Official estimates of the wounded based on proven casualties remained unrealistically smaller, as the names of those who survived were not put forward to the authorities. By 5 March 1920, the *sewa samiti* had the names of only two hundred wounded. Irving eventually managed to list 192, and the Government of India finally settled for a figure of two hundred.[31]

There are differing reports of Dyer's state of mind when he reached the Ram Bagh, which he did at about 6 p.m. To Major Inskip, after the firing and for the next few days, Dyer seemed 'calm and quite normal'. Though he appeared worried, he was rational and in command of himself. He may even have been rather pleased with his deed. Nehru (who collected evidence for the INC Inquiry) records a conversation reported between Dyer and the City Medical Officer,

Lieutenant-Colonel Smith, on Dyer's return, quoting Dyer to Smith: 'I have done it', and Smith replying: 'Give them one or two doses more'. Gandhi did not regard this hearsay as sufficiently reliable to publish in the inquiry report.

There is, however, some evidence that Dyer was considerably shaken by what he had done, and that he remained so for some time. Gerard Wathen, who met him at about 6 p.m., saw 'how distraught Dyer was'. He vehemently attacked Dyer when he heard what had happened, telling him India would never forget what he had done. Dyer replied that 'he had to decide quickly or his men would have been overpowered. He also said that he meant to strike hard as a lesson', and that he had been unable to stop the firing due to the noise in the Bagh, an excuse which he did not make later, perhaps as it was not really believable. Irving described his first meeting with Dyer to the writer Edward Thompson, who dined with him and F.G. Puckle, his relief, some time later: 'Dyer came to me all dazed and shaken up, and said, "I never knew that there was no way out". He explained that when the crowd did not scatter, but held its ground he thought it was massing to attack him, so kept on firing.' But Irving had his own grounds for deflecting attention from the deliberate nature of Dyer's act, which sprang from his absence from the scene, and is not perhaps to be relied on here in all aspects of what he said. As an explanation of Dyer's actions, Irving's suggestion is in any case inadequate; it explains neither why fire was opened in the first place, nor why it was continued for so long. His statement does, though, indicate something of Dyer's turbulent frame of mind on his return. Puckle added that six months later Dyer came through his station and dined with him, and told him: 'I haven't had a night's sleep since that happened. I keep on seeing it all over again.' Doris Price Jones, the daughter of Judge Brasher, in whose house Dyer was quartered at the time, similarly recalled: 'I well remember General Dyer walking up and down most of the night in an agitated manner, muttering, "I had to do it".' Most telling is Annie Dyer's testimony. Writing in 1927 to Brigadier-General Edmonds, she said: 'And for weeks he could hardly sleep at all from the nightmare memories of that scene.'

Others were also badly affected. Captain Crampton, the commander of the Gurkha contingent, 'always had a feeling of shame over the incident', and would not speak of it. Rehill took to the bottle after the massacre, for which he blamed himself according to his niece, and suffered appalling nightmares, ending as a shadow of the man he had been. Both Rehill and Plomer subsequently successfully covered up what they knew of the action in the Jallianwala Bagh.[32]

Fear of a violent backlash caused Dyer to have the Ram Bagh put in a state of defence, and the night was spent nervously. The brigade war diary records: 'Special precautions were taken during the night in case of reprisals.' Irving remembered: 'Evening [on 13th] had shut down by the time I got back, and I found the military making various arrangements for the safety of the civil station in case of a further attack. They were conducting it as in a state of warfare in the face of an enemy, and it was not proposed at that time to send out search parties in the city.' But this fear was misplaced; when Dyer, Morgan and Irving went through the town between 10.30 p.m. and midnight, in order to make sure, as Dyer reported next day, that 'my orders to inhabitants not being out of their houses after 20.00, had been obeyed … The city was absolutely quiet and not a soul to be seen'. While many were slowly dying in the Bagh, in the city, 'all was absolutely still'.[33]

Irving sent a coded wire to Lahore through police channels at 11.30 p.m. with only a very sketchy report of the day's arrests and mentioning 200 dead. Gerard Wathen, who saw this, and was by now growing extremely angry and anxious at the way affairs in Amritsar were being handled, demanded that Irving write a fuller report, which he did at 1 a.m. Using the car of a lecturer who had been visiting his college, a Mr Jacob, Wathen took it to Lahore himself, clutching a loaded revolver all the way. Just after 3 a.m. the couple burst in on Sir Michael O'Dwyer, who had just got to sleep, having come down from Simla that night, and gave him Irving's message. They also gave him an inaccurate verbal report of what had happened and demanded that the Lieutenant-Governor go to Amritsar to see things for himself. O'Dwyer dismissed their report as alarmist. He had no intention of visiting the city. J.P. Thompson, the Chief Secretary, and Commissioner Kitchin were called in, both wearing their pyjamas:

> Roused at 4.10 to go over to Government House. Wathen, Principal Khalsa College, had arrived in excited state about Amritsar. 'Only British troops fired. Shot men down like rabbits as they ran. Manjha up. Only thing that could save situation was the Lieutenant-Governor should disown action taken.'[34]

Wathen told the Lieutenant-Governor that he feared there would be a rising in the Manjha when the news of the massacre leaked out. O'Dwyer objected to being told his business by a college principal, and disbelieved Wathen's fears of a rising (rightly as it turned out; though, ironically, this was one of the principal reasons his Government gave for the declaration of martial law). Instead, he told Kitchin to return to Amritsar, and by his hand sent a message to Irving complaining of Wathen's lack of respect. He also phoned General Beynon, who so far had not heard from Dyer, and who, though he had heard at 11.45 p.m. that the civil authorities were getting reports of two hundred dead at Amritsar, had not taken steps to find out more, and was not to do so until he sent an aeroplane to Amritsar at dawn the next day.

In the city, the night was quiet, though not inactive; a party of Londons was sent to Jundiala, fifteen miles away, to bring in two isolated lady missionaries. They saw absolutely no one on the way. In the middle of the night, some of the people of the city somehow managed to seek permission from Dyer to bury their dead; he allowed this.[35] He sat down to write his report, only the second he had penned since his arrival in the city two days before. It was to be the first, and the shortest, of the three reports on the Jallianwala Bagh affair which he was destined to write, but it was the only report that the military authorities were to receive for the next four months, and so was the one upon which they based their initial considerations of what Dyer had done. Dyer's six hour delay in reporting the Jallianwala Bagh incident calls for some explanation: he may have been too shaken to write immediately, or he may have needed to get his thoughts in order. The latter seems more likely, as his report was brief, uninformative, and, whilst containing nothing that was strictly untrue, deliberately misleading in that it left out much of what might have inculpated him, both in terms of his intentions and of his actions.

In the report, which covered his activities in Amritsar after his arrival there on the 11th, Dyer described in detail his proclamation procession of the morning of the 13th, and states that though he had heard after midday that a meeting was planned in the Jallianwala Bagh, he did not believe it would take place. Being told at 4 p.m. that a meeting was being held, he sent picquets to hold the city gates, and marched to the Jallianwala Bagh. After enumerating the composition of his special force, he continued:

> I entered the JALLENWALLIAN BAGH by a very narrow lane which necessitated my leaving my armoured cars behind. On entering, I saw a dense crowd estimated at about 5000; a man on a raised platform addressing the audience and making gesticulations with his hands. I realized that my force was small and to hesitate might induce attack. I immediately opened fire and dispersed the crowd. I estimate that between 200 and 300 of the crowd were killed. My party fired 1650 rounds. I returned to my Headquarters about 18.00 hours.[36]

Missing from this is any discussion of Dyer's intentions in marching to the Bagh. The report carefully avoids mentioning the fact that no warning was given to the crowd, and does not state anything about the sustained length of firing nor about what happened afterwards to the casualties. Dyer introduces to the report the idea that he had already tried out on Gerard Wathen, that the fear of being overwhelmed was the cause of his immediately opening fire. If there is any falsehood in this report, it is here, for there is no indication from any of the other accounts of the action in the Bagh, those of Morgan, Briggs, Anderson, Rehill and Plomer, that there was such a fear at the initiation of, or during, the action. The circumstances that could be thought to come closest to this proffered explanation are the fire that was directed at groups of the crowd seeming to surge towards the troops, but this was incidental to, rather than causative of, the firing.

We need to bear two questions in mind when considering the explanations which we will now begin to encounter for what took place in the Jallianwala Bagh: first, what initiated the firing; and, secondly, why it went on for so long. Whilst the explanation given by Dyer's initial report might be accepted as an answer to the first, it cannot answer the second of these questions. In any case, in his subsequent written reports and evidence, Dyer himself was to reverse this position and would later categorically deny that he opened fire through fear of being overwhelmed. This was, however, the explanation that both General Beynon and Sir Michael O'Dwyer (and in fact all the civil servants of the Punjab Government) accepted at the time, as it was the first they were given, and they would continue to maintain it in the face of Dyer's later denials, and in the teeth of all evidence to the contrary, throughout the whole sorry aftermath of this affair.

It is clear that in this report Dyer intended to give the minimum information to his superiors, presumably because he feared what their reaction would be. We have seen enough of this kind of reporting from Dyer during his time in the Sarhadd to be familiar with the technique. Whilst he was sure in his own mind of the rightness of what he had done, he knew he had gone beyond any latitude allowed by the rules, and he could not yet know what his superiors would think of this. So he obfuscated. In doing so, he gained the approval of both the military and the civilian authorities, an approval that would cause them considerable embarrassment when it had to be withdrawn after the full facts became known.

It is not clear how Dyer sent this report to Lahore; it probably went by hand as the lines were down. Arriving at 16 Division at about 4 a.m., it persuaded General Beynon that the firing in the Bagh had been justified and he signified his approval of it. He was sufficiently aware of Dyer's character, however, to send an immediate response: 'General Officer Commanding Amritsar instructed not to take too drastic measures as he should now have situation well in hand.' In order, though, to bolster a subordinate who might now very well be out on a limb, he telephoned the Lieutenant-Governor to ask for his endorsement of Dyer's action. To his later regret, perhaps, though he would never acknowledge it, Sir Michael O'Dwyer gave his verbal approval. Beynon felt sufficiently uneasy in this matter to raise it again at O'Dwyer's conference at Government House that morning. He again secured O'Dwyer's approval for Dyer's action and had it recorded in the 16 Division War Diary. Even at that stage, it seems that General Beynon could see problems arising from the Jallianwala Bagh affair. Neither he nor Sir Michael O'Dwyer were ever to go back on the support they now gave. Beynon replied to Dyer's report: 'Your action correct and Lieutenant-Governor approves.'[37]

17

The Crawling Order

Violence continued around Amritsar over the night of 13–14 April. Stations, line and wires were attacked again in several places overnight and during the next day, cutting communications to Lahore. In the morning of 14th, people went about burying their dead. Many visited the Ram Bagh after 7 a.m. to request authority to do this, others to seek permission to open their shops. The funerals were allowed, as they had to be, but with the provisos that there were to be no processions and that mourners were to be restricted to eight per corpse. Dyer's Headquarters issued a terse proclamation: 'The inhabitants may burn or bury their dead as soon as they please. There must be no demonstration or disorder of any kind. The inhabitants must return to the city after the ceremony.'[1]

Commissioner Kitchin, and Donald, the Deputy Inspector-General of Police, came down again from Lahore by car, this time with an escort, and were in the lines by 8 a.m. Kitchin thoroughly approved of all Dyer had done, as he made plain at the subsequent inquiry:

Answer: Strong steps were necessary.

Question: What is your idea of strong steps?

Answer: Well, General Dyer took a strong step.

O'Dwyer had asked him before he left for Amritsar what he thought would be the effect of the shooting in the Jallianwala Bagh: 'I said in my opinion the trouble was over.' Yet Kitchin would not let well alone. Not content with what had been done the day before, he and Donald attempted to alarm Dyer with rumours of disturbances, this time telling him 'that the mutineers intended to hold another meeting around the Golden Temple'. They were trying to focus his attention on the Sikhs. To what end remains unclear; it is difficult to credit this report at this stage, or to know how they came by the information. Kitchin reported to Lahore at 9.30 a.m. to say that he had arrived safely in Amritsar, and that the road was clear, but made no mention at all of the news about the Temple. Fortunately, Dyer did not act precipitately this time, though Gerard Wathen later told his wife that he had been forced to argue with Dyer to prevent him bombing the temple. Following Wathen's intervention, Dyer instead summoned Sardar Arur Singh, the Golden Temple *sarbrah*, to the Ram Bagh to promise him that no harm would come to his temple and that troops would be used to protect it. Arur Singh brought with him Sardar Sundar Singh Majithia, another influential pro-British Sikh, and both assured Dyer that the Sikhs remained loyal. Dyer asked them to counter the rumours that were beginning to spread that the Temple had been attacked. Dyer's level-headed action meant that Kitchin's incitement to violent action did not have its intended result, and the bloodbath that would have ensued had the Golden Temple been attacked was avoided. This meeting was the start of a deliberate attempt to separate the Sikh community from the rest of the population. From this point on, Dyer worked assiduously to treat the Sikhs of the city and the Manjha with more consideration than he did the Muslim or Hindu inhabitants, and to bolster their relative position. This effort found fertile ground, as the Sikhs had largely stood apart from the Rowlatt agitation in Amritsar, and had for the most part remained loyal to the government across the province. The communal hatred between the Sikhs and the rest allowed the British an opportunity to divide and rule which they did not forego. The rumours of damage to the Temple which were being spread across the Punjab were intended to damage Sikh relations with the British, but they largely failed to do so because for once the authorities put much effort into getting the Government's case across to the population. The Army played a large part here; for example, 2nd Division sent four Sikh officers to Amritsar from the regiments around Rawalpindi to see that the Golden Temple had not been blown up, a fact they were able to report back to their units.[2]

That afternoon, Kitchin assembled about 150 of the chief men of the town in the public library and harangued them: 'You people want peace or war? ... The General will give orders today. The city is in his possession. I can do nothing. You will have to obey orders.' He stayed only for the opening of the meeting, and had made sure he had gone by the time Dyer entered, both graphically making the point that it was the latter, not Kitchin, who was in charge now. With Dyer entered Irving, Rehill and Plomer, and an escort of troops, and as Dyer stayed standing for his speech, the audience was forced to stand throughout. 'He rushed into the room, followed by others, all exceedingly angry, and he made a speech in Urdu':

> You people know well that I am a soldier and a military man, you want war or peace? And if you wish for war, the Government is prepared for war. And if you want peace, then obey my orders, and open all your shops, else I will shoot. For me the battlefield of France or Amritsar is the same.

Irving then spoke, advising all to comply with the General's orders, as 'the whole city is in his charge'. There were, unsurprisingly, no objections from the assembled worthies. Dyer agreed a request from the traders present that the shops be allowed to remain open until 10 p.m. (though he failed to alter the curfew, which was not to be relaxed from 8 to 10 p.m. for another ten days, so this was a promise he did not honour). He also promised that the city would be patrolled to protect them and that the water supply would be restored. The meeting closed, and Dyer marched back to the Ram Bagh. That evening, he posted fifty Gurkhas at the *kotwali*, and these immediately began to patrol all quarters of the city. A proclamation was made around the town to announce all this, and the shops opened the next day.[3]

Kitchin drove back to Lahore after he left the meeting, content that Amritsar was now again under control, even if things there had yet to be tidied up. As he did so, there were still dead bodies lying around the *hansli* in the Bagh; no one from either the military or civil government of the city made any attempt to ensure the site was cleared.[4]

Dyer was later to maintain that his action at the Jallianwala Bagh stopped the spread of insurrection in the Punjab. He was far from alone in making this claim, and from it sprang his reputation as the saviour of the Punjab and even, in its more extreme version, of India. It was this claim which, in the eyes of many of his British contemporaries, justified the shooting in the Bagh, and it was one widely accepted by the British in the Punjab. Irving believed it: 'The effect of this was electric. The news ended all danger of further disturbances in the district.' Kitchin agreed: 'All independent opinion is united that the blow struck on 13 April in Amritsar saved the central Punjab from anarchy, loot and murder.' Sir Michael O'Dwyer was of similar mind: 'I have no hesitation in saying that General Dyer's action that day was the decisive action in crushing the rebellion.' General Beynon ever afterwards maintained the view that 'the strong measures taken by General Dyer at Amritsar had a far reaching effect and prevented any further trouble in the Lahore Division Area'. Lieutenant-General Sir Havelock Hudson, the Adjutant General in India, tied himself up in knots before the subsequent inquiry trying to justify his statement that 'The result was that we had no more disturbances anywhere. The news of that was a very very great factor in stopping disturbances all over India.'

It is a claim, however, which General Hudson could not substantiate with any evidence under questioning and it is one contradicted by the chronology of events. It was not accepted by the Hunter Committee, the body later appointed to investigate the disturbances. An examination of the events in the hours and days after the shooting in the Jallianwala Bagh will make this clear. Whilst there is no doubt that Amritsar itself was terrified into immediate submission by the shooting, in the country areas around the city violence continued after the massacre. The railway station at Wagah on the line between Amritsar and Lahore was burnt on the night of the 13th, telegraph wires were cut, and the rails were pulled up, derailing the armoured train sent to deal with the outbreak. Another station at Jallo, closer to Lahore, was also burnt. The next day, on 14 April, there was violence at two Manjha villages, a *hartal* at Tarn Taran just south of Amritsar, and telegraph wires were cut in four places. At that point all violence did cease in Amritsar District, and this was probably due to the spreading fear of repression, but it was also due to the fact that throughout the Manjha most villagers had never taken any interest in the disturbances, and military columns marching through to 'pacify' the area found the people peacefully harvesting.

Further afield, as the reports of the shooting spread outwards like concentric ripples on a pond, violence accompanied them. The news reached Lahore on the evening of the 13th, well before either the Government or Army Headquarters there had reports, and thereafter unrest continued to spread across the Punjab. Attacks on telegraph lines across the province increased after the Jallianwala Bagh incident; on the 13th there were four, but on the 14th there were twelve, and seven on both the 15th and 16th. The attacks declined thereafter, but continued daily up until the 21st. Strikes by railway staff began after the massacre, on the 14th and 15th, and spread in subsequent days. At Gujranwala, sixty miles north of Lahore on the Grand Trunk Road, the station, telegraph office and post office, with the church and other buildings, were burned on 14 April, and the mob had to be bombed from the air before dispersing. Also that day, in Rohtak District, two hundred or more miles south east of Amritsar, and only twenty miles from Delhi, mobs attacked a train and damaged a bridge. *Hartals* occurred in many places that day, and wires were cut. On 15 April, violence occurred across Gujranwala District and in Gujrat, another forty miles to the north, where crowds attacking the station were driven off when the troops opened fire. *Hartals* and wire cutting continued across the province that day, and in Jullundur District *hartals* were observed in three places, though without violence. On the 16th, now three days after the massacre, mobs attacked government buildings in two villages in Gujranwala. *Hartals*, wire cutting and rail lifting, which led to the derailing of a train, spread to Jhelum, another forty miles north of Gujrat. All over the Punjab, *hartals* and wire cutting took place on 17 April, again on the 18th. More telegraph wires were cut on 19, 20, 21 and 22 April, and these attempts to cut British communications did not die out until the last case occurred on 2 May. In Jullundur, a signal station burned down on the night of 19 April, but this seems to have been an accident. Reports of strange itinerant preachers and *sadhus* continued to disturb Jullundur and Amritsar Districts for weeks. The situation in Lyallpur, eighty miles west of Lahore, was considered unstable enough as late as 24 April for martial law to be declared there. Indeed, martial law was declared in any part of the province only *after* the shooting in the Bagh, and it was justified at the time by the Punjab Government on the basis that it was designed to halt the spread of violence, violence which, according to Dyer's supporters, had been halted by his firing on the 13th.[5] From the record it is quite clear that the violence was a reaction to events in Amritsar, and that far from being 'the Saviour of the Punjab', Dyer's action at the Jallianwala Bagh was a major cause of the danger it was in.

The Government of India published Resolution Number 549 on 14 April. This set the tone for the administration's handling of the disturbances throughout the Punjab. It stated:

> It remains for the Governor-General in Council to assert in the clearest manner the intention of Government to prevent by all means, however drastic, any recurrence of these excesses. He will not hesitate to employ the ample military resources at his disposal to suppress organized outrage, rioting or concerted opposition to the maintenance of law and order ... To those servants of Government who are charged with the onerous responsibility of suppressing excesses against public peace and tranquility, the Governor-General in Council extends the fullest assurance of countenance and support.

H.D. Craik, Deputy Secretary of the Home Department, told the European Association on the following day that the Government would 'not hesitate to employ any action, however drastic, to protect the lives of its law-abiding citizens'. The Viceroy sent the provincial governors a message indicating that the Government would use any means to restore law and order, and that he would support them if they acted accordingly:

> On the 14th of April we published a Resolution in which we clearly laid down that we would not hesitate to employ any means at our disposal to suppress organized outrage, rioting or concerted opposition to the maintenance of law and order; and I informed the Heads of Local Governments that they might rely on my support in any action which they considered necessary to take for this purpose.[6]

As violence spread in the world outside, Amritsar, now pretty much cut off from the rest of the province by the British control of routes out of the city, was the calm at the eye of the storm. On the 15th, the garrison sent a column to suppress the *hartal* at Tarn Taran. Dyer began to detail off small parties of soldiers to travel onboard all trains routed through the Punjab, and to guard outlying stations and government offices. A radio set arrived to allow communications with 16 Division, and with Headquarters Northern Army at Peshawar. That day saw the return of the 1st/124th Baluchis to Lahore, with their Commanding Officer, Lieutenant-Colonel Morgan; they were to be replaced on the 16th by a party of 117 men of the 52nd Sikhs whom Dyer ordered down from Jullundur. More reinforcements were to follow from there on the 18th, as things were by then judged quiet enough in Jullundur for its garrison to be depleted. The new troops were 105 Gurkhas of the 1st Battalion, 7th Gurkha Rifles from Bakloh and a section of field guns with forty-six men of the 1093rd Battery, RFA.[7]

Yet despite the deathly quiet in Amritsar, on the morning of 15 April, the Government of India declared martial law there. In effect, this declaration legalised the *de facto* martial law the military had been exercising there since the 10th. Amritsar District was simultaneously proclaimed under section 15 of the Police Act, allowing the police greater powers of arrest and detention. The reasons for this introduction of martial law remain cloaked in shadows. It is clear that the Viceroy committed himself to it at the urging of Sir Michael O'Dwyer, and it seems that to a large degree the Government of India acquiesced in the proposal through panic, with little analysis of the need for the measure or understanding of O'Dwyer's aims in recommending it. The civil service at the centre, bitterly hostile to the Rowlatt agitators, was not inclined to oppose O'Dwyer, and the Viceroy, who was severely rattled in the early stages of what looked like a widespread revolt, was susceptible to his persuasion. Lord Chelmsford had told O'Dwyer by telephone on the 12th that if troops 'had to fire they should make an example', and that day the Government of India had warned the Governor of Burma to be prepared to accept political prisoners from India; they were clearly getting ready for repressive measures. The Resolution of the 14th makes it clear that the Viceroy considered he was facing a rebellion. Lord Chelmsford was thus receptive to O'Dwyer's demand of 13 April, that, as a 'state of open rebellion exists in parts of districts of Lahore and Amritsar', martial law should be declared there. O'Dwyer went up to Simla to lobby for this personally, and was granted his wish within the day. Martial law was declared under article 2 of Bengal regulation 10 of 1804; the courts were suspended and replaced by tribunals staffed by specially appointed judges. This slight amendment of the usual regulations, which strictly allowed only military courts to sit in martial law cases, was to mean that, although he was to be the martial law administrator of his district, Dyer never sat in judgment in a case brought by his officials.

O'Dwyer maintained that he sought the implementation of martial law to stop the spread of what he saw as a widespread and organised rebellion into the rural recruiting areas and into the Army, and to make it easier to deal with those arrested during the disturbances. Commissioner Kitchin explained the Punjab Government's reasoning:

> It was necessary to strike quickly and strike hard in order to save the rural people and above all to save the Army from infection ... Martial Law was necessary to provide summary courts for the clearance of the lock-ups which were full of arrests. Delay was most undesirable, and it was necessary to show at once that the rising had failed.

In fact, the day on which the Punjab Government applied for martial law was one in which control had already been recovered in both Lahore and Amritsar. Whilst violence was occurring elsewhere, martial law was not necessary to deal with the outbreaks of violence that occurred in these two places. The link between the suppression of violence and the imposition of martial law was tenuous; indeed, the Punjab Government was later to apply martial law in areas where the only violence was the cutting of telegraph wires. Fears of the spread of the violence were no doubt genuine, but the rural areas were not greatly affected, and the Army remained untouched. General Hudson was asked by the Hunter Committee:

> *Question*: With regard to the attempts to tamper with the Indian troops, I understood you to say that there was no organized or serious attempt in that way at all?

> *Answer*: I do not think so.

Whatever Sir Michael O'Dwyer believed, the Rowlatt agitation, and the violence that erupted after its suppression in Amritsar and Lahore, was not a repetition of the conspiracies he had faced before and during the war. The tragic fact was that he was bent on crushing a conspiracy that did not exist. Sir C.R. Cleveland, the officer of the Central Intelligence Department responsible for investigating this issue, came to this conclusion by June: 'I understand that the theory of widespread and deep conspiracy is not held in responsible quarters in the Punjab.' In July, the Home Department's Deputy Secretary, H.D. Craik, was asked to look for evidence of a conspiracy for Sir William Vincent, the Home Member, to use in debates in the Legislative Council. All he could come up with to support the conspiracy theory was the racially motivated attacks on individuals in Amritsar, where crowds had shouted '*Maro angrez!*'(Kill the English!), and a list of telegraph and railway line cutting which might have led an observer to conclude that there had been a coordinated plan of attack. The chronological record of violence did not justify this idea. There was never to be any improvement on this, and the Government abandoned the conspiracy theory. Sir Michael O'Dwyer, however, never did abandon it, but his intentions in seeking the imposition of martial law went well beyond the suppression of violence.

The key point of martial law as far as the Punjab Government was concerned was that the normal courts of justice were suspended for crimes committed during the disturbances. In their place, the new special commissions and tribunals were able to pass greater sentences based on easier rules of evidence, which required no confirmation of sentence and from which there was no appeal. Opponents of the Government could thus be punished in a way impossible under normal criminal law. O'Dwyer showed that this was the issue of most concern to him by applying to the Viceroy to backdate martial law to 30 March, long before the violence began and the first day of the *satyagraha* agitation. After some argument over the illegality of retrospective legislation, on 21 April the Government of India reluctantly agreed his request. O'Dwyer was thus able to sweep up all his political enemies, all of those who had been involved in the Rowlatt agitation. These were men who had been irritating, perhaps even dangerous, but who had not broken any law. In addition, he had a personal motive to deal so swiftly with his enemies, for he was within weeks of leaving his post; if he were to be able to deal finally with those who had opposed his rule, and so to be able to present his successor with a clean slate, he had to move fast.

This last supposition is, of course, conjectural, but it may account for the bitter and ultimately unsuccessful fight which O'Dwyer initiated as soon as martial law was declared to wrest control of its administration from the military. Inconceivable as it may seem, it really does appear that he thought he could bring down martial law upon his province, yet still remain in charge. The Viceroy, compliant in all else, would not yield in this; the rules were clear that martial law replaced the civil administration with a military one. To his immense chagrin, in his last few weeks in office, O'Dwyer had to take a back seat as a mere adviser to General Beynon. He did not find the cup of revenge he had filled quite so sweet to drink as he had imagined.[8]

Dyer was notified by General Beynon of the proclamation of martial law on 15 April, but the Viceroy's order in council had taken effect on the 13th, and it is probable that Dyer heard of it through Irving on that day or the next. Beynon told Dyer he would not need to convene courts or confirm findings, and instructed him to brief his officers to collect and prepare evidence for the use of the tribunals to be established. It took 16 Division another five days to set out the rules of martial law, which it published only in a proclamation of 19 April. By this, Dyer was appointed martial law administrator, with Major S.R. Shirley as his Area Officer, or Provost Marshal, for Amritsar District; the latter was entrusted with the administration of martial law on Dyer's behalf. General Beynon's proclamation listed sixteen new acts that were now made offences; these were in addition to the normal criminal offences which continued to be dealt with by the courts. The regulations were drafted widely enough to enable the easy prosecution of offenders; they were aimed at the prevention of disorder, to allow the military to impose discipline on the civilian population and to prevent the continuance of any political activity. They included provisions against 'being in arms against the State or inciting others to be in arms'; 'assisting or harbouring rebels'; 'failure to report gatherings of rebels'; 'use of language or issuing proclamations likely to foment rebellion or promote hostility between different classes of His Majesty's subjects'; 'convening or attending a meeting of more than five persons'; 'disobeying an order given by a civil military officer in the execution of his duty when administering martial law'; and the catch-all 'committing an act in prejudice of good order of public safety or calculated to hamper or mislead His Majesty's forces'. The Area Officer was empowered to try cases under these rules arising only after the 19th; Irving, Rudkin, Puckle, Beckett and Connor, all local civil servants, were gazetted with similar powers to deal with minor cases arising before the 19th. Major cases, which included the capital crimes of 10 April, were to be referred to the Martial Law Commission in Lahore. The martial law courts were also permitted to deal summarily with minor offences committed against normal law as the huge number of these cases had begun to swamp the regular courts. These new martial law courts were entitled to award punishment of up to two years' rigorous imprisonment, a fine of 1000 rupees, or both, and whipping.[9]

Unaware of this gathering cloud, Amritsar was getting back to normal. 'Everything was now perfectly quiet and the demeanour of the inhabitants of the city subdued. Practically all signs of the marked insolence which had been apparent from the 10th to the 13th disappeared.' A column marched through the city at 11 a.m. on 15 April. Water was restored during the day. The soldiers of the garrison, at first instructed to move about only in groups, soon found that it was safe to do so individually.[10]

Dyer drove up to Lahore on the 16th to attend a conference chaired by General Beynon at Government House, Sir Michael O'Dwyer being present but no longer in charge. The meeting was arranged to allow all the brigadiers and other senior officers of the division the chance to discuss the handling of martial law. After the conference, the Lieutenant-Governor, with his Chief Secretary, J.P. Thompson, took a few minutes to question Dyer about what had happened in the Jallianwala Bagh. Dyer told him that he feared his small force would be surrounded and cut off. After he fired the first volley, he explained, the crowd made a rush, and he had thought they were going to attack him or get behind him, so he kept on firing. He told O'Dwyer that he now felt he had been mistaken in this view, 'after seeing the place more fully'. Dyer was still developing the line he had initiated in his first report, but was now offering an explanation for the length of firing as well as for opening fire immediately. The account is no more convincing than before; as an explanation of an action covering a period of between ten and fifteen minutes firing, with multiple reloading, it can only have convinced those not too particular about the numbers he had killed.[11]

On 16 April, the Punjab Government applied for an extension of the Seditious Meetings Act to Jullundur. The Chief Secretary told the Home Department of the Government of India: 'undesirable meeting reported from Multan and provincial congress due to meet this week at Jullundur. Please sanction declaration of these two districts as proclaimed under Seditious Meetings Act, 1911.' This request was made despite the cancellation on the 14th of the Provincial Congress meeting planned in Jullundur due to the arrest in Lahore of its chairman. The extension was sanctioned, though there was at that stage little violence in Jullundur; wires were cut that day just outside the cantonment, as well as in two villages of the district, and sporadic *hartals* were still going on in a few places, but that was all. This was purely a move by the Punjab Government to prevent a political meeting. Dyer was told by 16 Division to organise an armoured train to patrol to the east of Jullundur that day.

Also on the 16th, the Chief Secretary told the Home Department that in Amritsar the 'situation is well in hand and confidence is being restored'. It was now being restored by the use of a great deal of force. From then until martial law was lifted on 9 June, a sustained pattern of oppression developed in the city. The police were in charge of all investigations, and handled all the evidence. They were spurred on both by a desire for revenge for the humiliations they had suffered in the city, as well as by the financial pickings which martial law offered; it gave almost unlimited scope for arrest and detention, and there were many allegations of police extortion made at this time. Dyer was not unaware of this and, characteristically, ordered those with complaints of corruption to approach him directly. None did, but by the time he left Amritsar in early May he had collected enough evidence against one policeman to mount a case for corruption. This was just the tip of the iceberg, for the police conducted daily arrests and searches, accompanied by brutality and, in some cases, torture to extract confessions.

Eighty-six people were arrested between 18 and 19 April, one hundred and fifty arrests were recorded on the 21st alone, and an order that all suspicious *sadhus* be arrested was issued on the 25th. Each wave of arrests was triggered by the confessions and information extracted from those arrested before. By 30 April a total of 350 people had been arrested. Many of these were held without trial; 193 of those arrested in the district were to be held for periods of up to seventy-nine days then released without any charges being brought. Allegations arose of sexual assault by the police on low-caste women and of their rough handling of some women in *purdah*, who were stripped of their veils and made to go outdoors. Dyer took interest only in the allegations of ill-treatment of Sikhs, doing his best to counter rumours of rape, and making much of an incident at the railway station where Sikh girls were questioned about their possession of *kirpans*, the knives prescribed by their religion, which they were allowed by the police to keep in their possession. All this police activity rapidly returned the city to an atmosphere of hatred and fear; the Area Officer complained that people would not give evidence or assist the police, and 'that there is no doubt that the inhabitants of the city and district became sullen and resentful as arrests and investigations proceeded'. Maulvi Gholam Jilani, *imam* of a mosque in Katra Garba Singh in the city, who had organised the party of boys dressed as Turks for the Ram Naumi procession of 9 April, was arrested three times and pressurised to give false evidence against Dr Kitchlew and Dr Satyapal. On the third occasion

Jowarhar Lal went in a phaeton [to the Gilwali Gate Police Lines]. Kesar Singh and armed constables took me in another carriage. They began to beat me without saying anything.

They beat me and beat me till I passed urine. Then they caused my trousers to be put off, and beat me severely with shoes and a cane … They beat me until I became senseless … Kesar Singh again took me into another room and beat me severely. Not content with that, *he pushed a stick into my anus* … I could not bear the agony and became unconscious.[12]

Most of this mistreatment was not at Dyer's order; the police, in theory under his command, were not really under his control, and it is clear that Plomer for one was intent on showing the city who was master. Within the military, the detailed handling of the martial law administration was the Provost Marshal's responsibility and Dyer himself was out of the city for much of the time; he led three marches, each of several days in duration, through the surrounding countryside to pacify, successfully, the Sikhs of the Manjha. All that said, however, it is the inescapable fact that Dyer was in charge. He gave the orders, and set the tone for the actions of his subordinates. His own behaviour gave them all the example they needed. When he was in the city, every few days starting on 15 April, he developed the habit of driving in state around the town in his car, escorted by large numbers of troops. On these tours, he would stop and take note of any locals who did not *salaam* him in proper military fashion. Dyer had asked Irving to spread the word that all should salute him: 'The General brought to my notice the fact that people were not salaaming him when he went out, and asked me to make it known that he should be salaamed.' Those who did not *salaam* were told to report at the Ram Bagh, where they were kept waiting in the sun all day, and sometimes detained overnight, and taught to salute. Har Gopal Khanna was one who failed to *salaam*;

On the 18th of April, 1919, while I was passing through Karmon Deori street, along with three other gentlemen, I saw some policemen on horseback, followed by some motor-cars, and I stopped on the side of the road. A motor-car, carrying some military officers passed by us, and stopped a few paces further. The gentleman sitting on the left side of the car, signalled me to go to him. On reaching there, I made a salute in the military fashion. The officer on the right of the car who, as we were afterwards told, was General Dyer, addressed me as follows:

Dyer: Have you forgotten to *salaam*?

Khanna: No Sir, I did not see you and I did not know the order.

Dyer: What is your trade?

Khanna: I am a Sub-Head in Chief Auditor's Office, North-West Railway. Lahore.

Dyer: You must present yourself at 9 a.m. tomorrow in the Ram Bagh garden.

An Indian officer, probably a Subedar, had, in the meanwhile, taken down my full address, after obtaining it from me. I took leave of the General with a salute, and asked Mr Plomer, City Superintendent of Police, who was standing by, as to whether I had to present myself to the Club House in the Ram Bagh garden, whereupon he ordered a constable on horseback to take me to the Kotwal Sahib … At the Kotwali, we passed the night, sitting or lying in the open, on the stairs, below the verandah, and a Gurkha guard was placed on us. At about 8.30 in the morning, we were marched to the Ram Bagh garden, surrounded by armed policemen. We were made to stand in the sun, on the tennis ground, and a military Hawaldar was deputed to teach us how to *salaam* properly … Then we were let off.[13]

On about 14 April, Dyer ordered all the lawyers of the town, about one hundred all told, to enrol as special constables, and instructed that they report daily to the Provost Marshal at 10 a.m., 1 p.m. and 5 p.m., supposedly so that they could be given instructions to pass on to the inhabitants. On one occasion, he held this meeting at the Ram Bagh whilst a flogging was going on next to the assembled pleaders. They were made to patrol the streets and ordered to inform on the citizens. Some were given manual labour. Because of this, they were unable to work as lawyers during this time and much resented what they regarded as a degrading and time-wasting occupation. Dyer maintained that the lawyers liked the job, but the record is full of their complaints. Dyer states that he let off the old lawyers from this duty after Irving asked for their release, but this does not seem to have happened. Lala Kanhyalal Bhatia, under whose name the Jallianwala Bagh meeting of the 13th had been advertised, and who was seventy-five years old, was detailed as a special constable on the 22nd

when there was no necessity for such an appointment for the maintenance of peace and order in the city. The police force was quite sufficient for the purpose, and as a matter of fact, the city was quiet on those days. In my old age I was made to work like a coolie, carrying tables and chairs from one place to another, and had to patrol the city in the hot sun. The abuse which was showered on us and the indignities to which we were put, added greatly to our sufferings. I cannot believe that our appointment was necessary for the maintenance of peace and order. The order was meant to punish us. The local Bar takes part in public affairs and it took a prominent part in the Rowlatt Act agitation. That is why the whole Bar was punished in this way.

Irving got Dyer to relax the order later; the members of the Bar were appointed ward officers rather than constables, with easier duties. This relaxation, and the fact that Dyer listened to Irving on this occasion, was unusual. Dyer seems to have consulted Irving as little as possible; the latter complained that he was 'formally in a worse position than if he had been political officer on the staff of the local commander as there he would have had the right to be consulted'.[14]

Unpleasant and petty as this treatment was, it was actually better than the treatment meted out under martial law to locals in other places in the Punjab, where physical punishments were often more frequently and more arbitrarily inflicted, and where 'unusual' punishments, more redolent of the public school than of government, were invented and applied by some British officers. The inhabitants of Amritsar were, however, totally cowed by these actions and gave no resistance. The city was patrolled daily from 17 to 20 April without further incident. Indeed, things were now more unsettled in Jullundur, though not greatly so; wires were cut on the 17th, and the district was proclaimed that day under Section 15 of the Police Act, to make it easier, perhaps, to arrest any members of the Punjab Congress who might still have been intent on assembling there. A few more wires were cut on the 18th, after which Jullundur fell as quiet as Amritsar. Gandhi, appalled by the violence his *satyagraha* had unleashed, made a public announcement suspending civil disobedience that day.[15]

The same day in Amritsar, Irving issued an *ishtihar* in Urdu giving an account of what had occurred in the city to date and warning the public to obey the military. Dyer does not seem to have taken notice of this, and Irving did not report it to the Hunter Committee, which did not record it. The note was the only proclamation made attempting to justify what had happened hitherto. It included the words:

> The General had issued an order that no meeting was to be held without *his* permission. When that order was disobeyed, the General went to the meeting accompanied by fifty soldiers … Seeing the soldiers, the people showed an attitude of defiance. On this the order to fire was given with the result that many were wounded and many killed … General Sahib will not, in future, put up with any kind of unrest.[16]

On 19 April, the party of 1st/9th Gurkhas who had continued to do duty in the city was at last permitted to continue its journey to Peshawar, and Dyer felt confident enough by then to order the restoration of the electricity supply. That day, he and Annie, who had driven down from Jullundur shortly before, visited Miss Sherwood in the fort, where she was still lying seriously ill. The sight of her injuries affected both of them deeply. Next day, at church parade in the civil lines, Dyer lectured the British troops of the garrison against taking unauthorised reprisals against Indians; he said that he believed that many of the British troops had become incensed by what had happened in the city, particularly to Miss Sherwood, though the timing of this lecture indicates that at least one of those who had become so incensed was himself. Irving states that he, too, was worried that some might seek reprisals:

> I think it right to say that the feeling among Europeans was desperately bitter, some civilians in the fort were saying what they would do to Indians when they got out, and I was seriously afraid of acts of reprisal.

At church, Dyer announced special provisions for what he called the 'sacred' spot where Miss Sherwood had been left for dead. He later visited the fort and repeated this order to the civilians there, presumably for their satisfaction. The orders were unique. Daytime picquets were to be placed at either end of the street where the assault had taken place (they were not required at night due to the curfew), and anyone wishing to proceed along the street between 6 a.m. and 8 p.m. was to be made to crawl the 150 yards of its length 'on all fours'. This was expanded in the deed by his soldiers, who made those subject to the order proceed 'lying flat on their bellies and crawling exactly like reptiles. The whole motion, therefore, had to be performed by the movement of the belly and arms'. One of those who did this recalled:

> I had to lie with my belly on the ground and move on my shoulders with the arms bent like a grasshopper's. The street is very long and hence it was very difficult and painful to crawl like that … If anybody raised his buttock in crawling he was kicked by the *goras* who patrolled the street. The street was patrolled by about eighteen *goras* who came at 6 in the morning and left at 8 in the evening for many days.[17]

The first to undergo this punishment were eleven people Dyer had arrested for failing to *salaam* him; these were 'by chance' taken to the street and made to crawl its length. Dyer explained later why he had instituted this order: 'We look upon women as sacred or ought to. I was searching my brain for a suitable punishment to meet this awful case ... I was closing the street to punish them.' Dyer always made it absolutely clear that the order was his idea, though one other possibility is mentioned by McCallum:

> During breakfast next day, 12 April, General Dyer talked about his drive round.[18] Much to his surprise and amusement he had found that the guard (British) at the place where the English lady had been beaten up, had told everyone that if they wanted to pass, they must crawl. I am convinced that General Dyer did not issue such an order.

It is just a possibility that Dyer took up an idea that had been thought up by his soldiers for their own amusement. That the soldiers did find it amusing is clear from the surviving photos of men of the 25th Londons prodding a crawling man along the street with a bayonet. Yet Dyer's report of August is too specific in the circumstances it describes to allow much weight to be given to McCallum's story; indeed his story begs the question as to why the guard was there at all. The street was not an important one. Dyer himself stated:

> I inspected the spot where Miss Sherwood ultimately fell, and I gave orders for a triangle to be erected there. I then posted two British picquets, one at each end of the street, with orders to allow no Indians to pass, that if they had to pass, they must go through on all fours.[19]

The order was another occasion upon which the Deputy Commissioner, Irving, showed his lack of mettle:

> I was not there at the time. He [Dyer] said he had issued it and asked whether it was all right. I asked him to make sure that no woman was involved and said I supposed it was all right. I understood then that it would block a single place. The next morning, after consideration, I advised him to modify it slightly ... I said it would probably be just as good and better in many ways if people were told to remove their shoes while passing the place.

Dyer took no notice – 'He however adhered to his order for which he said he was fully responsible' – though it does seem that the order was assumed by all not to apply to women. It remained in force until Sir Michael O'Dwyer heard of it and asked for its cancellation. It is notable that not a single supporter of Dyer could bring himself to support the crawling order; even the military found it impossible to justify. The Adjutant-General, Lieutenant-General Sir Havelock Hudson, stated in his evidence to the Hunter Committee: 'The order was of course an unusual one, and not one which might have been considered necessary by other officers in like circumstances. The Officer in Command at Amritsar will doubtless be prepared to justify his action should he be called upon to do so.' The order was rescinded sometime between 24 and 26 April. Dyer stated that he had not believed 'any sane man would voluntarily go through under these conditions ... therefore I thought nobody would crawl'. In fact, as he himself admitted, some forty-three people were made to crawl through the street, though he also maintained that some had to be prevented from doing so as they were mocking his order; one man was stopped after crawling through three times.

It was the humiliation of the order which struck Indians most deeply, but apart from the shame felt by those made to wriggle up the street on their bellies, the order effectively closed the street. The houses had no back doors and the inhabitants, who included those who had rescued Miss Sherwood, could not go out without climbing down from their roofs. Dyer claimed not to understand this, and also claimed that the inhabitants were able to go out at night when the picquets were withdrawn. The curfew which he himself had imposed began at 8 p.m., and was not relaxed to 10 p.m. until 25 April, so in effect the street was closed for twenty-four hours a day. No doctor, supplier or sweeper could call. The sick went untended, the rubbish and latrines piled up, and people were forced to sleep at their shops or elsewhere. The locals alleged that the soldiers fouled their well and temple, and ate its sacred pigeons. Kahan Chand, who was blind, stated:

> I have been blind for the last twenty years. I used to have meals occasionally in Kucha Kurrichhan. About 18 April, while I was groping my way into the street with the support

of a stick that I always carry, I was asked by a policeman to halt. On my begging him to let me proceed, I was told that I could do so only if I was willing to crawl over the whole length. I informed the policeman that I had been practically starving for the last two days, but he would not let me go. I then had to crawl on my belly, and had hardly gone a few yards when I received a kick on my back, and my stick slipped off my hands.

Rakha Ram, a shopkeeper living in the Kucha Duglan, stated:

He ordered me to turn back and crawl on my belly from the Kaurianwala well up to the place where he was sitting. So I had to go back and crawl on my belly all the distance from the house of Lala Bihari Lal to my own house. I could get nothing to eat in my house during the night, and when I wanted to go out the next morning on the 19th of April, the British soldiers again compelled me to crawl as before ... The soldiers eased themselves on our well in the bazaar also, so we could not draw water from it.[20]

Dyer determined to avenge the crime against Miss Sherwood by flogging in public the men he thought were responsible:

It seemed intolerable to me that some terrible punishment could not be meted out. Civil law was at an end and I searched my brain for some military punishment to meet the case. Shooting was, in my opinion, far too mild a punishment and it was for me to show that woman must be looked upon as sacred.

Six youths who were suspected (yet only in some cases later convicted) of the assault on Miss Sherwood were brought from the fort, and, ostensibly for disciplinary offences that they had committed whilst in custody, were lashed with thirty stripes on the frame of wood at the end of the street. The Provost Marshal claimed that the street was closed off at the time, but eyewitness accounts refute that.[21] Whilst flogging was not an uncommon punishment in India, the accounts of these floggings in the INC report make clear the reality of what Dyer had ordered. Pandit Salig Ram, a municipal employee, who lived nearby, stated:

I witnessed the flogging of six boys in front of Kucha Kurrichhan. Sundar Singh was the first to be fastened to the flogging post (tiktiki) and given thirty stripes. He became senseless after the fourth stripe, but when some water was poured into his mouth by a soldier, he regained consciousness; he was again subjected to flogging. He lost consciousness for the second time, but the flogging never ceased till he was given thirty stripes. He was taken off the flogging post, bleeding and quite unconscious. Mela was the second to be tied to the post. He too became unconscious after receiving four or five stripes. He was given some water, and the flogging continued. Mangtu was the third victim. He too got thirty stripes. While Mangtu was being flogged, I cried bitterly, and as I could not bear the sight any longer, I lost my consciousness. When I recovered my consciousness, I saw the six boys who had just received flogging, were bleeding badly. They were all handcuffed, and, as they could not walk even a few paces, they were dragged away by the Police. They were then taken to the Fort.[22]

When Dyer met Sir Michael O'Dwyer after the crawling order had been cancelled, the Lieutenant-Governor asked him what had led him to issue such an 'irregular and improper order'. True to form, and following the pattern of his earlier report to O'Dwyer about the Jallianwala Bagh, Dyer dissembled;

> He referred to his position at the time, that he had a certain number of British troops, he had the greatest difficulty in restraining them because they had seen English ladies savagely assaulted, they had known that their fellow countrymen had been killed and he thought they might break out of control; he therefore ordered this punishment to make an impression on their minds.

This account is unbelievable. Dyer was not the sort of officer to be pushed into anything by unruly subordinates and was too proud a man to have admitted it if he had been. Moreover, the assumption that it was somehow acceptable to treat a civilian population in this fashion simply to 'make an impression' on the minds of the troops speaks volumes about Dyer's view of the relationship between the two.[23]

O'Dwyer travelled down by armoured car to Amritsar with Kitchin, for the first time since the outbreak, on 20 April. This was the day Dyer instituted the crawling order, but Dyer does not seem to have told him about it when they met in the civil station. Dyer was by that stage using the Circuit House there as his Headquarters. O'Dwyer's was, indeed, a flying visit, and he did not think it necessary to take in the Jallianwala Bagh during his tour of the city. He claimed that it was 'undesirable' to go there as he could only travel with a military escort before and behind, and that no carriage could get through the passage. He clearly had no intention of seeing it. He was not alone in this; Irving hadn't been there either. The Lieutenant-Governor's cavalcade swept in one end of the town, past the burned out buildings, and out the other, before moving on to the fort. There he found eighty women and children still holed up in the four rooms that was all the shelter it provided, and listened, and gave a sympathetic ear, to their demands for justice to be meted out on those who had committed the crimes of the 10th. He saw Miss Sherwood, but at no stage did he meet any one from the city, a place for which he had little affection. He had written to the Viceroy a few days before: 'The Amritsar business cleared the air, and if there was to be a holocaust anywhere, and one regrets that there should be, it was best at Amritsar.' He then returned to Lahore, where his extension in office was to be announced the next day. He described his visit to the Viceroy, who himself at no stage in any of the disturbances had bestirred himself to visit the Punjab, let alone Amritsar:

> I motored down to Amritsar yesterday and spent some hours there, went through the city with the General Officer Commanding, Commissioner of Division and the troops. All were salaaming most profusely and they are thoroughly frightened. Lakhs of rupees

worth of property looted from the bank godowns is being thrown into the streets at night. A good deal has been found in the adjoining villages ... I think our prompt action in dominating Lahore and Amritsar by an overwhelming military force ... paralysed the movement before it had time to spread.[24]

The Army viewed it as vital that the recruiting grounds in the country districts be kept loyal. 16 Division had sent its first moveable column through the rural Manjha heading towards Amritsar from Ferozepore to its south as early as 13 April; the column reached the city ten days later. Dyer, along with the other Punjab Army commanders, was instructed by General Beynon at the conference in Lahore to take similar action locally. On 21 April, as the garrison had by then been reinforced sufficiently to allow troops to be detached for duties outside the city, he set out with the first of what was to be three columns that penetrated out into the countryside from the city, taking Irving with him. The column was an impressive force, with two hundred infantry (including one hundred men of the Londons) and twenty cavalry, and his two armoured cars. They went by train to Gurdaspur, some forty miles to the north east of Amritsar, where the local officials had called in the chief people of the area to a gathering at the school. Dyer and Irving harangued the local notables, denying that women had been raped or that the Golden Temple had been bombed. Gurdaspur was a town which had seen considerable unrest on the 13th and 14th, but had been quiet since. Commissioner Kitchin had ordered the collection of the names of those amongst its lawyers who had supported the *hartal* in the town, and this was done; their licences were revoked and they were later to be taken off to Lahore and held for two months.

Whilst the column spent the night there, Dyer and Briggs took their train and an escort to visit the Gurkha detachment at Pathankot another twenty miles further along the line. Back at Gurdaspur, the whole column slept the night in the train before travelling on to the next location they were to visit, Dhariwal, early the next day. There at 9 a.m. Dyer again addressed a meeting. With the help of the local police, five men were arrested for organising the local *hartal* and a government servant was arrested for behaving insolently (it is not recorded to whom, though one suspects it was to Dyer). The process was repeated that afternoon at Batala, the next stop, where two meetings were held, one of the dignitaries of the town, and the second of the rural *lambadars*. The train took the column back to Amritsar in the evening, and the prisoners it had collected were lodged in the Govindgarh Fort. 45 Brigade organised a similar, but smaller, flying column to visit villages in Jullundur District at the same time. It moved out on the 22nd, and stayed out until the 24th.[25]

On 23 April, in the Circuit House once more, Dyer wrote a full report for 16 Division on the riots in Amritsar; regrettably this has not survived. The Lieutenant-Governor designate, Sir Edward Maclagan, with W. M. Hailey of the

ICS, drove down from Lahore at about this time to meet Dyer, who told them that he had, at the Jallianwala Bagh, been 'preoccupied by the memory of standing instructions given to Army officers that, when called upon to aid the civil authorities, it was imperative to secure the safety of any detachments under their charge against attacks made by a hostile crowd.' Maclagan and Hailey accepted this explanation, but it is clear that Dyer was trying out a new version of his account on them, and one which subsequently he allowed to disappear, perhaps as it was paper thin. General Beynon conducted his first and only visit to Amritsar on the 24th. His Headquarters war diary gives the timings of his visit as 6 a.m. to 1.10 p.m., but 45 Brigade's war diary shows that Dyer had left Amritsar with another column in time to reach a village named Raja Sansee by 9 a.m., so they had little time together. Beynon did wish to see the Jallianwala Bagh. The street was not too narrow for the General, who was shown around by Dyer, who told him that he had had to open fire without warning and 'hit hard' as the place was 'a trap', and as his forces would have 'perished like a fly flattened on a wall' if he had hesitated. Beynon did ask Dyer why he had fired so long, and Dyer told him the story he had given O'Dwyer on the 16th, that the surging of the mob had made him think it was rushing his force. Beynon accepted this explanation.[26]

On his second expedition into the Sikh rural areas, Dyer took with him a senior Sikh priest, Mahant Siri Kirpa Singh of the important Guru Sat Sultani shrine. Irving went along again, and this time Dyer took even more troops. Two hundred and fifty infantry (again including a company of the Londons), twenty cavalry, some field guns and the armoured cars. They held a large *darbar* at the village of Raja Sansee, and there the *mahant* spoke to good effect to dispel rumours about the Temple. They then marched on to China Bugga, held a meeting there in the afternoon and camped around Canal Bungalow for the night. On the next day, the column went on to Atari, Dyer, escorted by the cavalry and an armoured car, visiting the mission at Ashrapur on the way. They held another large meeting in the evening, and the column camped for the night around the Public Works Department rest house. A British officer present with the column recorded his impression of what was happening, and was witness to some of the meetings that Dyer had with his old Sikh officers and men as the column progressed through the countryside:

> These old Sikh officers, in uniforms of bygone days, coming out of the villages to pay their respects to the General. With the help of the Indian officers whom they knew, and seeing their high priest with the column, the villagers soon began to realize they were being used or were meant to be tools in the hands of enemies of the Crown.

At Atari the next morning the names of eleven men implicated in the burning of Wagah Station were obtained from local informants. All of these were arrested by Irving, and the column arrested another five men who were found in possession of property stolen from the looted Amritsar banks. The column was back in the city in the afternoon of the 26th, Dyer returning through the small station of Chheharta, where the police had arrested thirty men for the attacks on the railway there. Back in Amritsar, he found that another company of 104 men from the 1st/7th Gurkhas had arrived from Bakloh. The garrison was still building up, and Battalion Headquarters of the Londons arrived the next day with Lieutenant-Colonel Hynes, their Commanding Officer. There was not enough space in the Amritsar barracks for all these troops, and the Londons were moved into the suburbs and billeted on families, travelling to work thereafter by requisitioned transport every day. They rather enjoyed this:

> As a result of this, most duties which required movement … were carried out in an almost sumptuous style … All the electric fans were also commandeered and fitted, in most cases, on the ceilings of the sleeping quarters. As usual the General looked to the comfort of the men under his command, and at Amritsar the Londons certainly had no reason to grumble on this score, even though the duties were stiff. [27]

The loss of their fans and means of transport was to figure largely in the complaints of Amritsar's inhabitants to the INC inquiry later in the year.

By the time Dyer got back to base, the first local martial law orders, thirteen in total, had been published by the Area Officer. These orders, issued in Dyer's name, were a supplement to the regulations published by 16 Division on the 19th. Why it was felt necessary to publish them now is unclear; the city had been under *de facto* martial law since the 10th, and, apart from the Jallianwala Bagh shooting, it had been completely quiet, supine in fact, ever since. The new orders were irritatingly petty, repressive in intent, designed to impose a military style of discipline upon the civilian population. It is true that two of them were relaxations of earlier orders: number one relaxed the curfew to the hours of 10 p.m. to 5 a.m, and number three increased the numbers permitted to accompany processions to ten, except for funerals, marriages and religious processions for which more were allowed. But numbers four and nine made it illegal to prevent shop owners opening their shops, and made it obligatory upon them to open them; in effect making *hartal* illegal. Number five prohibited the sale of third-class railway tickets, the only type open to most Indians. Number seven outlawed the carrying of a *lathi*; the size of the stick was not defined, and the police were to make use of this order to arrest people with walking sticks. Number eight made it unlawful to walk more than two abreast on a pavement. Number thirteen requisitioned all pedal cycles, which were ordered to be delivered to the fort by 27 April, and were henceforth reserved for the use of the military.[28]

Dyer was ordered by 16 Division to go out again into the rural areas on 28 April, this time to join the column that had come up from Ferozepore and which was now at Sursingh village, a place which was reported to be particularly disaffected. He took with him this time Irving's assistant, Puckle, and they both addressed the assembled *lambardars*, as before telling them that the Raj was not at an end, and warning them not to believe the rumours circulating about the Temple. That day, Dyer gave permission for the traditional Sikh *amarwas mela* to take place at Tarn Taran. He was still actively discriminating in favour of the Sikhs, and was at this time gathering together many of his old Sikh officers whom he sent out around the villages of the district to speak on his behalf. His staff in Jullundur were doing much the same; a column set out into the country on the 29th.[29]

At the Circuit House, on the 29th, Briggs received a call from the railway station, where the station master had found a suspiciously large numbers of *lathis*, 'very thick and heavy', on inbound trucks. He and Dyer went to take a look, and found a storehouse full to the roof, with more on the trucks. They inspected the records, and found that in the same period in 1918 only twelve bundles of staves had arrived; there were now 1056 bundles in the station, each of 200 canes, awaiting delivery to the city. They were 'not *lathis* but short sticks with curved handles'. Dyer believed these were intended to arm the *danda fauj* which he thought was to have been the army of the insurgents, and he and Briggs 'were very pleased at capturing what was evidently the enemy's arsenal'. More staves arrived from Saharanpur by 9 May, both '*lathis* and bamboo sticks'. There is no record, however, that the consignees were traced and no confirmation that these were for other than a genuine purpose. The large number was undoubtedly suspicious, and it is not beyond the bounds of possibility that someone in Amritsar had in fact been intent on arming anti-government mobs. The discovery of the *lathis* is one of the unsolved mysteries of the disturbances. Dyer kept one of them as a souvenir.[30]

In the evening of that day, Dyer and Briggs attended a 16 Division conference at Flagstaff House, Lahore, where General Beynon briefed his senior officers about his fears that there would be attempts by the 'rebels' to 'get at' the Indian troops. Dyer linked this in his own mind with the sweetmeats which he had heard had been given to the troops by the inhabitants of Amritsar. There were in fact no real attempts to subvert the troops during his time there, and Beynon's fears were unfounded. The Indian troops stayed solidly loyal throughout the Punjab disturbances. It was probably on that day that Dyer visited the Lieutenant-Governor to explain his actions over the crawling order. O'Dwyer put him in his place: 'I took him strongly to task.' It was perhaps also on that day that the Lieutenant-Governor prevented Dyer from imposing 'an enormous fine' on Amritsar in retribution for the events of the 10th; Dyer had perhaps raised the idea with him when they met. No doubt somewhat chastened, Dyer went on to Jullundur the next day, and in his Headquarters held a conference of his own commanders, all of whom assured him that their troops were loyal. He was back in Amritsar the same day, perhaps in time to watch some of the eight arrests that were made that day.

He continued his habit of parading through the city. The log records:

2 May: General Officer Commanding and cavalry and armoured car went through city. All being quiet and inhabitants most polite. All quiet during night. One arrest made.

4 May: General Officer Commanding with cavalry and armoured cars went through city at 1700 hours. Committee for civil damages held.

5 May: General Officer Commanding went into city with cavalry and armoured cars at 1800. Military Committee first meeting.[31]

More and more information came in concerning the corrupt behaviour of the police, and it began to widen the rift, already deep, between the military and the civilian authorities. Dyer put in train the case against an ex-sepoy constable who was alleged to have taken a bribe, but could not get it heard quickly, and it was eventually to fall to his successor as Martial Law Administrator, Lieutenant-Colonel Hynes, to bring the case to trial. Irving tried to have the case transferred to his court, but Hynes, clearly of similar mind to Dyer about the probity of the administration of local justice, would have none of it. He directed that it be heard by Major Shirley, who was ultimately to have to dismiss the charge for lack of evidence. The situation got so bad that Dyer complained of it to General Beynon, who in turn wired Army Headquarters on 8 May: 'Amritsar reports that the principal cause of discontent appears to be attitude of the Police. It is reported that the Police are extracting bribes under cover of Martial Law'. The Government of India put pressure on the Punjab Government to clear this up, and two more cases did finally come to trial. One, the case of a man named Ahmad Din, a head constable, who was accused of taking a bribe of 500 rupees, emerged after Dyer had left, and the man was successfully prosecuted and received a punishment of eighteen months' rigorous imprisonment. The most senior man prosecuted, Sub Inspector Khuda Baksh, eventually received a sentence of three years' rigorous imprisonment. J.P. Thompson recorded the talk of corruption in his diary for 29 July: 'Interesting talk with Kesho Ram, a loyal pleader of Amritsar. Spoke very strongly about behaviour of Police there and says that Plomer, the Eurasian DSP, is said to have made a lakh.' No evidence was ever obtained against Plomer, though his name reached the Home Department in Simla. If he made his fortune in the aftermath of the Punjab disturbances, he got away with it, as he went on leave in 1921 and disappeared.[32]

C.F. Andrews, Gandhi's aide and confidant, visited Amritsar in early May, the first of a stream of outsiders to visit the city once the restrictions on travel imposed by Sir Michael O'Dwyer had been relaxed. He wrote later:

> In those days, when I first came to Amritsar … I have seen with my own eyes just such a sudden rush of panic. I have also seen the police, at every corner, dominating the city. I have seen the long lines of cavalry patrolling the streets. I have understood from the lips of many witnesses, the terror which these forces have inspired.[33]

He was almost immediately arrested and deported from the province. There was to be no recurrence of political opposition in the city whilst Dyer was in charge.

Indeed, with all the political figures of the Rowlatt agitation locked up or on the run, the traditional heads of the religious and ethnic communities were beginning to reassert themselves, and to seek to reassure the British of their continued loyalty. Towards the end of April, Dyer was visited at the Circuit House by a crowd which came to thank him for restoring law and order and for saving the city from plunder. Briggs came out to take their messages to his Brigadier, and returned carrying Dyer's thanks, but the crowd would not leave without seeing Dyer, and in the end he was forced to come out to speak to them. He remembered that: 'I was thanked by thousands and the press on one occasion was greater than the Circuit House grounds could hold.'[34] Many, if not most, of those there that day must have been Sikhs, for by now the Sikh community, or at least those of it then in influential positions throughout the Punjab, had come out firmly on the Government side. The *Chief Khalsa Diwan*, the Sikh central governing body, issued a message to all Sikhs calling on them to abstain from any movement likely to disturb the peace of the country and to support the Government's efforts to restore law and order. Arur Singh, manager of the Golden Temple, along with seven other principal Sikh shrine managers, circulated a notice in early May that no aeroplane had touched the Temple, that no machine gun had been planted in it, and that no bombs had been dropped upon it.[35]

It was mutually advantageous, both to Dyer and to those then in power in the Sikh community in Amritsar, to make use of each other. Dyer supported the Sikhs both from his conviction that their community was loyal and from his personal affection for them. He was drawn to them in the way in which many British officers who served with them were drawn, to their martial, manly bearing and behaviour, and to the simplicity of their faith. He protected their Temple, honoured their *mahant*s, cultivated and employed their retired senior officers and toured their villages, and it is clear that he enjoyed doing this and was proud of his actions. In return, his Sikh troops held him in awe and affection, and the shrine managers and priests saw a man who was partial to their side. They happily did his bidding and kept their people away from political agitation and violence, making it clear through him to the Government that their community could be relied upon in a way that the Muslims and Hindus could not. Sikhs had not been prominent in the Rowlatt agitation in Amritsar; it is noteworthy that of the 291 Jallianwala Bagh dead whose *jat* can be identified, only twenty-two were certainly Sikhs. The Sikh leaders shamelessly flattered and humoured Dyer. At a ceremony sometime in late April, both he and Briggs were invited to the Golden Temple for the almost unheard of honour of being made honorary Sikhs. Annie later related what her husband told her of this ceremony (an account confirmed by the recollections of the Sikhs who were there at the time):

> 'Sahib', they said, 'you must become a Sikh even as Nikalseyn Sahib became a Sikh.'[36] The General thanked them for the honour, but he objected that he could not as a British officer let his hair grow long. Arur Singh laughed. 'We will let you off the long hair', he said. General Dyer offered another objection, 'But I cannot give up smoking'. 'That you must do', said Arur Singh. 'No', said the General, 'I am very sorry, but I cannot give up smoking.' The priest conceded, 'We will let you give it up gradually'. 'That I promise you', said the General, 'at the rate of one cigarette a year.'

Dyer and Briggs were presented with symbols of the Sikh faith, including the turban and *kirpan*, and were given a *siropa*. The *sarbrah* thanked them for their protection of the Temple. A few days later, as Dyer left Amritsar, bound for the Afghan War, the leading Sikhs of the city came to him to offer him ten thousand men to fight the Afghans, an offer he relayed to the Government but which was declined. There is evidence that a shrine was dedicated in his honour at the temple of Guru Sat Sultani.[37]

Martial law was a disastrous time for Amritsar. By the time it was lifted in June, the arrests that had been made in the city had resulted in major charges in the Lahore martial law tribunals against 298 persons. Of these, 218 were convicted. The punishments meted out by the tribunals were heavy. Fifty-one were sentenced to death, forty-six to transportation for life, 104 to imprisonment of between three and ten years, and eleven for lesser periods. The leaders of the Rowlatt agitation were particularly singled out. Dr Kitchlew and Dr Satyapal, whose arrest had sparked the conflagration, were sentenced by Mr Justice Broadway, before whom the cases against the Amritsar leaders were brought, to transportation for life to the Andaman Islands. Dr Muhammad Bashir, the organiser of the meeting in the Jallianwala Bagh, was sentenced to death and the forfeiture of all his property. On review, these sentences were reduced by the Government of India to two years' rigorous imprisonment for Kitchlew and Satyapal, and six for Bashir. In Amritsar itself, the martial law magistrates courts presided over by civilians dealt with twenty-two cases of minor crime, and tried 143 people, whilst the military magistrates dealt with twenty-six cases, such as breach of discipline, being out after hours, assault and refusal to give transport when requisitioned. Sixty persons were charged before the military courts, of whom fifty were convicted. Of these, twenty-six were whipped, though all but six were punished in private, as Dyer was prevented from using the flogging triangles he had erected in the open ground outside the walls.[38] But by then he had no longer any need to make the point he had intended. Amritsar was thoroughly cowed.

18

Thal

Whilst British attention was focussed on the agitation against the Rowlatt Acts, and on dealing with the Punjab disturbances which followed, an ominous situation was developing in Afghanistan. The Amir, Habibullah, had remained true to his treaty undertakings to the British during the First World War; he had not tried to establish relations with any foreign power and had kept Afghanistan neutral. After the war, however, he began to press for independence in foreign affairs, and sought, unsuccessfully, to send a representative to the Versailles peace conference. He had given shelter, but not support, to the various groups of Indian revolutionaries who had gravitated to Kabul over several decades. His balancing act was increasingly opposed, however, by both fundamentalist religious and nationalist elements. Within his own family, his brother, Nasrullah Khan, his third son, Amanullah, and the latter's mother, the senior queen, formed the Mashruta reform and war party, which had a mouthpiece in the sole newspaper in Kabul, the *Siraj-al-Akhbar*, a vociferously anti-British journal. On 19 February 1919, Habibullah was murdered whilst on a hunting trip, probably by Nasrullah Khan and the Commander-in-Chief of the Army, Nadir Khan. Nasrullah was proclaimed Amir, but Amanullah, back in Kabul, seized the treasury, and with its wealth succeeded by 27 February in deposing his uncle, who was to die shortly afterwards in prison. On 3 March, in a message to the Viceroy, Amanullah announced his succession to 'the free and independent Government of Afghanistan'; the Government of India chose to ignore the implications of this announcement. The new Amir quickly became unpopular, particularly in the army and amongst the Muslim clergy, who were antagonised by his treatment of his uncle, by the execution of Colonel Ali Raza, who was made a scapegoat for the murder of his father, and by the favour he showed the family of his in-laws, the Musahibans, particularly his father-in-law, Muhammad Tarzi, founder and proprietor of the *Siraj-al-Akhbar*. This last was now designated the Commissary for Foreign Affairs. By the start of April, the Amir's name began to be omitted from prayers in the mosques of Kabul, a sign he could not ignore.

Amanullah sought a foreign distraction to gain popularity at home, and he found his opportunity in the turmoil developing throughout March and April in India. Now, perhaps, with the British weak after the war, and distracted by India's internal problems, he might recover some of the territories his predecessors had lost across the Indus over the previous century. Perhaps now was also the time to throw off the British control of Afghan foreign affairs. He was assured by the Indian revolutionaries who clustered around his court, and who exaggerated the difficulties the British were facing in the Punjab, that India would surely now rise up in his support. In March, he issued a *firman* affirming the independence of Afghanistan and blaming his father's murder on British agents. On 13 April, the day on which Dyer's force was opening fire at the Jallianwala Bagh, Amanullah summoned tribal chiefs from the Frontier areas to a *darbar* in Kabul and told them that they should prepare for war. He appointed envoys to Teheran and Bokhara, openly breaching the treaty which reserved control of Afghan foreign affairs to the British, and began to send troops to the Frontier; the new Commander-in-Chief, Saleh Muhammad Khan, appeared at Dakka at the head of the Khyber Pass in late April with two companies and some guns, ostensibly on a frontier tour, and Nadir Khan, who had been restored to his rank of general, appeared further south at Matun in Khost Province, where he started to assemble forces brought forward from Ghazni. At a *darbar* held on 1 May, the Amir read aloud letters he had received from people in India complaining of British tyranny, and in his address he linked this with the British subjection of Baghdad and the Holy Places. Indian devotion in the war had been rewarded with cruelties and injustices, he said, and, although international law gave him no right to interfere, the Indians were justified in rising against their oppressors. 'It was a pity, he added, that the British considered no one but themselves to be human beings.' He declared he had ordered troops to the Frontier to prevent the Punjab disturbances spilling over into Afghanistan. Leaflets began to appear in British territory along the Frontier urging the tribes to rise up in defence of the faith, as the Egyptians, who were then in revolt against the British, were said to be doing: 'You should therefore use every possible means to kill British, continue to tear up railways and cut down the telegraph.'[1]

The Government of India had not expected that this deterioration in relations would lead to hostilities, but the Amir's pronouncements of 1 May alerted them to the danger.[2] They were still hoping that the Amir would take his activities only to a point short of war when, on 4 May, Afghan irregular forces occupied the small settlement at Bagh, which was on the British side of the Frontier inside the Khyber, and which controlled the water supply to the British station at Landi Kotal. The Afghans killed some labourers who were unlucky enough to be working there when they arrived. The Government of India ordered mobilisation on the 5th and halted all demobilisation of wartime troops. When the Amir refused to arrest Zar Shah, the Afghan commander at Bagh, as the British demanded, and cited the fact that he viewed the Rowlatt Acts as a 'tyrannical law' which prevented any extradition, war became inevitable. The Amir called a *loya jirga*, a gathering of all the tribes of Afghanistan, only the third in

Afghanistan's history, and declared a *jihad* against the British, who in turn declared war on the 6th.[3]

The Afghan plan was for an uprising behind British lines in Peshawar (a city which was full of Pathans, and which had been part of Afghanistan until the Sikhs had seized it a century before). Their army would then make three thrusts into India, a northern one down the Khyber, a second, central attack into the Kurram area, and a third, southern assault across the Frontier at Quetta. They hoped to take advantage of the disruption the disturbances in the Punjab had caused communications, but they were several weeks too late for this, as the imposition of martial law had already put the Punjab under military control. The Chief Commissioner of the North-West Frontier Province, Sir George Roos-Keppel wrote to Sir Michael O'Dwyer: 'What a blessing you got the Punjab in hand before this show started.' The Third Afghan War, which now broke out, had the unwanted side effect of delaying the lifting of martial law until peace was declared.

The rising in Peshawar was to have been coordinated by the Afghan post-master in the city, Ghulam Haider, who had been steadily subverting the inhabitants, and who boasted that he had about seven thousand men ready to rise on the 8th. He had travelled back from Jellalabad in Afghanistan on 4 May, his car loaded with leaflets saying that the Germans had restarted the war, and that India and China had risen against the British. Roos-Keppel caught wind of the conspiracy from an informer on the 7th and acted swiftly, turning off the water supply and surrounding the native city with troops the next day. He arrested the postmaster and his principal aides, and seized the large sums of money and propaganda which were concealed in his house, and this broke the conspiracy. The British also quickly dealt with the Afghan threat on the southern front by a pre-emptive seizure of the Afghan fort at Spin Boldak, just over the Frontier, and this deterred any further Afghan moves in the area. In the central Kurram area Nadir Khan hung back inside Afghanistan, giving no indications at first of his intentions. That left the Khyber front, where on 6 May the British Northern Army began to mobilise troops to eject the Afghans from Bagh.

The force was to be commanded by General Sir Arthur Barrett, the Commander-in-Chief of the Northern Army, who was based in Peshawar. The Indian Army's forces available to meet this emergency were weaker than at any time in the recent past. The First World War had drained many of India's units overseas, and many had yet to return, so overall strength was well down. The number of British troops in India had also fallen from an establishment of 75,000 to an actual strength of only 60,000; pre-war, there had been fifty-two battalions of British infantry, but in 1919 there were only eight regular and fifteen territorial battalions left. Of forty-five batteries of field artillery in India before the war, only nineteen were left, and of eleven horse batteries there were just two. Many of the men in these units were unfit; a territorial battalion of 16 Division, for instance, with a paper strength of 789, could muster only 380 fit men. The garrison units, meant for internal duties and largely composed of the old or unfit, were in a worse state. 16 Division had 249 garrison artillerymen of whom only thirty-eight were fit for duty, and of 539 men on the strength of its one garrison battalion only five were fit. The Indian units of the Army were similarly depleted. At the outbreak of the Afghan War, 124 battalions and eighty-nine squadrons of Indian troops were serving overseas. What was left of the Indian units of the Army was often a mix of the old who were about to be pensioned off, the infirm who were recovering from wounds and sickness, and new recruits. There was a scarcity of experienced officers to command the troops. Army Headquarters believed that, man for man, the tribesmen and Afghans were probably superior on the Frontier to their own soldiers, and that more troops would be needed to deal with the emergency than would have been required by the old professional pre-war Army.

Making things worse, the British units in India were often wartime units awaiting disbandment, and were full of those impatiently waiting to go home. Many did not want to fight another war, and the delay in demobilisation was highly unpopular, leading to individuals and units refusing to fight. There was a great deal of ill-feeling that those who had volunteered for service five years before had still not released, whilst those who had been conscripted later, but were workers from pivotal industries, had already gone home. At one point an entire brigade got out of the trains carrying it to the Frontier and encamped without order by the line; it had to be persuaded to go back to its duty. The Commander-in-Chief, General Sir Charles Carmichael Monro, was reduced to receiving a delegation from British Territorial NCOs to hear their views and explain why they had to serve on. In almost every case, however, the men did their duty and went off to yet another campaign. There was little else to do, as the huge increase in the responsibilities facing the British Army at the end of the war meant there was no immediate chance of reinforcement from home. The Army was tied down across the globe, in recently conquered Mesopotamia and Palestine, in the civil disturbances in Egypt and in Ireland, where the final death throes of British rule in the south had commenced, and in the vast spaces of the Russian Empire, where British troops were trying unsuccessfully to prop up the White Russian foes of Bolshevik revolution. At the start of the troubles, the Viceroy warned London that India might need reinforcing by up to 70,000 troops, a figure which seriously alarmed Field-Marshal Sir Henry Wilson, the Chief of the Imperial General Staff, who had only nine cavalry regiments and twenty battalions of infantry uncommitted, half of what Delhi estimated it might ask for. The Afghans had chosen their moment well. India would have to cope with this crisis, and by great effort it did so. By the end of the war, the Indian

Army had managed to mobilise 340,000 men and 158,000 animals to fight the Afghans.[4]

Dyer was in Amritsar on 4 May when he first heard of the growing trouble in Afghanistan. When war was declared two days later, 16 Division was not mobilised, being left initially to carry on its martial law duties in the Punjab, but it was placed in the general reserve, and 45 Brigade was thus declared to be part of the Afghanistan Field Force. Dyer was directed to divert his attentions to the forthcoming war and to hand over his responsibilities at Amritsar, so on the 7th he went by train way to the north of his area to inspect the defences at Dalhousie and Dhariwal, which were in the foothills of the Himalayas and not far from the Kashmir border. He returned not to Amritsar but to his Headquarters at Jullundur, taking Briggs, his Brigade Major, with him. Lieutenant-Colonel Hynes of the Londons was given charge of Amritsar. Annie had probably already returned to Jullundur; it is likely her stay in Amritsar was short, so the family was again together in Flagstaff House.

It was at this time that Annie saw how the shooting at the Jallianwala Bagh had scarred her husband. She wrote of this later to Brigadier-General Edmonds: 'For weeks he could hardly sleep at all from the nightmare memories of that scene.' This turmoil was not visible on the surface; Lieutenant-Colonel S.P. Williams saw him in Jullundur at the time and thought that, though he seemed worried, he remained rational and in command of himself; another who met him there, a civilian, J.W. Fletcher, thought much the same. But the shooting was beginning to prey severely on Dyer's mind. He could not shake off either the horror of what he had witnessed in the Bagh or doubt as to whether he had been right to fire upon the crowd. Alice Dyer, who was still with the family in Flagstaff House, recalled that on several occasions, in the weeks following his return from Amritsar, Dyer said to her: 'I thought of all those women and children in the fort … I had to do it.' This inner turmoil was self-generated; as yet there was no sign that he would cease to enjoy the approval of the Government, nor of any loss in support from his military superiors. He had the written and verbal backing of his immediate superior, General Beynon, and of the Lieutenant-Governor of the Punjab. Both had accepted his explanations of his action and of his motives in the Jallianwala Bagh. The Government of India, seemingly satisfied with the reports that they had received, had called for no new information. There was no enquiry underway, other than the continuing pursuit by the authorities of those involved in the Rowlatt agitation and the disturbances which had followed it. The reports of the prosecutions then underway in Lahore, and of the harsh sentences being meted out there, crossed his desk; as they satisfied Sir Michael O'Dwyer, they are very likely to have satisfied Dyer. There was no cause yet for concern on his part. It was his own conscience that was pricking him.

Nor was there much reason for Dyer to be worried about the political opponents of the Government, who during this period of martial law seemed to be on the run. The rigorous censorship exercised in the Punjab, coupled with the exclusion of reporters and lawyers from outside the province, meant that detailed news of what had happened there leaked out only very slowly. The Government had not hesitated to close down the local press; the editor of *The Tribune*, Mr Kalinath Roy, was sentenced to two years imprisonment and his paper was suspended for reporting on martial law. A report in the *Bombay Chronicle* led to a two year sentence for Gobardhan Das, its author, and the deportation of the editor of the paper, B.G. Horniman, who was a prominent member of Gandhi's *satyagraha* committee. Gandhi withdrew for a time from the limelight, ashamed of the violence, announcing that: 'I had called upon the people to launch upon civil disobedience before they had thus qualified themselves for it, and this mistake of mine seemed to me to be of a Himalayan magnitude.' Many Home Rule League members who had supported *satyagraha* had withdrawn their support as the violence spread. Swami Shraddhanand, who had spoken in the Delhi mosque, and was a leader of the Hindu *Arya Samaj*, publicly criticised Gandhi's policies, and even the moderate and mystic Sir Rabindranath Tagore urged him to abandon the campaign of passive resistance. By the end of May, Gandhi was politically isolated and it seemed as though his campaign had failed.

Yet there were growing signs that this retreat by the Government's enemies would be short-lived. The non-English press was beginning to fill with lurid and shocking detail of what had happened in the Punjab, and the All India Congress Committee began to campaign for an end to martial law. At their meeting of 20 to 21 April, they passed a resolution deploring and condemning 'all acts of violence against person and property, and life recently committed at Amritsar, Ahmedabad, Viramgam and other places'. Their strictures were too mild yet to worry either the Government or Dyer; the committee appealed 'to the people to maintain law and order and help in the restoration of public tranquility, and it requests the Government to deal with the situation in a sympathetic and conciliatory manner immediately reversing the present policy of repression'. They did, however, begin to campaign for an enquiry into what was happening in the Punjab, although they did not specifically mention the Jallianwala Bagh.

In England, where the Congress sent Vitthalbhai Patel and N.C. Kelkar to put their demands to the Secretary of State for India, Edwin Montagu, some notice was beginning to be taken by a few on the left of the state of affairs in the Punjab. The Labour Party, working with B.G. Tilak and the London Congress Committee, began to call for an end to martial law and for a public enquiry. A meeting was held by the Labour Party and the Indian Committee of the Workers Welfare League of India in Hyde Park on 1 May; they estimated that 300,000 attended the meeting (though this was an exaggeration), and 10,000 copies of a pamphlet by Robert Williams, Robert Smillie and George Lansbury called *Coercion, Repression and Butchery in India* were handed out there. It said: 'Indians are unarmed, yet they are bombed from aeroplanes and shot down with machine guns' and went on to express the 'demand for a public inquiry into these outrages'. Tilak spoke on the same subject to the British and India Society at the Caxton Hall on 3 May, and a meeting against the Rowlatt Acts was held on the 12th. Disquiet was beginning to spread across the party divide. On 9 May, London Indians met under the auspices of the Fabian Society to hear speeches by Tilak and by Commander Kenworthy, who was a Liberal MP and so a member of Montagu's own party. So far none of this protest had focussed on the shooting in the Jallianwala Bagh, and the figures involved were politically peripheral, so it is unlikely that Dyer feared that their call for an enquiry would eventually pose a threat to his position. He could not know, though, that Montagu had already made up his mind to hold an enquiry. On 1 May the Secretary of State wrote to the Viceroy:

> I am shortly going to telegraph you suggesting that it will be necessary to have an enquiry into the causes of and the treatment of the riots that have occurred in India. I do not mean by that that there is any reason to suppose that any Government did not handle the question as it should have been handled. But it always seems to me that one ought to investigate allegations of needless brutality in dealing with an *émeute*. [5]

Even the Government of India could now see the necessity for an enquiry into some of the allegations that were surfacing concerning the more excessive measures taken during martial law (particularly the floggings, the Jallianwala Bagh shooting and the bombing of crowds), but it set its face against a public or a wide-ranging enquiry, and fought through the next few months to retain the right to handle the issue in-house. This, they argued, would prevent any recrudescence of racial ill-feeling. Unfortunately, Montagu stated his intention to appoint an inquiry in a debate on Indian affairs in the House of Commons on 22 May, so the Government of India's position was undercut almost at the outset:

> As regards these troubles which I have been describing, as questions have been asked from time to time and resolutions have been moved demanding an enquiry, the Viceroy has always contemplated an enquiry. You cannot have disturbances of this magnitude without an enquiry into the causes and the measures taken to cope with these disturbances, but no announcement has been made of the enquiry up to this moment for this reason; let us talk of an enquiry when we have put the fire out.

The tussle over the form the inquiry should take resulted in delay to any announcement concerning it, so Dyer was not aware in early May that an enquiry was inevitable. He almost certainly was aware, though, that his position, along with those of all his fellows, was about to be bolstered by the Indemnity Bill with which the Government of India intended to protect its servants from prosecution for anything they had done under martial law. The Government realised that it needed to protect those who had been acting according to its resolution and directives of April, and by 4 May the Home Department resolved to enact an Indemnity Act.[6]

While hostilities commenced on the Frontier, and unsettling talk of an enquiry into the Punjab disturbances began to appear in the press, Dyer spent two weeks in Jullundur with time on his hands, waiting for orders to move which he was not sure would come. The war seemed likely to be over swiftly. On the Khyber front, the Afghans were swiftly ejected from British territory, and British troops crossed the Frontier to occupy Dakka on 13 May, going on to defeat the Afghan field army on the road to Jellalabad on the 17th. In that sector regular Afghan troops now ceased to play an active part in operations. The British believed the road was open for an advance on Jellalabad, and beyond that to the capital, Kabul.

It must have seemed to Dyer that once again he was being left to kick his heels in a backwater whilst others were winning laurels, but orders eventually came for 45 Brigade to move to Peshawar to relieve troops who were about to move forward into Afghanistan. With undoubted relief, Dyer entrained for the Frontier with his Headquarters on the morning of 23 May. His brigade had been augmented by a number of units from across the Punjab to bring it up to fighting strength. It still included his old friends the 1/25th Londons, with whom he had by now developed an affectionate rapport; they were still in Amritsar and now moved from there with the Brigade Signal Section. The 2nd/41st Dogras were posted to join him from Sialkote, the 2nd/72nd Punjabis were on their way from Multan and the 3rd/150th Infantry were now en route from Ambala.[7] The brigade's need for more than the usual three or four battalions arose from the weak strength of all these units; the Londons entrained at under half strength with just twenty officers and 270 men. These had been waiting to go home, but responded well to the call for all those who were fit to go to the war;

> It was gratifying, as it was pathetic, to notice the way in which almost every member of the battalion tried to get passed as medically fit for service, despite the fact that practically all of them had sworn that nothing would induce them to return to the Frontier if they, as individuals, could avoid it.[8]

The train carrying Dyer and his staff, led by the faithful Briggs, with Staff Captain Bostock and another officer named Bostock of the 11th Lancers as Orderly Officer, took some time to get to its destination as the war was disrupting traffic, and everyone slept in the carriages overnight. They arrived jaded and weary in Peshawar on the 24th, and the brigade set up at the racecourse camp.

Already there were the 2nd/72nd Punjabis and the 3rd/41st Dogras; the 3rd/150th Infantry and the Londons followed them in that afternoon. Local duties commenced immediately, and the brigade was used to relieve the picquets mounted across the city, a familiar duty for the Londons who had just had several weeks of this at Amritsar. Whilst Dyer's brigade was now in the theatre of war, it must have seemed as though once again he had drawn the short straw of the reserve; he must have foreseen a long period of dull duty holding the lines of communication.[9]

The situation then changed suddenly. The Afghan General Nadir Khan made an unexpected incursion from Matun, and, with a strong force of fourteen infantry battalions and forty-eight pieces of artillery carried by elephants, crossed the Frontier by roads thought to be impassable. This was in the central region between the forces massed on the road to Jellalabad and those at Quetta far to the south. Nadir Khan's point of attack was where the tribes of Waziristan bordered the Turis of the Kurram valley, a key point in the volatile tribal mosaic of the Frontier, which had until now been held, still according to Curzon's 'Close Border' policy, by tribal militias led by a tiny number of British officers. The British troops nearest to the Frontier were stationed some seventy-five miles back at Kohat. Many of the tribes in the region welcomed Nadir Khan and rose to join his forces, abandoning old hostilities to fight the British, with Shiranis and Kakars unexpectedly joining Mahsuds and Darwesh Khel Waziris. On 21 May, the British commander in Kohat, Major-General Eustace, ordered the evacuation of all remaining militia posts on the Tochi river to the south of the Kurram. He had not consulted the political authorities, and was taken aback by the immediate risings of the tribes around the posts he had abandoned. British officers were attacked by their men, and the survivors and those of their men who remained loyal had to fight their way out, pursued all the way by the tribes around them. By 26 May, the North and South Waziristan Militias had ceased to exist.

The next day the Afghan Army reached the British post at Thal on the Kurram river. Here were 65 Brigade and General Eustace, who had just arrived with reinforcements and found himself besieged with his troops. He had some 2000 men with four field guns, but had denuded much of the force at Kohat to achieve this, and the men at Thal managed to hold with difficulty a perimeter of some five miles of hastily built emplacements. Deploying about 3000 troops with an estimated 9000 tribesmen, two 100 mm. Krupp field howitzers and seven 75 mm. mountain guns, Nadir Khan held the upper hand, and proceeded to lay siege to Thal. He began to shell the garrison and already by the 28th had managed to set fire to the railway yard, the petrol dump, the forage for the animals and the wireless station. The local Frontier Constabulary, who were holding a post which overlooked the garrison's water supply, all deserted and the Afghans occupied their tower, which was only five hundred yards from the fort. By attacking Thal,

Nadir Khan also isolated the small British garrison at Parachinar to its north, which Eustace had just managed to reinforce. He had sent troops there on 7 May to support the Turi tribesmen, who, unlike their neighbours, were Shias, and had been loyal to the British since the Second Afghan War. 60 Infantry Brigade's two infantry battalions, guns and a squadron of cavalry held Parachinar. Had Thal fallen, these would have been prey to the Orakzais and Zaimukhts who lived in the mountains to the north east and who were on the verge of rising, watching to see how events would unfold. Nadir Khan's neat move endangered the flank of the British attack through the Khyber, for, as Eustace had seriously weakened the Kohat garrison, there was a risk that the Afghans might move on there and beyond, perhaps in the worst case threatening Peshawar itself. Eustace was to prove himself curiously supine in his defence of Thal; admittedly outnumbered, and faced by a force three times his size, he was not surrounded, for the Afghans had insufficient troops to encircle him and could not cut his communications back to Kohat, with which there was still morse communication back through the post at Hangu. Yet Eustace did not sally out against the Afghans, and allowed his troops to dig in around the fort at Thal, waiting to be rescued.[10]

When Peshawar heard the news of Nadir Khan's advance, Dyer's brigade was immediately stood to, and was relieved of its duties in Peshawar by 44 Brigade. On the next day, 27 May, the 3rd/150th went up to reinforce Kohat, though at that stage the seriousness of the situation at Thal had not yet become apparent, and Dyer's Headquarters received orders the following morning to proceed in another direction, to Jamrud, at the mouth of the Khyber. In this Northern Army was still following the plan to use them as reserve for the advance on Jelallabad. Within six hours of being issued that order was cancelled, however, and the brigade was redirected to Kohat. It moved there by train at 5 a.m. on the 29th, taking with it an extra company of 2/4th Border Regiment with two Lewis guns from the Peshawar garrison; these were to bring the Londons up to strength. The Londons recalled the chaos of the three-mile move from the racecourse to the station: '50 mules, 81 camels and 8 ox-drawn carts arrived for transport. Chaos to the station'. That day, Headquarters 16 Division, with the 2/6th Royal Sussex and the 1st/124th Baluchis, were ordered to Kohat, General Beynon being diverted there to take command of the newly named Kohat Kurram Force.

Before entraining for Kohat, Dyer was ordered to see the Commander-in-Chief Northern Army, General Sir Arthur Barrett, to receive orders for the relief of Thal. He was given these that evening, and afterwards he took his chance and raised with Barrett the subject of his conduct at the Jallianwala Bagh. Barrett was General Beynon's immediate superior, and so Dyer's second reporting officer, but Dyer had not met him at any time during or since his time in Amritsar. This was his first chance to explain himself, and to seek his Commander-in-Chief's views. Dyer told General Barrett that:

I had by then become aware that the influences which had inspired the rebellion were starting an agitation against those who had suppressed it … I told him that I wished, if possible, to be free from any anxiety about my action at Amritsar, which had so far been approved. He said: 'That's all right, you would have heard about it long before this, if your action had not been approved.'

This was greatly reassuring, and Dyer could go to war feeling that he had little to fear on this count. He would not have been aware, unless Barrett told him so then, that his Commander-in-Chief's own views were not far removed from his own. Barrett had only just penned, on 30 April, his own report to Army Headquarters on the Punjab disturbances. This was a strange, almost whimsical document that restricted itself to outlining Barrett's opinions, and gave neither chronology nor analysis of the events themselves. He saw, he wrote, the growth of racial hostility against the British and a decline in respect for the non-official English in India. He believed, as Dyer did, that the Punjab disturbances were a revolutionary plot:

> I think there is evidence to show the existence of a deeply laid and carefully planned conspiracy to overthrow the British power. It appears to have been intended to destroy our railway and telegraphic communications, to isolate our garrisons, cut off our supplies, and, with the assistance of disaffected Indian troops and police, to outnumber and overwhelm our scanty European forces.

He recommended that a collective penalty be imposed on towns like Amritsar and Kasur, that fixed sums be levied from the rich who had done nothing to prevent the outbreaks, and that 'no passenger or goods traffic to be booked, except on Government service, either to or from these towns, or any wayside station within twenty miles of them' as a punishment for the attacks on the railway. He made no constructive recommendations, and the Government wisely ignored his report.[11]

Dyer's brigade was again augmented for the forthcoming operations and formed the nucleus of what was now named the Thal Relief Column. He himself added to this some artillery pieces he took from the fort at Kohat, four of the six fifteen-pounder guns which were manned there by the Frontier Garrison Artillery. The column was ordered to assemble at Hangu just inside the administrative frontier, about twenty-six miles up the road between Kohat and Thal. When Dyer arrived at Kohat, some of his troops had already left there by rail for this point, and he had the additional guns transported there on lorries as there was no available train. With them he sent dummy guns made of tree trunks, carried on the trucks in an attempt to disguise his weakness in artillery. Whilst in Kohat, he was lucky enough to meet Eustace's GSO 1, who was on his way back to Thal from Peshawar, as well as the Inspector-General of Communications, who happened to be on tour in the area. Dyer was thus able to make detailed plans based on sound local and technical knowledge. The GSO 1 drafted Dyer's initial marching orders, and the Inspector-General placed sixty-two lorries at Dyer's disposal (lorries which had earlier been dedicated to move the troops forward up the Khyber), and set about organising troop trains. For once, Dyer's logistics were in the hands of experts. This was a vital element in the campaign, for there was only one route to Thal, a road with a small light railway running alongside it up the Miranzai valley. There was a very limited amount of engines and rolling stock available for this, so a careful organisation of transport and supply was the key to getting the troops to Thal as fast and as fit-to-fight as possible. The shortage of engines meant that they had to shuttle the troops forward turn by turn, and it was decided that the farthest that the railway could take the column was the station at Togh, after which those who could not be carried by lorry would have to march.

Dyer went forward to Hangu by car, and found there troops of the Kohat Mobile Column which had earlier formed up in preparation for a local attempt to relieve Thal. This was commanded by one of its unit Commanding Officers, Lieutenant-Colonel Houston of the 1st/69th Punjabis, who was now ordered to protect the concentration of Dyer's Relief Column. Dyer's Headquarters, packed into a lorry, followed him up the road on the 30th, whilst his units trickled in behind. The heat was intense, the small, overcrowded railway carriages were unbearably stuffy and cramped, and the lorries were exposed to the blazing sun throughout their journeys. Some of the Londons carried by truck collapsed with heat stroke as they sat. Reaching Hangu by noon, Dyer gathered his unit commanders and held an immediate orders group, instructing the column to move out to the next halt at Togh at 4 p.m. that day. Much of his force was still back at Kohat, and he ordered it to move without stopping straight through to Togh, which was a few miles further up the valley to the west. Dyer was also allocated some of the troops he found at Hangu, so that by the afternoon of the 30th his column consisted of the following:

Headquarters 45 Infantry Brigade

One squadron, 37th Lancers (from the troops at Hangu)

89th Battery Royal Field Artillery (from the troops at Hangu)

Four 15-pounder guns, Frontier Garrison Artillery (from Kohat)

One section 23 Mountain Battery (two mountain guns)

Half section No 57 Company, 1st Sappers and Miners (from the troops at Hangu)

One section Pack Wireless of 40th Signal Company (from the troops at Hangu)

Two armoured cars (from the troops at Hangu)

1/25th London Regiment

One company 2/4th Border Regiment (from Peshawar garrison)

2nd/41st Dogras

1st/69th Punjabis (from the troops at Hangu)

3rd/150th Infantry

265 men of 57th Rifles Frontier Force (from the troops at Hangu)

An ambulance unit

The 2nd/72nd Punjabis were left behind for the time being in Kohat. Despite the large number of its units, the column numbered only 2612 men. Getting these organised to move with their supplies and ammunition, which was partially deficient, delayed their departure for Togh until 5.30 p.m., and the troops, many of whom did not eat that day as they travelled up from Kohat, moved on the next four and a half hour stretch on an empty stomach. The last of the column did not make it to Togh until 1.30 the following morning, and none of them got much sleep that night. This was the first time the column had come together, and it was the last chance Dyer had to address them before they got close to the enemy. Beneath the myriad stars brightening the darkness of the desert night, and lit by the flickering light of low torches, he gathered together his sleepy and hungry troops and exhorted them to make a great effort to rescue their comrades in Thal. Afterwards, as the men slept fitfully, it was cold enough for ground frost to form on their blankets.[12]

Dyer was determined to reach Thal as soon as possible, and wanted to divide the remaining miles so that the shortest possible march would be left for the day they reached their objective, so enabling his troops to go into action fresh. He therefore decided to march as much of the route as possible on the 31st, a distance of eighteen miles to the campsite he had selected for that night. The day was horribly hot, 120 degrees Fahrenheit or 49 degrees Celsius, and to make things worse they would meet neither breeze nor water along the route. Although they set off as early as possible to avoid the heat, they had to breakfast before they moved, and so were not away before 4 a.m. and the troops suffered badly later in the day. The 2nd/41st Dogras provided the advance guard, and so marched largely free of the dust which enveloped the rest of the column. Many men of the Londons fell out on this march and had to be carried on the guns of the 89th Battery, the gunners giving up their seats and marching in their place. Other troops collapsed by the roadside and were picked up by the ambulance which travelled in the rear. Marching with his men, and only occasionally travelling in his car, Dyer was kept going by the wet towels his bearer, Alladad Khan, continually pressed round his head, but he eventually fell exhausted by the heat. Briggs got him under the shade of the car and sought water from the Londons, who were close by. Many of the men around him had no water to give, and were themselves unable to speak as their mouths and tongues had swollen from thirst. Yet by the afternoon the whole column finished the march, and they staggered into the new campsite, at the end of their tether but proud of themselves for getting there after all. The 2nd/41st reached the campsite at Darsamand, a *doaba* or stream junction, by noon, and the whole column was in by 4 p.m. Captain Briggs watched them march in, giving the men words of encouragement as they passed; the Londons proudly recorded that as Captain Briggs was 'not the man to have given praise where it was not due, and if, in his opinion, the troops finished "in excellent marching order", perhaps the Londons need not have felt ashamed.' There was little time to draw breath, as the column had to picquet the hills around the camp before entrenching it and only then settling down. It had been an epic march, and Dyer's troops had responded to his call, summoning up reserves of strength they had not known they possessed.

General Beynon joined Dyer at Darsamand, driving up behind the column by car, and gave him the latest intelligence. The Afghans were still reported to be in the positions around Thal which they had occupied from the first. They were still shelling the garrison, whose guns were outranged and could not hit back, and they had been reinforced by two more regiments which had marched in that day. So far, the Orakzai and the Zaimukht, along the edge of whose territory Dyer's column was marching, had not risen, and this news matched the column's experience of that day, for they had found no opposition on the road, and had passed flocks and herds, villages still occupied and corn being threshed. The railway line had been found intact so far, and the cavalry, which had pushed as far forward that day as the seven mile marker from Thal, had reported that the road was clear. The Political Officer attached to Dyer, Major Anson, recommended a speedy advance to keep the tribes quiet, an opinion which chimed nicely with Dyer's; on this campaign, even his relations with the Politicals worked towards, and not against, the success of his mission. From Darsamand, communications were opened with Eustace by heliograph to the nearby Fort Lockhart on the Samana Ridge, which was in radio communications with Thal. The column's own radio was no longer working, but by this indirect route Dyer told Eustace he would relieve him the next day. The column got as much rest as it could that night.[13]

At 5.50 a.m. on the morning of 1 June, the column set out on the last nine miles to Thal. As he reached the more open ground some miles short of the settlement, Dyer began to deploy his troops. He sent the 57th Rifles to hold the high ground to the left of the road, and when these were in place he pushed forward an advance guard under Lieutenant-Colonel Houston, who took with him the squadron of the 37th Lancers, most of his own 1/69th Punjabis and the two mountain guns; these reached the flat ground used as an aerodrome at milestone 58, two miles east of Thal, without encountering any enemy. Here they were shelled by the Afghan artillery, which had spotted a race between an armoured car and an aeroplane to get on the ground there first; both had to veer off as the shells struck the landing strip. The Afghans were also still shelling Thal. Behind the 1st/69th, the main body of Dyer's column followed up the road, the Londons bringing up the rear.

Dyer had good intelligence of the enemy's position and strength. The RAF had put planes in the air for the last few days, and two now dropped Dyer a message to say that his enemy were still where they had been the day before. Nadir Khan's forces had not closed up to Thal and he had not sought to make a direct assault on the garrison since he had arrived five days before. He had left his Headquarters and baggage some five miles to the west up the Azgol Khwar, the small valley down which his force had crossed the Frontier, and had split his force into three, placing about half of his regular forces, estimated at about 1500 men with nine guns, his two 3.8 inch howitzers and seven 2.9 inch guns, on the slopes of the Khapianga feature. This lay over the Kurram river and dominated Thal from just over a mile to its west. The other half, with four guns to their rear, were on the east side of the Kurram river, the British side, on the lower slopes of the Khadimakh feature, which overlooked Thal from the north west; these were the Afghan troops closest to the British garrison. With tribal levies, the forces on the Khapianga and Khadimakh features numbered about 9000 men. Also east of the Kurram were the Waziri, Khostwal and other tribal *lashkars* under the chief Malik Babrak Zadran, about 4000 in number, with two guns. They had occupied the high ground near the village of Muhammadzai, and overlooked Thal from about two miles to the south. All told the enemy had a strength of about 13,000, six times Dyer's force, and three times that of the combined British forces. One of Eustace's staff officers, Major Wylly, rode back to meet Dyer and confirmed this intelligence from the observations the garrison had made; this was the only action Eustace undertook towards meeting his relief. He had, by then, suffered about ninety casualties and was short of water, but his five-mile perimeter had not been seriously threatened. Despite this, Eustace made no move to assist Dyer's column.[14]

True to form, but in this case absolutely appropriately, Dyer determined to attack at once, and opened the action by ordering his artillery to bombard the village of Thal, which lay outside British lines in front of Eustace's position, and the tribal positions above Muhammadzai. He aimed to give Nadir Khan an impression of great strength, and to deceive him as to the object of his first assault, for he had by now determined to pick off the three Afghan positions one by one, and this needed time. The danger in this was that it allowed Nadir Khan time to concentrate his forces against the attack, but it was a logical choice. With Eustace's force inactive around the fort, Dyer did not have enough men or artillery to launch an assault on more than one position at a time, and the wide separation of the three Afghan positions meant that they were not mutually supporting and could come to each other's aid only with difficulty. He was still not quite sure which objective to take first, so he moved the main body of his column forward up the main road, and halted it around the aerodrome. He was now within a mile of the fort. It was about 9.30 a.m. and the sun was rising inexorably above them, making every task more and more difficult as the day wore on. But Dyer needed Eustace's help and advice before he could begin his assault, so he drove alone ahead of his force into the Thal garrison's perimeter to meet Eustace in the fort at 10 o'clock. He was back fifty minutes later, having clarified in his own mind that his first objective was to be the tribesmen under Babrak Zadran on the hills to the south. These were, Dyer thought, the most isolated of the enemy, as well as the least likely to resist a full-scale attack. A success on this flank would bring his guns into range of the Afghan artillery bombarding Thal, and he had arranged that Eustace's troops would give flanking fire as his attack went in.

In swift verbal orders, he directed Colonel Houston to lead the assault. Dyer was by now physically in a very bad way; at his orders group he collapsed with a blinding headache, and had to be restored by application of the brandy and aspirin which Briggs carried with him, and which had been prescribed for these eventualities by the brigade's medical officer. Houston, though, who was to win a DSO for this action, had been given sufficient to go on, and formed his force up for the attack. He found that his approach was across the stream of the Ishkalai Nala, which could be waded, then through flooded paddy fields to the foot of the hill, where there was a long, slow and difficult climb up the slopes of the feature. There were limited options for the climb, and the few paths available gave good targets for the tribal snipers crouching behind the rocks overhead. It took Houston until the end of the morning to get organised; at midday he led the 1st/69th off in determined fashion to the start line, followed at some distance behind by the 3rd/150th who were in support. The 2nd/41st Dogras and the Londons stayed in the valley as brigade reserve, whilst the artillery, protected by the 2/4th Borders, put down a bombardment on the tribal positions on the feature, helped by the aircraft which spotted the fall of shot from above. The tribesmen fled under the bursting shells, C and D Companies of the 1st/69th pulled up onto the ridge and charged the Afghan position with bayonets fixed. By 2 o'clock the position was in their hands. The tribesmen scattered in all directions, ceasing from that point to be an effective opposition and suffering casualties as they fled from the machine guns in Thal fort, which caught them on the skyline. The 1st/69th had only four men wounded in this action, and, while its C and D Companies consolidated on the position they had won, A and B Companies sent out patrols to follow up the fleeing enemy. They found their abandoned camp, an enormous conglomeration of tents and chaotically abandoned equipment, of a size sufficient, the troops reported, for an entire brigade. The intelligence of their numbers had not been wrong. The troops were unable to follow up the retreating tribesmen closely enough to prevent their escape, however, as the heat made any further exertion impossible. Dyer sent them a short but heartfelt message: 'Congratulations on the fine way the attacking troops took a very difficult hill to climb.'

By 3 p.m. the way was clear to move forward in the valley, and Dyer determined next to silence the Afghan guns. He sent a gun team of 89th Battery galloping forward below the recently taken high ground. In full view of both sides, they reached their intended position, swung around and came neatly to a halt, unlimbered the gun, and fired a single round at the most active enemy gun on the Khapianga feature. With an enormously lucky shot, they hit their target first time, destroying the Afghan gun to the loud cheers of the onlooking troops. More British guns then came into action and the rest of the Afghan artillery proved no match for them. By nightfall, Dyer's guns had put six of the seventeen Afghan guns out of action, and the rest had fallen silent, too apprehensive to fire and give away their positions.

During the afternoon, Dyer's main body stayed around the aerodrome, where it was ineffectually sniped at by the Afghans on the Khadimakh feature to the north. These were in stone sangars on a hill across the Sangroba river, but, wisely deciding that he was unable to accomplish more that day, Dyer let these be and consolidated what he had gained. He left two hundred men of the 3rd/150th to hold the feature just captured by the 1st/69th, and brought the latter back down the hill to rejoin the rest of his force at the aerodrome. There they dug in and got some rest overnight. General Beynon was soon back with the column that night, driving up again from Kohat. Suspicious of the lack of enemy resistance so far, he told Dyer's force to 'keep its eyes skinned'. There is evidence that the Afghan commanders had already been ordered to 'suspend hostilities until the door of discussion and communication is opened' with the British, but it was also clear that much of the Afghan force had already fled the field. Reports came in that evening that the force on the Khapianga heights had reduced to seven hundred regulars and a thousand tribesmen. The tribal leaders who had fled that day had abandoned Nadir Khan, making off to the south through the village of Biland Khel and taking with them two of his guns. The Afghans had not had any success in getting the other neighbouring tribes to rise; these had sat out the fight to see who would win, and they were now known to be resisting the *mullahs* who were urging them to join the Afghan force. Dyer's choice of Nadir Khan's tribal allies as his first target had achieved the desired political effect.[15]

Through that night, Dyer planned the next day's attack. His next objective was the Khadimakh feature upon which he planned a two-phase assault. The first, to start at 9 a.m., was to capture the low-lying hills closest to Thal and clear away the enemy within range of the garrison. He ordered this to be done by the 3rd/9th Gurkhas, who were to take the ridge on the left, and the 1st/151st Sikhs who were to assault that on the right. He took both these battalions from 65 Brigade, Eustace's garrison troops, command of which he was due to take the next morning when Eustace returned to Kohat. Perhaps Eustace had lost his nerve; his rank and his position should have meant that he took overall command. Instead, he handed over to Dyer and returned to Kohat as fast as he could.

On the morning of the 2nd, Dyer's attack went off exactly as planned. The guns opened up on the Afghan positions, firing now from both the aerodrome and the area of the fort. The two battalions formed up in a railway cutting under cover from view, then swiftly crossed the Sangroba river and climbed the hill to their front. With them went the men of the 2/4th Borders, who were ordered to take a third objective on the hill. Behind them in support, and sheltering in the railway cutting until their turn came, were the Londons and the 2nd/41st Dogras, whose task was to pass through the first wave and go on further up the hill to take the main Afghan positions. The 1st/69th and what was not already deployed of 3rd/150th remained at the aerodrome as reserve. Again, it was debilitatingly hot, but the troops advanced and climbed steadily. Aircraft again spotted for the guns, and bombed and machine-gunned a group of about four hundred Afghans they found on the northern slopes of the Khadimakh feature, causing them to flee.

Whilst the troops toiled slowly up the slope, a messenger arrived in Dyer's camp bearing a letter from Nadir Khan, who wrote that he had been ordered by his Amir to suspend hostilities, and asked for Dyer's reply. He seems to have been stalling for time; that morning, the Political Officer had been given information that the Afghans had again been reinforced overnight, this time by four battalions of regular infantry and a battery of guns. Dyer estimated that there were now some 19,000 men and thirteen guns still in the field opposed to him. He sent a message back in reply, a characteristic and rather fine one: 'My guns will give an immediate reply, and a further reply will be sent by the Divisional Commander, to whom the letter has been forwarded.' Nadir Khan's message went back to Kohat with General Eustace. In the meantime, Dyer's force pressed on up the hill. The Gurkhas and Sikhs reached the first Afghan positions, almost without opposition, and the enemy fled before them, not just from the first position, but from the main one higher up the hill as well, where a Gurkha rifleman captured an Afghan standard which he found hanging in their officers' mess tent. The Khadimakh feature had been abandoned. Thal was effectively relieved.

Dyer was not about to sit on his laurels and was determined not to let the enemy escape. At that point, too, he was still faced with the Afghan position on the Khapianga feature to the west of the Kurram river. He immediately pushed his artillery further up the Kurram valley to Mulla Rasul. There, screened by the cavalry and the armoured cars which went further up the east bank, the guns were in range of the Khapianga and able to shell the Afghan camp at Yusuf Khel. The cavalry and armoured cars could not move fast enough to come up with the enemy, who were in full flight and had dropped all they carried in their haste to escape. The aeroplanes flew across to the west bank of the Kurram, and later that evening reported that the Afghan camp was still in place, with thirty-nine tents visible, three miles west of the river. At this stage, Dyer realised that the enemy to the west of the Kurram had gone.

His hopes of cutting off the Afghan retreat dashed, Dyer again decided to halt his operations for the day. The heat was by now intense, the air rising from the rocks and shingle in shimmering waves, the ground too hot to touch. The Londons, who had not been in action, had thirty cases of heatstroke just climbing the hill, and every single able-bodied man of the battalion had to be employed carrying these down. The infantry could go no further, and Dyer again withdrew most of the men back down to the valley during the afternoon. His forces had only five casualties from artillery shrapnel and sniping during the day; they had got off remarkably lightly. The men were allowed to rest.

The officers, however, were not. Dyer held another orders group, and gave instructions for the next day. This was to be one of pursuit across the Kurram to the Afghan camp. He was intending to be extremely active. Major Anson reported to the political authorities that afternoon: 'General Officer Commanding Thal is to punish Wazir villages, Biland Khel, and Zaimukht village Dholragha and Hadmela as ample proof villagers joined *lashkar* and harrassed our communications.' Dyer had also requested authority from General Beynon to march north to the relief of the garrison at Parachinar, but this was denied, and the plan for punitive expeditions was ordered to be postponed. General Beynon told Dyer to rest his forces, and also gave him a ticking off for trying to take control of the aircraft which had been flying around Thal and which were under divisional control. Following his usual habit, Dyer had tried to coopt the pilots and give them instructions; he was firmly told not to address the pilots directly again. Ominously, signs of cholera began to appear amongst the troops inside Thal that day. The insanitary conditions that had developed inside the perimeter during the siege were beginning to have an effect.[16]

Early on 3 June, leaving, as he had been instructed, the bulk of his forces to rest, Dyer himself led out a small force of Lancers, guns, armoured cars and some men of the Londons and Borders carried in trucks. They drove up the riverbank and dismounted to cross the Kurram, marching on to the abandoned Afghan camp at Yusuf Khel. They found it had been left in such haste that all its equipment, including Nadir Khan's tent, stool and standard, was still there, along with about a thousand shells for the Afghan guns, and dead and wounded lying where they had been abandoned. Restrained by Beynon's order to let his men rest, Dyer left the camp in charge of the local villagers, a mistake as it turned out, as they were to pillage it almost completely that night. The small force then returned to Thal, taking the surviving Afghan wounded back with them. The heat was still such that the Londons had a heatstroke casualty onboard the trucks.

Dyer signalled Beynon asking for permission to follow the retreating Afghans across the border towards Nadir Khan's base at Matun, but Beynon refused this due to the armistice which was now imminent; that day, the negotiations which had been conducted with the Amir's envoys since 15 May were concluded, and an armistice was signed. No further pursuit was possible, though Beynon did allow preparations to be made for Dyer's column to move on to relieve Parachinar. Dyer was told now to try to make contact with Nadir Khan to arrange a local ceasefire, and to ensure that the terms of the armistice, which stipulated that Afghan troops would withdraw beyond twenty miles from all British troops, be observed. The war had ended in just twenty-nine days. In the relief of Thal, Dyer's column had lost one British officer and eleven Indian soldiers killed, one British officer, five British and seventy-six Indian soldiers injured, a total of ninety-four casualties. There was no estimate of the number of Afghans and tribesmen killed. Dyer's men could now relax somewhat, and began to be billeted about Thal in slightly less spartan circumstances than they had endured to date. The Londons found themselves in the Lord Roberts Mission Hospital.[17]

Next day, the Borders were sent back to Yusuf Khel with two hundred camels to retrieve the Afghan equipment, but found all of it gone, along with a heap of documents that had been left there the day before. The locals were blamed, and no doubt had been involved, but it is unlikely they could have spirited away so many artillery shells unaided. Perhaps some of Nadir Khan's troops were still at hand. Dyer went up with some of the Londons to see what was happening, and this led to a characteristic incident at the village of Pir Kasta. Dyer ordered the inhabitants to produce all the drinking water they had, as the dead camels in the streams running into the Kurram had forced the Medical Officer to stop the men drinking the river water. General Dyer, 'with a somewhat dubious smile, had a drink [of the water] thick as treacle'. He then sent for the village headman, the *lambardar*:

> The GOC was noted as being one of the finest linguists in India and it was difficult, if not impossible, to find a single dialect with which he was not completely familiar … Informality was the keynote of this particular little expedition, and the troops were all grouped on the ground beneath the tree, near which the General was interrogating the very uncomfortable Pathan and they gathered, from his many and amusing asides, that he was convinced that the villagers were the parties guilty of the looting at the Afghan

camp. He ended the conversation by curtly sending for a rope and on its arrival indicating very clearly that it was his intention to hang summarily the, by now, very frightened lambadar. While the General was deciding on the particular bough [the rifles were given up, and] it was a subject for discussion that evening, after the return to the perimeter, whether the General would have gone to the extreme had he not obtained the information he wanted.

While the Londons (not good judges of language themselves, but nevertheless clearly aware of Dyer's reputation) enjoyed the General playing to the crowd, they were well enough aware of his character from their time together at Amritsar to have harboured the suspicion that he was quite capable of carrying out his threat. Back in Thal, Dyer toured his troops, assembling them in turn to speak to them. He addressed the Londons and thanked them for their 'pluck under trying circumstances' and their services to him, and told them of the armistice which had been signed on 3 June.

The Thal Relief Column was now dissolved, and units began to prepare for their return to their parent formations. Instructions came from Kohat countermanding the orders of the day before, and detailing 65 Brigade to relieve Parachinar, so that 45 Brigade could stay where it was at Thal. In the afternoon, Dyer moved his Headquarters into the government rest house there. Here he ordered a commemorative plaque to be fixed to the wall, inscribed: 'Veni, Vidi, Vici. Dyer 1919', a true, if somewhat crass, memorial to what he had accomplished.[18] Rumours reached the Political Officer that night of an attack by the Orakzai tribe, so the men stood to, but no attack materialised. The first signs of cholera, spreading from the old garrison, began to appear in the brigade.

The next day, at 7 a.m., Dyer led out a column consisting of a company each of the 2nd/72nd Punjabis (who had by now reached Thal), the 3rd/150th Infantry and the 2nd/41st Dogras on a punitive expedition to the village of Biland Khel, whose inhabitants were believed to have supported the Afghans. This was the expedition he had earlier planned but had been prevented from executing. The village was in British territory across the Kurram, a few miles to the south of Thal, and the artillery shelled it for fifteen minutes before the troops entered. They spent the rest of the day destroying its towers and houses, and seizing the fodder and timber there; the loot needed three hundred camels to take it away. Five towers in the village were blown up, and a cave was searched, where it was found that the village women were taking refuge. They were released, and the cave was searched by one brave Indian bugler who went into it twice armed only with a knife; Dyer watched this, and recommended the man for the award of an IDSM. He was always good at recommending his men for gallantry awards, one of the reasons, perhaps, why they liked him as much as they did. Other outlying villages were then destroyed around Biland Khel, and although the local Pathans sniped from a distance at the troops, wounding a couple of men, the column got back to Thal that night having suffered no other casualties.[19]

General Beynon drove up from Kohat on the 6th to brief Dyer on what was to happen next. He detached the 2nd/41st Dogras from 45 Brigade and made it the Thal garrison, and he personally selected a site for a hospital in the fort. He stayed overnight, and the next day, in a private interview, congratulated Dyer on his conduct of the relief of Thal. The log recorded: 'General Dyer granted a formal interview by General Officer Commanding KK Force who congratulated General Dyer and the troops under him on the success of the operations.' A local man was found who was willing to act as a messenger to Nadir Khan, to whose message no formal reply had yet been sent. Beynon and the politicals had drafted a reply, and it was sent that afternoon. Their letter agreed the Amir's request for a cessation of hostilities on the condition that Nadir Khan withdrew twenty miles from British troops, and promised that, if he did so, the General Officer Commanding Thal would cease operations. Nadir Khan was given twenty-four hours to commence movements in compliance with this, and ninety-six hours to complete them, but, as it was not known where he was, how this was to be monitored was left unstated.

There was some reshuffling of lines that day, and 45 Brigade Headquarters moved from the rest house to the perimeter camp. The cavalry rode back to the Afghan camp at Yusuf Khel to find a gun carriage that had been spotted earlier, but it had been taken away and buried, it was believed, by the locals. General Beynon drove on to Parachinar, returning through Thal the next day, but this time going straight back to Kohat. When he got back to his Headquarters on the 8th, he was able to forward to Dyer a congratulatory telegram from General Sir Arthur Barrett, which Dyer had read out to his troops:

> The Force Commander congratulates General Dyer and all ranks which formed the THAL RELIEF COLUMN under his command on the success of their operations. The march of the Column to Thal was carried out with the greatest celerity and under the most trying conditions, and its success redounds to the credit of the Column.

Dyer issued his own order of the day to tell his men what he thought of their achievement:

> The General Officer Commanding wishes to thank all under his command for the manner in which they have borne fatigue, heat and discomfort, and for the gallant way they have responded to a call for an extra effort when he felt that they had already done more than enough to try the best. As a reward for these efforts our object has been completely accomplished with loss of only four wounded to us, and a heavy punishment to the enemy. I trust the Commanding Officers will take into consideration the difficult conditions under which we have been operating, and liberally bring to notice such officers and men who have done very exceptional work, though he realizes it will be

difficult to pick and choose where all have done so well. He feels proud to command such troops.

Some of his men were already beginning to depart. The Borders entrained for Kohat and on to Peshawar that day.

Dyer took Major Anson and drove up to Parachinar to see the situation there for himself on the 9th, returning the next day. On the 11th, a reply came back from Nadir Khan, addressed to his 'Honourable Friend, General Dyer Commanding the Forces at Thal', regretting that he had no power to negotiate on behalf of the Amir. In this messsage Nadir Khan made the irritating claim that he had been recalled during the fighting when victory was at hand for his forces. He further regretted that he was unable to comply with the armistice terms, and so it was up to General Dyer to attack or not. Now that the armistice had been signed, Nadir Khan could afford to thumb his nose at the British, who were not, he knew, about to follow him into his own country.

Cholera was by now spreading slowly among the troops. The first death occurred on the 12th, and by the 14th thirteen had died. This gave an impetus to reducing the numbers around Thal, but there were other reasons for a swift withdrawal. Both water and rations were scarce, and bad, and morale was sufferring. This gave Dyer the opportunity to make the kind of personal intervention he relished and for which his troops had reason to thank him. The log recorded:

> General Officer Commanding went to fort to see Supply Officer why men not receiving fresh meat and naturally discontented. Supply Officer said Political Officer had made arrangements but not received. General Officer Commanding said would guarantee food supply if Supply Officer would take it over. Went to Mamun 1406 and made arrangements. Animals vetted by veterinary officer at aerodrome. Men were in full rations for first time 1406 since 2905. General Officer Commanding arranged for onions to be supplied by Thal villagers from 1406.

The Londons entrained for Nowshera on the 13th. This was their last campaign, and they were soon to ship home to Devonport for their disbandment parade the following December. They made much of Sir Michael O'Dwyer's observation that they were the first British unit both to quell a 'mutiny' and to oppose a foreign invasion of India in one tour of duty.

Dyer carried on routine duties at Thal, inspecting posts and the railway and making recommendations for improvements to the defences. He was at Darsamand on the 16th, returning along the railway track to Thal to examine the line the next day. There had by now been 139 cases of cholera amongst his troops and a terrible toll of sixty-six deaths. The almost bloodless relief of Thal was rapidly being overshadowed by a lethal epidemic. The troops had to be got out, and the 2nd/41st Dogras left for Nowshera by train on the 16th, despite their earlier assignment to the garrison. Three days later, Brigade Headquarters and the 3rd/150th Infantry moved to Kohat. On the way, passing through Hangu, Dyer met Lieutenant-Colonel Morgan, whose battalion had been moved there some weeks before, and whom he had not met since their days together in Amritsar. Morgan recalled something which Dyer said to him which indicates that he had not, throughout all his time at Thal, been able to forget the Jallianwala Bagh. 'I met Dyer during the campaign and he said "I hear they want my blood for Amritsar".' Dyer did not stay long in Kohat, moving on to Nowshera, where he was joined within a day by some of his troops, the 2nd/72nd Punjabis and the gunners of the 27th Battery RHA. Cholera had followed them, two cases being diagnosed en route, but thankfully there was no outbreak in the more hygienic circumstances of the regular lines at Nowshera. The brigade was assembled again there by the 24th. A week later the Londons said farewell and left for Rawalpindi on the first stage of their long trip home.[20]

The Third Afghan War was a military victory for the British, whose opponents indeed had largely fled before them, but it was to prove a political defeat. At the peace treaty signed at Rawalpindi on 8 August that year, Afghanistan was granted what was in effect full independence, as the British surrendered their power to conduct Afghan foreign affairs. They were, in truth, too war-weary to want to make an issue of the matter. The Afghans certainly viewed this as a victory, and Amir Amanullah erected a column in Kabul which featured a lion crouching in chains. The war became known as the 'War of Liberation' and the treaty which concluded it was celebrated annually thereafter in August. Amanullah himself, after a period in power in which he proved himself to be a reforming, if erratic, ruler, was replaced in a coup by the same Nadir Khan who had been Dyer's opponent at Thal. Despite the peace, the Frontier remained inflamed, as the Afghans continued to urge the Mahsuds and the Waziri tribes to make trouble for the British right up until 1924.

From Nowshera, Dyer was summoned to Peshawar to meet General Barrett, who wished to give him his personal thanks and congratulations. Barrett had by now formed a very high opinion of Dyer. Later that month, he wrote formally to 16 Division a letter which he asked should be forwarded to Dyer:

> The efforts made by Brigadier-General Dyer from the time he arrived at Kohat were attended with full energy and competence. The manner in which he disposed of his troops, the full use he made of his artillery, the ardour he infused into his troops, denoted the hand of a Commander confident in his capacity and his troops. Brigadier-General Dyer in this episode has given further evidence of power of Command.

This was indeed a fair assessment. Dyer had faced an enemy who largely outnumbered him. To rescue the garrison at Thal before it succumbed to the grave danger of being encircled and destroyed, and before the surrounding tribes had come to the conclusion that British weakness made it worth their joining Nadir Khan, he had to march swiftly, deep through the mountainous desert of tribal territory, and this at the hottest, driest time of the year. He had done so with units depleted in strength and with troops who were in many cases unfit for war. He had inspired these men to give of themselves what little they had left. Having reached Thal in remarkably quick time, and still in good order, he conducted over two days a series of textbook brigade assaults on widely-spaced positions, held by an enemy which dominated all approaches from its high ground. Each assault necessitated a slow, arduous approach in the heat of the June sun. He had carefully husbanded the strength of his troops, setting them tasks they could and did achieve, then resting them. His forces had not suffered one reverse. He had seen his enemy flee before him, his troops had cleared them from all the British territory in his sector, and he had relieved Thal. He had done this at a cost of a handful of wounded men.

For Dyer, on this occasion, all the circumstances had combined to make his command a success. His operation was properly planned; he had the great good fortune to have Eustace's GSO 1 to help draft the initial orders. There was sound and plentiful intelligence available upon which to base the operation, intelligence gained by both the local politicals and from the air. The fortuitous presence of the Inspector General of Communications, and the assets already in place around Kohat, meant that the logistic support and transport for his force could be provided and coordinated by senior and expert staff. His superior commander, Beynon, was at all times close at hand to guide, restrain but not to interfere with him, and his Political Officer, Major Anson, was congenial and of similar mind, so there was no repetition of the unseemly squabbles of the Sarhadd. The commanding officers serving under him were an experienced group capable of handling troops according to the mission they had been set, so Dyer did not have to conduct detailed operations himself. It was not, however, just the team effort behind the relief of Thal which accounts for what was probably the most outstanding feat of arms in the whole Third Afghan War. Dyer deserves the credit for his sensible, methodical and thorough reduction of the Afghan position around Thal, for his use of all the arms in his force to their best effect, especially his artillery, and most of all for the leadership which drove the men under his command along the road to Thal, and then up the hill under the blazing sun when their comrades were falling around them from heatstroke and when not one of them could know that the Afghans, and particularly the tribesmen, would turn and run. It was a campaign well handled, one of which any soldier could justifiably have been very proud.

Though the reputation Dyer won at Thal was soon to be overshadowed by the infamy of the Jallianwala Bagh, and the success he had won was to prove all too fleeting, as he returned to the plains of the Punjab in June 1919, we may allow that he had reached the high point of his career and of his life. The last word can be left to the Viceroy, writing a year later to the King Emperor, George V: 'General Dyer at the outset of the last Afghan War commanded a column for the relief of Thal with great distinction.'[21] He did indeed.

19

Dalhousie and Jamrud

The Afghan campaign, brief though it had been, had proved a severer trial than Dyer's constitution could cope with. After his interview with General Barrett at Peshawar, he was given ten days' leave to recover, and he went to Dalhousie in the hills. Although no detail of his condition survives, it is likely that this was the first evidence of the arteriosclerosis which was thenceforth gradually to dominate his life. After his leave, only partially refreshed, he rejoined his brigade at Nowshera, finding there a letter awaiting him from the Adjutant-General ordering him to write a report on his actions at Amritsar. Similar letters were going out all over India, as the Government belatedly realised that it needed to prepare evidence for the inquiry which it had been forced to accept. It was now mid July, and, as he tried to piece together an account of what he had done, Dyer found that many of the key people who had been with him at the time were difficult to contact. Though Briggs was still with the brigade, and he had with him the log sheets giving the chronological account of its activities (a particularly important fact as it appears that Dyer had not kept a diary of his own at Amritsar), many of the others were at the Frontier or had gone on leave. Irving, for instance, was now in England.

In his convalescence at Dalhousie, Dyer found plenty of time to catch up on the papers, and so was able to read of the execration his acts were eliciting from the Indian community and the praise he was receiving from the British, most of whom were beginning to treat him as a hero. The issue of the Punjab disturbances was now dividing India down largely racial lines. Much of the British press supported the idea that the Punjab disorders had been a second Mutiny which had been nipped in the bud by the courageous action of Sir Michael O'Dwyer and his subordinates, chief among whom they singled out Dyer. His firing at the Jallianwala Bagh was widely credited with having stopped all subsequent violence, and with confining the outbreak to the Punjab. This school believed that Dyer had saved at least the Punjab if not the whole of India.[1]

The Indian press took the opposite view. Whether of moderate or extreme opinion, it considered martial law, and in particular the events at Amritsar, as an affront to the nation, and the methods used to suppress the disturbances as an indication of the real nature of British rule and of British racial prejudice. The crawling order particularly was seen as a racial insult. Gandhi treated it as more serious than the massacre in the Jallianwala Bagh itself. As censorship was lifted, and especially after 9 June 1919, when martial law was finally ended in Amritsar city, news of what had happened gradually seeped out. India was in shock, and anti-British feeling was now so acute that political relations between the two communities were rapidly breaking down.[2]

Whilst the Afghan War was being fought, the widely respected moderate Sir Rabindranath Tagore wrote to the Viceroy to surrender his knighthood, citing as his reason the 'insults and sufferings endured by our brothers in the Punjab'. Gandhi demanded a Royal Commission of Inquiry and began bombarding both the Government of India and Edwin Montagu in London with telegrams and letters. The All India Congress Committee meeting in Allahabad took up this call and passed a resolution on 8 June demanding an inquiry, for the first time specifically mentioning the Jallianwala Bagh. They reiterated this on 20 July, sending the moderate Sir Chettur Sankaran Nair to England to lobby for an inquiry; he had just resigned from the Viceroy's Executive Council in protest against the Government's refusal to repudiate the suppression in the Punjab. Congress also began relief work in the Punjab, led by Pandit Madan Mohan Malaviya, who was a member of the Imperial Legislative Council, and Swami Shraddhanand, and both of these began to collect and circulate stories of what had happened there. Motilal Nehru was in Amritsar in late June and wrote to his son, Jawarhalal, that he had seen badly decomposed bodies floating in the Jallianwala Bagh well; this was denied by the Government. Meetings began to be held all over the country to protest about what had happened at Amritsar.[3]

Despite this growing storm, the Government of India neither took alarm nor contemplated any change of course. They had, they thought, defeated what they still considered to have been an organised rebellion and had placed most of their more virulent opponents in gaol. The Government seemed in control of events, but Montagu's commitment to Parliament that there would be an inquiry could not be circumvented, so preparations went ahead, but very slowly; on 11 June, two days after martial law ended, the India Office asked the Government of India to submit proposals for its terms and composition.

In London, Edwin Montagu had not yet grasped the significance of the Jallianwala Bagh. Simla had reported the event to him just after it happened, but it had forwarded only Irving's initial report of two hundred casualties with a minimum of explanation, appending it to the bottom of their telegram of 15 April which had announced the first imposition of martial law, a subject much more likely to have caught the Secretary of State's eye. Montagu had missed further reports of the massacre, none of which were very clear, amongst the deluge of detail he was receiving about the disturbances. Follow up messages had clarified that the casualties had been deaths, but had not added details of how they had occurred, and the Viceroy had gone so far as to assure Montagu that 'the effect was salutary'. There had been no messages about the Jallianwala Bagh since April. Nor was Montagu much more enlightened by two office calls he received from Sir Michael O'Dwyer, who was in London having at last handed over his post and who went to see him on 30 June and 24 July. The two men had disliked each other intensely since Montagu's war-time visit to India, and Montagu was perfectly aware that O'Dwyer opposed his ideas for reform root and branch. O'Dwyer gave Montagu a version of the events in the Bagh based upon his own fifteen-minute interview with Dyer, and left Montagu believing that Dyer had acted out of fear of being overwhelmed. O'Dwyer did not tell Montagu that Dyer had fired without warning, nor did he mention for how long he had fired or what had happened to the casualties.

Montagu was better informed about the crawling order, as he had a full letter on the subject from Lord Chelmsford dated 7 May, which did not, however, arrive in London until 8 June. This woke Montagu up with a start. He immediately telegraphed:

> Dyer's judgment and temper have in my opinion proved so unreliable that I am of opinion that he cannot be fit to retain command. I consider in fact it very undesirable that he should continue in the Army of India. Unless the military authority has something to urge on his behalf beyond his previous excellent record of which I am not aware, I think you should relieve him of his command and send him to England.[4]

The Viceroy was not prepared to do this, being all too aware of pro-Dyer opinion in India and in any case resenting Montagu's detailed interference. He himself had failed to make any proper inquiry into the Amritsar events, indeed he had yet to set foot in the Punjab at all, so he was almost as in the dark about the firing at the Jallianwala Bagh as was the Secretary of State. He and the Commander-in-Chief in India both remained convinced that Dyer was worthy of their support and that the crawling order was not a mistake of judgment sufficient to ruin a career. Chelmsford replied to Montagu, again by letter, quite aware of the length of time it would take to reach him:

> I was extremely sorry to get your telegram with regard to Dyer, not that I think it was unnatural in the circumstances. I have had an opportunity of discussing the situation in the Punjab with the Bishop of Lahore, who reported ... Indian villagers saying ... that it was Dyer's prompt action which saved the situation from being infinitely worse. Moreover, since then, I have heard that Dyer administered Martial Law in Amritsar very reasonably and in no sense tyrannously. In these circumstances you will understand why it is that both the Commander-in-Chief and I feel very strongly that an error of judgment, transitory in its consequences, should not bring down upon him a penalty which would be out of all proportion to the offence and which must be balanced against the very notable services which he rendered at an extremely critical time. I should add

further that Dyer took part in the recent operations at Thal and again distinguished himself as a military leader of great push and determination.[5]

When Montagu received this, he reluctantly accepted the Viceroy's view. He clearly didn't like it; so, as he could not bring himself to issue a direct instruction to act, he rather characteristically confined himself to giving vent to his feelings in the reply he sent the Viceroy on 17 July:

> I have again deferred on this matter to your opinion. I should not have complained if Dyer had lynched those who attacked the lady missionary. It was the savage and inappropriate folly of the Order which roused my anger … I cannot admit that any service that Dyer has rendered anywhere can atone for action of this kind, and I am very much worried that he should have escaped punishment for an Order, the results of which are likely to be permanent.

Montagu and Chelmsford were an ill-matched pair: Montagu, an anxiety-ridden old woman whose best intentions were spoiled by his fussy involvement in every possible detail of business and by a lamentable tendency to nag; Chelmsford, a lofty patrician with a Merovingian disdain for interference in any business at all and a man in the hands of his own officials. Even by July, however, their failure to act had yet to have any political consequences. India was cowed, and little pressure on this issue had so far arisen in London. A few meetings had been held, but there was not yet much interest in the press or in Parliament.[6]

So, whilst there were clouds on the skyline, the political climate was not yet such as might give Dyer much cause for concern and he could spend July preparing his report. Before it was completed, he was summoned to Simla, where, on 2 August, the Commander-in-Chief in India, General Sir Charles Monro, formally congratulated him on his performance and that of his troops at Thal. Monro was often monosyllabic in his dealings with subordinates and made no comment on this occasion to Dyer about his actions in the Jallianwala Bagh, confining himself to reminding Dyer to write his report. He thus missed the chance to forewarn himself of the position Dyer was about to take up, a failure which was to involve him later in bitter accusations that he had abandoned a subordinate whose actions he had long condoned. Given the recent communications with London, to which he had been a party, it is likely that Monro at least gave Dyer the impression that he was not going to come to any harm for what he had done, and indeed the date of this interview, after Montagu's telegram acquiescing in the Viceroy's refusal to remove Dyer, is indicative that Monro had waited until he was sure on this issue before summoning Dyer to congratulate him. It is also very likely that, in his visit to General Headquarters, Dyer discussed the forthcoming inquiry with other senior officers and may very well have been made aware of their support. The Adjutant-General, Lieutenant-General Sir Havelock Hudson, for one, was to defend him publicly up until the inquiry. The

Quartermaster-General, Lieutenant-General Sir George Fletcher Macmunn, was also behind him.[7]

Whilst in Simla, Dyer was asked to meet Sir William Vincent, the Home Member of the Viceroy's Council, in effect the Home Secretary of India and the most senior civil servant in the Government. A member of Vincent's staff later recalled:

> I was on special duty in Vincent's department. He spoke to me almost immediately after seeing Dyer, and told me he had come away from the interview considerably disturbed by Dyer's refusal to face the fact that the propriety of his action might be challenged, and by his unshakable insistence that this action alone saved the Punjab from anarchy. Among the statements which, Vincent told me, caused him great uneasiness were: (1) Dyer's unhesitating admission that he had continued firing *after* the need to protect his small body of troops from being overwhelmed by numbers had disappeared, and *while* the mob was milling about in an endeavour to escape; (2) Dyer's assertion that he had kept on firing because he was determined to teach the mob a lesson which would crush further resistance in the Punjab: and that, with this end in mind, he had personally directed fire to the spots where the crowd was thickest: and (3) Dyer's statement that he would have gone on firing longer if he had had more ammunition. In describing the interview to me, Vincent took (3) – as I did – to mean that Dyer had fired all his ammunition away. Other highly-placed civilians who encountered Dyer at this period formed the same impression.[8]

This was the first airing of the line which Dyer was now determined to follow, and this account makes it clear that the Government of India had clear warning of the bombshell he was now intent on dropping. It is strange that Vincent did not think it necessary to do anything about this before Dyer testified before the enquiry, but his silence may very well have been taken by Dyer as acceptance of his explanation. Dyer had now received the verbal support of every military officer superior to him in the chain of command, had made plain what he had done to the most senior civil official in India, and had received no adverse reaction. He had very probably been made aware that the Viceroy had supported his actions to the Secretary of State. It really must have seemed to him that there was no danger left in making a clean breast of what he had done. He returned to Nowshera to complete his report with sufficient reassurance to muffle the nagging doubts that had not left him since his action in the Bagh.[9]

Despite this strengthened confidence in his position, his ill health gave signs of the internal conflicts which continued to plague him, for it now broke down again. He could no longer endure a prolonged stay in the heat of the plains and he was forced back to the cool of Dalhousie. Command of the brigade was now beyond his capabilities. He passed through Lahore on the way from Nowshera, and called on J.P. Thompson, Chief Secretary to the Punjab Government, who had been present in his April meeting with Sir Michael O'Dwyer and had heard the explanation he had given then for the shooting in the Bagh. This time he gave Thompson an entirely new account of what he had done, one word for word with what he had just told Sir William Vincent. This account, in all its minor personal detail, echoes the wording of the report he was in the process of writing, and Dyer may even have been trying out elements of this to see their effect. This undoubtedly alarmed Thompson, though not enough for him to say so or to take any action to limit the damage he might have foreseen. His diary for 8 August records:

> General Dyer called on me in morning, and had a long talk with him. He said he felt he knew what we were up against. He had first come back from sightseeing at Delhi and Agra. Was in Delhi on 30th when disturbances took place. Was spat at in Delhi and stoned in Ludhiana as car passed through. Reached Amritsar night of 11th. Spent 12th on going round with Deputy Commissioner from street to street, proclaiming that no meetings would be allowed. Was followed shortly afterwards by men going round with ghi-tin proclaiming that there was to be a meeting. Insisted on view that whole series of events should be regarded as one transaction. When his men entered the Jallianwala Bagh, and he saw the meeting in progress, his mind was made up in three seconds that it was his business to suppress the insurrection then and there. That was why he went on shooting … The men sometimes collected in knots instead of bolting and he thought they meditated attack. Did not attend to wounded; his ammunition was nearly exhausted, and his men could not have defended themselves if attacked. He seems to regard it as his mission, his religious duty, to kill the rebellion.[10]

The only echo in this new account of what he had earlier told O'Dwyer and Thompson was his mention that the crowd sometimes collected in knots making him think it was about to rush his force. This was to be the last time Dyer used this line; it survived here, perhaps, because Dyer was very well aware that when he had last spoken to Thompson it had been his principal defence. Thompson chose not to take note of the discrepancy in Dyer's stories, and later at the enquiry was to mention only his first interview with Dyer and not the second.

Back in England, the subject of the Punjab disorders was discussed in the House of Lords, when Earl Russell objected to the sentence of death passed on Harkishan Lal by the court trying martial law cases for Amritsar. Lord Sydenham made the first of what were to be many interventions on the issue, giving his view of the severity of the situation in the Punjab. He had been briefed well by Sir Michael O'Dwyer: 'It is the first time since those dark days', he said, referring to the Mutiny, 'that the cry "Kill the English" was raised.' Sydenham gave the House details of the assault on Miss Sherwood, quoting a friendly Indian saying: 'She is only an English Mission Miss, and she does no harm … but the mob shouted "She is English, kill her".' He went on, oblivious to the exaggeration in his words, 'But for the strong action of Sir Michael O'Dwyer there might have been no Europeans left in the Punjab'. Lord Sinha, the Indian peer who was Under-Secretary of State for India, gave a long and detailed reply to Lord Russell's question, but in his account of events in the Punjab left out all mention of the events of 13 April. The Jallianwala Bagh was thus not mentioned in the House, and there was again nothing here to cause Dyer alarm had he read accounts of the debate in the press.[11]

Dyer was still in Dalhousie when his brigade returned to the Kurram. The Mahsud part of the Frontier was once again in flames, and 45 Brigade had to deploy without its Commander. This removed the advice and clear head, as well as the personal friendship and support, of his Brigade Major, Captain Briggs, who went with the brigade. Dyer was left alone to finish his report, which he did on 25 August. Incredibly, this was the first formal report he had been asked to write about action in Amritsar four months before.

The report was posted to 16 Division marked up for General Beynon, who sent it onward up the chain of command. It is a strange document, in its organisation, in what it contains, and in Dyer's strikingly honest description of his motives for both the firing in the Jallianwala Bagh and for the crawling order. It tells a completely different story from that of his report of 14 April, and from the explanations he had given subsequently to Wathen, Irving, Sir Michael O'Dwyer and finally General Beynon. It is instead the story he had more recently given Sir William Vincent and J.P. Thompson. Rather than a military report, it is a manifesto based upon his personal circumstances and innermost thoughts. Dyer's language in the report is often inappropriate, redolent at times of the Book of Common Prayer rather than of service staff papers, and the report is heavily laden with his apocalyptic view of the rebellion with which he believed he had been destined to deal. Whilst the report purports to cover the events at Amritsar during the full period of his command there, it is in reality a plea in justification for the two major acts for which he was open to criticism. His initial paragraph makes this quite clear:

> It will be necessary for me to mention certain events which occurred prior to 11th April 1919, the date on which I reached Amritsar, to show why I considered it *my bounden duty to disperse by rifle fire* the unlawful and mutinous assembly in the Jallianwala Bagh on the 13th April 1919.

Dyer recognised that the issue at stake here was his own motivation for what he had done. He had, therefore, to show his state of mind and his beliefs at the time, as well as to show what sort of man he was so that he could justify his deeds. To this end he took the reader back to the occasions in 1918 and 1919 when he placated military and civilian trouble without the use of violence, and he described in some detail the anarchy he and his family saw during their holiday in Delhi in order to clarify that by the time he had arrived at Amritsar he believed

that 'A mutiny was in fact in full swing': the frequent use of the word 'mutiny' in
the report was not meant to indicate any contemporary military mutiny (for he
did not at any stage in 1919 consider that there was one) but rather his belief that
what the British had faced was a repeat of the Mutiny of 1857. He described what
he believed was his own forbearance in not opening fire on the crowds at the
Sultanwind Gate on the 12th, and in processing through the city making a
proclamation on the morning of the 13th. Despite this clemency, he heard news
that the 'seditionists' were to meet in the Bagh. 'I recognized that matters must
be critical and that all law, both civil and military, was set at defiance.' Marching
to the Bagh, he saw the crowd, and considered that there was no need to issue a
warning to them to disperse, for this was the same crowd that had erupted in
Amritsar on the 10th, and he had warned them that morning:

> My work that morning, in personally conducting the proclamation, must be looked upon
> as one transaction with what had now come to pass. There was no reason to further
> parley with the mutineers, evidently they were there to defy the arm of the law. The
> responsibility was very great. If I fired I must fire with good effect, a small amount of
> firing would have been a criminal act of folly. I had the choice of neglecting to do my
> duty, of suppressing a mutiny or of becoming responsible for all future bloodshed ...
> What faced me was the 'Danda Fauj'. The enemy had given me a fleeting opportunity of
> suppressing the mutiny there and then, and I must take advantage of it at once or lose it
> for ever. I fired and continued to fire until the crowd dispersed and I consider this is the
> least amount of firing which would produce the necessary moral and widespread effect,
> it was my duty to produce if it was to justify my action ... It was no longer just a question
> of dispersing the crowd but one of producing a sufficient moral effect, from a military
> point of view, not only on those who were present but more specially throughout the
> Punjab. There could be no question of undue severity. The mutineers had thrown out
> the challenge and the punishment, if administered at all, must be complete, unhesitating
> and immediate.

He did not assist the wounded as he needed to safeguard his troops, and as 'I had
to be most careful of not at the last giving up the victory'. The remainder of his
report, another four pages with twenty-six pages of appendixes, aimed to show
that his action at the Bagh immediately pacified the situation in the city and its
district, and that subsequently he was responsible for pacifying the Sikhs of the
rural areas. The report concludes with two letters supporting his case, written by
British clergymen working in the Punjab, who both stated that in their view the
firing at the Jallianwala Bagh prevented worse violence developing.

What Dyer included in the report is striking: a frank admission that there was
no warning given; that the firing went on so long not because it was necessary to
disperse the crowd but to create an impression in the Punjab; and that aid to the
wounded was not important. What is missing is equally striking: gone are the
stories of opening fire through fear of his small force being overwhelmed; of

continuing to fire because the mob was thought to be surging forward; and of mistakenly firing because he did not know that there was no way out. All the excuses, indeed, which Dyer had developed in the days following the shooting had now been jettisoned, and it was this which was to leave his staunchest supporters high and dry. Sir Michael O'Dwyer and General Beynon, though they never said so, must have felt very badly let down. Why, four months later, in the cool of the hills, and with time to reflect, did Dyer write as he did?

The explanation offered for this by Irving, and one that has been taken up since, is that Dyer now realised that he was being lionised for what he had done. He had read the extreme language expressed in his defence by much of British India, and he was, as Irving put it, 'trailling his coat', overstating and embroidering his case to maximise his achievement and the adulation he was receiving. It is difficult to accept this as an explanation for such a radical change in his story, for we are not dealing here with a question of degree of emphasis or exaggeration. Irving's suggestion assumes that Dyer was deliberately lying about both his motives and actions. Such is not, of course, an impossibility, and in any event we must accept that at least one set of Dyer's explanations was false. In this case, we need to seek the explanation which most closely fits all the circumstances and answers the major questions, and here it is clearly the evidence in the report which does so. It supports the indications of Dyer's intentions found in his words to Briggs, his choice of troops, his dismissal of his company commanders, the deployment of the police. His new account, and that alone, is able to explain convincingly why he fired without warning and then went on firing continuously over ten to fifteen minutes. His report makes it clear that he had intended to do both. For the rest of his life, whilst he might expand or justify the explanation he had written in his report of 25 August, he would never abandon it. There is no doubt that it was the true one.

Why did he make this explanation only now? It is probable that this was the first time he had felt safe enough to do so. All those in a position to object, it seemed to him, had approved what he had done. He was now the hero of the relief of Thal. What must have seemed like the whole of British India was behind him, and London had accepted that he would not be disciplined. He was as safe as it was possible to get, and there was now no more need to dissemble.

We do not have General Beynon's reaction to what Dyer wrote, but the surprise he later showed when he heard Dyer's evidence at the inquiry indicates that he may not have read the report carefully before forwarding it to Northern Army. He wrote his own report on 5 September, and in that included fulsome support for what Dyer had done:

> The wisdom of General Dyer's action has been fully proved by the fact that there has been no further trouble at Amritsar ... The strong measures taken by General Dyer at Amritsar had a far reaching effect and prevented any further trouble in the Lahore

Divisional area. His knowledge of the Indian and his popularity with the Sikhs did much to restore confidence and loyalty in the surrounding districts.[12]

Dyer's report reached General Headquarters in September and was forwarded to the Government of India for inclusion in its submissions to the Hunter Committee. It was seen in the Home Department by its Secretary, W.M. Hailey, who returned it to Dyer suggesting that the term 'rebels' should not be used; otherwise, Hailey seems not to have noticed the significance of the rest of the report. For a third time the Government was given warning of the storm about to break and for a third time they ignored it. Dyer duly replaced the word 'rebels' with 'mutineers' and 'seditionists', making no difference in meaning, and resubmitted the report. It was not scrutinised further.[13] The Viceroy was not shown it, and was to see it only in the following year.

Ironically, on very the day on which Dyer signed the report which would end his career, Major-General Beynon was signing a recommendation for the award to him of Companion of the Indian Empire. He wrote of Dyer:

> This officer, whose determination and push are well known, was entrusted with the relief of the garrison at Thal who were surrounded by a body of Afghans and tribesmen. He organised his relief column with supplies and transport and effected the object of his operations with remarkable skill. I consider that the rapidity of his movements prevented a serious rising of the ORAKZAI tribes to join the Afghan forces under NADIR SHAH.

After it reached Simla, the staff crossed out the CIE and inserted 'CSI', Companion of the Star of India. When it found its way finally to the desk of the Commander-in-Chief, he himself altered this to 'Recommended for CBE Military Division'.[14]

The subject of Dyer's actions at Amritsar first surfaced at meetings of the Imperial Legislative Council in September. The Indemnity Bill had reached the light of public debate, and the several days spent upon the subject served to reinforce Dyer's belief that he had nothing to fear in the way of official censure from Government or Army. The debates were acrimonious, with the Indian Members, particularly Pandit Madan Malaviya, who had recently returned from Amritsar, pressing hard to elicit details of the handling of the disturbances, and seeking to censure those in charge of the operation of martial law. The Indian Members failed to make an impression on the Government's position and their detailed questions and lengthy, emotionally charged speeches were treated with contempt by the official members of the council. Alone of the civilian official members, J.P. Thompson, the Chief Secretary of the Punjab, touched on the Jallianwala Bagh in his speech, and then only, with breathtaking effrontery, to quibble about the figures for the casualties, figures which his own administration had done so little to discover. The Adjutant-General, Lieutenant-General Sir Havelock Hudson, gave a stout and detailed defence of Dyer's action at the Bagh, basing his speech upon Dyer's explanation in his report of 14 April that he had opened fire immediately through fears for the safety of his small force. Hudson managed to avoid discussing either the length of firing or the failure to tend the wounded. He even did his best to justify the crawling order, ending his speech with a plea to support a man on the spot who had been faced with a hard decision, whom the Government had promised to support, and who had done his duty. The Indemnity Bill was passed, preventing any future court case, civil or criminal, against anyone who had acted to restore order. To the Government and its officials, this Act was absolutely necessary to prevent any action in the courts against those officers who had operated in the 'lawless' conditions of martial law, but to most Indians the Act was an attempt to pre-empt the forthcoming inquiry, and meant that any action against officials who had exceeded their authority was now impossible. The press reported the debates and the Government printed a copy of its record (though it did not print Pandit Madan Malaviya's speech). Here was public evidence, had Dyer needed it, that the Government would honour its commitment to its servants and that he had nothing to fear from censure. Any qualms he had felt in submitting his written report had been allayed.

Whilst the debates were underway, Dyer left Dalhousie, although he had been restored only to partial health, and rejoined his brigade on the plains. It had now moved to Chaklala, six miles east of Rawalpindi, where it was stationed in reserve for the ongoing Mahsud campaign. There was nothing at Chaklala save for one stone-built hut, and everyone lived and worked in tents. Remarkably, Annie and Alice joined him there. They had been without Ivon's support at Flagstaff House since the previous month when he, by now a captain, had been posted to the 1st Battalion Kashmiris, who were Imperial Service Troops stationed on the North West Frontier, part of the Kohat Kurram Force, coincidentally then at Thal. He was not to get back from there until the following May. Dyer still needed some nursing, so his wife and niece endured the spartan conditions in the camp and stayed with him. It must have reminded Annie of their days in Hong Kong. After about a month of this, in early October, 45 Brigade was posted up to Bannu on the Frontier, but Dyer was unable to go with it. His health was no longer up to an active tour of Frontier duty. Almost in tears, he bade a last farewell to his Headquarters, and especially to Captain Briggs, the young officer who had been with him throughout his command, and who had stood by him in the worst times at the Bagh and on the road to Thal. Briggs had become almost a son to Dyer, whose niece, Alice, had become engaged to be married to him. It was to be the last time they all met.

Dyer was now posted to Peshawar, to Northern Army, and shortly thereafter given command of 5 Brigade, which was part of 2nd (Rawalpindi) Division and which had its Headquarters in Jamrud Fort at the foot of the Khyber Pass. Dyer claimed later, in his statement to the Army Council, that 'I was promoted by being given permanent command of a Brigade'. As his appointment in 45 Brigade had always been 'temporary', this would have been true had he now been given a permanent command, but the *Indian Army List* records that Dyer was appointed 'Officiating General Officer Commanding', in other words that he was standing in for someone else. Due to the dangerous state of the Frontier, there was room in neither Jamrud nor Peshawar for Annie and Alice, so they returned to Jullundur, where they were still able to stay in Flagstaff House, as a new Commander had yet to be posted in to 45 Brigade. Annie must have been glad to have at least retained her home, for she herself was about to fall sick again. Perhaps the strain of the last few months had brought on a further attack of her old ailment, perhaps this was something new.[15]

The Indian National Congress was by now organising its own inquiry into the events in the Punjab. On 16 October, their investigation was mounted by Pandit Motilal Nehru (later to be replaced by M.R. Jayakar), C.R. Das and Swami Shraddhanand, with C.F. Andrews, Jawarhalal Nehru and Purushottam Das Tandon as workers. Gandhi joined it on 17 October when the order banning him from the Punjab was lifted. This inquiry was to prove of historic importance. The detail it accumulated of what had happened in the Punjab was immense, and, as the forthcoming Government inquiry was to confine itself almost entirely to interviewing officials, the Congress inquiry was to be the only one to give a voice to the victims of the repression. Congress later boycotted the official inquiry, so the evidence that it had gathered was never added to the Government record. This work brought Gandhi for the first time into contact with mainstream Congress politicians; on the committee, he met C.R. Das for the first time, 'and established that intimate relation which remained the most outstanding alliance in contemporary Indian public life'. Gandhi gradually came to dominate the proceedings, bringing his skills as a barrister to its work of questioning witnesses and recording statements. His methods were meticulous enough to upset his colleagues, who would have preferred to include the more lurid and unproven detail offered them, but Gandhi allowed the admission of evidence only if it could be proven as in a court of law, and was ruthless in steering clear of the many conspiracy theories that were offered the committee. The enquiry was a personal watershed for Gandhi: what he heard in the Punjab turned him from a loyal citizen of the Empire into an opponent of all its works. He wrote of this process: 'I came across tales of Government's tyranny and the arbitrary despotism of its officers such as I was hardly prepared for, and they filled me with deep pain.' The inquiry also brought him for the first time into contact with Jawaharlal Nehru, who took most of the evidence himself, and who was henceforth devoted to Gandhi.[16]

Preparations for the official inquiry were completed only by 14 October, when the Government of India published Resolution 2168, an order in council which announced its terms. The inquiry was 'to investigate the recent disturbances in Bombay, Delhi and the Punjab, their causes, and the measures taken to cope with them'. It was to be chaired by Lord Hunter, formerly Solicitor-General for Scotland in Asquith's Liberal administration, and now a Senator of the College of Justice in Scotland; he was by then on his way from England. He was described by one of his fellow inquiry members, General Barrow, as 'a mild man somewhat dazzled on his entry on a new stage' and became famed throughout India for going to sleep during a tiger hunt at Dehra Dun not long after his arrival. He was criticised by many British Indians for being without Indian experience, and for his lack of knowledge of Hindi, though as the procedures he chaired were in English, and as the rest of his committee were all old Indian hands, it is difficult to see that this was a real drawback. The committee was to have as members Mr Justice G.C. Rankin of Calcutta, Mr W.F. Rice of the Home Department, Major-General Sir George Barrow, General Officer Commanding Peshawar Division (who had been at Staff College with Dyer), Pandit Jagat Narayan, a lawyer and member of the Legislative Council of the United Provinces, Sir Chimanlal Harilal Setalvad, advocate of the Bombay High Court, Mr Thomas Smith, also a United Provinces Legislative Council member (the representative of the European Association appointed to deflect their calls for an inquiry into Irving's failure to warn the non-officials in Amritsar on 10 April), and Sardar Sahibzada Sultan Ahmed Khan, a lawyer and Government loyalist from Gwalior state. The inquiry's Secretary was Mr H.C. Stokes of the Home Department. Pandit Narayan had earlier crossed swords with Sir Michael O'Dwyer, and the Punjab Government unsuccessfully objected to his membership, whilst Setalvad had been excluded from the Punjab during the disturbances. Both were, despite Sir Michael O'Dwyer's views, eminent men. Setalvad was Vice-Chancellor of Bombay University, and was soon to be a judge. They were both later to be Ministers in the Governments of their two provinces. Montagu had managed to secure a balanced committee and to include much appropriate expertise and knowledge.

The committee, which quickly became known by the name of its chairman, but was also referred to as the Disorders Inquiry Committee, met initially in Delhi on 29 October. It was given a copy of all the written statements collected from those whom the Government of India considered should be witnesses. This was a restricted, even though a very large, list, and did not include the Government's opponents, anyone in gaol, or anyone drawn from the population upon which martial law had been imposed. As Montagu had succeeded in widening the scope of the committee's membership, so the Government of India had succeeded in controlling its access to evidence. To make matters even more one-sided, Congress boycotted the enquiry after 19 November and amongst its supporters only C.R. Das had time to give evidence. Witnesses were called in Delhi then in Lahore, Ahmedabad and Bombay. All but a few witnesses, those whose evidence was to include classified material, were examined in public, and witnesses were not on oath. This did not prevent them being subjected to severe, lengthy and rigorous examination based upon the written statements they had submitted; the committee did its homework well, and in the event managed to lay bare most of the omissions and anomalies in the evidence. Many witnesses, Sir Michael O'Dwyer in particular, objected to being scrutinised in this fashion, and reacted badly to being treated as if they were 'criminals' by Indian lawyers. They were not used to such rough treatment at the hands of men they regarded as their inferiors. Gandhi, who was present at some of the sessions, described the committee's method:

> Pandit Jagat Narain's cross-examination is extremely severe. I feel that at times it is harsher than it need be. Those who know him say that this is his usual manner. Having conducted criminal cases for a long time, he has got into this habit. Sir Chimanlal Shrestha also asks questions in great detail. Sahebzada Sultan Ahmed asks few questions, but these are very much to the point. The British members do not appear to be partial in their questions. The general feeling is that the members of the Committee are not such as would deliberately do injustice. Whether or not this is so, it is admitted by all that the Indian members are no 'yes-men'.[17]

Despite the restrictions placed on those whom they saw, the Hunter Committee did a thorough and rigorous job, and by its unrelenting questioning elicited a vast and dependable amount of evidence about what had happened in the Punjab. The fact that it was later criticised from both directions is a reasonable indication that it succeeded in doing its work well. The form of the inquiry was, however, one with many dangers for those who gave evidence before it. As there were no accused before the Hunter Committee, its witnesses were not accorded any of the legal rights that might otherwise have been granted them; and, as it was not a court, rules of procedure were not applied. Witnesses often found themselves floundering under hostile questioning; in their ill-considered responses they found blame apportioned to them, in their replies to leading questions they incriminated themselves, and in answering hypothetical sallies they made themselves look criminal or foolish. In such an enquiry, as Dyer would find, it was quite possible to be convicted of a crime of which you were not aware you were accused.[18]

20

The Hunter Committee

The Hunter Committee reached Lahore in November 1919 and spent several weeks examining all the principal witnesses for the events in Amritsar. They were by now well into their stride and had developed an efficient system of questioning. By the time Dyer appeared they were very well aware of much of the detail of the events which concerned him. They were also fully aware that India expected them to uncover the facts concerning the action in the Jallianwala Bagh and the crawling order, and that these were, in effect, the central part of their inquiry. Dyer was about to face a formidable interrogation.

He had faced some problems in preparing his notes for his evidence, as he was stuck in Jamrud and his original papers had gone with Briggs to Bannu. Briggs was now ill with appendicitis and unable to come to Lahore. He went into the operating theatre on the day Dyer appeared before the inquiry and died the day after from the peritonitis the operation revealed. What papers he had went with him to the grave. The news of his death affected Dyer badly; he was very fond of Briggs and was disturbed by the damage he feared from the loss of the papers. He said to Annie: 'Briggs has all the papers. What the deuce will happen to all my papers?' He was thus feeling ill-prepared when he appeared before the committee. There is evidence that his supporters, particularly General Beynon and even General Barrow, who knew him from their days together in Staff College and who did not like him much, aware of the nature of the questioning Dyer would face and of his tendency to irascibility, attempted to persuade him to be accompanied by legal council, but Dyer would have none of it. Beynon told him: 'There are on this Inquiry several extremely clever Indian lawyers, who are out to get you. For God's sake, stick to facts and keep your mouth shut.' Dyer had no intention of following this sound advice. He, too, was aware that the eyes of India were upon him. As Irving later told Edward Thompson, 'he was determined to fight'. This was not an occasion on which Dyer wanted to be seen to avoid answering questions or to dissemble the truth. On Thursday 19 November, he appeared before the committee.[1]

The session lasted all day, and each member of the committee took turns to question Dyer. The hearing was held in a public hall, and many of those attending were Indian students whose behaviour was called rowdy by some of the British who were present and who felt that Lord Hunter had insufficient control of the room. The students applauded the hostile and difficult questions put to witnesses by the three Indian members. Brigadier-General Sir John Smythe recalled: 'The proceedings of the Commission of Inquiry were a shambles, held in open court in conditions of noisy vituperation. The judge, speaking no Hindustani, was unable to keep order.' There were also later allegations that the Secretary left the minutes to Indian clerks and that the minutes got in such a muddle that the *Pioneer* reporter present, a Mr Watson, had to be called in to check the transcript against his notes. Dyer for one disputed some of the words attributed to him, although General Barrow later flatly contradicted him, stating that he clearly remembered the words Dyer denied having said.

Lord Hunter commenced the questioning, politely taking Dyer through the events at Amritsar and carefully establishing the chronology and the areas upon which Dyer might face criticism. Even in response to this gentle questioning Dyer was forthright; he admitted that 'there may have been a good many who had not heard the proclamation' of the morning among the crowd in the Bagh, and stated that he had not issued a warning to it before firing;

> At the time it did not occur to me. I merely felt that my orders had not been obeyed, that martial law was flouted, and that it was my duty to immediately disperse it by rifle fire … if my orders were not obeyed, I would fire immediately.

In regard to the length of firing, he said: 'I thought it my duty to go on firing until it dispersed. If I fired a little, the effect would not be sufficient. If I had fired a little, I should be wrong in firing at all.' He admitted that 'I think it quite possible that I could have dispersed them perhaps even without firing' and that he did not do this because 'then they would all come back and laugh at me, and I considered I would be making myself a fool'. The crowd he was facing in the Bagh was, he said, 'rebels who were trying to isolate my forces and cut me off from other supplies. Therefore I considered it my duty to fire on them and to fire well.' He had given the wounded no aid as the military situation did not allow it. He explained his view of the sacredness of women as his reason for issuing the crawling order and said that in his experience in the Army flogging was best done in public because of the impression it had on others.

Mr Justice Rankin took over the questioning. He was similarly courteous, but probed Dyer thoroughly, and the civility of his questions led Dyer to further admissions. Asked about whether he could have prevented the meeting in the Bagh, Dyer said that it could have been done; 'twenty men at each entrance would have been sufficient'. Rankin asked him his state of mind as he drove to the Bagh. Dyer replied: 'I had made up my mind. I was only wondering whether I should do it or whether I should not'. Rankin followed up: 'No question of having your forces attacked entered into your consideration at all?' Dyer replied: 'No. The situation was very serious. I had made up my mind that I would do all men to death if they were going to continue the meeting'. Rankin then asked him whether firing in order to make an impression beyond the Bagh was not 'a resort to what has been called "frightfulness"?' Dyer replied:

> No, I don't think so. I think it was a horrible duty for me to perform. It was a merciful act that I had given them chance to disperse. The responsibility was very great. I had made up my mind that if I fired I must fire well and strong so that it would have a full effect. I had decided if I fired one round I must shoot a lot of rounds or I must not shoot at all. My logical conclusion was that I must disperse the crowd which had defied the arm of the law. I fired and I continued to fire until the crowd dispersed.

Sir Chimanlal Setalvad was next, his tone again reasonable, measured, gently leading the witness but not hectoring or confusing him. He returned Dyer to the Jallianwala Bagh and started by probing his intentions: 'You made up your mind that if the meeting was going to be held you would go and fire?'

> When I heard that they were coming and collecting I did not at first believe that they were coming, but if they were coming to defy my authority, and really to meet after all I had done that morning, I had made up my mind that I would fire immediately in order to save the military situation.

Setalvad then offered Dyer a hypothetical question, one he foolishly answered: 'Supposing the passage was sufficient to allow the armoured cars to go in would you have opened fire with the machine guns?' 'I think probably yes.' 'In that case the casualties would have been much higher?' 'Yes'. He probed Dyer again on the issue of creating an impression upon the rest of the Punjab. Dyer answered: 'They had come out to fight if they defied me, and I was going to give them a lesson.' 'I take it that your idea in taking that action was to strike terror?' 'Call it what you like. I was going to punish them. My idea from the military point of view was to make a wide impression.' 'To strike terror not only in the city of Amritsar, but throughout the Punjab?' 'Yes, throughout the Punjab. I wanted to reduce their *moral*, the *moral* [sic] of the rebels.' Dyer went on to explain that he wished to prevent by this act 'more bloodshed, more looting, more lives lost ... I realized it was the only way of saving life'. His further clarification was almost childish in the naivety of its schoolboy language: 'I thought I would be doing a jolly lot of good and they would realize that they were not to be wicked.' Setalvad then elicited a statement of great callousness from Dyer about his treatment of the casualties: 'After the firing had taken place did you take any measures for the relief of the wounded?' 'No, certainly not. It was not my job. But the hospitals were open and the medical officers were there. The wounded only had to apply for help.'

General Barrow, who was next to question Dyer, put him questions deliberately framed to allow him to answer to his own advantage, particularly about the handover of civil authority and the implementation of martial law in Amritsar. He tried to get Dyer to put the shooting in the Jallianwala Bagh in the best light: 'You were convinced honestly in your own mind that when you fired on this crowd it was to prevent further trouble and bloodshed which might follow later on?' 'Absolutely, Sir.' 'The necessity for prompt action was so essential that there was no time for further reflection?' 'Yes, Sir.' 'And also perhaps you will agree with me that when one is faced with such a situation, it creates quite a different impression in one's mind to what it will when you are simply reading about it?' 'Quite true, Sir.'

This did little, however, to dispel the impression Dyer had already made. His respite was a short one, as Pandit Jagat Narayan took over the interrogation. His questions were shorter, sharper, coming in staccato bursts and leaving Dyer little time to think of his replies. Narayan pressed repeatedly if he didn't get the answer he wanted, niggling at small, seemingly irrelevant details, and highlighting the fact that Dyer had had six men flogged who had not been convicted of the Sherwood assault. His tone was peremptory – 'I want to know if any records have been kept' – and sneering – 'Is it not an extraordinary coincidence that ...?' Dyer became shorter and less forthcoming in his replies as this storm of questions beat about his head. He was getting tired by now and had to ask Narayan to repeat his questions. He became tetchy: 'I cannot go on wandering about these things ... I say yes.' 'There is no doubt in your mind?' 'There is doubt, that is why I am hesitating. I had so much to do. It is not quite fair to ask me what happened so long ago. I cannot answer you straight. I cannot remember.' Narayan's technique scored fewer points than his politer colleagues, but he did, towards the end of his very lengthy questioning, make a telling point on the issue of the curfew that prevented aid being given to the wounded in the Bagh. Dyer would not answer his question as to how the people could have aided the injured and collected their dead if there was a curfew in place. Narayan asked him this some six times, eliciting from Dyer only that 'I allowed them to go. That is quite enough.'

Towards the end of the afternoon, Sardar Sahibzada Sultan Ahmed Khan concluded the questioning. He was quiet, careful and polite. His questions concentrated on the legality of Irving's handover of complete authority in Amritsar and the issue of whether the Rowlatt agitation was a rebellion. Dyer stated that he thought that it was. The sardar finished with one telling point, clarifying that the inhabitants of the street closed by the crawling order had included those who had rescued Miss Sherwood, and that the curfew prevented anyone in the street moving when the picquet was off duty.[2]

It had been a very long day. Dyer had stood up to the questioning despite his ill-health and the evident hostility all around him, which must have been quite a shock to him. Watson of the *Pioneer* thought he 'seemed only like a man very weary, who gave up trying to put his case when he saw that it was useless'.

J.P. Thompson had also observed the day: 'General Dyer gave his evidence. Lasted whole day. He came thru' it very well, he was transparently honest. And he kept his temper.' Others disagreed, seeing that he lost his temper, as the transcript shows that he did. The *Pioneer* in its obituary in 1927 recalled: 'He was jeered by a gallery of students at the back of the improvised court and Lord Hunter signally failed to keep order or protect the witnesses against over-zealous cross examination ... that was fatal with a man of Dyer's temperament. He lost his temper.' Brigadier-General Sir John Smythe remembered that: 'General Dyer, baited beyond endurance made some very silly statements. In this respect he was his own worst enemy.' Dyer's supporters afterwards maintained that his loss of temper was the reason for the new line he took (which of course ignores the point that there was no discrepancy between Dyer's written statement, drafted with time for reflection, and his verbal evidence). Sir Michael O'Dwyer accepted in 1924 that Dyer's evidence was 'indefensible', but that he had been goaded into saying what he did, as it was not what he told him at the time. General Beynon said: 'I am sorry to say that the evidence he gave is quite different from what he was thinking and doing at the time', and that 'It was not an enquiry; it was an inquisition'. Beynon went on leave to Burma shortly afterwards, and told Sir Percy Craddock, its Governor:

> The Indian pleaders on the Committee were simply out for [sic] insulting the official witnesses and that Dyer had not a chance with astute lawyers of this kind, while Lord Hunter did nothing to save him from insult and annoyance.[3]

What is clear is that the effect of the questioning was to make Dyer stick to his guns. He gave the Hunter Committee an account of his actions that coincided with his report of 25 August and with the evidence surviving from the events themselves. His evidence to the inquiry, of course, failed to coincide with the differing explanations he had given of his actions to Wathen, Irving, Maclagan, Hailey, O'Dwyer and Beynon, and for these, particularly for the latter two, whose own support of Dyer was thereby called into question, it created great difficulty. To maintain their own positions they were now forced to deny the truth of what Dyer had said at the inquiry (and had written in his report of 25 August). In their view, his initial statements alone were reliable. Sir Michael O'Dwyer and General Beynon were to go on maintaining this for the rest of their lives. The Government of India had no such option. Dyer's statements made it clear that he had broken all the rules in a way that made it certain that he could not be defended officially.

Dyer's testimony split the Hunter Committee. Setalvad reported the argument that developed and which

> on occasions heated led to some unpleasantness, particularly because of the intolerant attitude adopted by Lord Hunter towards any difference of opinion. During one of the

discussions I had with Lord Hunter, he lost his temper and said: 'You people (meaning myself and my Indian colleagues) want to drive the British out of the country.' This naturally annoyed me very much and I said: 'It is perfectly legitimate for Indians to wish to be free of foreign rule and Indian independence can be accomplished by mutual understanding and good will. The driving out process will only become necessary if the British are represented in this country by people as short-sighted and intolerant as yourself.' After this, though under the same roof, we, the Indian Members, ceased to talk to Lord Hunter … The tension under the unpleasant atmosphere was too great and on the day we signed the report, I fell ill with a high fever.[4]

Dyer went back to Jamrud, but a few days later came back to Lahore to listen to General Beynon's evidence; he was relieved to hear Beynon support him stoutly. Afterwards, Dyer was given tea at Government House by Sir Edward Maclagan, the new Lieutenant-Governor, who congratulated Dyer upon his evidence and upon the way he had stood up for women. From what Dyer could see, support for his position had held firm. That night he travelled on to Delhi, as was recounted by Jawaharlal Nehru, who joined the train at Amritsar:

The compartment I entered was almost full and all the berths, except one upper one, were occupied by sleeping passengers. I took the vacant upper berth. In the morning I discovered that all my fellow-passengers were military officers. They conversed with each other in loud voices which I could not help overhearing. One of them was holding forth in an aggressive and triumphant tone and I soon discovered that he was Dyer, the hero of Jallianwala Bagh, and he was describing his Amritsar experiences. He pointed out how he had the whole town at his mercy and he had felt like reducing the rebellious city to a heap of ashes, but he took pity on it and refrained. He was evidently coming back from Lahore after giving his evidence before the Hunter Committee of Inquiry. I was greatly shocked to hear his conversation and to observe his callous manner. He descended at Delhi station in pyjamas with bright pink stripes, and a dressing gown.[5]

The evidence given before Hunter, being in public, was widely reported in the press in India and picked up in the London papers. The Indian National Congress also sent their own evidence to London for publication and their British Committee got a report out quickly. On 13 December, the *Daily Express* was the first British paper to quote Dyer's evidence, making much of the fact that he had stated that it was possible that he had killed between four and five hundred people in the Bagh. *The Times* carried a similar story two days later. Montagu, taken completely by surprise, was appalled. He immediately telegraphed the Viceroy to point out that this figure was considerably more than that announced in the Legislative Council on 10 September and by him in the Commons on 10 October. He sought confirmation from Chelmsford as to what the real figure was. On the 18th, the day that the Punjab Government Report on the disturbances at last arrived on his desk, Montagu again telegraphed Chelmsford, saying that the newspaper articles had 'created a very strong and very painful impression here'. He had been questioned in the House and had taken the line that the Government had to await the Hunter Committee's recommendations before taking action. Nevertheless, he felt that 'the fact will be an unforgettable one in the history of our administration in India'. The news had affected him deeply and he confided to Chelmsford that: 'I cannot keep my mind off the tragedy that occurred ... I ask myself whether I could not have done more than I did to prevent it.' Three days before, while answering questions in the House, Montagu was reduced to saying that he had known 'of no details of the circumstances until I saw the report in the newspapers'. This was clearly an inadequate answer; he had been left to dangle in the wind by the Viceroy, who had failed entirely to appreciate the political effect in London of what was going on in India. Instead of briefing Montagu and taking active steps to handle what was being revealed by the Hunter Committee, Chelmsford was still burying his head in the sand, trying to do nothing at all until the committee had reported. Montagu repeated to the Viceroy that reports of the Hunter Committee's hearings were causing 'great public perturbation', and that he was finding it hard not to take action before the committee's judgment was published. The English press, aside from the *Morning Post*, was almost unanimously hostile to Dyer. He concluded: 'Meanwhile it is assumed by me that Dyer is being employed in a manner which would not risk his reappearance in a similar role.'

This issue became more pertinent on 22 December, when Colonel Wedgwood, a member of his own party, asked Montagu in the House if Dyer had been relieved of his command and whether the Secretary of State had yet received an official report of his evidence. Montagu was forced to reply negatively to both. Wedgwood's speech was scathing: 'An English sportsman would take any amount of trouble or time to see that a wounded partridge was put out of its misery, but these wounded people were lying there for two days dying slowly.' Montagu could only reply that the issue was *sub judice*, and this at least ensured that the motion was not put to a vote. Badly stung, he very reasonably asked Chelmsford the next day whether, if he had been aware that Dyer fired on the crowd without warning, he had not thought of suspending Dyer from his command until the Hunter Committee's report and, if not, why not. He also asked him whether he had taken action to prevent a recurrence of actions like the crawling and salaaming orders. He added plaintively: 'Public opinion is very much inflamed and extremely difficult to keep steady. You are charged with not having sent me sufficient information ... Dyer's evidence has staggered me as much as anybody.' A week later he returned to the charge that there was a huge disparity between India's initial reports and what was now coming out at the Hunter Committee hearings. 'I have no wish to press for Dyer's removal from Command on the frontier;

I must, however, insist that pending report he shall not be employed in any place or capacity to deal with civil disturbances.'

The Viceroy continued to reply that nothing could be done until the Hunter Committee had reported. He had his own problems of public opinion to deal with and amongst the British in India these ran directly contrary to those pressing upon Montagu. The Viceroy would not act against the views of his own officials and of the vast majority of the Army without the shield which he hoped the Hunter Committee would afford him. Replying to Montagu, Chelmsford attempted to maintain the line that Dyer's reports of 14 April and 25 August were substantially compatible; he could do so as neither report was yet in Montagu's possession. Chelmsford also alleged that Sir Michael O'Dwyer had told Montagu all there was to know, which was more than a little disingenuous given that he was fully aware of the line O'Dwyer was taking. O'Dwyer made matters worse by writing to Montagu, vituperatively criticising the account he had given to the House of their meetings, and initiating a long row between the two men that erupted in the press when O'Dwyer copied his letter to two newspapers in the following June. Despite being pressed several times by the Secretary of State, the Viceroy would not even favour him with a personal opinion of Dyer's case. Montagu became so distraught that he suffered a nervous breakdown and retired to a nursing home from January to March 1920.[6]

The Government in London watched with alarm the collapse of mutual respect between the British and their Indian subjects. They understood that restoring this was vital for the success of the Montagu-Chelmsford reforms that were about to be launched. At this time they saw the festivities organised in India to celebrate the Allied victory in the First World War boycotted; the military processions passed down empty streets where the shops were closed in token of national mourning. It became clear in London that something had to be done urgently to restore the situation, even if merely to ensure the implementation of the reforms, for the Act embodying them was on its way through Parliament and gained the royal assent on 31 December. On the same day, the King Emperor issued a proclamation aimed at pouring oil on India's troubled waters by announcing an amnesty: clemency was given to those arrested and charged with political offences in the recent disturbances. This was widely welcomed in India by all communities, and, had it not been for the events which followed the publication of the Hunter Committee's report, it might very well have stabilised the situation sufficiently to put gradual reform back on course. At the Indian National Congress meeting held in Amritsar between 27 and 30 December, Montagu was complimented for his reforms, and resolutions were passed thanking George V for his proclamation, and welcoming the Prince of Wales, who was due to visit the following year. Congress's report into the Punjab disturbances had yet to be published, but its President, Motilal Nehru, referred to the lack of official condemnation of the Jallianwala Bagh shooting, and said: 'That is a revelation of official mentality which staggers me.' A resolution was passed demanding the removal of Dyer from his command. Gandhi was at this meeting of Congress for the first time, and it marked the beginning of his involvement in mainstream Congress politics.[7]

Dyer had gone back to work in Jamrud, but was so ill with jaundice shortly after Christmas that he was sent down to Jullundur, his skin a bright yellow colour. He was suffering from several complaints at this stage, some perhaps brought on by his inner turmoil and the stress of the last few months. He was, however, at last back at home with Annie, but ill-luck dogged him, for whilst recovering from his jaundice, he went for a walk in the very cold wind of the winter, which there swept down off the high Himalayas. He returned 'in terrible pain with gout in the head'. He relapsed into sickness and his nights were spent in delirium. Annie did not, though, give him the sleeping draught she had been given by his doctor, as she feared it would damage his heart. They were both aware by now that his heart was affected by his arteriosclerosis, and that his life was at risk.

Dyer felt he could no longer cope with his work and that he needed to go to England to recover his health; but when he applied for six months' leave he was told, on 30 January 1920, that it could not be granted unless he vacated his post in 5 Brigade. This he would not do, as were he to do so he would lose not only his rank but probably also all chance of another command. The forfeiture of pay would have struck the Dyers hard. This depressing news meant he had to try to soldier on where he was and to get well enough at least to occupy his post at Jamrud. That same day, however, an indication that he was not yet viewed with disfavour arrived in the form of a telegram from General Headquarters appointing him 'officiating in Command of the 2nd Division *vice* Major-General Sir Charles Dobell', who had been moved up to be officiating Commander-in-Chief Northern Command. This was not a promotion, though it was later claimed to be so by his supporters, but rather a temporary holding of the divisional command until it could be filled properly. In fact it was already being filled temporarily by Brigadier-General Caulfield. The telegram, though, was a restorative to the Dyers' morale. The thought that perhaps his work at Thal had not been forgotten, and that he might after all beat the ruling of the promotion board and become a major-general, must have passed through the Dyers' minds and have been the subject of cautious optimism at their dinner table. Others, after all, had been promoted for less.

Dyer's illness now snatched away the last chance he had of any preferment. General Headquarters realised that he was not fit enough to hold down the job, or even to move to the Frontier. On 14 February, before the end of his current bout of sick leave, and before he was due to move, the order was cancelled.

Brigadier-General Caulfield was left where he was and Major-General Sheppard was posted in permanently. This saddened Dyer, but cannot have surprised him; the 2nd Division at Rawalpindi was one of the most active commands in India, and in Dyer's state of health there was no possibility that he would have been able to cope. What is surprising is that he had been temporarily appointed at all. Within days of this disappointment, Dyer became so ill that he could no longer remain at home to be nursed by Annie, who was herself now too sick to manage him. Once more he found himself back in the hospital.[8]

As Dyer was lying gravely ill in Jullundur, the Hunter Committee produced their report, forwarding it to the Viceroy on 8 March. It was a massive document, nearly two hundred pages of text, with maps and photographs, and six thick volumes of evidence, two of which were classified secret and so were not published. As had been feared for some time by the Government of India, the report revealed that the committee had split down embarrassingly racial lines. All three Indian members had failed to agree with the remainder, and had produced a minority report. The two reports were to mirror almost exactly the divisions which had opened up in India, for most of the British community rejected the committee's condemnations of the excesses of martial law as pandering to the nationalists, whilst both moderate and nationalist Indians were united in rejecting what they saw as a whitewash.

Both reports were united on some points, and one of these was their view of Dyer and his actions. The majority findings, although gentler in their strictures, were perfectly sufficient by themselves to damn him. In respect of his opening fire without warning at the Bagh, the majority reported: 'Notice to disperse would have afforded those assembled in ignorance of the proclamation and other people also an opportunity to leave the Bagh, and should have been given.' The minority added that 'the proclamation [of 13 April] was unsufficiently promulgated, important portions of the town having been left out', and they highlighted Dyer's own view that he could have dispersed the crowd without firing at all. The length of firing also attracted both the majority and minority's condemnation: 'In continuing to fire for so long as he did it appears to us that General Dyer committed a grave error.' They also both roundly condemned Dyer's motive of 'producing a sufficient moral effect' in the rest of the Punjab: 'In our view this was unfortunately a mistaken conception of his duty ... continued firing upon that crowd cannot be justified because of the effect such firing may have upon people in other places.' In addition, the minority report highlighted the fact that there were innocent people among the crowd and that there had been no violence in the Bagh before the shooting.

Dyer's lack of attention to the wounded was not accepted as grounds for criticism by the majority: 'It has not been proved to us that any wounded people were in fact exposed to unnecessary suffering from want of medical treatment.'

The minority report disagreed strongly with this, saying that Dyer should either have taken steps himself to help the wounded or should have arranged that the civil authorities did so. The majority did not believe that Dyer had saved the situation in the Punjab or had averted another Mutiny, as they believed that there was not 'a conspiracy to overthrow British power'. The minority report went further, emphasising the negative effect the shooting had had on Indian opinion and comparing it to the Prussianism the British had just fought in Belgium and Flanders: 'We feel that General Dyer, by adopting an inhuman and un-British method of dealing with subjects of His Majesty the King Emperor, has done great disservice to the interest of British rule in India.'[9]

Neither Dyer nor even the Government of India had any warning of these findings, though General Headquarters seems to have had an inkling of what was to come (perhaps forewarned by Major-General Barrow). Three days earlier, still in the hospital in Jullundur, Dyer had received a telegram sent by General Headquarters to 2nd Division instructing them to send him to Delhi to report to the Commander-in-Chief on 9 March, and warning that he would be required in Delhi for some days. General Headquarters seems to have planned that he should be close at hand when the Hunter Report was published, but the medical officer in charge of the hospital spoiled this plan as he refused to allow Dyer to travel due to his ill health. His state was now so bad that a medical board held nearly two weeks later on 16 March recommended that he be granted six months' sick leave in England. Events were now in train, however, which would not be stayed by even the dire medical condition to which Dyer had been reduced. If he could travel to England, he could travel to Delhi, and it was there that he now had to go.

On 18 March, now a good ten days after the Hunter report had been made public, 2nd Division sent Dyer a further telegram, this time instructing him to be in Delhi on the 22nd, and to report to the Military Secretary (the general officer responsible for personnel matters) on the 23rd. Again the medical officer tried to prevent this, but the next telegram, and one that came immediately, was a personal one from the Commander-in-Chief, stating: 'If well enough to travel, kindly report yourself to the Military Secretary at Delhi at 10 o'clock on Tuesday morning next, the 23rd instant.' Dyer could scarcely resist this and he insisted on going. He was taken to the train by a medical officer, Captain Beamish, who accompanied him to Delhi.[10]

Strange as it may seem, even by the date of the telegram which summoned him to Delhi, Dyer's fate had yet to be decided. His file was swiftly circulating through the offices of the members of the Viceroy's Executive Council on 19 and 20 March.[11] Dyer's fate was woven as each senior official's opinion was added to the file. The key members of the Government of India had all read the Hunter Committee's reports, and they were now unanimous in agreeing that Dyer could no longer be supported; they disagreed now only on what to do with him.

G.S. Barnes and W.M. Hailey were alone amongst the council members in showing sympathy to Dyer. The former wrote that: 'Without doubt Dyer acted wrongly, but equally without doubt believed he was acting rightly'; the latter's view was that Dyer acted 'honestly, if mistakenly'. Hailey supported the suggestion that Dyer be placed on the unemployed list. M.A. Shafi, the only Indian Member of the Executive Council, gave his view that Dyer's action was deliberate, intended 'to kill and kill, so as to produce an effect'. He called for his dismissal from the service. C.H.A. Hill agreed that Dyer be retired from the service, and concurred with Shafi that Dyer was wrong because he sought a 'moral effect that would be produced in other parts of the province'. Significantly, one of the two Military Members, Lieutenant-General Sir Havelock Hudson, agreed that Dyer had showed 'an error of judgment in continuing to fire'. He believed he was 'unfit to be trusted any longer with the command of troops', but left any recommendation for action to the Commander-in-Chief. The most senior civilian, the Home Member, Sir William Vincent, depending upon J.P. Thompson for his description of Dyer as a 'very honest witness', gave his opinion that a military commander

> in such circumstances ought only to take into consideration the actual facts before him and not the possible effects in distant parts of the country or of the province of which he is not competent to judge ... The deliberate conclusion at which I have arrived is that in acting as he did he went beyond any reasonable requirement of the case. He showed a disregard for human life, a misconception of his duty, and his action was such that it would be unwise to allow him to continue to hold the responsible position which he is now occupying.

Vincent believed that the Indemnity Act did not protect Dyer, but ruled out a court martial or civilian prosecution. He was supported in his view by Sir George Lowndes, the Legal Member: the legal advice which the Government had obtained made it clear that a prosecution would be fraught with difficulty, and that it was very unlikely that a conviction could be secured in either a civil or a military court. Were a prosecution to fail, the Government of India would have to face the fact that Dyer might claim reinstatement, and this would be unacceptable to Indian opinion.

> He did not act with as much humanity as the case permitted. In this view I think he should be relieved of his command without delay and that he should be called upon to retire or be compelled to do so ... I cannot contemplate the retention of a man of his mentality and with his record in a position in which he might again do away with the lives of so many persons improperly.

The view of the Commander-in-Chief in India, General Monro, was the most significant, as the matter was passed to him to resolve. He wrote: 'The Government has a right to expect in a General Officer of General Dyer's experience a higher degree of self-restraint and the exercise of a cooler and more reasoned appreciation of the situation than was displayed by him on this occasion.' He agreed with Vincent that Dyer should retire from the Army, but he added a warning of the bad effects upon the sentiments of the service; he feared that Dyer would be seen by his brother officers as a martyr thrown by the politicians to nationalist wolves.

Lord Chelmsford's views are not recorded; perhaps, as Montagu had found, he had none, but his Executive Council prepared a memorandum which stated that:

> We can arrive at no other conclusion than that at Jallianwala Bagh General Dyer acted beyond the necessity of the case, beyond what any reasonable man could have thought to be necessary, and that he did not act with as much humanity as the case permitted. It is with pain that we arrive at this conclusion for we are not forgetful of General Dyer's distinguished record as a soldier and of his gallant relief of the garrison at Thal during the recent Afghan war. We must, however, direct the judgment above pronounced be communicated to His Excellency the Commander-in-Chief with the request that he take the appropriate action.

The matter was now in Monro's hands.[12]

Dyer reported to General Headquarters in Delhi on the due date, but was shown not to the Military Secretary's office but straight to that of the Commander-in-Chief. Outside in the anteroom he was met by General Hudson, who told him that he was to be deprived of his command, as the Commander-in-Chief agreed with the censure of the Hunter Committee. Dyer objected that, as he had not been tried, he should not be condemned, but Hudson told him that it was too late and asked Dyer not to make difficulties with the Commander-in-Chief as he 'is very much upset'. Dyer agreed that he would not do this. He entered the Commander-in-Chief's office and was told briefly by Monro to resign his post and that he would not be re-employed. Dyer left without speaking a word.

Thus, for all the right reasons, was initiated a travesty of due process. Dyer was removed from his post and placed on the unemployed list. This meant he was placed on half pay with no prospect of any employment and without any opportunity being given him to state his case. Whilst his final interview with Monro was conducted according to the more rigid code which applied in that day, and there could have been no possibility of Dyer's making a scene in front of his Commander-in-Chief, it remained the case that he had not had any charges against him aired at a hearing and had not been given any opportunity to reply to the Hunter Committee, the only tribunal before which he had appeared and whose report he had not been shown. In fact, he was not to see a copy of this until he returned to England. The matter was handled neither according to rule nor custom of the service. Monro and his staff thereby handed Dyer's supporters the issue on which they would fight his removal from his post and with which they would browbeat the Government in both Houses of Parliament. It was a sad, and rather cowardly, mistake.

Some idea of why Monro had dealt so monosyllabically with Dyer, and why he was so upset, was recounted later by General Molesworth, who was then on the staff of Sir Havelock Hudson and handled Dyer's paperwork. He recalled that from April to Dyer's appearance before the Hunter Committee, General Headquarters backed Dyer, and that all, including the Commander-in-Chief, believed that he had been justified in his actions, and that he had indeed saved the situation by them. His statements before the Hunter Committee had changed all this. 'Monro now considered that Dyer had showed a lack of wisdom, a foolhardiness, a lack of sensitivity that was inexcusable. He therefore decided he could no longer protect Dyer from political pressure.' Monro was so upset at this last interview with a man with whom he had served long before, and whom he had just congratulated for the relief of Thal, 'because he felt it so acutely that after a long and distinguished career in action, Dyer should have destroyed himself by failing to keep his mouth shut.'[13]

Dyer returned to Jullundur in a daze, a broken man. The decision he had been given by Monro had been a complete bolt from the blue. Every indication he had been given up until that point was that he enjoyed the support of the highest in the land. He went in to the Commander-in-Chief's office a hero twice over, first for saving the Punjab, some said all India, and then for saving Thal. He walked out having lost his post and his career. He had become a pariah, but it had not been explained to him why, and he had been given no chance to defend himself. The blow was crushing. His journey back home was a hollow nightmare of despair. When he got back to Jullundur, he was so ill that he was immediately hospitalised, and the doctors feared that his condition was so bad that they did not tell him that Annie was also seriously ill. He lay in bed in the military hospital alone, unable even to tell his wife what had happened, and unaware why she could not come to see him.[14]

Dyer threshed around in his mind for a way to soften the blow. Through the medical officer he applied to take the six months' sick leave he had been granted earlier, and to resign after that, but unsurprisingly this was not granted, and on 24 March he was instructed by letter to resign his appointment as soon as possible. Sometime about now, he must have told Annie that he was disgraced and that they were going back to England. He wrote on the 27th to the General Officer Commanding 2nd Division resigning his appointment as Brigadier-General Commanding the 5th Infantry Brigade. He applied to go to Jamrud to hand over his brigade and to Rawalpindi to withdraw his papers from the Alliance

Bank of Simla there, but even this was refused by the Commander-in-Chief Northern Command, who seems to have become nervous of leaving Dyer at liberty to travel about and issued an order restricting him to Jullundur. This extraordinary order, perhaps motivated by a desire to keep Dyer out of reach of the press and the public, was rescinded on 1 April, too late to allow Dyer to travel as he had asked. Passages were allotted to him and Annie to travel from Bombay on the 10th, but once more the Commander-in-Chief Northern Command intervened. This time it seems that he had the intention of meeting Dyer in Jullundur, and so ordered that he remain there, but this too was cancelled on the 2nd, and the two did not in fact meet. Humiliated by this treatment, the Dyers were at last allowed to leave. Worn down and ill, together they packed up their house and said their farewells. They were not able to say goodbye to Ivon; he had already left the 1st Kashmiris and was on leave in England, where two days after his parents left India, he married his fiancée, Phyllis, in their absence.[15]

On the evening of 6 April, their last day in Jullundur, Dyer and Annie set out for the station by car. When they got near to its approaches, they found their path lit up by flares under which stood *sepoys* of all the Indian regiments in the station standing at the salute. In the station forecourt was a large guard of honour of all the garrison's NCOs who had gathered without order. The station was thronged.

> Large numbers of officers, British and Indian, together with most of the ladies, were at the station to see them off. In fact it can be said that practically the whole station was there. Cheers and 'He's a jolly good fellow' nearly lifted off the station roof and effectively woke the other passengers. General and Mrs Dyer were visibly effected [sic] by the warmth of the send off. On the same afternoon, an address, very beautifully illuminated by a Jullundur lady artist, had been presented by a small deputation on behalf of over one hundred English ladies in the Punjab, the spokeswoman of whom addressed General Dyer as follows: 'Sir, We the undersigned wish to express our heartfelt gratitude for the firmness you displayed in the crisis which arose in this province last April. We deplore the loss of life which occurred, but we believe that it was your action which saved the Punjab and thereby preserved the honour and lives of hundreds of women and children. We trust, Sir, that you will understand that we, who would have suffered most had the outbreak spread, are not unmindful of what we owe you.'

The long journey onboard the Bombay Mail which took them to the port was a sad one. Captain Beamish accompanied them, as Annie was incapable of looking after her husband and was still very ill herself. Their travel had been arranged at such short notice that they had no bookings in Bombay, and they found accommodation only in the dormitory of a hostel, where they slept side by side in a room with many other travellers. They boarded the hospital ship *Assaye*, at first with Allah Dad Khan, their Poonchi bearer, but he was found onboard and ejected; Indian servants were not allowed on the ship. He sat and wept on the quayside. Beamish left them and the Dyers were finally alone. As the *Assaye* steamed out of the harbour, a crowd of people who had heard they were onboard cheered them from the docks. Neither of them would see India again. It was exactly a year since the outbreak of violence at Amritsar.[16]

Some few days before this, on 29 March, General Headquarters had written what they hoped would be a final line under Dyer's Indian career. Their telegram to the India Office ran:

> Reference to Commander-in-Chief's recommendation for rewards in connection with Afghan operations sent in advance by mail of March 4th 1920. In view of finding of Hunter Commission we consider recommendation made on behalf of Brigadier-General Dyer should be cancelled.

In London, with blue crayon, the word 'cancelled' was scrawled over the recommendation.[17]

21

The Army Council

The Hunter Report reached London by telegraph just before the Dyers' ship sailed from Bombay, and copies were immediately circulated for comment within the India Office. Sir Sankaran Nair, now permanently advising Montagu in London, minuted his views, which were highly critical of Dyer, to the Secretary of State on 10 April. Montagu was not about to allow any more time to be wasted in a process which had already driven him to distraction because of what he regarded as India's dragging its feet; he rapidly persuaded the Cabinet to appoint a committee 'to consider and advise on the Report of the Disorders Enquiry Committee (India) received from Lord Hunter'. He was to chair this, and its members were the amongst most senior in the Government, including Lord Birkenhead, the Lord Chancellor, Short, the Chief Secretary for Ireland, Milner, the Secretary of State for the Colonies, and Winston Churchill, Secretary of State for War, in whose department any consideration of action against Dyer would have to be conducted.[1]

Draft resolutions from the Government of India came over the telegraph lines over three days between 10 and 12 April. These were Delhi's comments on the Hunter Report and a statement of the Government of India's policy towards Hunter's recommendations. A few days later, on the 16th, the Viceroy dispatched a printed copy of the Hunter Report by sea, and with it a letter which was his first notification to Montagu that the Dyers were on their way home. At the least this was discourteous, Chelmsford washing his hands of the Dyer problem with no thought for the political problems Montagu was facing in London. At the worst, it was devious, as it tended to pre-empt action against Dyer other than that already taken. It was timed to arrive in London six days after the Dyers. In his letter, Chelmsford told Montagu:

> General Dyer also will probably be arriving about the same date. He is in a very bad way, and his condition is such that the doctors fear that any prolonged excitement may cause haemorrhage of the brain. Consequently, the Commander-in-Chief the other day, when he had an interview with him, had to confine it to a very brief space of time. He told Dyer that our judgment on him was that he had acted in excess of the requirements of the occasion at Jallianwala Bagh, and that he must therefore call upon him to resign. He also told him that it would be impossible for him to again hold command of troops in India. Since then General Dyer has resigned his command and gone home by Troopship on medical certificate.[2]

Montagu was becoming aware that it was not going to be possible to prosecute
Dyer, and so the view at which he had somewhat reluctantly arrived was not,
in the event, far removed from that of the Viceroy. His own Legal Adviser,
Sir Edward des Chamier, had advised him:

> The finding of the majority of the Committee amounts to a finding that the case falls
> within Exception 3 to Section 300 of the Indian Penal Code, and that he committed
> culpable homicide not amounting to murder … If he were prosecuted by Government
> the recent Indian Indemnity Act would, apparently, not protect him (see Section 6 of the
> Act) … General Dyer could not be tried by court martial anywhere for murder or
> manslaughter, because Amritsar is less than a hundred miles from Lahore, where there
> was a High Court competent to try him … I think he committed culpable homicide not
> amounting to murder according to Indian law and manslaughter according to English
> law, but it is notoriously difficult to obtain convictions in cases of this kind … I believe
> the jury would acquit.

The possibility of a court martial was rejected because the Army Act stated
that an offence of murder or manslaughter could not be tried by court martial
unless, *inter alia*, it was committed on active service. Whilst it was arguable that
duty in Amritsar had indeed been active service, it was the Government's view
that the Army Act's intention was that both offences must always be dealt with
by the civil power if civil courts were available.[3] The Legal Adviser warned,
however, that there was nothing to stop any private person bringing a case against
Dyer. If this happened, the Government was entitled to take over, then drop, the
case. Montagu accepted this, but still wished to take the matter further than what
had been done so far, the removal of Dyer to the unemployed list by the
Commander-in-Chief in India. In a note he drew up to clear his mind, he wrote:

(5) The Government of India is right to suggest not to try Dyer, but to suggest dismissal.[4]
Condemnation of his use of principle of terrorism must be stronger than Hunter.

(6) His Majesty can have no further use for the services of General Dyer … He leaves
the service a brave soldier whose fault is a misconception of the principles which
govern his profession.[5]

Montagu was also advised by his Military Secretary, Lieutenant-General Sir
A.S. Cobbe, of Dyer's personal circumstances. As an officer without employment,
Dyer was entitled to unemployed pay of £700 per annum, which he was entitled
to draw for up to five years. Cobbe presumed, however, that Dyer would elect to
retire; in this case, or in the case of compulsory retirement, he would receive a
pension. Dismissal from the service, which could only be effected by sentence of
a court martial or by the King, on the advice of the Secretary of State for War,
would mean the loss of his pension. Advice given to the Secretary of State for

War around the same time expanded this, and explained why Cobbe had assumed Dyer would opt to retire:

> Colonel Dyer, on relinquishing his Brigade in India, *automatically* passed to the half pay list and relinquished his rank of Brigadier-General. He will remain on the half pay list until he is further employed, but as the C. in C. in India has made a definite recommendation that he shall *not* be so further employed he *inevitably* must apply to retire because the half pay of his rank is £700 per annum and as he has already earned his full rate of Colonel's pension which is £900 per annum, he would thus lose £200 per annum as long as he remains on half pay.

The staff added that Dyer had to retire at the age of fifty-seven, which was in any case in about a year's time. So the options were four: to allow Dyer the choice to serve on; to allow him to retire; compulsorily to retire him; or to dismiss him. [6]

Cobbe's note also informed Montagu (eleven days after the event) that Dyer was on his way home: 'According to a telegram recently received, Brigadier-General Dyer has been invalided from India and is now on his way to this country on a hospital ship. It is not known whether he has vacated his Brigade Command or is on leave from it.' No one in India had thought fit to tell Montagu even this, or to give him any recommendation as to what to do with Dyer. Montagu brooded over this for two weeks before delivering a reprimand by telegram to the Viceroy, who was forced to make a lame apology:

> There was no desire to rush a decision as you outline in your telegram. The Commander-in-Chief knew that Dyer was in a bad state of health and likely to be invalided here. We thought in addition that it would be expedient for many reasons to get Dyer out of the country as soon as possible. He therefore sent for Dyer and informed him of his decision. He now realizes that the course he adopted was precipitate and that this action should have been deferred until your approval of our Resolution had been received. He regrets the embarrassment he has caused you ... I feel also that I am to blame in not making it clear to the Commander-in-Chief that no action would be taken ... until your consent had been received. As soon as I received on tour news from the Department of the action taken I wrote to you the same day. I see now that it would have been better if I had telegraphed.[7]

Speed was now essential to Montagu if he was to be able to complete management of the issue before Dyer reached England and became a focus for the opposition to the Government's Indian policies. Montagu, a Liberal, was well aware that most of the Conservative Party members of the ruling Liberal-Conservative coalition were bitterly hostile to Indian reform and to the Hunter Committee, which they believed was a sop to Indian revolutionaries. He knew that they would oppose any action being taken against Government servants involved in the suppression of the Punjab disorders. Stirred up by Sir Michael O'Dwyer and others of his persuasion in India, parliamentarians such as Lord Sydenham, Sir William Joynson-Hicks (who had toured India over the winter to gather ammunition to use against Montagu) and Sir Edward Carson were becoming increasingly dangerous to Montagu. He feared the effect their defence of Dyer might have on his reforms and on his attempts, embodied in the royal proclamation of the previous December, to bring some redress to satisfy Indian opinion. Joynson-Hicks, whom Montagu loathed with some passion, visited him on his return from India and threatened him with a letter to the press attacking Government policy over the Hunter Report. Montagu wrote the next day to Chelmsford: 'I had a visit yesterday from Joynson-Hicks. He is an intolerable person, and it is quite obvious that he has battened on all the reactionary talk he could find.' Montagu was also becoming worried about the opposition to any action against Dyer that was becoming evident in the senior ranks of the Army. This was no exaggerated anxiety. The Adjutant-General, General Creedy, had just minuted Churchill:

> I am totally opposed to 'frightfulness' as such, but in India and elsewhere the sole test of any action taken under Martial Law is that of necessity. Sir Michael O'Dwyer thought that General Dyer's action was necessary, and I hesitate to differ from the opinion of a man of his wide knowledge and experience … At the Jallianwala Bagh the crowd that General Dyer fired into was undoubtedly an unlawful assembly.[8]

The Army Council was an element in the equation totally beyond Montagu's control, but the course he had decided upon was to put himself, and Dyer's future, in their hands.

The Indian Disorders Committee, as the Cabinet Committee chaired by Montagu became known, met for the first time on 21 April 1920. Montagu opened the meeting with the statement that the most important subject for the consideration of the committee was the action taken by General Dyer at Amritsar on 13 April 1919, and urged:

> That if good relations were to exist between the Indian people and their Government a true announcement should be made by that Government in regard to General Dyer's action. The matter could not be brazened out. It would, however, be unwise for Government to direct a trial of General Dyer to be held. It would only result in exacerbation of feeling on both sides. Moreover, General Dyer's action should not form the basis of a criminal charge. The correct course would be to censure General Dyer and pronounce a judgment condemning his action in emphatic terms … General Dyer himself should be removed from employment though he should be allowed to retain his retiring allowance.

Montagu had by now abandoned his hope of having Dyer dismissed, but was still intent on having him compulsorily retired. The committee agreed that it was undesirable to allow a trial in India or the United Kingdom and that it would be impossible to try Dyer by court martial. The members accepted that they should condemn Dyer's failure to make a proclamation or exhibit a notice at the Jallianwala Bagh when he heard of the meeting, as well as his actions of opening fire without warning and continuing to fire for ten minutes. The committee met again on the 26th, though made no progress that day, as Montagu had not been able to prepare a draft resolution condemning Dyer. He was still discussing with Chelmsford the Government of India's draft resolutions, and the committee's draft would have to await the outcome of this.[9]

Eventually, agreement over the resolution was reached. The Government of India published their findings on the Hunter Report in a letter to Montagu dated 3 May 1920. This was their first public pronouncement upon the Hunter Report, which was by now some two months old. In their letter, they accepted that the civilian authorities had been at fault in handing over control of Amritsar to the military 'in such terms as to suggest that they did not intend to exercise supervision or guidance over the action of the military commander'. They censured Dyer severely, finding that:

> Orders prohibiting assemblies should have been promulgated more widely and in particular that notices might have been posted up at Jallianwala Bagh ... The Government of India agree with the Committee that General Dyer should have given warning to the crowd before opening fire ... General Dyer's action in continuing to fire on the crowd after it had begun to disperse was, in the opinion of the Government of India, indefensible. [They] cannot however accept this [Dyer's intention to intimidate lawless elements in the population] as a justification of the continued firing, which greatly exceeded the necessity of the occasion ... General Dyer exceeded the reasonable requirements of the case and showed a misconception of his duty which resulted in a lamentable and unnecessary loss of life ... We must express our great regret that no action was taken by the civil or the military authorities to remove the dead or give aid to the wounded.

The document made as little of the crawling order as it could in the circumstances. Adding it to the list of acts taken by the martial law authorities and criticised by the Hunter Report, they stated: 'The action of the officers mentioned was unjustifiable and in some cases inflicted unnecessary humiliation, resulting in ill-feeling which has been a serious embarrassment to the administration.' They singled out the flogging of the six men in the lane where Miss Sherwood was assaulted as 'highly improper', but pointed out that in moments 'of great crisis', such as Dyer faced, 'an officer may be thrown temporarily off the balance of his judgment', and that Dyer's action resulted, in their view, in 'an immediate discouragement of the forces of disorder'. They concluded, however:

We can arrive at no conclusion other than at Jallianwala Bagh General Dyer acted beyond the necessity of the case, beyond what any reasonable man could have thought to be necessary, and that he did not act with as much humanity as the case permitted. It is with pain that we arrive at this conclusion, for we are not forgetful of General Dyer's distinguished record as a soldier or of his gallant relief of the garrison at Thal during the recent Afghan war. We must however direct that the judgment above pronounced be communicated to His Excellency the Commander-in-Chief with the request that he will take appropriate action.[10]

They did not specify what that 'appropriate action' should be. Much was left to be disputed in England in the months ahead, but the Government of India's judgment, once published, made it impossible that Dyer could ever have been reinstated.

On the day that the Viceroy's judgment was telegraphed to London, Rex and Annie Dyer arrived at Southampton. They had endured a miserable journey on the *Assaye*. The troopship had been crowded and many of those it carried were very sick. As the number of nurses onboard was insufficient to cope with the wounded, the Dyers took over the duty of caring for some of the invalids. Annie made jellies for them on a camp stove in her cabin, and took a particular interest in nursing one very sick young officer named Smythe. His death and burial at sea further saddened their melancholy journey. There can have been little to think of other than the sick, their own illness, and the straits they were in. This was a bitter return to England indeed. Dyer made efforts not to be borne down by his situation. He gave a lecture to the ship's company on his campaign in the Sarhadd, something which was the seed, perhaps, for his later decision to publish his story. The fresh sea air was invigorating, and the spring weather passage was uneventful, so that, by the time the ship docked at Southampton, Dyer was in better health. Financially, though, he was not at all well off. He had relinquished his brigadier's rank and was now existing on the half pay of a colonel.[11]

Striding down the gangway onto the dockside at Southampton, Dyer was met by a reporter from the *Daily Mail*, whose cameraman captured Dyer's image that day for their readers and for posterity. Dyer strides towards the camera, dressed incongruously in solar topi and long, flapping greatcoat, whose ill-fitting size suggests that his illness had shrunken him from his former bulk, though the reporter did not see this: 'The general, burnt brick-red by thirty-five years' service in India, is thickset and fairly tall, with greying hair and kindly blue eyes.' Dyer gave the unnamed reporter both barrels, venting his feelings about the way he had been treated and what was happening in India. The long sea voyage, and the grievance which had festered throughout it, had released his inhibitions and overcome any thought of complying with service prohibitions about speaking to the press. The reporter wrote that he proceeded to state 'his case bluntly':

I shot to save the British Raj – to preserve India for the Empire, and to protect Englishmen and Englishwomen who looked to me for protection. And now I am told to go for doing my duty – my horrible, dirty duty … I had to shoot. I had thirty seconds to make up my mind what action to take, and I did it. Every Englishman I have met in India has approved my act, horrible as it was. What would have happened if I had not shot? I and my little force would have been swept away like chaff, and then what would have happened? … No one in authority condemned me for it. On the contrary, I was given command of another operation, as a result of which I was complimented … If I have done anything wrong, I should be court martialled, but there has been no suggestion of that. I have never been heard in my own defence.[12]

Dyer was no longer prepared to go quietly. He and Annie took the train for London, and by the end of the day were in a house they had hired at 33 Clarges Street off Piccadilly. Montagu had been right to make haste, but he had not been quick enough.

Two days later, on 5 May, the Indian Disorders Committee met for its third session. Montagu steered them to agree a draft text of the Government's findings on Hunter and the Government of India's Resolution. The committee also discussed Dyer's interview in the *Mail*, which was about to be raised in a Commons question. Moving fast, Montagu circulated the draft of the committee's conclusions the next day. It included a clear condemnation of Dyer:

The principles which have consistently governed the policy of His Majesty's Government in directing the nature, and the methods employed in the course of, military operations … may be broadly stated as the employment of no more force and destruction of life than is necessary … It must regretfully, but without the possibility of doubt, be concluded that Brigadier-General Dyer's action at the Jallianwala Bagh was in complete violation of this principle … The omission to give warning before fire was opened is inexcusable. Further, that Brigadier-General Dyer should have taken no steps to see that some attempt was made to give medical assistance to the dying and wounded was an omission from his obvious duty. But the gravest feature of the case against Brigadier-General Dyer is his avowed conception of his duty in the circumstances which confronted him. His Majesty's Government repudiate emphatically the doctrine of 'frightfulness' upon which Brigadier-General based his action … He was not entitled to select for condign punishment an unarmed crowd, which, when he inflicted that punishment, had committed no act of violence, had made no attempt to oppose him by force, and many members of which must have been unaware that they were disobeying his commands. [The crawling] order offended against every canon of civilised government … It is impossible to regard him as fitted to remain entrusted with the responsibilities which his rank and position impose upon him. The Commander-in-Chief should be instructed to remove Brigadier-General Dyer from his employment and to direct him to retire.

It was this last sentence which was to embroil both Montagu and Churchill (who supported its inclusion in the draft, apparently without taking the advice of his own department) with the Army Council, for it was not within any Commander-in-Chief's remit to order a brigadier-general to retire. Montagu wrote immediately to the Cabinet Office seeking to have the committee's conclusions tabled before the full Cabinet as soon as possible, and circulating the members of the Cabinet a copy each of the Hunter Report. He was still moving fast, and was still just ahead of the game. It seemed that Dyer had come home just too late to fight his case.[13]

The Indian Disorders Committee's conclusions arrived in the War Office and immediately raised a storm. Initially, this took the form of an assertion of the Army Council's prerogative; his staff pushed Churchill into writing to Montagu on 8 May objecting to the words 'to direct him to retire' and suggesting that this should be rendered 'retired or placed on retired list by the act of superior authority'. He returned to the issue three days later, asking Montagu to write to him:

> an official letter drawing attention to the conduct of Brigadier-General Dyer, forwarding the Report of the Hunter Committee and any other evidence on which you rely; and expressing in the text of the letter the view taken by yourself and by the Cabinet Committee. I will circulate these papers to the Army Council. I will then bring the matter before them at a special meeting on Friday next, and will acquaint you with their decision. Meanwhile let me make it clear that neither the Government of India, not the Commander-in-Chief in India, nor the Government here, nor the Secretary of State for India are competent to 'order Brigadier-General Dyer to retire' or to place him on the retired list. Such a process can only be achieved by the Army Council or by the authority of the Secretary of State for War overruling the Army Council after that body has expressed its opinion. On no account, therefore, must anything be published, either here or in India, until the matter has been put in a thorough order.

In effect, because Montagu had sought Dyer's compulsory retirement, he had allowed the Army Council the means to place a block on all progress in the case. On the 11th, Montagu wrote to Churchill the letter he had been asked for, which requested that Dyer 'be called upon to retire'. Had Montagu left this out, the Army Council would have had no part in the issue; he must have bitterly regretted later that he had not done so.

The conclusions of the Indian Disorders Committee were telegraphed to India on 6 May, and caused a further rift with the Viceroy, who demanded that the word 'frightfulness' be deleted. He believed that it had not been suggested that General Dyer acted from the mere 'lust of brutality' which he thought those words implied.[14]

Dyer had by now been in England for a week, time for him to draw breath after his voyage and after settling Annie into the rented house in Clarges Street. He was probably already in touch with supporters in the War Office who were feeding him information, for from now on it is clear that he had a good idea of what was going on regarding his case, although he was not told much about it officially. On 10 May, he wrote a letter to Lieutenant-General Cobbe, the Military Secretary at the India Office, who was the superior of any senior Indian Army officer such as Dyer who was on sick leave in England. In this letter he stated that he understood his case was about to be considered by the Army Council, and that 'I would ask that I be permitted to represent my case personally, attended, if necessary, by a legal adviser. I am of the opinion that I had not a proper opportunity during the Hunter Committee of fully representing my case.' He took the letter round to the India Office in person, and it was given immediately to Montagu (perhaps by some military member of the India Office staff who was aware of the need for urgency if Dyer were to be given any chance of preventing the call for his retirement).

The letter was in the nick of time. Montagu was about to go that afternoon to the Cabinet with the Indian Disorders Committee conclusions; he took Dyer's letter with him. Bonar Law was in the chair. Of the Indian Disorders Committee members, three were present, Montagu, Churchill and Birkenhead. Also there were Austen Chamberlain, the Chancellor of the Exchequer, and Lord Curzon, the Secretary of State for Foreign Affairs. Montagu informed the Cabinet that Dyer had appeared that morning at the India Office, and was seeking to put his case to the Cabinet. This was not a request made by Dyer in his letter, though he may have made it verbally when he called at the India Office, perhaps on being told that the Cabinet was about to discuss his case. It is possible that Montagu had misread or was exaggerating Dyer's request. The Cabinet declined to let Dyer appear before it. Those present were critical of the Indian Disorders Committee's conclusions, and spent much time amending its text in great detail. The Cabinet accepted its main recommendations, however, and by doing so ensured that the committee's conclusions now became Government policy. Dyer was not informed of this, nor that he had been refused permission to address the Cabinet. The Indian Disorders Committee met for the fourth time on 14 May to take into account the changes to its draft which had been directed by the Cabinet and to discuss the new wording of their conclusions. Montagu gave Chelmsford the news that they had agreed to amend the draft to reflect the concerns he had telegraphed earlier.[15]

By now the military staff in the War Office were considering the committee's conclusion that Dyer should be made to retire. The Director of Personnel Services, General B.E.W. Childs, sent Churchill a memorandum advising him that he believed that the Army Council was obliged to judge Dyer on his report of 25 August 1919 and not on the Hunter Report. This was in some way logical, as Dyer's report was the only military evidence the War Office had to hand. To disregard the Hunter Report, however, was to ignore everything which had caused the Government of India and Montagu to take action. Yet, incredibly, this is what the Military Members of the Army Council were to do. Childs also advised Churchill not to accede to Dyer's request to represent himself before them, or to allow him to be assisted by counsel. He confirmed that in law the Army Council were able to deal with Dyer, but that he had no right to demand a court martial, or even to seek an interview with a member of the Army Council unless he were called upon to retire. He sensibly recommended that the advice of the Commander-in-Chief in India, who had yet to inform the War Office of any aspect of this case, should be sought before proceeding further. A telegram was therefore sent seeking General Monro's view. He replied two days later, supporting the line taken by the Indian Disorders Committee: 'I directed Dyer to resign command of his brigade. I do not recommend this officer for further duties and I informed him that he can expect nothing further in India. He should be ordered to retire; beyond this I have no further recommendation.'[16] The Military Members did not find Monro's reticence particularly helpful, and they were not about to follow his recommendations.

Churchill had the issue of Dyer's case brought formally before the Army Council at its monthly meeting on 14 May, but discussion of the issue was deferred as General Monro's recommendation had not by then been received. The civil servants in the War Office were not displeased at the delay; they would, in fact, have preferred to leave the issue entirely to the India Office, as they could see that it was bound to lead to another rift between their Secretary of State and his senior Military Members. Churchill's office advised him that the Army Council had only to deal with Indian Army officers of the rank of colonel and above if they were called on to resign or retire, or if an appeal to the King had been submitted by such an officer. In Dyer's case, the Army Council was involved only as the Secretary of State for India had recommended he be placed on retired pay. They proposed that the Secretary of State for India be persuaded to withdraw his letter requesting this; if he would do that, the Commander-in-Chief in India's recommendation could be published and supported by the India Office, in which case the Army Council need do nothing. 'The question, therefore, is one *entirely* for the India Office.' That would still leave Dyer the options to remain on half pay, to apply to retire or to appeal to the King. If he were to do the latter, he would have to appeal through the Secretary of State for War, and with the Commander-in-Chief in India's recommendation; 'it would be an unheard of thing to question that officer's discretion either to relieve Colonel Dyer of his appointment or to recommend that he should not be further employed'.[17]

This neat scenario was not allowed to transpire. Churchill, as well as Montagu, wanted Dyer to be retired, so he ensured that the case came before the Army Council. It did so at a time when the relationship between the Secretary of State and the Chief of the Imperial General Staff, Field-Marshal Sir Henry Wilson, was under severe strain over a whole series of issues, principally Ireland. Wilson believed the policies being pursued by the Government coalition were endangering the Empire. He was an irascible man, and something of a blimp. His diaries expand on what happened the first time Churchill had raised the issue of Dyer on the 14th. Wilson resented being rushed into considering an issue for which he had only been sent the papers that morning; he refused to consider the matter at that meeting:

> Winston made a long speech, prejudging the case and in effect saying that the Cabinet, and he, had decided to throw out Dyer, but that it was advisable for the Army Council to agree. It appeared to me, listening, that the story was a very simple one. The Frocks have got India (as they have Ireland) into a filthy mess. On that the soldiers are called in, and act. This is disapproved of by all the disloyal elements, and the soldier is thrown to the winds. All quite simple … The Frocks have sat on it for eighteen months! After the Army Council, I had a short meeting of Military Members, at which I suggested it was our duty to protect a brother officer until he had been proved in the wrong by a properly constituted Court of Inquiry.

Churchill's failure to carry the Military Members with him was to cost him much unnecessary bother, and was to cost Montagu more. Churchill had been attending meetings of the Cabinet Committee considering Dyer for over three weeks, but had not given any of the details to the Military Members. On 15 May, the CIGS saw General Rawlinson, who was about to go out to India to take over from Monro, and told him:

> How clear I was that in the near future we should have many Dyer cases both in India and in Ireland, and that if we did not stand by our own soldiers we should lose their confidence. Then they would not act, and then we should lose the Empire. Rawly cordially agreed – up to the point of saying that, if Dyer was jettisoned by the Frocks without a proper military Court of Inquiry, he would not go as C. in C. to India.

Wilson began to swing the other Military Members behind his idea of a military inquiry: 'Discussed the Dyer affair again and I am glad to say they are all shaping to my proposal of a Court of Enquiry'. This was all very well from a military point of view, but the CIGS was now taking a line contrary to what had been Government policy since the Cabinet meeting of 10 May, and this was clearly going to be unacceptable to the Government, if it were not indeed unconstitutional. Nonetheless, the Military Members had two good points: Dyer had not been allowed to present his case to anyone, in India or England; and the Army Council had been left totally in the dark by the Commander-in-Chief in India and then bypassed by the India Office. In the heated atmosphere of the controversies in which they were already embroiled with Churchill and the Government, they were not about to allow themselves to be pushed around so obviously. The Military Members met privately before the informal Army Council meeting of 17 May. 'We agreed that we would not agree to Dyer being thrown out on the evidence before us, and we therefore suggested that the precedent of the Mesopotamian Inquiry should be followed where the accused were given the report and were asked to answer it.' Wilson recorded that at the Army Council Meeting:

> Winston tried again to rush a decision to remove Dyer from the Army, saying that it was only a matter of form. I at once said that I could not agree, that we had not sufficient evidence on which to form a judgment, and that we must ask Dyer to state a case ... Later, Winston sent for me and said that he was much upset by this 'pistol at his head by the Military Members' and that in future he would have to take precautions against these 'ambushes'. I said that he had only himself to thank ... He tried to argue, but the more he argued the more I put him in the 'muck heap'.[18]

One result of these arguments was that Churchill prevented any reply to Dyer's letter of the 10th. Dyer had been left kicking his heels, though he was doubtless being kept informed of what was going on. He wrote again on the 17th, this time a scruffy note on lined paper, asking that he be given a copy of the Hunter Report, which he still had not seen, so that he might answer it. The timing of this, on the same day Wilson suggested this idea to the Army Council, suggests strongly that someone senior amongst the Military Members was coordinating the affair; this does not seem to have been Wilson or his deputy, Harington, so it may have been Creedy, the Adjutant-General, though this can only be conjectural. Dyer wrote as before to General Cobbe at the India Office, and the letter was forwarded to the War Office two days later, having been seen by Montagu, who added a covering note objecting to Dyer being shown the report before it was presented to Parliament. This caused another argument in the War Office, where the Military Members' view that Dyer should be given a copy and be asked to make an answer to it was grudgingly accepted by Churchill. He still, however, allowed no reply to Dyer, who was to be left in limbo waiting for his answer for the next three weeks.[19]

On 18 May, at its fifth session, the Indian Disorders Committee, meeting in the Lord Chancellor's room in the Lords, agreed to Dyer's request to make a statement and to be given a copy of the Hunter Report. This led to a significant excision from paragraph 3 of the dispatch embodying the Cabinet's decision, the words 'has been called upon by the Army Council to retire'. They were replaced by 'the circumstances of the case have been referred to the Army Council'. Dyer's application to be allowed to state his case had prevented at the last minute the inclusion in the document embodying Government policy of the requirement that he be made to retire. The Military Members of the Army Council were thus allowed a free hand to frustrate Montagu and Churchill's intentions.[20]

The Dyer story was now beginning to leak into the press. The letter of which Joynson-Hicks had forewarned Montagu was published in the *Sunday Times* on 23 May, under the heading 'Amritsar. Hunter Commission Report. Shall General Dyer Be Sacrificed?' The letter reflected the briefings Joynson-Hicks had from Sir Michael O'Dwyer during his visit to India, which had excused Dyer's firing without warning on the grounds that there was fear that the crowd would surge forward, and which claimed that he carried on firing until it dispersed. The letter, clearly aimed at the Army Council, concluded: 'Do not condemn this man too hastily.'[21] The *Morning Post* went further the next day. In an article headed 'The Amritsar Episode. Some Sidelights on the Event', the paper wrote that the appointment of the Hunter Committee had been a great mistake. It blamed Chelmsford for giving way to Indian nationalists. The *Post*, which published considerable detail of Dyer's actions, had also been fed the O'Dwyer line. Dyer, the article maintained, had gone down a blind alley where he had found himself faced with a mob that could have rushed his force. He had fired on the mob which broke, ran, couldn't get out and surged back. Fearing that he was being enveloped, Dyer had continued to fire. General Dyer, the *Post* went on, was

an officer of high capacity in dealing with Indian troops. He is one of those men who have the special secret of getting Orientals to follow them anywhere and to do anything. On the strength of this he was sent after the War broke to the No Man's Land, nominally Persian, at the back of Afghanistan, where, with a perfectly nominal force, he kept order over several hundred square miles of villainous country, ostensibly in the interests of the Shah. [At Thal] he reached the place after a forced march in the frightful heat of June, the column having so thinned out that the General and his staff were leading with a few cavalrymen coming next behind. Of a man whose record is marked by such services we may safely say that he is neither a butcher nor of a character capable of being lured into atrocities under the influence of panic.[22]

These were signs that the opposition was becoming more organised, and Montagu pressed on with the revisions to the committee's conclusions as fast as possible. On 26 May, he published both the Viceroy's letter of 3 May and his own despatch, No. 108 (Public), which replied to Chelmsford and embodied the Cabinet's decision. Both documents were published as Command Paper 705, and the Hunter Report was published at the same time. This was now the published policy of the British Government. Montagu's despatch followed word for word the Indian Disorders Committee conclusions circulated on 6 May, as amended by the Cabinet, though the word 'frightfulness' was, as requested by the Viceroy, omitted. Dyer was severely censured:

It is certain that he made no attempt to ascertain the minimum amount of force he was compelled to employ, that the force which he actually employed was greatly in excess of that required to achieve the dispersal of the crowd, and that it resulted in lamentable and unnecessary loss of life and suffering.

Following the recent agreement to accept a statement of his case from Dyer, the concluding paragraph addressed to the Viceroy now read:

> You have reported to me that the Commander-in-Chief has directed Brigadier-General Dyer to resign his appointment as Brigade Commander, has informed him that he would receive no further employment in India, and that you have concurred. I approve this decision, and the circumstances of the case have been referred to the Army Council.[23]

The Government had published its policy, but this was far from putting an end to the controversy surrounding the subject, and Montagu's opponents, with their press arm, the *Morning Post*, were determined that it should not. The *Post* now began to campaign energetically on Dyer's behalf. In their coverage of the publication of the Hunter Report on the 27th, they called it 'An Unhappy Report' and alleged that the attitude of the Government was such as to encourage Dyer's enemies in India to mount a criminal prosecution of him. The *Post* returned to the subject the next day in an editorial headed: 'A Very Strange Story', a piece which made it clear that the opponents of Montagu's reforms saw Dyer's case as a means of mounting an attack on the Government:

> In the egregious Minority report, we have three native Indians condemning a British officer who was not on trial ... Under Mr Montagu's system of Government the country was on the verge of a second Mutiny. [We see] that it was saved by a soldier; and that the soldier has been relieved of his appointment and has been censured. [The Government has decided] to sacrifice General Dyer to the susceptibilities of the native agitators. These methods will lose India.

Other supporters of Dyer were also making themselves felt. The recently retired Roman Catholic Archbishop of Simla, the Right Reverend A.E.J. Kenealy, wrote under the heading 'The Punjab Rising. European Feeling in India. A Courageous Policy' that the Punjab disturbances had been:

> An anti-white man movement of so menacing and widespread a character [that had the military] hesitated they would have failed, and failure would have meant the general murder of European men, the outraging of women, the loot of public buildings and the desecration of Christian churches.

He added an oblique reference to the expected sexual assault upon European women (that in fact had never occurred, but his comment reflected contemporary European fears): 'An Oriental mob has peculiar proclivities.' He warned that making a scapegoat would prevent soldiers carrying out their duty in future, and concluded that soldiers 'saved the Punjab, and in the opinion of many, saved India'.

It was in the newspapers that Dyer claimed to have seen his first accounts of the Hunter Report; he still had not been given a copy, though it is quite likely that he had unoffically been shown one by now. He and Annie were still in the house in Piccadilly. They must have given up any hope of reinstatement; the publication of the Government's policy in Command 705 was enough to make it clear to them that this was now a lost cause. But the fight to avoid the disgrace of compulsory retirement was left to Dyer, and he was encouraged by his supporters to go on with this. He was no doubt advised by his contacts in the War Office that there still remained some hope of instituting a military inquiry; and, if that was done, he would at last get the trial he by now craved. If an inquiry were to be held, matters would be once again much more fluid, and there was no telling where they might end. By now it is likely that he was in touch with Montagu's political opponents in Parliament, and these allowed him some hope of redress in the debate which was to take place in the Commons. The period was one of sickly expectation, anxiety and continual disappointment. His and Annie's lives were in suspension, and they waited on the next turn of events to govern their days and to give them hope that they would one day get back to some form of normality. It was a seemingly endless, waking nightmare.[24]

The press coverage generated by the publication of the Hunter Report caused a flurry of letters to the papers in support of Dyer. In *The Times*, Lord Sydenham's letter of 1 June gave the detail of Dyer's case fed him by Sir Michael O'Dwyer: 'It may not be generally known that the Sikhs showed great admiration for General Dyer, and presented him with the *kara* wristlet, which is an emblem of their faith'. On the same day, Constance E.E. Tuting, who had been resident in the Punjab for twenty-four years, wrote to *The Times* that it was the opinion of all there that Dyer 'saved the Punjab at any rate, if not all India'. Friends there had told her that General Dyer was 'a most kindly British officer, to whom any sort of cruelty would be abhorrent'. She quoted one of these missionary friends: 'It has been real Bolshevism. The plan was to wipe out the white people', and cited another who had feared a repetition of the Cawnpore massacre of 1857. The religious were amongst the most alarmist and vociferous supporters of Dyer in India. Those who had served with him also weighed in on his behalf. One old soldier of the 25th Londons, in a letter headed 'The Relief of Thal, June 1, 1919', wrote on the anniversary of that event: 'The man who did this "on his own" was Brigadier-General R.E. Dyer CB. He is an officer under whom it was an honour to serve, both at Amritsar and in the Kurram.' Three days later, S.R. Purnell, who had been one of the missionaries rescued from an outstation by Dyer's troops on 14 April 1919, wrote that Dyer 'had stopped the rising'. Mr G. Morgan, the President of the European Association of India Council, telegraphed *The Times* on the 10th: 'General body of Europeans in India strongly uphold Dyer and condemn action of Government of India and Secretary of State'. In the *Morning*

Post of 1 June, Sir Henry Lovett, a retired civil servant and writer, stated: 'When General Dyer marched his small force to the Jallianwala Bagh, his mind was full of the consciousness of all that had preceded the gathering.' There were similar letters in many of the major papers, and there was little contrary opinion expressed in any of them.[25]

Dyer still had not had a reply from the War Office. On 8 June, the Cabinet heard that a question was about to be raised in the House by a Conservative MP, Rupert Gwynne, as to whether Dyer's case had been referred to the Army Council. The Indian Disorders Committee had been unable to reach agreement on an answer to this the day before, as the arguments in the Army Council had been leaked to the press, and it was certainly known to many Members of Parliament that the Military Members took a more lenient view of General Dyer's conduct than had commended itself to the Cabinet. The Cabinet agreed to answer in the affirmative and to state that the Commander-in-Chief in India had recommended that he should be retired. They also decided that Churchill should say that Dyer had requested he make a further written statement which the Army Council had agreed to consider. Churchill brought up the issue with the CIGS that afternoon: 'Winston told me of the Cabinet today about Dyer. He said the Cabinet were unanimous in their determination to fling Dyer out.' Wilson would not budge, and it was only at that point that Churchill authorised a letter in reply to Dyer's two of the month before.[26]

The Army Council met on 9 June, noted the Commander-in-Chief in India's recommendation, and agreed to take a written statement from Dyer, though they refused his permission to appear in person. General Sir Herbert Creedy, the Adjutant-General, wrote to Dyer forwarding a copy of the Hunter Report and asking for a written statement of his case. Dyer was still without the papers that had been lost with Briggs's death the year before, but with what he had he went to a firm of solicitors, Sharpe, Prichard & Co., who found him a barrister in the chambers of Reginald Hills and Austin Jones. He had probably already begun to prepare his statement, and the document he worked on with the lawyers was not to be the straightforward report that he had submitted in August, but rather a legal and political document aimed at swaying the minds of the powerful.[27]

That day, Sir Michael O'Dwyer hit the press with a letter revealing his argument with Montagu and alleging that the Secretary of State had misled Parliament by telling the Commons that he had not been informed of what had happened in the Bagh until he read the Hunter Report. The letter appeared in both the *Daily Telegraph* and the *Morning Post*. It was calculated to do the maximum damage. The *Morning Post* carried the letter under the banner 'The Hunter Committee – Report Condemned – Officers Prejudiced by Delayed Inquiry – Criticism by Sir Michael O'Dwyer'. O'Dwyer revealed that he had asked to appear before the Cabinet Committee but had been denied permission to do so, and said that he now intended to make public what he would have said to the Government had he been allowed to. He quoted the letter he had written Montagu in December 1919 in which he told him he had known of the events in the Bagh at the time and from the briefings he had given him when he visited his office. He added that:

> Dyer, at the first interview I had with him on the 16th of April, told me everything as frankly and fully as the limited time I could spare him (when there was rebellion all around) would allow ... I still adhere to my opinion that General Dyer's action at Amritsar on 13 April smashed the rebellion at its source, and thus prevented widespread bloodshed, rapine, and the murder of Europeans in the Punjab and probably elsewhere.

The charge of misleading the House was highly damaging to Montagu. The delay in the revealing of information about the Jallianwala Bagh was indeed a scandal, but one that should have been laid at the door of the Government of India, and in particular at the door of his accuser, Sir Michael O'Dwyer, rather than at that of the Secretary of State, but the latter found it very difficult to counter the charge whilst protecting the Viceroy as it was his duty to do. J.L. Maffey, Chelmsford's Private Secretary, who was in England on leave, wrote to the Viceroy on the 10th, having come up to town for the debate on Dyer promised in the House that day, but which was now postponed:

> It looks as if E.S.M. [Edwin Montagu] was funking the fence! Meanwhile Micky O'Dwyer has come out with a letter which will not make Montagu's task easier ... I shall not attend the dinner to O'Dwyer as I think he is giving himself over to the wrong people, and I do not think I ought to be there.

There was indeed a growing group of 'the wrong people', whose methods were getting dirtier, and Montagu was increasingly forced onto the defensive by them. They included Lord Sydenham, who was President of the Indo-British Association, a grouping opposed to reform in India, Joynson-Hicks, Carson and O'Dwyer. With Morgan, the President of the European Association of India, they reprinted O'Dwyer's letter to the press in the form of a pamphlet a few weeks later. Sydenham wrote in its introduction: 'The feeling of responsible Indians of all classes after the event was one of deep gratitude to Sir Michael O'Dwyer and to General Dyer for averting a grave disaster'. The group was being given covert assistance by the highest levels in the Army, as Field-Marshal Wilson's diary for 10th June makes clear:

> The Archbishop of Simla (Kincaly an RC) [sic] came to see me about Dyer ... told us that Dyer was perfectly right and if we threw him out we should lose India with untold murders and rape and chaos. I told him he ought to see Carson [Sir Edward Carson] and I telephoned to Carson and arranged for a meeting at 1 p.m. on Monday.[28]

While this was going on, Dyer and his lawyers were working on the statement. He wrote to the Military Secretary at the War Office on the 10th, promising the statement by the 16th, but five days later had to write again delaying this. The document was proving a complicated one to assemble. Sir Michael O'Dwyer carried on his harrying of the Government; he wrote to the War Office on the 11th asking that he be heard, and cheekily forwarding them his recent newspaper article. He was not given a hearing. He followed this up with a demand to be seen by the Prime Minister, but again failed to gain an appointment.[29]

Sir William Joynson-Hicks published another letter on 15 June, this time in *The Times*, one which chimed closely with the views of the Military Members of the Army Council. He suggested that Dyer insist upon a court martial or court of inquiry as he had been 'examined, cross-examined and tortured by three of the cleverest native lawyers'. He accused Montagu of withholding inform-ation on the disturbances during the passage of his Indian Reform Act, quoting Sir Michael O'Dwyer's claim to have told Montagu everything the previous year.[30]

The postponement of the Commons debate on Dyer, which was caused directly by the need for the Army Council to conclude its consideration of his case, was causing Montagu growing problems, as he explained to the Viceroy on the 16th:

> Our Indian debate has now been postponed till Monday fortnight to give the Army Council time to consider Dyer's case. If only we could have had it last week, I am convinced the whole thing would now be dying away. But as it is the right and left wings are hardening more and more while the centre is more and more losing all interest … However, if you will pray for me on the eventful day I will do my best, and I still think the event over means the end of the affair in sight.

Churchill explained the situation to Lord Curzon, who was to handle the issue in the Lords, on the 17th: 'My Dear Curzon, It is quite impossible to take a Dyer debate in H. of L. or H. of C. until the Army Council have received his reply and adjudicated upon it.' The delay began to fray Montagu's nerves. He wrote to Churchill on 22 June:

> It is rumoured that your Army Council proposes to say that they have not the information to deal with the Dyer case, and will wash their hands of it, throwing back the responsibility on His Majesty's Government. They are going to say that they have not seen Dyer's evidence before the Hunter Committee or the Hunter Report. If that be so, it is not my fault. I sent you copies and you had my official letter.

The Army Council had not seen the Hunter Report, but they did not believe that they needed to, so he was only partially right. He wrote again three days later complaining about rumours being spread that the troops would not fire in

Ireland as they feared censure after what had happened to Dyer. Churchill became increasingly irritated with Montagu's anxious fussing.[31]

It was not only Montagu who was getting wind of the Military Members' views, as they were becoming embarrassingly public. Lord Stamfordham, George V's Secretary, wrote to the Viceroy on behalf of the King Emperor on 23 June:

> You will, naturally, understand how much public opinion has been aroused by the outcome of the Hunter Committee and the action of General Dyer. Upon the latter, judgment is divided, and while on one side he is condemned for what is regarded as heartlessness, callousness and indifference to the value of human life; on the other side there are many who sum up their opinion in the words – 'Dyer saved India'. This latter view is strongly held by the Military Members of the Army Council, and I have heard it repeated by thoughtful men who have lately returned from India.[32]

The row within the War Office rumbled on. The CIGS recorded on 26 June:

> Winston and I discussed Dyer's case. There was a disgraceful article in the *Times* this morning saying the Military Members of the AC [Army Council] were over-riding the Cabinet. I told Winston that we MMs [Military Members] were very angry about this which is an absolute lie. The matter was referred to us by the Cabinet and we are now waiting for Dyer's information which won't be in for another week. I pressed Winston to put the matter straight and he promised to do so in the H. of C. on Monday.

The article in *The Times* had pointed out that the Government had already declared its policy, so the Army Council's action in reconsidering the issue could be considered unconstitutional;

> A constitutional question of a very serious importance is coming into view in connection with the case of General Dyer ... A committee of generals, presided over by Mr Churchill, in virtue of his office as Secretary of State for War, and assisted by two or three civil officials, are, if report be accurate, proceeding to reopen the whole case and to review the findings of the various civil authorities, including, presumably, even those of the Cabinet.

Who had tipped off *The Times* is unknown, but, as it decried what it called 'A growing tendency to lessen the authority of the civil power', it is worth noting that Churchill's interests were clearly served by it.

Wilson was right in his comment that the referral was the Cabinet's own doing, but fears of what the Army Council might now do, and in particular that the Military Members might exonerate Dyer, spread as far as India. The Viceroy telegraphed Montagu on the 25th:

> Telegrams received from home and published in European press here during the last few days suggest that the condemnation of General Dyer's action by HMG may be

modified as a result of the further consideration of his case by the Army Council. This seems unlikely but I feel that I should warn you that any such modification would have a disastrous effect on Indian opinion and largely intensify the racial feeling which O'Dwyer's recent letter has revived and greatly embittered.[33]

Dyer, or rather his lawyers, ended this fractious period of waiting on 3 July, when he submitted the statement they had drawn up. The document was a rather more sophisticated piece of work than Dyer had produced hitherto, and one which was very evidently the work of his lawyers. It bears signs that he himself did not check it thoroughly, including several small errors of fact regarding his personal circumstances: for instance, the statement says, at page 13, that he had thirty-four years' residence in India; this was merely his service there, he had lived there most of his life. The document was twenty-three pages long, and had attached to it as appendixes the report he had written on 14 April 1919, with the telegram signifying approval of his action by General Beynon and Sir Michael O'Dwyer; the statement of Captain Briggs which he had earlier attached to his report of 25 August (but which had not been published by the Hunter Committee due to Briggs's death); and the speech of General Hudson to the Legislative Council of September 1919 supporting his position.

Dyer's statement commenced by objecting to the irregular way he had been punished without being given the opportunity to defend himself, then left this strong ground and turned to his action at Amritsar. It made the claim that he opened fire in the Bagh without warning as 'Hesitation I felt would be dangerous and futile', a smooth combination by his lawyers of his initial statement that he feared for his force and his subsequent line that not firing on the crowd would not have served his purpose of punishing the rebels. It went on: 'groups appeared to be collecting as though to rush us', adding that he directed fire on these, but ceased fire when the crowd had dispersed. This managed to avoid any justification for the length of fire, and made use of elements that were factually correct, though subsidiary, to create a favourable impression.

After claiming that the action he took at the Jallianwala Bagh quietened the Punjab, the statement turned next to an explanation of his motives and to a rebuttal of the charge that he had used more than minimum force. Here a new element was introduced, one arising, unsurprisingly in the light of the involvement of lawyers, from the technicalities of the *Manual of Military Law*. The statement declared that, in Dyer's view of the situation, he was faced in Amritsar with a part of the insurrection which was going on throughout the Punjab, and that he was entitled to bear this in mind in dealing with the crowd in the Bagh. The term 'insurrection' was used advisedly; the *Manual of Military Law* recognised three states of civil disobedience: unlawful assembly, riot and insurrection. Whilst for the first two of these states mere dispersal 'is laid down as the proper course in a case of unlawful assembly', the *Manual* stated that 'the existence of an armed insurrection would justify the use of any degree of force necessary effectually to meet and cope with the insurrection'. It was, in the lawyers' view, therefore crucial for Dyer's presentation of his case for there to have been an insurrection; regrettably, the Hunter Committee, and by now the Government of India, had rejected this idea (though the opponents to the Government in England and in much of British India had not). This interpretation of the *Manual*, and of the regulations and customs of the service which flowed from it and which bound officers in his position, was an idiosyncratic one which did not bear examination. It was never one accepted by the Government or the Military, departing as it did from all the restraints of minimum force.* Nor, it has to be said, was a semantic quibble on the contents of the *Manual* likely to have occurred to Dyer when he faced the crowd in the Bagh.

The statement goes on to enumerate the circumstances in which Dyer found himself on 13 April, citing facts which were chosen to justify his belief in an insurrection. This includes several statements that are dubious; the claim that 'I knew of the cloud from Afghanistan, which broke three weeks later' does not accord with the fact that news of the Afghan threat reached Delhi only on 4 May 1919. The claim that, had Dyer not acted as he did, the mob would have 'destroyed all the European population, including women and children and all my troops, and involved in its ruin the law-abiding Indian population as well' is simply unbelievable.

The statement then attempted to counter the criticism that Dyer failed to warn the crowd before he opened fire. Whilst it nods again at the argument that had he done so he would have been overwhelmed, it goes on to repeat what he had said to the Hunter Committee:

> But apart from the imminent danger it was, in my view, futile and unnecessary to address the crowd because I was satisfied that it was a rebellious gathering and knew of the proclamations that had been issued and had assembled in defiance of them, and that no warning would induce them to disperse.

In this last remark, Dyer appears to have partially changed his mind since his appearance before the Hunter Committee, to which he had expressed confidence that he could have dispersed the crowd without force. The alteration may have been made to improve the appearance of his motives. The statement devotes space to attempting to prove that the crowd was not an innocent gathering but is unconvincing; the main point made here, that many of the members of the crowd were subsequently convicted of offences, was not something that could have been known at the time, and many of their convictions had in any case already been overturned as unsafe.

---

* For the arguments as to whether what Dyer did accorded with Military Law, see the Appendix, pp. 435–42.

The statement contains much detail trying to explain the crawling order, maintaining that Dyer was attempting to make the ground holy, and to ensure that 'no one was to traverse it except in a manner in which a place of special sanctity might naturally in the East be traversed'. It attempts to make light of the order as a 'most trivial incident'. The statement then attempts to rebut the charge that Dyer paid the wounded in the Bagh no attention, making it clear that he did not believe that those he was faced with there 'deserved the care of the authorities in the same way as would innocent sufferers', and repeating the words he had earlier used that 'the hospitals were open and the Indian medical officers were there'. It concludes defiantly: 'I submit there is no case whatever against me of any neglect of duty in regard to the wounded.' There is no mention here of the curfew that prevented any aid being given.

The statement lists in detail all the words of approval and condonation which Dyer had received from his superiors, both military and civil, since his time at Amritsar, and makes the exaggerated claim that he 'was promoted by being given permanent command of a Brigade', meaning 5 Brigade at Jamrud. This, as we have seen, was untrue and is not a statement that a senior officer could have expected his superiors to accept. The statement clearly had a wider audience, Parliament and the public, in mind.

The statement concludes with a record of Dyer's service, particularly stressing those actions he had taken in the past which showed him to be 'possessed of any feelings of humanity or regard for human life' and emphasising the acclaim he had received after the relief of Thal. It ends by claiming for Dyer the support that the Government of India had promised its officers in its resolution of April 1919.

Dyer's statement was, on the face of it, and particularly to those who had not read the earlier reports with which it was largely inconsistent, an impressive document. Yet it did not offer any convincing exculpation, nor did it deny Dyer's intent to open fire upon the crowd without warning, and to keep firing for ten minutes to create an effect. Its argument depended heavily upon an interpretation of military law that could not be acceptable to any British government. It excuses, lamely, but does not explain, the lack of assistance given to the wounded in the Bagh, and its explanations for the crawling order, whilst ingenious, are totally unconvincing. The document altered nothing of substance in the case and changed no one's mind. Its very existence served the purpose of saving Dyer from compulsory retirement, but its contents had no effect at the time, and have served since only to confuse the argument about Dyer's motivations.[34]

The statement had to be forwarded to the CIGS at Spa in Germany, where he was involved in the conferences still dragging on to rearrange post-war Europe. The papers reached him only two days later, but he had not the time to take any action on them due to his participation in the conference. His diary for 5 July records: 'The Dyer statement reached me this morning at 10 a.m. in an envelope without covering with a message of any sort, and I am so busy I have no opportunity at the moment to examine it.' This did not have the bad effect that Dyer's faction might have feared, as Wilson's military colleagues back in London were united in resisting the call for Dyer to be made to retire. Wilson's deputy, Major-General Sir C.H. Harington, organised several meetings of the Military Members before the Army Council meeting that took place on the 6th. Harington's background was typical of those involved in the consideration of Dyer's case, and accounts to a great extent for the views he expressed. His father had nearly been killed in the Mutiny in 1857; he had experience of crowd control duties and of firing at rioters in Belfast in 1898; and Captain Briggs, Dyer's Brigade Major, had been under his command when a subaltern. Harington was also so busy that he found time to study Dyer's statement for only four hours, and does not appear to have read any other document on the case. He drew up a paper based upon views which rejected the Government position in its entirety. He sent a précis of this to Wilson on the 4th. Speaking of Dyer, it stated, *inter alia*:

(a) That he certainly acted for the best and had reasonable grounds for action.

(c) That he appreciated the situation with sound judgment.

(e) That he gave ample warning.

(f) That it is ridiculous to suppose that he was faced by an innocent assembly.

(j) That he should be exonerated from any charge of inhumanity.

(m) That it was in substance the same mob which had defied all law and order during the previous two days.

(n) That if he had not taken strong and firm action his own force and the women and children would have been overwhelmed.

(w) That he should be freed from blame and censure.

Harington's preposterous document was little more than a précis of Dyer's statement, so close a rendering of it in places that it echoes its wording. Churchill naturally refused to accept this paper, and harangued the Army Council which met on 6 July, trying to persuade the Military Members to bend to what he stated was the will of the Cabinet, but after an hour he found himself unable to move them to accept his demand that Dyer be made to retire. Harington wrote to the CIGS after the meeting, telling Wilson that they had not yielded. A compromise was, however, achieved, as the Council's decision made no mention of a military inquiry and the idea was quietly dropped. Harington explained to Wilson that they had not been able to get around arguments deployed by Churchill:

We agree that there was an error of judgment. We can't get away from the fact that he went all out and meant to, as he condemns himself by saying if he had more troops he would have inflicted more. We cannot get away from C-in-C having removed him, sent him home … but we gained our point … that we do *not* agree that he should be retired, though we should not employ him.[35]

The month's delay represented by the referral of Dyer's case to the Army Council had produced no change to the current position. Montagu and Churchill had failed to force Dyer to retire. The delay had made, and would continue to make, things increasingly difficult for Montagu in the political arena, and was one of the factors which eventually combined to ruin him. When he met them in the House, his opponents had grown stronger because of this delay, and he had been weakened by his failure in the Army Council, as was made publicly clear by the decision which it now promulgated:

The Army Council have considered the report of the Hunter Committee together with the statement which Brigadier-General Dyer has, by their decision, submitted to them. They consider that, in spite of the great difficulties of the position in which this officer found himself on 13 April, 1919, at Jallianwala Bagh, he cannot be acquitted of an error of judgment. They observe that the Commander-in-Chief in India has removed Brigadier-General Dyer from his employment, that he has been informed that no further employment will be offered him in India, that he has in consequence reverted to half pay, and that the Selection Board in India have passed him over for promotion. These decisions the Army Council accept. They do not consider that further employment should be offered to Brigadier-General Dyer outside India. They have also considered whether any further action of a disciplinary nature is required from the Army Council. In view of all the circumstances they do not feel called upon, from the military point of view with which they are alone concerned, to take any further action.[36]

The next full Cabinet meeting took place on the 7th, the day after the Army Council met. Churchill presented the Army Council's decision, clearly an embarrassing defeat for himself and Montagu. The Cabinet conclusions record:

(1)   That on general grounds of public policy it was not necessary to retire General Dyer compulsorily from the Army.

(2)   That the Secretary of State for War should communicate the decision of the Army Council to the House of Commons that afternoon by means of Question and Answer, and in the event of a Supplementary Question should state that the Government proposed to take no further action.[37]

Churchill made this announcement in the House that afternoon. Though the decision was not yet transmitted officially to Dyer, he heard publicly that day that his hopes for an inquiry were dashed and that any lingering hope for reinstatement was to be disappointed. All that he had to hope for now was that he would be vindicated in the eyes of the world in the debates in Parliament which now at last could take place.

The next day, 8 July, was fixed for the Commons to debate his case, a debate which had been held over for more than a month. This was Dyer's last chance to overturn the censure of the Government and to defend his name. Much rode on this debate, much more than Dyer's personal future, and Montagu for one approached it with dread. The Viceroy wrote to him the day before:

> Tomorrow is the fateful day – 8 July – on which, as I understand, you are going to 'fight beasts at Ephesus' and I shall be thinking of you and wishing you all good luck in the debate. It will no doubt be a disagreeable debate.[38]

The Viceroy's words were percipient. It was to be a debate which destroyed Edwin Montagu's career.

22

Parliament

Much more hung upon the result of the debate which was about to take place in the House of Commons than Dyer's future. The debate was of political significance to the Government, which was at that point still the Liberal Unionist coalition led by Lloyd George that had governed during the war, though its Labour Party members had by now gone into Opposition. Though the 1918 election had given the Unionists, as the Conservative Party were then termed, a majority, they did not take power by themselves, and the 339 Coalition Unionists and 134 Coalition Liberals now supported the Government against twenty-six independent Liberals and sixty-three Labour Party members. The Government majority was therefore large enough to enable it to get its way in the Commons with little difficulty. The Dyer case, though, was different. In 1920, the Commons was not an assembly of men with moderate views; reaction was in the ascendant. Baldwin called the Members of that Parliament 'hard-faced men who looked as if they had done well out of the war'. A very large number of them had served in the Army or Navy and still used their military rank. They were temperamentally averse to Montagu both as a liberal reformer and because he was a Jew. Unrest in Egypt, the Bolshevik threat, and above all the collapse of British authority in Ireland, meant at the time that the maintenance of the Empire was an issue that had begun to divide the coalition, which was by now beginning to fray at the edges. This was scarcely surprising as its two factions divided on ideological grounds. The Montagu-Chelmsford reforms had been enacted in the teeth of opposition from much of the British Indian establishment, and these men had extensive links with the Conservative Party.

Complicating all the events of the time was the issue of Ireland, which was at the height of both its troubles and its destructive effect on British politics. Much of southern Ireland was now slipping out of English control, whilst in Ulster Sir Edward Carson and the Irish Unionists were fighting to keep Ireland within the Empire. Government policy on Indian issues tended to be viewed by the Unionists as part and parcel with the treachery they saw endangering the Empire everywhere. In the face of this, the Government aimed to keep the coalition together, to implement as much reformist policy as it could get away with, and in particular in India to ensure that the Montagu-Chelmsford reforms got off to as good a start as was possible in the circumstances. To both sides in the forthcoming debates, Dyer was symbolic of bigger issues; these would embitter the argument about his case and would ensure that there was no possibility of Parliament considering it upon its merits.

The Government realised early on that it would be necessary to hold a debate in the Commons on Dyer's case, as the issue was so contentious and as it had already attracted parliamentary interest. They understood the importance to their Indian policy of winning this debate and began to arrange that key figures of the Government would speak, both in the initial debate in the Commons and then later in the debate planned for the Lords. Montagu took the lead in this at first; back in June he had sought a commitment from Earl Curzon, the Foreign Secretary, that he would lead for the Government in the Lords. This had been unsuccessful, as Curzon had distanced himself from the issue and had suggested that Birkenhead, the Lord Chancellor, who had been a member of the Indian Disorders Committee and so was more up to date with the facts, make the major speech. Planning was taken out of Montagu's hands when the likely strength of opposition was realised. Bonar Law, Leader of the Commons and the *de facto* Deputy Prime Minister running affairs in the absence of Lloyd George, who was in Europe attending the international conferences continuing after the peace, took over management of the debate. He arranged that Montagu, as the Secretary of State for the responsible ministry, should open in the Commons; that Churchill, whose War Ministry was the other department of state involved, should stand ready to speak at an advantageous point later in the debate; and that he himself would speak last for the Government.[1]

As the days wore by, and as the Army Council consideration of Dyer's case imposed increasing delay in the date of the Commons debate, Montagu became more and more anxious about his speech. He had scarcely recovered from his nervous breakdown of the spring. Driven both by his deep moral revulsion at what Dyer had done, and by his earnest desire to salve the wounds of Indian public opinion and redress the wrongs they had suffered, he burned to censure Dyer in public. He felt a huge emotional responsibility for India, and he desperately feared letting its people down, but he knew the nature of the opposition he would face in the House, and approached his burden with trepidation. J.L. Maffey, the Viceroy's Secretary, met him several times in the weeks before the debate, and stayed the weekend with him in his country house in Norfolk. He reported Montagu's loss of confidence to the Viceroy. Montagu had gone so far as to ask Maffey whether he thought his own very presence jeopardised the reforms he was dedicated to introducing. He believed that his personality created attack, and feared that he, a Jew, might now be doing more harm than good. Maffey continued:

> The Hunter Debate hangs over him as a nightmare, and he evidently feels most keenly the bitter personal attacks to which he has been subjected. [He] wants to refute Sir

Michael O'Dwyer and to attack his administration. I persuaded him to drop it … He had prepared a good deal of rather violent stuff and did not care much for my line.[2]

Montagu was also aware of the way the press had skilfully played upon the gut feelings of Conservative Members; on 6 July the *Morning Post*'s editorial wrote of posters found at Lyallpur during the disturbances which, it said, had encouraged the dishonouring of European women.

> We do not wonder that the name of General Dyer is universally held in honour at the present moment by Englishwomen in Northern India. Who know what the situation was though they cannot talk of it … In a country where women are nothing better than chattels, where all feeling of chivalry is practically non-existent, and it is considered legitimate to cause pain and humiliation to the men by striking at the women, Englishmen decline, and rightly so, to take any chances where their wives and daughters are concerned … The justification of General Dyer must be their [the posters'] contents and his conviction that without swift and drastic action he was imperilling the safety and honour of hundreds of British women. He may not be excused in the eyes of the law, but posterity will say that he saved a situation the possible, if not probable, horrors of which cannot be exaggerated.

Dyer had not, of course, seen the Lyallpur posters, but it was true that the issue raised by the *Post* had been in his mind; it was, after all, one of British India's perennial fears. On the same day, the *Post* reprinted the report of the Dyers' emotional departure from Jullundur published in the *Pioneer* of 23 April.

Dyer's statement was rushed through the press by the Government and published along with the Army Council decision on the morning of 8 July. It came out as a Parliamentary Paper, Command 771, but it arrived too late for MPs to do more than scan it before they entered the House for the debate that afternoon. This, of course, gave further ammunition to the Government's enemies.[3]

The House met at 4 o'clock that afternoon to debate a question put by Sir Edward Carson ostensibly seeking to reduce Edwin Montagu's salary as Secretary of State by £100. Carson had been prepared carefully by Sir Michael O'Dwyer, who was in the House that day, sitting next to J.L. Maffey, on whose other side sat Dyer. It is probable that Carson had met Dyer prior to the debate to discuss his speech, and Mrs Dyer sat with Lady Carson. Maffey later described for Chelmsford the atmosphere in the crowded House before the debate started:

> There was plenty of excitement in the air and the old 'true-blue' service section rallied in force, determined to make more noise than their numbers justified, not very clear or caring greatly about the facts and greatly prejudiced by 'personal' considerations. To this body the only issues were: (a) Is it English to break a man who tried to do his duty? (b) Is

a British General to be downed at the bidding of a crooked Jew? Obviously it was necessary for Montagu to be very tactful and explanatory, very patient and very convincing. Winston Churchill took this line later. But Montagu? He was utterly deplorable. Some papers describe him as speaking with passion. All I saw was nervousness, pallor and lack of judgment in facing a passage of arms which he dreaded … But from the moment he began to speak I could feel antipathy to him sweeping all over the House.[4]

When he rose to open the debate, it was immediately clear that Montagu had not taken the advice he had been given to restrain his tone and stick to the facts. He launched directly into what he saw as the nub of the question at issue: whether the House would 'endorse the position of His Majesty's Government, of the Hunter Committee, of the Commander-in-Chief in India, and of the Army Council, or whether they will desire to censure them', but he then very rapidly lost control of the direction in which he was going, abandoned much of his prepared speech, and launched into an emotional tirade that alienated any sympathies his audience had retained. Unwisely, he swept past any reference to the facts of the case, and so never established exactly why Dyer had been censured, 'because,' as he said, 'the whole matter turns upon this, that it is the doctrine of terrorism'. He characterised the crawling order as 'racial humiliation', but failed to establish exactly what the order meant, which was a pity as most of those who opposed him had but a sketchy grasp of the facts of the case. He asked: 'Are you going to keep your hold on India by terrorism, racial humiliation and subordination, and frightfulness, or are you going to rest it upon the goodwill, and the growing goodwill, of the people of your Indian Empire?' The Conservative members were quite unwilling to accept any accusation of frightfulness unless it were proven to them, and, as it hadn't been, this caused an uproar from all sides. MPs began to shout interruptions and insults, drowning Montagu out, causing him in turn to try to outshout them. Cries of 'It saved a mutiny', 'What a terrible speech' and 'You are making an incendiary speech' threw Montagu off what remained of his thread, and he fell back on repetition. 'There is one theory upon which I think General Dyer acted, the theory of terrorism, and the theory of subordination', but this was interrupted by shouts of 'Bolshevism!' Passions became so high that Sir William Sutherland later reported to Lloyd George that many Tories seemed on the verge of physically assaulting Montagu; as he got excited, he became 'more Yiddish in screaming tone and gesture, and a strong anti-Jewish sentiment was shown by shouts and excitement among normally placid Tories'. Montagu concluded in what should have been a rousing finish but which amidst the baying of his opponents seemed at best to them an illogicality, at worst a misappropriation of the imperial faith by a man who was betraying it: 'I invite this House to choose, and I believe that the choice they make is fundamental to a continuance of the British Empire, and vital to the continuation, permanent as I believe it can be, to the connection between this country and India.'[5]

Austen Chamberlain, the Chancellor of the Exchequer, whose fellow Unionists were baiting Montagu, watched the debacle with dismay:

I hope that I shall not have such a House as confronted Montagu on Thursday, and that, if I do, I shall not handle it so maladroitly. With the House in that temper nothing could have been so infuriating to it as his opening remarks – no word of sympathy with Dyer, no sign that Montagu appreciated his difficulties, but as it were a passionate peroration to a speech that had not been delivered, a grand finale to a debate which had not begun … Our party has always disliked and distrusted him. On this occasion all their English and racial feeling was stirred to a passionate display – I think I have never seen the House so fiercely angry – and he threw fuel on the flames. A Jew, rounding on an Englishman and throwing him to the wolves – that was the feeling.[6]

Maffey revealed to Chelmsford the scale of Montagu's failure: 'When he sank back and buried his head in his hand I felt "There is a man who has done for himself".'[7]

Sir Edward Carson rose next, and the House fell quiet. Carson was all reason, politeness, a deliberate contrast with what had just gone before, a neat turning of the tables on an issue where the Liberal case was based upon the facts, and the Conservative case upon the emotions they aroused. The subject of Montagu's oratory was not, he claimed, the proper subject of that day's debate, which was rather the treatment of General Dyer, who had been removed from his post without trial. Here Carson took a very clever line, one which allowed him to pass by with little examination what it was that Dyer had been censured for, and allowed him to play upon the prejudices of his audience, particularly those with service connections. 'We may at least try to be fair, and to recognize the real position in which this officer is placed … General Dyer has a right to be brought within those principles of liberty' which Montagu had demanded be applied to Indians. Carson carefully quoted General Sir Havelock Hudson's speech to the Legislative Council in which he had offered such strong support for Dyer. He claimed that Dyer had faced what was 'at all events the precursor to a revolution', one which he considered was actually a single conspiracy covering Ireland, Egypt and India. 'Admit if you like in your armchair that he did commit an error of judgment, but was it such that alone he ought to bear the consequences?' If the House supported the censure of Dyer, 'you will never get an officer to carry out his duties towards his country … You must back your men.' Turning to his fellow Ulsterman, Sir Michael O'Dwyer, Carson stated that he was proud that 'it is not an Irishman who has thrown over his subordinate', cleverly stigmatising Montagu's treatment of Dyer as 'un-English'. His conclusion was a model of moderation. 'Censure a soldier who made a genuine mistake but do not break him.'

Bonar Law saw that things were now going very badly for the Government, and asked Churchill to speak next. Churchill had taken much care with the preparation of his speech, and had the facts to hand. He now deployed them in a way that Montagu had failed to do, and skilfully built upon them to show that the Government's censure of Dyer was imperative were it to be able to insist in the future that its servants meet the standards upon which any civilised government was built. More than this, the Government's censure had been a moral necessity. Dyer's deed had been 'an extraordinary event, a monstrous event, an event which stands in sinister isolation', and he had done something which no other English officer faced with a similar problem had ever done. This was so because Dyer had abandoned the principle of minimum force upon which all military aid to the civil power had to be based. Churchill elucidated this principle, and showed the House how it had to be applied: 'no more force should be used than is necessary to secure compliance with the law'; a commander had to 'confine himself to a limited and definite objective, that is to say to preventing a crowd doing something they ought not to do'. Dyer had gone beyond this, and had thereby laid himself open to the charge of 'frightfulness', a word Churchill used intentionally and advisedly, for it recalled the charges made against the Germans in the war. 'What I mean by frightfulness is the inflicting of great slaughter or massacre upon a particular crowd of people, with the intention of terrorizing not merely the rest of the crowd, but the whole district or country.' Batting aside those who were by now attempting to interrupt his flow, he turned Carson's claim of 'Englishness' back against him: 'I do not think that it is in the interests of the British Empire or of the British Army for us to take a load of this sort for all time upon our backs. We have to make it absolutely clear, some way or other, that this is not the British way of doing business.' Dyer had not saved British India; it was not in need of saving. Ironically, in light of the fight he had just lost, he described the Army Council decision that Dyer should not be retired as 'moderate and considered conclusions' and pointed out to the House that similar decisions had been frequently taken in the war, a time when officers were treated much more peremptorily than Dyer had been. Churchill's cogent yet passionately delivered speech persuaded many, and undid some of the damage Montagu had inflicted on his own side. It was a particularly well-wrought performance given Churchill's personal view of Dyer's guilt, a view which he revealed in a subsequent letter to Lord Crewe: 'My own opinion is that the offence amounted to murder, or alternatively manslaughter.'[8] Unlike Montagu, Churchill had kept his head, and by so doing saved the day for the Government.

Asquith, an ex-Prime Minister but now a lone voice on the backbenches, rose next to state that 'for the House of Commons to take upon itself, on behalf of the British Empire as a whole, the responsibility of condoning and adopting one of the worst outrages in the whole of our history' would be unsupportable.[9]

Speaking after Mr Spoor of the Labour Party, who called for Dyer to be tried, Lieutenant-General Sir Aylmer Hunter-Weston usefully outlined the provisions of Indian Army Regulations, and confirmed Churchill's reading that they called for the adoption of the principle of minimum force, and noted, echoing Asquith, that it would be contrary to all tradition to overturn the decisions of the Commander-in-Chief in India. He was followed by a more junior retired officer, Lieutenant-Colonel James, who put the opposite view of the Punjab tradition that decisions had to be left to the man on the spot, which he felt meant that Dyer had to be supported.

Nevertheless, since Churchill had spoken, the debate had flowed much the Government's way, but now Sir William Joynson-Hicks rose to speak. Joynson-Hicks, Jix to his friends, was a Conservative of the most reactionary tendency, and he had very early spotted that this was an issue with which both to bait the Government and to make his own name. He was, dangerously for the Government, an accomplished orator, and a man not averse to making the most of the facts he favoured and the least of those he did not. He had travelled to India over the previous winter on his own fact-finding mission, one in which he had met all that was most reactionary in British India, and had returned fortified by their complaints and fears. 80 per cent of Indian civil servants and 90 per cent of the Europeans in India supported Dyer, he claimed, without the slightest hint of being able to justify such a cavalier use of statistics. Montagu, by his actions over Amritsar, had 'utterly destroyed any little shred of confidence that was left to him' in India. Joynson-Hicks was 'convinced there was a real rebellion in the Punjab and that General Dyer saved India and us from a repetition of the miseries and cruelties of 1857'. His speech closely followed the O'Dwyer line. Dyer's small force would have been overwhelmed had he not acted as he did. Indians had thanked him, and he had been made a Sikh. 'I assert that General Dyer was and is today beloved of the Sikh nation.' Dyer was entitled 'to judge of what was necessary to be done in a military fashion' and he had acted in good faith to 'put an end to rebellion'. Joynson-Hicks appealed to the House to support those out in the Empire 'upholding our flag there under very great difficulties ... We must trust the men on the spot.' This was a hugely successful speech, warmly received by the House. Like Carson, he had avoided all discussion of the points upon which Dyer had been censured, and had brought to the House's mind whatever parts of the whole affair would most engage its sympathies. Joynson-Hicks was a man with a future which was to include the Home Office, and he was to build that future to a considerable extent on the approbation he received that day. He had managed to undo what Churchill had achieved.

The following speakers were largely hostile to the Government. Brigadier-General Surtees put the view of many in India: 'General Dyer, I think, realized and gauged accurately the temper with which he was confronted.' He warned that the debate would affect all the races ruled by the British, and that 'once you destroy British prestige, then the Empire will collapse like a house of cards'. The next speaker, a Mr Palmer, raised the level of tension in the House by several notches: 'there was', he asserted, 'a concerted attempt at revolution' in the Punjab, and Montagu's 'deplorable speech' had been 'an encouragement to disloyalists and those forces of disorder' which had been behind it. He had, he said, managed to get a copy of Dyer's statement at 8 o'clock that morning, and 'a more manly and splendidly frank and open statement I have never read'. With Joynson-Hicks, he claimed that 'patriotic Indian opinion was with General Dyer', reading to the House a letter he had received from a woman who was in Ahmedabad during the disturbances: 'the prompt action of General Dyer in the Punjab saved our lives'. Another of his correspondents had written: 'I have had the pleasure of serving under this General, and a better or more kind-hearted man you could not wish to meet. I went through the Amritsar and Lahore riots with the motor transport section … This General had only one alternative, and that was to deal with a firm hand. If he did not give the orders he gave, there would not be many of the garrison alive to-day to tell the truth.' Palmer then turned bitterly on Churchill, who was, he said, 'responsible for the loss of more lives than any man sitting in this house'. This deeply offensive jibe referred to Churchill's part in the Gallipoli campaign and the Antwerp raid in the recent war. Referring to Montagu's speech, Palmer said 'the whole tone and temper of that speech inflamed the Committee more than I have seen it inflamed in thirty-five years' experience'. He concluded that 'We feel that General Dyer has been sentenced without trial' and demanded an inquiry.

Hilton Young followed to support Montagu. He had been in Amritsar, and had passed through after Joynson-Hicks, but 'I did not receive the impression which he received'. He had found that all he met did support the Government and Sir Michael O'Dwyer, but 'there is a very large body of opinion – I will not attempt to evaluate it – which is not prepared to support the action of General Dyer at Jallianwala Bagh … General Dyer does not understand or appreciate … that the interpretation he has put upon the recognized principle [of minimum force] is an enormous extension of it'. It had now gone nine o'clock, and the House had been sitting feverishly for over five hours, but there was more to follow. A Liberal Member, Colonel Wedgwood, rose next, and tried to persuade the House that it should not think solely of Dyer but more of the honour of the country. 'He placed on English history the greatest blot since in days gone by we burned Joan of Arc.' The Conservative MP Rupert Gwynne followed, and again raised the level of antagonism in the Chamber. In a vituperative speech dripping with contempt for Montagu and Churchill, Gwynne said that General Dyer had not received justice and that, in comparison with Churchill's error at Gallipoli, Dyer's offence was slight. Montagu's conduct, he claimed, was a greater danger to India than Dyer's. He closed in on Montagu's inability to explain why he had not informed the House of the events at Amritsar at the time they had occurred, quoted a good deal of circumstantial detail to support his allegations, and accused Montagu of misleading the House. He alleged that Montagu had tried to cover up the whole issue. Montagu was stung to rise and interject, but could only produce incoherent cries of outrage by way of a defence. Gwynne resumed his seat, having successfully made Montagu look both foolish and guilty.

At the last, Bonar Law rose to sum up. He gently poured oil on the tumult that had arisen in the House, carefully and quietly picking out, as only Churchill had managed to do before him, the facts at issue. The Government's dispatch censuring Dyer was not, he pointed out, the work of Montagu alone, but of a Cabinet Committee upon which had sat most of the Government. He accepted of course that Dyer had been placed in a very difficult position, and that he had made a proclamation that was defied. He even went further than Dyer in accepting that he was in danger in the Bagh, as his troops were very few. Yet the Hunter Committee had been fair, he was sure, in finding two faults: first, that there had been no warning given before fire was opened. This point gave rise to loud laughter from the Conservative benches, and to shouts that Dyer had given six hours' notice, and that he felt he was about to be attacked. Bonar Law denied this, using Dyer's own words. 'He was determined to shoot right away. He himself said it.' The Hunter Committee's second criticism was of the length of firing, for which Bonar Law personally could see no justification. Again, he quoted Dyer's own words at length, and said that the principle of inflicting punishment for its effect on others which they revealed 'is a principle which ought to be repudiated'. He went on: 'No one accused him – at least I do not – of anything except a grave misconception as to what was his duty. The very fact that that view was expressed by a man of that kind makes it all the more necessary that it should be repudiated by the Government of this country.' Dyer had been treated as many generals had been in the war, and he had no right to a court martial. The Army Council had acted properly. 'I myself have discussed this with a good many soldiers. Nearly all of them share the view that no action ought to have been taken against General Dyer. But there is not one to whom I have spoken who has not taken the view that General Dyer was wrong. That is a fact.' He agreed that the Government must not make scapegoats of its servants, but neither could it 'support them however wrong they are'. Bonar Law had done his homework, and had adopted the right tone. He pulled the debate back to the tracks upon which Churchill had set it.

The House now divided. The Government won by 101 votes, though 119 of the 129 who voted against it were Unionist members of its own coalition. The House broke up in a muttered growl of 'Montagu, Resign! Resign!' He left the House a ruined man. Dyer left stony-faced, Annie in tears. She was comforted by Lady Carson, who told her not to worry: 'They call Edward much worse things.'[10]

The Dyers made their way back to Clarges Street. There was little for them left to do now but somehow to pick up the pieces of their lives, but where and how was not clear. It would have to be in England, but they had no roots there, no home to go to. They were not yet aware of it, but the *Morning Post* had already begun to alter their future fundamentally. On the day of the debate, the *Post* appealed for funds to assist Dyer with his defence costs. In the first twelve hours, £584 8s. 4d. was received at the paper's offices, and the mail the next day brought the beginning of what was to become a flood of letters and gifts in Dyer's support. On the 9th, alongside an article which analysed the debate in the House, and which in particular castigated Churchill, under the headline 'An Error of Judgment. A Study of Contrasts', the *Post* said that whilst Dyer's 'error' had killed 379 natives, Churchill's errors at Antwerp had cost 300 deaths and the capture of 2000 British soldiers, and at Gallipoli 41,211 killed and captured. The paper continued its call for funds for Dyer. In an article headed 'For General Dyer. The Man Who Saved India. Our Appeal to Patriots. A Splendid and Immediate Response', the paper appealed to those who

> realise the truth – that the lives of their fellow-countrymen in India hung upon the readiness of a General Dyer to act as he acted ... He is not only broken but financially crippled ... We forthwith propose to open a General Dyer fund, the subscriptions to which will serve a two-fold purpose; [to] relieve a gallant and despitefully used soldier of a grievous embarrassment [and to be] an assurance that some of his fellow countrymen at least extend to him their sympathy, their confidence, and their gratitude, and disassociate themselves from the mean and cowardly conduct of the politicians and the time-servers.

Anything above the costs of his defence was to be dedicated as a gift to Dyer 'to symbolize for him, in his enforced retirement, the goodwill of his friends'. Sir Edward Carson, said the *Post*, had already subscribed £20, and they published a letter from him complaining that Dyer had never had a trial. When news of this appeal, which had been made without his involvement, reached him, Dyer was not sure that it was something which he could accept; he may have been aware that as a serving officer he was not entitled to accept publicly subscribed funds. Perhaps, too, the appeal smacked of the political to him, and as such it may have been unwelcome. He consulted Sir Michael O'Dwyer, who advised him that it was the only way the public could show him their sympathy and their disgust at his treatment by the Government. Dyer accepted this advice and withdrew his objection.[11]

The appeal in the *Morning Post* was a snowball which quickly turned into an avalanche. The idea was probably not the *Post*'s own; in India a similar appeal had already begun. On 14 May, the *Pioneer* had carried letters in support of Dyer; one, written by 'A Would Be Subscriber', stating that Dyer and others had left

India with no mark of recognition for 'saving India from the horrors of another
'57' and suggesting that 'a fund be organized and public subscriptions called for
to enable a sword of honour with a suitable inscription thereon to be purchased
and presented to each of the officers'. This call was taken up across India,
particularly in the Punjab, where ladies formed a thirteen-member committee
under Mrs Florence Holland and began to collect funds intended to present both
a sword of honour and a purse to Dyer. Soon, it was a common sight throughout
India to see such women outside club doors with their collecting tins, sights
which infuriated most Indians who saw them. The English press in India, and
those who wrote to it, added to Indian indignation. The *Pioneer*'s letter page was
full of support for Dyer. Writing under the pseudonym 'Real Englishman', a
Government officer claimed that 'I have only met those who agree without
reserve that General Dyer not only did the only thing possible, but that by so
doing he certainly saved from death, and worse, many Englishmen and women
who were under his protection'. Another, signing himself only 'Fourteen Years in
India', wrote:

> I have never heard anything but praise and approval of Dyer's action [which] was the
> saving of a very dangerous situation at the time, and we all firmly believe that it promptly
> put a stop to prospects of still greater horror ... Everyone knows that no British soldier
> fires on unarmed men – no matter how great their number against how few – without
> very grave questioning and when it has to be done it can never be more than a horrible
> duty. This is simply one more case of a brave man doing his duty instead of hiding
> behind officialdom.

Very few voices put the other view in the British Indian Press. One who did,
'An Onlooker', wrote that 'We have not met a single Englishman or Englishwoman who does not feel a sense of irremovable shame both at the tragedy of
Jallianwala Bagh and at the excesses that were committed under martial law'. But
the few who opposed what Dyer had done were scarcely noticed by Indians. The
hurt being done by the majority of what was published was ground daily into
Indian wounds. The Indian press, on the other hand, was united in its criticism
of the debate and of the Army Council's decision. There were widespread calls
for Dyer to be punished, and many allegations, made by papers such as the
Bombay Chronicle, of British racial prejudice.[12]

Montagu was cast into deep depression by what had happened in the Commons,
and in particular by his own dismal failure. On 9 July he telegraphed India:

> The debate did not go satisfactorily yesterday. The majority of the Conservative Party
> were ruffled by the speech with which I opened the debate. I could not placate them and
> they voted against the Government. I spoke without notes and was very worried. This
> morning I am regretting that I may have let you and your Government down.

When he wrote a letter to the Viceroy on the 15th, he could scarcely bring himself to mention the debate, and Chelmsford was brought to chide him for failing to give him a full account. J.L. Maffey called to see Montagu some days later and wrote to the Viceroy:

> E.S.M. hung his head when I entered his office! You would have laughed. He said 'Well, I made an infernal mess of it!' He had worried silly and got really ill. For a week before the debate he had not slept. When he got to the House he felt that the utmost he could do was to put the issue in the way he did briefly to the House. Hostile interruptions rattled him. He made a mess of it!

Maffey's contempt was shared by Chelmsford. In a letter to Maffey that crossed the latter's account of his meeting Montagu, he made plain that his contempt had been of longstanding, and at last let something of his character creep out from under the stone where he consistently concealed it:

> No doubt the consummate orator is able to change the tone and style of his speech to the audience which he addresses, but that assumes he can gauge his audience, and I wonder if this is possible when the audience is Western and the speaker is Eastern… it is in matters of taste that the Jew so often fails … Poor Montagu has written me a most pathetic wail on the subject.

Chelmsford and Montagu now fell into a bitter and protracted argument about what India had told London, and whether the Government of India had changed its mind over Dyer. Chelmsford particularly objected to Montagu's reintroduction of the word 'frightfulness' he thought he had excised from government pronouncements, as well as to Churchill's statement that it was the Government of India's repeated condonation of Dyer that had prevented his punishment. None of these issues was ever to be resolved satisfactorily between them, and their relations, already bad, did not recover.[13]

To add to Montagu's discomfiture, he faced the fact that the Lords, who were much more conservative in their views than the Commons, were scheduled to debate Dyer, and until they did so the *Morning Post* for one was intent on not letting the issue die. On 10 July the paper was full of analysis and letters about the Commons debate. With some satisfaction, it reported the abandonment of the Government position by Conservative members of the coalition. It tried to stir trouble in the Army Council, decrying the fact that its civilian members outnumbered the military, and claiming that this was the cause of its acceptance of the censure upon Dyer. It carried a poem entitled 'Soldier or Politician', which included the lines

> 'Error of Judgment'! What can e'er dispense,
> A soldier from the guilt of that offence.

Its letters page carried another rehash of his position by Sir Michael O'Dwyer, who accompanied his letter with a subscription to the Dyer fund, and a letter from Mr Kennedy Jones, MP, who said 'It was not a riot that faced him; it was stark, naked rebellion'. The Duke and Duchess of Somerset lamented that 'It is a pity we have not a General Dyer in Ireland at the present time', and the Reverend D. Baldock opined that 'Anyone who has been working for his living in the East knows that General Dyer was right'. He was supported on the same page in this strangely un-Christian view by two fellow clerics. In another letter, Mr H. Sullivan elaborated on the *Post*'s subscription by suggesting the presentation of a sword of honour. The *Post* smugly reported that the *Globe* had come out in its support and was also collecting money.[14]

Now that the debate in the Commons, with its potential of an upset for the Government, was passed, the War Office at last informed Dyer of what he had long since read in the press and heard in Parliament. The Adjutant-General wrote to Dyer at his solicitor's address on the 14th: 'I am commanded to inform you that the Army Council have considered the report of the Hunter Committee together with the statement which you submitted by their direction on the 3rd instant.' The letter gave Dyer almost exactly the text of the Army Council resolution as published on the 8th. General Creedy did not expand on this, or add any explanation of the decision; it was never at any stage to be explained to Dyer by letter or to his face.[15]

The number of servicemen and civil servants wishing to subscribe to the Dyer fund, both at home and in India, was very soon sufficiently large to cause irritation and some alarm to both Governments. On 26 July, the Government of India issued a telegram to the provincial administrations informing them that such subscriptions contravened Indian Government Rules prohibiting subscriptions to political movements. This was greatly resented by many British Government servants. Chelmsford informed Montagu of this, and of his prohibition of official subscribers, on 30 July:

> Subscription lists for Dyer have been opened in this country and have been taken up energetically by Ladies' Committees, European Associations and some English newspapers, but Pickford, as Sheriff of Calcutta, made an appeal to drop the Dyer controversy because of its effects on racial feeling.

In England, Churchill was advised by General Creedy that a serving officer was 'forbidden to accept presents of money from public bodies or private individuals in recognition of services rendered in the performance of their duties', but he wisely chose to let this sleeping dog lie. Dyer was reckoned in any case to be bound to retire, so no instruction was issued to the Army at home. This was not to be the case in India, where the Government could not tolerate Army officers openly subscribing to the Dyer fund when their civilian counterparts had been prevented from doing so. On 9 August, the Indian Adjutant-General's Department wrote to all commands banning such subscriptions: 'The attention of officers should be drawn to King's Regulations paragraph 443, and it should be pointed out that to subscribe to Funds of this nature is contrary to such regulations and the customs of the service.' This was on occasion simply ignored; the *Pioneer*, which was coordinating fund-raising in India, printed a list of subscribers on 25 August which included a Brigadier-General Parker of Ootacamund, who gave £3, and 'The British and Gurkha Officers', Almora, who jointly donated £50. By that date, the total collected in India stood at £7480 15s.[16]

The tide of opinion amongst the British in India was hugely in Dyer's favour. The Viceroy warned Montagu:

> I must warn you that even as the matter stands I expect considerable agitation on the part of the European community with regard to Dyer's condemnation … It is idle to talk to them of Dyer having exceeded the necessities of the case or having been guilty of want of humanity. The one thing they consider is the fact that, in their opinion, his action saved both them and theirs.[17]

The military were generally pro-Dyer. Their thinking was almost universally in agreement with the views of the new Commander-in-Chief in India, Lord Rawlinson, who wrote to the CIGS in terms that were reminiscent of some of the schoolboy English Dyer had used before the Hunter Committee:

> The semi-educated native as well as the entirely stupid coolie takes clemency as proof of weakness. Ninety-nine per cent of the natives of India are children and must be treated as children.

Rawlinson wished, he wrote, for 'a good strong Viceroy with a birch to smack the naughty boys'. A more junior, but very representative, officer, Major-General Nigel Woodyatt, wrote that:

> The majority of my brother soldiers … feel, that whatever excesses or errors of judgment it may be thought he committed, his actions effected the immediate object in view, i.e. the suppression of the rebellion at its very centre, and were primarily approved by the highest authorities. This being so, no political or other influences should have induced the same authorities, later on, to reverse their judgment and let him down.

General Sir Herbert Lawrence, son of the Lord Lawrence who had established British rule in the Punjab and held it fast during the Mutiny, told Brigadier-General Edmonds:

> That in his opinion – which was general – Dyer had saved a massacre of Europeans and had nipped in the bud a serious outbreak. He agreed with me that Dyer had been brought into the world solely that he might be at Amritsar at that precise time; for no other

soldier of his rank would have been so fearless as to act as he did without thought of his own future, and have acted with such an understanding of 'the half devil and half child', as Kipling also born in India diagnosed the natives to be.[18]

Ethel Savi gave the similar view of many civilians in her novel *Rulers of Men*, which was set in contemporary India and published a few years later:

> They sacrificed a fine old soldier and killed British prestige in India, for ever; so that a captious minority might be appeased. Instantly sedition broke out afresh, encouraged by the weakness of the Government, and things have since gone from bad to worse. The Indians laugh in their sleeves at the Government, and think they can defy it. Disorder and violence continue unchecked, so that the natives imagine the Government dare not use force to repress outbreaks. General Dyer should have been upheld if India is to be successfully ruled … It has become a common saying among junior officials, 'If you don't fire on a mob out for serious mischief you'll be killed, and if you do, you'll be hanged'.

Fellow novelist Maud Diver wrote similarly in her book *Far to Seek*, published in 1921:

> Our people don't understand this new talk of 'Committee Ki Raj' [Rule by Committee] and 'Dyarchy Raj'. Too many orders make confusion. But they understand 'Hukm Ki Raj' [Rule by Order]. In fact, it's the general opinion that prompt action in the Punjab has fairly well steadied India – for the present at least.

Those establishment Indians who were seen to have betrayed the British position were the objects of particular ill-feeling. Sir Chimanlal Setalvad, who had resigned from the Viceroys' Executive Council, wrote:

> In those days, I received several anonymous letters abusing me for having condemned General Dyer. One person sent me a cutting from an English paper which had reproduced a photograph of Montagu. Across that cutting he had written in ink: 'A Typical Jew and a scoundrel like you.' He had erased the words in the caption 'the Hero of the Amritsar Debate' and substituted the words 'the Judas in the British Cabinet'.

The public subscriptions for the Dyer fund enraged Indians, who could not fail to contrast this with the fact that the Punjab Government was still 'haggling over doles to the widows and orphans of Jallianwala'. Compensation had yet to be paid to the victims of the shooting in the Bagh. Worse, the Punjab Government was pursuing recovery of the costs of military operations from the areas placed under martial law, and an impost of 1,850,000 rupees had been placed on Amritsar. The issue was hotly debated in the Punjab legislature, and was to drag on until 1921, by which time the sum had increased to 2,056,000 rupees. The compensation payments for the victims in Amritsar, when they came, were divisive. British dependants of those murdered were amply compensated, and they were to receive a total of 400,321 rupees; one alone, Mrs Stewart, whose husband had been murdered at his bank, was awarded the very large sum of 20,000 rupees. Those few Europeans who had been injured in Amritsar were awarded a total of 43,250 rupees. The dependants of those Indians killed in the Jallianwala Bagh got 500 rupees for each dead body. In total only 13,840 rupees was paid to them. The difference in the value the British placed upon each life was plain for all to see.[19]

Back in England, Dyer did what was expected of him and resigned on 17 July. He did so almost immediately on receipt of General Creedy's letter, for which he had doubtless been waiting. Yet his resignation was far from removing Dyer from the political field. The Commons had not forgotten him, and on 19 July a question was tabled in the House asking whether a statue had been erected to Dyer in the Golden Temple; the Viceroy was able to deny this a few days later.[20]

The Lords debate was now looming, scheduled for 19 July. Over the previous year, the Lords had made much of the running in raising Indian issues. Now, Lord Sydenham prepared the way for the debate, and set something of its tone, by asking in the Lords on the 14th if the Government of India resolution or their despatch of 3 May had been altered under pressure from the India Office, a question which evoked a flurry of telegrams between London and Simla, and an angry denial from Lord Chelmsford. Sydenham, an ex-Governor of Bombay, was the principal thorn in the Government's side on this issue in the Lords, working throughout hand-in-glove with Sir Michael O'Dwyer, whose line he consistently took.

The Government planned that Lord Sinha, an Indian peer and Montagu's Under-Secretary and spokesman in the Lords, would put the Government's case. Montagu drew up a paper for him giving the heads of objection to the motion which they would face:

1.   That the Government agreed that it was unfair to criticize Dyer's failure to make a proclamation closer to the Jallianwala Bagh on 13 April.

2.   That Dyer's opening fire without warning should be condemned.

3.   That Dyer's firing after the crowd had begun to disperse, and the unnecessary loss of life, should be condemned.

4.   The fact that Dyer had made no arrangements for the dead and wounded should be condemned.

5.   That the principle of terror should be rejected.[21]

On Monday 19 July, Viscount Finlay rose to move 'that this House deplores the conduct of the case of General Dyer as unjust to that officer, and as establishing a precedent dangerous to the preservation of order in face of rebellion'. The atmosphere in the Lords did not approach the heated antagonisms which had exploded in the Commons. Following their tradition, the Lords treated each other with respect and the arguments with greater rigour. This did not prevent, however, some personal attacks as the debate developed. Viscount Finlay was not an old India hand, so stumbled over some of the Indian detail of his speech, but he gave a workmanlike résumé of the O'Dwyer line. Dyer, he said, had been awarded 'a stigma which, I believe, is entirely undeserved', and this would have a dangerous effect on junior officers. He accepted without any reservation Dyer's case that his long firing was justified by its effect elsewhere, and rejected the idea that this was 'frightfulness'. 'This was not a case of frightfulness visited on innocent people.' He concluded that 'I think that the Secretary of State should have weighted his words more carefully before he put such a stigma as this upon a gallant officer whose humanity is beyond question'.

The major speech in reply was made by Lord Sinha. He made a much better job of this than his superior had managed in the Commons, and he spoke judiciously and in great detail. Wisely, he opened by deploring the incidents of violence by Indians during the disturbances. He strove to deny that the Government of India had changed its mind about Dyer at any stage, though found the going difficult here due to the apparent support Dyer had received in the Legislative Council debates of September. He took the unusual step of refuting in detail the allegations of a cover up made by O'Dwyer, reading out a letter from Sir Thomas Holderness, the Permanent Under-Secretary in the India Office who had retired in January. This contradicted Sir Michael O'Dwyer's accounts of his visits to Montagu, and supported Montagu's version of events, particularly that the details of the incident in the Bagh were unknown to him or the Viceroy before Dyer came before the Hunter Committee. Lord Sinha then turned to Dyer himself, and pointed out that he had been condemned by his own words, words not extracted by cross-examination but which were in the report he had written before he appeared at the Hunter Inquiry. Sinha repudiated for the Government Dyer's doctrine of intimidating others elsewhere in the Punjab by firing in the Bagh. He then took another swipe at Sir Michael O'Dwyer, cleverly differentiating what had happened in the Punjab from what had taken place in the rest of India, specifically praising Governors Harcourt Butler in the United Provinces and George Lloyd in Bombay, who, he said, did 'not interfere too hastily or too violently with an agitation of this nature'. His implications concerning Sir Michael O'Dwyer's administration were clear.

The Earl of Midleton, now a leading Irish Unionist, followed Lord Sinha; it was upon his estate that Dyer had played cricket as a boy. Dyer had, he believed, faced not a riot but a rebellion, and the Government of India was to blame for its failures at the time and for censuring its officers so tardily. Dyer's feat of arms at Thal, in the Noble Earl's mind, had wiped out any crime. The Marquess of Crewe, who had once been Secretary of State for India, and who had taken care to check the details of the case with Churchill, told the House that he believed the appointment of the Hunter Committee had been a mistake, and that the Government of India should have held its own inquiry. He wished to focus on Dyer's faults; he believed that Dyer's statement that all troops in his command were at risk if he didn't act was nonsense. The crowd in the Bagh was not all guilty and so had not been a legitimate target. The crawling order seemed to him 'an index of the unfitness of the particular man for the particular task'. What other Indian Army officer had done what Dyer did? 'General Dyer was a man who, having followed straitly and strictly the path of duty as he saw it, took a wrong turning.'

The Lord Chancellor, Lord Birkenhead, who had been a member of the Indian Disorders Committee, spoke next. He agreed that Dyer was 'a very gallant soldier; we are agreed that he had exhibited discretion, sobriety and resolution before the incidents now under discussion', but he believed that Dyer's conduct at the Bagh 'has never, so far as my knowledge of the history of the Empire extends, been approached in all our long, anxious and entirely honourable dealings with native populations'. To vote for the motion was to set the House against the Hunter Committee, the Government of India, the Commander-in-Chief in India, the Cabinet and the Army Council. This was something the House should not do. It was by now 8 p.m., and the Lords rose for dinner, to resume at 9.15. When it did, the debate continued, with most of the speakers Law Lords who were hostile to the Government, until the House adjourned for the night at 11 p.m.

The next day, the 20th, Viscount Milner, Secretary of State for the Colonies, opened for the Government. No injustice had been done to Dyer, he said. His original prejudices had all been in favour of the soldier, but he had found Dyer's case unsupportable. Every officer who acted in the wrong could not be supported by the authorities. The Commander-in-Chief in India had decided his fate, and this should be adhered to. Milner was followed by the Archbishop of Canterbury, Randall Davidson, who made a disappointing speech objecting to the case being discussed by Parliament at all. His words were surprisingly empty of any moral or Christian imperative. He thought of Dyer only as 'a brave, public-spirited patriotic soldier; but of a man whose policy and practice, as regards our administration in India, ran somewhat counter to what the greatest of our Indian administrators have taught us'.

Lord Sumner, a Law Lord, rose next. He considered that Dyer faced a rebellion not a riot, and that he had been placed at a disadvantage by being convicted by the Hunter Committee instead of at a trial. He believed that it was by the prestige of their name that the British held the Empire, and that the Government of India had weakened this and so the authority of its junior officers. Lord Buckmaster commented briefly that if the crowd had fallen to its knees in submission before him, on his own account Dyer would have continued firing. Lord Meston, another ex-Governor, defended the Government of India and denied that a mutiny had been averted as the Indian Army had remained completely firm. He spoke of the effect Dyer's action had: 'I have never seen nor heard such bitterness as was expressed to me when I re-visited that country last winter.' A vote against the motion would hasten the recovery of good will.

Earl Curzon, then Secretary of State for Foreign Affairs, spoke next, as impressive as he was upon all important occasions, and with a keen grasp of the facts unrivalled by most of the other peers who contributed to the debate. 'It is not the case that at any stage General Dyer was promoted ... I have it on the highest military authority ... he was merely continued in the status which he had previously enjoyed.' Curzon's knowledge of India allowed him to understand why the crawling order and the Jallianwala Bagh had so badly affected Indians. He justly pointed out that Dyer's explanation of his order that people should move on all fours as the street was a holy place was 'an absurdity ... The people of India do not go down on all fours in places of special sanctity'. The humiliation of the crawling order was impossible to excuse. He carefully described the Jallianwala Bagh scene using Dyer's own words, and objected to the principle of firing to frighten others. 'I profoundly mistrust the theory that General Dyer saved the Punjab by his exertions: I altogether deny that he saved India by his example.' He concluded 'General Dyer's conception of his duty was a wrong conception'.

The Government had intended that Curzon's persuasive speech would put a seal upon the debate, but this was not to be, for at this point the Marquess of Salisbury made an intervention, and it was not one in the Government's favour. He went on to make a speech containing several contentious statements and many errors of fact, ones obvious enough to cause several peers as to go so far as to interject whilst he was speaking, but he loftily ignored their interventions and concentrated his speech upon two factors which he said were inextricably linked: 'Let us never forget that this was a rebellion', and the idea that all 'punishment is deterrent'. Erroneous as both of these points were, and as pernicious as their linkage, he thereby managed to do the Government considerable damage:

> Do not let us think too much of General Dyer. I know that he did some things of which many of your Lordships do not approve. I agree. I do not approve of them myself, and much less do I approve of all that he said, though that is a minor matter. But what is the broad question? It is this; are officers to be supported by Government if they do their very best in positions of great difficulty? ... There is a need to teach Indians that self-government does not mean disorder. Order must be maintained.

Order was a cry around which the peers had little difficulty in rallying. The Lords divided: 129 were for the motion, eighty-six against, so the House was for Dyer. Most of the upper levels of the aristocracy there that day voted for Dyer; those content with Finlay's motion included eight dukes, six marquesses and thirty-one earls. Those not content included numbered no dukes, only two marquesses and nineteen earls. All but one of the Law Lords voted to support Dyer.

It was a humiliation for the Government and must have gladdened Dyer's heart when he heard the news. It was one more nail in Montagu's coffin. On 11 August he wrote to Chelmsford: 'I am infinitely depressed and nothing but a determination not to desert the policy for which you and I stand, gives me the heart to go on with my work.'[22]

The votes in both Houses had no effect on Government policy, though their victory in the Lords was a great boost to its opponents and was a clear indication of the growing power of the Conservative element in the coalition. The two debates had, however, longer lasting implications. For Edwin Montagu they were personally disastrous. After the debates, ninety-three Members of Parliament signed a petition calling on him to resign. He did not, but staggered on in his post, a lame duck increasingly at odds with Chelmsford and in less and less sympathy with his ministerial colleagues. In March 1922, when he committed the indiscretion of publishing Government of India papers without the Viceroy's authority, he had no goodwill left to save him, and he was peremptorily sacked by Lloyd George. In the election of 19 October that year, which saw the Conservatives take power and the almost total annihilation of the Liberals, he lost his seat, and he died in 1924 aged only forty-five. The coalition did not survive the election of 1922. Its Conservative wing had come to realise that it neither liked nor needed Lloyd George and his Liberals. So the rift which started with the Amritsar debates ended in Lloyd George's downfall, a Conservative landslide and the eclipse of British Liberalism.[23]

In India, there were even greater and more damaging ramifications. They were not foreseen at all by the Viceroy, who continued to the end of his tenure in April 1921 to have understanding neither of the people he ruled nor of the massive forces that had by then been unleashed in India. To the end, he paid greatest attention to the bureaucratic niceties of the system of rule he exemplified. After the debates, he telegraphed Montagu to say that he was disappointed with the result; while he liked Curzon's speech, which he thought 'powerful and sympathetic', he thought that 'the speech by Lord Sinha was not vigorous enough'. The fact that the debates and the British reaction to them had finally alienated the Indian political elite was something he entirely failed to notice.[24]

The Government of India's failure to deal publicly with the officials and military officers censured by the Hunter Report was to become a grievance both with Montagu in London, and, more importantly, with Indian opinion. Despite Sir Michael O'Dwyer's assertion that many loyal servants of the Government had their careers ruined in the months following the publication of the report, this was not widely seen to be so, largely because the Government of India refused to publish its findings or to publicise its actions. The Viceroy felt it impossible to proceed with rigour against officials who had done less wrong than Dyer, who had avoided all punishment other than loss of his employment and a public censure. In the event, the military ignored the Hunter Report's censure of any of its other officers, promoting at least one of them. General Beynon had resigned as early as 1919, but does not seem to have come under pressure to do so. He claimed that he resigned because of his disgust at the way Dyer had been treated, but this is difficult to square with the date he submitted his resignation, which was months before any change in the Government view of Dyer, and well before the publication of any censure. Beynon may have had other, personal, reasons for his departure of which there is now no trace.

Of the civilians criticised by the Hunter Report, Kitchin and Irving did not escape censure, despite a rearguard action on their behalf by the Punjab Government and strong support for them from Sir William Vincent. Eventually, on 13 September 1920, the Government of India sent its findings about both to the Punjab Government:

> The Government of India must express regret that Mr Kitchin made the mistake either of surrendering his authority too completely or of not making it clear to all concerned that his surrender of authority was restricted to purely military dispositions ... They consider that [Irving] should have maintained closer and more responsible touch with the Military Commander throughout the subsequent events. In particular, the Government of India think that the Deputy Commissioner should have remained with General Dyer on the afternoon of the 13 April, when, so far as can be ascertained from the evidence, it was known to both officers at least from 1 p.m. that preparations were being made to hold a meeting in the Jallianwala Bagh in defiance of the proclamation which had just been issued to them. The Government of India think that having this knowledge the Deputy Commissioner ought to have offered General Dyer the benefit of his advice and shared with him the responsibility for any action that might be necessary to disperse the proclaimed meeting. They consider it most unfortunate that the Deputy Commissioner left General Dyer at this critical moment, in order to attend to other business in the Fort ... Nor do they overlook the fact that it could not be foreseen by them that General Dyer would take action which was greatly in excess of the action that an officer of his standing and experience might have been expected to take ... They were nevertheless regrettable errors of judgment, and I am to request that the views of the Government of India indicated in this letter may be conveyed to both officers.

This was sufficient to ruin Kitchin's career, and he resigned. Irving, though, stayed on to earn an eventual knighthood. The tardiness of the Government's consideration of their cases was typical, as was the secrecy with which their considerations were recorded. There was absolutely no sense within the Government of India that it owed its subjects an explanation, let alone that it should persuade them of the rightness of its policies. This was ironic given the fact that many members of that Government were highly critical of what had happened in the Punjab, as their judgments on Kitchin and Irving, and as their views of O'Dwyer and his policies expressed elsewhere, show. One at least of the Viceroys' Executive Council, C.W. Gwynne, certainly had no illusions about Dyer, and was prepared to put his views before Chelmsford:

> [Dyer] knew there was a possibility of a gathering two or three hours before he marched to the Jallianwala Bagh and he had the Deputy Commissioner and various police officers with him all that time. One can only infer he thought he had absolute control, that he had made up his mind what he was going to do if the crowd assembled in spite of his proclamation and that he was not prepared to share his intentions with the civil officers or seek their advice. If General Dyer had been an ordinary person he would have consulted the Deputy Commissioner before he took action. But he was a person of peculiar mentalities, he believed he had a mission in Amritsar, the mission of saving the Punjab and India from the horrors of mutiny, and he was determined to carry out his mission, taking upon himself the complete responsibility. I do not think the Government can blame either the Commissioner or the Deputy Commissioner for the resultant catastrophe, which would probably not have occurred had they had to cooperate with any military officer other than General Dyer.

All of this was tremendously sensible. But it all took place in very slow time within the conclaves of Government, and was seen by no member of the public. No good could come of it at all.[25]

Outside the confines of the Government, British India was largely delighted by the Lords debate, believing that the peers had vindicated their views. Their press, and they themselves individually, made this quite plain to the Indians around them, and so reinforced the catastrophic effect upon Indian opinion which the rhetoric surrounding the arguments in both Houses and the press had achieved. Those who had been prepared to believe that British justice could be relied upon to right the wrongs of the Punjab were disappointed, and the belief held by hitherto loyal and moderate subjects in the moral code underlying British prestige largely evaporated. Gratitude for the King Emperor's Address and clemency, and for the Montagu-Chelmsford reforms, was replaced in Indian minds by a horrible realisation of the contempt in which they were held by many of their British rulers. In place of loyalty came mistrust; in place of a copying of British culture and ways came a rejection of everything British.

The process by which this occurred was a gradual one, upon which the House of Lords debate merely set the final seal. It can be traced in the effect of events upon Gandhi's opinions and policies; the change in his mind from loyal reformer to the leader of unrelenting non-cooperation was probably the most momentous long-term result of the events in the Punjab. Up until December 1919 he held fast to his belief in Dominion-style self-government for India within the Empire. 'Plassey laid the foundation of the British Empire, Amritsar has shaken it', he said, but he still welcomed the King Emperor's Address. But by January 1920, as a result of the discoveries he had made during the Amritsar enquiry, his mind had become irretrievably altered, and that month he marked the transformation by returning his Kaisar-i-Hind and South African War medals to the Government. He began then to speak of the British Government as an immoral, satanic organisation with which there could be no compromise, and he was not to change this view again.[26]

Other Indian leaders were affected gradually by the inept policies followed by the Government of India in the follow up to the disturbances and, in particular, in its response to the Hunter Report. London had made clear in the King Emperor's proclamation its desire for reconciliation. The Viceroy's Government had no such belief. Despite the fact that the judicial reviews of the martial law court judgments had revealed the unsafe nature of many of the convictions, and had been enormously critical of the way the trials had been conducted, the Government of India pressed on with many of the cases not covered by the amnesty. Appeals for some of them reached the Privy Council in London, and were rejected; this had a disproportionate effect on the Indian political classes, many of whom were lawyers, and in particular upon the Congress Chairman, Motilal Nehru, who had personally represented many of the accused himself without fee. At least two men Motilal considered innocent were hanged. The *Tribune* of 28 February 1920 stated that 'the rejection by the Privy Council of the Amritsar case had dealt a severe blow to the whole scheme of Reforms'. Motilal Nehru had also hoped that the Government would pursue liberal policies in implementation of the Reform Act, but he and his colleagues were to be disappointed. The Government still considered members of the Indian National Congress as rebellious opponents, and excluded their adherents from the advisory committee constituted to frame the rules for the implementation of Montagu's reforms. Motilal Nehru protested to Lloyd George about this in February 1920, but in vain.

On 14 February 1920 an appeal was launched for a Jallianwala Bagh Memorial Fund, and this was to play a part in Indian consciousness similar to that which the Dyer fund played in the British. 'We are glad to inform the public that the Jallianwala Bagh has now been acquired for the nation.' At a cost of 540,000 rupees, a committee including Gandhi, Madan Mohan Malaviya, Motilal Nehru, Swami Shraddhanand, Harkishan Lal, Kitchlew and Girdhari Lal purchased for the nascent Indian nation a focus of martyrology that would help to light and keep lit the flame of independent nationalism. The *Bombay Chronicle* of

16 February kicked off the national press coverage, which soon rivalled that which the *Morning Post* and the *Pioneer* achieved for Dyer. The next month, this campaign received a huge boost with the publication of the Congress Report into the suppression of the Punjab disorders. 'What a shock the country received on reading the gruesome revelations. The publication of some of the horrific havocs on life and honour caused widespread alarm and resentment.' The report was widely read throughout India. Impressive in tone and compiled with extreme care, mostly under the personal direction of Gandhi, the report provided evidence of the suffering caused by the suppression of the Punjab disturbances, and in particular by Dyer's actions in Amritsar. The Government of India ignored the Congress Report, but no part of it was ever proved false. The differences between the British and Indian approaches were now clear for all to see in the print of the Hunter and Congress Reports, and it was not a flattering comparison.[27]

In May, after the Hunter Report was published, Motilal Nehru wrote to his son Jawarharlal: 'My blood is boiling since I read the summaries you have sent. We must hold a special Congress now and raise a veritable hell for the rascals.' The All India Congress Committee met at Benares on 30 May; they indignantly protested about what Hunter had revealed, but more about its failure to take account of much revealed by their own report. Amongst the resolutions passed were:

3 (d) That Parliament be requested to take such steps as are necessary to place General Dyer, Colonel Johnson, Colonel O'Brien and Mr Bosworth-Smith before His Majesty's Court of Justice in Great Britain for the cruelties committed by them in April and May 1919 in Amritsar.[28]

7.   That the All-India Congress Committee deplores that the Report of the majority of the Hunter Committee should be tainted with racial bias and a desire to overlook and justify the manifest and proved grave acts of commission and omission of the Government of India and the Punjab Government and the many acts of inhumanity perpetrated by officers appointed during the Martial Law regime and that it should thus accentuate the tendency to count Indian life and honour as of little consequence.

They decided that a special Congress should be called to consider the matter. Gandhi wrote of his own feelings at the time:

To my amazement and dismay, I have discovered that the present representatives of the Empire have become dishonest and unscrupulous. They have no regard for the wishes of the people of India and they count Indian honour as of little consequence ... I can no longer retain affection for a Government so evilly manned as it is now-a-days.[29]

Reports of the debates in both Houses circulated all over the country, and Churchill's criticisms of Dyer's policy of 'frightfulness' were quoted 'from scores of platforms in India'. After the debates, Motilal Nehru felt sickened by British attitudes and withdrew from constitutional politics, moving from a position of opposition to Gandhi in his *satyagraha* days to one in which he was the only front-rank leader of Congress to support Gandhi at the Calcutta conference in August 1920. At this, Gandhi's call for non-cooperation, to include the surrender of all Government titles and offices, the boycott of all Government public functions, of Government schools and colleges, and of the new legislatures about to be established under the Montagu-Chelmsford constitution, was accepted. Immediately after that, Motilal Nehru resigned from the United Provinces Council, abandoned his practice at the bar, burned his foreign finery, and put on *khadi*, the homespun cloth worn by most of the poor of the country. His granddaughter, Indira Gandhi, recalled seeing as a three-year-old child the bonfire in the garden of his house, the Anand Bhawan in Allahabad, as Motilal burned his British furniture and his clothes. His son Jawarharlal reached a similar position, if somewhat sooner; he had collected much of the evidence at Amritsar. He wrote:

> This cold-blooded approval of that deed shocked me greatly. It seemed absolutely immoral, indecent; to use public school language, it was the height of bad form. I realized then, more vividly than I had ever done before, how brutal and immoral imperialism was, and how it had eaten into the souls of the British upper classes.[30]

Rabindranath Tagore was in London during the debates, and was appalled by their intemperate tone:

> The result of the debates in both Houses of Parliament makes painfully evident the attitude of mind of the ruling classes of this country towards India. It shows that no outrage, however monstrous, committed against us by agents of their Government, can arouse feelings of indignation in the hearts of those from whom our Governors are chosen. The unashamed condonation of brutality expressed in their speeches and echoed in their newspapers is ugly in its frightfulness. The feeling of humiliation about our position under the Anglo-Indian domination had been growing stronger every day for the last fifty years or more; but the one consolation we had was our faith in the love and justice of the English people, whose soul had not been poisoned by that fatal dose of power which could only be available in a Dependency where the manhood of the entire population had been crushed down into helplessness. Yet the poison has gone further than we expected, and it has attacked the vital organs of the British nation. I feel that our appeal to their higher nature will meet with less and less response every day.[31]

Gandhi reacted violently to the parliamentary debates. After the first, he wrote of Dyer and his fellows in *Young India*:

> His brutality is unmistakable. His abject and unsoldier-like cowardice is apparent in every line of amazing defence before the Army Council … Such a man is unworthy of

being considered a soldier … No doubt the shooting was 'frightful', the loss of innocent life deplorable. But the slow torture, degradation and emasculation that followed was much worse, more calculated, malicious and soul killing, and the actors who perform the deeds deserve greater condemnation than General Dyer for the Jallianwalla Bagh massacre. The latter only destroyed a few bodies but the others tried to kill the soul of a nation.[32]

By August, Gandhi had lost all sympathy with the British, and could no longer be even polite to them. He wrote to the Viceroy on the 2nd:

The punitive measures taken by General Dyer were out of all proportion to the crime of the people and amounted to wanton cruelty, and inhumanity, unparalleled in modern times; and your Excellency's light-hearted treatment of the official crime, your exoneration of Sir Michael O'Dwyer and Mr Montagu's dispatches and, above all, your shameful ignorance of the Punjab events and callous disregard of the feelings betrayed by the House of Lords, have filled me with the greatest misgivings regarding the future of the Empire, have estranged me completely from the present government and have disabled me from tendering, as I have hitherto tendered, my loyal cooperation.

Reconciliation had been ruined by the Government of India's insensitivity, and the British reaction to the Hunter Report had permanently disillusioned the educated men who formed much of India's political classes. Sir Michael O'Dwyer's resistance to reform could in truth be said to have beaten Montagu, but the price of this rearguard reaction was to be paid in the next thirty bitter years of Indian politics, and the eventual dissolution of the Indian Empire in acrimony and bloodshed. To say that Dyer's actions at Amritsar had ended the Raj is as exaggerated a claim as that which made him the 'Saviour of India'. It is, however, by no means an exaggeration to say that Dyer's actions were the major factor in a series of events which ensured that it was impossible for the British to leave India in 1947 with honour and with the affection or respect of their Indian subjects.[33]

23

Retirement

The debates in Parliament had placed a great strain on Dyer's health. Immediately after they were both over, he went up to Harrogate for the first professional treatment he had received in England. He was now a civilian, so this he had to pay for. The doctors confirmed his affliction as arteriosclerosis, for which there was little treatment available except rest and the avoidance of excitement. The possibility of a heart attack or stroke was to be ever-present now. After leaving Harrogate, the Dyers accepted an invitation from Sir Geoffrey Barton to stay a while in his house in Dumfries. There they could be well away from the controversies of the capital.[1]

As they gradually returned to a sense of normality in Scotland, and as they nursed each other back into some sort of health, the *Morning Post*'s appeal gathered momentum. By 3 August the fund had reached £15,899, and the *Post*'s correspondent in Calcutta had another £3000 in a bank account there. By the 14th, it had swelled to a total of £17,254 12s. 10d. Letters in support of Dyer continued to pour in. On 12 August, under the headline 'Feeling in the East. Sympathy with the General', the *Post* quoted some of them. The Reverend E.R. Guilford, who had been one of the authors of the two letters Dyer had quoted at the end of his report of 25 August 1919, wrote: 'He not only saved us (the English) but the rich city of Amritsar from being looted.' The paper cited the resolution passed by the Ex-Officers' Association of Calcutta, expressing their 'indignation and amazement at the unjust treatment of General Dyer'. The Reverend D.C. Macmichael of St Andrew's Scots Church, Colombo, praised the *Post* for standing up for Dyer. On 14 August, the *Post* printed a letter from 679 British women in India which had been addressed to the European Association of India:

> As Englishwomen who know India, and the risk to the lives and honour of Englishwomen at time of rebellion … We appeal to you to champion our cause, which is also that of all Europeans in India, with a view to getting it [the judgment against Dyer] revoked.

Again, the fear of rape provided a scarcely veiled motivation for their support. Behind the scenes, Sir Michael O'Dwyer began what was to be a two-year campaign of harassment of every official he could reach in India and England in an attempt to overturn the policy of the Government and to clear the names of those who had been censured. He was not to be successful, but he became increasingly embarrassing to the Government and on one occasion forced his way into Lloyd George's waiting room in Downing Street before being denied admittance. The Dyer fund climbed to £18,773 1s. 2d. in September.[2]

Coming back down from Scotland before the winter of 1920, the Dyers went to stay with their son, Geoff, for whom they had purchased a dairy farm named Ashton Field just outside Ashton Keynes in Wiltshire. It was just to the south of the Gloucestershire border and not far from Cirencester. Ivon had stuck to a career in the Indian Army after the war, so Geoff needed providing for first. It seems that Dyer bought the farm, or at least paid the deposit, with his own money, as the *Post*'s subscription was still growing and none had yet been given to him. On 27 October, the fund had reached £21,115 18s. 6d, and when Edwin Montagu was questioned in the Commons in November about the Government of India's attempts to prevent its officers subscribing, the fund stood at £24,626 6s. 2d.[3]

At that point, H.A. Gwynne, the editor of the *Morning Post*, could see that the flow of contributions to the fund was now slowing and that the time had come to close it to further subscriptions. He and the owner of his paper, Lilias, Countess Bathurst, whose father, Lord Glenesk, had been the *Post*'s founder, now sought to make as much political capital from the fund as they could. The obvious thing to do was to make a very large show of the presentation of the cheque to Dyer, and this, perhaps, is what Gwynne planned when he invited the Dyers to meet the paper's proprietors in October. Surprisingly, this was not a proposal acceptable to Dyer, who may have felt that he had been sufficiently exposed to political manipulation. It is also possible that he could not face any more publicity at so early a stage. Annie may have feared for the damage the excitement might do to her husband's health. They refused to participate, and so denied the *Post* the triumphal splash it had planned. Gwynne wrote to Lady Bathurst:

> I entirely fail to understand Dyer's and Mrs Dyer's attitude of ingratitude; for both seemed to me to be the kind of people who would appreciate to the full all that the *Morning Post* has done for them, and when an opportunity was given them of meeting the Proprietors of the paper I cannot understand why they did not show in an unmistakable way their appreciation of what has been done. I shall say nothing to Dyer of course; for even if I did it would be no good for he has missed an opportunity which, for a man of his upbringing and temperament is a failure to me quite inexplicable. I, like yourself, never look much for gratitude in anything one does, but you would expect a man of that sort to behave differently.[4]

What makes this somewhat strange is that the Dyers were now beginning to move in South Gloucestershire and Cirencester society, at the pinnacle of which were the Bathursts, whose seat was in Cirencester Park, and to whom the Dyers were, though perhaps only on the fringes of their acquaintance, becoming known. Dyer had begun to recover sufficiently to get out in local society. On 13 October, he was a guest of Mr Richard Mullings at the annual dinner of the Cirencester Bull Club, the town's Conservative dining society. Some sixty members and their guests assembled at the Fleece Hotel, the guests, not unusually for the time, mostly military men; Major-General Sir Louis Bols was the most senior, and spoke after dinner of his experiences in the Palestine campaign. After a good west country eight-course dinner of oxtail and tomato soup, boiled turbot and lobster sauce, saddle of mutton, venison in redcurrant jelly, jugged hare and roast pheasant, wine jellies and custards, the club drank through its customary toasts – 'Church and King', 'His Majesty's Naval, Military and Air Forces', 'Prosperity to the Club', 'The Unionist Cause', 'Absent Members', 'A Speedy End to All Our Grievances' and 'Lord Bathurst' (who was absent that day, though he supplied the venison and hares). With all present by now considerably mellowed, 'The Guests' was proposed by Lieutenant-Colonel Wrigley, and each of them was asked in turn to stand to make reply. The local paper reported that 'General Dyer, who was accorded a rousing reception, spoke with deep feeling, and at the close of his simple and soldierly speech the company rose and cheered him with enthusiasm'.[5]

By the middle of November, the Dyer fund stood at £24,626 6s. 2d. The Post, baulked of a public presentation of the money, decided to draw a line and on 6 December it announced that the fund was closed. By then, the fund's treasurer had received the enormous sum of £26, 317 1s. 10d. The money had come in from all over the globe, not just cheques or transfers, but in many forms: cash, items of jewellery, stamps, even books to be sold for the fund. Many of the British Indian newspapers had taken part in the subscription, and individual contributors had ranged from the aristocracy – the Duke of Westminster sent £100, the Earl of Harewood contributed – to the poor who sent a few pennies. Many wrote letters accompanying their gifts, and the Post had by the end accumulated a veritable mound of correspondence.

Beneath the headline 'A Debt Acknowledged', the Post's article stated that 'A soldier's honour has been vindicated, and the stigma of national ingratitude been to some extent removed'. Reporting the closure of the fund, it stated that the sums received had included £9360 subscribed in India, and that 'Many of the subscriptions that have been received have been accompanied with the words: "To the man who saved India"'. Dyer had been sent a cheque, and his letter of thanks was quoted in full by the Post:

> I am proud to think that so many of my fellow-countrymen and women approve of my conduct at Amritsar, and I accept the token of their approval in the spirit in which it is offered. On my part my conviction was, and still is, that I was bound to do what I did, not only with a view to saving the military situation and the women and children, but with a view to saving life generally. No hesitating or half-hearted measures would, under

the circumstances, have served the purpose. The act I was called upon to perform filled me with horror, but the great sympathy and approval accorded to me by thousands strengthened my convictions and were a great help at a time of extreme strain. The thousands of letters received by you as treasurer of the Fund and by myself privately form a memorial which I value very highly, and I would take this opportunity of expressing my great regret that it was impossible for me to answer them all personally. I am very grateful for the splendid support given me throughout by the *Morning Post*, not only in upholding the cause, but also in opening its columns to the Fund and so enabling a better estimate to be formed of the general trend of public feeling in this matter. It is difficult to find words in which sufficiently to thank all those who have helped me, and I can only hope that others in similar difficulties may meet with an equally generous response from their fellow-countrymen. Your obedient servant, R.E. Dyer.

The *Post* thanked the *Calcutta Statesman*, the *Rangoon Times and Press*, the *Civil and Military Gazette*, the *Englishman*, the *Madras Mail*, the European Association, the Madras Club and Mr S. Robson for their help with the subscription. It concluded that 'The mass of correspondence which has been received, and indeed all the documents relating to the fund, will be handed over to General Dyer for his perusal as time and opportunity afford.' Money continued to trickle in after this, and when all had been eventually forwarded to Dyer, he received about £28,000. He was now a man of independent means.[6]

Whether it was the enormous outpouring of support he received through the fund, or whether he had over the few months of rest in Scotland and England been able to recoup some of his spirits, by the start of 1921 Dyer had recovered his poise, and was setting about returning to the world from which he had to some degree withdrawn. His life at Ashton Field Farm was a pleasant enough one. The farm, a late eighteenth-century limestone building, was surrounded by trees and had a sheltered garden at the rear. A courtyard surrounded by the other farm buildings formed the front view of the house. Inside, the thick walls and beamed ceilings made the spacious rooms cool and quiet. The farm was a few miles out of the village, tucked away in flat, luscious dairy pasture; the pace of life was gentle there. At last Dyer had the space, and the time on his hands, to return to work on his range-finder, but it was to his despair that he now found the mathematical calculations more than he could handle. The calculations made his head ache and he was forced to abandon the work. The range-finder was destined never to see the light of day.

By now Dyer, and the political factions with which he had been thrown into contact during the days of the debate, had realised that in his fame and popularity lay a potential focus for opposition to the Government's policy in India. The first sign of Dyer's emergence into the political forum was the appearance of an article by him in the *Globe* of 21 January 1921, one of a series which that right-wing evening newspaper was running entitled 'The Peril to the Empire' for which

Lord Sydenham and Sir Michael O'Dwyer had been earlier contributors. It was Dyer's first outing into political writing, and his article, headlined 'India's Path to Suicide', was intended to refute the idea of self-rule for India. More a series of unsupported assertions than an argument, it was not a well-written piece and would have persuaded few who were not already of similar views. The article reveals the self-regarding and self-referring world in which Dyer was cocooned, a world which may have had some reality before the First World War and the Punjab disturbances but was now already gone. The opinions Dyer exposed to public view now bore little relation to the current situation in India and show a mind still set in the mould of the imperial romances he had read as a boy. The article commenced with the words: 'India does not want self-government. She does not understand it', and continued that to 'the massed millions of India … the Raj is immaculate, just and strong; to them the British officer is a Sahib, who will do them right and will protect them from enemies of all kinds'. Dyer believed that only he and his class could speak for India: 'It is only to an enlightened people that a free speech and a free Press can be extended. The Indian people want no such enlightenment.' He went on in similar vein:

> There should be an eleventh commandment in India – 'Thou shalt not agitate'. All that the cultivator and the factory worker want is just and clear laws applicable to all alike. He does not always know why his passions have been roused and whether he is being misled, who is there to tell him but the Sahib? And now it seems that the Sahib is not allowed to tell him. He does not want an exchange of rulers.
>
> Our politicians are forcing a growth in pretending to India that she is ready for Home Rule. It is cruel to pretend that she is now approaching the era of self-government. India will not be desirous or capable of self-government for generations, and when self-government does come, it will not be the leaders of revolt who will rule. The very names of most of the extremists smell in the nostrils of Indian manhood.
>
> Our politicians like playing with vital affairs; but India should lie beyond the sphere of their jugglery. Self-government for India is a horrible pretence which would set the people of the country at each other's throats long before the beginnings of constructive work were made possible. Under self-government, India would commit suicide; but our politicians would be guilty of murder as associates in the crime.

Dyer took the opportunity to repeat his belief that the Punjab disturbances had been a rebellion nipped in the bud, and ended with an appeal to the British public and a threat to the nationalists, both trailing clouds of the Old Testament:

> And with this confidence I say that the time will come to India very shortly when the strong hand will be exerted against the malicious perverters of good order. A new star has not arisen in the East; a new era will not come suddenly. Gandhi will not lead India to capable self-government. The British Raj must continue, firm and unshaken in its administration of justice to all men, to carry out the job it has taken in hand.[7]

This was no longer a view that anyone in the Government of India could take, let alone anyone in the Government in London. The era when these words might have reflected the way the world was, if it had ever existed in reality, was over, destroyed by the education and by the development the British themselves had brought to India, by the war and all that had happened since, and not a little by what Dyer himself had done. The Duke of Connaught was even then in India on an official visit, the principal aim of which was reconciliation. A few days after Dyer's article was printed, the Duke, on behalf of the King Emperor, opened the new Legislative Assembly that the Montagu-Chelmsford reforms had instituted. In his speech the Duke said: 'The shadow of Amritsar has lengthened over the fair face of India', and he expressed 'deep regret for the administration at the perpetration of these improper actions', promising India that 'any repetition would be forever impossible'. On that occasion, even the arch-conservative Sir William Vincent brought himself to express to the assembly 'deep regret that the canon of conduct for which the British administration stands had been violated by some of the acts of certain individual officers'. The whole tone of the British administration in India was changing. Chelmsford's replacement as Viceroy, Lord Reading, scandalised British India by making Amritsar his first visit after arriving in post. He visited the Jallianwala Bagh, and ordered an increase in the compensation paid to its victims. Dyer's views had been left behind.

It was about the time of the article in the *Globe* that Dyer began to take steps to remedy the discrepancy between the rank of colonel in which he had retired and the rank of brigadier-general to which he believed he was entitled. To all his supporters, he remained 'General Dyer', yet he was not so. He had lost his temporary rank when he forfeited command of 5 Brigade, and so was in reality now merely a colonel. The custom of the service was that those retiring after some years holding a temporary rank were granted the courtesy of using it thereafter, but such a privilege had not been accorded Dyer. Perhaps someone pointed this out to him; he may not have realised that he needed permission to go on calling himself 'General'. When he woke up to this, he wrote on 25 January 1921 to the War Office to apply to retain the honorary rank of brigadier.[8]

His letter initiated a bureaucratic rigmarole that was to last a year, and was to reopen the argument between Edwin Montagu at the India Office and the Army Council. It was very bad luck indeed for Dyer that the India Office was about to receive from the War Office the delegated power to grant the retention of honorary rank by brigadiers of the Indian Army. This was a result of a proposal the India Office itself had made to the War Office just two weeks before, a proposal entirely unconnected with Dyer's case, which had not been foreseen. The delegation of power was agreed, on the 18th, by the Secretary of State for War, who was by then no longer Churchill but Sir Worthington Laming

Worthington-Evans, one of those who had loudly heckled his predecessor during the Dyer debate of July. When Dyer's letter arrived, the War Office, perfectly correctly under the new circumstances, instructed him to make an application to the Under-Secretary of State at the India Office. Dyer did so on 9 February. The India Office was now caught in a trap of its own making and sought to stall for time. To start with, they adopted the line that the official delegation of authority from the War Office had not been made until 11 March, which was technically correct as the appropriate order had not been issued until then. This was, of course, after Dyer's application; after sitting on his request until 15 March, the India Office sent the documents back to the War Office asking that they take the necessary action. There, the Military Secretary circulated Dyer's papers on 1 April, seeking views from the Military Members of the Army Council. They were, he said, entitled to recommend that Dyer be granted the honorary rank of brigadier-general under article 81 of the royal warrant. This said:

> An officer upon whom the local or temporary rank of Brigadier-General, Major-General, Lieutenant-General, or General has been conferred in time of war under Article 66 may, if he is recommended by our Army Council, be granted on retirement the honorary rank of Brigadier-General, Major-General, Lieutenant-General, or General respectively.

It was the Military Secretary's view that, although the Army Council had told Dyer in their ruling of the previous July that they considered 'he had made an error of judgment', they had also carefully said then that they 'did not propose to take any disciplinary action'. There 'accordingly seems to be no reason why the honorary rank should be withheld'. The Military Members of the Council were of similar mind. On 12 April they wrote to the India Office advising them to publish Dyer's honorary rank in the *London Gazette* of 25 April, but the India Office, frightened of the public furore that might arise, would still not take the responsibility for this and asked the Army Council to do it. The publication date slipped by and Dyer's chance of keeping his rank was missed.[9]

Oblivious of all this, Dyer was now working on his book, *Raiders of the Sarhad*, the story of his campaign in East Persia which was to be published during the year. It may very well have been the preparations for this forthcoming publication that stimulated his desire to clarify his rank. The book was to be his claim to a place in history, and he will have wished to be remembered as a general, and to place, as he eventually did, that rank on its cover. He wrote the book in the peace of Ashton Field, unaided except for the help of his friend, secretary and typist, Miss Stout. The book reads very well as a military adventure of the 'Boy's Own' type it was intended to be, an intention Dyer made plain in its sub-title, *Being the Account of a Campaign of Arms and Bluff against the Brigands of the Persian-Baluchi Border during the Great War*. The sub-text, though, was the establishment of the Dyer myth and the demonstration to the public and to history of the bluff, honest and soldierly antecedents of the hero of the Punjab. That his account was selective, that it was in places dishonest, and that it concealed much of a campaign that had at times been considerably lacking in soldierly skill, was not something which his readers then and now, unaided by recourse to the files of the Public Record Office, could have been expected to discover for themselves. The book did its job, and, when H.F. & G. Witherby of High Holborn published it later in the year, it established an image of its author that was to last for nearly eighty years.[10]

Raiders of the Sarhad was launched with the help of a lecture series, one of which was recalled later by a correspondent to the *Evening Standard* who remembered Dyer lecturing in London: 'He was cheerful, interesting and even eloquent. But it was curious to see the way in which he was constantly on the verge of referring to Amritsar, and then restraining himself by what seemed to be almost a physical effort.' Dyer had not succeeded in laying his own ghosts. But, for the time being, his morale was bolstered by the continuing signs of support from well-wishers amongst the public, and by another event, this time one at which he, and we may assume also Annie, agreed to be present. Lord Sydenham, Chairman of the Indo-British Association, had been sent a memorial book of signatures collected by the committee of British women who had supervised the Dyer subscription campaign in India, and who asked him to present it to Dyer on their behalf. Sydenham says in his memoirs that: 'I felt it an honour to present to the General on April 8, 1921, a Memorial signed by the British women in India, who well understood what they owed to him.' It appears that he did not read its contents too closely, as this is probably the volume now in the possession of Dyer's great-grandson, Martin Dyer, which is entitled: 'Memorial to Brig. Gen. R.E.H. Dyer CB', bound in purple leather, decorated with the badge of the European Association of India as well as Dyer's crest, a ram's head above a coronet, with his motto 'Che Sara Sara'. Inside the cover is a list of the branches of the European Association with their addresses and the names of their officers. The Memorial is dedicated:

To Brigadier-General H.E.R. [sic] Dyer CB

We the three thousand four hundred and ninety-five residents of India, who have signed this Memorial realize the grave conditions of this country before and during the month of April 1919, desire to place on record and convey to you our considered opinion.

We believe that you were fully justified in looking beyond the immediate situation which faced you in Amritsar on April 13th, 1919; that the charges against your honour and humanity are utterly unfounded, and that you have received at the hands of those in authority the most unjust and unmerited treatment.

We are thankful that an occasion of great danger and responsibility found in you a man prepared to act without regard to personal consequences and we therefore wish to express to you our gratitude for your share in suppressing the rebellion in the Punjab as we consider that your courage and resolution saved India from a greater catastrophe.

We hope that the knowledge that you retain our confidence and support may in some measure compensate you for the injustice with which your active Military career has been terminated.

The signatures, names and addresses of the 3495 subscribers make up the rest of the volume. A gold watch was also presented to Dyer by his Indian admirers. Despite the intentions of the Dyer Fund Committee, a sword of honour was never presented, though the earlier reports that such was the intention have left echoes in various accounts which state that the intention was fulfilled.[11]

As Dyer continued returning to activity and better health, spending the year writing his book and lecturing groups upon his Sarhadd campaign, his application for honorary rank continued to spread ripples in the bureaucratic pond, ripples which eventually reached the Government. Edwin Montagu, in whose department Dyer's application had again by now come to rest, sought the Viceroy's views in May. The Viceroy replied that he thought it best that the request be deferred, on the grounds that any grant which appeared in the *Gazette* 'would revive bitterness' in India. Montagu supported a line to which he was in any case personally inclined, but the Army Council felt as little like conceding to the India Office's view as it had the year before. In June, they wrote to the India Office to support Dyer's application, bolstering their own preference for this course with the argument of precedent. This was actually firmer ground, for it had always been the case that a period of six months' satisfactory service in a higher rank had allowed retention of that rank on retirement, notwithstanding the fact that an officer might have been removed from a post for which he had been found not up to standard.

This was exactly what had happened to Dyer, and was indeed all that the Army Council's own decision of the previous July had allowed to happen to him. The Army Council now stated that they felt 'bound to consider the question from a military and not a political aspect, and, if they are overruled, they urge that this must be made public', pointing out that 'the recommendation of the Government of India that Colonel Dyer should be compulsorily retired was not approved by the Cabinet, and his retirement was voluntary'. Montagu, in whose hands the decision actually lay at that point, but who was unwilling to act against the War Office's advice, nevertheless wrote to object to their view. He was supported in this by two telegrams from the Viceroy which arrived in July. These claimed that the Government of India had always been asked to acquiesce in such grants in the past, and stated that in this case they refused to do so. Montagu's room for manoeuvre was not as great as he would have liked, as he was advised by his own department that, were he to reject the Army Council's view, they would be entitled to appeal to the Cabinet. His legal adviser also told him that it was possible that a refusal to grant honorary rank would be seen as 'further action of a disciplinary nature' which would run counter to the policy of inaction that the Cabinet had declared the previous year. Frustrated, Montagu wrote again on 21 July to the Army Council asking them to reconsider. They would not. They replied to the India Office on 21 September that it was 'their invariable custom, in granting honorary rank, to consider whether an officer's service has been satisfactory as a whole'. This, they evidently believed, Dyer's had been. By October, the issue was still unresolved, and a reply had not been sent to Dyer.[12]

The new Secretary of State for War, Worthington-Evans, was right behind his Military Members on this issue. In October, the issue reached his tray as his department had been unable to break the impasse. He wrote to Edwin Montagu on 6 October saying that he was in favour of recommending to the Cabinet that Dyer retain his rank. He pointed out that Dyer was universally called 'General Dyer' in India, so the award would have little practical effect there. Montagu would have none of it; on 12 October he replied that this would be 'a new provocation to India, and I am compelled to oppose this with all my power'. He viewed such a grant as a new reward for Dyer, whose 'service was marred by a blunder which is largely responsible for the condition of India today'.

Worthington-Evans began to prepare the ground with his ministerial colleagues for a fight in Cabinet. He wrote to Churchill, who was by now at the Colonial Office, seeking his support:

> I cannot agree to administer what is in effect further public reproof of Colonel Dyer by taking away from him a rank which the proper authorities recommend he should keep. The Army Council would have to explain publicly that if the rank is withheld, it is done entirely on political grounds, and this would be an impossible situation.

Churchill, surprisingly in view of his opinion of Dyer, agreed. In the light of the fact that the Army Council, in its judgment against Dyer, had set its face against taking any further action, and that this was now a policy confirmed by the Cabinet and announced in the House, he replied: 'It appears to me that to deprive Dyer of the rank which he held while on the active list would certainly amount to further action in this sense, and I shall therefore support you in resisting the proposal.'

The scene was set for a bruising confrontation in Cabinet, but at the last minute Montagu was saved the effort of fighting his corner. On 10 November, General Sir Claude Jacob, the Chief of the General Staff in India, who happened to be in London, called at the War Office and discussed Dyer with General Creedy, the Adjutant-General. Jacob was firmly of the view that Dyer should not be granted honorary rank due to the forthcoming visit to India of the Prince of Wales and the effect that this news might have on his visit. Clearly, the senior members of the Army in India were not numbered among Dyer's friends; the accusations of failing to support a subordinate, made against them all over India, had stung them badly, and it is likely that the military had been behind the Viceroy's rejection of Dyer's application from the first. In the face of this advice from one of the most senior soldiers in India, and in particular because of the linkage which he had cleverly made with the Royal Family, Creedy circulated to his colleagues a recommendation that the Army Council should withdraw its support for Dyer's retention of rank. The CIGS and the DCIGS concurred, though the QMG and the Military Secretary even now would not alter their minds. Although the issue had been pencilled in to go before the Cabinet in December, it was quietly dropped. As the Army Council's objections had vanished, Dyer's application could now be rejected by the India Office alone. It seems that they did not even do him the courtesy of a reply to his letter.[13]

There was, though, by now no real need to reply, for Dyer was lying in Cirencester Hospital, stricken by a stroke which had felled him while he was on the farm. The stroke partially paralysed him, adding to the loss of power he had already experienced in his lower limbs after the fall from his horse three years before, and thrombosis had set in subsequent to the stroke. It seemed to his doctors and to Annie that he was likely to die, for he signed his will in the hospital on 14 November, with his solicitor, R.W. Ellett, and Mary Warner, the hospital matron, as witnesses. The launch of an active public life as writer, speaker and campaigner had been more than his body could cope with. His arteriosclerosis, his continuing mental anguish and its resulting depression had caught up with him at last. From now on he would eke out the remainder of his life as an invalid, unable to walk, confined as a recluse to the farm, and with constant need of nursing and care. His brief resurgence was over.[14]

When he had recovered enough to be moved, he was taken to convalesce in Elmsleigh, the house of a doctor in the village of Bassett, just north of Southampton. An invitation from Countess Bathurst reached Annie there just after Christmas. She replied on 28 December:

Dear Lady Bathurst, Your kind invitation has followed me about and has only just reached me. I am so sorry to have been unable to come, but I cannot leave my husband at all. We are in a doctor's house here, and are very comfortable. It is such a relief to have a doctor on the spot. My husband is very feeble. He has had all the best advice, and there is nothing to be done but to try and ease suffering. He sees only his sisters now. Your son has not made his maiden speech yet, has he? I have been watching as well as I could but I have so little time. We are all looking for great things from him in the future. Yours sincerely, A. Dyer.[15]

The next few years are as complete a blank as Dyer's life had become. He and

Annie remained at Ashton Field, visiting no one, seeing family and perhaps a few close friends. Geoff managed the farm, and made a success of it. Probably using some of the money from the fund, he went into partnership in Cirencester some time in 1923 with Joshua Bower, a businessman from nearby Somerford Keynes. Together they set up a retail dairy outlet at 173–75 Cricklade Street in Cirencester, naming it the Gloucestershire Dairy. It did well, and the premises expanded to the rear in Ashcroft Road. Later, they opened shops and depots in other towns, and by 1926 the company was trading as the Gloucestershire Dairy Company Ltd, had three retail outlets in Cheltenham, as well as the one in Cirencester, and had acquired dairy farms at Cheltenham and Charlton Kings. The company had a depot at Imperial Lane, Cheltenham, where they processed and distributed their milk. Geoff bought Bower out at some point and continued the business on his own.

Ivon came home from India in March of 1923. He had spent most of his time in regimental duty in Waziristan on the Frontier leaving poor Phyllis back in the family lines.[16] They came home together, and their first son, Rex Mulroney, was born in August while they were on leave. He was christened in Newquay in Cornwall. It is unlikely that Rex Dyer was able to travel that far to be there, though Annie probably was. He had missed both his son's wedding and the christening of his grandson.[17]

For one final time in his lifetime, Dyer's deeds at Amritsar appeared once more in the public eye, this time as the key factor in something of which he was given no knowledge at all until it was over. In 1924, some three years after Dyer had been isolated from all society by his stroke, Sir Michael O'Dwyer went to law in London to sue the Indian politician Sir C. Sankaran Nair, who had published a book in India some two years before entitled *Gandhi and Anarchy*. Nair had been a member of the Viceroy's Executive Council until he had resigned in July 1919 in protest against the Viceroy's refusal to repudiate what had been done in the Punjab under martial law. He was a moderate, a supporter of the Montagu-Chelmsford reforms, and had become very much opposed to Gandhi's non-cooperation policies, which he wrote his book to attack. He had not, however, forgiven Sir Michael O'Dwyer for what had happened in the Punjab, and he took a side-swipe at him in the book: 'The conditions now have entirely changed. Before the reforms it was in the power of the Lieutenant-Governor, a single individual, to commit the atrocities in the Punjab which we know only too well.'[18]

Sir Michael O'Dwyer asked for a retraction, an apology, and the donation of £1000 to charities of his choosing. He saw the opportunity to vindicate himself and his subordinates in public in England – indeed he specifically stated after the trial that he had brought the case with the intention of vindicating Dyer –

but his choice of solicitors in the firm of Sir William Joynson-Hicks makes it plain that the case also had political objectives from the start. In the interview he gave after his victory at the trial, he was to claim that the case 'had vindicated British rule in India'. Nair refused to retract what he had written, denying that his words were defamatory, and said that they were true in fact and fair comment on a matter of public interest. He applied to have witnesses in his defence examined on commission in India. This took considerable time, but eventually one hundred and twenty-five witnesses were examined there during 1923. The case came before Mr Justice McCardie in the King's Bench Division on 30 April 1924. It was to last for five weeks.

O'Dwyer was represented by Mr Ernest Charles, KC and Sir Hugh Fraser; Nair by a team of three led by Sir Walter Schwabe. The jury of nine men and three women included, though it was not spotted by O'Dwyer's team, Harold Laski, a lecturer at the LSE and a friend of George Lansbury, the Labour MP active with the Indian National Congress. Sir Michael O'Dwyer called a very large number of witnesses, and the trial was a unique occasion, collecting together for the first time in one courtroom in London all those involved in the events in the Punjab five years before. Lord Chelmsford, by now First Lord of the Admiralty, was a witness, as was General Sir Charles Monro, who was now the Governor of Gibraltar. Major-General Sir William Beynon, who had been for several years in retirement, and A.J.W. Kitchin were also called, but Dyer was not. He would have been unable to attend, a fact perhaps convenient for Sir Michael O'Dwyer, as Dyer's outspoken self-justifications were what had largely sunk their side at the Hunter Committee. O'Dwyer's counsel were instead able to make play of his illness, Mr Charles telling the judge that Dyer was 'very ill – hopelessly', and giving the judge the impression he was dying. In the event, three more years were to remain to Dyer, but the court's sympathy was won from the start. Nair's team called fewer witnesses in England, among them Gerald Wathen, who had by then returned from the Punjab.

At the outset, Schwabe informed the court that the defence based their case upon the fact that Dyer's act had been an atrocity which had the consent and later the blessing of Sir Michael O'Dwyer. Dyer's action thus became one of two main points at issue. O'Dwyer was lucky in that McCardie was a judge somewhat notorious for his outspoken and reactionary comments on many topics of the day. He came to the trial with very fixed ideas of the nature of the violence in the Punjab, ideas which were similar to those of the plaintiff. At the beginning of the trial, McCardie told the jury 'that where the safety of the Indian Empire was in question and through that the safety of the British Empire, perhaps it might be necessary to do things which would not be justified in other circumstances'. This was Dyer's case in a nutshell, and the five weeks of the trial might as well have stopped there. From his comments at the trial, it is clear that McCardie shared

O'Dwyer's intention of vindicating Dyer: 'I wish to see that this man who is dying has a fair hearing from a living jury.'

During the trial, the judge frequently interrupted questioning to disagree with the defence counsel, and continually affirmed the justice of what Dyer had done. Questioning Wathen, who had said that he believed that Dyer should have warned the crowd in the Bagh and not fired for such a length of time, McCardie asked: 'Warning should have been given even if it were useless?' In an exchange directed at Sir Walter Schwabe, who was then trying to question O'Dwyer, the judge said: 'If General Dyer's force had been surrounded and destroyed, no one with the faintest imagination can doubt that Amritsar would have been delivered over to anarchy. You seem to be ignoring the appalling consequences.' On another occasion McCardie interjected: 'Can a man be said to be guilty of an atrocity when he is acting with complete integrity?' He openly disapproved of the Hunter Committee, and indicated that he thought the officials censured by the Government of India had been punished for reasons of political expediency.

General Beynon took the stand at one point and added perhaps the only fresh piece of information to emerge at the trial. He said that he had asked Dyer, after the latter had given evidence to the Hunter Committee, 'Why did you say that you went down with the intention of firing?' Dyer had replied: 'I intended to fire if necessary.' Beynon had retorted: 'That is not the impression which you have given the Committee.' The sting was, of course, in the word 'necessary'. From Dyer's own evidence to the Hunter Committee, it is clear that he viewed it 'necessary' to open fire if he found the crowd assembled in the Bagh when he got there. Beynon's assumption, following Dyer's earlier story and his knowledge of military regulations, was that what Dyer meant by 'necessary' was that he had to fire because of a danger to his force or to disperse the crowd. Beynon really had believed the original story Dyer had told him back in April 1919. It is clear that Dyer, cornered by his superior outside the committee room, had once more been reduced to quibbling and leaving a false impression.

Whatever the effect of McCardie's bias, he was entitled, as the Lord Chancellor later stated, to give his opinion of the facts, but, although this was not binding on the jury, this could not but have had an influence on their verdict. The court was his to display his opinions, and his behaviour gave no legal grounds to seek to overturn the proceedings, even though the trial was a travesty of partiality. On 4 and 5 June, McCardie summed up for over seven hours. He indicated to the jury that he preferred the testimony of the Europeans to that of the absent Indians. In the particular case of Dyer, his guidance was that 'I express my view that General Dyer, under the grave and exceptional circumstances, acted rightly, and in my opinion, upon his evidence, he was wrongly punished by the Secretary of State for India'. There was applause in the courtroom as he concluded. The jury declared eleven for Sir Michael O'Dwyer, one – Laski – against, and he was awarded £500 damages and costs, which were estimated at the enormous sum of £20,000. Dyer's supporters were henceforth to be able to claim, and very frequently did claim, that he had been vindicated in an English court of law.

In India the effect of the trial was predictable. The *Tribune* called the verdict 'a wanton misuse of judicial authority', and C.R. Das tried to propose a motion in the new Legislative Assembly to have Nair's costs paid from public funds, but was ruled out of order. The European press exulted in the vindication of their views. In London, both sides of the House of Commons again took issue over Dyer. A Labour Government was now in power, though a weak one as it was in a minority. Ramsay MacDonald had become Prime Minister in January 1924, and Lord Olivier was now at the India Office. In his first speech in the Lords on 26 February, the latter had blamed the Lords' 1920 resolution in favour of Dyer for the current obstructionist policies of the *swarajists*. Now, in the Commons, Colonel Sir Charles Yate asked from the Conservative benches that time be given to debate an Address to the Throne to 'revoke the censure passed upon General Dyer after the incomplete executive investigation of 1920'. Ramsay MacDonald refused to provide such time, saying rather misleadingly that 'the findings of the jury contained no suggestion that Dyer had been dealt with unfairly'. From the left, George Lansbury gave notice that he would seek to put in train an Address to the Throne to have McCardie removed from the bench on the grounds that he was unfitted to carry out the judicial duties attached to his high office. Such an Address would have needed the assent of both Houses, and the Cabinet, meeting on 18 June, was aware that it would not pass in the Lords. It was also a drastic step for the executive to seek to remove a member of the judiciary for expressing his opinion, and the Cabinet shied away from it. They were not content, though, simply to ignore McCardie's words, and the Cabinet left it to Ramsay MacDonald to deal with the matter. The Prime Minister addressed Lansbury's question in the House, and stated that: 'The learned judge was not informed as to what took place. As I have already stated, the Government completely associates itself with the decision by the Government (not merely the Secretary of State) of the day.'

With that, Dyer's case at last rested in Parliament. Lord Olivier sent a dispatch to India, emphasising that the Government adhered to the principle of the use of minimum force and that it maintained the view that it was not acceptable for an officer to take punitive action against one group of people which was designed to have an effect on others elsewhere. The Government of India repeated this in a proclamation. So the political furore surrounding Dyer at last came to an end, and although Sir Michael O'Dwyer spent the next three years agitating for Dyer's reinstatement, he could be successfully ignored. Dyer became lost slowly to public view.

After the trial, Sir Michael O'Dwyer wrote to Annie to tell her of the outcome, and she asked Rex's doctor if she could tell him the news. Dyer had heard nothing of the trial, all news of it being kept from him in case it excited him. The doctor believed that the good news would not be dangerous, and so Annie told him, and showed him the transcript of the trial with McCardie's charge to the jury. Dyer told his wife he was greatly consoled. The judgment may have eased his mind, but it did not still his doubts.[19]

Dyer's next two years passed uneventfully, with no change to his circumstances and little change to his health. There is evidence that the Dyers managed to maintain a circle of friends, and even to travel a little, attended by Geoff, who went with them to help his father and to take care of all the arrangements. Sometime in 1925 or 1926, Geoff began to court the daughter of Colonel and Mrs Seymour Paskin of the nearby Siddington Manor. Perhaps it was this that caused his parents, and particularly by this stage Annie, who had assumed control of all aspects of her husband's life, to think about moving out of the farm to leave Geoff to establish his own family home. In 1925, the Dyers took a lease of St Martin's Cottage in the village of Long Ashton, near Bristol, and left Ashton Field empty for Geoff. He married Margaret Paskin in late 1926 or early 1927. Why his parents chose a house at Long Ashton is unclear; perhaps they had contacts there, or knew the local landowners, the Smyths, who owned Ashton Court, the estate to which the cottage belonged.

St Martin's Cottage was about as secluded a home as it was possible to find. It was an old building, built prior to 1700, and had formed part of Kempe's School which had been opened in some neighbouring houses in the mid nineteenth century. At that stage the cottage had been a sanatorium for the pupils and then the headmaster's house. The school had closed at the start of the First World War, leaving the cottage free to be let. Kempe's School buildings lay around the end of a cul-de-sac leading off the main Bristol road which formed the village high street. Behind the school, and totally out of sight of the road, or even of the cul-de-sac, and reached only on foot by a narrow footpath squeezed between a hedge and a stone outhouse, lay St Martin's Cottage. Though itself secluded, it had a magnificent view out over the village and across the valley, countryside which ran uninterrupted as far as Bristol. Here, free from all prying eyes, and unseen even by the villagers, Dyer could sit in his chair in the garden when the days were fine. It was a place Annie seems deliberately to have chosen as a refuge from the world. The couple were visited here by Geoff and his wife Margaret, and occasionally, when they were home from India, by Phyllis and her two children, Rex and his sister, Eve, who was born in India in December 1924. Phyllis returned to England with the children by 1927, so was able to visit more often. The children's visits were one of the few things which enlivened the quiet into which their grandparents' lives had now fallen.[20]

Even at this late stage, Sir Michael O'Dwyer had not left off his campaign to persuade the Government to reinstate Dyer. He wrote in the *Edinburgh Review* and pressed Lord Birkenhead to act before Dyer died. Though the Government was by now a Conservative administration, they refused to act.

Beyond the walls of the secret garden surrounding the cottage, the village scarcely noticed that Dyer was there. He was later remembered by villagers being pushed about in a wheelchair. The local GP, Doctor Gordon Valentine, provided the expert care Dyer needed, and Nurse Grant, who came to work at the cottage, helped Annie with the heavy work of moving her increasingly immobile husband. For the most part, Dyer was a complete recluse, as the *Bristol Times*, with perhaps some exaggeration, recorded after his death:

> He just shut himself away from the world, his wife standing as guardian between him and the too cruel and curious public. Interviewers were never allowed to approach him, his wife dealt with all his correspondence and business, and though a few people in the immediate neighbourhood knew that he lived among them, none had ever seen him. Even the police of the district who passed daily round and about his house had never as much as caught a glimpse of him.

But this was not a quiet repose. There was nothing left to Dyer now but time, which stretched emptily hour by hour, day by day with nothing to keep his mind free of the demons that he had raised in Amritsar and which now returned to goad him in his seclusion. An unidentified friend, whose comments were syndicated by the Press Association at his death, made plain the torment that Dyer suffered in the long years when he had nothing to do but go over and over the events in Amritsar until he could not sleep:

> The stroke left him incapable of walking even, and five years followed of suffering with a tortured mind … He was broken hearted over the Amritsar affair. It played on his mind terribly, and to gain rest from his thoughts he used to read literally all day and night. When his eyes were too tired his wife, who was devoted to him, would read aloud. He always told me that if he were to react the Amritsar case a million times, he would always give the same order 'to fire' … He would relate how he had only eighty men against something like 20,000 Indians all armed with six foot poles leaded at the end … He would explain the incident in minutest detail again and again as if trying to relieve his mind, but never did he think he had made a mistake … 'It was the only thing a true soldier could have done in the circumstances', he would say, time and again … General Dyer was really the most kind-hearted and gentle man alive. He was just a big simple boy and hated to see others suffer … His grief was not only at having his career ruined. He was more concerned at having had to be the cause of so many deaths … Yet such was his gentle nature that after the inquiry and his return to England he would never allow a word of reprobation to be said in his hearing of any of the officers who had censured them. He always had a word of understanding for them, but with the politicians it was different. Those he never forgave, although he would never hear them run down in his

presence. He was never an embittered man, however, despite his ruined career. He was just a broken man. He was terribly sensitive and had a brilliant brain – more brilliant than anyone believed. He had a particular scientific turn of mind, and invented a field range-finder … He was so simple, so light-hearted and enthusiastic, so fond of outdoor sports and games. Then came the Amritsar incident, and afterwards he was a changed man. He lost his high spirits, his ardour, and enormous energies … We had hoped that with the present Government in power General Dyer would have been reinstated, but it is too late now … Then a fortnight ago he was taken with another stroke, and we knew the end was at hand.[21]

For over five years of unrelenting nightmare, Dyer remembered what he had done in the Jallianwala Bagh. What it was that fuelled his doubts Dyer never recorded, or, if he did write anything to explain himself in those years, Annie made sure it did not survive. All that is left now are his assertions that he saw it as his horrible duty to crush a rebellion that he feared would bring back the terrors of the great Mutiny of '57. Many others thought the same, but none then or since interpreted their duty as he did. Why, indeed, had Dyer seen his duty in this way, and why had he chosen, quite deliberately, to kill so many people in furtherance of it?

At this distance in time, and with the little documentation we have left, there can be no certainty in answering this question. To approach even a tentative solution we must use both Dyer's own words and the evidence from the course of his life. From these, three factors stand out to combine so fatally at Amritsar: Dyer's character; his view of the world and his place in it; and the situation upon which both these two came to bear in 1919.

Underlying everything was Dyer's unique and difficult personality. He was from boyhood an introverted character, shy and withdrawn, sensitive to criticisms and slights, at times almost cut off even from his military colleagues, who often failed to understand him. He could not endure being made fun of or belittled, and lacked the confidence to ignore threats to his position and to his public face. From his boyhood he was an outsider, a fish out of almost every water, forced to fight a very long and lonely corner against the world. He must have desperately wanted to belong. That the insecurity to which this gave rise could erupt in outbursts of fury and violence was well known to his contemporaries and does not surprise. Dyer had a very low flashpoint and an uncontrolled anger which he had no compunction about visiting upon his inferiors. This turned him, when it was sparked, into something of a bully, though he treated his subordinates very kindly when his temper was not aroused. In fact, he seems to have needed their approval and approbation, and to have gone out of his way to seek it, and to this end he developed an unattractive tendency to brag, to exaggerate and to mould facts to inflate his own myth. To form part of an image which he believed others would like and respect, he self-consciously emanated the impression of a simple, unsophisticated and honest soldier, which, though something of a smokescreen, was reinforced by his disingenuous and genuine lack of forethought and his frequent habit of opening his mouth then putting his foot in it.[22] He often acted as well as spoke without thought of the consequences, and thereby overshot the mark of what was reasonable to an extent which could place himself and others in peril. Often muddle-headed in considering the bigger picture, he was prone to misinterpret his mission and to exaggerate his part in it, and saw himself very much as a hero with a romantic role in the world. At times, this gave his actions the unreality of a drama in which the part he was playing came to substitute for the part he had in real life. This, too, could be highly dangerous to himself and to those affected by his performance.

He was ambitious, terribly frustrated that success had eluded him in his career, and desperately keen to prove to himself, and perhaps to the parents who had cut him off, that he could make a success of his life. He was ruthless in pursuit of any mission he set himself; any regulation or restraint that got in the way he would circumvent or ignore. He took his own advice and despised those who saw things differently, and would make up his own mind, independent of outside direction, then stick to it stubbornly. As he refused to listen to those advising against his plans, so he avoided any orders countermanding them from his superiors, and developed a habit of informing them of his intentions either too late or in too little detail for them to do anything to prevent them. When he had acted, he would report, in similar vein, only part of what he had done. This led him into paths of deception which were completely contrary to his public image and its reputation for honesty.

Dyer was far from being unintelligent in certain spheres, and indeed through much of his career he was pointed out as a modern, educated soldier. Where his interests lay, he had surprisingly creative intellectual gifts, and his development of the range-finder demonstrated technical and mathematical abilities of a high order. He was different here, a bit of a boffin, and it helped to set him further apart from his contemporaries, who did not understand his interests and wondered at his obsessive pursuit of them. In his propensity for the solution of mathematical calculations can be seen, perhaps, the operation of a mind that preferred to treat the problems the world presented as if they were equations which could be solved with absolute reliability, and which thus led to his adopting rational courses of action which were in reality far from reasonable.

Yet he was not at all deficient in emotions. With his family he was loving and kind. He was sweet with his children and very dear to his wife. He loved Annie devotedly from the day they met, and they clung together throughout his service, no matter what obstacle to his career their marriage might have posed and no matter what discomfort or even danger Annie faced in following him. Dyer had a chivalrously idealistic respect for womankind and placed them (as he certainly placed his wife, and probably as he had originally placed his mother) on a pinnacle. He was outstandingly good with his soldiers, to whose welfare he was genuinely dedicated, and to whom as individuals he showed compassion and concern for their careers. He related to his Indian soldiers in a way that few of his contemporaries could emulate. That, as well as the undeniable fact that he was a brave man, was why they liked and even venerated him.

Dyer's character made him what he was, but the way he behaved also stemmed from the way he saw the world and his own place in it. The system of beliefs by which he lived his life, those of a late nineteenth-century Army officer and of an Englishman whose entire life was lived in the isolated and segregated society of British India, reinforced the experiences which that life gave him. In India, he had been born into a society of outsiders, ruling yet fearing their Indian subjects. His whole life was spent in the service of a Raj which was under threat, a Raj which at its very apogee, at a moment when he himself was engaged in throwing its bounds ever wider, was beginning to slip away. As a child, he had been torn from his home, his family and all safety, and been sent to school where he remained in unremitting exile, and where he grew up enduring the imperial decay in Ireland. He had probably thought that he had escaped this when he secured his posting back to India, but this was never really to be so. When he returned home, he was cast out again after a very short time, and cut off forever from his family. As he saw the slow emancipation of India evolving before his eyes, he could, with justice, have feared that whatever security he had found was about to vanish with his whole way of life, as had the Protestant ascendancy in the Ireland of his youth. Beneath this quite rational fear lurked the deeper fears of what this might mean, fears generated by the carnage and defilement of the Mutiny, fears which he and his class had lived with all their lives. The horrors that this complete collapse of security might mean to Annie and his children were unbearable to think of.

And if India went, where did he have left to go? Not to an England where he was so much out of water. He felt truly an Indian, and loved both the country and its natives, though the latter only so far as they were loyal subordinates; here, imperial distance reinforced his natural aloofness. He had no racial prejudice, rather the reverse, and does genuinely seem to have preferred the company of inferiors in rank of any race; part of the awkwardness, perhaps, which prevented any close relationship with his equals. His prejudices were different, those of a soldier against everything civilian, and for those members of a settled hierarchy who knew their place and kept to it against those who placed themselves outside it. But woe betide any of these if they betrayed his trust or transgressed. The Empire was a hierarchy in which his place was the whole of his life. Although he was a Christian, and one whose language was scattered with biblical echoes, the Raj and India were in reality his religion, his 'bounden duty'.

So this insecure, self-opinionated, wrong-headed and violent man found himself in Amritsar facing what he believed was a challenge to his way of life and everything he thought it stood for. For over a decade he had been engaged in fighting Indian revolutionaries, and he, with most of British India at that stage, believed they were at the root of the disturbances then engulfing the Punjab. In Amritsar, he believed, he faced the core of an organised rebellion. The Indians then placed in his charge had shown the temerity to want to be free of the British, and had by their violence confirmed his worst fears for the future of his family and his caste; the logical conclusion to which he had come then was that the fate that had met the dead of 10 April was one which all of these would meet were he to show the slightest weakness. English womanhood had been ravished, the Raj attacked and shamed, and it was his duty, he thought, to prevent the collapse of all he held dear. He was afraid for the future, and he was very angry in the present, for he was being ridiculed, impotently followed by little boys beating the tin drums of his ignominy. His orders were being widely and publicly flouted. He felt the challenge personally, and he had never refused a challenge. Alone, as always, he made up his mind to face down this challenge whatever the consequences. All his experience, all his instincts, told him he must strike swiftly and hard against anyone who posed this threat. He would not consult, he needed no guidance, he would brook no obstacle, this was his moment and he would save the Punjab, India and his caste.

Dyer did not fire at the Jallianwala Bagh and impose the 'crawling' order because he was callous or bloodthirsty. Without a genuine emotional commitment to his caste and to the maintenance of their position, and his deep fear of what he thought faced his wife, his children and himself, he could not have reached his horribly mistaken rationalisation of what he felt he had to do, of 'my horrible, dirty duty', as he was ever after to call it.[23] This was something he could not express in words; who could? He let it slip, deliberately perhaps, on just one occasion, when he drafted his report of 25 August 1919. The words he chose then have puzzled readers of the report ever since, but they shine a light for once on Dyer's real motivation for the Jallianwala Bagh massacre:

> We cannot be very brave unless we be possessed of a greater fear ... My duty and my military instincts told me to fire.[24]

It was an extraordinary thing to write in a military report. It came from the depths of his soul. Dyer's conception of his duty arose from his fears. He had killed, and would forever believe he was justified in killing, to allay them.

On the night of 10 July 1927, a great storm caused the electricity to fail at the cottage, and the lights went out. Annie went into her husband with a candle, and found him very nervous and upset. Geoff and Ivon's wife Phyllis were staying with them that night, Ivon being in Mesopotamia with his regiment. The next day, Phyllis sat with her father-in-law, but he would not listen to her gentle words of comfort. The Jallianwala Bagh would not leave his mind even now:

> Thank you, but I don't want to get better. So many people who knew the condition of Amritsar say I did right … but so many others say I did wrong. I only want to die and know from my Maker whether I did right or wrong.

The end came later that day, when a stroke left him speechless. He gradually ebbed away, and died on Saturday 23 July with Annie next to his bed. His death certificate, certified by Dr Valentine gives the cause of death as '(a) Cerebral Haemorrage (b) Arterio Sclerosis'. In the certificate he was entitled 'Brigadier'. There was no post mortem. His family believed he died of a broken heart.

In the will he had signed nearly six years before and never altered, and which was given probate on 27 September, he left all his estate to Annie; it was not by then a grand sum, £11,941 1s. 1d., reduced after death duties to £6108 15s. 7d. It would seem that most of the fund had gone already to the boys. Annie had enough, though, with this and his pension to go on living quietly in St Martin's.[25]

The funeral service was held at All Saints' Church in the village, which was under a mile from the cottage. The coffin, draped in the Union Flag which had adorned Dyer's last Headquarters at Jamrud, was carried from the house and placed on a gun carriage drawn up in the cul-de-sac below the cottage for the short procession to the church. The gun carriage came from 75th Battery Royal Artillery, which was stationed in Somerset, and which provided an escort of eight men commanded by a sergeant. The service was conducted by the Reverend John Varley, the Vicar of Long Ashton, assisted by the Reverend Canon Yates, Vicar of St Mary's, Leigh Woods, the neighbouring parish. The mourners included many of the family. Annie led the list, supported by Phyllis, Geoffrey and Margaret. Alice, the niece who had been at Jullundur was there, with her brother Dr Douglas Dyer. Annie's mother, Mrs Ommaney, was present, as was Colonel Edward Richards, who, while Dyer had courted Annie, had courted her sister in India all those years before. Dr Valentine and Nurse Grant attended along with a smattering of local dignitaries; Colonel E.F. Knox represented the Bristol British Legion. One of Dyer's old Commanding Officers, Colonel Hamilton, of the 25th Punjabis, came with his wife; Dyer had been his second-in-command back in Rawalpindi in 1908. Wreaths were sent by Dyer's uncle James, his brother Edward, and by Geoff's parents-in-law, the Paskins. Others were from those who remembered his Indian days: Captain F.A.S. Clarke, whom Dyer had sent with reinforcements to Amritsar from Jullundur; anonymously, 'A Grateful Englishwoman who was in the Punjab in 1919'; another, 'From a grateful Englishwoman who was in India'. Flowers from Dyer's own garden were placed around his coffin.

The church was packed, and at the close of the service a bugler sounded the last post and reveille.[26]

Annie had stayed his support until the end. 'Upheld by a wife of dauntless spirit' was how *The Times* put it and such was indeed a just judgment. She would never cease to fight for the memory of her husband; as late as 1938, she was still taking up pen to the *Daily Telegraph* to give the lie, as she thought, to propaganda released by Goebbels's Nazi Party machine, an article in the *12-Uhr Blatt* of 15 November 1938, which had sought to use the Amritsar events to denigrate the British in India. She would never allow a slur to blemish his memory unchallenged. At the time Rex died, though, her life effectively stopped. She wrote later to thank Brigadier-General Edmonds for his letter of condolence:

> Up to the very end he said 'I should do just the same now'. His suffering is over and I can only be thankful for his rest, and very proud and grateful for all the expressions of admiration I have received. I am sorry to learn that you also have suffered. You can understand what the blank is to me.[27]

24

Epilogue

Grey skies blanketed London on Thursday 28 July 1927, and a steady rain fell upon the knots of people which formed in the late morning in Whitehall, lining the road from Wellington Barracks towards the Mall and huddling behind policemen in their dark waterproof capes. Dyer's body lay within the barracks in the Guards Chapel, having been brought that morning by road from Long Ashton, where it had spent the night in the church. A few people tried to gain entry to pay their respects, but they were stopped by the sentry on the gate and had to be content with standing outside. One, a white-haired old lady, carried a wreath with a card, which read: 'To the great, gallant, splendid, noble soldier, General Dyer, from a Major's daughter.' Two women who had been at Amritsar in 1919, perhaps recognised by the widow or others in the official funeral party assembling in the barracks, were allowed into the barrack forecourt as far as the steps of the chapel, where at 1.30 p.m. they watched Dyer's coffin being borne out by the eight Irish Guardsmen of the bearer party. The coffin was placed upon a gun carriage waiting in the rain and a procession formed up behind it, then followed it out of the gates and turned right in a slow progress towards Horse Guards.

The cortège made a colourful sight on that dull and wet afternoon. Behind a lone policeman on foot came the four horses drawing the gun carriage, each pair with a trooper of M Battery, Royal Horse Artillery, in braided blue tunics, polished black boots and busbies. Covering the coffin was Dyer's Union Jack, which had travelled with the body from Somerset, its colours of red, white and blue standing out boldly against the grey of the day. On top of the coffin glittered Dyer's sword and medals, and behind them the red and white plumes of his brilliant white solar topee fluttered in the slight breeze. At the front of the coffin lay an immense wreath of bright red carnations, subscribed by the old comrades of the 25th Battalion, the London Regiment, with a card which read: 'With the deepest respect and admiration of all ranks of the Battalion.' The Guardsmen of the bearer party marched on both sides of the carriage, resplendent in scarlet tunics and bearskins, their young lieutenant marching immediately behind the coffin with another, older, officer in wartime khaki service dress, Sam Browne belt and high, polished boots. Behind these walked the civilian mourners, sombre in black mourning, five pairs of men and women led by Annie Dyer, veiled, her arm supported by her brother-in-law, Colonel Edward Richards, and behind her

Ivon's wife, Phyllis, then Geoffrey and his wife Margaret. Dr Douglas Dyer and his sister, Alice, came next, then Annie's mother with the nurse, Miss Grant, and behind them three cars full of mourners. Last of all marched a throng of men on foot, fifty or more old soldiers of the Londons.[1]

The Press were out in force: every national and provincial paper covered the event that night or the next day, and the news was syndicated across the Empire. Among the reporters there, the representative of the *Yorkshire Post* commented that 'The unusual spectacle of a military funeral in the heart of London drew large crowds', and indeed there were many people standing in silence along the length of the route.[2] There was no band to provide music, only the tramp of marching feet, as the cortège moved slowly past the Guards Memorial then through Admiralty Arch into Trafalgar Square, where it made its way around the south side, past the watching statue of Sir Henry Havelock, the hero, appropriately, of the Mutiny which had overshadowed so much of Dyer's life. The carriage came to a halt before the west door of St Martin's in the Fields.

Awaiting the coffin on the church steps was a crowd of several hundred mourners and onlookers, sheltering from the rain under the portico or outside it under their own umbrellas.[3] The bearer party carefully unloaded the coffin and carried it up the steps, where they were met at the doors by the two officiating clergy, the Right Reverend L.H. Gwynne, Bishop in Egypt and the Soudan, and the Vicar of St Martin's, the Reverend William P.G. McCormick. Gwynne was a natural choice to conduct this service. His brother, Howell Gwynne, was editor of the *Morning Post*, and the Bishop had held the post of Deputy Chaplain General of the Forces in France in the Great War. He was a well-known missionary figure, a bishop since 1920, and his conservative political views had recently reached pubic notice when he had quarrelled with Field-Marshal Allenby, the British Commander-in-Chief in the Middle East, over the exclusion of Egyptians from the funeral of the assassinated British Sirdar of the Egyptian Army, General Sir Lee Stack. The Bishop had supported their exclusion.[4]

The clergy turned inside and preceded the coffin up the aisle whilst the congregation, which filled the broad aisles of the church to overflowing, sang the first hymn, 'Lead, Kindly Light'. St Martin's in the Fields was an appropriate setting for the ceremony, both in terms of the Baroque splendour of its early eighteenth-century architecture and of its national significance. In the centre of the capital on the east side of Trafalgar Square, close to Government and Court, it was the royal parish church. The arms of George I were emblazoned on the pediment above the west door, and that monarch's tenure of the first churchwarden's post in 1726 had initiated a long-lasting royal connection. At the time of Dyer's funeral, Queen Mary was a regular member of the congregation. St Martin's was also closely linked with the Admiralty Board, which, as did the Crown, retained a box in the chancel, and kept its own flag and a White Ensign at the rear of the nave.

The congregation that day reflected these connections. Many of them were military men: eleven generals, nineteen colonels, many more junior Army officers and officers of the other services. Two of these were family: Commander Hibbert representing his wife, Dyer's sister Alice, and Colonel Jack Gannon, Dyer's step-brother-in-law. Many of the others had been Dyer's colleagues. Major-General Sir William Beynon; Brigadier-General F.J. Moberly, Dyer's successor as Commandant of the 25th Punjabis, and by a strange twist of fate the official historian of his Sarhadd campaign; Colonel B.M. Hynes, Commanding Officer of 1/25th Battalion London Regiment, not there himself but represented by Captain C.A. Burt; Captain H. Hughes of the 56th Rifles, who had served under Dyer at Amritsar; Lieutenant-Colonel Smith, who had been the Civil Surgeon there in 1919, and who was representing Sir Michael O'Dwyer; another medical officer, that of Dyer's Brigade, Colonel Frederick Septimus Penny, who had treated him in the hospital at Jullundur; Lieutenant-General Sir Thomas Scott, who as Military Secretary to the Commander-in-Chief in India in 1919 had handled part of Dyer's case. The *Daily Telegraph* the next day reported that those present included 'the officer who said he had given the actual firing order that quelled the rioting', but didn't name him, so it is possible that they had been misled by someone seeking to claim the glory. There is no record of anyone who had been in the Bagh attending the funeral. It is clear, though, that many of those who had served with Dyer wished to register their support for him, as did large parts of the Army as a whole. The Royal Artillery, a corps with which Dyer had had no particular connection, made sure that its representation by Major-General Sir Richard Bannatine-Allason was publicly known.

Also there that day were many members of the imperial establishment. Major-General Sir Lionel Herbert, Chief Commissioner of the Andaman and Nicobar Islands; Sir George Arthur, private secretary to, and biographer of, Field-Marshal Lord Kitchener; Sir John Campbell, Director of Civil Supplies, United Provinces; Sir Bartle Frere, Chief Justice of Gibraltar; Sir Horace Mules, Head of the Karachi Port Trust; Sir Lionel Jacob, Secretary to the Government of India and Member of the Viceroy's Council. The Home Secretary of the day, by then Sir William Joynson-Hicks, informed the press that he was represented by Mr R.R. Millais. The historian and MP Sir Charles Oman was present. The Oriental Club was represented by its secretary, Colonel Cairns Wicks, who was the husband of Dyer's niece, Mary du Cane-Smith, and who represented Dyer's sister, Clare. The English Friends of Denmark League sent two representatives.[5] This was a gathering of much of British conservatism, although, it could fairly be said, of men of the second rather than of the very first rank. At the funeral of a mere brigadier-general, it was, however, an extraordinary congregation.

They sung the 23rd Psalm, then another hymn, 'The Strife is O'er.' Bishop Gwynne delivered the address, a funeral march was played, and finally a bugler sounded the last post and reveille from the balcony at the rear. At the last, the coffin was borne back down the aisle by the bearer party and once outside the church placed in a motor hearse for its final journey to Golders Green Crematorium. There were a very large number of wreaths from all over the world. One came from the officers and men of the 25th Punjabis, the regiment Dyer had commanded. Another bore the words: 'With deep and grateful thanks from one of the many hundreds of British women who owe their lives to this brave soldier in the riots of the Punjab, 1919'; another, 'from a few members of the Oriental Club', was sent 'In grateful remembrance of one who prevented grave trouble in India'. Rudyard Kipling's wreath bore the tribute: 'He did his duty as he saw it.' The wreaths and flowers were piled high on two cars and were taken after the service to be laid at the base of the Cenotaph in Whitehall, as Dyer himself had requested they should be.[6]

Outside the church the Press mingled with the crowd, collecting the names and comments of the congregation. One reporter interviewed Mr P.H. Nicol, Secretary of the 25th Londons Old Comrades' Association, who had been the Company Sergeant-Major of C Company of the Londons at Amritsar. He said of Dyer: 'He was one of the finest officers I have ever served under. We would have followed him anywhere.' His comrades felt the same. They were to record of him in their regimental history:

> It seems fitting to pay tribute to what is now, unfortunately, only the memory of one who was, in every sense of the word, a man – Brigadier-General R.E.H. Dyer, CB – who, as the result of brilliance and courage, doused, by his momentous decision, the rapidly growing flame which, generating from the Amritsar spark of the 10th April, 1919, assuredly was increasing to such a conflagration, throughout the length and breadth of India, as would have made the Mutiny of 1857 – terrible though it undoubtedly was – pale into insignificance … the man who, by his action that day, saved India for the Empire.[7]

This was not only the view of the regiment's officers, it was also that of the men. Sergeant Howgego, who was with Dyer at Amritsar, remembered fifty years later: 'General Dyer was a first class soldier condemned by people at home who knew nothing of India, his troops would have done anything and gone anywhere with him.'[8] The old comrades of the Londons present that day would have said similar words to Annie; it must have comforted her greatly. She did not linger long outside the church, and with a few other close mourners drove with her husband's body to Golders Green, where it was cremated. She had no memorial stone made to Dyer, and there is no known resting place of his ashes, though she did allow a memorial service to be held at Long Ashton the following week, on Wednesday 3 August.[9]

As the Press noticed, it had been an extraordinary funeral, a military parade through the heart of the capital with a service held in one of its most notable churches. This was not customary for even the most senior and eminent Army officers. It was a form of respect reserved for public heroes, but this funeral was that of a man who had retired in disgrace seven years before. We are left to speculate as to who arranged the political permission that would have been required to mount such a ceremony and to close the streets of the city, who provided the police on duty, and who was responsible for the provision of troops and gun carriage, and for allowing the body to rest in the Guards Chapel. The Conservatives were in power, and the members of the Government were now sympathetic to Dyer in a way none of its predecessors would have been. Joynson-Hicks was at the Home Office, and Worthington-Evans was still Secretary of State for War. It is probably to these two, particularly the former, that we may attribute the special treatment Dyer received. Neither, though, seems to have left any record of it. Perhaps events had to be handled too fast.[10]

The Press of the Empire covered both funerals, and in articles reviewed, praised or reviled Dyer's history according to their political complexion. From Rangoon to Tanganyika, Cork to Calcutta, Dyer was remembered and his name memorialised with an obituary in almost every paper. The *Morning Post* remembered him, typically, in articles headed: 'The Man Who Saved India' and 'He did his Duty'. The *Westminster Gazette* was one of many which took a contrary view, though few would utter much ill of the dead now: 'No British action, during the whole course of our history in India, has struck a severer blow to Indian faith in British justice than the massacre at Amritsar, and the attitude of official Anglo-India to it.'

In the conservative press appeared many letters of support for Dyer, many with reminiscences about him. The Reverend Norman Bennett, a garrison chaplain in Lucknow during the disturbances and an organiser of the Dyer fund there, wrote to the *Telegraph* from his vicarage at Crewkerne in Somerset: 'We were living in those days on the edge of a volcano, and it was absolutely essential that the strongest possible remedies should be taken if Europeans were to remain in India.'[11] An old soldier of the 25th Londons wrote from Weybridge to the *Daily Express*: 'He was one of the finest men I was ever privileged to know. His thoughts were always for those who served under him, but duty with him ever had first place … I am proud to have been a humble soldier in his command.'[12]

The Army had not forgotten Dyer, nor had much of it forgiven those who had insisted upon his disgrace. The *Army and Navy Gazette* said:

> The most that can in fairness be urged against him is that he did the right thing in the wrong way. But two wrongs don't make a right, and, whatever his mistakes, the Home and Indian Governments were to blame for their severe and unjust treatment of a brave and zealous officer and a loyal son of the Empire.[13]

Even those who had neither real need to remember him, nor anything worth saying, felt the need to satisfy their readers' desire for news of his death. The *Sporting Times* waxed into fantasy in an account which supposedly included recollection of the 1924 trial Dyer had been too ill to attend:

> It had been a dull morning, but as General Dyer went into the box to give evidence, sunlight broke into the drab Court, and lay like a benediction on the silver hair of the brave servant of the Empire.[14]

In India, the British Indian press continued its self-defeating campaign of rubbing salt in Indian wounds. The *Civil and Military Gazette* had a front page devoted to Dyer, and quoted Sir Michael O'Dwyer's words: 'General Dyer was the last man in the world to use force recklessly or until it was absolutely necessary.'[15]

Even with the funeral, the Dyer story was not yet quite over. Frustrated in his campaign to have Dyer rehabilitated, Sir Michael O'Dwyer now initiated a campaign to have a memorial built to honour his name. Oblivious of the fact that he had made himself so widely unpopular that the linking of his own name to such an appeal would, by that stage, be almost sufficient in itself to ensure its failure, he formed a Dyer Memorial Committee. As he explained later: 'Some of his friends and sympathizers suggested to his widow that his memory should be perpetuated in some practical form. Mrs Dyer asked a few people, of whom I am one, to advise her.' The committee set about seeking a suitable project. Perhaps Annie herself recalled that Lady Walker, widow of Sir J. Walker, who had been at one stage a partner with Dyer's father Edward in his brewery business, had endowed a small private hospital on land at Simla, and had opened it to the wives and families of Army officers. This seemed an ideal institution for a memorial to her husband, and the committee decided to endow a bed, or even a ward if funds were sufficient. It was not, though, intended to make a public appeal, as the committee, perhaps guided here by Annie's wishes, did not wish to reopen the public controversy. This did not stop them canvassing for money. Field-Marshal Sir Claude Jacob was asked personally for a contribution to the Dyer Memorial Fund by Sir William Beynon, who clearly had misappreciated his views. He refused.

In late October, the committee sent a telegram to the Walker Hospital to seek its views. Its members were probably unaware that the *ex-officio* President of the Committee of Management of the Walker Hospital was the Secretary to the Home Department of the Government of India, and so their telegram immediately found its way into the Viceroy's tray. Lord Irwin was by then Viceroy, and he sought information about the Dyer Memorial Committee from London. He told London that to add to what was by now the habitual embarrassment felt by the Government of India about the entire subject of Dyer, an additional complicating factor had arisen, for Indians had been admitted to the Walker Hospital for the first time that year. Increasing numbers of Indian officers now held the King's Commission, and a Dyer Ward would be at best an inappropriate place for their treatment.

Lord Birkenhead, the Secretary of State, telegraphed back that he advised the offer be declined by the hospital as to accept would leave them 'open to grave misconstruction'. So in January 1928 the Hospital Committee wrote back to the Dyer Memorial Committee to decline the offer, and to suggest that they might consider instead devoting their intended donation to an English institution for the benefit of families of Indian Army officers. Annie had no interest in a memorial in England. It is not clear why; perhaps this final disappointment over the benefaction may have made her decide that there was no fit place one could be raised. She wrote back herself to the Walker Hospital Committee to say that: 'The Memorial Committee agree that the controversy which might arise would be painful, and have therefore decided not to approach the Walker Hospital Committee in this matter.' There was to be no memorial. The controversy over Dyer was laid at last.

The Dyer Memorial Committee had approached Rudyard Kipling to write a dedication which they had hoped to place in the Walker Hospital. In the event, Kipling's ambiguous lines remain Dyer's only memorial:

These beds have been endowed as a lasting memorial to Brigadier-General R.E.H. Dyer, a brave man who in the face of a great peril did his duty as he saw it – 'he that observeth the clouds shall not reap'.[16]

Appendix

The Military and Legal Position Regarding the Action at the Jallianwala Bagh

Military theory in Dyer's day had yet to develop the complicated counter-insurgency doctrines which are the British Army's legacy of half a century of campaigns covering the withdrawal from Empire. In the early twentieth century, military doctrine was still based upon techniques developed during the period of aggressive imperial expansion. Dyer and his fellows in the Punjab did not have to hand the operation manuals and coloured cards giving rules of engagement with which their successors are now provided. That is not to say, however, that there were no rules to ensure that the military operated with restraint; there were, but they were looser in their formulation than those of the present, and they arose from, and were embedded in, a very different military outlook from that which prevails today. It is perhaps true to say that, whilst restraint was prescribed by the law and regulation, it was not something which the military believed gave them a moral or political advantage in a civil conflict. On the contrary, restraint was viewed in Dyer's day as an obstacle to the enforcement of military power.

As the principles of counter-insurgency campaigning had yet to be evolved, so had the military theory and methodology, what is nowadays called the 'military doctrine', which spring from them. In 1919, military theory lacked comprehensive definitions and descriptions of insurgency. The textbooks upon which the teaching of military schools was based, both before 1919 and for a considerable time after it, up until the Second World War in fact, would now be considered vague in their analysis, over-aggressive in their prescriptions and dangerous in the tactics which they taught.

According to generally accepted theory, counter-insurgency was one end of a continuous spectrum comprising all forms of warfare. It was seen very much as a uniquely military matter rather than as a civil or a policing one. At that time, the principal exponent of military doctrine covering insurgency was Colonel Charles Callwell, whose book, *Small Wars: Their Principles and Practice*, was used in military schools from its publication in 1898. Callwell divided wars into two categories, 'regular' and 'small'. Small wars, according to Callwell, could 'be said to include all campaigns other than those where both the opposing sides consist of regular troops' and so included what to modern eyes is the ragbag of 'wars of conquest', 'campaigns for the suppression of lawlessness' and 'punitive expeditions'. The linkage of these disparate types of warfare, some of which involved external enemies, others internal, reflected the experience of, and in turn had a considerable influence in forming the attitudes of, a generation of military officers who had spent their careers in wars of conquest (for instance in Upper Burma) and in punitive expeditions on the Empire's frontiers. This was very much the sort of experience which Dyer's career had given him. The linkage which Callwell established in the minds of his students between aggressive and very violent types of warfare, and the very different category of 'the suppression of lawlessness' was particularly regrettable, for it allowed the military officer to consider the types of enemy he faced in all these situations as one, and to adopt similar techniques for dealing with them.

Whilst Dyer never made this point in any of his public utterances, it is clear that the doctrine he had imbibed in his training, and the experiences which had shaped his career, formed the context in which he thought through the problems he faced at Amritsar. Significantly in this regard, Callwell specifically classed the 1857 Mutiny as a 'small war' and went on to say that wars of conquest and annexation usually passed into the suppression of insurrection and lawlessness at a later stage. As an example of this, Callwell cited a case of which Dyer was well aware: 'the same was the case in Upper Burma'. Here again, Callwell also made clear that 'small wars' included Indian Frontier campaigns, of which Dyer had enjoyed more than his share. Describing campaigns where 'no capital or political aim applies', by which he meant there was no conquest of enemy territory intended, Callwell wrote that there would instead be a tendency for a 'resort to cattle lifting and village burning', in which case such 'war assumes an aspect which may shock the humanitarian'.

> When, however, the campaign takes the form of quelling an insurrection, the object is not only to prove to the opposing force unmistakably which is the stronger, but also to inflict punishment on those who have taken up arms … Expeditions to put down revolt are not put in motion merely to bring about a temporary cessation of hostility. Their purpose is to ensure a lasting peace. Therefore, in choosing the objective, the overawing and not the exasperation of the enemy is the end to keep in view.

Callwell defined 'suppression of lawlessness' as 'the crushing of a populace in arms, the stamping out of widespread disaffection by military methods'. He also argued that against poorly armed and ill-disciplined natives a dramatic early blow would have a far more demoralising effect than against a regular opponent, and that over caution on the part of one's own side would encourage the enemy and endanger eventual victory in the campaign. He went on:

> It cannot be insisted upon too strongly that in a small war the only possible attitude to assume is, speaking strategically, the offensive … Enemy forces in small wars swell and contract according to the moral effect which is produced … The records of small wars show unmistakably how great is the impression made upon semi-civilized races by a bold and resolute procedure … and in no campaign has this spirit been more constantly evinced [than in the] Indian Mutiny.

We are a long way here from the acceptance of restraint later evolved for operations in aid of the civil power. Even when he wrote, however, Callwell's theories sat uncomfortably with the requirements of the law, and with the military regulations based upon them. Military theory was at dangerous variance with military law. When considering Dyer's appreciation of the situation he faced at Amritsar, and his plans for dealing with it, this is a factor which has to be borne in mind.[1]

The confusion which military theory showed in relation to aid to the civil power was to some degree mirrored by ambiguities in British law. The British constitution recognised war and peace, but did not take account of any situation which lay at any stage between the two. It had long been recognised in law that martial law would take the place of civil law if the latter became unworkable, but martial law was regarded as, in effect, no law, as an absence of law, and there was no legislation which embodied its procedures or guided its operation. The law recognised only that martial law was 'the exercise of the will of the military commander'. Despite this, however, those responsible for the administration of martial law were not free in British law to act as they pleased. Although during his exercise of martial law powers an officer was almost untouchable, he had to be aware that his actions would be measured later against the precepts of common law, the pragmatic, limited application of traditional legal doctrines, of opinion and of precedent. Contrary to military theory, the law saw it as an officer's aim to contain, not to extirpate, lawlessness, using minimal rather than exemplary force. A.V. Dicey's *Introduction to the Study of the Law of the Constitution* (1885), which was considered as an authority on the subject, emphasised the common law principle of 'necessary force', a force no more and no less than was absolutely necessary for the restoration of the peace. In his examination of the use of military power, Dicey did not distinguish different principles at work 'in the case of invasion, insurrection, riot or generally any violent resistance to the law'. 'Necessary', or minimum force as it was more usually known, applied to all; a state of martial law did not alter this. So, whilst the administration of martial law had to be left in an emergency to the designated commander on the spot, and he was entitled to make his own rules as he went along, he knew very well that he would have to justify his actions subsequently when civil law had been restored. This was the reason why Acts of Indemnity were customarily passed at the end of any period of martial law, as they were by the Government of India in 1919, in order to prevent an officer being called to account by those he had harmed in the legitimate pursuit of the restoration of the peace. These Acts of Indemnity did not, though, free any officer who had committed a crime, including using force going beyond what his duty could reasonably be expected to require, from subsequently being held to account.[2]

The law was embodied for the Army in the *Manual of Military Law*, and in particular in its chapter on 'Summary of the Law of Riot and Insurrection'. This divided situations in which the military might find itself coming to the aid of the civil power into three: unlawful assembly, which was designated a meeting which would seem to 'persons of reasonable firmness and courage' to 'endanger the public peace and raise fears and jealousies among the King's subjects'; riot, defined as 'a tumultuous disturbance of the peace' which had intent to execute its private ends 'in a violent and turbulent manner to the terror of the people'; and insurrection, which differed from riot only in that it involved 'some enterprise of a *general and public nature*' and an intention 'to levy war against the King'. In relation to dispersing an unlawful assembly, the *Manual* stated: 'The principle is that so much force only is to be used as is sufficient to effect the object in view, namely the dispersion of the assembly.' In the case of riot, the *Manual* indicated that a soldier might use firearms to suppress a riot if used 'in the fair and honest execution of his duty', but added that this 'can only be excused by the necessity of self-protection, or by the circumstance of the force at the disposal of the authorities being so small that the commission of some felonious outrage ... cannot be otherwise prevented'. Turning to insurrection, the *Manual* stated that: 'In such cases the use of arms may be resorted to as soon as the intention of the insurgents to carry their purpose by force is shown by open acts of violence, and it becomes apparent that immediate action is necessary.'

The *Manual* discussed the opening of fire on mobs which had an insurrectionary intent; a non-violent political meeting, it said, 'should be interfered with as little as may be'. For a violent assemblage, 'force should be repelled with force, care being taken to avoid any unnecessary bloodshed or injury'. The *Manual* considered the amount of force that should be used in each of the three cases, and prescribed that the use of firearms should be avoided in dispersing unlawful assemblies or riots wherever possible. However, 'an armed insurrection would justify the use of any degree of force necessary effectually to meet and cope with the insurrection'. The *Manual* also advised that 'an officer, therefore, in all cases where it is practicable, should place himself under the orders of a magistrate'. The three appendixes to this chapter of the *Manual* all expanded on the principle of the use of minimum force. The third, an opinion of the Law

Officers in 1911, discussing officers' responsibilities, said that: 'Should it be necessary for them to use extreme measures they should, whenever possible, give sufficient warning of their intention.'[3]

British legal principles applied in India and were embodied in local statutes and regulations. The law which governed the use of military force was enacted in the Code of Criminal Procedure, which made no distinction between unlawful assembly, riot and insurrection, and dealt with the dispersal of crowds under provisions for dealing with 'Unlawful Assemblies'. Sections 127, 128 and 131 of the code laid upon any magistrate and military officer the duty of dispersing any assembly which was unlawful, or any group of 'five or more persons likely to cause a disturbance to the public peace'. Section 131 of the code allowed a military officer to disperse a crowd when no magistrate could 'be communicated with', though it laid upon such an officer the responsibility of placing himself under a magistrate's orders when he could; 'but if, while he is acting under this section, it becomes practicable for him to communicate with a magistrate, he shall do so, and shall thenceforward obey the instructions of the magistrate, as to whether he shall or shall not continue such action'. Section 128 of the code (which also applied to military officers acting where there was no magistrate) stated:

> If upon being so commanded, any such assembly does not disperse, or if, without being so commanded, it conducts itself in such a manner to show a determination not to disperse, any magistrate or officer in charge of a police station may proceed to disperse such an assembly by force.

Section 130 of the code stated:

> A magistrate may require any commissioned or non-commissioned officer to disperse an assembly by military force ... Every such officer shall obey such a requisition in such a manner as he thinks fit; and in so doing he shall use as little force, and do as little injury, to persons and property, as may be consistent with dispersing the assembly and arresting and detaining such persons.

Part Two of *Army Regulations, India*, issued in 1918, which were extant in 1919, and which embodied rules concerning 'Unlawful Assemblies' which had remained unchanged in the many editions of the regulations published since the previous century, included four paragraphs devoted to this subject. Paragraph 572 stated: 'The following sections of the Code of Criminal Procedure lay down the course to be adopted in dispersing illegal assemblies', then reprinted in full sections 127–32 of the Criminal Code. Army Regulations, India, following the code, made no distinction between unlawful assembly, riot and insurrection, and referred only to the first. The index, under 'Riot', referred the reader to paragraphs 571–74, the paragraphs headed 'Unlawful Assemblies'. The index to the *Regulations* does not mention insurrection at all.

As Lieutenant-General Sir Aylmer Hunter-Weston told the Commons during the Dyer debate, paragraph 573 of the Regulations, the only paragraph which makes any addition to the provisions of the Criminal Code cited in paragraph 572, stated that when an Officer Commanding Troops acted under a magistrate in accordance with Section 130,

> or determines that it is necessary under Section 131, to disperse an assembly by force, he will, before taking action, adopt the most effectual means possible to explain that the fire of the troops will be effective. If it be found necessary to fire he will personally order such a minimum number of files to fire as he considers the circumstances of the case demand. Care must be taken not to fire on persons separated from the crowd, nor over the heads of the latter. The firing must be carried out with steadiness and be stopped the moment it becomes unnecessary.[4]

We can rely upon it that most of this was known to Dyer. It is certain that the principle of minimum force, which is the key feature of all the statutes and the regulations based upon them, was also known to him. He made much in his statements that, as a junior officer, he had instructed military law in Army schools:

> I had had special occasion and opportunity to study principles in this connection, as for five years I held the staff appointment of Deputy-Assistant Adjutant-General for instruction in military law, and the administration of martial law during civil disturbances was necessarily a subject of study by me in that capacity.[5]

He was better educated than most of his peers, having spent two years at Staff College, where the subject was covered in detail. Brigadier-General Edmonds, Dyer's fellow student at the Staff College, later made this clear:

> We had been carefully instructed at the Staff College that when soldiers are called out in the aid of the civil power, the Riot Act must be read and no more force used than is absolutely necessary: thus in the case of a riot, if called on to fire by a magistrate, first only a single round should be fired; if this had no effect, five rounds might be fired; and so on.[6]

So, was Dyer, by his action at the Jallianwala Bagh, guilty of breaking the law and military regulations? Dyer's lawyers made the best case that they were able that he was not guilty. They presented this in the statement they prepared for the Army Council in 1920, and based it upon the distinction made in the *Manual of Military Law* between an unlawful assembly, a riot and an insurrection. The point they sought to establish was that the crowd in the Jallianwala Bagh was not an unlawful assembly or a riot, which had to be dispersed using the rules of minimum force, but was part of an insurrection. This, they claimed, directly quoting the *Manual of Military Law*, 'would justify the use of any degree of force necessary effectually to meet and cope with the insurrection'. It was therefore important for them to establish that there was an insurrection, which is why the statement they prepared does its utmost to prove that there was a planned rebellion. Regrettably for their case, the Hunter Committee found no trace of such a planned insurrection, and by the time of the preparation of Dyer's statement, the idea had been quietly allowed to drop even by its supporters in the Government of India. Dyer's case was based upon a misreading of the state of affairs in the Punjab. It could not stand on fact.

Dyer's lawyers, perhaps recognising that the findings of the Hunter Committee could not be easily overturned, attempted to go beyond this. Using the *Manual of Military Law*, they attempted to make the case that Dyer's honest belief in the existence of such an insurrection was sufficient to exonerate him. Their case, however, was as badly based in law as it was in fact. The reading they chose to make of the *Manual*'s sections on insurrection was highly selective. They ignored the *Manual*'s caveat of the need for 'care being taken to avoid any unnecessary bloodshed or injury', a caveat which the *Manual* specifically applied to insurrection. They ignored entirely the principle of minimum force, which underlay the common law and every consideration in the *Manual of Military Law*. Their assertion that a state of insurrection gave a commander *carte blanche* to act as he judged fit, and that it permitted him to apply any degree of force in order to create an example sufficient to impress those taking part in an insurrection wherever they might be, is not supported by the *Manual*. Significantly, Dyer's lawyers made no mention of the Code of Criminal Procedure nor of Army Regulations, India, both of which governed specifically what Dyer did at Amritsar, presumably because these both undermined their case. Neither of these made any distinction between unlawful assembly and insurrection, and both applied the principle of minimum force to the dispersal of all assemblies. Dyer's lawyers could not justify their case. Their highly selective reading of British law was as unacceptable to the British Government of the day as it had been to their predecessors and as it has been to their successors ever since.

An examination of the issues upon which Dyer was censured, made against the provisions of British and Indian law, Military Law and *Army Regulations, India*, will clarify the legality of his actions. In relation to the firing, Dyer was censured because:

1. He opened fire without warning. This was contrary to the *Manual of Military Law* and to Army Regulations, India. Dyer's defence that the proclamation he made in the city on the morning of the Jallianwala Bagh firing was sufficient to fulfil the requirement to give warning could not succeed, because the people warned in the morning and the afternoon could not be proven to be the same people, and in fact were not the same. Many who were fired upon had not been warned.

2.   He opened fire on a crowd which was not indulging in violent behaviour and was not threatening him, when there was, in his own belief, as he later told the Hunter Committee, a possibility that he could have dispersed the crowd by other means. The crowd had also not given any indication when he arrived at the Jallianwala Bagh that it had any 'determination not to disperse.' This was contrary to Military Law, to the Code of Criminal Procedure and to Army Regulations, India.

3.   He maintained fire longer than was necessary to disperse the crowd. This was contrary to British Law, the *Manual of Military Law*, the Code of Criminal Procedure and Army Regulations, India.

Each of these actions laid Dyer open to prosecution. It was for these reasons that the Legal Adviser to the India Office, followed, as they made their own judgments, by Edwin Montagu and Winston Churchill, believed that Dyer had been guilty of manslaughter or murder. It is also why not one expert military writer on imperial policing and counter-insurgency, from Dyer's day to the present, has been able to bring himself to acquit Dyer of both a breach of law and of a catastrophic failure of judgment.[7]

Yet it remains the case that we are able to make this judgment that Dyer contravened the law in large part only because he said that he did so; in this, in his report of 25 August 1919, in his evidence to the Hunter Committee, and even in his statement of 1920, Dyer condemned himself out of his own mouth. Had he stuck to his original explanations, that he had opened fire immediately because he believed his force was threatened, and that he fired for as long as did because he feared that the crowd was about to rush his men, and maintained that line throughout the course of all the explanations he was called upon to give, such a professed intention would have saved him. For all the law and regulations depended upon a judgment of what was the minimum force necessary to disperse a crowd, and the judgment of the man on the spot was indisputable in these matters. When Dyer informed his superiors immediately after the shooting that he had fired because he had made such judgments, they accepted and approved of what he had done. It was his later admissions of what he had really intended which made it impossible for the Government of India to approve what he did. A man's judgment and intentions were all that there was to prove his guilt or innocence, and Dyer made plain that his were criminal.

Major-General Nigel Woodyatt, who met Dyer shortly before he left India for the last time, and discussed the affair with him, was in this sense right when he said: 'I told him plainly, that I considered he was bound to get the worst of it; *not so much for what he had done, but for what he had said.*'[8]

Glossary

Arya Samaj	Aryan Society
ashram	retreat
atta	wheat flour
ayah	nurse
bagh	garden, open space in a town
Baisakhi, Vaisakhi	Sikh new year's day
bania	sweeper
bhusa	fodder
bo	leader of a band of Burmese
box-wallah	businessman, person in commerce or trade
buzurg	prophet
chaprasi	bearer
Chief Khalsa Diwan	Sikh Central Committee
chota	lower, smaller
chota sahib	little sir
chuddah, chador	cloth mantle, shawl
dacoit	bandit
danda fauj	army armed with staves
darbar, durbar	meeting, council
darbar sahib	Golden Temple
dharmsala	religious association
dhobi	laundryman
duggiwalla	bamboo cart
doaba	stream junction, confluence of two streams
faryad	request, prayer or petition for clemency
fatwah	decree by Muslim religious authority
feu de joie	celebratory firing of weapons in volleys on parade
firman	decree
ghari	vehicle
ghazi	Muslim warrior
ghi	ghee, butter fat
godown	warehouse
gora	white man, British

gul-bibi	rose lady
gurdwara	Sikh temple
halwai	seller of sweets
hartal	a period of religious penance, also commonly a general strike and closure of business
havildar	Indian sergeant
howdah	elephant saddle
imam	Muslim priest
ishtihar	notice
jai	long live
jat	caste, tribe
jihad	Muslim holy war
jingal	musket
jirga, jirgah	council
khadi	homespun cloth
khalsa	Sikh religious community
khan	tribal chief
khassadar	footman
khel	section of a tribe
khilafat	Caliphate, the supreme leader of the Muslim faithful, the Turkish Sultanate
khud	cliff, hillside; jungle, wilderness
khukuri, kukri	knife, the traditional Gurkha weapon
kirpan	knife prescribed by the Sikh religion
kotwali, kotwal sahib	municipal police station
lakh	one hundred thousand
lambardar	village headman
lashkar	armed band, fighting men
lathi	stick, stave
loya jirga	Afghan grand assembly
mahant	Sikh priest
mahout	elephant rider and keeper
malik	tribal leader
mandir	temple
maulvi	Muslim cleric, religious leader
mela	fair
mir	city or town ruler
mullah	Muslim cleric, religious leader
Mussulman, Mussleman	Muslim
naib tahsildar	deputy *tehsildar*
nali	open drains, sewers

nullah	stream bed
pandit	Hindu priest, member of a Brahmin priestly caste
panka	fan
peepul	type of tree
picquet	guard or observation post or detachment
poorbeia	native of the plains of the state of Oudh
prahu	Malay boat with sail and a single outrigger
praya	waterfront
purdah	behind the veil, in seclusion
ram naumi	birthday of the Hindu god Ram
Rangar	Musulman (Muslim) Rajput
sadhu	wandering Hindu ascetic
saheb, sahib	Sir, Lord
salam, salaam	salute
samadhi	tomb
sangar	stone emplacement
sarbrah	temple manager
sardar	tribal chief
sarkar, sirkar	the Government of India
satyagraha	Gandhi's pledge of non-violent resistance, 'soul force'
satyagraha sabha	*satyagraha* committee
sepoy	Indian soldier
sewa samiti	service committee
shikari	huntsman
sirkar, sarkar	the Government of India
siropa	robe of honour
snakehead	smuggler of people
sowar	cavalry trooper, rider
subedar, subadar	Indian captain
subadar major	Indian major
swami	Hindu religious leader
swaraj	self rule
sultan	sultan, Muslim ruler; captain
tehsildar	junior local government official
thanadar	district officer
thika ghari	hired trap, small carriage
tiktiki	flogging frame
tonga	horse-drawn taxi
topi	hat, helmet
Vaisakhi, Baisakhi	Sikh new year's day
waqt	time

Notes

Notes to Chapter 1: Simla

1 Ian Colvin, *The Life of General Dyer* (London: Blackwood, 1929), p. 1; Dyer family tree, in the possession of Martin Dyer; Owen Rutter, *The Pirate Wind: Tales of the Sea-Robbers of Malaya* (Singapore: Oxford University Press 1991), p. 30; Steven Runciman, *The White Rajahs: A History of Sarawak from 1841–1946* (Kuala Lumpur: S. Abdul Majeed, 1992), p. 40.

2 Dyer family tree; *Pioneer Mail and Indian News*, 2 May 1902, p. 26, with Edward Dyer's obituary; Colvin, *Dyer*, p. 2; Captain James Dyer sent a wreath to General Dyer's funeral ceremony at Long Ashton, *Bristol Times*, 28 July 1927. Lord Hailey papers, MSS Eur E220/57.

3 W.H. Carey, *A Guide to Simla: With a Descriptive Account of the Neighbouring Sanitaria* (Calcutta: Wyman, 1870), p. 76; website of Mohan Meakin Ltd, *www.goldeneagletrading. com/india/india.html.*

4 Carey, *Guide to Simla*, p. 8.

5 Dyer family tree; *Dictionary of National Biography, 1922–1930*, ed. J.R.H. Weaver (Oxford University Press: Oxford, 1976), p. 280. Rex Dyer's birth was not registered; his birth date is given in the *Indian Army List*, July 1906, and again by Colvin, *Dyer*, p. 4.

6 Carey, *Guide to Simla*, p. 76; Onkar Chand Sud, *The Simla Story (The Glow and After-Glow of the Raj): A Sketch Book* (Simla; Maria Brothers, 1992), p. 10; F. Beresford Harrop, *Thacker's New Guide to Simla* (Simla: Thacker, Spinks & Co., 1925).

7 Edward Buck, *Simla, Past and Present* (Bombay: The Times Press, 1925), p. 214; Carey, *Guide to Simla*, p. 36; *Towelle's Handbook and Guide to Simla* (Simla: Station Press, 1890), list of Simla houses (no page number); Sud, *Simla Story*, p. 179.

8 Patt Barr and Ray Desmond, *Simla: A Hill Station in British India* (London: Scolar Press, 1978), p. 23.

9 Barr and Desmond, *Simla*, p. 22; Dennis Kincaid, *British Social Life in India* (Newton Abbot: Readers Union, 1974), p. x.

10 Michael Edwardes, *Bound to Exile: The Victorians in India* (London: Victorian (and Modern History) Book Club, 1969), p. 194; Malcolm Yapp, *The British Raj and Indian Nationalism* (London: Harrap, 1977), p. 26; Vipin Pubby, *Shimla Then and Now* (New Delhi: Indus Publishing, 1996), p. 80; J.M. Kenworthy, *India: A Warning* (London: Elkin Mathews & Marrot, 1931), pp. 9–14; Nirad C. Chaudhuri, *The Continent of Circe: Being an Essay on the Peoples of India* (London: Chatto & Windus, 1965), p. 122.

11 Colvin, *Dyer*, p. 16.

12 *Pioneer Mail and Indian News*, 2 May 1902, p. 26; Colvin, *Dyer*, pp. 6 and 16.

13 Carey, *Guide to Simla*, p. 95; Colvin, *Dyer*, pp. 6–7.

14 Colvin, *Dyer*, pp. 5–6.

15   Carey, *Guide to Simla*, p. 50.

16   Buck, *Simla, Past and Present*, p. 131. The school website, www.bishopcotton.edu/gallery.htm, has the current school motto 'Overcome evil with good' and the school song, one verse of which goes:

> And so from those who have gone before, to those who are yet to come,
> We pass our motto loud and clear, all evil overcome
> As true as is a brother's love, as close as ivy grows,
> We'll stand four square throughout our lives to every wind that blows.

17   Website of Bishop Cotton School, Shimla, 'School History', *School Home Page*, no date, www.bishopcotton.edu/gallery.htm (25 November 2001); Buck, *Simla, Past and Present*, p. 131; Barr and Desmond, *Simla*, p. 26; Sud, *The Simla Story*, p. 65; Colvin, *Dyer*, p. 6; private communication to the author from Mr Kabir Mustafi, Headmaster, Bishop Cotton School, 15 January 2002.

18   F.S.L. Lyons, *Ireland since the Famine* (London: Collins/Fontana, 1979).

Notes to Chapter 2: Cork and Sandhurst

1   Detail of Dyer's time at Midleton College is taken from Midleton College, 'School History', *School Home Page*, no date www.midletoncollege.com (25 November 2001); Trevor West, *Midleton College, 1696–1996: A Tercentenary History* (Midleton, County Cork: Midleton College, 1996); Brian D. Cairns, 'The Reverend Canon Thomas Moore MA LLD, Headmaster of Midleton College, 1863–1882', *Midleton College Magazine* (no date); Ian Colvin, *The Life of General Dyer* (London: Blackwood, 1929), pp. 8–10.

2   Detail of events in Ireland at this time is taken from F.S.L. Lyons, *Ireland since the Famine* (London: Collins/Fontana, 1979); E. Strauss, *Irish Nationalism and British Democracy* (Westport, Connecticut: Greenwood Press, 1951); G.M. Young, *Victorian England* (London: Folio Society, 1999).

3   Dyer's life in Dublin is covered in Colvin, *Dyer*, pp. 10–11. Detail of the Royal College of Surgeons is taken from John David Henry Widdess, *The Royal College of Surgeons in Ireland and its Medical School, 1784–1966* (Edinburgh: E. & S. Livingstone, 1967).

4   For detail of the Sandhurst of the day, see Alan Shepperd, *The Royal Military Academy Sandhurst and its Predecessors* (London: Country Life Books, 1980), pp. 35–98; John George Smyth, *Sandhurst* (London: Wiedenfeld & Nicolson, 1961), pp. 98–113 and 258–62; Michael Yardley, *Sandhurst: A Documentary History* (London: Harrap, 1987), pp. 40–45. The surviving record of Dyer's attendance at Sandhurst is in the *Royal Military College Gentleman Cadet Register, 1884–85*; information contained therein communicated to the author by letter dated 16 May 2002 from Dr P.J. Thwaites, Curator, the Sandhurst Collection. Dyer's report is mentioned by Colvin, *Dyer*, p. 11.

5   For the military's attitudes to their own status and their place in society, see Corelli Barnett, *Britain and Her Army, 1509–1990* (Harmondsworth: Penguin, 1974); Gwyn Harries-Jenkins, *The Army in Victorian Society* (London: Routledge & Kegan Paul, 1977), p. 8.

6   Dyer's commission is in the Dyer Papers, 9012–55, National Army Museum, item 1. It is inscribed 'Reginald Edward Harry Dyer, Gent, Lieutenant Land Forces' and signed 'Victoria

RI,' countersigned 'W.H. Smith', and effective from the '29th Day of August 1885'. It was 'Signed at St James's Twentieth Day of August 1885 in the Forty-Ninth Year'. On the outside is written 'Commission R.E.H. Dyer, Gent., Lieutenant Land Forces – The Queen's (Royal West Surrey Regiment). 28.8.85.' The effective date of 29 August 1885 is confirmed in the *Army List* for September 1885, and India Office, L/MILITARY/10/100, fol. 142, which contains Dyer's leave record in 1891.

Notes to Chapter 3: Ireland and Burma

1   For detail of Dyer's time in Ireland with 1st Battalion Queen's, see Ian Colvin, *The Life of General Dyer* (London: Blackwood, 1929), pp. 11–12; John Davis, *The History of the Second, Queen's Royal Regiment, Now The Queen's (Royal West Surrey) Regiment*, v (London: Eyre & Spottiswoode, 1906), pp. 176–77.

2   The troubles in Belfast in 1886 are covered in L.P. Curtis, *Coercion and Conciliation in Ireland, 1880–1892: A Study in Conservative Unionism* (London: Oxford University Press, 1963), pp. 123–25; James Loughlin, *Gladstone, Home Rule and the Ulster Question, 1882–93* (Atlantic Highlands, New Jersey: Humanities Press International, 1987), pp. 128–67 and 225–26; Nicholas Mansergh, *The Irish Question, 1840–1921* (London: George Allen & Unwin, 1975), p. 210.

3   India Office, L/MILITARY/10/100, fol. 142; Colvin, *Dyer*, p. 12;

4   For detail of the first phase of the Third Burma War, see Anil Chandra Banerjee, *Annexation of Burma* (Calcutta: A. Mukherjee, 1944), pp. 317–21; Edmund Charles Browne, *The Coming of the Great Queen: A Narrative of the Acquisition of Burma* (London: Harrison & Sons, 1888), pp. 189–90 and 271–85; George Ludgate Bruce, *The Burma Wars, 1824–1886* (London: Hart-Davis MacGibbon, 1973), pp. 154–61; John F. Cady, *A History of Modern Burma* (New York: Cornell University Press, 1958), pp. 133–34; John Leroy Christian, *Modern Burma: A Survey of Political and Economic Development* (Berkeley: University of California Press, 1942), p. 37; S.W. Cocks, *Burma under British Rule* (Bombay: K & J. Cooper, 1920), pp. 52–60; Joseph Dautremer, *Burma under British Rule* (London: T. Fisher & Unwin, 1916), pp. 70–75; A. Ruxton MacMahon, *Far Cathay and Farther India* (London: Hurst & Blackett, 1893), pp. 16–18; John Marks, *Forty Years in Burma* (London: Hutchinson, 1917), p. 228; Sir J.G. Scott, *Burma from the Earliest Times to the Present Day* (London: T. Fisher & Unwin, 1924), pp. 333–42; D.P. Singhal, *British Diplomacy and the Annexation of Upper Burma* (2nd edn, Singapore: South Asian Publishers, 1981), pp. 98–138; A.T.Q. Stewart, *The Pagoda War: Lord Dufferin and the Fall of the Kingdom of Ava, 1885–6* (Newton Abbot: Victorian (& Modern History) Book Club, 1974), pp. 78–184; Frank N. Trager, *Burma: From Kingdom to Republic. A Historical and Political Analysis* (London: Pall Mall, 1966), pp. 40–44; Henry M. Vibart, *The Life of General Sir Harry N.D. Prendergast (The Happy Warrior)* (London: Eveleigh Nash, 1914), pp. 271–312; Dorothy Woodman, *The Making of Burma* (London: Cresset, 1962).

5   Rudyard Kipling, *Rudyard Kipling's Verse: The Definitive Edition* (London: Hodder & Stoughton, 1986), pp. 56–57.

6   For British conduct in the war, see Grattan Geary, *Burma, after the Conquest, Viewed in its*

Political, Social and Commercial Aspects from Mandalay (London: Sampson Low, Marston, Searle, & Rivington, 1886), pp. 230–49; Maung Htin Aung, *The Stricken Peacock: Anglo-Burmese Relations, 1752–1948* (The Hague: Martinus Nijhoff, 1965), pp. 94–95; Maung Htin Aung, *A History of Burma* (New York: Columbia University Press, 1967), pp. 266–67; Maung Htin Aung, *Lord Randolph Churchill and the Dancing Peacock: British Conquest of Burma, 1885* (New Delhi: Manohar, 1990), pp. 73–215. MacMahon, *Far Cathay and Farther India*, p. 17: 'Overzealous efforts to stamp out dacoity by shooting and flogging men and burning villages, coupled with a want of readiness to pardon offenders who repented of the evil of their ways, hardened men of this stamp and aggravated the difficulty.'

7   Lockhart was posted in on 3 September 1886; India Office L/MILITARY/7/9176, Army Headquarters, Simla, orders. He had a very high reputation as an energetic and successful commander in Burma.

8   The British campaign in 1886–87 is covered in Charles Haukes Todd Crosthwaite, *The Pacification of Burma* (London: Frank Cass, 1912; reprinted in 1968), pp. 14–72; Mortimer Durand, *The Life of Field-Marshal Sir George White*, 2 vols (Edinburgh: William Blackwood, 1915), i, pp. 340–52; Alleyne Ireland, *The Province of Burma: A Report Prepared on Behalf of the University of Chicago* (New York: Houghton, Mifflin, 1907), pp. 45–56; John Nisbet, *Burma under British Rule – and Before*, 2 vols (London: Archibald Constable, 1901), i, pp.105–48. India Office, L/MILITARY/7/9178, Major-General White's dispatch, 10 March 1887, records Colonel Holt's arrival as 18 November 1886.

9   India Office, L/MILITARY/7/9178, dispatch, 10 March 1887.

10   Operations around Pyinmana, and those which involved 2nd Queen's, are covered in Army Headquarters India, *Frontier and Overseas Expeditions from India*, v, *Burma* (Simla: Government of India, 1907), pp. 252–66; Davis, *The History of the Second, Queen's Royal Regiment*, v, pp. 148–66; J. George Scott and J. P. Hardiman, *Gazetteer of Upper Burma and the Shan States*, 5 vols (Rangoon: Government of Burma, 1900), i, pp. 117–73.

11   India Office, L/MILITARY/7/9176, telegram the Government of India, Fort William, Viscount Cross, Secretary of State for India, 23 November 1886.

12   Roberts's account of his campaign in Burma is in Field-Marshal Lord Roberts of Kandahar, *Forty-One Years in India: From Subaltern to Commander-in-Chief*, 2 vols (London: Richard Bentley & Son, 1897), pp. 415–16 and 491–93; see also Nisbet, *Burma under British Rule – and Before*, i, p. 148.

13   Nisbet, *Burma under British Rule – and Before*, i, p. 124.

14   Davis, *The History of the Second, Queen's Royal Regiment*, v, p. 149.

15   Scott and Hardiman, *Gazetteer of Upper Burma and the Shan States*, i, p. 153.

16   India Office, L/MILITARY/7/9178, Major-General White's dispatch, 10 March 1887.

17   India Office, L/MILITARY/7/9178, Major-General White's dispatch, 10 March 1887, detailed list of engagements in Burma.

18   Kipling, *Rudyard Kipling's Verse*, pp. 255–62.

19   The course of events in 1887 is traceable in the weekly reports sent to the India Office by the Viceroy, found in India Office, L/MILITARY/7/9180.

20   Dyer's medals are in the National Army Museum. This medal is the India General Service Medal, 1854, and the two clasps he was awarded were Burma 1885–87 and Burma 1887–89. The medal is inscribed 'Lieut., 2d Battalion. R.W.Surr.R.' His service is shown in the *Indian*

Army List, July 1919, p. 282, War Services: 'Burma 1886–87 – Operations of the 3rd Brigade, Medal with two clasps.'

21 Brigadier-General Sir James Edmonds papers, EDMONDS III/2, in the Liddell Hart Centre, King's College London, p. 18.

22 The only source for this incident is Colvin, *Dyer*, p. 14.

Notes to Chapter 4: *The Black Mountain*

1 Website of Mohan Meakin Ltd, *www.goldeneagletrading.com/india/india.html*; Ian Colvin, *The Life of General Dyer* (London: Blackwood, 1929), p. 18.

2 Dyer family tree, in the possession of Martin Dyer.

3 *Indian Army Lists*, April 1897, p. 152, January 1888, p. 313, *Army List*, December 1888, pp. 274 and 740a. He retained his seniority from the British service, with a commissioning date of 29 August 1885. The date of his appointment to the Bengal Staff Corps was 30 August 1887; both shown in *Indian Army List*, July 1896, p. 155; Colvin, *Dyer*, pp. 14–15, 28.

4 Quoted in Philip Mason, *A Matter of Honour: An Account of the Indian Army, its Officers and Men* (London: Jonathan Cape, 1974), pp. 346–47.

5 John Gaylor, *Sons of John Company: The Indian and Pakistani Armies, 1903–91* (Tunbridge Wells: Parapress, Into Battle Series, 1996), p. 6; India Office, L/MILITARY/7/17007, Bengal Army Return, 1887–88, p. 49. There is no extant regimental history of the 39th; India Office, L/MILITARY/7/17007, Bengal Army Returns, 1887–88, p. 62, and 1888–89, p. 118.

6 Ommanney family tree, in the possession of Martin Dyer; *Army Register of Marriages*, 1888, p. 101, Family Records Centre, Islington.

7 Ommanney family tree.

8 There is no marriage certificate. The sole source for the story of courtship and marriage is Colvin, *Dyer*, pp. 15–18.

9 Ian Colvin letter to G.W. Blackwood, 25 January 1929, Blackwood Papers.

10 India Office, L/MILITARY/10/100, fol. 142, shows him as Wing Officer, 29th Bengal Infantry; *Indian Army List*, January 1889, p. 313: 'Lieutenant Staff Corps, 29th Bengal Infantry; Wing Officer 29th Punjabis 28 April 1888'.

11 Gaylor, *Sons of John Company*, p. 338; Colvin, *Dyer*, p. 21. Mason, *A Matter of Honour*, pp. 348, 384; India Office, L/MILITARY/7/17007, p. 61. The 29th did not produce a regimental history, so we do not have their own view of themselves.

12 Colvin, *Dyer*, p. 23.

13 The background to the Black Mountains and its tribes is in Sir William Barton, *India's North-West Frontier* (London: John Murray, 1939), p. 37; Edward E. Oliver, *Across the Border: or Pathan and Biloch* (London: Chapman and Hall, 1890), p. 314.

14 For the Hindustani Fanatics, see James W. Spain, *The Pathan Borderland* (The Hague: Mouton, 1963), pp. 87 and 105. The Piarai Saiyids were spelled by the British variously Parari or Piari Sayyids, Sayids, Saiyads or Sayuds.

15 The lead up to the 1888 campaign is in C. Collin Davies, *The Problem of the North-West Frontier, 1890–1908; With a Survey of Policy since 1849* (Cambridge University Press: Cambridge, 1932), pp. 60–78; J.G. Elliott, *The Frontier, 1839–1947: The Story of the North-*

West Frontier of India (London: Cassell, 1968), p. 125; *Frontier and Overseas Expeditions from India: Compiled in the Intelligence Branch of the Division of the Chief of Staff, Army Headquarters, India*, i, *Tribes North of the Kabul River* (Simla: Government Monotype Press, 1907), pp. 95–96, 139–44.

16 India Office, L/MILITARY/7/14688, telegram McQueen to the Adjutant-General India, 19 June 1888.

17 India Office, L/MILITARY/7/14688, report of the Board of Inquiry held by Major Thompson, 3rd Sikhs.

18 Major-General W.K. Elles wrote from the Adjutant-General's branch, Army Headquarters to the Secretary to the Government of India on 2 July: 'Although Major Battye acted most injudiciously in ascending the Black Mountain, the Commander-in-Chief believes from what he knew of Major Battye's chivalrous nature that he refrained from opening fire upon the enemy, when he found himself near them, from a feeling that he did not want to invite an attack, and that as he was within British territory he hoped his inaction would be understood. It was of course an error of judgment and shewed a want of appreciation of the Pathan character unaccountable in an officer who had served for so many years in the Punjab Frontier Force', India Office, L/MILITARY/7/14688.

19 For the events of 1888, and the decision to send the expedition, see A.H., Mason, *Report on the Black Mountain and Adjacent Independent Territory* (Simla: Government of India, 1888), pp. 80–82, and H.C. Wylly, *From the Black Mountain to Waziristan* (London: Macmillan, 1912), pp. 42–45. The scheme of operations issued by Major-General E.F. Chapman for the Quartermaster-General in India on 2 September 1888 was blunter in its objective, which was simply 'to punish', India Office, L/MILITARY/7/14688.

20 India Office, L/MILITARY/7/14688, the scheme of operations issued by Major-General E.F. Chapman for the Quartermaster-General in India on 2 September 1888.

21 Of Number 2 Battery, 1st Brigade Scottish Division Royal Artillery; India Office, L/MILITARY/7/14688.

22 India Office, L/MILITARY/7/14688, Despatch of Major-General McQueen, 19 November 1888, appendix B; Brigadier-General Galbraith's Despatch, 4 November 1888.

23 Colvin, *Dyer*, p. 21.

24 Telegram from the Viceroy to the India Office, 25 October 1888, India Office, L/MILITARY/7/14688.

25 The operations are covered in Michael Barthorp, *The North-West Frontier: British India and Afghanistan. A Pictorial History, 1839–1947* (Poole, Dorset: Blandford Press, 1982); *Frontier and Overseas Expeditions from India*, i, pp. 145–56; and H.L. Nevill, *Campaigns on the North-West Frontier, 1849–1908* (London: John Murray, 1912), pp. 95–100. India Office, L/MILITARY/7/14688 has day-by-day detail.

26 Sotheby's, *Orders, Medals and Decorations* (London: sale catalogue, Tuesday 18 December 1990).

27 *Indian Army List*, July 1919, p. 282, 'War Services'.

28 India Office, L/MILITARY/7/17007, p. 116.

Notes to Chapter 5: The Relief of Chitral

1   India Office, L/MILITARY/7/17021 gives the annual report on 25th Punjabis for 1911–12, then commanded by Dyer, and includes confidential reports he had written on his officers; on Captain G.W. Atkins, he comments that he is a good officer but is in debt, and of Lieutenant A. Flagg that his debt hampers his performance.

2   T.L. Hughes, 'Man of Iron: A Biography of Major-General Sir William Beynon' (unpublished typescript in the Gurkha Museum, Gm: Acc. No 94–10–9 H3), p. 2.

3   India Office, L/MILITARY/7/17007.

4   Ian Colvin, *The Life of General Dyer* (London: Blackwood, 1929), p. 28; Brigadier-General R.E.H. Dyer, *The Raiders of the Sarhad* (London: Witherby, 1921), p. 138; *Report from Brigadier-General R.E.H. Dyer to the General Staff, 16th (Indian) Division,* 25 August 1919, in the Dyer papers in the National Army Museum, 6, p. 7; *Indian Army Lists,* January 1893, p. 643, October 1903, p. 757: 'passed Punjabi (obligatory) exam'.

5   Colvin, *Dyer,* p.22.

6   *Army List,* January 1889, p. 740; *Indian Army List,* January 1889, p. 313.

7   Colvin, *Dyer,* p.22, letter to Colvin from Captain Man Singh, an instructor under Dyer at the time.

8   The only source for this is Colvin, *Dyer,* pp. 23–24. Colvin assigns this incident to the time of the 29th's march to the Black Mountain campaign. I do not believe that this can be correct. The story makes it clear that Dyer was the sole British officer present at the time, and that he was detained in Nowshera by the subsequent court case. Neither circumstance fits a deployment of the whole battalion to active service.

9   Colvin, *Dyer,* p. 25.

10 India Office, L/MILITARY/7/17007; Colvin, *Dyer,* p. 21.

11 Colvin, *Dyer,* p. 31.

12 Colvin, *Dyer,* p. 25.

13 India Office, L/MILITARY/7/17007, p. 238, report for 1891.

14 India Office, L/MILITARY/10/100, fol. 142; Dyer's leave record for 1891, dated 14 January 1890 (this is an error, and should have been written 1891); *Indian Army List,* January and July 1891; Colvin, *Dyer,* p. 31.

15 Colvin, *Dyer,* p. 31. We have only Colvin's word for this as no records of non-Engineer officers' course results survive at Chatham; personal communication to the author from Ms Rebecca Cheney, Curator, Royal Engineers Museum, Chatham, 20 August 2002.

16 Dyer is shown in the *Army List,* April 1892, p. 744, as 'Lieutenant Indian Staff Corps'; India Office, L/MILITARY/7/17007, p. 238; Major Donovan Jackson (Invicta), *India's Army* (London: Sampson Low, Marston, 1940), p. 348; *Indian Army Lists,* January and July 1891; Colvin, *Dyer,* p. 31; it is evident that Colvin was working from a diary kept by either Rex or Annie Dyer as the dates he gives are precise. Regrettably, no diary survives.

17 *Indian Army List,* January 1893, p. 326: 'Quartermaster 29 December 1891'.

18 *Indian Army* List, January 1893, p. 632: 'Officer's Extra Certificate Musketry'; Colvin, *Dyer,* p. 31.

19 Papers of Brigadier-General W.D. Villiers-Stuart, in the Gurkha Museum, Winchester, autobiographical account, 1918, no page number.

20   India Office, L/MILITARY/7/17007, p. 284.

21   India Office, L/MILITARY/7/17008, p. 74.

22   Colvin, *Dyer*, p. 32.

23   Colvin, *Dyer*, p. 32; *Indian Army List*, January 1895, p. 384: 'Quartermaster on furlough'; *Gazette of India*, January to June 1894, p. 153, no. 260: 'The undermentioned officers are granted leave out of India under article 704, Army Regulations, India, vol. i, part 1: Lieutenant R.E.H. Dyer, Indian Staff Corps, Wing Officer and Quartermaster, 29th (Punjab) Regiment of Bengal Infantry, for one year. Pension service – 9th year commenced 29th August, 1893.'

24   Basil Liddell Hart papers, LH11/1938/6, Liddell Hart Centre, King's College London, B.H.L.H. 5.1.38, 'Talk with General Edmonds (lunch at the Athenaeum) 5.1.38'.

25   Birth certificate Y508034, '8 March 1895, Brooke House, West Malling, Ivan Reginald, son of Reginald Edward Harry Dyer, Lieutenant 29th Punjaub Native Infantry, and Frances Annie Trevor Dyer formerly Ommanney'; Family Record Centre; India Office, L/MILITARY/14/1025.

26   G.J. and Frank E. Younghusband, *The Relief of Chitral* (London: Macmillan, 1895), p. 53.

27   W.G.L. Beynon, *With Kelly to Chitral* (London: Edward Arnold, 1896); Lionel T.C. James, *With the Chitral Relief Force* (Calcutta: The 'Englishman Press', 1895); H.C. Thomson, *The Chitral Campaign* (London: William Heinemann, 1895); Younghusband, *The Relief of Chitral*.

28   The political background to the Chitral campaign is taken from Michael Barthorp, *The North-West Frontier: British India and Afghanistan. A Pictorial History, 1839–1947* (Blandford Press: Poole, Dorset, 1982), p. 103; Sir William Barton, *India's North-West Frontier* (London: John Murray, 1939), pp. 29 and 102.

29   This account of the Chitral Relief Force is taken from J.G. Elliott, *The Frontier, 1839–1947: The Story of the North-West Frontier of India* (London: Cassell, 1968), p. 141; *Frontier and Overseas Expeditions from India: Compiled in the Intelligence Branch of the Division of the Chief of Staff, Army Headquarters, India*, i, *Tribes North of the Kabul River* (Simla: Government Monotype Press, 1907), pp. 59, 521–24, 548–51; John Harris, *Much Sounding of Bugles: The Siege of Chitral, 1895* (London: Hutchinson, 1975); Charles Miller, *Khyber: British India's North West Frontier. The Story of an Imperial Migraine* (London: Macdonald and Jane's, 1977), p. 263–64; H.L. Neville, *Campaigns on the North-West Frontier, 1849–1908* (London: John Murray, 1912); H.C. Wylly, *From the Black Mountain to Waziristan* (London: Macmillan, 1912).

30   India Office, L/MILITARY/7/6886, *An Official Account of the Chitral Expedition 1895 Compiled under the Orders of the Quarter Master General in India by Captain W.R. Robertson, 3rd Dragoon Guards*. (Calcutta: the Government of India, 1898), tables I and II, Strengths as at 8 April and 1 May 1895.

31   General Sir Bindon Blood, *Four Score Years and Ten: Sir Bindon Blood's Reminiscences* (London: G. Bell, 1933), p. 264.

32   India Office, L/MILITARY/7/6886, *An Official Account of the Chitral Expedition*, p. 83.

33   India Office, L/MILITARY/7/17008, p. 272; the report is dated 12 January 1896, after the 29th were back at Meerut.

34   India Office, L/MILITARY/7/6912, *Chitral Blue Book*, pp. 10–11.

35 India General Service Medal, 1895, clasp 'Relief of Chitral 1895', inscribed 'R.E.H. Dyer Lieut., 29th Bl. Infy', collection in the National Army Museum; *Indian Army List*, July 1919, p. 282, War Services.

36 C. Collin Davies, *The Problem of the North-West Frontier, 1890–1908: With a Survey of Policy since 1849* (Cambridge; Cambridge University Press, 1932).

Notes to Chapter 6: *Staff College and the Mahsud*

1 Ian Colvin, *The Life of General Dyer* (London: Blackwood, 1929), p. 33; Staff College record card for Lieutenant R.E.H. Dyer, 29th Punjab Infantry, personal communication to the author from Mr Stephen Connolly, Curator, Staff College Museum, 24 May 2002.

2 Edmonds papers, 3/2/1–27, Autobiographical Notes, p. 10; Dyer Papers, 9012–55, National Army Museum, 2 – Staff College 'Names and addresses of the Professors, and Officers Students, 1897'.

3 Edmonds papers, 3/2/1–27, Autobiographical Notes, pp. 8–9, 20.

4 Dyer was promoted captain on 29 August 1896; *Army List*, October 1896, p. 744, which also shows him at the Staff College; *Indian Army List*, April 1897, p. 152, Staff College entry p. 367.

5 Edmonds papers, 3/2/1–27, Autobiographical Notes, p. 7.

6 *Owl Pie*, the Staff College Magazine, 1956. It should be noted that by 'Generals' Edmonds also means Brigadier-Generals.

7 Colvin, *Dyer*, p. 34.

8 Edmonds papers, 3/2/1–27, Autobiographical Notes, p. 17–20. Dyer was promoted captain in August 1896, so Edmonds's estimate of the date is a little out. Basil Liddell-Hart records Edmonds telling him this story almost verbatim in 1938. Edmonds added that he had told the Commandant that he had spent money on a crammer; Basil Liddell Hart papers, LH11/1938/6, Liddell Hart Centre, King's College London, B.H.L.H. 5.1.38, 'Talk with General Edmonds (lunch at the Athenaeum) 5.1.38'. The students worked in groups which came together voluntarily and were known as 'syndicates.'

9 Staff College record card for Dyer; *Army List*, February 1898, p. 78, psc list; *Indian Army List*, April 1898, p. 687, psc list.

10 India Office, L/MILITARY/7/3425. Colvin, *Dyer*, p. 34, gives an entirely different report: 'This officer has shown great force of character, and I shall expect to hear of him again.' If this is made up, and not a quote from a report issued to Dyer but now missing, this is the only occasion upon which Colvin is discovered writing a falsehood.

11 *Army Quarterly Review*, 10 September 1927.

12 Colvin, *Dyer*, pp. 34–35; at the end of 1896.

13 *Indian Army List*, April 1898, p. 367; 'Wing Officer 29th'.

14 India Office, L/MILITARY/7/17008, pp. 310, 366.

15 Colvin, *Dyer*, pp. 25–27.

16 Colvin, *Dyer*, p. 35.

17 Variously written also as Kala Drosh or Kila Darosh.

18 India Office, L/MILITARY/7/17008, p. 415.

19 Colvin, *Dyer*, pp. 29, 35. Colvin quotes this information from a letter he received from an Indian Officer of the Regiment, Captain Man Singh, Bahadur.

20 Colvin, *Dyer*, pp. 29–30.

21 Colvin, *Dyer*, p.35.

22 *Indian Army List*, July 1899, p. 367 'at Depot'.

23 India Office, L/MILITARY/7/17008, p. 502.

24 *Indian Army List*, October 1903, p. 377 'Present appointment in regiment 1 May 1900'; July 1906, p. 339, 'Double Company Commander appointed 1 May 1900'.

25 Colvin, *Dyer*, p. 36.

26 India Office, L/MILITARY/7/17009, p. 160.

27 *Army List*, November 1901, p. 27; 'Bengal Command, District Staff, Deputy Assistant Adjutant-General (for instruction) Captain R.E.H. Dyer Indian Staff Corps, psc'; *Indian Army List*, October 1903, pp. 11–12: 'D.A.A.G. for Instruction Chakrata, 6 March 1901 to 6 March 1906', p. 26: 'Meerut District staff'; Colvin, *Dyer*, p. 37.

28 Colvin, *Dyer*, p. 37.

29 Dyer papers, 18; the signature on the letter is indecipherable, so there is no indication of the writer's name. It was written from Glentor, Fort William, on 6 October 1929; Colvin sent it to Annie Dyer.

30 *Indian Army List*, October 1903, p. 135, 'Substantive Major, 29 August 1903'.

31 Command 771 – *Parliamentary Papers* (Commons), 1920, vol. 8 (*Reports*, vol. 4. 'Army'), 'Disturbances in the Punjab. Statement by Brig.-General R.E.H. Dyer', p. 5.

32 *Indian Army List*, July 1908, p. 335, '"Q" (qualified in tactical fitness for command)'; Colvin, *Dyer*, p. 42.

33 Colvin, *Dyer*, p. 37.

34 Olaf Caroe, *The Pathans, 550 BC–AD 1957* (London: Macmillan, 1958), pp. 397, 401.

35 The background to the 1901–2 Mahsud campaign is taken from Michael Barthorp, *The North-West Frontier: British India and Afghanistan. A Pictorial History, 1839–1947* (Poole, Dorset: Blandford Press, 1982), p. 147; Sir William Barton, *India's North-West Frontier* (London: John Murray, 1939), pp. 52, 72, 211–15; Richard I. Bruce, *The Forward Policy and its Results* (London: Longman, Green, 1900); C. Collin Davies, *The Problem of the North-West Frontier, 1890–1908: With a Survey of Policy since 1849* (Cambridge: Cambridge University Press, 1932), pp. 116–28; J.G. Elliott, *The Frontier, 1839–1947: The Story of the North-West Frontier of India* (London: Cassell, 1968), p. 240; Colin Enriquez, *The Pathan Borderland: A Consecutive Account of the Country and People On and Beyond the Indian Frontier from Chitral to Dera Ismail Khan* (Calcutta: Thacker, Spink 1921); Charles Miller, *Khyber: British India's North-West Frontier. The Story of an Imperial Migraine* (London: Macdonald and Jane's, 1977), pp. 295–98; H.L. Nevill, *Campaigns on the North-West Frontier, 1849–1908* (London: John Murray, 1912), p. 326; André Singer, *Lords of the Khyber: The Story of the North-West Frontier* (London: Faber & Faber, 1984), pp. 167–71.

36 India Office, L/MILITARY/7/16820, telegram Viceroy to India Office, 29 November 1901.

37 L.W. Shakespear, *History of the 2nd King Edward's Own Goorkha Rifles* (Aldershot: Gale & Polden, 1950), p. 121.

38 India Office, L/MILITARY/7/16820, telegram Viceroy to India Office, 9 December 1901.

39 Colvin, *Dyer*, p. 37.

40   This account of the Mahsud expedition is taken from Army Headquarters India, *Frontier and Overseas Expeditions from India*, ii, *North-West Frontier Tribes between Kabul and Gumal Rivers* (Simla: Government of India, 1908), pp. 436–45; H.C. Wylly, *From the Black Mountain to Waziristan* (London: Macmillan, 1912), pp. 47–472.

41   *Indian Army List*, July 1919, p. 282, War Services; Sotheby's, *Orders, Medals and Decorations* (London: sale catalogue, Tuesday 18 December 1990), clasp 'Waziristan 1901–2'.

Notes to Chapter 7: *Chakrata and Chungla Gully*

1   Ian Colvin, *The Life of General Dyer* (London: Blackwood, 1929), pp. 38–39.

2   *Pioneer Mail and Indian News*, 2 May 1902, p. 26.

3   Colvin, *Dyer*, p. 38, credits the plan that led to this capture to Dyer, which is unlikely considering his temporary position in 4th Brigade Headquarters.

4   Colvin, *Dyer*, p. 38; David Gilmour, *Curzon* (London: John Murray, 1994), pp. 228–29, 243–44.

5   Colvin, *Dyer*, pp. 39–41.

6   *Gazette of India*, January to June 1904, Government General Orders Military Department, vi: 'The King has approved of the following promotions among officers of the Indian Army, and admissions to the Indian Army made by the Government of India: Captains to Major dated 29th August 1903: Reginald Edward Harry Dyer.'

7   Philip Mason, *A Matter of Honour: An Account of the Indian Army, its Officers and Men* (London: Jonathan Cape, 1974), p. 344.

8   *Indian Army List*, July 1908, p. 335, 'Q' (qualified in tactical fitness for command); Colvin, *Dyer*, p. 42.

9   The Military Member of the Viceroy's Council was an officer of the rank of major-general who was adviser to the Viceroy and was independent of the Commander-in-Chief, something abhorrent to the strong-willed Kitchener.

10   Alan J. Guy and Peter B. Boyden, eds, *Soldiers of the Raj: The Indian Army, 1600–1947* (London: National Army Museum, 1997), p. 16.

11   David Omissi, *The Sepoy and the Raj: The Indian Army, 1860–1946* (London: University of Hull, 1994), p. 206.

12   Donovan Jackson (Invicta), *India's Army* (London: Sampson Low, Marston, 1940), p. 552; John Gaylor, *Sons of John Company: The Indian and Pakistani Armies, 1903–91* (Tunbridge Wells: Parapress, Into Battle Series, 1996), p. 338.

13   India Office, L/MILITARY/7/17011, L/MILITARY/7/17012 and L/MILITARY/7/17013, review reports on 29th Punjabi Infantry and 29th Punjabis 1902–3, 1903–4 and 1904–5 respectively. Sir Bindon Blood's criticism was aimed at Mullins, the Commanding Officer; Major-General Pearson, Commander Derajat Brigade, reported on him: 'Is inclined to do work that it would be better to delegate to his subordinates. I am not prepared as yet to recommend him for promotion.'

14   Colvin, *Dyer*, p. 42.

15   His postings in the early part of 1906 are confusing. The *Army List*, in the volume for June 1905, manages to show him on the strength of two units simultaneously, that of his own

regiment as a double company commander, and that of the 20th Punjabis without a post. As he was on leave at the time, these may have been paper postings against which his name was held; there is no evidence he was ever actually with the 20th. Both the *Army List* of April 1906 and the *Indian Army List* of July 1906 show him back in the 29th as a double company commander

16 *Army List*, June 1905, p. 1317: 'attached 20th Duke of Cambridge's Own Infantry (Brownlow's Punjabis)', also p. 1326: 'Double Company Commander 29th Punjabis'; *Army List*, April 1906: 'attached 20th Duke of Cambridge's Own Infantry (Brownlow's Punjabis)'; *Army List*, May 1906, 'Double Company Commander 29th'; *Indian Army List* July 1906, p. 339: 'Double Company Commander 29th Punjabis appointed 1 May 1900'.

17 India Office, L/MILITARY/7/17015, p. 153.

18 India Office, L/MILITARY/7/17015, p. 153.

19 India Office, L/MILITARY/7/17016.

20 Colvin, *Dyer*, p. 42.

21 Colvin, *Dyer*, p. 43; *Army List*, March 1907, p. 26: 'Deputy Assistant Adjutant-General Headquarters Northern Command Rawalpindi, 1 June 1906'. The last *Army List* this entry appears in is the volume for March 1908.

22 Colvin, *Dyer*, pp. 43–44; India Office, L/MILITARY/7/1111–25.

23 India Office, L/MILITARY/7/17045, p. 26.

24 Colvin, *Dyer*, p. 50. Colvin states that this is 'one of Dyer's few surviving letters', so he must have seen a few more. This letter is the only fully extant letter to his family that we have. The only other fully extant letters are two handwritten letters to the India Office of 1920 and 1921 concerning his case.

25 D.L. Choudhary, *Violence in the Freedom Movement of Punjab (1907–1942)* (Delhi: B.R. Publishing, 1986), p. 69; Gilmour, *Curzon*, pp. 322–24; Percival Spear, *A History of India*, ii (London: Penguin, 1986), pp. 175–76.

26 India Office, L/MILITARY/7/17045, p. 28.

27 Colvin, *Dyer*, p. 51. The change is seen in the *Army List*, November 1907, where Dyer first appears as second-in-command of the 25th, and exits the 29th. J.E. Shearer, *A History of the 1st Battalion, 15th Punjab Regiment, 1857–1937* (Aldershot: Gale & Polden, 1937), p. 93, shows Dyer joining the 25th in 1907.

Notes to Chapter 8: The Zakka Khel

1 John Gaylor, *Sons of John Company: The Indian and Pakistani Armies, 1903–91* (Tunbridge Wells: Parapress, Into Battle Series, 1996), p. 338; J.E. Shearer, *A History of the 1st Battalion, 15th Punjab Regiment, 1857–1937* (Aldershot: Gale & Polden, 1937), p. 93. Shearer's work includes the regimental history of the 25th, which became 1st Battalion 15th Punjabis in the reorganisation of 1922. It is their only regimental history.

2 India Office, L/MILITARY/7/17016.

3 Shearer, *1st Battalion, 15th Punjab Regiment*, p. 36; this account agrees with that in India Office, L/MILITARY/7/16842, 12 February 1908.

4 Ian Colvin, *The Life of General Dyer* (London: Blackwood, 1929), p. 29; Arthur Swinson,

Six Minutes to Sunset: The Story of General Dyer and the Amritsar Affair (London: Peter Davies, 1964), p. 195, quotes evidence from the next generation of the Dyer family that Rex spoke six languages; in addition to English, we have record of Hindustani, Persian, Punjabi, Pushtu and French.

5 Moberly went on to reach the rank of brigadier-general, and was one of the authors of the official histories of the First World War compiled by Brigadier Edmonds. Strangely, in his volumes on the campaigns in East Persia, Moberly was to find himself writing on Dyer.

6 *Army List*, April 1908, p. 1322: 'Second-in-Command to Commandant Brevet Colonel A. Hamilton, Rawalpindi, 25th Punjabis'; *Indian Army List*, July 1908, p. 98: '25th Punjabis'; ibid., p. 335: 'Second-in-Command to Brevet Colonel A. Hamilton'. No appointment date is shown.

7 *Indian Army List*, June 1911, p. 50: 'Date of completion of last staff appointment 1 February 1908'.

8 James W. Spain, *The Way of the Pathans* (London: Robert Hale, 1962), p. 57.

9 India Office, L/MILITARY/7/16842, telegram Viceroy, Calcutta, to Secretary of State for India, 8 February 1908.

10 Detail of the Zakka Khel and the lead up to the campaign of 1908 is taken from William Barton, *India's North-West Frontier* (London: John Murray, 1939), p. 73; C. Collin Davies, *The Problem of the North-West Frontier, 1890–1908: With a Survey of Policy since 1849* (Cambridge: Cambridge University Press, 1932), pp. 135–47; Donovan Jackson (Invicta), *India's Army* (London: Sampson Low, Marston, 1940), p. 350; Charles Miller, *Khyber: British India's North-West Frontier. The Story of an Imperial Migraine* (London: Macdonald and Jane's, 1977), pp. 301–2; James Spain, *The Pathan Borderland* (The Hague: Mouton, 1963), p. 180; Arthur Swinson, *North-West Frontier: People and Events, 1839–1947* (London: Hutchinson, 1967), p. 261.

11 India Office, L/MILITARY/7/16842, telegram Viceroy (Lord Minto) to Secretary of State for India (Lord Morley), 15 February 1908.

12 India Office, L/MILITARY/7/16842, telegrams Viceroy (Lord Minto) to Secretary of State for India (Lord Morley), 13 and 15 February 1908.

13 'Zakka Khel Force Strength Return and Organisation', attached to a minute addressed to the Under Secretary of State, India Office, unsigned, probably by the Military Secretary, India Office, dated 12 February 1908; India Office, L/MILITARY/7/16842.

14 Shearer, *1st Battalion, 15th Punjab Regiment*, pp. 38–39.

15 This account of the Zakka Khel campaign is taken from Army Headquarters India, *Frontier and Overseas Expeditions from India*, ii, Supplement A: Operations against the Zakka Khel Afridis, 1908 (Simla: Government of India, 1908), pp. 9–11; Michael Barthorp, *The North-West Frontier: British India and Afghanistan. A Pictorial History, 1839–1947* (Poole, Dorset: Blandford Press, 1982); William Barton, *India's North-West Frontier* (London: John Murray, 1939), pp. 73–74; Davies, *Problem of the North-West Frontier*, pp. 148–49; H.L. Nevill, *Campaigns on the North-West Frontier, 1849–1908* (London: John Murray, 1912), p. 332; D.S. Richards, *The Savage Frontier: A History of the Anglo-Afghan Wars* (London: Macmillan, 1990); H.C. Wylly, *From the Black Mountain to Waziristan* (London: Macmillan, 1912), p. 339.

16 Sotheby's, *Orders, Medals and Decorations* (London: sale catalogue, Tuesday 18 December 1990); medal in the collection of the National Army Museum, inscribed: 'R.E.H. Dyer

Major, 25th Pjbis'; *Indian Army List*, July 1919, p. 282: 'War Services: NW Frontier of India, 1908 – Operations in the Zakka Khel country – Medal with clasp'.

17   Shearer, *1st Battalion, 15th Punjab Regiment*, p. 39.

18   *Specifications of Inventions: Printed under the Patents, Designs, and Trade Marks Act 1883, 1908* (London: Patent Office Sales Branch, 1909), xlviii and lxix, patents 9559 of 1908 and 13,746 of 1908; Shearer, *1st Battalion, 15th Punjab Regiment*, p. 39.

19   *Specifications of Inventions: Printed under the Patents, Designs, and Trade Marks Act 1883, 1908* (London: Patent Office Sales Branch, 1910), cviii and cxxxvi, patents 21,456 and 27,022 of 1908.

20   India Office, L/MILITARY/7/17017.

21   Colvin, *Dyer*, pp. 51–52.

22   *Specifications of Inventions: Printed under the Patents, Designs, and Trade Marks Act 1883, 1909* (London: Patent Office Sales Branch, 1910), xxii, patent 4227 of 1909.

23   *Specifications of Inventions: Printed under the Patents, Designs, and Trade Marks Act 1883, 1909* (London: Patent Office Sales Branch, 1910), xxii, patent 5169 of 1909.

24   Colvin, *Dyer*, p. 52; India Office, L/MILITARY/9/509.

25   Colvin, *Dyer*, p. 46.

26   *Specifications of Inventions: Printed under the Patents, Designs, and Trade Marks Act 1883, 1910* (London: Patent Office Sales Branch, 1911), lxii, patent 12,238 of 1910.

27   *Army List*, May 1910, p.1322: 'Major, Commandant 25th Punjabis, Multan. Major F.J. Moberly, D.S.O., p.s.c., Second-in-Command'; ibid., June 1910, pp. 1213 and 1322: 'Lieutenant-Colonel 25 February 10'; *Indian Army List*, June 1911, p. 59a: 'Lieutenant-Colonel 25 February 1910'; ibid., p. 335: 'Commandant appointed 25 February 1910'.

28   India Office, L/MILITARY/7/17018.

29   Shearer, *1st Battalion, 15th Punjab Regiment*, p. 93.

30   *Gazette of India*, Government General Orders Military Department, January to June 1910, 424.

31   Shearer, *1st Battalion, 15th Punjab Regiment*, p. 93.

32   India Office, L/MILITARY/7/17019; Colvin, *Dyer*, p. 327.

33   Colvin, *Dyer*, p. 55.

34   Colvin, *Dyer*, p. 47.

35   Those elected rather than appointed or holding office *ex officio*.

36   Percival Spear, *A History of India* (Harmondsworth, Middlesex: Penguin, 1986), p. 179.

37   Colvin, *Dyer*, p. 55; Shearer, *1st Battalion, 15th Punjab Regiment*, p. 40; Sotheby's, *Orders, Medals and Decorations* (London: sale catalogue, Tuesday 18 December 1990); medal: 'Delhi Durbar, 1911 (unnamed)', in the collection of the National Army Museum.

38   Shearer, *1st Battalion, 15th Punjab Regiment*, p. 93. In the photograph are Captain G.W.Atkins, Lieutenant N.G.R. Coats, Lieutenant R.G. Gardner, Captain H.R.A. Hunt, Major F. Martin, by then the Second-in-Command, standing next to Dyer, Major W.E. Paleologus, Captain De L. W. Passy, Captain C.B. Riley, Lieutenant C.N. Steel, the Quartermaster, Captain C.H. Tyrrell, and Lieutenant H.R.O. Walker, the Adjutant.

39   *Specifications of Inventions: Printed under the Patents, Designs, and Trade Marks Act 1883, 1911* (London: Patent Office Sales Branch, 1913), xciv, patent 18,616 of 1911.

40   India Office, L/MILITARY/7/17021, p. 233. Dyer's reports on his officers are also given.

Almost all of them were reported on well; Captain C.B. Riley, Captain H.R.A. Hunt, Captain B.C. Penton ('working for Staff College'); Captain De L.W. Passy, Captain C.H. Tyrrell, Captain G.W. Atkins (though the latter was 'in debt'), Lieutenant C.N. Steel (Quartermaster), Lieutenant H.R.O. Walker, Lieutenant S.W. Finnis ('trying for Political Department'), Lieutenant R.G. Gardner ('Championship golf shield for two years') and Lieutenant N.G.R. Coats ('Signals Officer') are all in this category. Only one junior officer was reported on badly, Lieutenant A. Flagg, who was in debt, 'which hampers his performance'.

Notes to Chapter 9: Hong Kong

1   India Office, L/MILITARY/7/17021, p. 233; Review Report for 25th Punjabis; Lieutenant-General Pearson, Commander 3rd (Lahore) Division: 'Not inspected owing to move to China'; Lieutenant-General James Willcocks, Commanding Northern Army: 'Battalion left for China very suddenly and before I could get an opportunity of seeing it.'

2   National Archives of India, Foreign and Political, External B, March 1912, 690–93, 'Despatch of Indian Troops to Hong Kong', p. 7, telegrams, 11 January 1912.

3   National Archives of India, Foreign and Political, External B, March 1912, 690–93, 'Despatch of Indian Troops to Hong Kong', p. 5, telegram, 13 January 1912, from Major-General Grover, Secretary to Government of India, to the Quartermaster-General in India.

4   Ian Colvin, *The Life of General Dyer* (London: Blackwood, 1929), p. 56.

5   National Archives of India, Foreign and Political, External B, March 1912, 690–93, 'Despatch of Indian Troops to Hong Kong', p. 8, telegram, 23 January 1912, Major-General Grover to Quartermaster-General in India. The authority came a day after the ship had sailed, so either verbal authority had been given before, or, which is unlikely, Dyer had pre-empted the decision.

6   War Office, WO106/27, 25 January 1912, telegram 02234, Army Headquarters, Simla to Secretary of State for War.

7   War Office, WO106/27, 112, 26 January 1912, telegram from the Government of India to Hong Kong.

8   Of their party, the press named Rex and Annie Dyer, Major Poleologus (sic), Major and Mrs F. Martin, Captain and Mrs Riley, with their child, Captains Penton, Passy and Tyrrell, Lieutenants Flag, Steel, Walker, Gardner and Coats, and Lieutenant-Colonel Norman of the Indian Medical Services, the 25th's Medical Officer, and his wife. There was also a Mr Newman (probably a warrant officer of the Supply and Transport Corps), with his wife and children; *Hong Kong Daily Press*, 8 February 1912; *Army List*, March 1912, p. 1322 and *Indian Army List*, April 1912, first show Dyer in Hong Kong.

9   *Hong Kong Daily Press*, 3 April and 24 May 1912.

10   It was reported on 1 May 1912 that there had been 330 fatal cases of plague so far that year; a week later another column reported that 122 fatal cases of plague had occurred in that week alone. Plague went on until the next year, but the outbreak of smallpox was coming to an end by May; on the 13th of that month, it was reported in the press that there were only six cases that week; *Hong Kong Daily Press*, 1, 7 and 13 May 1912.

11 *Hong Kong Daily Press*, 23 March 1912.

12 *Hong Kong Daily Telegraph*, 30 May 1913. Mr G.N. Orme, District Officer, reported that 62.13 inches of rain had fallen in 1912 in Tai Po (across the hills of the New Territories from Lai Chi Kok) against an average of 99.4 inches for the previous six years. The first rice crop was good in June 1912, but the second in September to October was poor due to drought. The Fan Ling golf course development that year had included the construction of the clubhouse, and the road between Tai Po and Fan Ling had been started, whilst reclamation was made at Tai Po.

13 Background to Hong Kong in 1912 is taken from Geoffrey Robley Sayer, *Hong Kong, 1862–1919* (Hong Kong: Hong Kong University Press, 1975), pp. 104–10, 111–20.

14 Colvin, *Dyer*, p. 56; J.E. Shearer, *A History of the 1st Battalion, 15th Punjab Regiment, 1857–1937* (Aldershot: Gale & Polden, 1937), p. 41.

15 *Specifications of Inventions: Printed under the Patents, Designs, and Trade Marks Act 1883, 1912* (London: Patent Office Sales Branch, 1914), xxii, patent 19,201 of 1912.

16 *Hong Kong Daily Press*, 27 June 1912, report of 1460 plague deaths to date in 1912.

17 Colvin, *Dyer*, pp. 56, 58; *Hong Kong Daily Press*, 1 August 1912.

18 *Hong Kong Daily Press*, 22 August 1912; National Archives of India, Foreign and Political, External B, October 1912, 118, 'Expedition from the Hong Kong Garrison against a gang of pirates in the vicinity of Macao', 24 August 1912, telegram from the War Office announcing that the Army Council had approved the Colonial Office letter concerning the expedition including 400 Indian troops against pirates in conjunction with the Portuguese Macao and Chinese Governments.

19 India Office, L/MILITARY/7/17022.

20 *Specifications of Inventions: Printed under the Patents, Designs, and Trade Marks Act 1883, 1912* (London: Patent Office Sales Branch, 1914), xxii, patent 28,206 of 1912; India Office, L/MILITARY/9/509.

21 Colvin, *Dyer*, p. 47.

22 Regrettably, all Dyer's notes used by Colvin have vanished, and there is no record in the Royal Arsenal at Woolwich of any of these transactions. The models and paperwork associated with such projects were housed in the Royal Artillery Institute Library and Archive, which was destroyed with all its contents by a V Bomb in 1944; personal communication to the author by Mr Paul Evans, Librarian, Firepower, the Royal Artillery Museum, 19 March 2002.

23 Photograph in the possession of Martin Dyer; *Specifications of Inventions: Printed under the Patents, Designs, and Trade Marks Act 1883, 1913* (London: Patent Office Sales Branch, 1915), civ, patent 20,771 of 1913.

24 Colvin, *Dyer*, pp. 48–49.

25 The 25th had continued their training throughout the year, and had taken part in garrison exercises in January, forming part of Blue forces with the 26th Punjabis, pitted against a Red force of a composite battery of mountain artillery and the 8th Rajputs. On 16 April, Lieutenant N.G.R. Coats had taken over as Quartermaster from the long-serving Captain C.N. Steel, whose next job indicated that he had done well in his previous post; on 24 April, he had been appointed officiating Adjutant vice Captain H.R.O. Walker, who had proceeded on three months' leave. In the next month the alarming news had arrived by telegram

from Singapore that the troop ship *Assaye*, carrying reinforcements from Bombay, including one Indian Officer and some other ranks of the 25th, had caught fire off the coast of the Malay States. Luckily, none of the regiment's men had been injured, and the ship had managed to limp back to Singapore where she was repaired and again sent on her way to Hong Kong. Captain C.H. Tyrrell had taken over as an officiating double company commander on 22 May in place of Captain C.B. Riley who went home on leave. A parade of eight hundred men including a detachment of the 25th had marched past the Governor on the Hong Kong Cricket Ground to celebrate the King's Birthday on 2 June, headed by General Anderson, who had been about to leave post; this had been his last major parade. The battalion had gained first place in the China Command Athletic Meeting held in the winter months, and had also won the United Services Recreation Club Hockey Tournament, which they were to retain until they departed. The epidemic of bubonic plague had continued, but was diminishing; by 24 April, only thirty-three cases of plague had been registered in Hong Kong since 1 January, although the summer weather caused another outbreak, and by 19 August this had caused 296 fatalities. The previous year's drought had been over-compensated by a particularly wet summer, and the colony had been struck by two typhoons of unusual violence. The first had come close to Hong Kong, reaching land at a spot across the Pearl River to the west of the colony, just south of Macao. It had battered Hong Kong on 17 August, flooding the *praya* in Wanchai to a depth greater than at any time since 1900. Three yachts had been driven ashore, telegraph wires fell, a house collapsed, and there had been over twenty deaths. A second storm had struck on 19 September, the centre of the typhoon this time further away, some fifty miles from the colony, and so there was less damage. Both typhoons had caused severe problems in the shacks and canvas at Lai Chi Kok. There had been more piracy in Hong Kong waters; the steamer *Tai On* had been attacked underway between Hong Kong and the West River. *Hong Kong Daily Press*, 23 December 1912, 9 July, 18 and 19 August 1913; *Hong Kong Telegraph*, 14 January, 17 and 24 April, 19 and 27 May, 3 June, 25 July, 1, 8, 18 and 28 August, 9, 12 and 19 September 1913.

26 Sayer, *Hong Kong, 1862–1919*, p. 113.

27 Shearer, *1st Battalion, 15th Punjab Regiment*, pp. 42 and 93. There is an unnamed photograph of a Sikh Havildar-Major in the possession of Martin Dyer which may be the new Subadar-Major taken some years before; if so, it indicates that Rex Dyer held him in some affection.

28 *Hong Kong Telegraph*, 10 October 1913; Philip Mason, *A Matter of Honour: An Account of the Indian Army, its Officers and Men* (London: Jonathan Cape, 1974), p. 344.

29 *Hong Kong Telegraph*, 10 October 1913.

30 There was, though, the occasional reminder that life in Hong Kong was not wholly secure. That year the steamer *Tai On* was again attacked by pirates, but this time the crew attempted to resist. She was burned to the waterline, and two hundred passengers lost their lives. This prompted Sir Henry May to add to his emergency powers of arrest and deportation, and the police and Royal Navy were directed to crack down on banditry; Sayer, *Hong Kong, 1862–1919*, p. 113.

31 *Specifications of Inventions: Printed under the Patents, Designs, and Trade Marks Act 1883, 1913* (London: Patent Office Sales Branch, 1915), civ, patent 20,771 of 1913.

32 General Kelly's report on the 25th shows that their health in the bad climate and disease of

Hong Kong was good, but that their arms and equipment had not been so well looked after, and the staff officers who had accompanied him on his inspection had found 'rifles not satisfactory, 225 being unserviceable'. The humidity and temporary storage at Lai Chi Kok had perhaps taken their toll. The battalion's new Quartermaster, Coats, was also perhaps not so much on the ball as his predecessor Steel had been. Kelly, however, assessed the 25th as highly effective: 'The unit is most efficient and fit in every way for active service'; Dyer's own reports stated: 'Captain C.B. Riley – good, seeking instruction musketry post in Indian school'; this was a man after Dyer's own heart. 'Captain H.R.A. Hunt – Very Good double company commander. At Staff College now'. Allowing his young officers to try for Staff College was one of Dyer's priorities, which must have added to his popularity. 'Captain de L.W. Passy – Very Good and Very popular'. 'Captain C.H. Tyrrell – methodical and intelligent, recommended for staff college list'. 'Captain G.W. Atkins – gifted, able, intelligent, monetary difficulties needing constant supervision. Not recommended for staff college'. 'Captain A. Flagg – Money difficulties prevent him doing self justice'. 'Captain C.N. Steel – good Quartermaster, unassuming'. 'Captain H.R.O. Walker – one of the best officers in the regiment, recommended for Staff College'. 'Lieutenant R.G. Gardner – Adjutant recently appointed. Possesses force of character, not passed for promotion'. 'Lieutenant N.G.R. Coats – Now Quartermaster, hardworking, good. Fond of sport and popular with the men'. India Office file L/MILITARY/7/17023.

33   *Hong Kong Daily Press*, 10 April 1912; Sayer, *Hong Kong, 1862–1919*, pp. 120, 153; India Office, L/MILITARY/9/509 and L/MILITARY/14/1025.

34   Colvin, *Dyer*, p. 59.

35   Measures for the pre-planned 'Precautionary Period' were immediately put in place, and the Royal Navy began to inspect ships visiting the harbour from 2 August. A 'Plan for the Defence of Hong Kong Harbour' had been issued by General Kelly as Operational Order 1 in 1913. It called for the two reinforcement battalions, 25th and 26th Punjabis, to form an 'additional fortress reserve' and on mobilisation the 25th were to move to 8th Rajput's lines at Whitfield Barracks in Kowloon. They were allocated for this move three launches and two lighters to take them from Lai Chi Kok to Kowloon Public Pier; War Office, WO/32/5345, Hong Kong. Report on the Operations from the Outbreak of War to the End of 1914, by Major-General Kelly, Commanding His Britannic Majesty's Troops in China, 3 February 1915, to Secretary, War Office. Transmitted by the Governor Sir F.H. May, 15 January 1915, to Lord Kitchener; War Office, WO/32/5316, Defence of Hong Kong Harbour, Operational Order 1, 4 October 1913.

36   War Office, WO/95/5441, South China Command, War Diary, Hong Kong Headquarters, General Staff.

37   General Kelly had several changes of mind about where to locate the 25th. On 3 August, his Headquarters published a map with both 25th and 26th shown together at Quarry Point in the east of Hong Kong Island. This plan survived only twenty-four hours; on the next day, when modifications were ordered for the Defence Scheme in the event of war, the 25th were ordered to Happy Valley; War Office, WO/95/5441, South China Command, War Diary, Hong Kong Headquarters, General Staff.

38   War Office, WO/95/5441, South China Command, War Diary, Deputy Assistant Director Supplies and Transport, August 1914 to July 1915.

39   Colvin, *Dyer*, p. 59.

40   War Office, WO/32/5345, Hong Kong, Report on the Operations from the Outbreak of War to the End of 1914.

41   Shearer, *1st Battalion, 15th Punjab Regiment*, p. 43.

42   War Office, WO/95/5441, South China Command, War Diary, Eastern Section 1914 August to 1915 July, 19 August: 'information received 25th Punjabis to be located Happy Valley and detached from General Reserve'.

43   *Hong Kong Daily Press*, 19 August 1914.

44   Dyer went over to inspect the new lines on 24 September. He was not impressed with them, and made an immediate request for the Government to forego officers' payment for rent; it is probable that none of his officers had been charged for the makeshift quarters in Lai Chi Kok, and he could see no reason why wartime service should increase their financial burden; War Office, WO/95/5441, South China Command, War Diary, Deputy Assistant Director Supplies and Transport, August 1914 to July 1915. The 25th had 29,151 cubic feet of their heavy baggage stored in Holt's Wharf at the time.

45   War Office, WO/95/5441, South China Command, War Diary, Eastern Section 1914 August to 1915 July.

46   Shearer, *1st Battalion, 15th Punjab Regiment*, p. 43.

47   War Office, WO/95/5441, South China Command, War Diary, Eastern Section 1914 August to 1915 July.

48   War Office, WO/32/5345, Hong Kong, Report on the Operations from the Outbreak of War to the End of 1914.

49   We do not have the date of the end of Dyer's command. *Indian Army List*, July 1914, p. 403, shows the planned date of completion of tenure as 24 February 1915 after five years' regimental command, but Dyer left two months before this. Shearer, *1st Battalion, 15th Punjab Regiment*, p. 93, states only that Dyer's command ended in 1914.

50   War Office, WO/32/5345, Hong Kong, Report on the Operations from the Outbreak of War to the End of 1914.

51   India Office, L/MILITARY/7/17024.

52   *Indian Army List*, January 1915, p. 9: 'General Staff Officer Grade 1, Lucknow temporary, 2 December 1914' (perhaps he was posted initially to Lucknow, or held there on paper only; this could also be a mistake); ibid., p. 15: 'GSO 1 temporary to 2nd (Rawalpindi) Division'; p. 403 still shows him as Commanding Officer 25th Punjabis with end of tenure as 24 February 1915; ibid., p. 493, shows him as: 'GSO 1st Grade 2nd Division temporary'. Colvin, *Dyer*, p. 59, records that he arrived in Rawalpindi on 13 December.

Notes to Chapter 10: *The First World War*

1   *Army List*, March 1915, p. 68: 'GSO1 2nd Rawalpindi Division to General Officer Commanding Major-General Sir G.C. Kitson. (temporary)'; ibid., p. 2097, also shows him still as Commandant 25th Punjabis. J.E. Shearer, *A History of the 1st Battalion, 15th Punjab Regiment, 1857–1937* (Aldershot: Gale & Polden, 1937), p. 93, shows he was a lieutenant-colonel on staff duty from 1914–15.

2   Ian Colvin, *The Life of General Dyer* (London: Blackwood, 1929), pp. 60–61.

3   Sir Michael O'Dwyer, *India as I Knew It, 1885–1925* (London: Constable, 1925), p. 213.

4   India Office, L/MILITARY/14/1025.

5   Henry Landau, *The Enemy Within: The Inside Story of German Sabotage in America* (London: G.P. Putnam's Sons, 1937), pp. 28–32.

6   O'Dwyer, *India as I Knew It*, pp. 128–201.

7   S.L. Menezes, *Fidelity and Honour: The Indian Army from the Seventeenth to the Twenty-First Century* (New Delhi: Viking, Penguin Books, 1993), pp. 267–68.

8   Hari Singh, *Gandhi, Rowlatt Satyagraha and British Imperialism: Emergence of Mass Movements in Punjab and Delhi* (Delhi: Indian Bibliographies Bureau, 1990), p. 34; Richard J. Popplewell, *Intelligence and Imperial Defence: British Intelligence and the Defence of the Indian Empire, 1904–1924* (London: Frank Cass, 1995), pp. 4–332.

9   *Army List*, September 1916: 'Colonel 3 June 1915'; the *Gazette of India*, January to December 1920, however, shows that his substantive rank dated from a year later: 'The promotion of the undermentioned Officers, Ind. Army, to the rank of Colonel, as notified in the *Gazette* of 25 August 1916, 18 November 1916, 25 October 1917, 22 February 1918, and 22 May 1918, is antedated as follows: Colonel (temporary. Brigadier-General) R.E.H. Dyer to 5 March 1916.'

10   Seistan, the older form of the name of the Persian region, was written Sistan in Persian at the time, and is usually written in that form now. Except in quotations, such as the name of the Seistan Field Force, Sistan will be used in the text.

11   Reginald Edward Harry Dyer, *Raiders of the Sarhad: Being an Account of a Campaign of Arms and Bluff against the Brigands of the Persian-Baluchi Border during the Great War* (London: H.F. & G. Witherby, 1921).

Notes to Chapter 11: Sistan

1   F.J. Moberly, *Operations in Persia, 1914–1919* (London: Her Majesty's Stationery Office, 1987), p. 149.

2   Detail on German activities in Persia and Afghanistan is taken from Henry Landau, *The Enemy Within: The Inside Story of German Sabotage in America* (London: G.P. Putnam's Sons, 1937); S.L. Menezes, *Fidelity and Honour: The Indian Army from the Seventeenth to the Twenty-First Century* (New Delhi: Viking, Penguin Books, 1993), p. 267; Sir Michael O'Dwyer, *India as I Knew It, 1885–1925* (London: Constable, 1925), pp. 128–201; Richard J. Popplewell, *Intelligence and Imperial Defence: British Intelligence and the Defence of the Indian Empire, 1904–1924* (London: Frank Cass, 1995), pp. 4–332.

3   Detail on the campaign in East Persia is taken from W.E.R. Dickson, *East Persia: A Backwater of the War* (London: Edward Arnold, 1924), pp. 40–43; Moberly, *Operations in Persia*, p.149ff. The Army Headquarters logs for the East Persia campaign are in India Office, L/MILITARY/17/5/4137 to 4144. Dyer's headquarters produced a daily log, which is in War Office, WO 95/5415, *War Diary Sistan Field Force, 1915–1920*, which only commences in May. Dyer's two dispatches, one on the capture of Jihand Khan, the other on operations in August, are printed in War Office, WO 106/56. The principal correspondence recorded in

the Foreign and Political Department of the Government of India is found in Lord Chelmsford's papers in the India Office, MSS Eur E 264/54. The files in the National Archives of India are mostly still classified 'Secret'. One file that is open has some detail: Foreign and Political, April 1916, 1–106, 'Mekran Disturbances'. Dyer's own account is in Reginald Edward Harry Dyer, *Raiders of the Sarhad: Being an Account of a Campaign of Arms and Bluff against the Brigands of the Persian-Baluchi Border during the Great War* (London: H.F. & G. Witherby, 1921), which is closely followed by Ian Colvin, *The Life of General Dyer* (London: Blackwood, 1929), chapters 8/13. Various regimental histories also cover the period, particularly J.A.C. Kreyer and G. Uloth, *The 28th Light Cavalry in Persia and Russian Turkistan, 1915–20* (Oxford: Slatter & Rose, 1926) and C.L. Proudfoot, *We Lead: The 7th Light Cavalry, 1784–1990* (New Delhi: Lancer International, 1991), which are histories of the 28th Light Cavalry; W.B.P. Tugwell, *History of the Bombay Pioneers, 1777–1933* (London; Sidney Press, 1938), which is a history of the 12th Pioneers; and National Archives of India: Military Miscellany Bound Volume Notes, vol. 8, *Digest of Services of 106th Hazara Pioneers*. 19th Punjabis, unfortunately, left no regimental history.

4   The correct rendering is Baloch, but the spelling Baluch was, and is still, frequently used by most writers and will be used in the text.

5   Detail on East Persia is taken from C. Edmund Bosworth, 'The Sarhadd Region of Persian Baluchistan from Mediaeval Islamic Times to the Mid-Twentieth Century', in *Studia Iranica*, 31 (2002), fascicle 1, pp. 79–102; Sir Frederic Goldsmid, *Eastern Persia: An Account of the Journeys of the Boundary Commission, 1870–71–72*, 2 vols (London: Macmillan, 1876); Sir T. Hungerford Holdich, *The Indian Borderland, 1880–1900* (London: Methuen, 1901), pp. 314–39, 392; Philip Carl Salzman, *Black Tents of Baluchistan* (Washington, DC: Smithsonian Institute Press, 2000), p. 317.

6   The Sarhadd was often spelled Sarhad by the British, but the former rendering, correct then and now, will be used in the text except in quotations.

7   According to Dyer, the Damanis had three sections, the Yar-Muhammadzay, the Ismailzay and the Gamshadzay, though the British Political Agents were considerably confused by the tribal organisation in the Sarhadd, and this remains open to some doubt. Though the tribesmen were undoubtedly Baluch, the names of the three sections, ending in –zay, are Pushtu, and may indicate some allegiance to the Afghan monarchy at some stage. The Kurds Dyer met are not the Kurds of present-day Kurdistan but a group of nomadic people of uncertain provenance, perhaps Brahuis.

8   Chelmsford Papers, in the India Office collection of the British Library, MSS Eur E 264/54d/485.

9   Dyer was posted on paper to the post of Commander Rawalpindi Station, an administrative post commanding the garrison there, and one under General Kitson's control, which the latter would have needed to cover whilst Dyer was away in Persia; *Indian Army List*, April 1917, pp. 8, 15: '24 February 1916, Commander Rawalpindi Station'. There is no evidence he ever performed any of duties attached to this post.

10   Dyer, *Raiders of the Sarhad*, p. 18.

11   Colvin, *Dyer*, p. 68; Dyer, *Raiders of the Sarhad*, pp. 18–20. Allan gained a reputation in the campaign; Kreyer and Uloth, *The 28th Light Cavalry in Persia and Russian Turkistan*, p. 54, call him 'a distinguished driver'.

12   Colvin, *Dyer*, p. 69. The letter also included details of Dyer's life insurance and shares, and the fact that he had sent Annie furs and a jewel from Rawalpindi, so was almost a will, perhaps not surprising given the circumstances. The fact that Dyer, who had not long been a colonel, was in possession of a Rolls Royce, and obviously had some wealth to bequeath, may indicate that he had inherited some money from his father.

13   Dyer, *Raiders of the Sarhad*, p. 28.

14   Dyer, *Raiders of the Sarhad*, pp. 23–29; India Office, L/MILITARY/17/5/4137, War Diary, Army Headquarters, India, Persia, vol. 16 (from 1 to 31 March 1916); entries 41,739 and 41,964.

15   Kreyer and Uloth, *The 28th Light Cavalry in Persia and Russian Turkistan*, p. 53.

16   Ian Colvin, *The Life of General Dyer* (London: Blackwood, 1931), p. xvi note 2.

17   E.P. Yeates, 'General Dyer: Some Recollections', *Blackwoods Magazine* (December 1927), p. 793.

18   India Office, MSS Eur E 264/54(a), 26–27; National Archives of India, Foreign and Political, April 1916, 1–106, 'Mekran Disturbances'. At this stage the Government of India were enthusiastic about getting the Sarhaddis under control. A.H. Grant, Secretary in the Foreign and Political Department, minuted the file on 11 March: 'I told Army Department that it was most desirable for Colonel Dyer to come to any arrangement possible with the Sarhadd Sardars through the political authorities. It would be a pity to miss any chance of getting them on our side'.

19   Vasht was the spelling used by some British writers for the town of Washt, the Baluchi form, or Khwash, the Persian, which was the chief town of the Sarhadd. India Office, L/MILITARY/17/5/4137, entry 42190 – 6 March 1916, Dyer to CGS.

20   For instance, on 29 April, the Agent to the Governor General in Baluchistan telegraphed the Government of India: 'I concur in need of dominating Damanis, until they have atoned for past misdeeds'; India Office, MSS Eur E 264/54 (b), 145.

21   India Office, MSS Eur E 264/54(a), proceeding 25 (really proceeding 31).

22   28th Light Cavalry were deployed, from north to south: A Squadron at Birjand; D Squadron split between Neh and Bandan; Regimental Headquarters under Major Claridge, who was shortly to take over as Commanding Officer from Wilkely, and C Squadron with Force Headquarters at Nasratabad; and B Squadron split between Robat and Saindak. The gun section was from 25th Mountain Battery and had only two guns, deployed at Kacha. 19th Punjabis were missing one double company, and were deployed with 332 men in Nasratabad and to its north, and 258 men in Robat and Kacha in the south. The 12th Pioneer's machine gun section had six machine guns only, deployed two at Birjand, two at Nasratabad and two at Robat.

23   400 in Nasratabad and to its north, and 200 to the south.

24   Proudfoot, *We Lead: The 7th Light Cavalry*, p. 35; Moberly, *Operations in Persia*, p. 155; India Office, MSS Eur E 264/54(a), proceeding 99, 31 March 1916.

25   Sipi was Nasratabad Sipi, in the centre of the cordon and the previous location of its Headquarters. Major Keyes was the Consul at Sibi, which was south of Dyer's area.

26   India Office, L/MILITARY/17/5/4137, entry 42528; National Archives of India, Foreign and Political, April 1916, 1–106, 'Mekran Disturbances'.

27   His title, Sarhadd-dar, literally holder of the Sarhadd, is obscure, and may represent a

temporary appointment for this occasion. There is no record of an official permanently appointed by the Khan of Kalat in this role. Dyer usually writes his name Shukar Khan.

28 The British usually wrote this Jhalawan.

29 Moberly, *Operations in Persia*, p. 156; War Office, WO 106/56, *Commander-in-Chief in India Despatch*, p. 3.

30 India Office, L/MILITARY/17/5/4137, entry 42528, Dyer to CGS: 'Political is my present source of information almost entirely which is wrong as Captain Landon is quite up to organizing a separate source at my disposal.'

31 In Persian this is rendered as Rigi, and so they are known as such in some sources. Reki will be used in this text except in quotations.

32 Dyer, *Raiders of the Sarhad*, pp. 33–36.

33 Salzman, *Black Tents of Baluchistan*, p. 317.

34 Juma Khan was sardar of the Ismailzay section of the Damani Baluch.

35 Jiand Khan, also written Jiyand Khan (both Persian forms of his name), and Jihand Khan (his actual Baluch name), was the sardar of the Yar-Muhammadzay section of the Damani Baluch, and was recognised as the principal sardar of the Damani tribe. Jihand will be used in the text except in quotations.

36 India Office, L/MILITARY/17/5/4137, entry 42282.

37 Dyer, *Raiders of the Sarhad*, pp. 23, 51. The affair obviously made an impression on Dyer's troops, as it is recorded in both Tugwell, *History of the Bombay Pioneers*, p. 405, and Kreyer and Uloth, *The 28th Light Cavalry in Persia and Russian Turkistan*, p. 54; Colvin, *Dyer*, pp. 115–16.

38 India Office, L/MILITARY/17/5/4137, entry 44660, 21 March 1916, General Officer Commanding to CGS.

39 Dyer, *Raiders of the Sarhad*, pp. 47–48, 50. Brigadiers were accorded the rank of general until after the end of the war.

40 India Office, L/MILITARY/17/5/4137, entry 42587, Viceroy (Army) to SSI: 'Decided to raise status of commander of troops Sistan to Colonel on the Staff and Lieutenant-Colonel R.E.H. Dyer has been appointed to this post. Commander-in-Chief in India recommends the grant to Dyer of temporary rank of Brigadier-General with effect from 24 February.' Entry 42556, S.S.I. to Viceroy, sanctions this. *Army List*, April 1916, p. 2658a: 'Temporary Brigadier-General, 21st [sic] February 1916'; ibid., September 1916, p. 2658: 'Temporary Brigadier-General, 24th February 1916 whilst Colonel on Staff Indian'.

41 Moberly, *Operations in Persia*, p. 149.

42 India Office, MSS Eur E 264/54 (b), proceeding 219.

43 Dyer, *Raiders of the Sarhad*, p. 47.

44 This is usually written Sarawan. Sarawan and Jahlawan are the two major provinces of the Khanate of Kalat.

45 Usually written Makran, and the latter will be used in the text except in quotations. Makran is the southernmost province of the Khanate of Kalat.

46 India Office, MSS Eur E 264/54 (b), proceedings 219, 231, 273, and MSS Eur E 264/54 (c), proceeding 10.

47 India Office, L/MILITARY/17/5/4137, entries 46252 dated 30 March, and 46337 dated 31 March 1916.

48   Tugwell, *History of the Bombay Pioneers*, p. 406.

Notes to Chapter 12: The Sarhadd

1   Reginald Edward Harry Dyer, *Raiders of the Sarhad: Being an Account of a Campaign of Arms and Bluff against the Brigands of the Persian-Baluchi Border during the Great War* (London: H.F. & G. Witherby, 1921), p. 55.

2   India Office, MSS Eur E 264/54 (b), proceeding 187.

3   Ian Colvin, *The Life of General Dyer* (London: Blackwood, 1929), p. 91 note 1. He calls him Khan Bahadur Shukker Khan; Dyer, *Raiders of the Sarhad*, p. 57. Although Dyer seems to have liked this man, he got his name wrong; this was not unusual for him. In his book, he spelled the name of his subordinate, Yeates, 'Yates', and he managed to spell Major Landon 'Landen'.

4   Nasratabad Sipi, written sometimes by the British as Sipeh. Sipi will be used in the text except in quotations.

5   F.J. Moberly, *Operations in Persia, 1914–1919* (London: Her Majesty's Stationery Office, 1987), p. 156; C.L. Proudfoot, *We Lead: The 7th Light Cavalry, 1784–1990* (New Delhi: Lancer International, 1991), pp. 34–36; India Office, MSS Eur E 264/54 (b), proceeding 69, telegram Consul Seistan to Simla, 16 April 1916; ibid., proceeding 90, 22 April 1916.

6   The Yar-Muhammadzay were also known as the Yar-Ahmadzay. Their name was written in a multitude of forms by the British. Yar-Muhammadzay will be used in the text except in quotations.

7   Percy Molesworth Sykes, *Ten Thousand Miles in Persia: or Eight Years in Iran* (London: John Murray, 1902), p. 354.

8   Dyer, *Raiders of the Sarhad*, p. 59.

9   Dyer, *Raiders of the Sarhad*, pp. 57–62; India Office, L/MILITARY/17/5/4138, entry 49782, telegram General Officer Commanding Seistan to CGS, 15 April 1916.

10   The Gamshadzay were rendered Gomshadzai and other forms by the British. Gamshadzay will be used in the text except in quotations.

11   Khalil Khan is also rendered Halil Khan. The former will be used in the text except in quotations.

12   Ismailzay was also rendered Ismailzai and in other forms by the British. Ismailzay will be used in the text except in quotations.

13   One assumes Dyer used an interpreter for all his speeches, and even his conversations, as he had hardly any Baluchi and his Persian seems to have been too limited for business purposes. The Baluch would not have spoken Urdu, Hindustani, Punjabi or Pushtu, the other languages used by Dyer. It is probable that the interpreters were Shakar Khan, the Sarhadd-dar, and Idu, the Reki, who would have thereby been given some influence over what was said, and so over the flow of information and the course of events.

14   Moberly, *Operations in Persia*, p. 164; India Office, L/MILITARY/17/5/4138, entry 49951, 21 April 1916; Proudfoot, *We Lead: The 7th Light Cavalry, 1784–1990*, p. 39; Dyer, *Raiders of the Sarhad*, p. 99.

15   India Office, L/MILITARY/17/5/4138, entry 50796, 24 April 1916.

16 W.B.P. Tugwell, *History of the Bombay Pioneers, 1777–1933* (London; Sidney Press, 1938), p. 407.

17 Dyer, *Raiders of the Sarhad*, pp. 92–97.

18 India Office, L/MILITARY/17/5/4138, entry 51126, 28 April 1916.

19 India Office, L/MILITARY/17/5/4138, entry 51261, 29 April 1916.

20 India Office, MSS Eur E 264/54 (b), proceeding 150.

21 India Office, MSS Eur E 264/54 (b), proceeding 224.

22 War Office, WO 106/56, *Despatch by General Sir Charles Monro, Commander-in-Chief in India, on Operations on India's Frontiers, 1916*, p. 2.

23 India Office, MSS Eur E 264/54 (b), proceedings 156 and 201.

24 The Narui was a sub-section of the Ismailzay which had attacked the post at Sipi on 20 April. Dyer spells it 'Nahruis' a few lines further on, though these are the same people.

25 This should be Major Landon, whom Dyer seems to have promoted locally when he took him onto his staff; India Office, MSS Eur E 264/54 (b), proceeding 187.

26 India Office, MSS Eur E 264/54 (c), proceedings 9 and 64.

27 War Office, WO 95/5415, 2 May 1916.

28 Dyer, *Raiders of the Sarhad*, pp. 98–101.

29 India Office, MSS Eur E 264/54 (b), proceeding 203.

30 Dyer, *Raiders of the Sarhad*, p. 99; A.C. Kreyer and G. Uloth, *The 28th Light Cavalry in Persia and Russian Turkistan, 1915–20* (Oxford: Slatter & Rose, 1926), p. 61; Proudfoot, *We Lead: The 7th Light Cavalry, 1784–1990*, p. 39; Tugwell, *History of the Bombay Pioneers*, p. 408. All have the story of the 'dash to Khwash'.

31 His Headquarters log sheets commence at this time.

32 India Office, L/MILITARY/17/5/4139, entry 52217, 3 May 1916.

33 War Office, WO 95/5415, 4 May 1916; Kreyer and Uloth, *The 28th Light Cavalry in Persia and Russian Turkistan*, p. 61.

34 India Office, MSS Eur E 264/54 (b), proceeding 82.

35 Dyer, *Raiders of the Sarhad*, pp. 105–21; Tugwell, *History of the Bombay Pioneers*, p. 408.

36 Dyer, *Raiders of the Sarhad*, pp. 134–36.

37 India Office, L/MILITARY/17/5/4139, entry 54193, 14 May 1916.

38 War Office, WO 95/5415, 19 May 1916.

39 India Office, L/MILITARY/17/5/4139, entry 52971, 9 May 1916; MSS Eur E 264/54 (b), proceeding 223, 9 May 1916.

40 India Office, MSS Eur E 264/54 (c), proceeding 5. Dyer's spelling of the names of the tribes and men with which he was dealing is erratic. The Yarmuhammadzais or Yarmahomedzais are the Yar-Muhammadzay, and the Gamshazai or Gomshadzais are the Gamshadzay. The telegram cipher has garbled the word Gwgieh.

41 India Office, MSS Eur E 264/54 (b), proceeding 251. On 22 June, Sykes telegraphed Simla asking 'should not Dyer be keeping me informed?', MSS Eur E 264/54 (c), proceeding 103.

42 India Office, MSS Eur E 264/54 (b), proceeding 221; L/MILITARY/17/5/4139, entry 55713, 24 May.

43 India Office, MSS Eur E 264/54 (b), proceeding 234.

44 India Office, MSS Eur E 264/54 (c), proceeding 180.

45 Kreyer and Uloth, *The 28th Light Cavalry in Persia and Russian Turkistan*, p. 61.

46   War Office, WO 95/5415, 24, 26 and 28 May 1916; India Office, L/MILITARY/17/5/4139, entry 56782, 30 May; Dyer, *Raiders of the Sarhad*, p. 143; Moberly, *Operations in Persia*, p. 164.

47   War Office, WO 95/5415, 30 and 31 May, 1 June 1916; Moberly, *Operations in Persia*, p. 168; Dyer, *Raiders of the Sarhad*, pp. 139–42. In the latter, Dyer has two photos of the *darbar*, one of which clearly shows Major-General Grover, but as the latter is characteristically not mentioned in the text or caption, there is nothing at all in Dyer's book to indicate that anyone senior to him was present that day.

48   Dyer, *Raiders of the Sarhad*, p. 141.

49   War Office, WO 95/5415, 4 June 1916.

50   India Office, L/MILITARY/17/5/4140, entry 59527, 14 June 1916.

51   India Office, MSS Eur E 264/54 (c), proceeding 31.

52   India Office, L/MILITARY/17/5/4140, entry 60493, 19 June 1916; MSS Eur E 264/54 (c), proceedings 102, 106, 115, 119.

53   War Office, WO 95/5415, 3, 5 and 12 June 1916; Dyer, *Raiders of the Sarhad*, p. 143.

54   Dyer, *Raiders of the Sarhad*, p. 153.

55   Dyer, *Raiders of the Sarhad*, p. 159.

56   War Office, WO 106/951, report 147, Army Headquarters, MOI 18/33 F/Opns, *Report from the General Officer Commanding Sistan Field Force, Capture of Jiand (Damani) 14 June 1916*, 19 June 1916, is Dyer's full report to Army Headquarters on the incident, which they had printed. The incident is covered almost word for word in Dyer's log in War Office, WO 95/5415, 13–15 June 1916. Dyer's own account is in Dyer, *Raiders of the Sarhad*, pp. 152–61. Yeates's account is identical in Tugwell, *History of the Bombay Pioneers*, p. 409.

57   War Office, WO 95/5415, 19 June 1916.

58   Alfred Draper, *The Amritsar Massacre: Twilight of the Raj* (London: Buchan & Enright, 1985), p. 23.

59   India Office, L/MILITARY/17/5/4140, entry 60330, 18 June 1916; Dyer, *Raiders of the Sarhad*, pp. 162–64. Dyer maintains in his book that it was Army Headquarters which ordered the return of the prisoners to Quetta, but the log makes clear that he initiated the idea. The reason for this deception is made clear in subsequent events.

60   National Archives of India, Military Miscellany Bound Volume, Notes, vol. 8, *Digest of Services of 106th Hazara Pioneers*, 'An Account of the Part Taken in the Operations against the Damanis by a Detachment of 106th Hazara Pioneers 1916', by V. Moore-Lane, p. 1; India Office, L/MILITARY/17/5/4140, entry 60369; MSS Eur E 264/54 (c), proceeding 96.

61   Molesworth Sykes, *Ten Thousand Miles in Persia*, pp. 92–93.

62   Dyer, *Raiders of the Sarhad*, pp. 165–70.

63   Dyer, *Raiders of the Sarhad*, p. 137; War Office, WO 95/5415, 24 June 1916.

64   Dyer, *Raiders of the Sarhad*, pp. 148–52. It may well never have happened as Dyer describes it; there is no record of the court martial in the log, and in his book Dyer places the episode of the letters a few weeks earlier than it happened. He is not reliable here.

65   Dyer, *Raiders of the Sarhad*, p. 175.

66   War Office, WO 95/5415, 25–30 June 1916; India Office, MSS Eur E 264/54 (c), proceeding 203; Moberly, *Operations in Persia*, p. 184; Proudfoot, *We Lead: The 7th Light Cavalry, 1784–1990*, p. 39; Tugwell, *History of the Bombay Pioneers*, p. 410; Dyer, *Raiders of the Sarhad* pp. 171–80. Dyer maintains in his book that he was ordered to send the prisoners with an

escort to meet the 106th Pioneers. This is contradicted by Moberly, and there is no record of any such order in any of the records.

67   War Office file, WO 95/5415, 30 June 1916: 'The whole of June the authority of the General Officer Commanding has been delegated to Lieutenant-Colonel Dale, 19th Punjabis, at Kacha to enable him to deal with all troops of the Sistan Field Force other than those at Khwash.' This notes that there was no telegraph to Khwash, and that a letter from there took 3 days to reach Kacha.

68   India Office, MSS Eur E 264/54 (c), proceeding 170.

69   India Office, L/MILITARY/17/5/4140, entries 62430 and 62888; MSS Eur E 264/54 (c), proceedings 172 and 204.

70   India Office, MSS Eur E 264/54 (c), proceedings 181 and 205.

71   India Office, MSS Eur E 264/54 (c), proceeding 245.

72   India Office file, MSS Eur E 264/54 (c), proceeding 148. Dyer's tone throughout his account of this incident in *Raiders of the Sarhad* is similarly self-exculpatory. He turns his march to Kamalabad into a successful prevention of a movement by Khalil Khan's tribe to join Jihand Khan. There is no record in the logs of any such movement, which, at a date one or two days after the escape of the tribesmen, would have been surprisingly early. In the book, he also claims that he heard of Jihand's escape whilst he was at Kamalabad, and that he then hastened back to Khwash, which he feared was now under threat. He thus turns the story of his march back to Khwash into another 'race for Khwash' against Jihand, which he claims he won. His own headquarters log makes plain he heard of the ambush on Captain James only when he got back to Khwash. In his book, he also claims that Captain James's party was rescued by the wireless party which arrived in the nick of time; the log shows Colonel Claridge meeting James on 1 July, but only meeting the wireless party on 3 July further up the road near Ladis. One can only assume Dyer included this piece of misinformation to fit with his story of hearing of the second attack whilst he was at Kamalabad, as a rescue by the wireless detachment would have explained why he himself did not go back to rescue James; War Office, WO 95/5415, 1 and 3 July 1916.

Notes to Chapter 13: Khwash

1   War Office, WO 95/5415, 2, 4 and 7 July 1916; Reginald Edward Harry Dyer, *Raiders of the Sarhad: Being an Account of a Campaign of Arms and Bluff against the Brigands of the Persian-Baluchi Border during the Great War* (London: H.F. & G. Witherby, 1921), p. 182; India Office, MSS D978, *Operations against the Damani and Gamshadzai Tribes, 12th–25th July, 1916*, case 2409 F.operations (Simla: Government of India, 1918).

2   War Office, WO 95/5415, 8 and 9 July 1916; Dyer, *Raiders of the Sarhad*, pp. 182–83.

3   India Office, MSS Eur E 264/54 (c), proceeding 258.

4   India Office, MSS Eur E 264/54 (c), proceeding 246.

5   The Sar-i Mulan valley was also known as the Gilikoh valley. The Sar-i Drukan range was also known as the Gilikoh hills.

6   National Archives of India, Military Miscellany Bound Volume, Notes, vol. 8, *Digest of Services of 106th Hazara Pioneers*, 'An Account of the Part Taken in the Operations against

the Damanis by a Detachment of 106th Hazara Pioneers 1916', by V. Moore-Lane, p. 2; India Office, MSS Eur E 264/54 (d), proceeding 301.

7   Dyer, *Raiders of the Sarhad*, pp. 190–91.

8   Ian Colvin, *The Life of General Dyer* (London: Blackwood, 1929), pp. 104, 327; Dyer, *Raiders of the Sarhad*, pp. 186–87; India Office, MSS D978, *Operations against the Damani and Gamshadzai Tribes*.

9   A.C. Kreyer and G. Uloth, *The 28th Light Cavalry in Persia and Russian Turkistan, 1915–20* (Oxford: Slatter & Rose, 1926), p. 68.

10 War Office, WO 95/5415, 16, 17, 18 and 19 July 1916; India Office, MSS Eur E 264/54 (d), proceeding 301; Dyer, *Raiders of the Sarhad*, pp. 191–92; C.L. Proudfoot, *We Lead: The 7th Light Cavalry, 1784–1990* (New Delhi: Lancer International, 1991), pp. 40–41; F.J. Moberly, *Operations in Persia, 1914–1919* (London: Her Majesty's Stationery Office, 1987), p. 185.

11 Guz was on the road to the Gamshadzay territory.

12 India Office, MSS Eur E 264/54 (d), proceeding 301; War Office, WO 95/5415, 19 and 20 July 1916; Dyer, *Raiders of the Sarhad*, pp. 194–96. Yeates, in his account in W.B.P. Tugwell, *History of the Bombay Pioneers, 1777–1933* (London; Sidney Press, 1938), pp. 412–13, indicates the retreat was planned to draw the Baluch on, and that on the 20th they fell for it: 'Accordingly next day we withdrew, hotly pursued by the exulting tribesmen.'

13 India Office, MSS Eur E 264/54 (d), proceeding 301; ibid., L/MILITARY/17/5/4141, entry 66712; War Office, WO 95/5415, 21 July 1916; Kreyer and Uloth, *The 28th Light Cavalry in Persia and Russian Turkistan*, pp. 67–68; Proudfoot, *We Lead: The 7th Light Cavalry, 1784–1990*, p. 41; Moore-Lane, *Digest of Services of 106th Hazara Pioneers*, pp. 3–4.

14 Major E.P. Yeates, 'General Dyer: Some Recollections', *Blackwoods Magazine* (December 1927), p. 795.

15 War Office, WO 95/5415, 22–29 July 1916; India Office, MSS Eur E 264/54 (c), proceeding 341, and (d), proceedings 194 and 301; ibid., L/MILITARY/17/5/4141, entries 66854 and 68528; Kreyer and Uloth, *The 28th Light Cavalry in Persia and Russian Turkistan*, pp. 68–71; Tugwell, *History of the Bombay Pioneers, 1777–1933*, p. 413; Moore-Lane, *Digest of Services of 106th Hazara Pioneers*, p. 5; Proudfoot, *We Lead: The 7th Light Cavalry, 1784–1990*, p. 41; Dyer, *Raiders of the Sarhad*, pp. 201–8.

16 War Office, WO 95/5415, 30 July 1916.

17 Colvin, *Dyer*, p. 78, note 1, quoting a letter to Colvin from Lieutenant-Colonel Landon.

18 India Office, MSS Eur E/264/54 (d), proceeding 300; Kreyer and Uloth, *The 28th Light Cavalry in Persia and Russian Turkistan*, p. 74; India Office, MSS Eur D978, *Report of an Action near Khwash, 28 July 1916* (Simla: Government of India, 1918).

19 War Office, WO 95/5415, 30 July 1916.

20 War Office, WO 95/5415, 2 August 1916.

21 Moberly, *Operations in Persia, 1914–1919*, p. 191.

22 India Office, MSS Eur E/264/54 (d), proceedings 182, 191, 216.

23 Yeates, 'General Dyer: Some Recollections', p. 794.

24 India Office, MSS Eur E/264/54 (d), proceeding 191.

25 War Office, WO 106/56, *Despatch by Brigadier-General General R.E.H. Dyer, General Officer Commanding, Sistan Field Force on the Operations against the Damanis (1st-24th August 1916)* (Simla: Government Central Press Branch, 1916), p. 1.

26 War Office, WO 95/5415, 4 and 5 August 1916; India Office, MSS Eur E/264/54 (d), proceeding 239.

27 War Office, WO 106/56, *Despatch by Brigadier-General General R.E.H. Dyer*, p. 1; Dyer, *Raiders of the Sarhad*, pp. 209–13; Kreyer and Uloth, *The 28th Light Cavalry in Persia and Russian Turkistan*, pp. 71–72.

28 Kreyer and Uloth, *The 28th Light Cavalry in Persia and Russian Turkistan*, p. 72.

29 India Office, L/MILITARY/17/5/4142, entry 70795, 6 August 1916; ibid., MSS Eur E/264/54 (d), proceeding 212.

30 War Office, WO 106/56, *Despatch by Brigadier-General General R.E.H. Dyer*, p. 2.

31 War Office, WO 95/5415, 7 and 8 August 1916.

32 India Office, L/MILITARY/17/5/4142, entry 70164.

33 War Office, WO 95/5415, 7 August 1916; ibid., WO 106/56, *Despatch by Brigadier-General General R.E.H. Dyer*, p. 2.

34 War Office, WO 106/56, *Despatch by Brigadier-General General R.E.H. Dyer*, pp. 2–3.

35 India Office, MSS Eur E/264/54 (d), proceeding 216, 7 August 1916; ibid., L/MILITARY/17/5/4142, entry 71173. The cypher has corrupted the text, which is transcribed as in the record.

36 India Office, MSS Eur E/264/54 (d), proceeding 182; ibid., L/MILITARY/17/5/4142, entry 71113.

37 War Office, WO 106/56, *Despatch by Brigadier-General General R.E.H. Dyer*, pp. 4–6.

38 War Office, WO 95/5415, 8–12 August 1916; India Office, MSS Eur E/264/54 (d), proceeding 302; ibid., L/MILITARY/17/5/4142, entries 71697 and 72874.

39 India Office, MSS Eur E/264/54 (d), proceeding 225.

40 War Office, WO 95/5415, 13–15 August 1916; India Office, MSS Eur E/264/54 (d), proceeding 363; War Office, WO 106/56, *Despatch by Brigadier-General General R.E.H. Dyer*, p. 3.

41 Tugwell, *History of the Bombay Pioneers, 1777–1933*, p. 414.

42 War Office, WO 95/5415, 15 and 16 August 1916; Kreyer and Uloth, *The 28th Light Cavalry in Persia and Russian Turkistan*, p. 73; Dyer, *Raiders of the Sarhad*, pp. 216–18; India Office, L/MILITARY/17/5/4142, entry 73560; ibid., MSS Eur E/264/54 (d), proceedings 313 and 363; Proudfoot, *We Lead: The 7th Light Cavalry, 1784–1990*, pp. 41–42; Moore-Lane, *Digest of Services of 106th Hazara Pioneers*, p. 6; War Office, WO 106/56, *Despatch by Brigadier-General General R.E.H. Dyer*, p. 3.

43 India Office, MSS Eur E/264/54 (d), proceeding 339.

44 India Office, MSS Eur E/264/54 (d), proceedings 320 and 340.

45 War Office, WO 95/5415, 17–24 August 1916; Kreyer and Uloth, *The 28th Light Cavalry in Persia and Russian Turkistan*, p. 73; War Office, WO 106/56, *Despatch by Brigadier-General General R.E.H. Dyer*, p. 3.

46 India Office, MSS Eur E/264/54 (d), proceedings 162, 163, 167, 199, 207 and 487.

47 War Office, WO 95/5415, 26 August–9 September 1916; India Office, L/MILITARY/17/5/4142, entry 77920; Moore-Lane, *Digest of Services of 106th Hazara Pioneers*, p.6.

48 India Office, MSS Eur E/264/54 (d), proceeding 437.

49 Colvin, *Dyer*, p. 115. He does not name his source.

50 India Office, L/MILITARY/17/5/4142, entries 74968 and 75145; ibid., MSS Eur E/264/54 (d), proceedings 368 and 393.

51 India Office, MSS Eur E/264/54 (d), proceeding 418.

52 India Office, L/MILITARY/17/5/4143, entry 76071.

53 War Office, WO 95/5415, 29 August, 3, 4 and 9 September 1916; India Office, L/MILITARY/17/5/4143, entry 76871.

54 India Office, L/MILITARY/17/5/4143, entries 79312 and 80012.

55 India Office, MSS Eur E/264/54 (d), proceeding 501.

56 India Office, MSS Eur E/264/54 (d), proceeding 497.

57 Moberly, *Operations in Persia, 1914–1919*, p. 214; War Office, WO 95/5415, 26 September 1916.

58 W.E.R. Dickson, *East Persia: A Backwater of the War* (London: Edward Arnold, 1924), p. 47.

59 Dyer, *Raiders of the Sarhad*, p. 219.

60 War Office, WO 95/5415, 19, 22, 25, 26 and 30 September 1916; India Office, L/MILITARY/17/5/4143, entries 80985 and 81066.

61 War Office, WO 95/5415, 1 and 14 September 1916.

62 India Office, MSS Eur E/264/54 (d), proceedings 442, 463 and 464.

63 India Office, L/MILITARY/17/5/4143, entries 76897 and 80640.

64 India Office, MSS Eur E/264/54 (e), proceeding 10.

65 War Office, WO 95/5415, 27 September 1916; India Office, MSS Eur E/264/54 (e), proceeding 10. This is the subject of the last official dispatch signed by Dyer, and printed later by Army Headquarters as WO 106/56, *Report from the General Officer Commanding Sistan on the Action against Gunrunners at Kalmas, 26 September 1919*, Serial 63, GS Branch Case 16001, Simla 1916. The incident did not involve Dyer, and the report was prepared by his staff, and so involved him only in its signature.

66 India Office, L/MILITARY/17/5/4144, entries 82921 and 85001; Moberly, *Operations in Persia, 1914–1919*, p. 214; Moore-Lane, *Digest of Services of 106th Hazara Pioneers*, p. 6.

67 Dyer, *Raiders of the Sarhad*, p. 219.

68 Dyer never managed to spell Yeates's name properly.

69 India Office, L/MILITARY/17/5/4143, entry 75538.

70 War Office, WO 95/5415, 15 September 1916.

71 India Office, L/MILITARY/17/5/4143, entries 75833, 76130 and 78065.

72 India Office, MSS Eur E/264/54 (d), appendix I to notes.

73 India Office, MSS Eur E/264/54 (d), proceeding 519.

74 India Office, MSS Eur E/264/54 (d), proceeding 520.

75 India Office, L/MILITARY/17/5/4141, entry 63333.

76 India Office, MSS Eur E/264/1, 25 May 1920.

77 War Office, WO 95/5415, 4, 5 and 6 October 1916; India Office, L/MILITARY/17/5/4143, entry 78065; ibid., L/MILITARY/17/5/4144, entry 83344; ibid., MSS Eur E/264/54 (d), proceeding 485; ibid., MSS Eur E/264/54 (e), proceeding 57.

78 Tugwell, *History of the Bombay Pioneers, 1777–1933*, p. 415.

79 Yeates, 'General Dyer: Some Recollections', pp. 794–95.

80 India Office, MSS Eur E 264/15, no. 46a, 25 November 1916.

81 Reza Shah is rendered in many forms.

82 India Office, MSS Eur E 264/54 (d), appendix v to notes part ix, 'List of Tribes in the Sarhad, Sardars etc'.

83   India Office, MSS Eur D978, *Operations against the Damani and Gamshadzai tribes*; Philip Carl Salzman, *Black Tents of Baluchistan* (Washington, DC: Smithsonian Institute Press, 2000), p. 317.

84   India Office, MSS Eur E/264/1, 25 May 1920.

Notes to Chapter 14: Abbottabad and Jullundur

1   Onkar Chand Sud, *The Simla Story (The Glow and After-Glow of the Raj): A Sketch Book* (Simla; Maria Brothers, 1992), p. 117.

2   Ian Colvin, *The Life of General Dyer* (London: Blackwood, 1929), pp. 114–15.

3   *Indian Army List*, July 1919, p. 282: 'War Services: The War of 1914–18, Despatches, London Gazette, 31 October 1917; C.B. 4 June 1917'. The Despatches, in which Dyer's name is merely listed with those named for south-east Persia, are in War Office, WO 106/56, *Despatch by General Sir Charles Monro, Commander-in-Chief in India, on Operations on India's Frontiers, 1916*, 23 July 1917 (Simla: Government Press), p. 9. The 'Grant of the Dignity of a Companion (Military Division) of the Order of the Bath to Colonel (Temporary Brigadier-General) Reginald Edward Harry Dyer' is in the Dyer Papers, 9012-55, National Army Museum, item 3. The outside is signed 'George R.I.', and annotated '3rd class. Given at St. James's 4th of June 1917 in the 8th year'. Item 5–1 of the Dyer Papers is his Mention in Despatches: 'The War of 1914–1918, Indian Army, Col. (T./Brig-Gen.) R.E.H. Dyer was mentioned in a Despatch from General Sir Charles Monro dated 23 July 1917 for 'gallant and distinguished services in the Field'. It was signed 'Winston S. Churchill, Secretary of State for War. War Office, Whitehall, 1 March 1919'.

4   Colvin, *Dyer*, p. 114; India Office, L/MILITARY/14/1025.

5   *Indian Army List*, January 1917, p. 8: 'Colonels on Staff Commanding Brigades: Brigadier-General Dyer Abbottabad temporary'; ibid., p. 16; *Army List*, p. 69: 'Brigade Commander Abbottabad Brigade (Colonel on staff) (temporary)'.

6   Sir Michael O'Dwyer, *India as I Knew It, 1885–1925* (London: Constable, 1925), pp. 177–82; Richard J. Popplewell, *Intelligence and Imperial Defence: British Intelligence and the Defence of the Indian Empire, 1904–1924* (London: Frank Cass, 1995), pp. 186–87.

7   National Archives of India, Military Department, Reports and Returns: Casualties, Proceedings, 1885–1886, May 1917, part B, 'Dyer riding accident 29 March 1917 at Camp Akora'. The file is missing, so only its title survives; Colvin, *Dyer*, p. 115.

8   Brigadier-General W.D. Villiers-Stuart papers in the Gurkha Museum, Winchester, 'Autobiography', 1917, no page number.

9   Colvin, *Dyer*, p. 117.

10   War Office, WO32/21403, September 1921, untitled précis prepared for the Army Council on the issue of Dyer's retention of the rank of brigadier-general; *Army List*, July 1917, p. 166 shows him as a colonel; *Indian Army Lists*, July 1917, October 1917 and January 1918 show him as a colonel with no appointment. Ivon's service is in India Office, L/MILITARY/14/1025.

11   Colvin, *Dyer*, p. 117; India Office, L/MILITARY/14/1025.

12   Robin James Moore, *Liberalism and Indian Politics, 1872–1922* (London: Edward Arnold, 1966), p. 115; Robin James Moore, *The Crisis of Indian Unity, 1917–40* (Oxford: Clarendon

Press, 1974), pp. 1–2; L.S.S. O'Malley, *The Indian Civil Service, 1601–1930* (London: John Murray, 1931), p. 222.

13 *Indian Army List*, October 1918, pp. 12 and 25: 'Commander Jullundur as Colonel on the Staff Commanding a Brigade 12 March 1918'; ibid., p. 121, 'Brigadier-General 12 March 1918'; *Army List*, May 1919: 'Colonel (temporary Brigadier-General) R.E.H. Dyer, C.B., Brigade Commander Jullundur Brigade (45th Infantry Brigade)'; *Gazette of India*, January to June 1918, Memoranda, p. 931: 'Colonel R.E.H. Dyer, C.B., Indian Army, to be temporary Brigadier-General whilst commanding a Brigade in India, 12 March 1918.'

14 Sir George Barrow, *The Life of General Sir Charles Carmichael Monro* (London: Hutchinson, 1931), p. 207.

15 C.W. May, *History of the 2nd Sikhs, 12th Frontier Force Regiment, 1846–1933* (Jubbulpore: E.C. Davis, 1933), p. 65; Liddle Collection (1914–1918), in the Brotherton Library, University of Leeds, IND 10, 'Amritsar,' Letter from R. Moray Graham to the Editor, *Readers Digest*, 30 July 1984; Roger Perkins, *The Amritsar Legacy: Golden Temple to Caxton Hall. The Story of a Killing* (Picton: Chippenham, 1989), p.72; Colvin, *Dyer*, p. 119.

16 *The London Cyclist Battalion*, compiled by the History Committee of the 26th Middlesex (Cyclist) Volunteer Rifle Corps and the 25th (City of London) Cyclist Battalion, the London Regiment (London: Forster Groom, 1932), p. 162.

17 Liddle Collection, IND 15, Corporal C.J. Davis diary, 6 July 1918. Davis was a clerk in the Londons who kept a diary. India Office, L/PS/15/41, H168.

18 Colvin, *Dyer*, p. 120; India Office, L/MILITARY/9/509.

19 Colvin, *Dyer*, p. 125; *Report from Brigadier-General R.E.H. Dyer, Commanding 45th Brigade, to the General Staff, 16th (Indian) Division*, 25 August 1919, in the Dyer papers in the National Army Museum, p. 1; also in the *Hunter Report*, Evidence, vol. iii, p. 201.

20 *Report from Brigadier-General Dyer*, 25 August 1919, p. 1; *The London Cyclist Battalion*, p. 163; Colvin, *Dyer*, p. 125.

21 *The London Cyclist Battalion*, p. 163.

22 *The London Cyclist Battalion*, p. 164; Liddle Collection, IND 15, Corporal Davis, diary, 12 November 1918.

23 Colvin, *Dyer*, pp. 120–24. At the end of the War, Dyer received the standard British War Medal and Victory Medal (both engraved with his name in the rank of brigadier-general); National Army Museum Collection; Sotheby's, *Orders, Medals and Decorations* (London: sale catalogue, Tuesday 18 December 1990).

24 Arthur Swinson, *Six Minutes to Sunset: The Story of General Dyer and the Amritsar Affair* (London: Peter Davies, 1964), p. 165; Swinson had the information verbally from the Dyer family. In August 1917 seven Indians already in the Army were granted King's commissions. In 1918 a commissioning programme began at the Indore Cadet School (Daly Military College). Thirty-nine cadets were commissioned in December 1919; John Gaylor, *Sons of John Company: The Indian and Pakistani Armies, 1903–91* (Tunbridge Wells: Parapress, Into Battle Series, 1996), p. 22.

25 *Tribune*, 7 July 2001. Meakin, Edward Dyer's rival, was a founding shareholder of the club. Regrettably, the *Tribune*'s article records that the club, with all its records, had just burned to the ground, which was the occasion for the publication of the article.

26 Colvin, *Dyer*, p. 119.

27 H. Ulric S. Nisbet, 'Diaries and Memories of the Great War: England–France–Flanders–India', in the Imperial War Museum, 78/3/1. Nisbet wrote up his earlier notes well after the events they describe, hence his reference to Amritsar.

28 Colvin, *Dyer*, p. 126.

29 R. Moray Graham, Letter to Liddle, 2 December 1984, Liddle Collection, IND 10. Underlining in the original.

30 Liddle Collection, IND 15, Davis Diary, 25 December 1918.

31 Nisbet, 'Diaries and Memories of the Great War', 1 January 1919. Liddle Collection, IND 15, Davis Diary, 1 January 1919: 'Proclamation Parade on Brigade Parade ground. *Feu de joi* and March Past done excellently. Congratulated on turn out by Commanding Officer.'

32 Nisbet, 'Diaries and Memories of the Great War', 18 January 1919.

33 Colvin, *Dyer*, p. 126; Dyer family tree, in the possession of Martin Dyer.

34 H.W. Hale, *The Political Trouble in India, 1917–1937* (Allahabad: Chugh Publications, 1974), p. 60.

35 H.H. Dodwell and V.D. Mahajan, eds, *The Cambridge History of India: The Indian Empire, 1858–1918 and 1919–1969* (New Delhi: S. Chand, 1964), vi, p. 764; Vincent A. Smith, *The Oxford History of India*, ed. Percival Spear (Oxford: Clarendon Press, 1958), p. 785; B.G. Horniman, *Amritsar and Our Duty to India* (London: T. Fisher Unwin, 1920), pp. 53–64.

36 Sir Verney Lovett, *A History of the Nationalist Movement in India* (London: John Murray, 1921), p. 186; P.E. Roberts, *History of British India under the Company and the Crown* (London: Oxford University Press, 1952), p. 592.

37 Hale, *The Political Trouble in India*, p. 60; Claude H. Van Tyne, *India in Ferment* (New York: D. Appleton, 1923), p. 140.

38 Judith M. Brown, *Gandhi's Rise to Power* (Cambridge: Cambridge University Press, 1972), p. 160; Sumit Sarkar, *Modern India, 1885–1947* (London: Macmillan, 1989), p. 187; H.C.E. Zacharias, *Renascent India: From Ram Mohan Roy to Mohandas Gandhi* (London: George Allen & Unwin, 1933), p. 188.

39 Sir Stanley Reed, *The India I Knew, 1897–1947* (London: Odhams Press, 1952), pp.72–73.

40 K.T. Paul, *The British Connection with India* (London: Student Christian Movement, 1928), pp. 133–34; Sir Verney Lovett, *India* (London: Hodder & Stoughton, 1923), p. 206.

41 L.F. Rushbrook Williams, ed., *India in 1919* (Calcutta: Government of India, 1920), also published as *A Report Prepared for Presentation to Parliament in Accordance with the Requirements of the 26th Section of the Government of India Act (5 and 6 George V, Chap. 61)*, pp. 24–28; Satish Chandra Mittal, *Freedom Movement in Punjab (1905–29)* (Delhi: Concept, 1977), pp. 116–17; O'Malley, *The Indian Civil Service*, p.136; Henry Whitehead, *Indian Problems in Religion, Education, Politics* (London: Constable, 1924), p. 303; P.C. Bamford, *Histories of the Non-Co-operation and Khilafat Movements* (Delhi: Deep Publications, 1974), p. 10.

42 John S. Hoyland, *The Case of India* (London: J.M. Dent & Sons, 1929), p. 14; T.N. Jagadisan, *V.S. Srinavasa Sastri* (New Delhi: the Government of India, 1969), p. 29; D. Graham Pole, *India in Transition* (London: Leonard and Virginia Woolf at the Hogarth Press, 1932), p. 40; C.S. Ranga Iyer, *India: Peace or War?* (London: Harrap, 1930), pp. 85–86; Nirad C. Chaudhuri, *Autobiography of an Unknown Indian* (London: Picador, 1999), pp. 401–2; Sir

Chimanlal Setalvad, *Recollections and Reflections: An Autobiography* (Bombay: Padma, 1946), p. 299.

43 M.K. Gandhi, *Young India, 1919–1922* (Madras: Tagore & Co, 1922), p. 7; Gandhi, *An Autobiography* (London: Penguin, 2001), p. 410.

44 John Gallagher, Gordon Johnson and Anil Seal, eds, *Locality, Province and Nation: Essays on Indian Politics, 1870–1940* (London: Cambridge University Press, 1973), pp. 29, 123–27; Brown, *Gandhi's Rise to Power*, pp. 160–65; R. Kumar, ed., *Essays on Gandhian Politics: The Rowlatt Satyagraha of 1919* (Oxford: Clarendon Press, 1971), pp. 5–7; H.N. Mitra, ed., *Punjab Unrest Before and After* (Calcutta: N.N. Mitter, 1920), p. 42; B.N. Pandey, *The Break-Up of British India* (London: Macmillan, 1969), pp.105–6; Sumit Sarkar, *Modern India*, p. 188.

45 Kumar, *Essays on Gandhian Politics*, p. 8.

46 V.N. Datta, ed., *New Light on the Punjab Disturbances in 1919: Volumes VI and VII of Disorders Inquiry Committee Evidence*, 2 vols (Simla: Indian Institute of Advanced Study, 1975) (the text of the original is in India Office, L/MIL/17/12/42 and in Cabinet Office, Cab 27/93), pp. 23, 236–37; Hari Singh, *Gandhi, Rowlatt Satyagraha and British Imperialism: Emergence of Mass Movements in Punjab and Delhi* (Delhi: Indian Bibliographies Bureau, 1990), pp. 12–17; M.L. Darling, *The Punjab Peasant in Prosperity and Debt* (London: Oxford University Press, 1928), p. 279; Sir Reginald Craddock, *The Dilemma in India* (London: Constable, 1929), p. 184.

47 Datta, *New Light on the Punjab Disturbances*, p. 20; Kumar, *Essays on Gandhian Politics*, p. 255; M.R. Jayakar, *The Story of My Life*, 2 vols (Bombay: Asia Publishing House, 1958), i, pp. 278–79.

48 Brown, *Gandhi's Rise to Power*, pp. 185–86; Prithvis Chandra Ray, *Life and Times of C.R. Das: The Story of Bengal's Self-Expression. Being a Personal Memoir of the Late Deshbandhu Chitta Ranjan and a Complete Outline of the History of Bengal for the First Quarter of the Twentieth Century* (London: Oxford University Press, 1927), p. 157.

49 Brown, *Gandhi's Rise to Power*, p. 231, quoting Harcourt Butler's letter of 14 April 1919 to his mother.

50 Brown, *Gandhi's Rise to Power*, p. 164; P.C. Bamford, *Histories of the Non-Co-operation and Khilafat Movements* (Delhi: Deep Publications, 1974), p. 4.

51 Bamford, *Histories of the Non-Co-operation and Khilafat Movements*, pp. 8–9; Command 534 – *Parliamentary Papers* (Commons), 1920, vol. 14 (*Reports* vol. 6. 'East India (Punjab Disturbances).'). 'Reports on the Punjab Disturbances, April 1919', p. 38–47; Singh, *Gandhi, Rowlatt Satyagraha and British Imperialism*, pp. 147–52; Datta, *New Light on the Punjab Disturbances*, p. 18.

52 Nisbet, 'Diaries and Memories of the Great War', 18 March 1919; *Report from Brigadier-General Dyer*, 25 August 1919, p. 1; Colvin, *Dyer*, pp. 125–26.

53 Colvin, *Dyer*, p. 126.

54 Colvin, *Dyer*, p. 128; Mrs Annie Dyer, letter to Brigadier-General Edmonds, 9 August 1927, papers of Brigadier-General Sir James Edmonds in the Liddell Hart Centre, King's College London; *Report from Brigadier-General Dyer*, 25 August 1919, pp. 1–2.

55 Colvin, *Dyer*, pp.129–35, elaborates this to 'a large tree with its branches still on it'; *Report from Brigadier-General Dyer*, 25 August 1919, p. 2, calls it 'a large fragment of wood'; Annie Dyer, letter to Brigadier-General Edmonds, 9 August 1927.

56   *Report from Brigadier-General Dyer*, 25 August 1919, p. 2; Command 771 – *Parliamentary Papers* (Commons), 1920, vol. 8 (*Reports*, vol. 4, 'Army'.), 'Disturbances in the Punjab, Statement by Brigadier-General R.E.H. Dyer'; also in India Office, L/MIL/17/12/43; Captain Briggs's statement, p. 24.

57   Reports on the Punjab Disturbances, April 1919, pp. 2, 20, 40–41; Colvin, *Dyer*, p. 139; *Report from Brigadier-General Dyer*, 25 August 1919, p. 2; Command 771, Disturbances in the Punjab, Statement by Dyer, p. 24.

58   Hari Singh, *Gandhi, Rowlatt Satyagraha and British Imperialism*, p. 151; Reports on the Punjab Disturbances, April 1919, pp. 2, 44–45; Command 681- *Parliamentary Papers* (Commons), 1920, vol. 14: *Reports*, vol. 6, 'East India (Disturbances in the Punjab, etc)'. 'Report of the Committee Appointed by the Government of India to Investigate the Disturbances in the Punjab, etc'. (the Hunter Report), vol. iii, p. 173, Evidence of Mr Obaidullah, Sub-Inspector of Police, Kotwali, Amritsar; Liddle Collection, IND 15, Davis Diary, 6 April 1919.

59   *Report from Brigadier-General Dyer*, 25 August 1919, p. 2; Colvin, *Dyer*, pp. 160–61.

60   Hunter Report, Evidence, vol. iv, p. 57, Evidence of General Beynon; Command 771: Disturbances in the Punjab, Statement by Dyer, p. 19; Colvin, *Dyer*, p. 160.

61   Nisbet, 'Diaries and Memories of the Great War', Introduction. He refers to his old self in the introduction in the third person; Philip Ernest Richards, *Indian Dust: Being Letters from the Punjab* (London: George Allen & Unwin, 1932), pp. 181–82.

Notes to Chapter 15: Amritsar

1   Command 534: *Parliamentary Papers* (Commons), 1920, vol. 14, *Reports*, vol. 6, 'East India (Punjab Disturbances)'. 'Reports on the Punjab Disturbances, April 1919', p. 1; Sir J.P. Thompson papers, in the British Library, MSS Euro F 13731, draft by Sir Michael O'Dwyer, 'Notes on the Amritsar Shooting', 24 December 1919; Command 681: *Parliamentary Papers* (Commons), 1920, vol. 14, *Reports*, vol. 6, 'East India (Disturbances in the Punjab, etc)'. 'Report of the Committee Appointed by the Government of India to Investigate the Disturbances in the Punjab, etc.' (the *Hunter Report*), p. 19; Beryl Dhanjal, *Amritsar* (London: Evans Brothers: London, 1994), p. 36.

2   *Report from Brigadier-General R.E.H. Dyer, Commanding 45th Brigade, to the General Staff, 16th (Indian) Division*, 25 August 1919, in the Dyer papers in the National Army Museum (also in the *Hunter Report*, Evidence, vol. iii, appendix xiii), p. xx; Hunter Report, p. 19; H.N. Mitra, ed., *Punjab Unrest Before and After* (Calcutta: N.N. Mitter, 1920), p. 87.

3   V.N. Datta, ed., *New Light on the Punjab Disturbances in 1919: Volumes VI and VII of Disorders Inquiry Committee Evidence*, 2 vols (Simla: Indian Institute of Advanced Study, 1975) (the text of the original is in India Office, L/MIL/17/12/42 and in Cabinet Office, Cab 27/93), p. 166, evidence of Sir Michael O'Dwyer, and marginal note.

4   Mrs Melicent Wathen papers in the possession of the Reverend Mark Wathen, Diary, 2 April 1919 and Mrs Wathen's MS account, 'Amritsar 1919'.

5   Toufique Kitchlew, *Saifuddin Kitchlew: Hero of Jallianwala Bagh* (New Delhi: National Book Trust, 1987), pp. 1–21; Sir Michael O'Dwyer, *India as I Knew It, 1885–1925* (London:

Constable, 1925), p. 271; *Hunter Report*, pp. 19–20 and Evidence, vol. iv, p. 320, statement of General Beynon; Wathen papers, letters from Mrs Wathen to her mother, 6 April 1919, and to her brother, Walter, 18 April 1919.

6 *Hunter Report*, p. 20; Command 534: *Reports on the Punjab Disturbances*, pp. 2, 20 and 47; Wathen papers, Diary, 9 April 1919, letters from Mrs Wathen to her mother, 14 April 1919, and to her brother, Walter, 18 April 1919, and Mrs Wathen's MS account, 'Amritsar 1919', p. 3.

7 Datta, *New Light on the Punjab Disturbances*, p. 166, evidence of Sir Michael O'Dwyer.

8 Command 534: *Reports on the Punjab Disturbances*, p. 2; *Hunter Report*, p. 20, and Evidence, vol. iv, p. 320, statement of General Beynon; *Datta, New Light on the Punjab Disturbances*, pp. 272–73, statement of the Government of the Punjab; *Report of the Commissioners Appointed by the Punjab Sub-Committee of the Indian National Congress*, 2 vols (Bombay: Karnatak Press, 1920), ii, part iii; Hari Singh, *Gandhi, Rowlatt Satyagraha and British Imperialism: Emergence of Mass Movements in Punjab and Delhi* (Delhi: Indian Bibliographies Bureau, 1990), pp. 147–48.

9 O'Dwyer, *India as I Knew It*, p. 271; Kanji Dwarkadas, *India's Fight for Freedom 1913–1937: An Eye Witness Story* (Bombay: Popular Prakashan, 1966), p. 107; Command 705: *Parliamentary Papers* (Commons), 1920, vol. 14, *Reports*, vol. 6, 'East India (Disturbances in the Punjab, etc)'. 'Correspondence between the Government of India and the Secretary of State for India on the Report of Lord Hunter's Committee', p. 16; Hunter Report, p. 20, and Evidence, vol. iv, p. 321. Sir Charles Gwynn, *Imperial Policing* (London: Macmillan, 1934), p. 58, describes the order to arrest the ringleaders without reinforcements as 'like poking a stick into a wasps' nest without taking steps to stupefy the insects'.

10 Wathen papers, Diary, 10 April 1919, letter from Mrs Wathen to her mother, 14 April 1919, and Mrs Wathen's MS account, 'Amritsar 1919', p. 5. Charles Townshend, *Britain's Civil Wars: Counterinsurgency in the Twentieth Century* (London: Faber & Faber, 1986), p. 136, castigates the inadequacy of arrangements for the picquets at the railway line. Massey was a very junior officer for the responsibility he held that day.

11 *Hunter Report*, p. 21, exonerates Irving of fault for this, but the European Association thought otherwise. Their long campaign for an enquiry was successfully deflected by the Government of India which appointed of one of their members to the Hunter Committee; National Archive of India, Home Political, part A, October 1919, proceedings 421–24.

12 Command 534: *Reports on the Punjab Disturbances*, pp. 2–5, 47; Datta, *New Light on the Punjab Disturbances*, pp. 272–76, 374–78, statement of the Government of the Punjab; ibid., pp. 792–93, statement of Sir Michael O'Dwyer; ibid., p. 1051, memorandum submitted by the Government of India; *Hunter Report*, pp. 21–27, 88, and Evidence, vol. iii, pp. 3–4, evidence of Miles Irving, and annex A, p. 8; p. 43, evidence of F.A. O'Connor; pp. 46–50, evidence of Captain Massey and p. 191, statement; pp. 78–79, evidence of C.G. Farquhar and, p. 197, statement; p. 92, evidence of Khwaja Yusuf Shah, Khan Bahadur; p. 163, evidence of A.J.W. Kitchin; ibid., vol iv, statement of General Beynon, p. 321; *Report from Brigadier-General Dyer*, 25 August 1919, annex A, statement of Captain Massey, pp. i–ii; appendix xv, p. xxiii; India Office, L/MILITARY/17/5/3079, War Diary, Army Headquarters, India, vol. 51, 10 April 1919; Mitra, *Punjab Unrest Before and After*, p. 84; Winston Churchill papers in the Churchill Archives Centre, Churchill College, Cambridge, CHAR 16/47 B, letter from

Edwin Montagu, 25 June 1921, appendix, list of firing, serials 20–23; Akshaya K. Ghose, *Lord Chelmsford's Viceroyalty: A Critical Survey* (Madras: Ganesh, 1921), p. 20; Kapil Deva Malaviya, *Open Rebellion in the Punjab (with Special Reference to Amritsar)* (Allahabad: Abhudaya Press, 1919), pp. 15, 22–28, 35, 61; Malcolm Darling papers, boxes xiii and xiv in the Cambridge South Asian Archive, letter to E.M. Forster, 1 July 1919; M.R. Jayakar, *The Story of My Life*, 2 vols (Bombay: Asia Publishing House, 1958), i, p. 280; Sergeant Reginald Mortimer Howgego papers in the India Office, British Library, MSS EUR C 340/8, letters to Mr Graham Lord of the *Sunday Express*, 28 May 1978, and to Alfred Draper, 21 October 1978; *Civil and Military Gazette*, 'Punjab Disturbances', 2nd edn, April 1919, pp. 1–13; National Archive of India, Home Judicial, Part B Proceedings, June 1919, 247–50; ibid., deposit, June 1919, 23, Report on the rioting at Amritsar on 10 April 1919; Pandit Pearay Dattatreya Mohan, *The Punjab 'Rebellion' of 1919 and How it Was Suppressed: An Account of the Punjab Disorders and the Working of Martial Law*, ed. Ravi M. Bakaya, 2 vols (New Delhi: Gyan Publishers, 1999), pp. 294–74 and Supplement; Alfred Nundy, *Political Problems and Hunter Committee Disclosures* (Calcutta: 'The Publisher', 1920), p. 160; Frank McCallum, 'Amritsar, 1919: A Bystander's View', *Indo-British Review*, 16, no. 1 (March 1989) (also in the Imperial War Museum, the Liddle Collection, Brotherton Library, Leeds University, the British Library and the Gurkha Museum), p. 31; F.S. Poynder, *The 9th Gurkha Rifles, 1817–1936* (London: Royal United Service Institution, 1937), p. 166.

13   *Hunter Report*, p. 26; *Daily Express*, 23 January 1920, interview with Miss Sherwood.

14   Gerard Wathen was a friend of Malcolm Darling, then a member of the ICS serving in the Punjab (whose wife knew Miss Sherwood), and of E.M. Forster, and was at Cambridge with them both. It is probable that Forster based the character of Fielding in *A Passage to India* upon Wathen, who was a man whose tolerant fairness and great common sense allowed him to straddle both communities in the city. Wathen believed that this was the case; personal communication from the Reverend M. Wathen, Gerard Wathen's son, to the author 2 December 2002.

15   *Report from Brigadier-General Dyer*, 25 August 1919, annex A, p. iii, statement of Captain Massey; Wathen papers, Diary, 10 April 1919; 'Amritsar: By an English Woman', by an anonymous writer, *Blackwoods Magazine* (April 1920), 441–46.

16   Datta, *New Light on the Punjab Disturbances*, pp. 377, 1075; Command 534: *Reports on the Punjab Disturbances*, p. 5; *Hunter Report*, p. 32, and Evidence, vol. iii, p. 121, evidence of Brigadier-General Dyer; *Civil and Military Gazette*, 'Punjab Disturbances', p. 11.

17   *Report from Brigadier-General Dyer*, 25 August 1919, p. 2; *Hunter Report*, Evidence, vol. iii, p. 114, evidence of Brigadier-General Dyer; ibid., vol. iv, p. 320–21, report of General Beynon.

18   Command 771: *Parliamentary Papers* (Commons), 1920, vol. 8, *Reports*, vol. 4, 'Army', 'Disturbances in the Punjab, Statement by Brigadier-General R.E.H. Dyer' (also in India Office, L/MIL/17/12/43), p. 24, report of Captain Briggs; *Hunter Report*, Evidence, vol. iii, p. 114, evidence of Brigadier-General Dyer; *Report from Brigadier-General Dyer*, 25 August 1919, p. 2.

19   Ian Colvin, *The Life of General Dyer* (London: Blackwood, 1929), pp. 161–62; Command 534: *Reports on the Punjab Disturbances*, p. 48; *Hunter Report*, p. 26; *The London Cyclist Battalion*, compiled by the History Committee of the 26th Middlesex (Cyclist) Volunteer

Rifle Corps and the 25th (County of London) Cyclist Battalion, the London Regiment (London: Forster Groom, 1932), p. 173; Datta, *New Light on the Punjab Disturbances*, p. 378, report from Officer Commanding Amritsar to 16 Division, 11 April 1919; Command 771: *Disturbances in the Punjab, Statement by Brigadier-General R.E.H. Dyer*, p. 24, report of Captain Briggs.

20 War Office, WO/95/5414, War Diaries, 2/6th Royal Sussex and 1/124th Baluchis, 10 April 1919; *Hunter Report*, p. 192, statement of Captain Massey; p. 321, report of General Beynon, p. 321; Datta, *New Light on the Punjab Disturbances*, p. 375; *Report from Brigadier-General Dyer*, 25 August 1919, annex A, p. iii, statement of Captain Massey; O.A. Chaldecott, *The Tenth Baluch Regiment: The First Battalion, Duchess of Connaught's Own (Late 124th D.C.O. Baluchistan Infantry) and the Tenth Battalion (Late 2/124th Baluchistan Infantry)* (Bombay: Times of India Press, 1935), p. 164.

21 Datta, *New Light on the Punjab Disturbances*, p. 374, Government House Diary, 10 April 1919; p. 792, statement of Sir Michael O'Dwyer; *Hunter Report*, Evidence, vol. iii, pp. 220, 223, statement of A.J.W. Kitchin; Arthur Swinson, *Six Minutes to Sunset: The Story of General Dyer and the Amritsar Affair* (London: Peter Davies, 1964), p. 210.

22 *Hunter Report*, pp. 27, 31–32; Evidence, vol. iii, pp. 157, 163 and 172, evidence of A.J.W. Kitchin; National Archives of India, Home Political, part A, September 1920, 95–96.

23 *Hunter Report*, p. 27; Evidence, vol. iii, pp. 8–9, 13, evidence of Miles Irving; p. 48, evidence of Captain Massey and, p. 192, statement; p. 157, evidence of A.J.W. Kitchin and, p. 223, statement; Datta, *New Light on the Punjab Disturbances*, pp. 377–78; *Report from Brigadier-General Dyer*, 25 August 1919, annex A, p. iii; *Civil and Military Gazette*, 'Punjab Disturbances', p. 15; War Office, WO 95/5414, War Diary, 1/124th Baluchis, 10–11 April 1919; Wathen papers, Mrs Wathen's MS account, 'Amritsar 1919', p. 8.

24 Datta, *New Light on the Punjab Disturbances*, p. 375–76, telegrams from Kitchin to Lahore, 10 April 1919, and from Sir Michael O'Dwyer to Amritsar, 11 April 1919; War Office, WO 95/5413, War Diary, 16 Division, 10–11 April 1919.

25 Colvin, *Dyer*, p. 162; Datta, *New Light on the Punjab Disturbances*, p. 378; McCallum, 'Amritsar, 1919', p. 31; War Office, WO 95/5414, War Diary, 1/124th Baluchis, 11 April 1919.

26 *Hunter Report*, p. 321, report of General Beynon; Datta, *New Light on the Punjab Disturbances*, p. 378; War Office, WO 95/5413, War Diary, 16 Division, 11 April 1919.

27 Wathen papers, letter from Mrs Wathen to her brother, Walter, 18 April 1919, and Wathen Diary, Friday 11 April 1919, *Hunter Report*, Evidence, vol. vi, p. 378, telegram Officer Commanding Amritsar to Aviation Branch, Lahore, 11 April 1919.

28 *Hunter Report*, p. 27, Evidence, vol. iii, p. 13, evidence of Miles Irving.

29 *Report from Brigadier-General Dyer*, 25 August 1919, appendix xv, p. xxiii.

30 *Hunter Report*, Evidence, vol. iii, p. 13, evidence of Miles Irving; pp. 158, 172, evidence of A.J.W. Kitchin; Datta, *New Light on the Punjab Disturbances*, p. 377, telephone message Kitchin to Lahore 11 April 1919.

31 Pearay Mohan, *The Punjab 'Rebellion' of 1919 and How it Was Suppressed*, p. 127; Datta, *New Light on the Punjab Disturbances*, p. 376; Wathen papers, letter from Mrs Wathen to her brother, Walter, 18 April 1919 and Mrs Wathen's MS account, 'Amritsar 1919', p. 9.

32 Datta, *New Light on the Punjab Disturbances*, p. 377, telegram from Kitchin to Lahore,

11 April 1919; *Hunter Report*, p. 6, evidence of Miles Irving; p. 48, evidence of Captain Massey; p. 158, evidence of A.J.W. Kitchin and, p. 223, statement.

33 Wathen papers, Diary, 11 April 1919.

34 Malaviya, *Open Rebellion in the Punjab*, p. 16.

35 *Hunter Report*, p. 28; Evidence, vol. iii, p. 163, evidence of A.J.W. Kitchin and, p. 222, statement; War Office, WO 95/5414, War Diary, 1/124th Baluchis, 11 April 1919.

36 Datta, *New Light on the Punjab Disturbances*, pp. 376–77. Yet he later told the Hunter Committee: 'On 11th April, Amritsar was in rebellion. That was the position simply we were in', Evidence, vol. iii, p. 159. The possible subversion of the troops worried others, too; Lister, Telegraph Superintendent at Amritsar, complained that evening that some of the Baluch troops were being insubordinate, but there was nothing in the complaint; ibid., p. 378.

37 *Hunter Report*, pp. 33, 99–100; Evidence, vol. iii, pp. 21, 30, evidence of Miles Irving; p. 48, evidence of Captain Massey; p. 110, evidence of Dr Muhammad Abdullaf Fauq, private practitioner, Amritsar: 'Members of the *satyagraha* were asked to keep order' at a meeting appointing volunteers to do so on the 11th'; *INC Report*, p. 5; *Report from Brigadier-General Dyer*, 25 August 1919, appendix xv, 45 Brigade War Diary, 11–12 April 1919.

38 *Hunter Report*, Evidence, vol. iii, p. 223, evidence of A.J.W. Kitchin; Datta, *New Light on the Punjab Disturbances*, p. 793, statement of Sir Michael O'Dwyer.

39 Morgan seems to have held local rank; General Beynon regarded him as a major, but his contemporaries gave him the title of lieutenant-colonel.

40 M.H.L. Morgan, 'The Truth about Amritsar: By an Eye Witness', 72/22/1 T, in the Imperial War Museum, p. 3; War Office, WO 95/5413, War Diary, 16 Division, 11 April 1919.

41 *Report from Brigadier-General Dyer*, 25 August 1919, p. 2; Command 771: *Disturbances in the Punjab, Statement by Brigadier-General R.E.H. Dyer*, appendix A, p. 24, statement of Captain Briggs; *Hunter Report*, Evidence, vol. iii, p. 114, evidence of Brigadier-General Dyer.

42 *Hunter Report*, Evidence, vol. iv, p. 231, evidence of General Beynon; Morgan, 'The Truth about Amritsar', p. 3.

43 Command 534: *Reports on the Punjab Disturbances*, pp. 20, 49; Command 771: *Disturbances in the Punjab, Statement by Brigadier-General R.E.H. Dyer*, p. 24, statement of Captain Briggs; *Hunter Report*, Evidence, vol. iii, p. 114, evidence of Brigadier-General Dyer; ibid, vol. iv, p. 320, statement of General Beynon; *Report from Brigadier-General Dyer*, 25 August 1919, pp. 2, xxiii; *The London Cyclist Battalion*, p. 182; H.C. Wylly, *History of the Queen's Royal Regiment*, vol. 7 (Aldershot: Gale & Polden, n.d.), p. 144.

44 Colvin, *Dyer*, pp. 162–63.

45 Colvin, *Dyer*, p. 164.

46 *Report from Brigadier-General Dyer*, 25 August 1919, p. 2; *Hunter Report*, Evidence, vol. iii, p. 9, evidence of Miles Irving.

47 *Report from Brigadier-General Dyer*, 25 August 1919, appendix i, p. xiii; *Hunter Report*, Evidence, vol. iii, pp. 122, 125, evidence of Brigadier-General Dyer.

48 War Office, WO 95/5414, War Diary, 1/124th Baluchis, 11 April 1919; Chaldecott, *The Tenth Baluch Regiment*, p. 164; Morgan, 'The Truth About Amritsar', p. 4.

49 *Report from Brigadier-General Dyer*, 25 August 1919, pp. 2–3; annex A, p. iii, statement of Captain Massey; appendix v, p. xiv; appendix xiii, p. xx, Troop Strength; appendix xiv,

p. xxii, Report on Operations; appendix xv, War Diary, p. xxiii; Command 771: *Disturbances in the Punjab, Statement by Brigadier-General R.E.H. Dyer*, pp. 24–25, statement of Captain Briggs; Datta, *New Light on the Punjab Disturbances*, p. 1074, statement to the Legislative Council by J.P. Thompson; *Hunter Report*, Evidence, vol. iii, p. 49, evidence of Captain Massey and, p. 192, statement; p. 114, evidence of Brigadier-General; Rupert Furneaux, *Massacre at Amritsar* (London: George Allen & Unwin, 1963), p. 72.

50 *Report from Brigadier-General Dyer*, 25 August 1919, p. 3; appendix xv, p. xxiii, 45 Brigade War Diary; *Hunter Report*, Evidence, vol. iii, p. 115, evidence of Brigadier-General; Command 771: *Disturbances in the Punjab, Statement by Brigadier-General R.E.H. Dyer*, p. 25, statement of Captain Briggs; War Office, WO 95/5414, War Diary, 1/124th Baluchis, 12 April 1919; McCallum, 'Amritsar, 1919', p. 32.

51 *Hunter Report*, Evidence, vol. iii, p. 117, evidence of Brigadier-General Dyer; *Report from Brigadier-General Dyer*, 25 August 1919, appendix v, p. xiv.

52 *Hunter Report*, Evidence, vol. iii, p. 223, evidence of A.J.W. Kitchin.

53 Command 771: *Disturbances in the Punjab, Statement by Brigadier-General R.E.H. Dyer*, p. 25, statement of Captain Briggs; *Hunter Report*, Evidence, vol. iii, p. 114, evidence of Brigadier-General Dyer; *Report from Brigadier-General Dyer*, 25 August 1919, p. 3.

54 Datta, *New Light on the Punjab Disturbances*, p. 378.

55 Command 771: *Disturbances in the Punjab, Statement by Brigadier-General R.E.H. Dyer*, p. 25, statement of Captain Briggs; *Hunter Report*, Evidence, vol. iii, p. 115, evidence of Brigadier-General Dyer; *INC Report*, vol. 2, p. 7, evidence of Girdhari Lal.

56 The gate was known to the locals as the Sultan Pind Darwaza.

57 *Report from Brigadier-General Dyer*, 25 August 1919, pp. 3, 6; appendix xiv, p. xxii, Report on Operations; appendix xv, War Diary, p. xxiii; Command 771: *Disturbances in the Punjab, Statement by Brigadier-General R.E.H. Dyer*, p. 25, statement of Captain Briggs; *Hunter Report*, Evidence, vol. iii, p. 30, evidence of Miles Irving; p. 49, evidence of Captain Massey; pp. 115, 130, evidence of Brigadier-General Dyer; ibid., vol. iv, p. 321, report of General Beynon; War Office, WO 95/5413, War Diary 16 Division, 12 April 1919; ibid., WO 95/5414, War Diary, 1/124th Baluchis, 12 April 1919; National Archives of India, Home Political, Deposit, October 1919, 62.

58 Malaviya, *Open Rebellion in the Punjab*, pp. 31–32.

59 McCallum, 'Amritsar, 1919', p. 32; *The London Cyclist Battalion*, p. 176; *Hunter Report*, Evidence, vol. iii, p. 158, evidence of A.J.W. Kitchin.

60 *Report from Brigadier-General Dyer*, 25 August 1919, p. 3; appendix ii, pp. xiii, xxvi; *Hunter Report*, Evidence, vol. iii, p. 115, evidence of Brigadier-General Dyer; Command 771: *Disturbances in the Punjab, Statement by Brigadier-General R.E.H. Dyer*, p. 14 and p. 25, statement of Captain Briggs.

61 *Report from Brigadier-General Dyer*, 25 August 1919, appendix ii, p. xiii; Command 771, *Disturbances in the Punjab, Statement by Brigadier-General R.E.H. Dyer*, p. 25, statement of Captain Briggs; *Hunter Report*, p. 28; Evidence, vol. iii, p. 126, evidence of Brigadier-General Dyer; p. 223, statement of A.J.W. Kitchin; McCallum, 'Amritsar, 1919', p. 32; Datta, *New Light on the Punjab Disturbances*, p. 379, telegram Irving to O'Dwyer, 14 April 1919.

62 *Times*, 1924, transcript of the Sir Michael O'Dwyer versus Sir C. Sankaran Nair trial, May 1924, evidence of Rup Lal Puri taken on commission in the Punjab.

63   *Report from Brigadier-General Dyer*, 25 August 1919, appendix xiv, p. xiv; appendix xv, 45 Brigade War Diary, pp. xxiii-xxiv; *Hunter Report*, p. 28; Evidence, vol. iii, p. 6, evidence of Miles Irving; pp. 115, 136, evidence of Brigadier-General Dyer; ibid., vol. iv, pp. 321–22, report of General Beynon; Datta, *New Light on the Punjab Disturbances*, p. 276, statement of the Punjab Government; p. 379, telegrams; Command 771: *Disturbances in the Punjab, Statement by Brigadier-General R.E.H. Dyer*, p. 25, statement of Captain Briggs; *Reports on the Punjab Disturbances*, pp. 20, 50; War Office, WO 95/5413, War Diary 16 Division, 12 April 1919; *INC Report*, ii, pp. 2 and 6, evidence of Girdhari Lal; p. 56, evidence of Lala Kanhylal Bhatia; Satish Chandra Mittal, *Freedom Movement in Punjab (1905–29)* (Delhi: Concept, 1977), p. 126; Raja Ram, *The Jallianwala Bagh Massacre: A Premeditated Plan* (Chandigarh: Panjab University Publication Bureau, 2nd edn 1978), p. 78; Hari Singh, *Gandhi, Rowlatt Satyagraha and British Imperialism*, p. 161; Pearay Mohan, *The Punjab 'Rebellion' of 1919 and How it Was Suppressed*, i, p. 133.

64   *Hunter Report*, Evidence, vol. iii, p. 122, evidence of Brigadier-General Dyer.

65   *Hunter Report*, Evidence, vol. iii, p. 128, evidence of Brigadier-General Dyer.

66   *Hunter Report*, Evidence, vol. iii, p. 223, evidence of A.J.W. Kitchin.

67   Datta, *New Light on the Punjab Disturbances*, pp. 250, 277, 577; *Reports on the Punjab Disturbances*, p. 5; *Hunter Report*, Evidence, vol. iii, p. 16, evidence of Miles Irving; *Civil and Military Gazette*, 'Punjab Disturbances', p. 16.

68   Datta, *New Light on the Punjab Disturbances*, p. 254; *Hunter Report*, Evidence, vol. iii, p. 7, evidence of Miles Irving; pp. 115–16, evidence of Brigadier-General Dyer.

69   Datta, *New Light on the Punjab Disturbances*, p. 379.

Notes to Chapter 16: The Jallianwala Bagh

1   Command 681: *Parliamentary Papers* (Commons), 1920, vol. 14, *Reports*, vol. 6, 'East India (Disturbances in the Punjab, etc)'. 'Report of the Committee Appointed by the Government of India to Investigate the Disturbances in the Punjab, etc.' (the *Hunter Report*), Evidence, vol. iii, p. 118, evidence of Brigadier-General Dyer.

2   Command 534: *Parliamentary Papers* (Commons), 1920, vol. 14, *Reports*, vol. 6, 'East India (Punjab Disturbances)'. 'Reports on the Punjab Disturbances, April 1919', pp. 5, 49–50, 52; V.N. Datta, ed., *New Light on the Punjab Disturbances in 1919: Volumes VI and VII of Disorders Inquiry Committee Evidence*, 2 vols (Simla: Indian Institute of Advanced Study, 1975) (the text of the original is in India Office, L/MIL/17/12/42 and in Cabinet Office, Cab 27/93), pp. 277, 379, 795; *Report from Brigadier-General R.E.H. Dyer, Commanding 45th Brigade, to the General Staff, 16th (Indian) Division*, 25 August 1919, in the Dyer papers in the National Army Museum (also in the *Hunter Report*, Evidence, vol. iii, appendix xiii), appendix v, p. xiv; War Office, WO 95/5413, War Diary 16 Division, 13 April 1919; ibid., WO 95/5414, War Diary, 1/124th Baluchis, 14 April 1919 (wrongly entered from 13 April); War Diary 2/6th Royal Sussex, 13 April 1919; India Office, L/MILITARY/17/5/3079, Army Headquarters War Diary, entry 26049; *The London Cyclist Battalion*, compiled by the History Committee of the 26th Middlesex (Cyclist) Volunteer Rifle Corps and the 25th (City of London) Cyclist Battalion, the London Regiment (London: Forster Groom, 1932), p. 177.

3   M.H.L. Morgan, 'The Truth About Amritsar: By an Eye Witness', 72/22/1 T, in the Imperial
    War Museum, p. 6.

4   *Hunter Report*, p. 111; Evidence, vol. iii, p. 6, evidence of Miles Irving; pp. 114–15, 125–26,
    128, evidence of Brigadier-General Dyer; p. 181, statement of Miles Irving.

5   *Hunter Report*, p. 111; Evidence, vol. iii, p. 122, evidence of Brigadier-General Dyer; vol. iv,
    p. 322, report of General Beynon; *Report from Brigadier-General Dyer*, 25 August 1919,
    appendix iii, p. xiii, Proclamation No. 2.

6   The drum may have been a ghee tin.

7   *Report from Brigadier-General Dyer*, 25 August 1919, pp. 3, 6; appendix xiv, p. xxii, Report on
    Operations; appendix xv, p. xxiv, 45 Brigade War Diary; Command 771: *Parliamentary
    Papers* (Commons), 1920, vol. 8, *Reports*, vol. 4, 'Army', 'Disturbances in the Punjab, Statement
    by Brigadier-General R.E.H. Dyer' (also in India Office, L/MIL/17/12/43), p. 7; annex A, p. 25,
    statement of Captain Briggs; *Hunter Report*, p. 111, map 4; Evidence, vol. iii, p. 67, evidence
    of Malik Fateh Khan, Naib-Tahsildar, Amritsar; p. 116, evidence of Brigadier-General Dyer;
    p. 152, evidence of Lala Jowahar Lal, Inspector of Police, CID, Punjab; p. 173, evidence of
    Obaidullah, Sub-Inspector of Police; War Office, WO 95/5414, War Diary, 1/124th Baluchis,
    14 April 1919 (wrongly entered from 13 April); *Report of the Commissioners Appointed by the
    Punjab Sub-Committee of the Indian National Congress*, 2 vols (Bombay: Karnatak Press,
    1920), ii, p. 6, evidence of Girdhari Lal; Kapil Deva Malaviya, *Open Rebellion in the Punjab
    (with Special Reference to Amritsar)* (Allahabad: Abhudaya Press, 1919), pp. 17–18; Satish
    Chandra Mittal, *Freedom Movement in Punjab (1905–29)* (Delhi: Concept, 1977), p. 125.

8   *Report from Brigadier-General Dyer*, 25 August 1919, p. 3; appendix xiv, p. xxii, Report on
    Operations; Command 771: *Disturbances in the Punjab, Statement by Brigadier-General
    R.E.H. Dyer*, p. 25, statement of Captain Briggs; *Hunter Report*, Evidence, vol. iii, pp. 116,
    126, evidence of Brigadier-General Dyer evidence; War Office, WO 95/5414, War Diary,
    1/124th Baluchis, 14 April 1919 (wrongly entered from 13 April).

9   *INC Report*, ii, p. 64, evidence of Khusal Singh; *Report from Brigadier-General Dyer*,
    25 August 1919, p. 4; appendix xiv, p. xxii, Report on Operations; p. xxiv, appendix xv, War
    Diary Amritsar; Command 771: *Disturbances in the Punjab, Statement by Brigadier-General
    R.E.H. Dyer*, p. 8; *Hunter Report*, Evidence, vol. iii, p. 117, evidence of Brigadier-General
    Dyer; *INC Report*, i, p. 50; ii, p. 58, evidence of Maulvi Gholam Jilani; J.P. Thompson papers,
    MSS Euro F 137/13 in the British Library, Diary, Saturday 9 August 1919; Malaviya, *Open
    Rebellion in the Punjab*, p. 4.

10 Ian Colvin, *The Life of General Dyer* (London: Blackwood, 1929), pp. 168, 170.

11 *Report from Brigadier-General Dyer*, 25 August 1919, p. 4; appendix xii, p. xxi; appendix xiii,
    p. xxii; appendix xv, p. xxiv, War Diary Amritsar; Command 771: *Disturbances in the Punjab,
    Statement by Brigadier-General R.E.H. Dyer*, p. 25, statement of Captain Briggs; *Hunter
    Report*, Evidence, vol. iii, p. 116, evidence of Brigadier-General Dyer; Morgan, 'The Truth
    about Amritsar', p. 4; *INC Report*, ii, p. 1, evidence of Girdhari Lal; War Office, WO 95/5414,
    War Diary, 1/124th Baluchis, 14 April 1919 (wrongly entered from 13 April); F.S. Poynder,
    The 9th Gurkha Rifles, 1817–1936 (London: Royal United Service Institution, 1937), p. 166;
    Arthur Swinson, *Six Minutes to Sunset: The Story of General Dyer and the Amritsar Affair*
    (London: Peter Davies, 1964), pp. 45, 200, letter from Major-General R.D. Inskip; *Times
    Literary Supplement*, 20 February 1964, letter from General Jackie Smyth.

12 Brigadier-General Sir James Edmonds papers in the Liddell Hart Centre, King's College London, Mrs Dyer letter to Brigadier-General Edmonds, 9 August 1927.

13 Command 771: *Disturbances in the Punjab, Statement by Brigadier-General R.E.H. Dyer*, p. 25, statement of Captain Briggs; *Report from Brigadier-General Dyer*, 25 August 1919, p. 3; *Hunter Report*, Evidence, vol. iii, p. 116, evidence of Brigadier-General Dyer; Mrs Melicent Wathen papers in the possession of the Reverend Mark Wathen, Diary, 18 April 1919; letter from Mrs Wathen to her brother, Walter, 18 April 1919.

14 *Hunter Report*, Evidence, vol. iii, p. 7, evidence of Miles Irving; p. 117, evidence of Brigadier-General Dyer; Datta, *New Light on the Punjab Disturbances*, p. 379, telegram Irving to O'Dwyer, 14 April 1919; Swinson, *Six Minutes to Sunset*, p. 197.

15 *Hunter Report*, Evidence, vol. iii, pp. 117, 122, evidence of Brigadier-General Dyer; *Report from Brigadier-General Dyer*, 25 August 1919, p. 4; appendix xv, p. xxiv, War Diary Amritsar; Command 771: *Disturbances in the Punjab, Statement by Brigadier-General R.E.H. Dyer*, annex A, p. 25, statement of Captain Briggs; Alfred Draper, *The Amritsar Massacre: Twilight of the Raj* (London: Buchan & Enright, 1985), p. 87; Sergeant Reginald Mortimer Howgego papers in the India Office, British Library, MSS EUR C 340, letter to Alfred Draper, 21 October 1978.

16 *Hunter Report*, Evidence, vol. iii, p. 123, evidence of Brigadier-General Dyer.

17 *Hunter Report*, Evidence, vol. iii, p. 126, evidence of Brigadier-General Dyer; Command 771: *Disturbances in the Punjab, Statement by Brigadier-General R.E.H. Dyer*, annex A, p. 25, statement of Captain Briggs; Brigadier-General Sir John, Smyth, *The Only Enemy* (London: Hutchinson, 1959), p. 102, states that he was told by Briggs that Dyer planned to use an armoured car to stand on to address the crowd.

18 *Hunter Report*, Evidence, vol. iii, p. 38, evidence of Superintendent Plomer; p. 41, evidence of Chief Superintendent Rehill; p. 117, evidence of Brigadier-General Dyer; Datta, *New Light on the Punjab Disturbances*, pp. 277–78, statement of Punjab Government; *Report from Brigadier-General Dyer*, 25 August 1919, appendix xiv, p. xxii, Report on Operations; Command 771: *Disturbances in the Punjab, Statement by Brigadier-General R.E.H. Dyer*, annex A, p. 25, statement of Captain Briggs; *INC Report*, ii, p. 70, evidence of Lala Guranditta; p. 72, evidence of Lala Parmanand; Draper, *The Amritsar Massacre*, p. 87, from a letter from Sergeant Anderson; Satish Chandra Mittal, *Freedom Movement in Punjab (1905–29)* (Delhi: Concept, 1977), p. 127; Malaviya, *Open Rebellion in the Punjab*, p. 18; J.P. Thompson papers, *Diary*, 8 August 1919; Frank McCallum, 'Amritsar, 1919: A Bystander's View', *Indo-British Review*, 16, no. 1 (March 1989) (also in the Imperial War Museum, the Liddle Collection, Brotherton Library, Leeds University, the British Library and the Gurkha Museum), p. 32: 'I gathered the following at the time and in conversations later from then Jemadar Jitbahadur (later Subedar Major): "He told us to double through the narrow road leading to an open square and then said Gurkhas right, 59th left, fire". Personally I cannot say if the above is absolutely accurate but Jitbahadur was a very honest and straightforward Gurkha.'

19 *Hunter Report*, Evidence, vol. iii, p. 123, evidence of Brigadier-General Dyer; Command 771: *Disturbances in the Punjab, Statement by Brigadier-General R.E.H. Dyer*, p. 8; annex A, p. 25, statement of Captain Briggs; J.P. Thompson papers, Diary, 8 August 1919; Morgan, 'The Truth about Amritsar', p. 8; R Moray Graham, letter to Alfred Draper, 25 October

1984, in the Liddle Collection (1914–1918) in the Brotherton Library, University of Leeds, IND 10, 'Amritsar'; Swinson, *Six Minutes to Sunset*, p. 210; Malaviya, *Open Rebellion in the Punjab*, p. 6; *Times Literary Supplement*, 9 April 1964, quoting a letter from 'a British SNCO' (Sergeant Anderson) to Rupert Furneaux.

20   *Times Literary Supplement*, 19 March 1964, letter from John D. Tyson reporting his friend James Peddie ICS.

21   *Hunter Report*, Evidence, vol. iii, pp. 127, 131, evidence of Brigadier-General Dyer; *INC Report*, ii, p. 8, evidence of Girdhari Lal; Draper, *The Amritsar Massacre*, p. 88.

22   *INC Report*, ii, p. 139, evidence of Maulvi Gholam Jilani.

23   Malaviya, *Open Rebellion in the Punjab*, p. 62.

24   Dyer later told Gerard Wathen that the noise had prevented his stopping the firing, though this would only have been the case for a very short time, as in that short firing line any firers who carried on could have been physically stopped; private communication from the Reverend Mark Wathen (Gerard's son) to the author, 21 July 2002; Smythe, *The Only Enemy*, p. 103; *Observer*, letter from General Sir John Smythe, 13 April 1975; *Times Literary Supplement*, 9 April 1964, quoting a letter from 'a British SNCO' (Sergeant Anderson) to Rupert Furneaux.

25   *Hunter Report*, Evidence, vol. iii, p. 41, evidence of Chief Superintendent Rehill; pp. 153–54, statement of Lala Jowahar Lal; *INC Report*, ii, p. 8, evidence of Girdhari Lal; Draper, *The Amritsar Massacre*, p. 87; *Times Literary Supplement*, 9 April 1964, quoting a letter from 'a British SNCO' (Sergeant Anderson) to Rupert Furneaux.

26   *Hunter Report*, Evidence, vol. iii, p. 38, evidence of Superintendent Plomer; Morgan, 'The Truth about Amritsar', p. 8. Morgan, whose memory was not accurate on all points, put the opposite view: 'We remained until the Jallianwala Bagh was absolutely empty and this meant some minutes'; J.P. Thompson papers, Diary, 8 August 1919. Thompson also reports a conversation with a Mr Stewart on Monday 14 July, who 'tells me that when the troops had been firing for some time at the Jallianwala Bagh, Dyer turned to one of the men by him and said "Do you think they've had enough?" And then he went on "No, we'll give them four rounds more".' Lord Hailey papers, MSS Eur E220/57, p. 3.

27   *Hunter Report*, p. 31; Evidence, vol. iii, pp. 118, 127, evidence of Brigadier-General Dyer; *Report from Brigadier-General Dyer*, 25 August 1919, p. 5; Command 771: *Disturbances in the Punjab, Statement by Brigadier-General R.E.H. Dyer*, p. 18; Draper, *The Amritsar Massacre*, p. 90; *Times Literary Supplement*, 9 April 1964, quoting a letter from 'a British SNCO' (Sergeant Anderson) to Rupert Furneaux.

28   *Hunter Report*, Evidence, vol. iii, p. 118, evidence of Brigadier-General Dyer; *Report from Brigadier-General Dyer*, 25 August 1919, p. 5; appendix xiv, p. xxii, Report on Operations; appendix xv, p. xxiv, War Diary Amritsar. Dyer used a rough rule of thumb, that one casualty could be achieved for every six rounds fired; J.P.Thompson papers, Diary, 8 August 1919: 'His estimate of between 200–300 killed was based on experience in France which pointed to one in six killed as result of rifle fire.' The total of rounds fired is confirmed in part by McCallum, 'Amritsar, 1919', p. 32, who was detailed off by Captain Crampton to count the empty cartridge cases in the Gurkhas' possession. He found 923, just over half the total fired. Major Inskip counted the rounds left in the possession of his Frontier Force detachment when they returned; *Times Literary Supplement*, 6 February 1964, letter from

Swinson, and 20 February 1964, letter from Brigadier-General Smythe, who got the information from Briggs, saying men fired an average of thirty-three rounds, which was half what they carried.

29   *INC Report*, ii, pp. 70–71, evidence of Mohamed Ismail.

30   *INC Report*, ii, p. 73, evidence of Sardar Partap Singh.

31   *Report from Brigadier-General Dyer*, 25 August 1919, appendix xiv, p. xxii, Report on Operations; *Hunter Report*, pp. 29, 116–17; Evidence, vol. iii, pp. 7, 29, evidence of Miles Irving evidence; p. 62, evidence of Mr Burton; Datta, *New Light on the Punjab Disturbances*, pp. 80–81, 122, evidence of J.P. Thompson; pp. 174, 211, evidence of Sir Michael O'Dwyer; Command 534: *Reports on the Punjab Disturbances*, p. 6; National Archives of India, Home Political, Deposit, September 1919, 23; ibid., part A, February 1920, 347–358; ibid., part A, April 1920, 317–18; Churchill papers, in the Churchill Archives Centre, Churchill College, Cambridge, CHAR 16/47 B, Edwin Montagu letter to Winston Churchill, 25 June 1920, appendix 2, 'Casualties', Mittal, *Freedom Movement in Punjab*, p. 128; J.P. Thompson papers, Diary, 20 April and 15 November 1919. Estimates of the types of people who died give a guide to the composition of the crowd; of 291 named dead with jat (caste) names, 186 were Hindus, twenty-two Sikhs, thirty-nine Muslims and forty-four unknown; Kamlesh Mohan, *Militant Nationalism in the Punjab, 1919–1935* (New Delhi: Manohar, 1985), p 29.

32   *Report from Brigadier-General Dyer*, 25 August 1919, appendix xiv, p. xxii, Report on Operations; *Hunter Report*, Evidence, vol. iii, p. 49, evidence of Captain Massey; Wathen papers, Diary, 18 April 1919: 'At tiffin time'; private communication from the Reverend Mark Wathen (Gerard's son) to the author, 21 July 2002; Edmonds papers, 2/2, letter from Mrs Dyer, 9 August 1927, p. 2; A.A. Mains, 'General Dyer and Amritsar', *9th Gurkha Rifles Newsletter*, 59 (1992), p. 15; Roger Perkins, *The Amritsar Legacy: Golden Temple to Caxton Hall. The Story of a Killing* (Chippenham: Picton, 1989), pp. 183, 191; Draper, *The Amritsar Massacre*, p. 17; Edward Thompson, *A Letter from India* (Faber & Faber: London, 1932), pp. 102–4; Swinson, *Six Minutes to Sunset*, p. 199; Hari Singh, *Gandhi, Rowlatt Satyagraha and British Imperialism: Emergence of Mass Movements in Punjab and Delhi* (Delhi: Indian Bibliographies Bureau, 1990), p. 165, quoting Motilal Nehru's confidential notebook, 31 August 1919, 'Collection of Evidence and Other Work,' Note Book, ii, p. 35, Motilal Nehru papers, Nehru Memorial Museum and Library.

33   *Hunter Report*, Evidence, vol. iii, p. 27, evidence of Miles Irving; pp. 118, 134, evidence of Brigadier-General Dyer; *Report from Brigadier-General Dyer*, 25 August 1919, appendix xiv, p. xxii, Report on Operations; appendix xv, p. xxiv, War Diary, Amritsar; *Datta, New Light on the Punjab Disturbances*, p. 380, Irving report to Lahore, 14 April 1919; Morgan, 'The Truth about Amritsar', p. 6; Command 771: *Disturbances in the Punjab, Statement by Brigadier-General R.E.H. Dyer*, annex A, p. 25, statement of Captain Briggs; *The London Cyclist Battalion*, p. 180.

34   *Hunter Report*, Evidence, vol. iii, p. 223, statement of A.J.W. Kitchin; vol. iv, p. 322, report of General Beynon; Datta, *New Light on the Punjab Disturbances*, p. 78, evidence of J.P. Thompson; p. 130, evidence of Sir Michael O'Dwyer; pp. 379–80, 795–96; J.P. Thompson papers, Diary, 13 and 14 April 1919; War Office, WO 95/5413, War Diary 16 Division, 14 April 1919; Sir Michael Francis O'Dwyer, *India as I Knew It, 1885–1925* (London: Constable, 1925), p. 283; Wathen papers, letter from May to 'Aunt Annie', 20 April 1919.

35 *Report from Brigadier-General Dyer*, 25 August 1919, appendix v, p. xvi; *The London Cyclist Battalion*, p. 181.

36 *Report from Brigadier-General Dyer*, 25 August 1919, appendix xiv, p. xxii, Report on Operations. This is datelined 21.00 11 April 1919 to GENSTAFF DIVISION, B-21. It is the report same as the differently headed report at Command 771: *Disturbances in the Punjab, Statement by Brigadier-General R.E.H. Dyer*, appendix C, Report on Operations, 21.00, 14 April 1919, to GENSTAFF DIVISION. Both headings are missing elements; I suggest they both should read 'Report on Operations 21.00 11 April 1919 to 23.59 14 April 1919', as they cover that period and as he wrote it immediately after he got back from visiting the city before midnight.

37 *Hunter Report*, p. 31; Evidence, vol. iii, p. 127, evidence of Brigadier-General Dyer; vol. iv, p. 322, report of General Beynon; Datta, *New Light on the Punjab Disturbances*, p. 79, evidence of J.P Thompson; p. 131, evidence of Sir Michael O'Dwyer, and, p. 796, statement; *Report from Brigadier-General Dyer*, 25 August 1919, appendix viii, p. xvii; Command 771: *Disturbances in the Punjab, Statement by Brigadier-General R.E.H. Dyer*, p. 20; appendix D, p. 28; War Office, WO 95/5413, War Diary 16 Division, 14 April 1919; O'Dwyer, *India as I Knew It*, p. 286; J.P. Thompson papers, memorandum by Sir Michael O'Dwyer, 'Notes on the Amritsar Shooting', 24 December 1919. O'Dwyer did backtrack slightly; see Montagu papers in Trinity College Cambridge, AS3/4/59 (1), notes on Hunter Report, 11 March 1920, p. 3, PS. (1): 'Both his superior officers General Beynon and I as Head of the Civil Government approved of it at the time *as reported to us* (the death casualties were then put at 200).'

Notes to Chapter 17: The Crawling Order

1 Command 681: *Parliamentary Papers* (Commons), 1920, vol. 14, *Reports*, vol. 6, 'East India (Disturbances in the Punjab, etc)'. 'Report of the Committee Appointed by the Government of India to Investigate the Disturbances in the Punjab, etc.' (the *Hunter Report*), Evidence, vol. iii, pp. 118, 134, evidence of Brigadier-General Dyer; V.N. Datta, ed., *New Light on the Punjab Disturbances in 1919: Volumes VI and VII of Disorders Inquiry Committee Evidence*, 2 vols (Simla: Indian Institute of Advanced Study, 1975) (the text of the original is in India Office, L/MIL/17/12/42 and in Cabinet Office, Cab 27/93), p. 381; *Report from Brigadier-General R.E.H. Dyer, Commanding 45th Brigade, to the General Staff, 16th (Indian) Division*, 25 August 1919, in the Dyer papers in the National Army Museum (also in the *Hunter Report*, Evidence, vol. iii, appendix xiii), p. 5, puts this on 13 April, but it is dated the 14th; appendix vi, p. xvii; appendix xv, War Diary Amritsar, p. xxiv.

2 *Hunter Report*, Evidence, vol. iii, p. 118, evidence of Brigadier-General Dyer; pp. 163, 165, evidence of A.J.W. Kitchin, and, p. 223, statement; Datta, *New Light on the Punjab Disturbances*, p. 380; *Report from Brigadier-General Dyer*, 25 August 1919, pp. 6-7; appendix x, p. xvii; appendix xv, p. xxiv, War Diary Amritsar; Command 771: *Parliamentary Papers* (Commons), 1920, vol. 8, *Reports*, vol. 4, 'Army', 'Disturbances in the Punjab, Statement by Brigadier-General R.E.H. Dyer' (also in India Office, L/MIL/17/12/43), annex A, p. 25, statement of Captain Briggs statement; Mrs Melicent Wathen papers in the possession of

the Reverend Mark Wathen, Diary; War Office, WO95/5413, 16 Division War Diary, 19 April 1919.

3 *Report from Brigadier-General Dyer*, 25 August 1919, p. 6; Dyer puts the opening of the shops on the 14th, so some may have opened that night; appendix ix, p. xvii; appendix xv, p. xxiv, War Diary Amritsar; Command 771: *Disturbances in the Punjab, Statement by Brigadier-General R.E.H. Dyer*, annex A, p. 25, statement of Captain Briggs statement; Datta, *New Light on the Punjab Disturbances*, p. 279.

4 *Report of The Commissioners Appointed by the Punjab Sub-Committee of the Indian National Congress*, 2 vols (Bombay: Karnatak Press, 1920), ii, pp. 9–10, evidence of Girdhari Lal, who gives the texts of the speeches in Urdu and English; *The Times*, 4 June 1920, letter from S.R. Purnell.

5 *Hunter Report*, pp. 31, 55; Evidence, vol. iii, p. 7, evidence of Miles Irving, and, p. 181, statement; p. 222, statement of A.J.W. Kitchin; vol. iv, pp. 322, 325, report of General Beynon; Datta, *New Light on the Punjab Disturbances*, p. 133, evidence of Sir Michael O'Dwyer, and, pp. 796–97, statement; pp. 278, 379, statement of the Punjab Government; p. 901, memorandum of the Government of India; pp. 1143, 1147–48, evidence of Lieutenant-General Sir Havelock Hudson; *Report from Brigadier-General Dyer*, 25 August 1919, p. 4; appendix xv, p. xxiv, War Diary Amritsar; Command 534: *Parliamentary Papers* (Commons), 1920, vol. 14, *Reports*, vol. 6, 'East India (Punjab Disturbances)'. 'Reports on the Punjab Disturbances, April 1919', pp. 6, 53–67; Command 705: *Parliamentary Papers* (Commons), 1920, vol. 14, *Reports*, vol. 6. 'East India (Disturbances in the Punjab, etc)'. 'Correspondence between the Government of India and the Secretary of State for India on the Report of Lord Hunter's Committee', p. 9; Sir George Barrow, *The Life of General Sir Charles Carmichael Monro* (London: Hutchinson, 1931), p. 194; War Office, WO95/5413, 16 Division War Diary, 20–22 April 1919; J.P. Thompson papers, MSS Euro F 137 in the British Library, Diary, 21 April 1919.

6 *Hunter Report*, pp. 64–65, 72–73; Evidence, vol. iii, p. 118, evidence of Brigadier-General Dyer; Datta, *New Light on the Punjab Disturbances*, pp. 250, 279, 524, 579, 795, 897–98; pp. 1122–24, Resolution by the Government; Command 534: *Reports on the Punjab Disturbances*, pp. 7, 56; War Office, WO95/5413, 16 Division War Diary, 15 April 1919; Sir Michael O'Dwyer, *India as I Knew It, 1885–1925* (London: Constable, 1925), p. 280; Kanji Dwarkadas, *India's Fight for Freedom, 1913–1937: An Eye Witness Story* (Bombay: Popular Prakashan, 1966), p. 107; *Secret Papers from the British Royal Archives*, eds P.N. Chopra, Prabha Chopra and Padshma Jha (Delhi: Konark Publishers, 1998), p. 105, letter from the Viceroy to George V; Peter G. Robb, *The Government of India and Reform: Policies Towards Politics and the Constitution, 1916–1921* (Oxford: Oxford University Press, 1976), p. 180.

7 *Report from Brigadier-General Dyer*, 25 August 1919, appendix xiii, p. xx; appendix xv, p. xxiv; India Office, L/MILITARY/17/5/3079, entry 26969; War Office, WO95/5413, 16 Division War Diary, 14 April 1919; ibid., WO95/5414, 1/124th Baluch War Diary, 14 April 1919; M.H.L. Morgan, 'The Truth about Amritsar: By An Eye Witness', 72/22/1 T, in the Imperial War Museum, p. 6; Frank McCallum, 'Amritsar, 1919: A Bystander's View', *Indo-British Review*, 16, no. 1 (March 1989) (also in the Imperial War Museum, the Liddle Collection, Brotherton Library, Leeds University, the British Library and the Gurkha Museum), pp. 32–33; O.A. Chaldecott, *The Tenth Baluch Regiment: The First Battalion*,

Duchess of Connaught's Own (Late 124th DCO Baluchistan Infantry) and the Tenth Battalion (Late 2/124th Baluchistan Infantry) (Bombay: Times of India Press, 1935), p. 164.

8   *Hunter Report*, pp. 64–65; Evidence, vol. iii, p. 136, evidence of Brigadier-General Dyer; p. 222, statement of A.J.W. Kitchin statement; Datta, *New Light on the Punjab Disturbances*, appendix xx, pp. 579–85, statement of Punjab Government; p. 1143, evidence of Lieutenant-General Hudson; National Archives of India, Home Political, Deposit, August 1919, 53, memorandum, 24 June 1919; ibid., deposit, October 1919, 28, memorandum, 18 July 1919.

9   *Hunter Report*, pp. 76–78, 170; Evidence, vol. iii, p. 182, evidence of Miles Irving; Datta, *New Light on the Punjab Disturbances*, p. 580; Command 534: *Reports on the Punjab Disturbances*, p. 7; *Report from Brigadier-General Dyer*, 25 August 1919, annex B, pp. iv, vii, Report on Operation of Martial Law in the Amritsar Area.

10 *Hunter Report*, Evidence, vol. iii, p. 121, evidence of Brigadier-General Dyer; Datta, *New Light on the Punjab Disturbances*, p. 1075; *The London Cyclist Battalion*, compiled by the History Committee of the 26th Middlesex (Cyclist) Volunteer Rifle Corps and the 25th (City of London) Cyclist Battalion, the London Regiment (London: Forster Groom, 1932), p. 180; *Report from Brigadier-General Dyer*, 25 August 1919, appendix xv, p. xxiv, War Diary Amritsar.

11 Datta, *New Light on the Punjab Disturbances*, p. 120, evidence of J.P. Thompson; p. 173, evidence of Sir Michael O'Dwyer; *Report from Brigadier-General Dyer*, 25 August 1919, p. 7; J.P. Thompson papers, Diary, 16 April 1919; *Morning Post*, 9 June 1920, pp. 7–8, letter from Sir Michael O'Dwyer.

12 *Hunter Report*, pp. 79–80; Evidence, vol. iii, p. 118, evidence of Brigadier-General Dyer; Datta, *New Light on the Punjab Disturbances*, pp. 281, 577; *Report from Brigadier-General Dyer*, 25 August 1919, p. 7; annex B, p. vi, Report on Operation of Martial Law in the Amritsar Area; appendix xv, p. xxv, War Diary Amritsar; Command 534: *Reports on the Punjab Disturbances*, pp. 8, 54, 59 (the latter wrongly shows Jullundur proclaimed on 16 April); India Office, L/MILITARY/17/5/3079, Army Headquarters War Diary, 16 April 1919, entries 26714, 26969, 28692; War Office, WO95/5413, 16 Division War Diary, 16, 21 and 25 April 1919; National Archives of India, Home Political, part B, May 1919, 551–605, proceeding 583; *Tribune*, 7 November 1919, letter from C.F. Andrews letter; C.F. Andrews papers, 1/D-28, NMML; *INC Report*, ii, p. 139, evidence of Maulvi Gholam; *Civil and Military Gazette*, 'Punjab Disturbances', 2nd ed., April 1919, p. 25; Vinay Lal, 'The Incident of the Crawling Lane; Women in the Punjab Disturbances of 1919', *Genders*, 16 (Spring 1993), pp. 35–60.

13 *Hunter Report*, Evidence, vol. iii, p. 16, evidence of Miles Irving; p. 127, evidence of Brigadier-General Dyer; *Report from Brigadier-General Dyer*, 25 August 1919, p. 9; appendix xv, p. xxiv, War Diary, Amritsar; *INC Report*, ii, p. 120, evidence of Har Gopal Khanna.

14 *Hunter Report*, Evidence, vol. iii, pp. 118, 135, 136, evidence of Brigadier-General Dyer; pp. 182–183, statement of Miles Irving; *INC Report*, ii, pp. 56–57, evidence of Lala Kanhyalal Bhatia; *Report From Brigadier-General Dyer*, 25 August 1919, appendix vii, p. xvii.

15 Command 534: *Reports on the Punjab Disturbances*, pp. 60–61; *Report from Brigadier-General Dyer*, 25 August 1919, appendix xv, p. xxiv, War Diary Amritsar.

16 Datta, *New Light on the Punjab Disturbances*, p. 104, evidence of J.P. Thompson evidence; Rupert Furneaux, *Massacre at Amritsar* (London: George Allen & Unwin, 1963), p. 88; Kapil

Deva Malaviya, *Open Rebellion in the Punjab (with Special Reference to Amritsar)* (Allahabad: Abhudaya Press, 1919), p. 43.

17 Datta, *New Light on the Punjab Disturbances*, p. 1074, speech of J.P. Thompson; McCallum, 'Amritsar, 1919', p. 33; Malaviya, *Open Rebellion in the Punjab*, p. 38, interview with man living in the Dugglan ki gali (Dugglan Alley); Ian Colvin, *The Life of General Dyer* (London: Blackwood, 1929), p. 196; Edmonds papers, letter from Annie Dyer to Edmonds, 9 August 1927; National Archives of India, Home Political, Deposit, October 1919, 62, Irving Report.

18 This date must be wrong. McCallum left Amritsar on the day of the order being issued, and had been out of the city between about 15 and 18 April in Lahore. It is possible, though that McCallum picked up a remark made by Dyer just before he issued the order.

19 *Report from Brigadier-General Dyer*, 25 August 1919, pp. 7, 9; Datta, *New Light on the Punjab Disturbances*, p. 281, statement of Punjab Government; the Punjab Government sought to portray the order in a better light, and gave the following incorrect statement: 'The houses had back exits and the picquets were on duty only between 6 a.m and 8 p.m'; *Hunter Report*, Evidence, vol. iii, pp. 120–21, 123, evidence of Brigadier-General Dyer; M.R. Jayakar, *The Story of My Life*, 2 vols (Bombay: Asia Publishing House, 1958), i, p. 286; J.P. Thompson papers, *Diary*, 29 July 1919; Edmonds papers, letter from Annie Dyer to Edmonds, 9 August 1927, p. 1; McCallum, 'Amritsar, 1919', p. 32; Sergeant Reginald Mortimer Howgego papers, in the India Office, British Library, MSS EUR C 340; one of the photographs is of three British soldiers prodding with bayonets a man crawling in the street.

20 *Hunter Report*, p. 83; Evidence, vol. iii, p. 12, evidence of Miles Irving; pp. 117, 136, 139, evidence of Brigadier-General Dyer; Datta, *New Light on the Punjab Disturbances*, pp. 134, 137–38, evidence of Sir Michael O'Dwyer, and p. 279, statement; p. 1104, speech by Lieutenant-General Hudson; Command 534: *Reports on the Punjab Disturbances*, p. 8; *Report from Brigadier-General Dyer*, 25 August 1919, p. 9; National Archives of India, Home Political, deposit, October 1919, 62, Irving report; *INC Report*, ii, pp. 126–27, evidence of Kahan Chand; p. 128, evidence of Rakha Ram; Edwin Montagu papers in Trinity College Cambridge, undated minute, AS3/4/5 584 (2); Edwin Montagu papers in the British Library, MSS Eur D 523/8, letter from Sir Michael O'Dwyer to the Viceroy, 1 May 1919.

21 *Hunter Report*, Evidence, vol. iii, pp. 121, 123–24, 139, evidence of Brigadier-General Dyer; Datta, *New Light on the Punjab Disturbances*, p. 281, statement of Punjab government; p. 1153, evidence of Lieutenant-General Hudson, shows that, although a military punishment, flogging had been reserved to the discretion in each case of the Commander-in-Chief for the previous two years; *Report from Brigadier-General Dyer*, 25 August 1919, p. 9; annex B, p. iv, Report on Operation of Martial Law in the Amritsar Area; Command 534: *Reports on the Punjab Disturbances*, p. 8.

22 *INC Report*, ii, pp. 131–32, evidence of Pandit Salig Ram.

23 Datta, *New Light on the Punjab Disturbances*, p. 137, evidence of Sir Michael O'Dwyer.

24 *Hunter Report*, Evidence, vol. iii, p. 26, evidence of Miles Irving; Datta, *New Light on the Punjab Disturbances*, pp. 130, 174, evidence of Sir Michael O'Dwyer, and, pp. 799–800, statement; Montagu papers in the British Library, letter from Chelmsford, 30 April 1919; Chelmsford Papers, vol. 24, roll no. 11, no. 273, Nehru Memorial Museum and Library, letter O'Dwyer to Viceroy, 26 February 1920; National Archives of India, Home Political,

part B, May 1919, 551–605, proceeding 581; ibid., part B, May 1919, 148–178, letter O'Dwyer to Viceroy, 21 April 1919.

25 *The London Cyclist Battalion*, p. 182; O'Dwyer, *India as I Knew It*, p. 293; *Hunter Report*, Evidence, vol. iii, p. 119, evidence of Brigadier-General Dyer; vol. iv, pp. 322, 333, report of General Beynon; *Report from Brigadier-General Dyer*, 25 August 1919, p. 7; appendix xi, p. xviii; appendix xv, p. xxv, War Diary Amritsar; Command 771: *Disturbances in the Punjab, Statement by Brigadier-General R.E.H. Dyer*, annex A, p. 26, statement of Captain Briggs; War Office, WO95/5413, 16 Division War Diary, 23 April 1919.

26 *Hunter Report*, Evidence, vol. iv, p. 336, report of General Beynon; Command 534: *Reports on the Punjab Disturbances*, p. 64; *Report from Brigadier-General Dyer*, 25 August 1919, appendix xxv, p. xxv, War Diary Amritsar; War Office, WO95/5413, 16 Division War Diary, 23 and 24 April 1919; Colvin, *Dyer*, pp. 193–94.

27 *Hunter Report*, Evidence, vol. iii, p. 119, evidence of Brigadier-General Dyer; vol. iv, appendix xviii, p. 337, report of General Beynon; *Report from Brigadier-General Dyer*, 25 August 1919, p. 7; appendix xii, p. xviii; appendix xxv, p. xxv, War Diary Amritsar; *The London Cyclist Battalion*, pp. 182–83; Colvin, *Dyer*, p. 201.

28 *Report from Brigadier-General Dyer*, 25 August 1919, p. viii, an abbreviated text; Malaviya, *Open Rebellion in the Punjab*, p. 100–17, quoting the martial law orders in full with the signature; Pandit Pearay Dattatreya Mohan, *The Punjab 'Rebellion' of 1919 and How It Was Suppressed: An Account of the Punjab Disorders and the Working of Martial Law*, ed. Ravi M. Bakaya, 2 vols (New Delhi: Gyan Publishers, 1999), p. 35, quotes part of the text in full.

29 *Hunter Report*, Evidence, vol. iii, p. 119, evidence of Brigadier-General Dyer; *Report from Brigadier-General Dyer*, 25 August 1919, p. 8; Command 771: *Disturbances in the Punjab, Statement by Brigadier-General R.E.H. Dyer*, annex A, p. 26, statement of Captain Briggs; War Office, WO95/5413, 16 Division War Diary, 26 and 28 April 1919; National Archives of India, Home Political, part B, May 1919, 551–605.

30 *Hunter Report*, Evidence, vol. iii, p. 132, evidence of Brigadier-General Dyer; *Report from Brigadier-General Dyer*, 25 August 1919, p. 3; appendix iv, p. xiv; Command 771: *Disturbances in the Punjab, Statement by Brigadier-General R.E.H. Dyer*, annex A, p. 26, statement of Captain Briggs; J.P. Thompson papers, Diary, 8 August 1919; National Archives of India, Home Political, part B, June 1919, proceedings 408–31.

31 *Hunter Report*, Evidence, vol. iii, p. 119, evidence of Brigadier-General Dyer; *Report from Brigadier-General Dyer*, 25 August 1919, p. 8; appendix xxv, p. xxv, War Diary Amritsar; War Office, WO95/5413, 16 Division War Diary, 29 April 1919; ibid., WO95/5414, Headquarters 45 Brigade War Diary, 1–7 May 1919; O'Dwyer, *India as I Knew It*, pp. 300, 323; Hugh Tinker, *The Ordeal of Love: C.F. Andrews and India* (Delhi: Oxford University Press, 1979), p. 153; Morgan, 'The Truth about Amritsar', p. 2, contradicts the line that there was no attempt to subvert troops. Morgan was based in Lahore and recalled: 'My own suberdar-major [sic] brought me a letter from the rebels telling him now was the time to murder all the British Officers.'

32 *Hunter Report*, Evidence, vol. iii, p. 118, evidence of Brigadier-General Dyer; *Report from Brigadier-General Dyer*, 25 August 1919, annex B, p. vii; Command 534: *Reports on the Punjab Disturbances*, p. 8; National Archives of India, Home Political, part B, May 1919, 274; ibid., deposit September 1919, 12, which shows that allegations of corruption continued

throughout the summer; ibid., deposit, October 1919 16; J.P. Thompson papers, Diary, 29 July 1919; Roger Perkins, *The Amritsar Legacy: Golden Temple to Caxton Hall: The Story of a Killing* (Chippenham: Picton, 1989), p. 182.

33 V.N. Datta, and S.C. Mittal, eds, *The Sources of National Movement*, i, *January 1919 to September 1920: Protests, Disturbances and Defiance* (New Delhi: Allied Publishers, 1985), p. 166, quoting letter C.F. Andrews to the *Tribune*, 5–7 November 1919, from C.F. Andrews papers, 1/D-28, NMML.

34 *Report from Brigadier-General Dyer*, 25 August 1919, p. 5; Colvin, *Dyer*, p. 193.

35 India Office, L/MILITARY/17/5/3079, War Diary, Army Headquarters, India, 21 April 1919, entry 28865; National Archives of India, Home Political, part B, May 1919, 184; Sitaramayya B. Pattabhi, *The History of the Indian National Congress (1885–1935)* (Bombay: Padma Publications, 1946), i, p. 171.

36 General John Nicholson, who had died in the siege of Delhi during the Mutiny and had inspired his own band of religious fanatics despite his own evangelical Christianity.

37 *Report from Brigadier-General Dyer*, 25 August 1919, p. 8; *Civil and Military Gazette*, 25 January 1920; *Pioneer*, 23 January 1920; *Tribune*, 9 May 1925; *Akali*, 17 December 1921; H.S. Bhatia and S.R. Bakshi, *Encyclopaedic History of the Sikhs and Sikhism* (New Delhi: Deep & Deep, 1999), v, 'National Movement and the Sikhs: The Martyrdom Tradition', p. 86; G.S. Chhabra, *Advanced Study in the History of the Panjab*, 2 vols (Ludhiana: Prakash Brothers, 1962), ii, pp. 440–41; Mohinder Singh, 'Gurdwara Reform Movement', in Ravi Dayal, ed., *We Fought Together for Freedom: Chapters from the Indian National Movement* (Delhi: Oxford University Press, 1995), p.107; Kamlesh Mohan, *Militant Nationalism in the Punjab, 1919–1935* (New Delhi: Manohar, 1985), p. 29; Khuswant Singh, *A History of the Sikhs*, ii, *1839–1964* (Delhi: Oxford University Press, 1984), p. 167; Mohinder Singh, *The Akali Struggle: A Retrospect* (New Delhi: Atlantic Publishers, Macmillan, 1988), pp. 14–16; Sangat Singh, *The Sikhs in History* (New Delhi: Uncommon Books, 1996), p. 157; Colvin, *Dyer*, p. 202.

38 *Hunter Report*, Evidence, vol. iii, p. 120, evidence of Brigadier-General Dyer; p. 183, statement of Miles Irving; Command 534: *Reports on the Punjab Disturbances*, pp. 7–8; *Report from Brigadier-General Dyer*, 25 August 1919, p. 9; annex B, p. iv, Report on Operation of Martial Law in Amritsar Area; B.G. Horniman, *Amritsar and Our Duty to India* (London: T Fisher Unwin, 1920), p. 133; National Archives of India, part B, June 1919, 408–31, has many details of individual punishments; Pearay Mohan, *The Punjab 'Rebellion' of 1919 and How It Was Suppressed*, ii, pp. 352–74; supplement I, 'Statement showing Sentences passed by Martial Law Commission together with the Orders of Government'.

Notes to Chapter 18: Thal

1 The political and military background to this chapter is taken from Ludwig W. Adamec, *Afghanistan, 1900–1923* (Berkeley: University of California Press, 1967), pp. 108–22; Ludwig W. Adamec, *Dictionary of Afghan Wars, Revolutions and Insurgencies* (London: Scarecrow Press, 1996), p. 229–31; Michael Barthorp, *The North-West Frontier: British India and Afghanistan. A Pictorial History, 1839–1947* (Poole, Dorset: Blandford Press, 1982),

pp. 156–57; Sir William Barton, *India's North-West Frontier* (London: John Murray, 1939), p. 142; J.G. Elliott, *The Frontier, 1839–1947: The Story of the North-West Frontier of India* (London: Cassell, 1968), p. 50; Arnold Fletcher, *Afghanistan: Highroad of Conquest* (Ithaca: Cornell University Press, 1965), pp. 185–95; Sir W. Kerr Fraser-Tytler, *Afghanistan: A Study of Political Developments in Central and Southern Asia*, revised by Sir M.C. Gillett (London: Oxford University Press, 1967); T.A. Heathcote, *The Afghan Wars, 1839–1919* (London: Osprey, 1980), pp. 170–96; T.A Heathcote, *The Military in British India: The Development of British Land Forces in South Asia, 1600–1947* (Manchester: Manchester University Press, 1995), p. 232; Keith Jeffery, *The British Army and the Crisis of Empire, 1918–22* (Manchester: Manchester University Press, 1984), pp. 2–10, 16, 100–1; Sir George MacMunn, *Afghanistan: From Darius to Amanullah* (London: G. Bell, 1929), p. 258–69; Charles Miller, *Khyber: British India's North-West Frontier. The Story of an Imperial Migraine* (London: Macdonald and Jane's, 1977), pp. 317–26; G.N. Molesworth, *Afghanistan 1919: An Account of Operations in the Third Afghan War* (London: Asia Publishing House, 1962), pp. 22–26, 115–22; T.R. Moreman, 'Passing it On': The Army in India and the Development of Frontier Warfare, 1849–1947' (PhD Thesis, London University DX195607, 1997), pp. 168–73; Edgar O'Ballance, *Afghan Wars, 1839–1992: What Britain Gave Up and the Soviet Union Lost* (London: Brassey's, 1993), pp. 52–61; James W. Spain, *The Pathan Borderland* (The Hague: Mouton, 1963), p. 230; Arthur Swinson, *North-West Frontier: People and Events, 1839–1947* (London: Hutchinson, 1967), pp. 268–71; Sir Percy Sykes, *A History of Afghanistan*, (London: Macmillan, 1940), ii, pp. 264–69; *The Third Afghan War, 1919: Official Account* (Calcutta: Government Press, 1926), pp. 13–14, 18 note, 59–61; Robert John Wilkinson-Latham, *North-West Frontier, 1837–1947* (London: Osprey, 1977); Donald N. Wilber, *Afghanistan: Its People, its Society, its Culture* (New Haven: Human Resources Area Files Press, 1962), p. 20; L.F. Rushbrook Williams, ed., *India in 1919* (Calcutta: Government of India, 1920), pp. 8–9.

2   V.N. Datta, ed., *New Light on the Punjab Disturbances in 1919: Volumes VI and VII of Disorders Inquiry Committee Evidence*, 2 vols (Simla: Indian Institute of Advanced Study, 1975) (the text of the original is in India Office, L/MIL/17/12/42 and in Cabinet Office, Cab 27/93), p. 1153, appendix to evidence of General Hudson, information obtained from Lieutenant-Colonel F.C. Isemonger: 'The date on which trouble first began to be anticipated on the North-West Frontier was 1 May 1919.'

3   Datta, *New Light on the Punjab Disturbances*, pp. 1127–28, evidence of General Hudson; Command 534: *Parliamentary Papers* (Commons), 1920, vol. 14, *Reports*, vol. 6, 'East India (Punjab Disturbances)'. 'Reports on the Punjab Disturbances, April 1919', p. 66.

4   Datta, *New Light on the Punjab Disturbances*, pp. 1128–30, evidence of General Hudson; Ian Colvin, *The Life of General Dyer* (London: Blackwood, 1929), pp. 206–7.

5   Brigadier-General Sir James Edmonds papers in the Liddell Hart Centre, King's College London, 3/2/171, letter from Annie Dyer to Edmonds, 9 August 1927; Arthur Swinson, *Six Minutes to Sunset: The Story of General Dyer and the Amritsar Affair* (London: Peter Davies, 1964), p. 195, quoting personal communication from Alice Dyer, and, p. 199, quoting letters from Lieutenant-Colonel Williams and Mr Fletcher; V.N. Datta, and S.C. Mittal, eds, *The Sources of National Movement (January 1919 to September 1920): Protests, Disturbances and Defiance* (New Delhi: Allied Publishers, 1985), i, pp. 98, 102–4; Sitaramayya B. Pattabhi, *The History of the Indian National Congress (1885–1935)* (Bombay: Padma Publications, 1946),

i, p. 172; Montagu papers in the British Library, MSS Eur D 523/3; Peter G. Robb, *The Government of India and Reform: Policies towards Politics and the Constitution, 1916–1921* (Oxford: Oxford University Press, 1976), p. 192; B.G. Horniman, *Amritsar and Our Duty to India* (London: T. Fisher Unwin, 1920), p. 176; Alfred Nundy, *Political Problems and Hunter Committee Disclosures* (Calcutta: 'The publisher', 1920), p. 130; John Gallagher, Gordon Johnson and Anil Seal, eds, *Locality, Province and Nation: Essays on Indian Politics, 1870–1940* (London: Cambridge University Press, 1973), p. 127; D.G. Tendulkar, *Mahatma: Life of Mohandas Karamchand Gandhi* (Delhi: The Publications Division, Government of India, 1960), i, pp. 259–60.

6 Robb, *The Government of India and Reform*, pp. 182, 192–99; Datta and Mittal, *The Sources of National Movement*, i, pp. 107, 110; Command 705: *Parliamentary Papers* (Commons), 1920, vol. 14, *Reports*, vol. 6, 'East India (Disturbances in the Punjab, etc)'. 'Correspondence between the Government of India and the Secretary of State for India on the Report of Lord Hunter's Committee', p. 9.

7 Command 681: *Parliamentary Papers* (Commons), 1920, vol. 14, *Reports*, vol. 6, 'East India (Disturbances in the Punjab, etc)'. 'Report of the Committee Appointed by the Government of India to Investigate the Disturbances in the Punjab, etc.' (the *Hunter Report*), Evidence, vol. iii, p. 119, evidence of Brigadier-General Dyer; *Report from Brigadier-General R.E.H. Dyer, Commanding 45th Brigade, to the General Staff, 16th (Indian) Division*, 25 August 1919, in the Dyer papers in the National Army Museum (also in the *Hunter Report*, Evidence, vol. iii, appendix xiii), p. 8; Command 771: *Parliamentary Papers* (Commons), 1920, vol. 8, *Reports*, vol. 4, 'Army'. 'Disturbances in the Punjab, Statement by Brigadier-General R.E.H. Dyer' (also in India Office, L/MIL/17/12/43), appendix A, p. 26, statement of Captain Briggs. Detail in the remainder of this chapter of the activities of 45 Brigade, its signal section and the 1/25th Londons is taken from War Office, WO 95/5414, 45 Brigade War Diary, 23 May to 29 June 1919; ibid., 1/25th Londons War Diary, 23 May to 5 July 1919; ibid., 45 Brigade Signal Section War Diary, 24 May to 20 June 1919; also from War Office, WO95/5389, Headquarters 16 Division War Diary, 27 to 31 May 1919; also from War Office, WO 95/5413, Headquarters 16 Division War Diary 1 to 12 June 1919, and appendix III, telegrams; also from War Office, 106/56, 'Report by Brigadier-General R.E.H. Dyer, etc, on the Operations for the Relief of Thal, May–June 1919', file no. 4747-F, Operations (Simla: Government Monotype Press, 1919); also from *The London Cyclist Battalion*, compiled by the History Committee of the 26th Middlesex (Cyclist) Volunteer Rifle Corps and the 25th (City of London) Cyclist Battalion, the London Regiment (London: Forster Groom, 1932), pp. 190–209.

8 *The London Cyclist Battalion*, p. 184.

9 *Report From Brigadier-General Dyer*, 25 August 1919, p. 8; Liddle papers, in the Brotherton Library of the University of Leeds, INDIAN 15, Lance-Corporal Charles J. Davis, Diary, 23–26 May 1919; Colvin, *Dyer*, p. 216. Detail of units of 45 and 65 Brigade for the rest of this chapter are taken from L. MacGlasson, *Diary of the 2/4th Battalion the Border Regiment, 1914–19* (Carlisle: Charles Thurnam & Sons, 1920), pp. 20–21; H.C. Wylly, *The Border Regiment in the Great War* (Aldershot: Gale & Polden, 1924), p. 244; R.D. Palsokar, *A Historical Record of the Dogra Regiment: A Saga of Gallantry and Valour, 1858–1981* (Faizabad: Dogra Regimental Centre, 1982), p. 144; 'Extract of Brigadier-General R.E.H. Dyer CB Association with 2nd/41st Dogra', private communication to the author through

USI India, January 2003; *Regimental History of the 4th Battalion, 13th Frontier Force Rifles (Wilde's)*, anon. (Frome: Butler & Tanner, 1932), p. 178; *Chronicle*, 12 August 1930, 'Short Histories of Indian Regiments, 2nd Battalion 2nd Punjab Regiment: The Old 69th', pp. 2–4; 'Extract of Brigadier-General R.E.H. Dyer CB Association with 69th Punjabis', private communication to the author through USI India, January 2003; O.A. Chaldecott, *The Tenth Baluch Regiment: The First Battalion, Duchess of Connaught's Own (Late 124th D.C.O. Baluchistan Infantry) and the Tenth Battalion (Late 2/124th Baluchistan Infantry)* (Bombay: Times of India Press, 1935); F.S. Poynder, Stevens and P. Choudhuri, *9 Gurkha Rifles: A Regimental History (1817–1947)* (New Delhi: Vision Books, 1984), p. 88.

10   Colvin, *Dyer*, p. 212.

11   Command 771: *Disturbances in the Punjab, Statement by Brigadier-General R.E.H. Dyer*, p. 20; Colvin, *Dyer*, p. 216; National Archive of India, Home Political, deposit, August 1919, 53.

12   Colvin, *Dyer*, pp. 216–18.

13   Chelmsford papers in the British Library, MSS Eur E 264/55g, Afghan War, item 380, proceeding 147, p. 62, Report from Commissioner North-West Frontier, 1 June 1919.

14   Colvin, *Dyer*, pp. 220–21.

15   Colvin, *Dyer*, p. 229; Chelmsford papers, MSS Eur E 264/55g, Afghan War, item 399, proceeding 166, Report from Commissioner North-West Frontier, 3 June 1919, relaying report from Major Anson of 10 p.m., 1 June.

16   Colvin, *Dyer*, pp. 222–23; 'Extract of Brigadier-General Dyer Association with 2nd/41st Dogra'; Chelmsford papers, MSS Eur E 264/55g, Afghan War, item 406, proceeding 173, p. 72, Report from Commissioner North-West Frontier, 3 June 1919, relaying report from Major Anson.

17   Colvin, *Dyer*, pp. 223–28.

18   Roger Perkins, *The Amritsar Legacy: Golden Temple to Caxton Hall. The Story of a Killing* (Chippenham: Picton, 1989), p. 105; telephone conversation between Perkins and the author, March 2002. The source for this information was a retired British Gurkha officer who went to Thal later but did not want to be identified and told Perkins this in private.

19   Chelmsford papers MSS Eur E 264/55g, Afghan War, item 420, proceeding 187, p. 78, and item 428, proceeding 195, p. 84, Reports from Commissioner North-West Frontier, 5 and 6 June 1919, relaying reports from Major Anson of 5 June.

20   Lieutenant-Colonel M.H.L. Morgan, 'The Truth About Amritsar: By an Eye Witness', in the Imperial War Museum, p. 6.

21   Command 771: *Disturbances in the Punjab, Statement by Brigadier-General R.E.H. Dyer*, p. 22; Colvin, *Dyer*, p. 229; *Secret Papers from the British Royal Archives*, ed. by P.N. Chopra, Prabha Chopra and Padshma Jha (Delhi: Konark Publishers, 1998), p. 197, Chelmsford to George V, 25 May 1920.

Notes to Chapter 19: Dalhousie and Jamrud

1   John Dove, *The Letters of John Dove*, ed. Robert Henry Brand (London: Macmillan, 1938), p. 75, letter to Brand, 24 April 1919.

2   Nirad C. Chaudhuri, *Autobiography of an Unknown Indian* (London: Picador, 1999), pp. 403–4.

3   V.N. Datta, ed., *New Light on the Punjab Disturbances in 1919: Volumes VI and VII of Disorders Inquiry Committee Evidence*, 2 vols (Simla: Indian Institute of Advanced Study, 1975) (the text of the original is in India Office, L/MIL/17/12/42 and in Cabinet Office, Cab 27/93), p. 3–4; Chelmsford Papers, 1919, vol. 22, roll no. 10, no. 554 (a), in the Nehru Memorial Museum and Library, letter Tagore to Viceroy 31 May 1919; Sitaramayya B. Pattabhi, *The History of the Indian National Congress (1885–1935)* (Bombay: Padma Publications, 1946), i, pp. 166, 171–72; Peter G. Robb, *The Government of India and Reform: Policies towards Politics and the Constitution, 1916–1921* (Oxford: Oxford University Press, 1976), p. 201; V.N. Datta and S.C. Mittal, eds, *The Sources of National Movement*, i, *(January 1919 to September 1920): Protests, Disturbances and Defiance* (New Delhi: Allied Publishers, 1985), p. 130; C.S. Ranga Iyer, *India: Peace or War?* (London: Harrap, 1930), p. 86; Jawarharlal Nehru, *An Autobiography* (Delhi: Oxford University Press, 1985), p. 42; Reginald Reynolds, *The White Sahibs in India* (London: Martin Secker & Warburg, 1937), p. 185; Judith M. Brown, *Gandhi's Rise to Power* (Cambridge University Press: Cambridge, 1972), p. 232; K.P.S. Menon, *C. Sankaran Nair* (Delhi: The Government of India Publication Division, 1967), pp. 103–4.

4   National Archives of India, Home Political, Part B, May 1919, 551–605, proceedings 558, 561, 566, 583; Chelmsford papers in the British Library, MSS Eur E 264, 264/1, 264/10/217, 616, 264/22; Montagu papers in the British Library, MSS Eur D 523, 523/8, and in Trinity College, Cambridge, MSS AS3/4/83 (1), 30/31 December 1919; Sir Algernon Rumbold, *Watershed in India, 1914–1922* (Athlone Press: London, 1979), p. 176.

5   Chelmsford papers, 264/1, 264/5; Montagu papers in the British Library, 523/8.

6   Chelmsford papers, 264/5; T.N. Jagadisan, ed., *Letters of the Right Honourable V.S. Srinavasa Sastri* (London: Asia Publishing House, 1963); Sir Surendranath Banerjea, *A Nation in the Making: Being the Reminiscences of Fifty Years of Public Life* (Calcutta: Oxford University Press, 1962), p. 304.

7   Datta, *New Light on the Punjab Disturbances*, pp. 1102–4, speech of General Hudson, and pp. 1143, 1147, evidence; General Sir Henry (Harry) Crichton Sclater, papers in the Liddell Hart Centre, King's College London, letter from Macmunn, 14 June 1920.

8   *Times Literary Supplement*, 6 February 1964, statement by the unnamed reviewer of Rupert Furneaux's *Massacre at Amritsar* (London: George Allen & Unwin, 1963).

9   *Report from Brigadier-General R.E.H. Dyer, Commanding 45th Brigade, to the General Staff, 16th (Indian) Division*, 25 August 1919, in the Dyer papers in the National Army Museum (also in the *Hunter Report*, Evidence, vol. iii, appendix xiii), p. 1; Command 771: *Parliamentary Papers* (Commons), 1920, vol. 8, *Reports*, vol. 4, 'Army'. 'Disturbances in the Punjab, Statement by Brigadier-General R.E.H. Dyer' (also in India Office, L/MIL/17/12/43), p. 20; Ian Colvin, *The Life of General Dyer* (London: Blackwood, 1929), pp. 228–29.

10   J.P. Thompson papers, in the British Library, F/137/13, Diary, 8 August 1919. The original version was much abbreviated and has been expanded here.

11   National Archives of India, Home Political, deposit, September 1919, 33; Parliamentary Debates, House of Lords, Official Report, vol. 36, no. 76, pp. 489–501, 6 August 1919.

12   Command 681: *Parliamentary Papers* (Commons), 1920, vol. 14, *Reports*, vol. 6, 'East India

(Disturbances in the Punjab, etc).' 'Report of the Committee Appointed by the Government of India to Investigate the Disturbances in the Punjab, etc.' (the *Hunter Report*), Evidence, vol. iv, pp. 322, 325, report of General Beynon; Command 771: *Disturbances in the Punjab, Statement by Brigadier-General R.E.H. Dyer*, p. 20.

13   Colvin, *Dyer*, p. 331.

14   India Office, L/MILITARY/7/946; Chelmsford papers, 264/13, telegram no. 9 from Viceroy to Montagu, 2 July 1920. The reason for these changes is not given, but may have had something to do with the numbers of each award available to be allocated at the time.

15   *Indian Army List*, January 1920, p. 25: 'Officiating General Officer Commanding 5th Infantry Brigade', no date of appointment; Colvin, *Dyer*, pp. 229–30; Command 771: *Disturbances in the Punjab, Statement by Brigadier-General R.E.H. Dyer*, p. 20; India Office, L/MILITARY/14/1025.

16   *Hunter Report*, pp. iv, 78; Datta, *New Light on the Punjab Disturbances*, pp. 1049–1119; Command 771: *Disturbances in the Punjab, Statement by Brigadier-General R.E.H. Dyer*, appendix B, pp. 26–27; Command 705: *Parliamentary Papers* (Commons), 1920, vol. 14, *Reports*, vol. 6, 'East India (Disturbances in the Punjab, etc)'. 'Correspondence between the Government of India and the Secretary of State for India on the Report of Lord Hunter's Committee', p. 10; India Office, L/PO/6/4; Montagu papers in Trinity College, AS3/4/52 (1); Kapil Deva Malaviya, *Open Rebellion in the Punjab (with Special Reference to Amritsar)* (Allahabad: Abhudaya Press, 1919); Sarvepalli Gopal, *Jawaharlal Nehru: A Biography* (London: Jonathan Cape, 1975), i, p. 36; Pattabhi, *The History of the Indian National Congress*, i, pp. 172–76; Prithvis Chandra Ray, *Life and Times of C.R. Das: The Story of Bengal's Self-Expression. Being a Personal Memoir of the Late Deshbandhu Chitta Ranjan and a Complete Outline of the History of Bengal for the First Quarter of the Twentieth Century* (London: Oxford University Press, 1927), p. 157; Robb, *The Government of India and Reform*, p. 201; H.S. Bhatia and S.R. Bakshi, *Encyclopaedic History of the Sikhs and Sikhism* (New Delhi: Deep and Deep, 1999), p. 114; Om Prakash Ralhan, *Jawaharlal Nehru and National Affairs (14 November 1889–14 August 1947)* (New Delhi: Anmol Publications, 1993), pp. 6–8; Datta and Mittal, *The Sources of National Movement*, i, pp. 142, 161–62; M.K. Gandhi, *An Autobiography* (London: Jonathan Cape, 2001), pp. 429, 437; M.R. Jayakar, *The Story of My Life* (Bombay: Asia Publishing House, 1958), i, pp. 320–26; Nehru, *An Autobiography*, pp. 42–43; N.R. Phatak, *Source Material for a History of the Freedom Movement in India* (Bombay: Government of Maharashtra, 1965), iii, part i, pp. 235–36.

17   *Hunter Report*, pp. iii–iv; Command 705: *Correspondence between the Government of India and the Secretary of State for India*, p. 2; Sir Valentine Chirol, *India Old and New* (London: Macmillan, 1921), p. 179; Sir Arthur Cunningham Lothian, *Kingdoms of Yesterday* (London: John Murray, 1951), p. 54; Sir George de S. Barrow, *The Fire of Life* (London: Hutchinson, 1941), p. 227; Bhatia and Bakshi, *Encyclopaedic History of the Sikhs and Sikhism*, p. 118, quoting a letter from Gandhi, Navajiwan, 23 November 1919; Rumbold, *Watershed in India*, p. 183.

18   Rumbold, *Watershed in India*, p. 176; Command 771: *Disturbances in the Punjab, Statement by Brigadier-General R.E.H. Dyer*, pp. 4, 20.

Notes to Chapter 20: *The Hunter Committee*

1   Sir George Barrow, *The Life of General Sir Charles Carmichael Monro* (London: Hutchinson, 1931), p. 210; T.L. Hughes, 'Man of Iron: A Biography of Major-General Sir William Beynon' (unpublished typescript in the Gurkha Museum, Gm: Acc. No. 94–10–9 H3), p. 138; Edward Thompson, *A Letter from India* (London: Faber & Faber, 1932), p. 104; Ian Colvin, *The Life of General Dyer* (London: Blackwood, 1929), pp. 237–38; Sir Algernon Rumbold, *Watershed in India, 1914–1922* (London: Athlone Press, 1979), p. 176; Arthur Swinson, *Six Minutes to Sunset: The Story of General Dyer and the Amritsar Affair* (London: Peter Davies, 1964), p. 126, relates a story that the doctor who operated upon Briggs told Alice at a dance that Indians had put ground glass in Briggs's food. This story is difficult to credit.

2   Command 681: *Parliamentary Papers* (Commons), 1920, vol. 14, *Reports*, vol. 6, 'East India (Disturbances in the Punjab, etc).' 'Report of the Committee Appointed by the Government of India to Investigate the Disturbances in the Punjab, etc.' (the *Hunter Report*), Evidence, vol. iii, pp. 139–141, evidence of Brigadier-General Dyer; Colvin, *Dyer*, pp. 237–50; Hughes, 'Man of Iron', p. 137.

3   Colvin, *Dyer*, p. 248; J.P. Thompson papers, in the British Library, F/137/13, Diary, 19 November 1919; Hughes, 'Man of Iron', p.137; Rupert Furneaux, *Massacre at Amritsar* (London: George Allen & Unwin, 1963), p. 119; *Pioneer Mail*, 29 July 1927; V.N. Datta and S.C. Mittal, eds, *The Sources of National Movement (January 1919 to September 1920): Protests, Disturbances and Defiance* (New Delhi: Allied Publishers, 1985), i, p. 177, quoting Sir Reginald Craddock letter to Viceroy, 23 December 1919 in the Chelmsford Papers, vol. 22, roll no. 10, no. 848 (a), NMML, pp. 603–4.

4   Sir Chimanlal Setalvad, *Recollections and Reflections: An Autobiography* (Bombay: Padma, 1946), p. 311–12.

5   Jawarharlal Nehru, *An Autobiography* (Delhi: Oxford University Press: Delhi, 1985), p. 43. Nehru states this was towards the end of 1919, but, as far as is known, Dyer did not go to Delhi until March 1920. The pyjamas on the platform may be an indication that Dyer was travelling as a sick man, and so this latter was perhaps the occasion.

6   National Archives of India, Home Political, deposit, 11 March 1920; Datta and Mittal, *The Sources of National Movement*, i, p. 170, quoting letter V.J. Patel to G.N. Mishra, 20 November 1919, in AICC papers, file 3, 1919, NMML; Montagu papers in the British Library, MSS Euro D 523/3, and in Trinity College, Cambridge, AS3/4/85 (1); Chelmsford papers in the British Library, MSS Euro E 264/5, 264/11; India Office, L/PO/6/8; Thompson papers in the British Library, MSS Euro F 137/31O; P. Ralhan and Suresh K. Sharma, eds, *Documents on Punjab* (New Delhi: Anmol Publications, 1994), v, pp. 60, 63; Sir Algernon Rumbold, *Watershed in India, 1914–1922* (Athlone Press: London, 1979), p. 183.

7   M.R. Jayakar, *The Story of My Life*, 2 vols (Bombay: Asia Publishing House, 1958), i, p. 295; Prithvis Chandra Ray, *Life and Times of C.R. Das: The Story of Bengal's Self-Expression. Being a Personal Memoir of the Late Deshbandhu Chitta Ranjan and a Complete Outline of the History of Bengal for the First Quarter of the Twentieth Century* (London: Oxford University Press, 1927), appendix G, p. 305; B.N. Pandey, *Nehru* (London: Macmillan, 1976), p. 73; A.M. Zaidi, Shaheda Ghufran Zaidi, Abdul Moid Zaidi, Naushaba Firdos Alvi and Amin Ahmed, eds, *The Encyclopaedia of Indian National Congress: Emergence of Gandhi*

(Delhi: S. Chand, 1979), vii, pp. 451–530; Reginald Reynolds, *The White Sahibs in India* (London: Martin Secker & Warburg, 1937), p. 185.

8   Command 771: *Parliamentary Papers* (Commons), 1920, vol. 8, *Reports*, vol. 4, 'Army'. 'Disturbances in the Punjab, Statement by Brigadier-General R.E.H. Dyer' (also in India Office, L/MIL/17/12/43), p. 20; Colvin, *Dyer*, pp. 250–53; *Dictionary of National Biography, 1922–1930*, ed. J.R.H. Weaver (Oxford: Oxford University Press, 1976), p. 280; Sir Michael Francis O'Dwyer, *India as I Knew It, 1885–1925* (London: Constable, 1925), p. 321; Barrow, *The Life of General Monro*, pp. 207, 218.

9   *Hunter Report*, pp. iii, 29–31, 111–15; Command 705: *Parliamentary Papers* (Commons), 1920, vol. 14, *Reports*, vol. 6, 'East India (Disturbances in the Punjab, etc)'. 'Correspondence between the Government of India and the Secretary of State for India on the Report of Lord Hunter's Committee', p. 2.

10   Colvin, *Dyer*, pp. 253–55.

11   The Executive Council was, in effect, India's Cabinet comprising the Viceroy's closest advisers.

12   National Archives of India, Home Political, June 1920, A, quoted in V.N. Datta, *Jallianwala Bagh* (Ludhiana: Lyall Book Depot and V.K. Arora, Kurukshera University Books, 1969), p. 131.

13   Swinson, *Six Minutes to Sunset*, p. 200.

14   Command 771: *Disturbances in the Punjab, Statement by Brigadier-General R.E.H. Dyer*, p. 3; Colvin, *Dyer*, pp. 254–55.

15   India Office, L/MILITARY/14/1025.

16   *Indian Army List*, April 1920, shown with no post. Brigadier-General L.W.Y. Campbell was by then 5 Brigade Commander; Colvin, *Dyer*, pp. 255–59; Alfred Draper, *The Amritsar Massacre: Twilight of the Raj* (London: Buchan & Enright, 1985), pp. 214–15; Datta, *Jallianwala Bagh*, p. 135; *Pioneer*, 23 April 1920.

17   India Office, L/MILITARY/7/946. Dyer's Mention in Despatches was, though, awarded. The certificate is in Dyer papers, 5–2, in the National Army Museum: 'The Afghan war, 1919. Indian Army. Col. (T./Brigadier-General) R.E.H. Dyer, CB, was mentioned in a dispatch from His Excellency General Sir C.C. Monro, GCB, GCSI, GCMG, ADC, dated 1 November, 1919, for gallant and distinguished services in the field.' Ironically, in view of what was to happen, it was signed 'Winston S. Churchill, Secretary of State for War, War Office, Whitehall, 3 August, 1920'. The MID rosette was displayed on his India General Service medal, 1908, Edward VII, for which a second clasp, 'Afghanistan North-West Frontier 1919' had been awarded. The medal is in the collection of the National Army Museum; Sotheby's, *Orders, Medals and Decorations* (London: Sale Catalogue, 18 December 1990).

Notes to Chapter 21: The Army Council

1   Cabinet Papers, Cab 23/21 – C. 19(20) 120420, item 4; Montagu papers in Trinity College, Cambridge, AS3/4/77(1).

2   Chelmsford papers in the British Library, MSS Eur E264/6, p. 77; Cabinet Office, Cab 27/91.

3   Churchill papers in Churchill College, Cambridge, Char 16/48A, 17 July 1920, letter from Churchill to Lord Crewe, quoting section 45(1) (a) of the Army Act.

4   It had not, in fact, done this, only recommending that he be directed to retire, the next level down in the punishments available.

5   Cabinet Office, Cab 27/91; Montagu papers in Trinity College, AS3/4/75 (1), minute by Montagu dated 19 April 1920; ibid., AS/3/4/74.

6   Cabinet Office, Cab 27/91, note by the Military Secretary, 21 April 1920; Winston Churchill papers, Char 16/60–1, unsigned, undated minute to Churchill; Montagu papers in Trinity College, AS3/4/69, letter from General Cobbe to Mr Dawson, 21 April 1920.

7   Cabinet Office, Cab 27/91, note by the Military Secretary, 21 April, two telegrams from the Viceroy to Montagu, 6 May 1920.

8   Montagu papers in the British Library, MSS Eur D 523/4; War Office, WO 32/21403, 19 April 1920.

9   Cabinet Office, Cab 27/91.

10 Command 705: *Parliamentary Papers* (Commons), 1920, vol. 14, *Reports*, vol. 6, 'East India (Disturbances in the Punjab, etc).' 'Correspondence between the Government of India and the Secretary of State for India on the Report of Lord Hunter's Committee', pp. 7, 8, 18, 21.

11 Ian Colvin, *The Life of General Dyer* (London: Blackwood, 1929), pp. 258–60; *Army List*, July 1920, pp. 166, 181b.

12 *Daily Mail*, 4 May 1920, pp. 7–8.

13 Cabinet office, Cab 27/91, especially Indian Disorders Committee Conclusions, 6 May 1920, pp. 1–5; War Office, WO32/21403; Montagu papers in Trinity College, AS/3/3/95 (1) 7/5/20, Montagu to Lieutenant-Colonel Sir Maurice Hankey, and AS/3/3/94.

14 Churchill papers, Char 16/47 A, Char 16/52 A; War Office, WO32/21403; Cabinet Office, Cab 27/91; Montagu papers in Trinity College, AS3/4/43; ibid., AS3/4/62 (1), 11 May 1920; ibid., AS3/4/31 (1), 13 May 1920; ibid., AS 3/4/58 (1), undated and unsigned minute, probably to the Secretary of State from the Military Secretary at the India Office.

15 Montagu papers in Trinity College, Cambridge, AS3/3/42 (1), 14 May 1920; War Office file WO32/21403; Cabinet office files 27/91; 23/21, C.26 (20), Item 3, Indian Disorders, p. 82, 10 May 1920; Colvin, *Dyer*, p. 261.

16 Montagu papers in Trinity College, AS3/4/9; ibid., AS3/4/60, 13 May 1920; War Office, WO32/21403, 15 May 1920. General Childs based his advice on *King's Regulations*, paragraph 255.

17 War Office, WO 163/25, p. 7, item 2 (84418/3), minutes of the 267th Meeting of the Army Council, 14 May 1920; Churchill papers, Char 16/60.

18 Sir C.E. Callwell, *Field-Marshal Sir Henry Wilson: His Life and Diaries* (London: Cassell, 1927), p. 237; Field-Marshal Sir Henry Wilson papers in the Imperial War Museum, HHW2/36–43, including correspondence with Monro, and microfilm of his diary, DS/MISC/80, reels 8 and 9.

19 War Office, WO 32/21403; Colvin, *Dyer*, p. 264.

20 Cabinet Office, Cab 27/91.

21 *Sunday Times*, 23 May 1920, p. 8

22 *Morning Post*, 24 May 1920, p. 6.

23 Command 705: *Correspondence between the Government of India and the Secretary of State for India on the Report of Lord Hunter's Committee*, pp. 23-25.
24 *Morning Post*, 27 May 1920, pp. 6-7; ibid., 28 May, p. 6; *The Times*, 26 May 1920, p. 8; Colvin, *Dyer*, p. 265.
25 *The Times*, 1, 4 and 10 June 1920; *Morning Post*, 1 June 1920, p. 4.
26 Cabinet Office, Cab 23/21; ibid., Cab 34(20), p. 232, 8 June 1920 and draft conclusions; Callwell, *Field-Marshal Sir Henry Wilson*, p. 237; Churchill papers, Char 22/3.
27 War Office, WO 32/21403, letter from the Adjutant-General to Dyer, 9 June 1920; ibid., WO 163/25, p. 8, minutes of Army Council's 268th Meeting, 9 June 1920; Colvin, *Dyer*, p. 277.
28 *Morning Post*, 9 June 1920; Montagu papers in Trinity College, AS3/4/28 (1), 15 June 1920; ibid., AS3/4/85 (1), letter from Sir T.W. Holderness, 30 June 1920; Sir Michael Francis O'Dwyer, *The Punjab Disturbances of April 1919: Criticism of the Hunter Committee Report* (London: Indo-British Association, 1920); Chelmsford papers, E264/16–577b; Wilson papers, HHW2/36–43, microfilm of the diary, DS/MISC/80, reels 8 and 9.
29 War Office, WO 32/21403.
30 *The Times*, 15 June 1920, p. 12.
31 Chelmsford papers, E264/6, p. 45, letter no. 12, 16 June 1920; Churchill papers, Char 16/47B.
32 Chelmsford papers, E264/1.
33 Wilson papers, HHW2/36–43, microfilm of the diary, DS/MISC/80, reels 8 and 9; *The Times*, 26 June 1920; Churchill papers, Char 16/47B.
34 Command 771: *Parliamentary Papers* (Commons), 1920, vol. 8, *Reports*, vol. 4. 'Army'. 'Disturbances in the Punjab, Statement by Brigadier-General R.E.H. Dyer' (also in India Office, L/MIL/17/12/43); War Office, WO 32/21403, *Manual of Military Law* (London: HM Stationery Office, 1914), pp. 216–33; Churchill papers, Char 16/48A.
35 Wilson papers, HHW2/36–43, microfilm of the diary, DS/MISC/80, reels 8 and 9; Keith Jeffery, *The Military Correspondence of Field-Marshal Sir Henry Wilson, 1918–1922* (London: Bodley Head, 1985), quoting correspondence from Major-General Sir C.H. Harington, DCIGS, 4–7 July 1920, pp. 184–87; War Office, WO 163/25, p. 10, minutes of the 270th Meeting of the Army Council, 6 July 1920.
36 War Office, WO 32/21403; ibid., WO 163/25, p. 10, minutes of the 270th Meeting of the Army Council, 6 July 1920.
37 Cabinet Office, Cab 27/91; ibid., Cab 23/22; ibid., Cab 39(20); War Office, WO 32/21403.
38 Chelmsford papers, E264/6, p. 156, letter no. 29, 7 July 1920.

Notes to Chapter 22: Parliament

1 Montagu papers in Trinity College, Cambridge, AS/3/3109 (1), 24 June 1920; ibid., AS/3/3/108 (1), 25 June 1920; Churchill papers in Churchill College, Cambridge, Char 2/110–49, 50, 55, 57, 59, 25 June to 7 July 1920; A.J.P. Taylor, *England, 1914–1945* (London: The Folio Society, 2000), pp. 109–41.
2 Chelmsford papers in the British Library, MSS Euro E264/16, 643a, letter from J.L. Maffey to Chelmsford, 1 July 1920.

3   *Morning Post*, 6 July 1910, pp. 6–7; ibid., 9 July 1920; War Office, WO32/21403, 8 July 1920.

4   *Parliamentary Debates, Official Report (Hansard)*, 5th series vol. 131 – *Second Session of the Thirty-First Parliament – House of Commons – Seventh Volume of Session, London 1920* – 'Punjab Disturbances. Lord Hunter's Committee. Army Council and General Dyer. Mr Montagu's Statement', pp. 1706–1814; Ian Colvin, *The Life of General Dyer* (London: Blackwood, 1929), pp. 296–304; Sir Michael Francis O'Dwyer, *India as I Knew It, 1885–1925* (London: Constable, 1925), p. 325; Chelmsford papers, E264/16, 662a, letter from J.L. Maffey to Chelmsford, 10 July 1920.

5   Montagu papers in Trinity College, AS3/4/7 (1) 586 (4); Martin Gilbert, *Winston S. Churchill, 1916–1922* (London: Heinemann, 1975), iv, p. 401.

6   Sir Charles Petrie, *The Life and Letters of Sir Austen Chamberlain* (London: Cassell 1940), ii, pp. 152–53.

7   Chelmsford papers, E264/16, 662a, letter from J.L. Maffey to Chelmsford, 10 July 1920.

8   Churchill papers, Char 9/60; ibid., Char 16/48A, 17 July 1920; Gilbert, *Winston S. Churchill*, iv, p. 401.

9   V.N. Datta and S.C. Mittal, eds, *The Sources of National Movement*, i, *(January 1919 to September 1920): Protests, Disturbances and Defiance* (New Delhi: Allied Publishers, 1985), p. 273.

10   Sir Algernon Rumbold, *Watershed in India, 1914–1922* (London: Athlone Press, 1979), p. 201; *Morning Post*, 10 July 1920; Chelmsford papers, E264/16, 662a, letter from J.L. Maffey to Chelmsford, 10 July 1920; Colvin, *Dyer*, p. 304.

11   *Morning Post*, 8–9 July 1920; O'Dwyer, *India as I Knew It*, p. 325.

12   *Pioneer*, 14 May 1920, p. 43; Chelmsford papers, E264/13, no. 102, 16 July 1920; Alfred Draper, *The Amritsar Massacre: Twilight of the Raj* (London: Buchan & Enright, 1985), p. 237.

13   Chelmsford papers, E264/6, no. 14, pp. 50–52, 15 July 1920; ibid., no. 32, pp. 175–76, 28 July 1920; ibid., E264/13, no. 54a, telegrams to Chelmsford, 10 and 15 July 1920; ibid., E264/16, no. 319, letter Chelmsford to Maffey, 4 August 1920 and no. 719a, letter Maffey to Chelmsford, 18 August 1920.

14   *Morning Post*, 10 July 1920.

15   War Office, WO 32/21403, 14 July 1920.

16   National Archives of India, Home Political, part A, 414–16, July 1920, telegram 26 July 1920, quoting Rule 22 of the Government Servants' Conduct Rules; ibid., deposit, December 1920, 64, quoting Army Order; War Office, WO 32/21403, 14 July 1920, quoting King's Regulations 443A, and 27 July 1920; Chelmsford papers, E264/13, no. 167, 30 July 1920, telegram Chelmsford to Montagu.

17   Chelmsford papers, E264/6, no. 22, p. 114, 19 May 1920.

18   Brigadier-General Sir James Edmonds papers, in the Liddell Hart Centre, King's College London, 3/2/19–20.

19   M.K. Gandhi, *Young India, 1919–1922* (Madras: Tagore, 1922), p. xlvi; Sir Valentine Chirol, *India Old and New* (London: Macmillan, 1921), p. 199; David Omissi, *The Sepoy and the Raj: The Indian Army, 1860–1946* (London: University of Hull, 1994), p. 194; Nigel Woodyatt, *Under Ten Viceroys: Reminiscences of a Gurkha* (London: Herbert Jenkins, 1922), p. 293; Ethel Winifred Savi, *Rulers of Men* (London: G.P. Putnam's Sons, 1925), p. 327; Peter G. Robb, *The Government of India and Reform: Policies towards Politics and the Constitution,*

1916–1921 (Oxford: Oxford University Press, 1976), p. 215; Maud Diver, *Far to Seek: A Romance of England and India* (Edinburgh: William Blackwood, 1921), pp. 260, 390; Satya M. Rai, *Punjabi Heroic Tradition, 1900–1947* (Patiala: Punjabi University, 1978), p. 122, quoting National Archives of India, Home Political, part A, February 1921, 312–38; Satish Chandra Mittal, *Freedom Movement in Punjab (1905–29)* (Delhi: Concept, 1977), p. 142; G.S. Chhabra, *Advanced Study in the History of the Panjab* (Ludhiana: Prakash Brothers, 1962), ii, p. 431; Sir Chimanlal Setalvad, *Recollections and Reflections: An Autobiography* (Bombay: Padma, 1946), p. 313.

20   *London Gazette*, 10 September 1920, p. 9148; *Indian Army List*, November 1920, p. 1885; Chelmsford papers, E264/13, 19 and 20 July 1920.

21   Colvin, *Dyer*, pp. 306–07; O'Dwyer, *India as I Knew It*, p. 325; Datta and Mittal, *The Sources of National Movement*, i, p. 279; Rumbold, *Watershed in India*; *Parliamentary Debates, Official Report (Hansard)*, 5th Series, vol. xli, *Second Session of the Thirty-First Parliament – House of Lords, Third Volume of Session, London, 1920*, pp. 222–374; Montagu papers in Trinity College, AS3/4/47 599(1); Chelmsford papers, E264/13, no. 71, 15 July 1920, telegram Montagu to Chelmsford; ibid., no. 107, 17 July 1920, telegram Chelmsford to Montagu; Bal Ram Nanda, *Gokhale, Gandhi and the Nehrus: Studies in Indian Nationalism* (London: George Allen & Unwin, 1974), p. 55.

22   Churchill papers, Char 16/48 A, 16 and 17 July 1920; Chelmsford papers, E264/6, no. 18, pp. 66–68, 11 August 1920, letter Montagu to Chelmsford.

23   Rumbold, *Watershed in India*, p. 202; S.D. Wayley, *Edwin Montagu: A Memoir and an Account of his Visits to India* (London: Asia Publishing House, 1964), p. 285; *Observer*, 6 April 1975, Sir Dingle Foot, 'Massacre that Started the Ending of the Raj'.

24   Chelmsford papers, E264/13, no. 167, 30 July 1920, telegram Chelmsford to Montagu.

25   O'Dwyer, *India as I Knew It*, p. 327; National Archives of India, Home Political, part A, September 1920, 95–96, in particular p. 22, Letter H. McPherson, Secretary to the Government of India, Home Department, to the Chief Secretary, Punjab Government, 13 September 1920; Chelmsford papers, E264/6, no. 41, p. 220, 6 October 1920, letter Chelmsford to Montagu; Montagu papers in the British Library, MSS Euro D 523/4, 28 October 1920, letter Montagu to Chelmsford.

26   Durga Das, *India from Curzon to Nehru and After* (London: Collins, 1969), p. 71; William W. Emilsen, 'Wrestling the Serpent: Gandhi, Amritsar and the British Empire', *Religion*, 24 (1994), p. 143; Prem Vati Ghai, *The Partition of the Punjab, 1849–1947* (New Delhi: Munshiram Manoharlal, 1986), appendix 3, p. 177, quoting National Archives of India, Foreign and Political, deposit, February 1921, 72. Lord Hailey papers, MSS Eur E220/57, p. 6.

27   O.P. Ralhan, and Suresh K. Sharma, eds, *Documents on Punjab* (New Delhi: Anmol Publications, 1994), v, p. 370; S.R. Mehrotra, *India and the Commonwealth, 1885–1929* (London: George Allen & Unwin, 1965).

28   The officers named were accused of martial law abuses elsewhere in the Punjab.

29   Sitaramayya B. Pattabhi, *The History of the Indian National Congress (1885–1935)* (Bombay: Padma Publications, 1946), i, p. 198; Datta and Mittal, *The Sources of National Movement*, i, p. 264; Reginald Reynolds, *The White Sahibs in India* (London: Martin Secker & Warburg, 1937), p. 185; Judith M. Brown, *Modern India: The Origins of an Asian Democracy* (Oxford:

Oxford University Press, 1985), p. 211, quoting M.K. Gandhi in *Young India*, 9 June 1920; Judith M. Brown, *Gandhi's Rise to Power* (Cambridge: Cambridge University Press, 1972), p. 244.

30   B.N. Pandey, *Nehru* (London: Macmillan, 1976), p. 82; B.R. Nanda, *The Nehrus: Motilal and Jawaharlal* (London; George Allen & Unwin, 1962), p. 175; Satya M. Rai, *Legislative Politics and Freedom Struggle on the Panjab, 1897–1947* (New Delhi: Indian Council of Historical Research, 1984), p. 94; Sarvepalli Gopal, *Jawaharlal Nehru: A Biography*, 3 vols (London: Jonathan Cape, 1975), i, p. 147; John Keay, *India: A History* (London: Harper Collins, 2000), p. 477.

31   Rabindranath Tagore, *Letters to a Friend*, ed. by C.F. Andrews (London: George Allen & Unwin, 1929), London, 22 July 1920.

32   Gandhi, *Young India*, 14 July 1920.

33   Edward Thompson, *The Reconstruction of India* (London: Faber & Faber, 1930); V.N. Datta, 'Jallianwala Bagh', in Ravi Dayal, ed., *We Fought Together for Freedom: Chapters from the Indian National Movement* (Delhi: Oxford University Press, 1995), p.100.

Notes to Chapter 23: Retirement

1   Ian Colvin, *The Life of General Dyer* (London: Blackwood, 1929), p. 308.

2   *Morning Post*, 2, 12, 14 August and 7 September 1920, p. 6; Sir Michael Francis O'Dwyer, *India as I Knew It, 1885–1925* (London: Constable, 1925), pp. 328–29.

3   Colvin, *Dyer*, p. 308; *Wiltshire and Gloucestershire Independent*, 30 July 1927; *Wiltshire and Gloucestershire Standard*, 30 July 1927; *Morning Post*, 27 October and 11, 13 November 1920; A. Lindsay Kelly, ed., *Kelly's Directory of the County of Wiltshire*, 1923 (London: Kelly's Directories, 1923), p. 27.

4   Glenesk-Bathurst papers in the Brotherton Library, Leeds University Library, MS Dep 1990/1/2501, letter H.A. Gwynne to Lady Bathurst, 12 October 1920.

5   *Wiltshire and Gloucestershire Standard*, 16 October 1920 and 30 July 1927; *Wiltshire and Gloucestershire Independent*, 30 July 1927; Bull Club, Cirencester, papers, in the Cirencester Bingham Library, A3 and A3a.

6   *Morning Post*, 27 October, 3, 13 November and 6 December 1920; Alfred Draper, *The Amritsar Massacre: Twilight of the Raj* (London: Buchan & Enright, 1985), pp. 237–38; Colvin, *Dyer*, pp. 305–6. Regrettably, the correspondence, seen by Colvin, no longer survives.

7   Colvin, *Dyer*, p. 308; *Globe*, 21 January 1921.

8   War Office, WO32/21403, letter from Dyer to the Assistant Military Secretary for the Military Secretary, 25 January 1921.

9   War Office, WO32/21403, undated précis of events relating to Dyer's application, post July 1921; ibid., letter from the Assistant Military-Secretary to Dyer, 3 February 1921; letter from Dyer to Under-Secretary of State for India, 9 February 1921; ibid., 84418/5, minute 1, Military-Secretary to Adjutant-General, Quartermaster-General, Deputy Chief of the Imperial General Staff, 1 April 1921; India Office, L/MILITARY/7/16018, letters War Office to India Office, 18 January and 11 March 1921; note by St G. Bull, 17 December 1921.

10 Brigadier-General R. E. H. Dyer, *Raiders of the Sarhad: Being an Account of a Campaign of Arms and Bluff against the Brigands of the Persian-Baluchi Border during the Great War* (London: H.F. & G. Witherby, 1921); Colvin, *Dyer*, p. 67, note 1.

11 Lord Sydenham of Combe, *My Working Life* (London: John Murray, 1927), p. 389; Brian Bond, 'Amritsar 1919', in *History Today*, October 1963, vol. 13, no. 10, p. 669; Sir Penderel Moon, *The British Conquest and Dominion of India* (London: Duckworth, 1989/90); items in the possession of Martin Dyer. The watch has regrettably been stolen.

12 War Office, WO32/21403, undated précis of events relating to Dyer's application, post July 1921; ibid., minute, 28 July 1921; ibid., letter Army Council to Under-Secretary of State, India Office, 21 September 1921; ibid., memorandum Secretary of State for War to the Cabinet, 36A, 21 November 1921; India Office, L/MILITARY/7/16018, minute by Military Secretary at the India Office 16 July 1921; ibid., minute by Legal Adviser to the India Office, 18 July 1921.

13 War Office, WO32/21403, letters from the Secretary of State to Montagu, 6 October 1921, and to Churchill, 10 October 1921; ibid., minute by the Adjutant-General, 10 November 1921; ibid., letter Montagu to Worthington-Evans, 12 October 1921; Churchill papers in Churchill College, Cambridge, Char 16/72, letter Worthington-Evans to Churchill, 10 October 1921, quoting Army Order 376 of 1918, and reply of 19 October 1921; India Office, L/MILITARY/7/16018.

14 Colvin, *Dyer*, p. 308; Court Service, Probate Registry, York, Dyer will dated 14 November 1921, probate granted 27 September 1927; *Dictionary of National Biography, 1922–1930*, ed. J.R.H. Weaver (Oxford: Oxford University Press, 1976), p. 280; *Daily Telegraph*, 27 July 1927; *Leeds Mercury*, 27 July 1927; *Wiltshire and Gloucestershire Standard*, 30 July 1927. George Pollock, *Mr Justice McCardie: A Biography* (London: John Lane, 1934), p. 135, states that Dyer fell off his horse, which looks like a conflation of the 1918 accident with the 1921 stroke, though it is possible Dyer was afflicted as he rode at Ashton Field.

15 Glenesk-Bathurst papers, 1990/1/3064, letter Mrs Dyer to Lady Bathurst, 28 December, no year given.

16 He was to serve on until the Second World War, reaching the rank of major.

17 Bailey and Woods, eds, *Baily and Woods' Cirencester Directory for the Year 1923, 1924, 1925, 1926, 1927* (Cirencester: Baily and Woods; 1923–27); *Wiltshire and Gloucestershire Independent*, 30 July 1927; A. Lindsay Kelly, ed., *Kelly's Directory of the Counties of Somerset and Gloucester with the City of Bristol, 1927* (London: Kelly's Directories, 1927).

18 Sir C. Sankaran Nair, *Gandhi and Anarchy* (Indore: Holkar State (Electric) Printing Press, 1922), p. 47.

19 Cabinet Office, Cab 23/48, Cab 38(24), 13, 18 June 1924, p. 196; India Office, L/PO/6/12; Colvin, *Dyer*, pp. 310–13; O'Dwyer, *India as I Knew It*, pp. 334–68; Pollock, *Mr Justice McCardie*, pp. 133–36; Rupert Furneaux, *Massacre at Amritsar* (London: George Allen & Unwin, 1963), p. 166; Arthur Swinson, *Six Minutes to Sunset: The Story of General Dyer and the Amritsar Affair* (London: Peter Davies, 1964), pp. 164–77; Draper, *The Amritsar Massacre*, pp. 247–63; H.C.E. Zacharias, *Renascent India: From Ram Mohan Roy to Mohandas Gandhi* (London: George Allen & Unwin, 1933), p. 234; Mark Naidis, 'Amritsar Revisited', *The Historian*, vol. 21, no. 1 (1958), p. 15; *Daily Telegraph*, *The Times*, *Morning Post*, May–June 1924.

20   Colvin, Dyer, p. 316; *Wiltshire and Gloucestershire Independent*, 30 July 1927; *Wiltshire and Gloucestershire Standard*, 30 July 1927; information given to the author by Miss Ruth Poole of Long Ashton, in part quoting the *Bristol Directory, 1925*, and M.L. Bonnington, 'Long Ashton: Our Village', p. 53; Dyer family tree in possession of Martin Dyer; *The Times*, 24 July 1927; India Office, L/MILITARY/14/1025.

21   *Bristol Times*, 25 July 1927; *Daily Mail*, 25 July 1927; *Daily Telegraph*, 25 July 1927; *Leeds Mercury*, 25 July 1927; *The Scotsman*, 25 July 1927; *Wiltshire and Gloucestershire Independent*, 30 July 1927.

22   J.P. Thompson, for instance, reporting watching Dyer give evidence to the Hunter Committee, entered in his diary for 19 November 1919: 'General Dyer gave his evidence. Lasted whole day. He came through it very well, he was transparently honest'; J.P. Thompson papers in the British Library, MSS Euro F 137, Diary.

23   *Daily Mail*, 4 May 1920.

24   *Report from Brigadier-General R.E.H. Dyer, Commanding 45th Brigade, to The General Staff, 16th (Indian) Division*, 25 August 1919, in the Dyer papers in the National Army Museum (also in the *Hunter Report*, Evidence, vol. iii, appendix xiii), p. 5.

25   Colvin, *Dyer*, pp. 316, 337; Court Service, Probate Registry, York, death certificate, 25 July 1927, given at Long Ashton, Somerset; ibid., Dyer's will, 14 November 1921, probate granted 27 September 1927; Swinson, *Six Minutes to Sunset*, p. 209; *Rangoon Times*, 30 July 1927; Sergeant Reginald Mortimer Howgego papers, in the India Office, British Library, MSS EUR C 340/8, letter to *Radio Times*, 27 August 1978, regarding the BBC programmes 'The Amritsar Massacre', 23 and 25 August 1978: 'Somewhere about 1930 we attended from Ipswich a reunion of 25 London. General Dyer's son was a guest and he said his father died of a broken heart.' Annie Dyer was to live at St Martin's Cottage until at least 1938.

26   Colvin, *Dyer*, p. 316, note 1; Draper, *The Amritsar Massacre*, pp. 265–66; *Bristol Press*, 28 July 1927; *Bristol Times*, 28 July 1927.

27   *The Times*, 24 July 1927; *Daily Telegraph*, 19 November 1938; Edmonds papers in the Liddell Hart Centre, King's College London, II/2/171, letter from Annie Dyer to Edmonds, 9 August 1927.

Notes to Chapter 24: Epilogue

1   *Bristol Press*, 29 July 1927; *Calcutta Statesman*, 29 July 1927; *Daily Express*, 29 July 1927; *Daily Mirror*, 29 July 1927; *Daily Telegraph*, 29 July 1927; *Evening Standard*, 28 July 1927; *Morning Post*, 29 July 1927, photograph; Dyer papers in the National Army Museum, photograph no. 325762, Sport and General Press Agency Ltd; *Westminster Gazette*, 29 July 1927; Alfred Draper, *The Amritsar Massacre: Twilight of the Raj* (London: Buchan & Enright, 1985), pp. 264–66.

2   *Yorkshire Post*, 29 July 1927.

3   Dyer papers, photograph no. 325759.

4   *Army and Navy Gazette*, 4 August 1927; H.C. Jackson, *Pastor on the Nile: Being Some Account of the Life and Letters of Llewellyn H. Gwynne, Formerly Bishop in Egypt and the Sudan and Deputy Chaplain-General in France in the First World War* (London: SPCK, 1960), pp. 2, 186, 190.

5   *Army and Navy Gazette*, 4 August 1927; *Bristol Press*, 29 July 1927; *Daily Telegraph*, 29 July 1927; *Morning Post*, 29 July 1927; *The Times*, 29 July 1927; *Westminster Gazette*, 29 July 1927.

6   *Calcutta Statesman*, 29 July 1927; *Eastern Daily Press*, 29 July 1927; *Westminster Gazette*, 29 July 1927; Ian Colvin, *The Life of General Dyer* (London: Blackwood, 1929), p. 316; Derek Sayer, 'British Reaction to the Amritsar Massacre, 1919–1920', *Past and Present*, 5, no. 131, May 1991, p. 158; Arthur Swinson, *Six Minutes to Sunset: The Story of General Dyer and the Amritsar Affair* (London: Peter Davies, 1964), p. 209.

7   P.W. Ellis, Indian Papers, in the Imperial War Museum, 75/2/1, Home Address Book of 1/25th Battalion the London Regiment; *Bristol Press*, 29 July 1927; *The London Cyclist Battalion*, compiled by the History Committee of the 26th Middlesex (Cyclist) Volunteer Rifle Corps and the 25th (City of London) Cyclist Battalion, the London Regiment (London: Forster Groom, 1932), pp. 167, 178.

8   Sergeant Reginald Mortimer Howgego papers in the India Office, British Library, MSS EUR C/3408, letter to Alfred Draper, 21 October 1978.

9   Colvin, *Dyer*, p. 316; *Wiltshire and Gloucestershire Independent*, 30 July 1927.

10 I have found no record in the National Archives or the British Library to explain this issue. Neither the papers of Joynson-Hicks nor those of Worthington-Evans contain any reference to the funeral; Sir Worthington Lamington Worthington-Evans papers, MS Eng Hist c. 890–940, in the Bodleian Library, Oxford; personal communication to the author from Viscount Brentford, 19 November 2002.

11 *Daily Telegraph*, 28 July 1927; *Morning Post*, 25 July 1927; *Westminster Gazette*, 25 July 1927.

12 *Daily Express*, 30 July 1927; C.J. Davis papers, INDIAN 15, Liddle Collection (1914–18), in the Brotherton Library, University of Leeds.

13 *Army and Navy Gazette*, 31 July 1927.

14 *Sporting Times*, 29 July 1927.

15 *Civil and Military Gazette*, 26, 27 July 1927.

16 India Office, L/PO/6/36A, telegram Viceroy to Secretary of State for India, 4 November 1927; ibid., telegram Secretary of State to Viceroy, November 1927; ibid., letter Sir Michael O'Dwyer to Sir M. Seton, 5 December 1927; telegrams Viceroy to Secretary of State for India, 14 January and 14 March 1928; Alfred Draper, *The Amritsar Massacre: Twilight of the Raj* (London: Buchan & Enright, 1985), p. 267.

Notes to Appendix

1   Charles E. Callwell, *Small Wars. Tzheir Principle and Practice* (London: HMSO, 1906), pp. 21–28, 41, 72–78; Brian Bond, *Victorian Military Campaigns* (London: Tom Donovan, 1994), pp. 17–24.

2   *Encyclopaedia Britannica* (London: Encyclopaedia Britannica, 1926), pp. 790–92.

3   *Manual of Military Law* (London: HMSO, 1914), chapter xiii, pp. 216–33.

4   India Office, L/MILITARY/7/556, Army Regulations, India, vol. ii, Regulations and Orders for the Army (Calcutta: the Government of India Army Department, 1918), p. 121; V.N. Datta, ed., *New Light on the Punjab Disturbances in 1919: Volumes VI and VII of Disorders*

Inquiry Committee Evidence, 2 vols (Simla: Indian Institute of Advanced Study, 1975) (the text of the original is in India Office, L/MIL/17/12/42 and in Cabinet Office, Cab 27/93), pp. 254–55, statement of the Punjab Government; Command 681: *Parliamentary Papers* (Commons), 1920, vol. 14, *Reports*, vol. 6, 'East India (Disturbances in the Punjab, etc).' 'Report of the Committee Appointed by the Government of India to Investigate the Disturbances in the Punjab, etc' (in India Office, L/MIL/17/12/42, in Cabinet Office, Cab 27/92 – 27/93 and in War Office, WO 32/21403) (the *Hunter Report)*, pp. 32–33; *Parliamentary Debates, Official Report (Hansard)*, 5th series, vol. 131 – *Second Session of the Thirty-First Parliament – House of Commons – Seventh Volume of Session, London 1920*, p. 1743; Kapil Deva Malaviya, *Open Rebellion in the Punjab (with Special Reference to Amritsar)* (Allahabad: Abhudaya Press, 1919), pp. 44–46.

5   Command 771: *Parliamentary Papers* (Commons), 1920, vol. 8, *Reports*, vol. 4, 'Army'. 'Disturbances in the Punjab. Statement by of Brigadier-General R.E.H. Dyer, CB' (also in India Office, L/MIL/17/12/43), p. 5.

6   Brigadier-General Sir James Edmonds papers, in the Liddell Hart Centre, King's College London, 3/2/20.

7   Charles Townshend, *Britain's Civil Wars: Counterinsurgency in the Twentieth Century* (London: Faber & Faber, 1986), pp. 13–21, 137–38; Sir George Barrow, *The Life of General Sir Charles Carmichael Monro* (London: Hutchinson, 1931), pp. 188–90; Sir Charles W. Gwynne, *Imperial Policing* (London: Macmillan, 1934), pp. 3–37, 60–63; A.A. Mains, 'General Dyer and Amritsar', *9th Gurkha Rifles Newsletter*, p. 15; Thomas R. Mockaitis, *British Counterinsurgency, 1919–60* (London: Macmillan, 1990), pp. 21–27; David Omissi, *The Sepoy and the Raj: The Indian Army, 1860–1946* (London: University of Hull, 1994), p. 217.

8   Command 771: *Disturbances in the Punjab: Statement by Brigadier-General R.E.H. Dyer*, p. 12; Nigel Woodyatt, *Under Ten Viceroys: Reminiscences of a Gurkha* (London: Herbert Jenkins, 1922), p. 292.

Bibliography

OFFICIAL RECORDS

BRITISH ARMY

Army Lists, 1884–1921.

The Manual of Military Law, War Office (His Majesty's Stationery Office: London, 1914).

Register of Marriages, 1889, Family Records Centre, Islington.

Royal Military College Gentleman Cadet Register, 1884–85, in the Sandhurst Collection, at the Royal Military Academy Sandhurst.

BRITISH GOVERNMENT (in the National Archive, Kew)

Cabinet Office

Cabinet Conclusions (Minutes)

Cab 23/10, War Cabinet Meeting 556.

Cab 23/21, Cabinet conclusions, April to June 1920.

Cab 23/22, Cabinet conclusions, July 1920.

Cab 23/48, Cabinet conclusions, June 1924.

Cabinet Memoranda

Cab 24/1/2/57 (CP 351 and 374).

Cab 24/78 (GT7139, 18 April 1919).

Cab 24/93.

Cab 24/105 (CP 1240).

Cab 24/106 (CP 1306).

Cabinet Papers

Cab 27/91–93, Proceedings of the Cabinet Committee on the Indian Disorders, 1920.

War Office

WO/32/5316, Defence of Hong Kong Harbour.

WO/32/5345, Hong Kong: Report on the Operations from the Outbreak of War to the End of 1914.

WO 32/21403, Request by Colonel R.E.H. Dyer, CB, IA, for Honorary Rank of Brigadier-General on Retirement.

WO 95/5389, War Diary of North-West Frontier Force, May 1919.

WO 95/5413, War Diary of 16 (Indian) Division, March–August 1919.

WO 95/5414, War Diary of 1/25th Battalion London Regiment, May–June 1919; War Diary of 45 Brigade Signal Section, No. 40 (Division Signals) Company, May–June 1919; War Diary of Headquarters 45 Brigade, May 1919; War Diary of 2/6th Royal Sussex Regiment, April 1919; War Diary of 1/124th Baluchistan Infantry, April 1919.

WO 95/5415, War Diary Sistan Field Force, 1915–20.

WO/95/5441, South China Command: Hong Kong, Headquarters, General Staff.

WO/95/5444, South China Command: Hong Kong.

WO106/27, Rebellion in China, Reinforcement to Hong Kong.

WO 106/56, *Dispatch by Brigadier-General R. E. H. Dyer General Officer Commanding, Sistan Field Force on The Operations against the Damanis (1–24 August 1916)*, serial 23, General Staff, India, case no. 15616, Simla, 1916 (also in L/MIL/17/13/26 and MSS Eur D978); *Report by Brigadier-General R.E.H. Dyer, Commanding 45th Infantry Brigade on the Operations for the Relief of Thal, May–June 1919*, serial no. 37, file no. 47, 47-F, Operations, Simla, 1919 (also in L/MILITARY/7/16924 and L/MIL/17/14/65); *Report from the General Officer Commanding Sistan on the Action against Gunrunners at Kalmas, 26 September, 1919*, serial 63, GS Branch, case 16001, Simla, 1916 (also in MSS Eur D978); *Despatch by General Sir Charles Monro, Commander-in-Chief in India, on Operations on India's Frontiers, 1916* (Simla: Government Press, 23 July 1917).

WO 106/951, *Report from the General Officer Commanding Sistan Field Force, Capture of Jiand (Damani) 14 June 1916*, report 147, Army Headquarters, MOI 18/33 F/Opns.

WO 163/25, Minutes of the Proceedings of and Precis Prepared for the Army Council for the Year 1920.

WO 163/26, Minutes of the Proceedings of and Precis Prepared for the Army Council for the Year 1921.

WO 163/33, Minutes of the Proceedings of and Precis Prepared for the Army Council for the Year 1927.

GOVERNMENT OF INDIA
(in the India Office Records in the Oriental and India
Office Collection of the British Library)

Military Proceedings

L/MIL/7/550–56, Army Regulations, India, ii (1904–18).

L/MIL/7/946, Afghan War awards.

L/MIL/7/1111–25, range-finders.

L/MIL/7/3425, Staff College reports.

L/MIL/7/6886–6912, operations for the relief of Chitral.

L/MIL/7/9170–178 and 9181, operations in Burma.

L/MIL/7/14688, the Black Mountain expedition.

L/MIL/7/16018, honorary rank of brigadier-general.

L/MIL/7/16820, Mahsud blockade, 1901–2.

L/MIL/7/16842, Zakka Khel operations.

L/MIL/7/17007–19 and 21–24, annual reports on Indian Army units (1887–1915).

L/MIL/7/17045, reports on staff officers,1907.

L/MIL/7/16924, *Report by Brigadier-General R.E.H. Dyer on the Operations for the Relief of Thal, May–June 1919* (Simla, 1919) (also in L/MIL/17/14/65 and WO 106/56).

L/MIL/9/509, applications for transfer to the Indian Army.

L/MIL/10/100, Indian Army officers leave records.

L/MIL/14/1025, Major I.R. Dyer, 3/5th Mahratta Light Infantry, personal file.

L/MIL/17/5/3079, War Diary, Army Headquarters, India, vol. 51 (1–30 April 1919).

L/MIL/17/5/4057–4065, War Diary, Army Headquarters, India, Third Afghan War.

L/MIL/17/5/4115, General War Diary, Frontier Operations, April–May and June–September 1919.

L/MIL/17/5/4137–44, War Diary, Army Headquarters, India, Persia, vols 16–23 (1 March–31 October 1916).

L/MIL/17/12/40, reports on the Punjab Disturbances, April 1919.

L/MIL/17/12/41, *Reports on the Punjab Disturbances, April 1919*, printed report on Amritsar District, Government of the Punjab (extracted from Command 534).

L/MIL/17/12/42, *Report of Committee Appointed by the Government of India into Disturbances in Punjab*, printed Hunter Report (Command 681).

L/MIL/17/12/43, *Disturbances in Punjab: Statement by Dyer* (Command 771).

L/MIL/17/13/26, *Despatch from Dyer as GOC Seistan Field Force, on Operations against the Damanis, 1–24 August 1916* (also in WO 106/56 and MSS Eur D978).

L/MIL/17/14/65, *Report by Dyer as GOC 45 Infantry Brigade on Operations for the Relief of Thal, May–June 1919* (also in L/MILITARY/7/16924 and WO 106/56).

Photographs
39/(44–104), Amritsar riot damage, 1919.

Private Office
L/PO/6/4, Hunter Committee establishment.
L/PO/6/8, Sir Michael O'Dwyer correspondence with India Office and Prime
   Minister, 1919–20.
L/PO/12, *Nair v. O'Dwyer.*
L/PO/6/36A, Dyer memorial.

Miscellaneous
L/PS/41, H168/1918, Decorations and Honours.
MSS Eur D978, Military reports, Indian corps, Sistan and East Persia. *Report of
   Action near Khwash, 28 July 1916. Operations against the Damani and
   Gamshadzai Tribes, July 12th–29th, 1916,* case 2409 F operations (Simla:
   Government of India, 1918).

PATENT OFFICE
(in the British Library)

*Abridgements of Specifications, Class 97(i): Optical Systems and Apparatus,
   Period 1909–15* (London: His Majesty's Stationery Office, 1922).
*Specifications of Inventions: Printed under the Patents, Designs, and Trade Marks
   Act 1883, 1908* (London: Patent Office Sales Branch, 1909), xlviii.
*Specifications of Inventions: Printed under the Patents, Designs, and Trade Marks
   Act 1883, 1908* (London: Patent Office Sales Branch, 1910), lxix.
*Specifications of Inventions: Printed under the Patents, Designs, and Trade Marks
   Act 1883, 1908–13* (London: Patent Office Sales Branch, 1910–15); cviii, cxxxvi,
   1908; xxii, 1909; lxii, 1910; xciv, 1911; xcvii, 1912; civ, 1913.

GOVERNMENT OF INDIA
(in the National Archives of India, Delhi)

Foreign and Political Department
External B, March 1912, nos 690–93, despatch of Indian troops to Hong Kong.
External B, October 1912, no.118, expedition from the Hong Kong Garrison
   against a gang of pirates in the vicinity of Macao.
April 1916, nos 1–106, Mekran disturbances.

Home Department, Judicial
A Series
October 1919, nos 228–50, composition of mob in Amritsar, Privy Council appeals
   of Bugga, Kali Nath Roy and others sentenced by the Martial Law Commissions.

B Series

June 1919, nos 247–50, petitions for mercy from Sundar Singh and Vilayati, sentenced to death by the Martial Law Commission, in connection with the Amritsar (Miss Sherwood) case.

Home Department, Political

A Series

June 1919, nos 517–25, Silk Letter internees.

July 1919, nos 170–71, article 'Sikhs and the Riots' in *Khalsa Advocate*.

October 1919, nos 187–97, appointment of Hunter Committee.

October 1919, nos 421–24, proposal to appoint a committee to report on the adequacy of the measures taken by the civil authorities for the protection of the European population at Amritsar on 10 April 1919.

November 1919, nos 288–95, proceedings of the Indemnity Bill in the Imperial Legislative Council.

February 1920, nos 347–58, report to the Secretary of State of the detailed casualties which occurred during the disturbances in the Punjab. Discussion on the evidence given by Brigadier-General Dyer before the Disorders Inquiry Committee.

February 1920, nos 421–33, memorandum submitted by the Government of India to Disorders Inquiry Committee.

April 1920, nos 269–80, printing of Evidences taken before Hunter Committee.

April 1920, nos 317–18, report to the Secretary of State of the total number of persons wounded at Jallianwala Bagh.

June 1920, nos 126–64, spread of unrest outside Amritsar following Jallianwala Bagh.

June 1920, nos 235–79, papers regarding the publication of the Hunter Committee Report.

July 1920, nos 414–16, decision that any subscriptions made by Government servants to the General Dyer Fund should be held to be barred by Rule 22 of the Government Servants' Conduct Rules.

August 1920, no. 19, firing on a 'mixed holiday crowd' by General Dyer has greatly prejudiced the British reputation in Europe, America and India.

September 1920, nos 95–96, enquiry into the action of the officers responsible for abdication of civil authority at Amritsar during the Punjab disturbances.

B Series

January–June 1919, no. 43, release of prisoners who have served their sentences.

May 1919, no. 124, disturbances instigated by pan-Islamic propaganda.

May 1919, nos 148–78, daily reports for April 1919 from the Punjab Government on the disturbance in the Punjab connected with the *satyagraha* movement.

May 1919, no. 184, contradiction of the false rumours about bombing of the
Golden Temple at Amritsar.

May 1919, no. 274, report that the principal cause of discontent in Amritsar and
the Punjab generally appears to be the attitude of the police who are
extracting bribes under the cover of martial law.

May 1919, nos 551–605, communication to Local Governments, etc., of a daily
summary of events in connection with the recent disturbances in India.

May 1919, nos 673–85, probable connection of disturbances in Egypt
and India.

June 1919, no. 23, report on the rioting at Amritsar on 10 April 1919.

June 1919, nos 408–31, daily reports of the Punjab Government in connection
with the disturbances in that province.

October 1919, nos 328–29, questions and answers in the Imperial Legislative
Council regarding the use of firearms at Amritsar.

January 1920, no. 513, Muslim and Hindu combination in unrest.

February 1920, no. 373, secret memoranda put before the Hunter Committee
by J.P. Thompson as Chief Secretary to Punjab Government.

April 1920, nos 118–20, allegations made by Dr Satyapal regarding the torture
of citizens at Amritsar.

Deposits

April 1919, no. 49, fortnightly report on the internal political situation for the
second half of March 1919.

June 1919, no. 23, report on the rioting at Amritsar on the 10 April 1919.

July 1919, no. 47, fortnightly reports on the internal political situation for the
second half of April 1919.

July 1919, no. 48, fortnightly reports on the internal political situation for the
first half of May 1919.

July 1919, no. 71, detail of 10 April 1919 events at Amritsar.

August 1919, no. 53, report from the General Officer Commanding, Northern
Command, Rawalpindi, in connection with the recent disturbances in India,
and suggestions for the adoption of certain precautionary measures to deal
with similar disturbances in future.

September 1919, no. 12, report by a CID officer regarding certain allegations of
police corruption at Amritsar during recent disturbances.

September 1919, no. 23, report from the Punjab Government giving the
approximate death-rate during the recent disturbances at Amritsar.

September 1919, no. 33, official report received from the India Office regarding
the House of Lords discussion on the Punjab disturbances.

October 1919, no. 16, allegations of police corruption at Amritsar during the
period of the existence martial law.

October 1919, no. 28, lists of incidents connected with the recent disorders showing that they were anti-British and anti-Government and that the rioting was not sporadic but an organised rebellion.

October 1919, no.31, total number of casualties at the Jallianwala Bagh.

October 1919, no. 62, report by Mr Miles Irving, Deputy Commissioner, Amritsar, with regard to allegations made by Pandit M.M. Malaviya against the local authorities and police at Amritsar.

December 1919, no.22, suggestion by the Punjab Government for granting pensions to dependants of the killed in Jallianwala Bagh.

February 1920, nos 347–58, report of detailed casualties.

March 1920, no. 11, papers regarding the publicity of the Hunter Committee Report: question of action taken against General Dyer.

June 1920, nos 124–64, request for General Dyer to resign.

August 1920, no. 19, letter from Mr Dobbs, regarding the Jallianwala Bagh crowd, contradicting General Dyer's statement of defence.

December 1920, no. 64, Army order passed regarding officers subscribing to the General Dyer Fund.

Military

Military Miscellany, bound volume, notes, vol. 8, Digest of Services of 106th Hazara Pioneers.

Publications

Army Regulations, India, ii, *Regulations and Orders for the Army* (Calcutta: The Government of India Army Department, 1918).

East India: North-West Frontier. Mahsud-Waziri Operations, 1902 (London: HMSO, 1903).

East India: North-West Frontier. Papers Regarding Orakzai, Zakka Khel and Mohmand Operations (London: HMSO, 1908).

East India: Afghanistan. Papers Regarding Hostilities with Afghanistan, 1919 (London: HMSO, 1920).

Frontier and Overseas Expeditions From India: Compiled in the Intelligence Branch of the Division of the Chief of Staff, Army Headquarters, India: vol. i, *Tribes North of the Kabul River* (Government Monotype Press: Simla, 1907); vol. ii, *Tribes between Kabul and Gomal Rivers* (1908); *Zakka Khel Afridis* (1908) and *Supplement*; vol. v, *Burma*.

The Disorders Inquiry Committee: Evidence Taken Before the Disorders Inquiry Committee, vol. iii, Amritsar (Calcutta: The Government of India, 1920) (extract from Command 681).

The Third Afghan War, 1919: Official Account (Government Press: Calcutta, 1926).

Indian Army List (Calcutta: Government of India, Military Department, 1888–1921).

PARLIAMENTARY PAPERS

Command 534: *Parliamentary Papers* (Commons), 1920, vol. 14, *Reports*, vol. 6,
  'East India (Punjab Disturbances)'. 'Reports on the Punjab Disturbances,
  April 1919'.
Command 610: *Royal Proclamation*, December 1919.
Command 681: *Parliamentary Papers* (Commons), 1920, vol. 14, *Reports*, vol. 6,
  'East India (Disturbances in the Punjab, etc)'. 'Report of the Committee
  Appointed by the Government of India to Investigate the Disturbances in the
  Punjab, etc.' (the *Hunter Report*).
Command 705: *Parliamentary Papers* (Commons), 1920, vol. 14, *Reports*, vol. 6.
  'East India (Disturbances in the Punjab, etc)'. 'Correspondence between the
  Government of India and the Secretary of State for India on the Report of
  Lord Hunter's Committee'.
Command 771: *Parliamentary Papers* (Commons), 1920, vol. 8, *Reports*, vol. 4,
  'Army', 'Disturbances in the Punjab, Statement by Brigadier-General
  R.E.H. Dyer'.
Parliamentary Debates, Official Report (Hansard), 5th series vol. 131 – *Second
  Session of the Thirty-First Parliament – House of Commons – Seventh Volume
  of Session, London 1920* – 'Punjab Disturbances. Lord Hunter's Committee.
  Army Council and General Dyer. Mr Montagu's Statement'.
Parliamentary Debates, Official Report (Hansard), 5th Series, vol. xli, *Second
  Session of the Thirty-First Parliament – House of Lords, Third Volume of
  Session, London, 1920.*

PRIVATE PAPERS

Barrow, Lieutenant-General Sir George de S., in the Imperial War Museum.
Beynon, Major-General Sir William, in the British Library, MSS Eur
  D 830.
Birkenhead, Lord, papers as Secretary of State for India, 1924–28, in the British
  Library, MSS Eur D 703.
Blackwood (*Blackwood's Magazine*), in the National Library of Scotland, MS
  30/598.
Brentford, Viscount (Sir William Joynson-Hicks), private papers in the
  possession of Viscount Brentford.
Bull Club, Cirencester, in the Bingham Library, Cirencester, A3 and A3a.
Butler, Sir Harcourt, in the British Library, MSS Eur F 136.
Campbell of Kilberry, in the National Register of Archives (Scotland), NRAS
  886, NRAS 10124.
Chelmsford, Viscount, in the British Library, MSS Eur E 264.

Churchill, Sir Winston Spencer, in the Churchill Archives Centre, Churchill College, Cambridge.

Darling, Sir Malcolm, in the Cambridge South Asian Archive, boxes xiii and xiv.

Dyer, Brigadier-General R.E.H., in the National Army Museum, 9012–55, and in the possession of Martin Dyer.

Edmonds, Brigadier-General Sir James, in the Liddell Hart Centre, King's College, London, 3/2.

Ellis, P.W., Indian papers, in the Imperial War Museum, 75/2/1.

Glenesk-Bathurst family papers, in the Brotherton Library, Leeds University Library, MS Dep. 1990/1.

Hailey, Lord, in the British Library, MSS Eur E220, 57, 58.

Heard, Lieutenant-Colonel John Arthur Edward, in the Liddell Hart Centre, King's College London, outsize box 1 of 2.

Howgego, Sergeant Reginald Mortimer, in the India Office, British Library, MSS Eur C 340.

Liddell Hart, Captain Basil, in the Liddell Hart Centre, King's College London, LH11/1938/6.

Liddle Collection (1914–1918), in the Brotherton Library, University of Leeds, IND 10 Amritsar.

McCallum, Brigadier-General Frank M., in the Cambridge South Asian Archive, in the Gurkha Museum, in the Liddle Collection of the Brotherton Library, University of Leeds, and in the Imperial War Museum.

Monro, General Sir Charles Carmichael, in the British Library, MSS Eur D 783.

Montagu, Edwin Samuel, correspondence and papers in Trinity College, Cambridge, AS1/12/142, AS/3/3/93–108, AS3/4/1–86 and papers as Secretary of State for India in the British Library, MSS Eur D 523.

Morgan, Lieutenant-Colonel M.H.L., 'The Truth about Amritsar: By an Eye Witness', in the Imperial War Museum, 72/22/1 T.

Nisbet, Captain H. Ulric S., 'Diaries and Memories of the Great War: England-France-Flanders-India', in the Imperial War Museum, 78/3/1.

Rawlinson, General Lord, in the Churchill Archives, Churchill College, Cambridge, RWLN.

Roberts, Field-Marshal Lord, in the National Army Museum, London.

Ross, Colonel Harry, in the British Library, MSS Eur B 235.

Sclater, General Sir Henry (Harry) Crichton, in the Liddell Hart Centre, King's College London, albums.

Scott, James Alexander, in the British Library, MSS Eur A181.

Sydenham, Viscount, in the British Library, Add. MSS 50831–41.

Thompson, Sir J.P., in the British Library, MSS Euro F 137.

Villiers-Stuart, Brigadier-General W.D., in the Gurkha Museum, Winchester.

Wathen, Mrs Melicent, in the possession of the Reverend Mark Wathen.

White, Field-Marshal Sir George, in the British Library, MSS Eur F 108.

Wilson, Field-Marshal Sir Henry, in the Imperial War Museum, HHW2/36–43, correspondence with General Monro; microfilm of the diary, DS/MISC/80, reels 8 and 9.

Wood, Rev. J.A., in the Cambridge South Asian Archive, box 51.

Worthington-Evans, Sir Worthington Laming, Bart, in the Bodleian Library, MSS Eng Hist c 890–940, d 424–27, e 319–20, f 26.

NEWSPAPERS AND PERIODICALS

Aberdeen Journal, 25 July 1927.

Army and Navy Gazette, 31 July, 4 August 1927.

Army and Quarterly Review, 10 September 1927.

Associated Press (Simla), 2 October 1915.

Belfast Newsletter, 25 July 1927.

Birmingham Dispatch, 25 July 1927.

Birmingham Gazette, 25 July 1927.

Birmingham Herald, 28 July 1927.

Birmingham Post, 25 July 1927.

Blackburn Telegraph, 25 July 1927.

Bristol Press, 29 July 1927.

Bristol Times, 25, 28, 29, 30 July 1927.

British Weekly, 28 July 1927.

Calcutta Statesman, 14, 20 July 1920; 29 July 1927.

Cardiff Daily News, 25 July 1927.

Cardiff Mail, 25 July 1927.

Christian World, 28 July 1927.

Civil and Military Gazette, 13, 14 April, 10 July 1919; 25 January 1920; 26–27, 31 July 1927.

Cork Examiner, 25 and 27 July 1927.

Daily Chronicle, 27 May 1920.

Daily Express, 13 and 16 December 1919; 23 January, 20 and 21 July 1920; 3 March 1924; 25, 29 and 30 July 1927.

Daily Herald, December 1919; 3 April, 5 May 1920; 25 July 1927.

Daily Mail, 4, 27 May 1920; March and April 1924; 25 and 29 July 1927.

Daily Mirror, 25, 27, 28 and 29 July 1927.

Daily News, December 1919; 27 May, 7 September 1920; 25, 27, 29 July 1927.

Daily Sketch, 25 and 29 July 1927.

Daily Standard, 29 July 1927.

Daily Telegraph, 13 December 1919; 27 May, 9 June 1920; 1 March 1921; March and April 1924; 25, 28 and 29 July 1927; 19 November 1938.

Devon Gazette, 25 July 1927.

Dublin Independent, 25 July 1927.

Dundee Courier, 25 July 1927.

East London Dispatch, 26 and 27 July 1927.

Eastern Daily Press, 29 July 1927.

Edinburgh Review, July 1927.

Egyptian Gazette, 25 July 1927.

Empire News, 30 July 1927.

Englishman, 25 and 29 July 1927.

Evening Standard, 27 May 1920; 25 and 26 July 1927.

Frontline: Indian National Magazine, 1–14 November 1997.

Glasgow Bulletin, 25 and 26 July 1927.

Glasgow Herald, 28 August 1920; 25 and 28 July 1927.

Glasgow Record, 25 July 1927.

Glasgow Times, 25 and 29 July 1927.

Globe, 21 January 1921.

Hong Kong Daily Press, 24 January, 8 February, 23 March, 3 April 1912; 1, 7, 13, 21 and 24 May, 5 and 27 June, 1 and 4 July, 1 and 22 August, 23 December 1912; 18 and 19 August 1914.

Hong Kong Telegraph, 7 and 14 January, 17 and 24 April, 19, 27 and 30 May, 3 June, 25 July, 1, 8, 18 and 28 August, 9, 12 and 19 September, 29 October 1913.

India National Herald, 25 July 1927.

Irish Times, 25 and 27 July 1927.

Londonderry Chronicle, 25 July 1927.

Leeds Mercury, 25 July 1927.

Lincoln Echo, 25 July 1927.

Liverpool Courier, 25 July 1927.

Liverpool Post, 25 July 1927.

Madras Mail, 25 July 1927.

Manchester Dispatch, 25 July 1927.

Manchester Guardian, 25 July 1927.

Morning Post, 1 December 1919; 24, 27 and 28 May, 1 June, 6, 8, 9 and 10 July, 2, 5, 12 and 14 August, 7, 15 and 22 September, 27 October, 3, 11, 13 and 30 November, 6 December 1920; 2 June, 7 November 1921; 16 May 1924; 25, 26, 27, 28, 29 and 30 July 1927; 3 February 1930.

Near East, 29 July, 4 August 1927.

Newcastle Chronicle, 28 July 1927.

Norwich Press, 25 July 1927.

Nottingham Guardian, 25 and 28 July 1927.

Observer, 11 July 1920; 16 October 1927; 13 April 1965; 6 April 1975.

Outlook, 5 August 1927.

Pall Mall Gazette, 20 and 21 July 1920.

Penang Gazette, 25 July 1927.

Pioneer Mail and Indian News, 2 May 1902; 1–31 December 1919; 2 and 23 April, 14 May, 1 July–31 August 1920; 27–30 July 1927.

Rangoon Times, 30 July, 10 August 1927.

Record, 28 July 1927.

Reynolds, 31 July 1927.

Saturday Review, 12 January 1935.

Scotsman, 25 and 27 July 1927.

Sheffield Independent, 25 July 1927.

Sheffield Telegraph, 25 and 28 July 1927.

Simla Times, 3 April 1919 to 12 August 1920.

South Bristol Free Press, 30 July 1927.

South Wales Echo, 29 July 1927.

Spectator, 17 July 1920.

Sporting Times, 29 July 1927.

Stafford Sentinel, 25, 28 and 29 July 1927.

Star, 25 July 1927.

Statesman (Calcutta), 1 March–30 April, 5 and 18 June 1919; 1–31 August 1920; 25 and 29 July 1927.

Sunday Express, 20 June 1920.

Sunday Times, 23 May 1920, 31 July 1927, 29 January 1961.

Sussex Daily News, 25 July 1927, 2 August 1927.

Tanganyika Times, 29 July 1927.

Times, 19 April, 15 and 16 December 1919; 11 January, 9 and 28 February, 26 and 27 May, 1, 3, 4, 8, 9, 10, 14, 25 and 26 June, 2, 5, 8, 9, 12, 13, 16, 19, 20 and 21 July, 5 August 1920; March and April 1924; 24, 25, 28, 29 and 31 July 1927.

Times Literary Supplement, 9 January, 6 and 20 February, 5 and 19 March, 9 and 30 April, 14 May 1964.

Times of India, 16 April, 17 May, 1–31 December 1919; 3 May, 1 July–31 August 1920, 25, 26 and 29 July 1927.

Tribune, 11 April, 21 March, 7 November, December 1919; 14 January 1921; 13 April 1922; 9 May 1925; 13 and 14 April 1961; 22 September 1968; 13 April 1969; 13 April 1975; 13 April 1976; 24 October 1977; 12 April 1981; 10 April 1994; 7 July 2001.

Wakefield Express, 30 July 1927.

Western Evening News, 25 July 1927.

Western Press, 25 and 27 July 1927.

Westminster Gazette, 27 May, 25, 27 and 29 July 1927.

Wiltshire and Gloucestershire Independent, 30 July 1927.
Wiltshire and Gloucestershire Standard, 16 October 1920; 30 July 1927.
Workers Life, 29 July 1927.
York Herald, 23, 25 and 28 July 1927.
Yorkshire Post, 25 and 29 July 1927.

BOOKS

Adamec, Ludwig W., *Afghanistan, 1900–1923* (Berkeley: University of California Press, 1967).

Adamec, Ludwig W., *Dictionary of Afghan Wars, Revolutions and Insurgencies* (London: Scarecrow Press, 1996).

Ahmad, Syed Nur, *From Martial Law to Martial Law: Politics in the Punjab, 1919–1958*, ed. Craig Baxter, trans. Mahmud Ali (Lahore: Vanguard Books, 1985).

Ali, Imran, *The Punjab under Imperialism, 1885–1947* (Princeton, New Jersey: Princeton University Press, 1988).

The Amritsar Massacre, 1919: General Dyer in the Punjab (London: Uncovered Editions, The Stationery Office, 2000).

Anderson, David M. and David Killingray, eds, *Policing the Empire: Government, Authority and Control, 1830–1940* (Manchester: Manchester University Press, 1992).

Andrews, C.F. and Girija K. Mookerjee, *The Rise and Growth of Congress in India (1832–1920)* (Delhi: Meenaskshi Prakashan, 1967).

Argov, Daniel, *Moderates and Extremists in the Indian Nationalist Movement, 1883–1920: With Special Reference to Surendranath Banerjea and Lajpat Rai* (London: Asia Publishing House, 1967).

Azad, Abul Karim, *India Wins Freedom* (Hyderabad: Orient Longman, 1991).

Bahadur, Krishna Prakash, *History of the Freedom Movement in India* (New Delhi: Ess Ess Publications, 1989).

Bailey and Woods, eds, *Baily and Woods' Cirencester Directory for the Years 1920, 1921, 1922, 1923, 1924, 1925, 1926, 1927, 1928, 1929* (Cirencester: Baily and Woods; 1920–29).

Baker, Christopher, Gordon Johnson and Anil Seal, eds, *Power, Profit and Politics: Essays on Imperialism, Nationalism and Change in Twentieth-Century India* (Cambridge: Cambridge University Press, 1981).

Bakshi, S.R., *The Jallianwala Bagh Tragedy* (Delhi: Capital Publishers, 1982).

Bamford, P.C., *Histories of the Non-Cooperation and Khilafat Movements* (Delhi: Deep Publications, 1974).

Banerjea, Sir Surendranath, *A Nation in the Making: Being the Reminiscences of Fifty Years of Public Life* (Calcutta: Oxford University Press, 1962).

Banerjee, Anil Chandra, *The Annexation of Burma* (Calcutta: A. Mukherjee, 1944).

Barnett, Corelli, *Britain and her Army, 1509–1970* (London: Penguin, 1970).

Barr, Patt, and Ray Desmond, *Simla: A Hill Station in British India* (London: Scolar Press, 1978).

Barrier, N. Gerald, and Harbans Singh, *The Punjab Past and Present: Essays in Honour of Dr Ganda Singh* (Patiala: Punjabi University, 1976).

Barrow, Sir George de S., *The Life of General Sir Charles Carmichael Monro* (London: Hutchinson, 1931).

Barrow, Sir George de S., *The Fire of Life* (London: Hutchinson, 1941).

Barthorp, Michael, *The North-West Frontier: British India and Afghanistan. A Pictorial History, 1839–1947* (Poole, Dorset: Blandford Press, 1982).

Barton, Sir William, *India's North-West Frontier* (London: John Murray, 1939).

Beloff, Max, *Imperial Sunset: Britain's Liberal Empire, 1897–1921* (New York: Alfred A. Knopf, 1970), i.

Bence-Jones, Mark, *The Viceroys of India* (London: Constable, 1982).

Bernays, Robert, *Naked Fakir* (London: Gollancz, 1931).

Beynon, W.G.L., *With Kelly to Chitral* (London: Edward Arnold, 1896).

Bhatia, H.S., ed., *Martial Law: Theory and Practice* (New Delhi: Deep & Deep, 1979).

Bhatia, H.S., and S.R. Bakshi, *Encyclopaedic History of the Sikhs and Sikhism*, 6 vols (New Delhi: Deep & Deep, 1999), v and vi.

Bigham, Charles Clive, Viscount Mersey, *The Viceroys and Governors-General of India, 1757–1947* (London: John Murray, 1949).

Blacker, L.V.S., *On Secret Patrol in High Asia* (London: John Murray, 1922).

Blood, Sir Bindon, *Four Score Years and Ten: Sir Bindon Blood's Reminiscences* (London: G. Bell, 1933).

Bolt, Christine, *Victorian Attitudes to Race* (London: Routledge & Kegan Paul, 1971).

Bond, B., ed., *Victorian Military Campaigns* (London: Tom Donovan, 1994).

Brecher, Michael, *Nehru: A Political Biography* (London: Oxford University Press, 1959).

Brockway, A. Fenner, *India and its Government* (London: Labour Publishing Co., 1921).

Brockway, A. Fenner, *The Indian Crisis* (London: Victor Gollancz, 1930).

Browne, Edmund Charles, *The Coming of the Great Queen: A Narrative of the Acquisition of Burma* (London: Harrison & Sons, 1888).

Brown, R. Grant, *Burma as I Saw It, 1889–1917: With a Chapter on Recent Events* (London: Methuen, 1926).

Brown, Hilton, ed., *The Sahibs: The Life and Ways of the British in India as Recorded by Themselves* (London: William Hodge, 1948).

Brown, Judith M., *Gandhi's Rise to Power: Indian Politics, 1915–1922* (Cambridge: Cambridge University Press, 1972).

Brown, Judith M., *Modern India: The Origins of an Asian Democracy* (Oxford: Oxford University Press, 1985).

Bryant, J.F., *Gandhi and the Indianization of the Empire* (Cambridge: J.Hall, 1924).

Bruce, George Ludgate, *The Burma Wars, 1824–1886* (London: Hart-Davis MacGibbon, 1973).

Bruce, Richard I., *The Forward Policy and its Results* (London: Longman, Green, 1900).

Buck, Edward John, *Simla, Past and Present* (Bombay: The Times Press, 1925).

Cady, John F., *A History of Modern Burma* (New York: Cornell University Press, 1958).

Callwell, Charles E., *Small Wars: Their Principle and Practice* (London: HMSO, 1906).

Callwell, Sir C.E., *Field-Marshal Sir Henry Wilson: His Life and Diaries*, 2 vols (London London: Cassell, 1927), ii.

Calvert, H., *The Wealth and Welfare of the Punjab* (Lahore: Civil and Military Gazette Press, 1922).

Cannadine, David, *Ornamentalism: How the British Saw Their Empire* (London: Penguin, 2001).

Carey, W.H., *A Guide to Simla: With a Descriptive Account of the Neighbouring Sanitaria* (Calcutta: Wyman, 1870).

Caroe, Olaf, *The Pathans, 550 BC–AD 1957* (London: Macmillan, 1964).

Carthill, Al., *The Lost Dominion* (Edinburgh: William Blackwood, 1924).

Caveeshar, Sardul Singh, *India's Fight for Freedom: A Critical Survey of the Indian National Movement since the Advent of the Mahatma Gandhi in the Field of Indian Politics* (Lahore: National Publications, 1936).

Chaldecott, O.A., *The Tenth Baluch Regiment: The First Battalion, Duchess of Connaught's Own (Late 124th DCO Baluchistan Infantry) and The Tenth Battalion (Late 2/124th Baluchistan Infantry)* (Bombay: Times of India Press, 1935).

Chand, Duni, *Ulster of India: or Analysis of the Punjab Problem* (Lahore: 1936).

Chand, Tara, *History of Freedom Movement in India* (Delhi: Publications Division, Ministry of Information and Broadcasting, 1961), iii.

Chand, Tara, *1921 Movement: Reminiscences* (New Delhi: Publications Division, Ministry of Information, 1971).

Chaudhuri, Nirad C., *The Continent of Circe: Being an Essay on the Peoples of India* (London: Chatto & Windus, 1965).

Chaudhuri, Nirad C., *Autobiography of an Unknown Indian* (London: Picador, 1999).

Chhabra, G.S., *Advanced Study in the History of the Panjab*, 2 vols (Ludhiana: Prakash Brothers, 1962), ii.

Chintamani, Sir C. Yajneswara, *Indian Politics since the Mutiny* (London: George Allen and Unwin, 1940).

Chirol, Sir Valentine, *India: Old and New* (London: Macmillan, 1921).

Chirol, Sir Valentine, *India* (London: Ernest Benn, 1926).

Chopra, P.N., Prabha Chopra and Padshma Jha, eds, *Secret Papers from the British Royal Archives* (Delhi: Konark Publishers, 1998).

Choudhary, D.L., *Violence in the Freedom Movement of Punjab (1907–1942)* (Delhi: B.R. Publishing, 1986).

Christian, John Leroy, *Modern Burma: A Survey of Political and Economic Development* (Berkeley: University of California Press, 1942).

Cocks, S.W., *A Short History of Burma* (London: Macmillan, 1910).

Cocks, S.W., *Burma under British Rule* (Bombay: K. and J. Cooper, 1920).

Cole, D.H., *Imperial Military Geography* (London: Sifton Praed, 1936).

Colvin, Ian, *The Life of General Dyer* (London: Blackwood, 1929; 2nd edn, London: Blackwood, 1931).

Condon, W.E.H., *The Frontier Force Rifles* (Aldershot: Gale & Polden, 1953).

Condon, W.E.H., *The Frontier Force Regiment* (Aldershot: Gale & Polden, 1962).

Coupland, Sir Reginald, *Britain and India, 1600–1941* (London: Longmans, Green, 1944).

Coupland, Sir Reginald, *The Indian Problem, 1833–1935: The First Part of a Report on the Constitutional Problem in India Submitted to the Warden and Fellows of Nuffield College, Oxford* (London: Oxford University Press, 1945).

Craddock, Sir Reginald, *The Dilemma in India* (London: Constable, 1929).

Crosthwaite, Sir Charles Haukes Todd, *The Pacification of Burma* (London: Frank Cass, 1912).

Cumming, Sir John, *Political India, 1832–1932: A Cooperative Survey of a Century* (London: Oxford University Press, 1932).

Curtis Jr, L.P., *Coercion and Conciliation in Ireland, 1880–1892: A Study in Conservative Unionism* (London: Oxford University Press, 1963).

Darby, H.C., and H. Fullard, eds, *The New Cambridge History of India* (Cambridge: Atlas, 1970), xiv.

Darling, Malcolm Lyall, *The Punjab Peasant in Prosperity and Debt* (London: Oxford University Press, 1928).

Das, Durga, *India from Curzon to Nehru and After* (London: Collins, 1969).

Datta, V.N., *Amritsar Past and Present* (Amritsar: Municipal Committee, 1967).

Datta, V.N., *Jallianwala Bagh* (Ludhiana: Lyall Book Depot and V.K. Arora, Kurukshera University Books, 1969).

Datta, V.N., ed., *New Light on the Punjab Disturbances in 1919: Volumes VI and VII of Disorders Inquiry Committee Evidence*, 2 vols (Simla: Indian Institute

of Advanced Study, 1975) (the text of the original is in India Office, L/MIL/17/
12/42 and in Cabinet Office, Cab 27/93).

Datta, V.N., *Ideology of the Political Elite in Punjab (1900–1920)* (Kurukshetra;
Kurukshetra University, 1977).

Datta, V.N., and S.C. Mittal, eds, *The Sources of National Movement*, i *(January
1919 to September 1920): Protests, Disturbances and Defiance* (New Delhi:
Allied Publishers, 1985).

Datta, V.N. and S. Settar, eds, *Jallianwala Bagh Massacre* (Delhi: Pragati
Publications, 2000).

Dautremer, Joseph, *Burma under British Rule* (London: T. Fisher & Unwin,
1916).

Davies, Cuthbert Collin, *The Problem of the North-West Frontier, 1890–1908:
With a Survey of Policy since 1849* (Cambridge: Cambridge University Press,
1932).

Davis, John, *The History of the Second, Queen's Royal Regiment, Now The Queen's
(Royal West Surrey) Regiment*, (London: Eyre & Spottiswoode, 1906), iv.

Dayal, Ravi, ed., *We Fought Together for Freedom: Chapters from the Indian
National Movement* (Delhi: Oxford University Press, 1995).

De Schweinitz, K., *The Rise and Fall of British India: Imperialism as Inequality*
(London: Methuen, 1983).

Dhanjal, Beryl, *Amritsar* (London: Evans Brothers, 1994).

Dickson, W.E.R., *East Persia: A Backwater of the War* (London: Edward Arnold,
1924).

Dictionary of National Biography, 1922–1930, ed. by J.R.H. Weaver (2nd edn,
Oxford: Oxford University Press, 1976).

Diver, Maud, *Far to Seek: A Romance of England and India* (Edinburgh: William
Blackwood, 1921).

Dixon, Norman, *On the Psychology of Military Incompetence* (London: Pimlico,
1994).

Dodwell, H.H., and V.D.Mahajan, eds, *The Cambridge History of India: The
Indian Empire, 1858–1918 and 1919–1969* (2nd edn, New Delhi: S. Chand,
1964), vi.

Dove, John, *The Letters of John Dove*, ed. Robert Henry Brand (London:
Macmillan, 1938).

Draper, Alfred, *The Amritsar Massacre: Twilight of the Raj* (London: Buchan &
Enright, 1985).

Dunbar, Sir George, *India and the Passing of Empire* (London: Nicholson &
Watson, 1951).

Durand, Sir Mortimer, *The Life of Field-Marshal Sir George White*, 2 vols
(Edinburgh: William Blackwood, 1915), i.

Dutt, R. Palme, *India Today* (London: Victor Gollancz, 1940).

Dwarkadas, Kanji, *India's Fight for Freedom, 1913–1937: An Eye Witness Story* (Bombay: Popular Prakashan, 1966).

Dyer, Reginald Edward Harry, *Raiders of the Sarhad: Being an Account of a Campaign of Arms and Bluff against the Brigands of the Persian-Baluchi Border during the Great War* (London: H.F. & G. Witherby, 1921).

Edwardes, Michael, *A History of India from the Earliest Times to the Present Day* (London: Thames and Hudson, 1961).

Edwardes, Michael, *The Last Years of British India* (London: Cassell, 1963).

Edwardes, Michael, *British India: A Summary of the Nature and Effects of Alien Rule, 1772–1947* (London: Sidgwick & Jackson, 1967).

Edwardes, Michael, *Bound to Exile: The Victorians in India* (London: Victorian (and Modern History) Book Club, 1969).

Edwardes, Michael, *Nehru: A Political Biography* (London: Allen Lane, 1971).

Elliott, J.G., *The Frontier, 1839–1947: The Story of the North-West Frontier of India* (London: Cassell, 1968).

Enriquez, Colin, *The Pathan Borderland: A Consecutive Account of the Country and People On and Beyond the Indian Frontier from Chitral to Dera Ismail Khan* (Calcutta: Thacker, Spink 1921).

Farwell, Byron, *Armies of the Raj: From the Great Indian Mutiny to Independence, 1858–1947* (London: Viking, 1990) .

Fein, Helen, *Imperial Crime and Punishment: The Massacre at Jallianwala Bagh and British Judgment, 1919–1920* (Honolulu: University Press of Hawaii, 1977).

Fischer, Louis, *The Life of Mahatma Gandhi* (London: Grafton, 1986).

Fletcher, Arnold, *Afghanistan: Highroad of Conquest* (Ithaca: Cornell University Press, 1965).

Fraser-Tytler, Sir W. Kerr, *Afghanistan: A Study of Political Developments in Central and Southern Asia*, revised by Sir M.C. Gillett (London: Oxford University Press, 1967).

Furneaux, Rupert, *Massacre at Amritsar* (London: George Allen & Unwin, 1963).

Gallagher, John, Gordon Johnson and Anil Seal, eds, *Locality, Province and Nation: Essays on Indian Politics, 1870–1940* (London: Cambridge University Press, 1973).

Gandhi, Mohandas Karamchand, *Young India, 1919–1922* (Madras: Tagore, 1922).

Gandhi, Mohandas Karamchand, *Source Material for a History of the Freedom Movement in India Collected from Bombay Government (and Government of India) Records, 1818–1947* (Bombay: Government Press, 1957).

Gandhi, Mohandas Karamchand, *The Collected Works of Mahatma Gandhi* (Delhi: Government of India, 1967), xx–xxii.

Gandhi, Mohandas Karamchand, *An Autobiography* (2nd edn, London: Penguin, 2001).

Garratt, G.T., *An Indian Commentary* (London: Jonathan Cape, 1928).

Gaylor, John, *Sons of John Company: The Indian and Pakistani Armies, 1903–91* (Tunbridge Wells: Parapress, 1996).

Geary, Grattan, *Burma, after the Conquest: Viewed in its Political, Social and Commercial Aspects from Mandalay* (London: Sampson Low, Marston, Searle and Rivington, 1886).

Ghai, Prem Vati, *The Partition of the Punjab, 1849–1947* (New Delhi: Munshiram Manoharlal, 1986).

Ghose, Akshaya K., *Lord Chelmsford's Viceroyalty: A Critical Survey* (Madras: Ganesh, 1921).

Gilbert, Martin, *Winston S. Churchill, 1916–1922* (London: Heinemann, 1975), iv.

Gilmour, David, *Curzon* (London: John Murray, 1994).

Golant, William, *The Long Afternoon: British India, 1601–1947* (London: Hamish Hamilton, 1974).

Gopal, Sarvepalli, *Jawaharlal Nehru: A Biography*, 3 vols (London: Jonathan Cape, 1975), i.

Gopal, Sarvepalli, *Selected Works of Jawaharlal Nehru* (New Delhi: Orient Longman, 1972), i.

Gould, Tony, *Imperial Warriors: Britain and the Gurkhas* (London: Granta Books, 1999).

Greenberger, Allen J., *The British Image of India: A Study in the Literature of Imperialism, 1880–1960* (London: Oxford University Press, 1969).

Griffiths, Percival J., *The British Impact on India* (London: Macdonald, 1952).

Griffiths, Sir Percival, *Modern India* (London: Ernest Benn, 1965).

Griffiths, Sir Percival, *To Guard My People: The History of the Indian Police* (London: Ernest Benn, 1971).

Gupta, Anandswarup, *The Police in British India, 1861–1947* (New Delhi: Concept Publishing, 1979).

Gupta, Dharam Chand, *Indian National Movement and Constitutional Development* (Delhi: Vikas, 1973).

Guy, Alan J, and Peter B Boyden, eds, *Soldiers of the Raj: The Indian Army, 1600–1947* (London: National Army Museum, 1997).

Gwynn, Major-General Sir Charles W., *Imperial Policing* (London: Macmillan, 1934).

Hale, H.W., *The Political Trouble in India, 1917–1937* (Allahabad: Chugh Publications, 1974).

Hall, D.G.E., *Burma* (London: Hutchinson, 1950).

Harries-Jenkins, Gwyn, *The Army in Victorian Society* (London: Routledge & Kegan Paul, 1977).

Harris, John, *Much Sounding of Bugles: The Siege of Chitral, 1895* (London: Hutchinson, 1975).

Harrop, F. Beresford, *Thacker's New Guide to Simla* (Simla: Thacker, Spinks & Co., 1925).

Harvey, Godfrey Eric, *Outline of Burmese History* (Calcutta: Longmans, Green, 1947).

Harvey, G.E., *British Rule in Burma, 1824–1942* (London: Faber & Faber, 1946).

Heathcote, T.A., *The Indian Army: The Garrison of British Imperial India, 1822–1922* (Newton Abbot: David & Charles, 1974).

Heathcote, T.A., *The Afghan Wars, 1839–1919* (London: Osprey, 1980).

Heathcote, T.A., *The Military in British India: The Development of British Land Forces in South Asia, 1600–1947* (Manchester: Manchester University Press, 1995).

Heimsath, C.H., *A History of the Freedom Movement, 1906–1936* (Karachi: 1961), parts 1 and 3.

History of the 4th Battalion 13th Frontier Force Rifles (Wilde's) (anonymous author) (London: Butler & Tanner, 1930).

Holdich, Sir T. Hungerford, *The Indian Borderland, 1880–1900* (London: Methuen, 1901).

Hopkirk, Peter, *The Great Game: The Struggle for Empire in Central Asia* (New York: Kodansha International, 1992).

Horne, E.A., *The Political System of British India: With Special Reference to the Recent Constitutional Changes* (Oxford: Clarendon, 1922).

Horniman, B.G., *Amritsar and Our Duty to India* (London: T. Fisher Unwin, 1920).

Horniman, B.G., and Helena Normanton, *The Agony of Amritsar and the Reign of Terror in the Punjab* (London: British Committee of the Indian National Congress, 1920).

Horniman, B.G., *British Administration and the Amritsar Massacre* (Delhi: Mittal Publications, 1984).

Hoyland, John S., *The Case of India* (London: J.M. Dent & Sons, 1929).

Htin Aung, Maung, *The Stricken Peacock: Anglo-Burmese Relations, 1752–1948* (The Hague: Martinus Nijhoff, 1965).

Htin Aung, Maung, *A History of Burma* (New York: Columbia University Press, 1967).

Htin Aung, Maung, *Lord Randolph Churchill and the Dancing Peacock: British Conquest of Burma, 1885* (New Delhi: Manohar, 1990).

Hughes, T.L., 'Man of Iron: A Biography of Major-General Sir William Beynon' (unpublished typescript in the Gurkha Museum, Gm: Acc. No 94–10–9 H3: Stoke Poges, 1975).

Indian National Congress Punjab Subcommittee, *Report of the Commissioners Appointed by the Punjab Sub-Committee of the Indian National Congress*, 2 vols (Bombay: Karnatak Press, 1920).

Ireland, Alleyne, *The Province of Burma: A Report Prepared on Behalf of the University of Chicago*, 2 vols (New York: Houghton, Mifflin, 1907).

Iyer, C.S. Ranga, *India: Peace or War?* (London: Harrap, 1930).

Jackson, Donovan (Invicta), *India's Army* (London: Sampson Low, Marston, 1940).

Jackson, H.C., *Pastor on the Nile: Being Some Account of the Life and Letters of Llewellyn H. Gwynne, Formerly Bishop in Egypt and the Sudan and Deputy Chaplain-General in France in the First World War* (London: SPCK, 1960).

Jagadisan, T.N., ed., *Letters of the Right Honourable V.S. Srinavasa Sastri* (London: Asia Publishing House, 1963).

Jagadisan, T.N., *V.S. Srinavasa Sastri* (New Delhi: the Government of India, 1969).

Jallianwala Bagh: A Watershed in the Freedom Movement (Chandigarh: Department of Information and Public Relations, Punjab, 1994).

James, David, *Lord Roberts* (London: Hollis and Carter, 1954).

James, Lionel, L.T.C., *With the Chitral Relief Force* (Calcutta: The Englishman Press, 1895).

James, Lawrence, *Raj: The Making and Unmaking of British India* (London: Little, Brown, 1997).

Jayakar, M.R., *The Story of My Life*, 2 vols (Bombay: Asia Publishing House, 1958), i.

Jeffery, Keith, *The British Army and the Crisis of Empire, 1918–22* (Manchester: Manchester University Press, 1984).

Jeffery, Keith, *The Military Correspondence of Field-Marshal Sir Henry Wilson, 1918–1922* (London: Bodley Head, 1985).

Judd, Denis, *The British Raj* (Hove: Wayland, 1972).

Judd, Denis, *Empire: The British Imperial Experience from 1765 to the Present* (London: Harper Collins 1996).

Kaye, Sir Cecil, *Communism in India with Unpublished Documents from National Archives of India (1919–1924)*, ed. Subodh Roy (Calcutta: Editions India, 1971).

Keay, John, *India: A History* (London: Harper Collins, 2000).

Keith, Arthur Berriedale, *A Constitutional History of India, 1600–1935* (New York: Barnes & Noble, 1926).

Kelly, A Lindsay, ed., *Kelly's Directory of the Counties of Somerset and Gloucester with the City of Bristol, 1927* (London: Kelly's Directories, 1927).

Kendall, Patricia, *India and the British: A Quest For Truth* (London: Charles Scribner, 1931).

Kenworthy, J.M., *India: A Warning* (London: Elkin Mathews and Marrot, 1931).

Kiernan, V.G., *The Lords of Human Kind: European Attitudes towards the Outside World in the Imperial Age* (Harmondsworth: Penguin, 1969).

Kincaid, Dennis, *British Social Life in India* (Newton Abbott: Readers Union, 1974).

Kipling, Rudyard, *Rudyard Kipling's Verse: The Definitive Edition* (London: Hodder & Stoughton, 1986).

Kitchlew, Toufique, *Saifuddin Kitchlew: Hero of Jallianwala Bagh* (New Delhi: National Book Trust, 1987).

Kreyer, J.A.C., and G. Uloth, *The 28th Light Cavalry in Persia and Russian Turkistan, 1915–20* (Oxford: Slatter and Rose, 1926).

Kripalani, J.B., *Gandhi: His Life and Thought* (Delhi: Publications Division, Ministry of Information & Broadcasting, 1991).

Kulke, Hermann and Dietmar Rothermund, *A History of India* (London: Croom Helm, 1986).

Kumar, R., ed., *Essays on Gandhian Politics: The Rowlatt Satyagraha of 1919* (Oxford: Clarendon Press, 1971).

Kumar, Ravindra, *Selected Documents of Lala Lajpat Rai, 1906–1928* (New Delhi: Anmol Publications, 1992), ii.

Landau, Captain Henry, *The Enemy Within: The Inside Story of German Sabotage in America* (London: G.P. Putnam's Sons, 1937).

Lawrence, Sir Walter Roper, *The India We Served* (London: Cassell, 1928).

Leigh, Maxwell Studdy, *The Punjab and the War* (Lahore: Punjab Government, 1922).

Lindsay, D.M., *Regimental History of the 6th Royal Battalion, 13th Frontier Force Rifles (Scinde), 1843–1923* (Aldershot: Gale & Polden, 1926).

Lindsay, D.M., *Regimental History of the 6th Royal Battalion, 13th Frontier Force Rifles (Scinde), 1843–1934* (Aldershot: Gale & Polden, 1935).

The London Cyclist Battalion, compiled by the History Committee of the 26th Middlesex (Cyclist) Volunteer Rifle Corps and the 25th (County of London) Cyclist Battalion, the London Regiment (London: Forster Groom, 1932).

Longer, V., *Red Coats to Olive Green: A History of the Indian Army, 1600–1947* (New Delhi: Allied Publishers, 1974).

Lothian, Sir Arthur Cunningham, *Kingdoms of Yesterday* (London: John Murray, 1951).

Loughlin, James, *Gladstone, Home Rule and the Ulster Question, 1882–93* (Atlantic Highlands, New Jersey: Humanities Press International, 1987).

Lovett, Sir Verney, *A History of the Nationalist Movement in India* (London: John Murray, 1921).

Lovett, Sir Verney, *India* (London: Hodder & Stoughton, 1923).

Low, D.A., ed., *Congress and the Raj: Facets of the Indian Struggle, 1917–47* (London: Heinemann, 1977).

Lyons, F.S.L., *Ireland since the Famine* (London: Collins/Fontana, 1979).

MacGlasson, L., *Diary of the 2/4th Battalion the Border Regiment, 1914–19* (Carlisle: Charles Thurnam and Sons, 1920).

MacKenzie, John M., ed., *Popular Imperialism and the Military, 1850–1950* (Manchester: Manchester University Press, 1992).

MacMahon, A. Ruxton, *Far Cathay and Farther India* (London: Hurst & Blackett, 1893).

MacMunn, Sir George, *Afghanistan: From Darius to Amanullah* (London: G. Bell, 1929).

MacMunn, Sir George, *The Romance of the Indian Frontiers* (London: Jonathan Cape, 1933).

MacMunn, Sir George, *Turmoil and Tragedy in India: 1914 and After* (London: Jarrolds, 1935).

MacMunn, Sir George, *The History of the Sikh Pioneers (23rd, 32nd, 34th)* (London: Sampson Low, Marston 1936).

Majumdar, R.C., H.D. Raychaudhuri and Kalikinkar Datta, *An Advanced History of India* (London: Macmillan, 1950).

Majumdar, Ramesh Chandra, *History of the Freedom Movement in India*, 3 vols (Calcutta: Firma K.L. Mukhopadhyay, 1963), iii.

Majumdar, R.C., ed., *Struggle for Freedom: The History and Cultures of the Indian People* (Bombay: Bharatiya Vidya Bhavan, 1969), xi.

Malaviya, Kapil Deva, *Open Rebellion in the Punjab (With Special Reference to Amritsar)* (Allahabad: Abhudaya Press, 1919).

Malik, Ikram Ali, *A Book of Readings on the History of the Punjab, 1799–1947* (Lahore: Research Society of Pakistan, 1970).

Mansergh, Nicholas, *The Irish Question, 1840–1921* (London: George Allen and Unwin, 1975).

Marks, John E., *Forty Years in Burma* (London: Hutchinson, 1917).

Martial Law Administration in the Punjab Described by Official Witnesses (Madras: Madras Liberal League, 1920).

Martineau, G.D., *A History of the Royal Sussex Regiment: A History of the Old Belfast Regiment and the Regiment of Sussex, 1701–1953* (Chichester: Moore and Tillyer, 1955).

Masani, R.P., *Britain in India: An Account of British Rule in the Indian Subcontinent* (Bombay: Oxford University Press, 1960).

Mason, Philip, *Patterns of Dominance* (London: Oxford University Press, 1971).

Mason, Philip, *A Matter of Honour: An Account of the Indian Army, its Officers and Men* (London: Jonathan Cape, 1974).

Mason, A.H., *Report on the Black Mountain and Adjacent Independent Territory* (Simla: Government of India, 1888).

Masselos, Jim, *Nationalism on the Indian Subcontinent: An Introductory History* (Melbourne: Nelson, 1972).

Maurice, Sir Frederick, *The Life of General Lord Rawlinson of Trent* (London: Cassell, 1928).

Maxwell, R.M., ed., *Villiers-Stuart Goes to War* (Edinburgh: Pentland, 1990).

May, C.W., *History of the 2nd Sikhs, 12th Frontier Force Regiment, 1846–1933* (Jubbulpore: E.C. Davis, 1933).

Mehrotra, S.R., *India and the Commonwealth, 1885–1929* (London: George Allen and Unwin, 1965).

Mehrotra, S.R., *A History of the Indian National Congress* (New Delhi: Vikas, 1995).

Menon, K.P.S., *C. Sankaran Nair* (Delhi: The Government of India Publication Division, 1967)

Menezes, S.L., *Fidelity and Honour: The Indian Army from the Seventeenth to the Twenty-First Century* (New Delhi: Viking, Penguin Books, 1993).

Meston, Lord, *Nationhood for India* (London: Oxford University Press, 1931).

Metcalf, Thomas R., *The Aftermath of Revolt: India, 1857–1870* (London: Oxford University Press, 1965).

Metcalf, Thomas R., *The New Cambridge History of India* (New Delhi: Cambridge, 1998), iii, part 4, *Ideologies of the Raj*.

Miles, C.W., *The Zakka Khel and Mohmand Expeditions* (Rawalpindi: Egerton Press: 1909).

Miller, Charles, *Khyber: British India's North-West Frontier. The Story of an Imperial Migraine* (London: Macdonald and Jane's, 1977).

Mishra, Shree Govind, *History of the Freedom Movement in India (1857–1947)* (New Delhi: Uppal, 1993).

Mitra, H.N., ed., *Punjab Unrest Before and After* (Calcutta: N.N. Mitter, 1920).

Mittal, Satish Chandra, *Freedom Movement in Punjab (1905–29)* (Delhi: Concept, 1977).

Moberly, Frederick James, *Operations in Persia, 1914–1919* (London: Her Majesty's Stationery Office, 1987).

Mockaitis, Thomas R., *British Counterinsurgency, 1919–60* (London: Macmillan, 1990).

Mohan, Kamlesh, *Militant Nationalism in the Punjab, 1919–1935* (New Delhi: Manohar, 1985).

Mohan, Kamlesh, Bhupinder Singh Tasser Sehgal and R.D. Sharma, eds, *Jallianwala Bagh: A Saga of Sacrifice* (Chandigarh: Sahitya Academy, 1995)

Mohan, Pandit Pearay, *The Punjab 'Rebellion' of 1919 and How it was Suppressed: An Account of the Punjab Disorders and the Working of Martial Law*, ed. Ravi M. Bakaya, 2 vols (New Delhi: Gyan Publishers, 1999).

Molesworth, G.N., *Afghanistan, 1919* (London: Asia Publishing House, 1962).

Moon, Sir Penderel, *Divide and Quit* (London: Chatto & Windus, 1961).

Moon, Sir Penderel, *Gandhi and Modern India* (London: English Universities Press, 1968).

Moon, Sir Penderel, *The British Conquest and Dominion of India* (London: Duckworth, 1989).

Moore, Robin James, *Liberalism and Indian Politics, 1872–1922* (London: Edward Arnold, 1966).

Moore, Robin James, *The Crisis of Indian Unity, 1917–40* (Oxford: Clarendon Press, 1974).

Moorhouse, Geoffrey, *India Britannica* (London: William Collins, 1983).

Moraes, Frank, *Witness to an Era: India, 1920 to the Present Day* (London: Wiedenfeld & Nicholson, 1973).

Moreland, W.H., and Sir Atul Chandra Chatterjee, *A Short History of India* (4th edn, London: Longmans, Green, 1957)

Morris, James, *Farewell the Trumpets: An Imperial Retreat* (London: Faber & Faber, 1979).

Naidis, Mark, *India: A Short Introductory History* (New York: Macmillan, 1966).

Nair, Sir C. Sankaran, *Gandhi and Anarchy* (Indore: Holkar State (Electric) Printing Press, 1922).

Nanda, Bal Ram, *Mahatma Gandhi: A Biography* (London: Unwin, 1965).

Nanda, B.R., *The Nehrus: Motilal and Jawaharlal* (London; George Allen & Unwin, 1962).

Nanda, B.R., *Motilal Nehru* (Delhi: the Government of India Publications Division, 1970).

Nanda, B.R., *Gokhale, Gandhi and the Nehrus: Studies in Indian Nationalism* (London: George Allen and Unwin, 1974).

Narain, Savita, *The Historiography of the Jallianwala Bagh Massacre, 1919* (South Godstone, Surrey: Spantech and Lancer, 1998).

Nehru, Jawarharlal, *An Autobiography* (Delhi: Oxford University Press, 1985).

Nevill, H.L., *Campaigns on the North-West Frontier, 1849–1908* (London: John Murray, 1912).

Nisbet, John, *Burma under British Rule – and Before*, 2 vols (London: Archibald Constable, 1901), i.

Nundy, Alfred, *The Present Situation with Special Reference to the Punjab Disturbances* (Dehra Dun: The Garhwali Press, 1919).

Nundy, Alfred, *Political Problems and Hunter Committee Disclosures* (Calcutta: 'The Publisher', 1920).

Nundy, Alfred, *Indian Unrest, 1919–20* (Dehra Dun: Garhwali Press, 1921).

O'Ballance, Edgar, *Afghan Wars, 1839–1992: What Britain Gave up and the Soviet Union Lost* (London: Brassey's, 1993).

O'Dwyer, Sir Michael Francis, *The Punjab Disturbances of April 1919: Criticism of the Hunter Committee Report* (London: Indo-British Association, 1920).

O'Dwyer, Sir Michael Francis, *India as I Knew It, 1885–1925* (London: Constable, 1925).

Oliver, Edward E., *Across the Border: or Pathan and Biloch* (London: Chapman and Hall, 1890).

O'Malley, L.S.S., *The Indian Civil Service, 1601–1930* (London: John Murray, 1931).

O'Malley, L.S.S., ed., *Modern India and the West* (London: Oxford University Press, 1941).

Omissi, David, *The Sepoy and the Raj: The Indian Army, 1860–1946* (London: University of Hull, 1994).

Osburn, Arthur, *Must England Lose India? (The Nemesis of Empire)* (London: Alfred A. Knopf, 1930).

Pal, Bipin Chandra, *Memories of My Life and Times*, 2 vols (Calcutta: Bipinchandra Pal Institute, 1973).

Palsokar, R.D., *A Historical Record of the Dogra Regiment: A Saga of Gallantry and Valour, 1858–1981* (Faizabad: Dogra Regimental Centre, 1982).

Pandey, B.N., *The Break-Up of British India* (London: Macmillan, 1969).

Pandey, B.N., *Nehru* (London: Macmillan, 1976).

Panikkar, K.M., *A Survey of Indian History* (London: Asia Publishing House, 1960).

Pattabhi Sitaramayya, B., *The History of the Indian National Congress* (Bombay: Padma Publications, 1946), i.

Paul, K.T., *The British Connection with India* (London: Student Christian Movement, 1928).

Perkins, Roger, *The Amritsar Legacy: Golden Temple to Caxton Hall. The Story of a Killing* (Chippenham: Picton, 1989).

Petrie, Sir Charles, *The Life and Letters of the Right Hon. Sir Austen Chamberlain*, 2 vols (London: Cassell 1940), ii.

Phatak, N.R., *Source Material for a History of the Freedom Movement in India*, 3 vols (Bombay: Government of Maharashtra, 1965), iii, part 1.

Philips, C.H., *India* (London: Hutchinson's University Library, 1949).

Philips, C.H., H.L. Singh and B.N. Pandey, *The Evolution of India and Pakistan, 1858 to 1947: Select Documents* (London: Oxford University Press, 1962), iv.

Polak, H.S.L., H.N. Brailsford and Lord Pethick-Lawrence, *Mahatma Gandhi* (London: Odhams Press, 1949).

Pole, D. Graham, *India in Transition* (London: Leonard and Virginia Woolf at the Hogarth Press, 1932).

Pollock, George, *Mr Justice McCardie: A Biography* (London: John Lane, 1934).

Popplewell, Richard J., *Intelligence and Imperial Defence: British Intelligence and the Defence of the Indian Empire, 1904–1924* (London: Frank Cass, 1995).

Poynder, F.S., *The 9th Gurkha Rifles, 1817–1936* (London: Royal United Service Institution, 1937).

Poynder, F.S., Lieutenant-Colonel Stevens and P. Choudhuri, *9 Gurkha Rifles: A Regimental History (1817–1947)* (New Delhi: Vision Books, 1984).

Proudfoot, C.L., *We Lead: The 7th Light Cavalry, 1784–1990* (New Delhi: Lancer International, 1991).

Pubby, Vipin, *Shimla Then and Now* (New Delhi: Indus Publishing, 1996).

Rai, Lajpat, *The Political Future of India* (New York: B.W. Huebsch, 1919).

Rai, Lala Lajpat, *Agony of Punjab* (Madras: Tagore and Co, 1920).

Rai, Lala Lajpat, *Autobiographical Writings*, ed. Vijaya Chandra Joshi (Delhi: University Publications, 1965).

Rai, Satya M., *Legislative Politics and Freedom Struggle in the Panjab, 1897–1947* (New Delhi: Indian Council of Historical Reasearch, 1984).

Rai, Satya M., *Punjabi Heroic Tradition, 1900–1947* (Patiala: Punjabi University, 1978).

Ralhan, O.P., *Indian National Movement: Punjabi Martyrs of Freedom*, 5 vols (New Delhi: Anmol Publications, 1994), i.

Ralhan, O.P., and Suresh K. Sharma, eds, *Documents on Punjab* (New Delhi: Anmol Publications, 1994), iv and v.

Ralhan, Om Prakash, *Jawaharlal Nehru and National Affairs (14 November 1889–14 August 1947)* (New Delhi: Anmol Publications, 1993).

Ram, Raja, *The Jallianwala Bagh Massacre: A Premeditated Plan* (Chandigarh: Panjab University Publishing Bureau, 1978).

Ray, Prithvis Chandra, *Life and Times of C.R. Das: The Story of Bengal's Self-Expression. Being a Personal Memoir of the Late Deshbandhu Chitta Ranjan and a Complete Outline of the History of Bengal for the First Quarter of the Twentieth Century* (London: Oxford University Press, 1927).

Raychoudhary, S.C., *History of Modern India (From 1707 AD to Present Times)*, 2 vols (Delhi: Surjeet, 1981), ii.

Reed, Sir Stanley, *The India I Knew, 1897–1947* (London: Odhams Press, 1952).

Regimental History of the 4th Battalion, 13th Frontier Force Rifles (Wilde's) (anonymous author) (Butler & Tanner: Frome, 1932).

Reynolds, Reginald, *The White Sahibs in India* (London: Martin Secker & Warburg, 1937).

Richards, D.S., *The Savage Frontier: A History of the Anglo-Afghan Wars* (London: Macmillan, 1990).

Richards, Philip Ernest, *Indian Dust: Being Letters from the Punjab* (London: George Allen & Unwin, 1932).

Robb, Peter G., *The Government of India and Reform: Policies towards Politics and the Constitution, 1916–1921* (Oxford: Oxford University Press, 1976).

Roberts, Field-Marshal Lord, *Forty-One Years in India: From Subaltern to Commander-in-Chief*, 2 vols (London: Richard Bentley, 1897).

Roberts. P.E., *History of British India under the Company and the Crown* (London: Oxford University Press, 1952).

Ronaldshay, the Earl of, *The Heart of Aryavarta: A Study of the Psychology of Indian Unrest* (London: Constable, 1925).

Roy, Manabendra Nath, *India in Transition* (Geneva: J.B. Target, 1922).

Rumbold, Sir Algernon, *Watershed in India, 1914–1922* (London: Athlone Press, 1979).

Runciman, Steven, *The White Rajahs: A History of Sarawak from 1841 to 1946* (Kuala Lumpur: S. Abdul Majeed, 1992).

Rutherford, V.H., *Modern India: Its Problems and their Solutions* (London: The Labour Publishing Company, 1927).

Rutter, Owen, *The Pirate Wind: Tales of the Sea-Robbers of Malaya* (Singapore: Oxford University Press 1991).

Saini, B.S., *The Social and Economic History of the Punjab, 1901–1939 (Including Haryana and Himachal Pradesh)* (Delhi: Ess Ess Publications, 1975).

Salzman, Philip Carl, *Black Tents of Baluchistan* (Washington, DC: Smithsonian Institute Press, 2000).

Sardesai, S.G., *India and the Russian Revolution* (New Delhi: Communist Party, 1967).

Sareen, Tilak Raj, *Russian Revolution and India, 1917–1921* (New Delhi: Sterling Publishers, 1977).

Sareen, Tilak Raj, *Indian Revolutionary Movement Abroad (1905–1921)* (New Delhi: Sterling Publishers, 1979).

Sarkar, Sumit, *Modern India, 1885–1947* (London: Macmillan, 1989).

Savi, Ethel Winifred, *Rulers of Men* (London: G.P. Putnam's Sons, 1925).

Sayer, Geoffrey Robley, *Hong Kong, 1862–1919* (Hong Kong: Hong Kong University Press, 1975).

Scott, J. George, and J.P. Hardiman, *Gazetteer of Upper Burma and the Shan States*, 5 vols (Rangoon: Government of Burma, 1900), i.

Scott, Sir J.G., *Burma from the Earliest Times to the Present Day* (London: T. Fisher & Unwin, 1924).

Segal, Ronald, *The Crisis of India* (London: Jonathan Cape, 1965).

Setalvad, Sir Chimanlal, *Recollections and Reflections: An Autobiography* (Bombay: Padma, 1946).

Sethi, R.R., *The Cambridge History of India* (Delhi: S. Chand, 1958), vi, *The Last Phase, 1919–1947*.

Shakespear, L.W., *History of the 2nd King Edward's Own Goorkha Rifles* (Aldershot: Gale & Polden, 1950).

Shatabdi, Ardh, *Jallianwala Bagh* (New Delhi: Government of India, Publications Division, 1969).

Shearer, J.E., *A History of the 1st Battalion, 15th Punjab Regiment, 1857–1937* (Aldershot: Gale and Polden, 1937).

Shepperd, G. Alan, *The Royal Military Academy Sandhurst and its Predecessors* (London: Country Life Books, 1980).

Shirer, William L., *Gandhi: A Memoir* (London: Abacus, 1981).

Simson, H., *British Rule and Rebellion* (Edinburgh: William Blackwood & Sons, 1937).

Singer, André, *Lords of the Khyber: The Story of the North-West Frontier* (London: Faber and Faber, 1984).

Singh, Fauja, *Who's Who Punjab Freedom Fighters* (Patiala: Punjabi Unversity, 1972), i.

Singh, Gopal, *A History of the Sikh People (1469–1988)* (New Delhi: World Book Centre, 1979).

Singh, Gurshuran, and Balraj Saggar, *Jallianwala Bagh (Who's Who)* (Chandigarh: Punjab State University, 1996).

Singh, Gursharan, Parm Bakshish Singh, Devinder Kumar Verma and Raj Krishan Ghai, eds, *Jallianwala Bagh: Commemoration Volume and Amritsar Our Duty to India* (Patiala: Punjabi University, 1997).

Singh, Harbans, ed., *The Encyclopaedia of Sikhism* (Patiala: Punjabi University, 1997).

Singh, Hari, *Gandhi, Rowlatt Satyagraha and British Imperialism: Emergence of Mass Movements in Punjab and Delhi* (Delhi: Indian Bibliographies Bureau, 1990).

Singh, Khuswant, *A History of the Sikhs* (Delhi: Oxford University Press, 1984), ii.

Singh, Mohinder, *The Akali Movement* (Delhi: Macmillan, 1978).

Singh, Mohinder, *The Akali Struggle: A Retrospect* (New Delhi: Atlantic Publishers, Macmillan, 1988).

Singh, Mohinder, ed., *History and Culture of Panjab* (New Delhi: Atlantic, 1988).

Singh, Sangat, *The Sikhs in History* (New Delhi: Uncommon Books, 1996).

Singhal, D.P., *British Diplomacy and the Annexation of Upper Burma* (2nd edn, Singapore: South Asian Publishers, 1981).

Smith, Vincent A., *The Oxford History of India,* ed. Percival Spear (3rd edn, Oxford: Clarendon Press, 1958).

Smith, William Roy, *Nationalism and Reform in India* (Port Washington, New York: Kennikat Press, 1973).

Smyth, Brigadier-General Sir John, *The Only Enemy* (London: Hutchinson, 1959).

Smyth, Sir John George, *Sandhurst* (London: Wiedenfeld and Nicolson, 1961).

Sotheby's, *Orders, Medals and Decorations* (London: Sale Catalogue, 18 December 1990).

Spain, James W., *The Way of the Pathans* (London: Robert Hale, 1962).

Spain, James W., *The Pathan Borderland* (The Hague: Mouton, 1963).

Spear, Percival, *India: A Modern History* (Ann Arbor, Michigan: University of Michigan, 1961).

Spear, Percival, *A History of India*, 2 vols (Harmondsworth, Middlesex: Penguin Books, 1986).

Stewart, A.T.Q., *The Pagoda War: Lord Dufferin and the Fall of the Kingdom of Ava, 1885–6* (Newton Abbot: Victorian (and Modern History) Book Club, 1974).

Stokes, S.E., *National Self-Realisation* (Madras: S. Ganesan, 1921).

Strauss, E., *Irish Nationalism and British Democracy* (Westport, Connecticut: Greenwood Press, 1951).

Sud, Onkar Chand, *The Simla Story (The Glow and After-Glow of the Raj): A Sketch Book* (Simla; Maria Brothers, 1992).

Sunderland, Jabez Thomas, *India in Bondage* (New York: Lewis Copeland, 1920).

Suntharalingam, R., *Indian Nationalism: An Historical Analysis* (Delhi: Vikas Publishing, 1983).

Swinson, Arthur, *Six Minutes to Sunset: The Story of General Dyer and the Amritsar Affair* (London: Peter Davies, 1964).

Swinson, Arthur, *North-West Frontier: People and Events, 1839–1947* (London: Hutchinson, 1967).

Sydenham of Combe, Lord, *My Working Life* (London: John Murray, 1927).

Sykes, Percy Molesworth, *Ten Thousand Miles in Persia or Eight Years in Iran* (London: John Murray, 1902).

Sykes, Sir Percy, *A History of Afghanistan* (London: Macmillan, 1940), ii.

Tagore, Rabindranath, *Letters to a Friend*, ed. C.F. Andrews (London: George Allen & Unwin, 1929).

Talbot, Ian, *Punjab and the Raj, 1849–1947* (New Delhi: Manohar, 1988).

Tandon, Prakash, *Punjabi Century, 1857–1947* (London: Chatto and Windus, 1961).

Taylor, A.J.P., *England, 1914–1945* (London: Folio Society, 2000).

Taylor, H.A., *Jix: Viscount Brentford. Being the Authoritative and Official Biography of the Rt Hon. William Joynson-Hicks, First Viscount Brentford of Newick* (London: Stanley Paul, 1933).

Tendulkar, D.G., *Mahatma: Life of Mohandas Karamchand Gandhi*, 8 vols (Delhi: The Publications Division, Government of India, 1960), i.

Tennyson, Jesse F., *The Story of Burma* (London: Macmillan, 1946).

Thompson, Edward, *A History of India* (London: Ernest Benn, 1927).

Thompson, Edward, *The Other Side of the Medal* (London: Leonard and Virginia Woolf at The Hogarth Press, 1930).

Thompson, Edward, *The Reconstruction of India* (London: Faber and Faber, 1930).

Thompson, Edward, *A Letter from India* (London: Faber and Faber, 1932).

Thompson, Edward, and G.T. Garratt, *Rise and Fulfilment of British Rule in*

India (London: Macmillan, 1934).

Thomson, H.C., *The Chitral Campaign* (London: William Heinemann, 1895).

Thornton, A.P., *The Imperial Idea and its Enemies* (London: Macmillan, 1966).

Tidrick, Kathryn, *Empire and the English Character* (2nd edn, London: I.B. Tauris, 1992).

Tinker, Hugh, *The Ordeal of Love: C.F. Andrews and India* (Delhi: Oxford University Press, 1979).

Tomlinson, B.R., *The Political Economy of the Raj, 1914–1947: The Economics of Decolonization in India* (London: Macmillan, 1979).

Towelle's Handbook and Guide to Simla (Simla: Station Press, 1890).

Townshend, Charles, *Britain's Civil Wars: Counter-Insurgency in the Twentieth Century* (London: Faber & Faber, 1986).

Trager, Frank N., *Burma: From Kingdom to Republic. A Historical and Political Analysis* (London: Pall Mall, 1966).

Trevelyan, Lord Humphrey, *The India We Left* (London: Macmillan, 1972).

Trevelyan, Raleigh, *The Golden Oriole: Childhood, Family and Friends in India* (London: Secker and Warburg, 1987).

Tugwell, W.B.P., *History of the Bombay Pioneers, 1777–1933* (London; Sidney Press, 1938).

Tully, Mark, and Satish Jacob, *Amritsar: Mrs Gandhi's Last Battle* (London: Jonathan Cape, 1985).

Tyne, Claude H. Van, *India in Ferment* (New York: D. Appleton, 1923).

Vasantha, Madhava K.G., *History of the Freedom Movement in India (1857–1947)* (New Delhi: Navrang, 1995).

Vibart, Henry Meredith, *The Life of General Sir Harry N.D. Prendergast (The Happy Warrior)* (London: Eveleigh Nash, 1914).

Wayley, Sir David, *Edwin Montagu: A Memoir and an Account of his Visits to India* (London: Asia Publishing House, 1964).

West, Trevor, *Midleton College, 1696–1996: A Tercentenary History* (Midleton, County Cork: Midleton College, 1996).

Whitehead, Henry, *Indian Problems in Religion, Education, Politics* (London: Constable, 1924).

Who Was Who, 1916–1928 (London: Adam & Charles Black, 1947).

Widdess, John David Henry, *The Royal College of Surgeons in Ireland and its Medical School, 1784–1966* (Edinburgh: E. and S. Livingstone, 1967).

Wilber, Donald N., *Afghanistan: Its People, its Society, its Culture* (New Haven: Human Resources Area Files Press, 1962).

Wilkinson-Latham, Robert John, *North-West Frontier, 1837–1947* (London: Osprey, 1977).

Williams, L.F. Rushbrook, ed., *India in 1919* (Calcutta: Government of India, 1920).

Williams, L.F. Rushbrook, ed., *India in 1920* (Calcutta: Government of India, 1921).

Wilson, Frederick William, *The Indian Chaos* (London: Eyre and Spottiswoode, 1932).

Wint, Guy, *The British in Asia* (London: Faber and Faber, 1947).

Wolpert, Stanley A., *Massacre at Jallianwala Bagh* (New Delhi: Penguin, 1988).

Wolpert, Stanley A., *A New History of India* (New York: Oxford University Press, 1993).

Woodcock, George, *Gandhi* (London: Collins, 1972).

Woodman, Dorothy, *The Making of Burma* (London: Cresset, 1962).

Woodruff, Philip, *The Men Who Ruled India: The Guardians* (London: Jonathan Cape, 1954).

Woodyatt, Nigel, *Under Ten Viceroys: Reminiscences of a Gurkha* (London: Herbert Jenkins, 1922).

Woolacott, J.E., *India on Trial: A Study of Present Conditions* (London: Macmillan, 1929).

Wylly, H.C., *From the Black Mountain to Waziristan* (London: Macmillan, 1912).

Wylly, H.C., *The Border Regiment in the Great War* (Aldershot: Gale and Polden, 1924).

Wylly, H.C., *History of the Queen's Royal Regiment* (Aldershot: Gale and Polden, n.d.), vii.

Wylly, H.C., *Regimental History of the 3rd Battalion 2nd Punjab Regiment* (Aldershot: Gale and Polden, 1927).

Wyrall, Everard, *The History of the Somerset Light Infantry (Prince Albert's), 1914–1919* (London: Methuen, 1927).

Yapp, Malcolm, *The British Raj and Indian Nationalism* (London: Harrap, 1977).

Yardley, Michael, *Sandhurst: A Documentary* (London: Harrap, 1987).

Young, G.M., *Victorian England* (London: Folio Society, 1999).

Younghusband, G.J., and Frank E. Younghusband, *The Relief of Chitral* (London: Macmillan, 1895).

Zacharias, H.C.E., *Renascent India: From Ram Mohan Roy to Mohandas Gandhi* (London: George Allen and Unwin, 1933).

Zaidi, A.M., Shaheda Ghufran Zaidi, Abdul Moid Zaidi, Naushaba Firdos Alvi and Amin Ahmed, eds, *The Encyclopaedia of Indian National Congress: Emergence of Gandhi* (Delhi: S. Chand, 1979), vii.

ARTICLES

'Amritsar: By an English Woman', by an anonymous writer, *Blackwoods Magazine* (April 1920), pp. 441–46.

Bond, Brian, 'Amritsar, 1919', *History Today*, 13, no. 10 (1963), pp. 666–76.

Bosworth, C. Edmund, 'The Sarhadd Region of Persian Baluchistan from Mediaeval Islamic Times to the Mid-Twentieth Century', in *Studia Iranica*, 31 (2002), pp. 79–102.

Bowden, Tom, 'The Amritsar Incident', *British Army Review*, no. 60 (1978), pp. 13–19.

Brown, Judith, 'Imperial Façade: Some Constraints upon and Contradictions in the British Position in India, 1919–1935', *Transactions of the Royal Historical Society*, 26 (1976), pp. 35–52.

Cairns, B.D., 'The Reverend Canon Thomas Moore, Headmaster of Midleton College, 1863–1882', *Midleton College Magazine* (no date).

Cowland, C.J., 'Amritsar and After: Extracts from a Letter to Colonel Mains', in *7th Duke of Edinburgh's Own Gurkha Rifles Regimental Journal* (1985), p. 101.

Datta, V.N., 'Jallianwala Bagh', in *We Fight Together for Freedom: Chapter from the Indian National Movement*, ed. by Ravi Dayal (Delhi: Oxford University Press, 1995), pp. 78–1040.

Emilsen, William W., 'Wrestling the Serpent: Gandhi, Amritsar and the British Empire', *Religion*, 24 (1994), pp. 143–53.

Krishna, G., 'The Development of the Indian National Congress as a Mass Organization, 1918–1923', *Journal of Asian Studies*, 25, no. 3 (1966), pp. 413–30.

Lal, Vinay, 'The Incident of the Crawling Lane: Women in the Punjab Disturbances of 1919', *Genders*, 16 (1993), pp. 35–60.

McCallum, Frank, 'Amritsar, 1919: A Bystander's View,' *Indo-British Review*, 16, no. 1 (1989), pp. 31–33 (copied in McCallum papers).

Mains, A.A., 'General Dyer and Amritsar', *9th Gurkha Rifles Association Newsletter*, 58 (1992).

'Martial Law', in *Encyclopaedia Britannica* (London: Encyclopaedia Britannica, 1926), pp. 790–92.

Naidis, Mark, 'Amritsar Revisited', *The Historian*, 21, no. 1 (1958), pp. 1–17.

Sayer, Derek, 'British Reaction to the Amritsar Massacre, 1919–1920', *Past and Present*, 131 (May 1991), pp. 130–64.

Tomlinson, B.R., 'India and the British Empire, 1880–1935', *Indian Economic and Social History Review*, 12, (1975), pp. 337–80.

Yeates, E.P., 'General Dyer: Some Recollections', *Blackwoods Magazine* (1927), pp. 793–95.

THESES

Moreman, T.R., ' "Passing it On": The Army in India and the Development of Frontier Warfare, 1849–1947' (unpublished doctoral thesis, University of London, DX195607, 1997).

WEBSITES

Anon., 'Churchill and the Amritsar Massacre'. No date. *http:// Lachlan.bluehaze.com.au/Churchill/amritsar.htm* (25 November 2001).

Anon., 'A Spark of Revolution: Bhagath Singh'. No date. *www.freeindia.organise/biographies/freedomefighters/bhagathsingh/page4.htm* (4 February 2002).

Basarke, Alice, 'Origins of Non-Violence Movement in India', *Khalsa Pride*. No date. *www.khalsapride.com/articles/3.htm* (25 November 2001).

Bishop Cotton School, Shimla, 'School History', *School Home Page*. No date. *www.bishopcotton.edu/gallery.htm* (25 November 2001).

Forgotten History Foundation, 'Amritsar Massacre (1919): What Happened?' No date. *www.forgottenhistory.org/exhibits/amritsar.htm* (25 November 2001).

Midleton College, 'School History', *School Home Page*. No date. *www.midletoncollege.com* (25 November 2001).

Mohan Meakin Ltd, 'Company History', *Company Website*. No date. *www.goldeneagletrading.com/india/india.html* (25 November 2001).

Saint Stephen's College, 'History: A Brief Historical Account', *School Web Page*. No date. *www.ststephens.edu/history* (5 February 2002).

Sikh History, 'Jallianwala Bagh', *Sikh History*. No date. *www.sikh-history.com/ sikhhist/events/jbagh.htm* (25 November 2001).

Singh, Brigadier Hardit, 'The Amritsar Tragedy'. July 1984. *www.sikh- institute.org/u2–2.aoss-articles/28.july.htm* (25 November 2001).

Index

Ranks shown in the index are the highest mentioned in the text.